HISTORY OF THE GREAT WAR

BASED ON OFFICIAL DOCUMENTS

BY DIRECTION OF THE HISTORICAL SECTION OF THE COMMITTEE OF IMPERIAL DEFENCE

ORDER OF BATTLE
OF DIVISIONS

• PART 3a •

New Army Divisions (9-26)

Compiled by

MAJOR A. F. BECKE

R.F.A. (Retired), Hon. M.A. (Oxon.)

The Naval & Military Press Ltd

Reproduced by kind permission of the Central Library,
Royal Military Academy, Sandhurst

Published by
The Naval & Military Press Ltd
Unit 10, Ridgewood Industrial Park,
Uckfield, East Sussex,
TN22 5QE England
Tel: +44 (0) 1825 749494
Fax: +44 (0) 1825 765701
www.naval-military-press.com
www.military-genealogy.com
© The Naval & Military Press Ltd 2007

ORDER OF BATTLE OF DIVISIONS

*In reprinting in facsimile from the original, any imperfections are inevitably reproduced
and the quality may fall short of modern type and cartographic standards.*

Printed and bound by Antony Rowe Ltd, Eastbourne

PREFACE

Orders of Battle for the fifteen regular British divisions were given in Part 1 of this series. Parts 2-A and 2-B contained the Orders of Battle of five mounted divisions and fourteen 1st-line and fourteen 2nd-line Territorial Force divisions, as well as three home-service divisions (71st–73rd) and the 74th and 75th Divisions.

The present Part (3-A) includes the Orders of Battle of eighteen New Army divisions (9th–26th). Succeeding Parts of this series, each giving about fifteen divisions, will contain : the remainder of the New Army divisions (3-B) ; and the Australian, Canadian, New Zealand, and Indian divisions (4-A and B). The series will be concluded with a volume dealing with G.H.Q.s, Armies, and Corps.

All the eighteen New Army divisions dealt with in this Part were War Time formations ; not a single one, nor any of the units, was in existence at the outbreak of the Great War. These eighteen divisions of Kitchener's Armies were engaged in six of the principal theatres of war : they fought on the Western Front in France and Belgium ; as well as in Italy, in Gallipoli, in Macedonia, and in Egypt and Palestine ; and they included the only British division which served and fought in Mesopotamia.

Each of the twelve divisions of the First and Second New Armies had a distinguishing territorial or other title in addition to the number allotted to it ; but the six divisions of the Third New Army were only numbered, like regular divisions of the original B.E.F.

No unit or formation of the first three New Armies kept its war diary until embarkation orders arrived. In consequence, there is no official record of the troubles and difficulties of the early days of these new divisions. Nevertheless it is necessary to stress the shortage of clothing, equipment, and arms and the lack of sufficient trained instructors which almost every unit had to face from the day of its formation, a shortage which, in several of the divisions, lasted all through 1914. Even in the divisions of the First New Army these deficiencies were very real ; they naturally became more serious and were increasingly felt in the divisions of the Second and Third New Armies. All spare clothing, equipment, and arms were used up almost at once, and for trained instructors the last-formed of the divisions had to rely largely on officers and n.c.o.s who had been wounded in the early fighting and had recovered sufficiently to report for duty.

Divisional histories, routine orders (when they existed), regimental histories, and private accounts have been used for the compilation of the short narrative which deals with the formation of each division, and the special difficulties which had to be surmounted before it was ready to embark for a theatre of war. Considering the general unpreparedness of the country for participation in a great war, it is remarkable that all but one of these eighteen newly-raised divisions should have been able to leave England within fourteen months of the declaration of war. The remaining division began embarkation in December, 1915.

The Field Artillery of the First and Second New Armies was at first organized in the same way as the Field Artillery of the original B.E.F.—in four 3-battery brigades, each battery consisting of 6 guns or howitzers (see Tables). In January 1915, however, it was decided that all the Field Artillery of the New Army divisions should consist of 4-battery brigades, and that each battery should be a 4-gun or 4-howitzer battery.* The Field Artillery of the divisions of the Third New Army was organized in the latter fashion (see Tables), and all the Field Artillery of the divisions of the first three New Armies went overseas organized in this way. Consequently, in May 1915, when the New Army divisions began to arrive in France, the seventh different divisional field artillery establishment appeared on the Western Front.

---

*W.O. letter, No. 20/Artillery/3818 A.G. 6, d/d 6.1.1915.

i

Even in 1916 the establishment of 18-pdrs. with British divisions on the Western Front still varied ; at the same time there were available in France a number of un-attached 4.5-in. howitzer batteries. The variation in divisional artillery establishments had caused difficulties ; and, as mixed field artillery brigades (guns and howitzers) had already been adopted in practice, it was proposed, in February 1916 to have a uniform divisional artillery establishment on the Western Front—mixed brigades of 18-pdrs. and 4.5-in. howitzers—and the 6-gun 18-pdr. battery was to be universally adopted as soon as possible. In due course the 4-gun 4.5-in. howitzer batteries were also to become 6-gun batteries. The conversion was eventually carried out (see Tables) ; in January 1917 the final step was taken and the 4.5-in. howitzer batteries were increased to 6 pieces each. From that time until the end of the Great War all the British divisions serving on the Western Front had identical field artillery establishments.

As in the previous parts of this series, the lists of Commanders and Staff Officers do not show temporary changes due to absences on short leave, at short courses, or at schools of instruction.

In the Divisional Tables each considerable change in composition is shown. In any case the organization of the division is given for each year, and at one or more important periods in its history.

The numerous reorganizations and redesignations of the field artillery brigades and batteries are given in the notes to the various tables.

In the lists of Battles and Engagements occasional deviations have been made from the lists given in the *Report of the Battles Nomenclature Committee* (published in 1921), in order to include actions of which a division has reason to be proud. In every case, after the battle in which a division fought, the Corps and Army in which the division served at the time is given in square brackets. If a division did not happen to be engaged during a whole year in some specific action then only the year is shown, but this signifies that the division was on active service in the field during this period.

In the lists, the words " Action " and " Affair " have been omitted and only the date and name of these engagements are given.* The periods when the divisional artillery, engineers, and pioneers were left in the line, after the relief of a division, are not shown.

Neither the attachments of Army field artillery brigades† to a division, nor the attachment of R.G.A. brigades, are shown in the General Notes to the Tables. All other attachments are given either in the Tables or in the General Notes. In order that the Tables shall be as clear as possible, the numerous notes are printed on the page following each Table.

The proclamation of the 11th August 1914, calling for the addition of 100,000 men to His Majesty's Regular Army is given on p. 2. In addition, Appendix 1 (at the end of this Part) gives a short description of the steps taken on the outbreak of War to augment the Regular Army.

Appendices 2, 3, 4, and 5 give the War Establishments of 14th (Light) Division (England), 1915 ; 14th (Light) Division (France), 1918 ; 23rd Division (Italy), 1918 ; and 10th (Irish) Division (Palestine), 1918. Appendices 6, 7, 8, and 9 give the War Establishments of 11th (Northern) Division (Gallipoli), 1915 ; 26th Division (Macedonia), 1915 ; 26th Division (Macedonia), 1918 ; and 13th (Western) Division (Mesopotamia), 1918.

In the present Part a new feature has been introduced. The total battle casualties of the division, as recorded in its war diaries, are given at the conclusion of each divisional narrative. To Mr. H. A. Cordery my grateful thanks are due for his labours in extracting

---

*The Actions of Villers Bretonneux, 24th and 25th April 1918, would appear as " 24 and 25 April, Villers Bretonneux."

†Formed in France early in 1917, after the final reorganization of the divisional artilleries.

these illuminating figures. A Table showing the total battle casualties of each British division, as well as its casualties for each year of the Great War, will be given as an appendix to the next Part (3-B).

Each divisional story was submitted for comment to the General Officer who commanded the division at the end of the Great War ; in addition, copies were sent to any officer who had served for a long period with the division. I am very grateful to all the divisional commanders and other officers who have assisted in checking and correcting these tables and for providing additional information. I am glad to record my gratitude for the considerable assistance which I have received both from the War Office Library and from " R " (Records), War Office. Without the help of the latter I should have been unable to recover many of the dates.

I am also greatly indebted to the Staff of the Historical Section (Military Branch) for the skilled help which they have given me on all occasions. In particular, my most grateful thanks are due to Mr. S. Woolgar for the continuous and valuable assistance which he has given me during the compilation of this Part.

Any corrections or amendments to these Tables should be sent to the Secretary, Historical Section, Committee of Imperial Defence, Audit House, Victoria Embankment, E.C.4.

A. F. B.

September **1938**.

CONTENTS

LIST OF ABREVIATIONS

NOTE.—For the period of the Great War the titles of regiments have been taken from the 1914-1918 Army Lists.

A.

(A.-A.)	(Anti-Aircraft).
A.-A. & Q.-M.-G.	Assistant-Adjutant & Quarter-Master-General.
A.C.C.	Army Cyclist Corps (Home Service).
A. & S.H.... ...	Argyll & Sutherland Highlanders.
A.F.A. Bde. ...	Army Field Artillery Brigade.
A.H.Q.	Army Head-Quarters.
Amb. or Ambce.	Ambulance.
Ammn. Coln. ...	Ammunition Column.
Ammn. Park ...	Ammunition Park.
A.R.O.	Army Routine Order.
Arty.	Artillery.
A.S.C.... ...	Army Service Corps.
A.T.	Army Troops.
A.T. Carts ...	Army Transport Carts.
Aux.	Auxiliary.

B.

B.A.C.	Brigade Ammunition Column.
Bde.	Brigade.
Bedf.	Bedfordshire Regiment.
Bedf. Yeo.... ...	Bedfordshire Yeomanry.
B.E.F.	British Expeditionary Force.
Berks.	Berkshire.
B.F.T.	British Forces in Turkey.
B.-G., R.A. ...	Brigadier-General, Commanding Royal Artillery.
B.-G., R.H.A. ...	Brigadier-General, Commanding Royal Horse Artillery.
B.L.	Breech-loader.
B.L.C.	B.L. Converted.
Bn.	Battalion.
Bord.	Border Regiment.
Br.-Gen.	Brigadier-General.
Bty.	Battery.
Bucks.	Buckinghamshire.
Buffs	Buffs (East Kent Regiment).
B.W.	Black Watch (Royal Highlanders).
B.W.I.	British West Indies Regiment.

C.

Camb.	Cambridgeshire Regiment.
Cam. H.	Cameron Highlanders.
Cav.	Cavalry.
C.B.	Cavalry Brigade.
C.C.S.	Casualty Clearing Station.
cd.	command.
C.D.M.T. Coy. ...	Cavalry Divisional Mechanical Transport Company.
Cdn.	Canadian.
C.F.A.	Combined Field Ambulance.
C.G.	Coldstream Guards.
Ches.	Cheshire Regiment.
C.I.	Central India.
Col.-Cdt.	Colonel-Commandant.
Comp.	Composite.
Conn. Rang. ...	Connaught Rangers.
Co.	County.
Coy.	Company.
Cos.	Companies.
C.R.E.	Commanding Royal Engineers.
C.R.H.A.	Commanding Royal Horse Artillery.

D.

d.	died.
D.A.C.	Divisional Ammunition Column.
D.C.L.I.	Duke of Cornwall's Light Infantry.
D.E. Coy.	Divisional Employment Company.
Detnt.	Detachment.
Devon.	Devonshire Regiment.
D.G.	Dragoon Guards.
Dgns.	Dragoons.
Disembkd.... ...	Disembarked.
Disembkn. ...	Disembarkation.
Div.	Division.
Divnl.... ...	Divisional.
D.L.I.... ...	Durham Light Infantry.
D.M.C.	Desert Mounted Corps.
D. of L. Own Yeo.	Duke of Lancaster's Own Yeomanry.
d. of w.	died of wounds.
Dorset	Dorsetshire Regiment.
D.P.	Drill-pattern.
Duke's	Duke of Wellington's (West Riding Regiment).

E.

E.	East ; or Eastern.
E.E.F.	Egyptian Expeditionary Force.
E. Lanc.	East Lancashire Regiment.
Embkd.	Embarked.
Emplnt. or Emplynt. ...	Employment.
Eng.	Engineers.
Entg. Bn.	Entrenching Battalion.
Essex	Essex Regiment.
E. Surr.	East Surrey Regiment.
evacd.	evacuated.
E. York.	East Yorkshire Regiment.

F.

Fd.	Field.

G.

(G.)	(Graduated Battalion).
Garr. Gd.	Garrison Guard Battalion.
G. B. or Garr. Bn. ...	Garrison Battalion.
Gds.	Guards.
G.G.	Grenadier Guards.
G.H.Q.	General Head-Quarters.
Glam.	Glamorganshire.
Glouc.	Gloucestershire Regiment.
G.O.C.	General Officer Commanding.
Gord. H.	Gordon Highlanders.
Gr. How.	Green Howards (Alexandra, Princess of Wales's Own Yorkshire Regiment).
G.S.O.1.	General Staff Officer (1st Grade).

H.

(H.)	(Howitzer).
H.A.C.	Honourable Artillery Company.
H.A.G.	Heavy Artillery Group.
Hants.	Hampshire Regiment.
H.A.R.	Heavy Artillery Reserve.
H.B.	Heavy Battery.

ix

H.D. Trps.	Home Defence Troops.
Hereford.	Herefordshire.
Herts.	Hertfordshire Regiment.
H.L.I.	Highland Light Infantry.
Home Cties.	Home Counties.
Househ'd.	Household.
How. Bde.	Howitzer Brigade.
How. Bty.	Howitzer Battery.
H.Q.	Head-Quarters.
Hsrs.	Hussars.
H.T.	Horse Transport.
H.T.M.B.	Heavy Trench Mortar Battery.
Hy. Bde.	Heavy Brigade.
Hy. Bty.	Heavy Battery.
Hy. Bty. A.C.	Heavy Battery Ammunition Column.

I.

I.G.	Irish Guards.
Ind.	Indian.
Inf.	Infantry.
Ir.	Irish.
It.	Italian.

K.

k. or kd.	Killed.
K.E. Horse	King Edward's Horse.
K.G.O.	King George's Own.
King's	King's (Liverpool Regiment).
K.O.	King's Own (Royal Lancaster Regiment).
K.O.S.B.	King's Own Scottish Borderers.
K.O.Y.L.I.	King's Own (Yorkshire Light Infantry).
K.R.R.C.	King's Royal Rifle Corps.
K.S.L.I.	King's (Shropshire Light Infantry).

L.

Lcrs.	Lancers.
Leic.	Leicestershire Regiment.
Leic. Yeo.	Leicestershire Yeomanry.
Leins.	Leinster Regiment.
L.F.	Lancashire Fusiliers.
L.G.	Life Guards.
L.I.	Light Infantry.
Linc.	Lincolnshire Regiment.
L.N.L.	Loyal North Lancashire Regiment.
L. of C.	Line of Communications.
Lond.	London Regiment.
Loyal	The Loyal Regiment (North Lancashire).
L.R.B.	London Rifle Brigade.
L.S.	London Scottish.
L.Sec.	Left Section.

M.

Manch.	Manchester Regiment.
Med.	Medium.
M.E.F.	Mediterranean Expeditionary Force [Gallipoli].
M.G.C.	Machine-Gun Corps.
M.G. Coy.	Machine-Gun Company.
M.G. Sec.	Machine-Gun Section.
M.G. Sqdn.	Machine-Gun Squadron.
M.I.	Mounted Infantry.
Midd'x.	Middlesex Regiment.
Midld.	Midland.
Mk.	Mark.
M.M.G.	Motor Machine Gun.
Mobn.	Mobilization.
Mob. Vety. Sec.	Mobile Veterinary Section.
Mon. or Monm'th.	Monmouthshire Regiment.
Montgom.	Montgomeryshire.
M.T.	Mechanical Transport.
Mtd.	Mounted.
Mtn.	Mountain.

N.

N.	North ; or Northern.
Newf'dld.	Newfoundland.
N.F.	Northumberland Fusiliers.
N. Irish H.	North Irish Horse.
N.M. Fd. Coy.	North Midland Field Company.
Norf.	Norfolk Regiment.
Northants. Yeo.	Northamptonshire Yeomanry.
North'bn.	Northumbrian.
North'd.	Northumberland.
North'n.	Northamptonshire Regiment.
N. Som.	North Somerset.
N. Staff.	North Staffordshire Regiment.
N.S.W.	New South Wales.
N.Z. & A.	New Zealand and Australian.

O.

O. & B.L.I.	Oxfordshire & Buckinghamshire Light Infantry.
Offrs.	Officers.
O.R.	Other ranks.

P.

(P.)	(Pioneers).
P.E.	Peace Establishment.
Pemb.	Pembrokeshire.
P.P.C.L.I.	Princess Patricia's Canadian Light Infantry.
P.O. Rif.	Post Office Rifles.
Provl.	Provisional.
P.W.O.	Prince of Wales's Own.

Q.

Q.O.O. Hsrs.	Queen's Own Oxfordshire Hussars.
Q.O.R.R. Staff. Yeo.	Queen's Own Royal Regiment, Staffordshire Yeomanry.
Q.O.R.W.K.	Queen's Own (Royal West Kent Regiment).
Queen's	Queen's (Royal West Surrey Regiment).
Q.V. Rif.	Queen Victoria's Rifles.
Q.W. Rif.	Queen's Westminster Rifles.

R.

R.	Royal.
R.A.F.	Royal Air Force.
R.A.S.C.	Royal Army Service Corps.
R.B.	Rifle Brigade.
R. Berks.	Royal Berkshire Regiment.
R. Cdn. H.A. Bde.	Royal Canadian Horse Artillery Brigade.
R.D.F.	Royal Dublin Fusiliers.
R.E.	Royal Engineers.
Regt.	Regiment.
R.F.	Royal Fusiliers.
R.F.A.	Royal Field Artillery.
Rfts.	Reinforcements.
R.G.A.	Royal Garrison Artillery.
R. Guern. L.I.	Royal Guernsey Light Infantry.
R.H.A.	Royal Horse Artillery.
R.H.G.	Royal Horse Guards.
Rid.	Riding.
R. Innis. F.	Royal Inniskilling Fusiliers.
R. Ir. F.	Royal Irish Fusiliers.
R. Ir. Regt.	Royal Irish Regiment.
R. Ir. Rif.	Royal Irish Rifles.
R.M.F.	Royal Munster Fusiliers.
R.M.L.I.	Royal Marine Light Infantry.
R.N.A.C.D.	Royal Naval Armoured Car Division.
R.N.D.	Royal Naval Division.
R. Scots	Royal Scots (Lothian Regiment).
R. Sec.	Right Section.
R.S.F.	Royal Scots Fusiliers.
R. Suss.	Royal Sussex Regiment.
R.W.	Royal Warrant.
R. War.	Royal Warwickshire Regiment.
R.W.F.	Royal Welsh Fusiliers.
R.W.K.	Queen's Own (Royal West Kent Regiment).

S.

S.	South ; or Southern.
S.A. or S. Afr.	South African.
S.A.A. Sec. ...	Small-Arm-Ammunition Section.
S.B.	Siege Battery.
S.B.A.C. ...	Siege Battery Ammunition Column.
Sco. Rif. ...	The Cameronians (Scottish Rifles).
Sea. H. ...	Seaforth Highlanders.
Sec. or Secn. ...	Section.
S.G.	Scots Guards.
Sher. For. ...	Sherwood Foresters (Nottinghamshire & Derbyshire Regiment).
Sig.	Signal.
S. Irish H.	South Irish Horse.
S. Lanc. ...	South Lancashire Regiment.
S. & M.	Sappers & Miners.
S.M. Fd. Coy.	South Midland Field Company.
Som. L.I. ...	Somerset Light Infantry.
Sqdn. ...	Squadron.
S. Staff. ...	South Staffordshire Regiment.
Suff.	Suffolk Regiment.
S.W.B.	South Wales Borderers.

T.

T.A.	Territorial Army.
T.C.	Training Cadre.
T. & S. Coln. ...	Transport & Supply Column.

T—continued.

Tempy.	Temporary.
T.F.	Territorial Force.
T.M. Bty.	Trench Mortar Battery.
Trp.	Troop.

U.

U.K.	United Kingdom.

V.

Vety.	Veterinary.

W.

W.	West ; or Western.
w. or wd.	wounded.
War.	Warwickshire.
W.E.	War Establishment.
Welsh...	Welsh Regiment.
W.G.	Welsh Guards.
Westld. & Cumbld. Yeo.	Westmorland and Cumberland Yeomanry.
Wilts.	Wiltshire Regiment.
Worc....	Worcestershire Regiment.
W. Rid.	West Riding.
W. York.	West Yorkshire Regiment.

Y.

Y. & L.	York & Lancaster Regiment.
Yeo.	Yeomanry.

A typhoon always gives warning of its approach, but not of its exact path.

1

Your King and Country Need You.

A CALL TO ARMS.

An addition of 100,000 men to his Majesty's Regular Army is immediately necessary in the present grave National Emergency.

Lord Kitchener is confident that this appeal will be at once responded to by all those who have the safety of our Empire at heart.

TERMS OF SERVICE.

General Service for a period of 3 years or until the war is concluded.

Age of Enlistment between 19 and 30.

HOW TO JOIN.

Full information can be obtained at any Post Office in the Kingdom or at any Military Depot.

God Save the King!

9TH (SCOTTISH) DIVISION

G.O.C.

27 August, 1914	... ...	Major-General C. J. MACKENZIE.
11 October, 1914	... ...	Br.-Gen. S. W. SCRASE-DICKENS (acting).
26 October, 1914	... ...	LT.-Gen. Sir C. FERGUSSON, Bt.
31 December, 1914	... ...	Br.-Gen. S. W. SCRASE-DICKENS (acting).
21 January, 1915	... ...	Major-General H. J. S. LANDON.
9 September, 1915	... ...	Major-General G. H. THESIGER (killed, 27/9/15).
27 September, 1915	... ...	Major-General E. S. BULFIN (tempy.).
28 September, 1915	... ...	Major-General W. T. FURSE.
2 December, 1916	... ...	Major-General H. T. LUKIN.
4 March, 1918	... ...	Br.-Gen. H. H. TUDOR (acting).
13 March, 1918	... ...	Major-General C. A. BLACKLOCK.
16 March, 1918	... ...	Br.-Gen. H. H. TUDOR (acting).
2 p.m., 24 March, 1918	...	Major-General C. A. BLACKLOCK.
28 March, 1918	... ...	Major-General H. H. TUDOR.

G.S.O. 1.

7 Sept., 1914...Captain G. E. B. STEPHENS
(acting).
7 Jan., 1915...Lt.-Col. C. H.
DE ROUGEMONT.
24 July, 1915...Lt.-Col. F. A. BUZZARD.
4 Sept., 1915...Lt.-Col. S. E. HOLLOND.
26 Feb., 1916...Lt.-Col. P. A. V. STEWART.
28 Dec., 1917...Lt.-Col. T. C. MUDIE.

A.-A. and Q.-M.-G.

12 Sept., 1914...Captain P. R. C.
COMMINGS (acting).
2 Nov., 1914...Colonel A. V. PAYNE.
14 Mar., 1915...Lt.-Col. R. F. UNIACKE
(killed, 27/5/15).
27 May, 1915...Captain P. R. C.
COMMINGS (acting).
6 June, 1915...Lt.-Col. A. A. McHARDY.
30 Aug., 1916...Lt.-Col. A. C. JEFFCOAT.

B.-G., R.A.

30 Sept., 1914...Br.-Gen. E. H. ARMITAGE.
28 Jan., 1916...Lt.-Col. A. H. CARTER
(acting).
1 Feb., 1916...Br.-Gen. H. H. TUDOR.
6 Sept., 1916...Lt.-Col. G. A. S. CAPE
(acting).
6 Oct., 1916...Br.-Gen. H. H. TUDOR.
16 Mar., 1918...Lt.-Col. W. McLEAN
(acting ; wounded, 21/3/18).
21 Mar., 1918...Lt.-Col. M. MUIRHEAD
(acting).
25 Mar., 1918...Br.-Gen. H. H. TUDOR.
28 Mar., 1918...Lt.-Col. M. MUIRHEAD
(acting).
6 April, 1918...Br.-Gen. A. R.
WAINEWRIGHT.

C.R.E.

9 May, 1915...Lt.-Col. H. A. A.
LIVINGSTONE (wounded, 26/9/15).
26 Sept., 1915...Major G. R. HEARN
(acting).
26 Oct., 1915...Lt.-Col. C. M. CARPENTER.
27 Jan., 1916...Lt.-Col. E. BARNARDISTON
(wounded, 17/7/16).
17 July, 1916...Major G. R. HEARN
(acting).
23 Sept., 1916...Lt.-Col. G. R. HEARN.
10 Feb., 1918...Major F. D.
NAPIER-CLAVERING (acting).
18 Feb., 1918...Major T. G. BIRD (acting).
24 Feb., 1918...Major F. D.
NAPIER-CLAVERING (acting)
1 Mar., 1918...Lt.-Col. H. C. B.
HICKLING.

B

26th BDE.

21 Sept., '14...Br.-Gen. H. R. KELHAM.
16 Nov., '14...Br.-Gen. E. G. GROGAN.
31 May, '15...Br.-Gen. A. B. RITCHIE.
5 Dec., '16...Br.-Gen. J. KENNEDY.
27 July, '18...Br.-Gen. Hon. A. G. A. HORE-RUTHVEN, V.C.
5 Nov., '18...Br.-Gen. H. G. HYSLOP.
[12 Nov., '18...Lt.-Col. R. CAMPBELL (acting).
22 Nov., '18...Br.-Gen. Hon. A. G. A. HORE-RUTHVEN, V.C.]

27th BDE.

27 Aug., '14...Br.-Gen. W. E. SCOTT-MONCRIEFF.
7 Jan., '15...Br.-Gen. C. D. BRUCE (captured, 25/9/15).
26 Sept., '15...Lt.-Col. H. E. WALSHE (acting).
14 Oct., '15...Br.-Gen. H. E. WALSHE (sick, 14/3/16).
17 Mar., '16...Br.-Gen. G. F. TROTTER (injured, 2/5/16).
2 May, '16...Lt.-Col. W. J. B. TWEEDIE (acting).
6 May, '16...Br.-Gen. S. W. SCRASE-DICKENS.
21 Oct., '16...Br.-Gen. F. A. MAXWELL, V.C. (killed, 21/9/17).
21 Sept., '17...Lt.-Col. H. D. N. MACLEAN (acting).
23 Sept., '17...Br.-Gen. W. D. CROFT.

28th BDE.

9 Sept., '14 ⎫
6 May, '16 ⎬ Br.-Gen. S. W. SCRASE-DICKENS.
(28th Bde. was broken up and ceased to exist on 6/5/16.)

SOUTH AFRICAN BDE.

(The Bde. was formed in S. Africa in Aug., 1915. The Bde. left S. Africa on 26/9/15 ; reached England on 13/10/15 ; left England on 30/12/15 ; arrived in Egypt on 10/1/16 ; left Egypt 13–15/4/16 ; disembkd. at Marseille on 20/4/16 ; and joined 9th Div. between 22/4–11/5/16.)

[11 Aug., '15]...Br.-Gen. H. T. LUKIN.
2 Dec., '16...Br.-Gen F. S. DAWSON (captured, 24/3/18).
25 Mar., '18...Lt.-Col. B. YOUNG (acting).
1 April, '18...Br.-Gen. W. E. C. TANNER.

(S. African Bde. left 9th Div. on 13/9/18, and the Bde. joined 66th Div. on 23/9/18.)

28th BDE.

(The Bde. was formed on 11/9/18.)

11 Sept. '18...Br.-Gen. J. L. JACK.

GENERAL NOTES

The following Units also served with the 9th (Scottish) Division :—

ARTILLERY :—508 **(H.) Battery, R.F.A. (4, 4·5″ Hows.),** see note 27.

9th Heavy Battery was formed on 6/9/14 at Woolwich. Personnel remained under canvas and the Heavy Battery was used as a depôt until February, 1915. On 9/5/15 the Heavy Battery mobilized at Bordon and on 10/5/15 drew gunsights. The Heavy Battery disembkd. at le Havre on 12/5/15, left 9th Div. on 16/5/15, and on 18/5/15 joined H.A. Reserve and went into action near Armentières. On 11/6/15 the Heavy Battery joined XVI Heavy Artillery Bde., R.G.A.

INFANTRY :—

2/R.S.F., from 26/4/18 (see note 46).

9/Sco. Rif., from 21/4/18 (see notes 34 and 47).

3/4/Queen's, disembkd. at le Havre on 1/6/17, joined S.A. Inf. Bde. on 6/6/17, was transferred to 12th Div. on 23/7/17, and joined 62nd Bde., 21st Div., on 9/8/17. Between 3–11/2/18 Bn. was broken up and drafted.

3/4/Q.O.R.W. Kent, disembkd. at le Havre on 1/6/17, joined S.A. Inf. Bde. on 6/6/17 ; was attached to 101st Bde., 34th Div., on 15/6/17, to 103rd Bde., 34th Div., on 18/6/17 ; and on 22/6/17 Bn. joined 51st Bde., 17th Div., and worked as pioneers. On 3/8/17 Bn. joined 52nd Bde., 17th Div., and between 5–10/2/18 Bn. was broken up and drafted.

3/10/Middlesex, disembkd. at le Havre on 1/6/17, joined S.A. Inf. Bde. on 6/6/17. Bn. left S.A. Inf. Bde. on 23/7/17 and joined 10th Bde., 4th Div., on 2/8/17. On 20/2/18 Bn. became 11/Entrenching Bn.

MACHINE GUN UNITS :—**Nos. 7 and 11 Motor M.G. Bties. (I.M.M.G. Bde.),** from 7/10–8/11/18.

No. 104 Bn., M.G. Corps, from 21/9–7/10/18 ;
and

C Coy., No. 104 Bn., M.G. Corps, from 7/10–8/11/18.

OTHER UNITS :—**20th Sanitary Section,** went to France with 9th Div. and disembkd. at le Havre on 13/5/15. On 29/3/17 the Section was transferred from 9th Div. to Army Troops, Third Army.

9th Div. Motor Ambce. Workshop, went to France with 9th Div. and disembkd. at Rouen on 10/5/15. By April, 1916, the Workshop was absorbed by Divnl. Supply Coln.

On 22/2/18 the reorganization of the 9th Division on a 9-battalion basis was completed ; and by 7/3/18 the pioneer battalion (9/Sea. H.) had been reorganized on a 3-company basis.

NOTE
South African Inf. Bde.

On 24/4/18, owing to casualties in action, 1/, 2/, and 4/S.A. Inf. Bns. were amalgamated and formed S.A. (Comp.) Regt. On 31/8 and 1/9/18, 1/, 2/, and 4/S.A. Inf. Bns. were reformed.

(Whilst serving in the 9th Division the Bde. was also known as 28th (S. African) Bde.).

B*

Dates	INFANTRY			ARTILLERY						Engineers	Signal Service	Pioneers	M.G. Units	Field Ambulances	Mobile Vety. Secn.	Divnl. Emplnt. Coy.	Divnl. Train
				Field Artillery		Bde. Ammn. Colns.	Trench Mortar Bties.		Divnl. Ammn. Coln.								
	Brigades	Battalions and attached Units	Mounted Troops	Brigades	Batteries		Medium	Heavy		Field Cos.	Divnl. Signal Coy.						
1914 October (England)	26th ...... 27th 28th	8/B.W., 7/Sea. H., 8/Gord. H., 5/Cam. H.	9th Div. Cyclist Coy.[1]	L[2] .... LI[2] .... LII[2] .... LIII (H.)[2]	160, 161, 162 163, 164, 165 166, 167, 168 169 (H.), 170 (H.), 171 (H.)	L B.A.C. LI B.A.C. LII B.A.C. LIII (H.) B.A.C.	...	...	9th D.A.C.	63rd 64th	9th	...	...	27th 28th 29th	21st[3]	...	9th[4]
		11/R. Scots, 12/R. Scots, 6/R.S.F., 10/A. & S.H.															
		6/K.O.S.B., 9/Sco. Rif., 10/H.L.I., 11/H.L.I.															
1915 September (France)	26th ...... 27th ...... 28th[8]	8/B.W., 7/Sea. H., 8/Gord. H.,[5] 5/Cam. H.	B. Sqdn.[12] 1/Glasgow Yeo. 9th Div. Cyclist Coy.[13]	L[2]; 14 .... LI[2]; 15 .... LII[2]; 16 .... LIII (H.)[2];17	A, B, C, D A, B, C, D A, B, C, D B (H.), C (H.), D (H.)	L B.A.C. LI B.A.C. LII B.A.C. LIII (H.) B.A.C.	...	...	9th D.A.C.	63rd 64th 90th[18]	9th	9/Sea. H. (P.)[19]	10th Motor M.G. Bty.[20]	27th 28th 29th[21]	21st	...	9th
		11/R. Scots, 12/R. Scots, 6/R.S.F.,[6] 10/A. & S.H.[7]															
		6/K.O.S.B.,[9] 9/Sco. Rif.,[10] 10/H.L.I.,[11] 11/H.L.I.[11]															
1916 June (France)	26th ...... 27th ...... South African[24]	8/B.W., 7/Sea. H., 5/Cam. H., 10/A. & S.H.; 26th Bde. M.G. Coy.[22]; 26th T.M. Bty.[23]	...	L[4]; 25 .... LI[5]; 26 .... LII[16]; 27 .... LIII[17]; 28	A, B, C; D (H.) A, B, C; D (H.) A, B, C; D (H.) A, B, C	...[31]	X.9[29] Y.9[29] Z.9[29]	V.9[30]	9th D.A.C.[31]	63rd 64th 90th	9th	9/Sea. H. (P.)	...	27th 28th S.A.Fd. Amb.[32]	21st	...	9th
		11/R. Scots, 12/R. Scots, 6/K.O.S.B.,[9] 9/Sco. Rif.[10]; 27th Bde. M.G. Coy.[22]; 27th T.M. Bty.[23]															
		1/S.A. Inf., 2/S.A. Inf., 3/S.A. Inf., 4/S.A. Inf.; 28th Bde. M.G. Coy.[22]; S.A.T.M. Bty.[23]															
1917 June (France)	28th ...... 27th ...... South African	8/B.W., 7/Sea. H., 5/Cam. H., 10/A. & S.H.;[33] 26th M.G. Coy.; 26th T.M. Bty.	...	L .... LI	A, B, C; D (H.)[36] A, B, C; D (H.)[37]	...	X.9 Y.9 Z.9[38]	V.9[39]	9th D.A.C.	63rd 64th 90th	9th	9/Sea. H. (P.)	197th[40] M.G. Coy.	27th 28th S.A. Fd. Amb.	21st	212th[41]	9th
		11/R. Scots, 12/R. Scots, 6/K.O.S.B., 9/Sco. Rif.;[34] 27th M.G. Coy.; 27th T.M. Bty.															
		1/S.A. Inf., 2/S.A. Inf., 3/S.A. Inf.,[35] 4/S.A. Inf.; 28th M.G. Coy.; S. Afr. T.M. Bty.															

	26th	27th	South African[2] / 28th[45]		Artillery batteries	L	LI		N.9 / Y.9	9th D.A.C.	63rd 64th 90th	9th	9/Sea. H. (P.)	No. 9 Bn. M.G.C.	27th 28th Fd. Amb.	21st	212th	9th
1918 March (France)	8/B.W., 7/Sea. H., 5/Cam. H.; 26th T.M. Bty.	11/R. Scots, 12/R. Scots, 6/K.O.S.B.; 27th T.M. Bty.	1/S.A. Inf., 2/S.A. Inf., 4/S.A. Inf.; S.Afr. T.M. Bty.	...	A, B, C; D (H.) / A, B, C; D (H.)	L	LI	...	N.9 / Y.9	9th D.A.C.	63rd 64th 90th	9th	9/Sea. H. (P.)	No. 9 Bn.[42] M.G.C.	27th 28th S.A. Fd. Amb.[44]	21st	212th	9th
1918 October (France)	8/B.W., 7/Sea. H., 5/Cam. H.; 26th T.M. Bty.	11/R. Scots, 12/R. Scots, 6/K.O.S.B.; 27th T.M. Bty.	2/R.S.F.,[46] 9/Sco. Rif.,[47] R. Newfdld. Bn.,[48] 28th T.M. Bty.[49]	...	A, B, C; D (H.) / A, B, C; D (H.)	L	LI	...	N.9 / Y.9	9th D.A.C.	63rd 64th 90th	9th	9/Sea. H. (P.)	No. 9 Bn. M.G.C.	27th 28th 2/1/E. Lanc.[50]	21st	212th	9th

NOTES

1 Cyclist Coy. was formed at Aldershot on 1/12/14.

2 Bties. were raised as 6-gun batteries and numbered. By Feb., 1915, all Bdes. were reorganized as 4-battery brigades; the batteries all became 4-gun batteries, and were lettered A, B, C, D in each Brigade.

3 Joined Div. in England, and went to France on 10/5/15 with the Div.

4 The Cos. were numbered 104, 105, 106, and 107 Cos. A.S.C.

5 Bn. left 28th Bde. on 6/5/16 and on 7/5/16 joined 44th Bde., 13th Div., near Bethune. On 11/5/16, 8/ and 10/ Gord. H. were amalgamated and became 8/10/Gord. H. in 44th Bde.

6 Bn. left 27th Bde. on 6/5/16 and on 7/5/16 joined 45th Bde., 15th Div., near Bethune. On 13/5/16, 6/ and 7/R.S.F. were amalgamated and became 6/7/R.S.F. On 21/2/18 6/7/R.S.F. joined 59th Div. as the Pioneer Bn. On 18/6/18 Bn. joined 16th Div. On 20/8/18 Bn. amalgamated with 18/Sco. Rif., and on 2/7/18, 18/Sco. Rif. joined 48th Bde., 16th Div.

7 Bn. was transferred from 27th Bde. to 26th Bde. on 6/5/16.

8 Bde. was broken up and ceased to exist on 6/5/16.

9 Bn. was transferred from 28th Bde. to 27th Bde. on 6/5/16.

10 Bn. was transferred from 28th Bde. to 27th Bde. on 6/5/16.

11 The 2 Bns. were attached to S. African Bde. from 6-14/5/16, and they joined 46th Bde., 15th Div., on 14/5/16. On 16/5/16 10/ and 11/H.L.I. amalgamated and became 10/11/H.L.I.

12 Sqdn. left Cupar on 11/5/15, arrived le Havre on 13/5/15, and concentrated with 9th Div. at St. Omer on 15/5/15. Sqdn. left 9th Div. and joined V Corps Cav. Regt. on 10/5/16.

13 Coy. left the Div. on 26/5/16, and joined II Corps Cyclist Bn.

14 Bde. was reorganized on 21/2/16: D was transferred to LIII; and B (H.)/LIII joined L and became D(H.)/L.

15 Bde. was reorganized on 21/2/16: D was transferred to LIII; and D. (H.)/LIII joined LI and became D (H.)/LI.

16 Bde. was reorganized on 21/2/16: D was transferred to LIII; and C (H.)/LIII joined LII and became D (H.)/LII.

17 LIII(H.) landed in France on 11/5/15 with A (H.), B (H.), C (H.), and D (H.). On 14/8/15 A (H.) and 1 subsecn. of LIII(H.) B.A.C. left 9th Div. and became A (H.)/CXXIX (H.) in 27th Div. On 21/2/16 LIII(H.) was reorganized; B (H.), C (H.), and D (H.) were transferred to L, LII, and LI respectively; and D/L, D/LI, and D/LII joined LIII and became A, B, and C/LIII.

18 Joined Div. in England in Jany., 1915, from 23rd Div., and went to France on 12/5/15, with 9th Div.

19 Attached to Div. from 3/12/14. Bn. became Pioneers, and went to France on 10/5/15, with the Div.

20 Joined 9th Div. on 30/4/15; went to France with Div. and served with Div. until June, 1916. Between 4-11/8/16 Bty. left Div., and on 16/7/16 came under IX Corps.

21 Fd. Ambce. left Div. on 29/5/16; it reached Rouen on 30/5/16.

22 The Bde. M.G. Cos. were formed: 26th by 29/1/16; 27th on 23/12/15; and 28th on 1-3/1/16. On 6/5/16 28th M.G. Coy. was transferred to S. African Bde.

23 The Bde. T.M. Bties. were formed: 26th by 15/5/16; 27th by July, 1916; and S. African by 13/8/16.

24 S. African Bde. H.Q. and 4 Bns. left Alexandria, 13-15/4/16, and disembkd. at Marseille on 20/4/16. Bde. H.Q. reached Hazebrouck on 22/4/16 and reported to 9th Div. The four Bns. arrived in 9th Div. as follows: 3/S.A. and 2/S.A. on 23/4/16; 1/S.A. on 24/4 and 11/5/16; and 4/S.A. on 11/5/16.

25 On 8/9/16 A and B were made up to 6 18-pdrs. each by B/LIII; and C was made up by 1 sec. C/LIII.

26 On 11/9/16 A and B were made up to 6 18-pdrs. each by A/LIII; and C. was made up by 1 sec. C/LIII.

27 In Septr., 1916, B was broken up: 1 sec. made up A to 6 guns, and 1 sec. made up C. In Nov., 1916, 508 (H.) joined LII. On 8/1/17 LII became an A.F.A. Bde.; D. (H.) left LII and R. Sec. made up D/L to 6 hows., and L. Sec. made up D/LI; 1 sec. D (H.)/CLVIII joined and made up 508 (H.) to 6 hows., and 508 (H.) then became D/LII. (On 8/1/17 No. 2 Sec., 9th Div. A.C. became LII A.F.A. B.A.C.) On 15/3/17 122 Bty. joined LII and completed the Bde.

28 LIII was broken up between 8-11/9/16; B and 1/2 C joined L, and A and 1/2 C joined LI, to make up the 18-pdr. batteries in L and LI to 6 guns each.

29 The Medium T.M. Bties. joined by April, 1916.

30 The Heavy T.M. Bty. joined by May, 1916.

31 B.A.C.s were abolished and the D.A.C. was reorganized on 14 and 15/5/16.

32 S.A. Fd. Ambce. reached Abbeville on 11/5/16; and joined 9th Div. on 18/5/16, near Steenwerck.

33 Bn. left 9th Div. on 15/2/18, and joined 97th Bde., 32nd Div., on 17/2/18.

34 Bn. left 9th Div. on 5/2/18 and joined 43rd Bde., 14th Div. On 21/4/18 Bn. rejoined 9th Div., and by 23/4/18 it was posted to S.A. Bde. (Also see n. 47.)

35 Bn. was disbanded between 13-22/2/18 and was drafted to the 1/, 2/, and 4/S.A. Inf. Bns. The surplus went to VII Corps Rft. Camp.

36 On 9/1/17 D/L was made up to 6 hows. by R. Sec., D/LII.

37 On 9/1/17 D/LI amalgamated with L. Sec., D/LII, and the 6-gun how. bty. became D/LI on 10/1/17.

38 On 18/2/18 Z was broken up between X and Y.

39 On 3/2/18 V was transferred to VII Corps Hy. Arty.

40 The M.G. Coy. disembkd. at le Havre on 16/12/16; it joined 9th Div. on 19/12/16 at Montenescourt.

41 Coy. was formed by 23/8/17.

42 S. African Bde. (with T.M. Bty.) left 9th Div. on 13/9/18, and was under VII Corps until 22/9/18. Bde. joined 66th (2/E. Lanc.) Div. on 23/9/18.

43 Bn. was formed on 1/3/18; it consisted of 26th, 27th, 28th, and 197th M.G. Cos.

44 S. African Fd. Amb. left 9th Div. on 22/9/18 and joined 66th (2/E. Lanc.) Div. on same day.

45 Bde. was formed on 11/9/18.

46 Bn. went to France in 1914 with 21st Bde., 7th Div. (with 21st Bde.) was transferred to 30th Div. on 19/12/15; and, on arrival, Bn. joined 90th Bde. On 7/4/18 Bn. left 30th Div. and joined 120th Bde., 40th Div.; on 25/4/18 Bn. left 40th Div. and joined S. African Bde., 9th Div., on 20/4/18. On 13/9/18 Bn. was transferred to 28th Bde.

47 Posted to S. African Bde. on 23/4/18 (see n. 34), Bn. on 13/9/18 was transferred to 28th Bde.

48 Bn. left 88th Bde., 29th Div., on 29/4/18 and joined G.H.Q. Troops. On 13/9/18 Bn. joined 28th Bde.

49 Bty. formed, and joined 28th Bde., on 11/9/18.

50 Fd. Amb. served with 66th (2/E. Lanc.) Div. until 22/6/18, and it was then attached to 27th (Am.) Div. until it joined 9th Div. on 26/9/18.

9TH (SCOTTISH) DIVISION

FORMATION, BATTLES, AND ENGAGEMENTS

This New Army Division had no existence before the outbreak of the Great War.

Great Britain declared war on Germany at 11 p.m. on Tuesday, the 4th August 1914, and on the 5th August Field-Marshal Earl Kitchener of Khartoum was appointed Secretary of State for War. On the 6th August Parliament sanctioned an increase of 500,000 men for the Regular Army, and a proclamation headed : " Your King and Country need you. A Call to Arms," was published on the 11th August (see page 2). This proclamation asked for an immediate addition of a hundred thousand men to the Regular Army, and the men were required to enlist for 3 years or the duration of the War. Army Order No. 324, issued on the 21st August 1914, and amended by Army Order No. 382 of the 11th September authorized the addition of six divisions (9th–14th) and Army Troops to the Regular Army.* This augmentation became the First New Army (see Appendix I), and the 9th (Scottish) Division was formed towards the end of August, 1914.

After enlistment the men went to their depôts ; they were then sent on to training camps in the Salisbury Training Centre, and in September the 9th Division assembled around Bordon. At first the scarcity of arms, munitions, and equipment added to the difficulties of training ; but as the deficiencies were overcome intensive training for war began and in due course unit training was followed by divisional field manoeuvres. On the 5th May 1915, Field-Marshal Earl Kitchener inspected the 9th Division on Ludshott Common, and on the 7th May embarkation orders were received. The Division crossed to France between Sunday the 9th and Wednesday the 12th May, and by noon on Saturday the 15th May the Division was concentrated in billets to the south-west of St. Omer.

Throughout the remainder of the Great War the 9th Division served on the Western Front in France and Belgium and was engaged in the following operations :—

1915

25–29 September ...	...	**Battle of Loos** [I Corps, First Army].

1916

BATTLES OF THE SOMME

1–13 July ...	...	...	**Battle of Albert** (In Corps Reserve on 1/7) [XIII Corps, Fourth Army].
3 July ...	...	...	**Capture of Bernafay Wood** (27th Bde.).
14 July ...	...	...	**Battle of Bazentin Ridge** [XIII Corps, Fourth Army].
14–18 July ...	...	...	**Attack of Longueval** (26th and S.A. Bdes.).
15–19 July ...	...	...	**Battle of Delville Wood** [XIII Corps, Fourth Army].
10–18 October	...	...	**Battle of the Transloy Ridges** [III Corps, Fourth Army].
12–18 October	...	...	**Attacks on the Butte de Warlencourt.**

1917

9–15 April ; and 30 April–10 May			**BATTLES OF ARRAS.**
9–14 April ...	...	...	**First Battle of the Scarpe** [XVII Corps, Third Army].
3 and 4 May	...	...	**Third Battle of the Scarpe** [XVII Corps, Third Army].
18–23 Sept. ; and 11–25 Oct.			**BATTLES OF YPRES.**
20–23 September	...	...	**Battle of the Menin Road Ridge** [V Corps, Fifth Army].
12 October ...	...	...	**First Battle of Passchendaele** [XVIII Corps, Fifth Army].
30 December	...	...	**Welch Ridge** (10/A. and S.H., 26th Bde.) [VII Corps, Fifth Army].

---

* Army Order No. 324 of 21/8/14 numbered the six divisions of the First New Army : 8th (Light)–13th (Western) ; but Army Order No. 382 of 11/9/14 directed that the 8th (Light) Division was to be renumbered 14th (Light) Division. In consequence of Army Order No. 382 the Divisions of the First New Army were the 9th (Scottish)–14th (Light) ; in this way the 9th (Scottish) Division became the senior New Army Division.

1918

21–27 March	**FIRST BATTLES OF THE SOMME.**
21–23 March	**Battle of St. Quentin** [VII Corps, Fifth Army].
24 and 25 March	**First Battle of Bapaume** [VII Corps, Third Army].

BATTLES OF THE LYS

10 and 11 April	**Battle of Messines** [IX Corps, Second Army].
13–15 April	**Battle of Bailleul** [XXII Corps, Second Army].
17–19 April	**First Battle of Kemmel Ridge** [XXII Corps, Second Army].
25 and 26 April	**Second Battle of Kemmel Ridge** [XXII Corps, Second Army].
29 April	**Battle of the Scherpenberg** (S. African Bde., under 49th Div.) [XXII Corps, Second Army].

19 July	**Capture of Meteren** [XV Corps, Second Army].

THE ADVANCE TO VICTORY

18 August	**Capture of Hoegenacker Ridge** [XV Corps, Second Army].

THE FINAL ADVANCE IN FLANDERS

28 Sept.–2 Oct.	**Battle of Ypres** [II Corps, Second Army].
14–19 October	**Battle of Courtrai** [II Corps, Second Army].
25 October	**Ooteghem** [II Corps, Second Army].

On the 26th and 27th October the 9th Division was relieved by the 31st Division, and the 9th Division then moved back to reorganize in billets in the Lys valley near Harlebeke. On the 5th November H.M. the King of the Belgians inspected the 9th Division on the ex-German aerodrome near Harlebeke. On the 10th the Division moved into Harlebeke and Cuerne, and it was occupying the same billets when hostilities ceased at 11 a.m. on the 11th November.

On the 12th November the Division was informed that it would advance to the Rhine. On the 14th the advance began, and on the 23rd and 24th November divisional head-quarters occupied Mont St. Jean. On the 4th December the Division entered Germany and on the 13th the Rhine was crossed at Mulheim. The 9th Division then settled down in billets and was responsible for the left divisional sector of the Cologne bridgehead.

In 1919 demobilization began, and education and recreational training were under-taken. On the 14th February the Division was warned that a Lowland Division would be formed from the 9th Division and the existing battalions would be replaced by battalions from other divisions. On the 22nd February the moves began ; and on the 16th March 1919, the history of the 9th (Scottish) Division came to an end when the Division was re-named Lowland Division. During the Great War the 9th (Scottish) Division lost 52,055 killed, wounded, and missing.

9

10TH (IRISH) DIVISION

G.O.C.

24 August, 1914	Lieut.-General SIR B. T. MAHON.
16 August, 1915	Br.-Gen. F. F. HILL (acting).
19 August, 1915	Major-General W. E. PEYTON.
23 August, 1915	Lieut.-General SIR B. T. MAHON.
18 November, 1915	Br.-Gen. L. L. NICOL (acting).
20 December, 1915	Major-General J. R. LONGLEY.
12 July, 1916	Br.-Gen. L. L. NICOL (acting).
24 September, 1916	Major-General J. R. LONGLEY.
11 June, 1918	Br.-Gen. E. M. MORRIS (acting).
18 August, 1918	Major-General J. R. LONGLEY.

G.S.O. 1.

25 Aug., 1914...Lt.-Col. J. G. KING-KING (tempy.).
14 Jan., 1915...Lt.-Col. J. G. KING-KING.
5 Sept., 1915...Lt.-Col. G. E. LEMON.
29 Dec., 1915...Lt.-Col. H. L. KNIGHT.
16 June, 1917...Lt.-Col. H. F. SALT.
18 Feb., 1918...Lt.-Col. W. E. DAVIES.

A.-A. and Q.-M.-G.

22 Aug., 1914...Captain C. E. HOLLINS (acting).
23 Aug., 1914...Colonel D. SAPTE.
26 Jan., 1916...Lt.-Col. C. W. PEARLESS.
24 Jan., 1918...Lt.-Col. E. R. O'HARA.

B.-G., R.A.

8 Oct., 1914...Br.-Gen. A. J. ABDY.
11 Feb., 1915...Br.-Gen. G. S. DUFFUS (sick, 26/10/15).
26 Oct., 1915...Lt.-Col. F. E. L. BARKER (acting).
4 Nov., 1915...Br.-Gen. F. B. JOHNSTONE.
25 Nov., 1915...Lt.-Col. F. E. L. BARKER (acting).
29 Nov., 1915 to 14 Dec., 1915...Br.-Gen. F. E. L. BARKER (to B.-G., R.A., 13th Div.).

[11 Oct.,1915]...Br.-Gen. A. B. HELYAR (from B.-G., R.A., 13th Div.).*
26 Feb., 1916...Br.-Gen. W. B. EMERY.
11 June, 1918...Lt.-Col. A. ROSS HUDSON (acting).
20 Aug., 1918...Br.-Gen. W. B. EMERY.

C.R.E.

22 Sept., 1914...Lt.-Col. F. K. FAIR.
15 Jan., 1916...Major A. S. HOLME (acting).
11 Feb., 1916...Lt.-Col. E. M. S. CHARLES.

---

* Br.-Gen. A. B. Helyar had been B.-G., R.A., 13th Division, from 12/10/14. 13th Div. R.A. Hd. Qrs. became 10th Div. R.A. Hd. Qrs. on 14/12/15.

29th BDE.

26 Aug., '14...Br.-Gen. R. J. COOPER
(wounded, 10/8/15).
11 Aug., '15...Lt.-Col. H. F. N. JOURDAIN
(acting).
13 Aug., '15...Lt.-Col. Q. G. K. AGNEW
(acting).
10 Sept., '15...Lt.-Col. H. F. N. JOURDAIN
(acting).
22 Sept., '15...Br.-Gen. R. S. VANDELEUR
(sick, 8/6/17).
8 June, '17...Lt.-Col. J. CRASKE
(acting).
28 July, '17...Br.-Gen. R. S. VANDELEUR.
9 June, '18...Lt.-Col. E. H. WILDBLOOD
(acting).
12 June, '18...Br.-Gen. C. L. SMITH, V.C.
12 June, '18...Lt.-Col. E. H. WILDBLOOD
(acting).
21 Aug., '18...Br.-Gen. C. L. SMITH, V.C.

30th BDE.

26 Aug., '14...Colonel L. L. NICOL.
24 Sept., '14...Br.-Gen. L. L. NICOL.
18 Nov., '15...Lt.-Col. P. G. A. COX
(acting).
20 Dec., '15...Br.-Gen. L. L. NICOL.
12 July, '16...Lt.-Col. V. T. WARSHIP
(acting).
9 Aug., '16...Br.-Gen. A. D.
MACPHERSON.
28 Feb., '17...Lt.-Col. P. G. A. COX
(acting).
23 April, '17...Br.-Gen. A. D.
MACPHERSON (sick, 7/5/17).
7 May, '17...Lt.-Col. F. A. GREER
(tempy.).
6 July, '17...Br.-Gen. F. A. GREER.

31st BDE.

26 Aug., '14...Br.-Gen. F. F. HILL.
16 Aug., '15...Lt.-Col. M. J. W. PIKE (acting).
19 Aug., '15...Br.-Gen. F. F. HILL (sick, 21/8/15).
21 Aug., '15...Lt.-Col. M. J. W. PIKE (acting).
6 Sept., '15...Br.-Gen. J. G. KING-KING.
30 Dec., '15...Br.-Gen. E. M. MORRIS.
11 June, '18...Br.-Gen. W. B. EMERY (tempy.).
20 Aug., '18...Lt.-Col. A. V. ALEXANDER (acting).
30 Aug., '18...Br.-Gen. E. M. MORRIS.

GENERAL NOTES

The following Units also served with the 10th (Irish) Division :—

MOUNTED TROOPS :—1 Sqdn., South Irish Horse, from May–July, 1915, at Basingstoke. Sqdn. left when 10th Division embkd. for Gallipoli.

ARTILLERY :—LVIII Bde., R.F.A. (11th Div. Arty.), served under 10th Division Artillery at Suvla from 16/8–18/12/15, covering the Left Flank.

10th Heavy Battery (4, 60-pdrs.), joined 10th Div. from Woolwich in March, 1915. In May the Division moved to England and the Hy. Bty. was stationed at Basingstoke. The Hy. Bty. embkd. at Devonport on 5/7/15, landed at Alexandria on 19/7/15, re-embkd. at Alexandria on 22/7 and 3/8/15, and on 5/8/15 the Hy. Bty. collected at Mudros. On 9 and 10/8/15 the Hy. Bty. disembkd. at Suvla and was in action under 11th Div. covering the Right Flank at Suvla until 1–6/12/15, when the Hy. Bty. re-embkd. at Suvla and went to Mudros. The Hy. Bty. reached Alexandria on 3/1/16. On 25/2/16 the Hy. Bty. moved to Port Said and joined Canal Defence Force. The Hy. Bty. left Canal on 30/11/16, joined XCVI H.A. Group on 3/4/17, was transferred on 6/9/17 to C H.A. Group, and on 29/11/17 10th Hy. Bty. rejoined XCVI H.A. Group. (In April, 1918, XCVI H.A. Group became XCVI Bde., R.G.A.)

15th Heavy Battery (4, 60-pdrs.), was raised for 15th Div. ; but on 10/8/15 at Suvla the Hy. Bty. was attached to 10th Div. and the Hy. Bty. was in action covering the Left Flank. From 1/10/15, after 10th Div. left Suvla, 15th Hy. Bty. remained in action at Suvla under B.G., R.A., 10th Div., until 15–19/12/15 when 15th Hy. Bty. re-embkd. The Hy. Bty. reached Alexandria on 21/1/16 and rejoined XX H.A. Group. The Hy. Bty. (in XX H.A.G.) went to el Ferdan on 24/2/16. On 14/5/16 XX H.A. Group H.Q. left for Macedonia, disembkg. at Salonika on 9/6/16 ; but 15th Hy. Bty. remained in Canal Defences and joined XCVI H.A. Group on 3/4/17. On 12/12/17 15th Hy. Bty. joined C H.A. Group in Palestine. (On 25/4/18 C H.A. Group became C Bde., R.G.A.)

2nd Mountain Battery (6, 2·75″ Guns), disembkd. at Salonika on 29/12/15 (from France), and Bty. was attached to 10th Div. 30/12/15–7/2/16. On 7/2/16 Bty. was transferred to 27th Div. On 18/6/16 2nd Mtn. Bty. joined the re-formed III Mtn. Arty. Bde.

Hong Kong and Singapore Mountain Battery, was attached from 1/9–26/10/18.

IV (Highland) Mtn. Bde. (Argyllshire Mtn. Bty. and Ross and Cromarty Mtn. Bty.), went overseas with 29th Div. From 13/8/15 Bde. was in action at Suvla under 10th Div. (Argyllshire Mtn. Bty. from 8/8/15). After 1/10/15, when 10th Div. left Suvla, the Mtn. Bde. remained in action at Suvla under B.G., R.A., 10th Div. until the evacuation in Dec., 1915. Mtn. Bde. returned to Egypt in Dec., 1915 ; embkd. on 6/8/16 at Alexandria (for Macedonia), and disembkd. at Salonika on 10/8/16.

Divnl. Trench Mortar Bty., was formed on 17/10/17 from the Inf. Bde. T.M. Bties. The Divnl. T.M. Bty. was broken up on 9/6/18.

ENGINEERS :—133rd Fortress Coy., was attached to 10th Div. from 27–29/7/15.

INFANTRY :—38/R.F. Bn. mobilized at Plymouth on 20/1/18, embkd. at Southampton on 5/2/18, disembkd. at Cherbourg on 6/2/18, embkd. at Taranto on 25/2/18, and disembkd. at Alexandria on 1/3/18. Bn. was attached to 31st Bde., 10th Div. (in Palestine) from 11/6–17/7/18 ; Bn. was then transferred to 60th Div. On 13/8/18 Bn. was transferred to Aus. Mtd. Div.

MACHINE-GUN UNIT :—13th Motor-Machine-Gun Battery, served with 10th Div. in England from 4/5/15 ; but M.G. Bty. did not accompany 10th Div. overseas in July, 1915.

OTHER UNITS :—21st Sanitary Section, joined 10th Div. in England ; went overseas with 10th Div. in July, 1915 disembkd. at Mudros on 29/7/15, and on 31/7/15 the Section was transferred to I.G.C.

52nd Sanitary Section, went overseas with 52nd (Lowland) Div. and landed at Mudros on 27/7/15. In Oct., 1915 the Section sailed for Macedonia and (on landing at Salonika) was attached to 10th Div. The Section (with 10th Div.) returned to Alexandria on 19/10/17, and on 22/10/17 the Section rejoined 52nd (Lowland) Div.

18th Sanitary Section, joined 52nd (Lowland) Div. at Mudros in Oct., 1915. The Section served with 52nd Div. until 24/10/17 ; the Section was then transferred to 10th Div., and the Section served with the 10th Div. for the remainder of the War.

10th Division Motor Ambce. Workshop, joined 10th Div. in England and served with Div. until July, 1915 when Div. embkd. for Gallipoli. The Workshop remained in England with 10th Div. Train (see note 4).

10TH (IRISH) DIVISION

Dates	INFANTRY Brigades	Battalions and attached Units	Mounted Troops	ARTILLERY — Field Artillery Brigades	Field Artillery Batteries	Bde. Ammn. Colns.	Trench Mortar Bties. Medium	Heavy	Divnl. Ammn. Coln.	Engineers Field Cos.	Signal Service Divnl. Signal Coy.	Pioneers	M.G. Units	Field Ambulances	Mobile Vety. Secn.	Divnl. Emplnt. Coy.	Divnl. Train
1914 October (Ireland)	29th 30th 31st	5/R. Ir. Regt.,[11] 6/R. Ir. Rif., 5/Conn. Rang., 6/Leins. 6/R.M.F., 7/R.M.F., 6/R.D.F., 7/R.D.F. 5/R. Innis. F., 6/R. Innis. F., 5/R. Ir. F., 6/R. Ir. F.	10th Div. Cyclist Coy.[1]	LIV[2] LV[2] LVI[2] LVII (H.)[2]	172, 173, 174 175, 176, 177 178, 179, 180 181 (H.), 182 (H.), 183 (H.)	LIV B.A.C. LV B.A.C. LVI B.A.C. LVII (H.) B.A.C.	...	...	10th D.A.C.[3]	65th 66th	10th	...	...	30th 31st 32nd	25th	...	10th[4]
1915 August (Gallipoli)	29th 30th 31st	10/Hants.,[5] 6/R. Ir. Rif., 6/Leins. 6/R.M.F., 7/R.M.F., 6/R.D.F., 7/R.D.F. 5/R. Innis. F., 6/R. Innis. F., 5/R. Ir. F., 6/R. Ir. F.	10th Div. Cyclist Coy.	LIV[2] ; [6] LV[2] ; [7] LVI[2] ; [8] LVII (H.)[2] ; [9]	A, B, C, D A, B, C, D A, B, C, D A (H.), B (H.), C (H.), D (H.)	LIV B.A.C. LV B.A.C. LVI B.A.C. LVII (H.) B.A.C.	...	...	...[3]	65th 66th 85th[10]	10th	5/R. Ir. Regt. (P.)[11]	...	30th 31st 32nd	25th	...	...[4]
1916 September (Macedonia)	29th 30th 31st	10/Hants.,[12] 6/R. Ir. Rif., 5/Conn. Rang., 6/Leins. ; 29th Bde. M.G. Coy.[13] 6/R.M.F., 7/R.M.F.,[14] 6/R.D.F., 7/R.D.F. ; 30th Bde. M.G. Coy.[13] 5/R. Innis. F., 6/R. Innis. F., 5/R. Ir. F., 6/R. Ir. F.[15] ; 31st Bde. M.G. Coy.[13]	10th Div. Cyclist Coy.[16]	LIV[6] ; [17] LVII[18] LXVIII[19]	A, B, C A, B, C ; D (H.) A, B, C ; D (H.)	LIV B.A.C. LVII B.A.C. LXVII B.A.C. LXVIII B.A.C.	...	...	10th D.A.C. [20]	65th 66th 85th	10th	5/R. Ir. Regt. (P.)	...	30th 31st 32nd	25th	...	10th[21]
1917 June (Macedonia)	29th 30th 31st	6/R. Ir. Rif., 5/Conn. Rang., 1/Leins.,[22] 6/Leins. ; 29th M.G. Coy.; 29th T.M. Bty.[23] ; S.A. Sec.[24] 1/R. Ir. Regt.,[25] 6/R.M.F., 6/R.D.F., 7/R.D.F. ; 30th M.G. Coy.; 30th T.M. Bty.[23] ; S.A. Sec.[24] 5/R. Innis. F., 6/R. Innis. F., 2/R. Ir. F.,[26] 5/R. Ir. F., 31st M.G. Coy.; 31st T.M. Bty.[23] ; S.A. Sec.[24]	...	LIV[27] ; [28] LVII[17] ; [28] LXVIII[18]	A, B, C A, B ; D (H.)[41] A, B ; D (H.)[40] A, B ; D (H.)[40]	LIV B.A.C.[27] LVII B.A.C.[28] LXVII B.A.C.[29] LXVIII B.A.C.[29]	...	...	10th D.A.C. [29]	65th 66th 85th	10th	5/R. Ir. Regt. (P.)	...	30th 31st 32nd	25th	...	10th[30]

Date	Bde.	Battalions	Artillery Bdes.	Batteries	D.A.C.	Field Ambulances	Pioneers	Div. units	M.G.	C.F.A.			
1917 October (Palestine)	29th	6/R. Ir. Rif.,[31] 1/Leins.,[32] 5/Conn. Rang.,[32] 1/Leins.,[33] 6/Leins.,[33] 29th M.G. Coy.,[57] 29th T.M. Bty.	LXVII ...... LXVIII ...... CCLXIII[41]	A, B; C (H.)[40]	10th D.A.C.	65th[42] 66th 85th	5/R. Ir. Regt. (P.)[43]	10th	...	30th[44] 31st[44] 32nd[44]	25th	...	10th
	30th	1/R. Ir. Regt.,[34] 6/R.M.F.,[34] 6/R.D.F.,[34] 7/R.D.F.,[35] 30th M.G. Coy.,[57] 30th T.M. Bty.		A, B; C (H.)[40]									
	31st	5/R. Innis. F.,[37] 6/R. Innis. F.,[38] 2/R. Ir. F.,[39] 5/R. Ir. F.,[39] 31st M.G. Coy.,[57] 31st T.M. Bty.		73; C (H.)[40]									
1918 August (Palestine)	29th	1/Leins., 1/54/Sikhs,[45] Grenadiers,[46] 2/151/Inf.;[47] 29th T.M. Bty.	LXVII ...... LXVIII CCLXIII	A, B; C (H.)	10th D.A.C.	86th 85th 18th Coy.,[55] 3/S. & M.	2/155 (P.)[56]	10th	No. 10 Bn., M.G.C.[57]	154 C.F.A.[58] 165 C.F.A.[59] 166 C.F.A.[60]	25th	...	10th
	30th	1/R. Ir. Regt.,[48] 38/Dogras,[48] 46/Punjabis,[49] 1/Kashmir Rif.;[50] 30th T.M. Bty.		A, B; C (H.)									
	31st	2/R. Ir. F., 2/42/Deoli,[51] 74/Punjabis,[52] 2/101/Grenadiers,[53] 31st T.M. Bty.		75,[54] 494,[41] C (H.)									

NOTES

1 The Cyclist Coy. was formed late in 1914; it went to Gallipoli with the 10th Div.

2 Btes. were all raised on the 6-gun basis and numbered. By Feb., 1915, all Bdes. were reorganized on 4-battery Bdes. the Btes. all became 4-gun batteries and were lettered A, B, C, D in each Bde.

3 The D.A.C. did not go overseas with the 10th Div.

4 The Train did not go overseas with the 10th Div. Train served overseas with 22nd Div.; it consisted of 108, 109, 110, and 111 Cos., A.S.C.

5 Bn. was formed after the outbreak of the Great War; and was attached to 10th Div., in Ireland, as Army Troops. Bn. joined 29th Bde., before embkn., to replace 5/R. Ir. Regt. (see n. 11).

6 LIV Bde. never landed in Gallipoli. Bde. embkd. at Devonport on 7/7/15, disembkd. at Alexandria on 21/7/15, embkd. at Alexandria on 9/8/15, reached Mudros on 13/8/15, returned to Alexandria on 24/8/15, left Alexandria on 23/8/15, reached Mudros on 1/9/15, and disembkd. at Mudros on 11/9/15. Bde. embkd. at Mudros on 5/10/15 and disembkd. at Salonika on 10/10/15. LIV B.A.C. arrd. on 22/10/15. On 20/7/16 D/LIV left and became A/LVII.

7 Bde. embkd. at Devonport on 7/7/15, disembkd. at Alexandria on 19/7/15, embkd. at Alexandria on 16/8/15, disembkd. at Mudros on 28/8/15, and landed at Suvla on 30/8/15. Bde. reached Mudros again on 22/12/15, and disembkd. at Alexandria on 3/1/16. LIV now left 10th Div.; joined 13th Div., and went with 13th Div. to Mesopotamia. LIV landed near Basra on 17/3/16.

8 Bde. embkd. at Devonport on 8/7/15, disembkd. at Alexandria on 20/7/15, embkd. at Alexandria on 9/8/15, reached Mudros on 13/8/15; and C & D landed at Helles on 23/8/15 and A & B followed on 17/10/15. Bde. left Helles and reached Mudros on 6/11/16. LVI left 10th Div. and returned to Egypt, disembarking at Alexandria on 14/1/16. On 30/1/16 LVI reached Port Said. Bde. joined 13th Div. in Feb., 1916, and went with 13th Div. to Mesopotamia in Feb., 1916.

9 Bde. embkd. at Southampton on 2/8/15, disembkd. at le Havre on 3/8/15, embkd. at Marseille on 5/8/15, and A (H.) and D (H.) landed at Suvla on 16/8/15. A and D were in action at Suvla until they re-embkd., 8–15/12/15. A (H.) and D (H.) then left LVII (H.) and the 10th Div. On 16/12/15 A (H.) and D (H.) landed at Helles and they were in action at Helles until they embkd. and left Helles on 30 and 31/12/15. Bde. H.Q. and B (H.), C (H.), and B.A.C. remained at Mudros, and went to Macedonia in Dec., 1915, with 10th Div., disembkg. at Salonika on 13/12/15. On 19/5/16 A (H.)/CXVII (H.) (from 26th Div.) joined LVII (H.) and became A (H.)/LVII (H.). Between 20–23/7/16 A (H.)/LVII became D (H.)/LXVII; B (H.)/LVII became D (H.)/LXVIII; and C (H.)/LVII became D (H.)/LVII; also D/LIV, D/LXVII, and D/LXVIII joined and became A, B, and C/LVII.

10 Fd. Coy. joined Div. in England, in Jan., 1915, from 21st Div.; and Fd. Coy. landed at Suvla on 7/8/15.

11 Bn. (from 29th Bde.) became Pioneer Bn. in England, and Bn. landed on 7/8/15.

12 On 2/11/16 Bn. was transferred to 82nd Bde., 27th Div.

13 The M.G. Cos. were formed: 29th and 30th on 10/5/16; and 31st on 11/5/16.

14 On 3/11/16 Bn. was absorbed by 6/R.M.F.

15 On 2/11/16 Bn. was absorbed by 5/R. Ir. F.

16 On 7/12/16 Cyclist Coy. joined XVI Corps Cyclist Bn.

17 On 27/12/16 C was broken up; 1 sec. joined A and 1 sec. joined B, completing A and B to 6 guns each.

18 LXVII Bde. was formed in Sept., 1914, for 13th Div. and Bde. concentrated with 13th Div. at Deepcut in Feb., 1915. Bde. embkd. on 15/6/15 and disembkd. at Alexandria on 29/6/15. On 9/10/15 Bde. re-embkd. at Alexandria, disembkd. at Salonika on 13–17/10/15, and joined 10th Div. On 23/7/16 D Bty. left Bde. and became B/LVII; and A (H.)/LVII joined Bde. and became D (H.)/LXVII. On 26/12/16 B was divided between A and C, making each up to 6 guns, and C then became B.

19 LXVIII was formed in Sept., 1914, for 13th Div. Bde. concentrated with 13th Div. at Deepcut in Feb., 1915. Bde. embkd. on 18/6/15 and disembkd. at Alexandria on 4/7/15. On 10/10/15 Bde. re-embkd. at Alexandria, disembkd. at Salonika on 13–15/10/15 Bde. and joined 10th Div. On 31/7–2/8/16 D Bty. left Bde. and became C/LVII, and B (H.)/LVII joined Bde. and became D (H.)/LXVIII. On 27–29/12/16 A was divided between B and C, making each up to 6 guns, and C then became A.

20 Formed for 29th Div.; D.A.C. embkd. with 29th Div. but was left in Egypt. In Oct., 1915, D.A.C. was transferred to 10th Div., embkd. for Salonika. On 23/10/15, D.A.C. lost 100 men and all animals and equipt. Animals, vehicles, and equipt. were made up from 42nd D.A.C. (in Egypt), and deficiency in personnel was made up from B.A.C.s. On 4/3/16 29th D.A.C. became 10th D.A.C.

21 Train (formed from Lowland Div. T. and S. Coln.) went to Egypt with 52nd (Lowland) Div. In Oct., 1915, Train embkd. for Salonika, disembkd. on 19 and 20/10/15, and became 10th Div. Train on 22/10/15. Train consisted of 475, 476, 477, and 478 Cos., A.S.C.

22 Bn. joined on 2/11/16, from 82nd Div.

23 T.M. Btes. were formed as follows:—No. 7 Stokes Mortar Bty. was formed on 2/10/16 and attached to 29th Bde. it became 29th T.M. Bty. on 8/12/16; No. 8 Stokes Mortar Bty. was formed on 28/9/16 and attached to 30th Bde., it became 30th T.M. Bty. on 8/12/16; 31st T.M. Bty. was formed on 17/10/16.

24 S.A. Secs. were attached to Inf. Bdes.: 29th by 13/9/16; 30th by 24/10/16; and 31st by 9/10/16. At Moascar (Egypt), on 25/9/17, 29th, 30th, and 31st Bde. S.A. Secs. rejoined 10th D.A.C.

25 Bn. joined on 3/11/16, from 82nd Bde., 27th Div.

26 Bn. joined on 2/11/16, from 82nd Bde., 27th Div.

27 Bde. (A, B, C Batteries, 4 guns each) and B.A.C. was transferred on 29/8/17 to 28th Div. Between 9–27/10/19 Bde. was absorbed by XCVIII Bde. (in 28th Div.).

[TURN OVER]

NOTES—contd.

28 Bde. and B.A.C. left 10th Div. on 28/8/17 and came under XII Corps. In Sept., 1917, LVII and B.A.C. joined 26th Div.

29 On 25/9/17 D.A.C. was reformed at Moascar (Egypt). D.A.C. was made up by LXVII and LXVIII B.A.C.s, 2 other sections, and the 3 Bde. S.A. Secs. (n. 24).

30 In Oct., 1916, the Train was organized in Wheel and Pack Echelons. Wheel Cos. retained their numbers (n. 21), but on 31/10/16 the 4 Pack Cos. were numbered 840, 841, 842, and 843. On 1 and 2/9/17, the Train was reorganized in 4 Wheel Cos. only, numbered, as before: 475, 476, 477, and 478.

31 Bn. was disbanded and drafted on 15/5/18.

32 Bn. left 10th Div. on 29/4/18, embkd. at Port Said on 23/5/18, disembkd. at Marseille on 1/6/18, joined 107th Bde., 66th Div., on 22/7/18, and Bn. was transferred to 199th Bde., 66th Div. on 28/8/18.

33 Bn. left 10th Div. on 2/5/18, embkd. at Port Said on 23/5/18, disembkd. at Marseille on 1/6/18, and joined 198th Bde., 66th Div., on 20/7/18. On 12/9/18 Bn. was disbanded and drafted.

34 Bn. left 10th Div. on 30/4/18, embkd. at Alexandria on 23/5/18, disembkd. at Marseille on 1/6/18, and on 5/6/18 Bn. was absorbed by 2/R.M.F. in 94th Bde., 31st Div. On 15/7/18 2/R.M.F. joined 160th Bde., 50th Div.

35 Bn. left 10th Div. on 27/5/18, embkd. at Alexandria on 3/7/18, disembkd. at Taranto on 8/7/18, joined 197th Bde., 66th Div., on 21/7/18, and Bn. was transferred to 198th Bde., 66th Div., on 10/9/18.

36 Bn. left 10th Div. on 30/4/18, embkd. at Alexandria on 23/5/18, disembkd. at Marseille on 1/6/18, and on 6/6/18 Bn. was absorbed by 2/R.D.F. in 94th Bde. 31st Div. On 15/7/18, 2/R.D.F. joined 149th Bde., 50th Div.

37 Bn. left 10th Div. on 28/5/18, embkd. at Alexandria on 17/6/18, disembkd. at Taranto on 22/6/18, and joined 198th Bde., 66th Div., at Abancourt on 19/7/18.

38 Bn. left 10th Div. on 2/5/18, embkd. at Port Said on 23/5/18 disembkd. at Marseille on 1/6/18, and on 16/7/18 Bn. joined 151st Bde., 50th Div.

39 Bn. left 10th Div. on 30/4/18, embkd. at Port Said on 18/5/18, disembkd. at Marseille on 27/5/18, and on 24/8/18 Bn. joined 48th Bde., 16th Div. On 27/8/18 Bn. absorbed 11/R. Ir. F.

40 By 3/10/17 the lettering of the howitzer batteries in LXVII and LXVIII was changed from 2 (H.) to C (H.).

41 Bde. was formed at Moascar on 27/9/17. On 11/10/17 CCLXIII joined 10th Div. at Rafa, and on the same day D (H.)/LVII joined from Alexandria and became C (H.)/CCLXIII. On 15/3/18, 424 joined CCLXIII at Nabi Eyub.

42 Fd. Coy. joined 3rd (Lahore) Div. between 14-20/7/18.

43 Pioneer Bn. left 10th Div. on 1/4/18, embkd. (with 52nd Div.) at Alexandria on 10/4/18, disembkd. at Marseille on 17/4/18, and on 14/7/18 Bn. joined 50th Div. as Pioneer Bn.

44 On the Indianization of the 10th Div. the 3 Fd. Ambces. handed over transport, equipt., and personnel to 154 C.F.A., 166 C.F.A., and 105 C.F.A., between 17 to 19/5/18; and the remdr. of 30, 31, and 32 Fd. Ambces. left for the Base on 20/5/18.

45 Bn. mobd. at Nowshera on 21/1/18, embkd. at Karachi on 17/2/18, disembkd. at Suez on 1/3/18, and went to Tell el Kebir. Bn. joined 29th Bde. on 27/4/18.

46 On 4/9/16, 101/Grendrs. disembkd. at Suez from East Africa and joined 29th Ind. Inf. Bde. in Suez Canal Defences. 2/101/Grendrs. was formed in Feb., 1917 (n. 53), and henceforward 101/Grendrs. was known as 1/101/Grendrs. On 10/4/17 Bn. was transferred to 49th Ind. Inf. Bde. (Br.-Gen. E. R. B. Murray) and joined Bde. at Kubri. On 18/1/18 Bn. was transferred to 20th Ind. Inf. Bde. at Gaza, and on 30/4/18 1/101/Grendrs. joined 29th Bde., 10th Div.

47 On 30/5/18 Bn. was formed near Jaffa from Cos. of 51/ and 53/Sikhs and 56/Punjabis. (Coy. of 54/Sikhs joined on 10/6/18.). On 10/6/18 Bn. joined 29th Bde.

48 Bn. (from Aden) disembkd. at Suez on 10/2/18 and went to Tell el Kebir. On 29/4/18 Bn. joined 30th Bde.

49 Bn. embkd. at Karachi on 19/2/18, disembkd. at Suez on 4/3/18, and went to Tell el Kebir. On 25/5/18 Bn. joined 30th Bde.

50 Bn. embkd. at Karachi on 5/2/18, re-embkd. on 11/2/18, disembkd. at Suez on 23/2/18, and went to Tell el Kebir. On 30/4/18 Bn. joined 30th Bde.

51 Bn. mobd. at Sibi on 12/2/18, embkd. at Karachi on 13/5/18, disembkd. at Suez on 22/5/18, and went to Tell el Kebir. Bn. joined 10th Div. on 24/6/18, and joined 31st Bde. on 18/7/18.

52 Bn. (from Bannu) embkd. at Karachi on 10/2/18, disembkd. at Suez on 25/2/18, and went to Tell el Kebir. On 29/4/18 Bn. joined 31st Bde.

53 Between 3-28/2/17 Bn. was formed near Suez; Bn. was made up partly from a draft which arrived from India on 3/2/17, and partly from a draft furnished by 1/101/Grendrs. On formation 2/101/Grendrs. joined 29th Ind. Inf. Bde. On 10/4/17 Bn. was transferred to 49th Ind. Inf. Bde. and joined Bde. at Kubri. On 19/1/18 Bn. was transferred to 20th Ind. Inf. Bde. and joined Bde. at Gaza. On 5/4/18 Bn. was attached to Impl. Service Cav. Bde. at Gaza; and on 1/5/18, 2/101/Grendrs. joined 31st Bde., 10th Div.

54 75 was attached to D.M.C. from 1/9-10/10/18.

55 Coy. was transferred from 3rd (Lahore) Division and joined 10th Div. between 10-17/7/18.

56 Bn. was formed on 12 and 13/6/18 from A Coy. 121 (P.), W. Coy., 1/23/Sikh (P.), C. Coy., 2/32/Sikh (P.), and A Coy., 2/23/Sikh (P.). Pioneer Bn. served with 60th Div. from 28/6-19/7/18, and joined 10th Div. on 19/7/18. Pioneer Bn. was attached to 53rd Div. from 31/8/18 until after the Breakthrough. In Oct., 1918, the Bn. moved forward and was employed on the Damascus Road near Tiberias.

57 Bn. was formed on 7/5/18; it was composed of 29th, 30th, and 31st M.G. Cos.

58 Fd. Ambce. (from Meerut) embkd. at Karachi on 5/3/18, disembkd. at Suez on 17/3/18, and went to Tell el Kebir. Fd. Ambce. joined 10th Div. on 17/5/18, and it was converted to C.F.A. on same day.

59 On 17/5/18 Fd. Ambce. joined 10th Div., and it was converted to C.F.A. on 18/5/18.

60 On 13/5/18 Fd. Ambce. joined 10th Div., and it was converted to C.F.A. on 19/5/18.

10th (IRISH) DIVISION

FORMATION, BATTLES, AND ENGAGEMENTS

This New Army Division had no existence before the outbreak of the Great War.

A proclamation was issued on the 11th August 1914, asking for an immediate addition of 100,000 men to the Regular Army (see Narrative 9th Division and Appendix I). Army Order 324 of the 21st August (amended by Army Order 382 of the 11th September) authorized the addition of six divisions (9th–14th) and Army Troops to the Regular Army. This augmentation formed the First New Army, and late in August 1914, the 10th (Irish) Division began to assemble in Ireland. The infantry of the Division was composed of battalions of all the Irish line regiments, the men were of all classes, creeds, and political opinions, and in August 1915, when the 10th Division went into action in Gallipoli, it had the honour of being the first Irish Division to take the field in War.

At first there was a shortage of arms and equipment. Rifles (of various marks) and bayonets were soon obtained, but the artillery had to undertake most of the preliminary training with " quaker guns " and very few horses. In 1915 the Division moved to the Curragh, Newbridge, and Kildare ; brigade training was then undertaken. In May the Division crossed over to England, concentrated around Basingstoke, and began its final training. On the 28th and 29th May, H.M. the King saw the 10th Division, and on the 1st June Field-Marshal Earl Kitchener inspected the Division in Hackwood Park.

On the 27th June the Division was ordered to prepare for service in Gallipoli ; divisional headquarters embarked at Liverpool on the 9th July, and by the end of the month the bulk of the division had collected on the Island of Lemnos. On the 6th August the troops embarked at Mudros, and on the 6th and 7th the Division (less the 29th Brigade, which was operating with the Anzac Corps) landed at Suvla and assaulted the Turkish position.

For the remainder of the Great War the 10th (Irish) Division served in Gallipoli, Macedonia, Egypt, and Palestine and was engaged in the following operations :

1915

BATTLES OF SUVLA

6–10 August	**Battle of Sari Bair** (29th Bde.) [Godley's Force, A. & N.Z. A.C.].
6–15 August	**The Landing at Suvla** [IX Corps].
Night, 7/8 August	**Capture of Chocolate Hill** (31st Bde. and 7/R.D.F., 30th Bde.) [Hill's Force, IX Corps].
21 ; and 27 and 28 August	**Hill 60** (10/Hants. and 5/Conn. Rang., 29th Bde.) [Cox's Force, A. & N.Z.A.C.].

On the 29th September the 10th Division (less that part of its artillery which had disembarked at Suvla) was ordered to prepare to move from Suvla. On the 30th the divisional headquarters, the three infantry brigades, field companies, pioneers, cyclist company, and field ambulances embarked and reached Mudros on the 1st October. By the 2nd the Division had collected in camps near Mudros and was engaged in making up deficiencies. On the 4th October 29th Inf. Bde. began to embark for Macedonia ; the Brigade disembarked at Salonika between the 5th–10th October, and it was followed by the rest of the division. By the 24th October the bulk of the division (400 officers and 13,000 men) had landed at Salonika, and 13th Division Artillery Headquarters and two 18-pdr. brigades joined to replace the 10th Division Artillery, which had been left in action at Suvla. On the 29th October a mobile force under Br.-Gen. Nicol (30th Inf. Bde.) left by train for the interior and detrained at Gevgeli and Bogdanci (west of Lake Dojran).

RETREAT FROM SERBIA

7 and 8 December	**Kosturino.**

1916

30 September–2 October ...	**The Karajaköis** (29th Bde.) [XVI Corps].
3 and 4 October	**Capture of Yeniköi** (30th Bde.) [XVI Corps].

1917

On the 18th August the 10th Division received orders to concentrate at Salonika ; embarkation began on the 1st September and the first units of the Division reached Ismailia on the 5th ; on the 22nd the first units left Moascar for Rafah, and by the 8th October all the units (except R.A. Hd. Qrs., LXVII Bde., R.F.A., and the D.A.C.) had left Moascar for the front. On the 16th October the Division completed its assembly at Rafah ; 10th Division then joined XX Corps.

1–7 November	...	...	**Third Battle of Gaza** [XX Corps].
6 November...	...	...	**Capture of the Sheria Position** (31st Bde.) [XX Corps].
9 December ...	...	...	**Capture of Jerusalem** [On left of XX Corps].
27 December	...	...	**Defence of Jerusalem** [XX Corps].

1918

8–12 March ...	...	...	**Tell 'Asur** [XX Corps].

Between April and June the 10th Division was Indianized (see Table and notes).*

THE FINAL OFFENSIVE

THE BATTLES OF MEGIDDO

19–21 September ...	...	**Battle of Nablus** [XX Corps].

On the 23rd September the 30th Infantry Brigade moved forward, and on the 24th 46/Punjabis occupied Tubas and blocked the road to Beisan. On conclusion of its active operations in Palestine the 10th Division was employed on salvage work, and in the middle of October the Division concentrated near Tul Karm with divisional headquarters at el Mas'udiye. The Division was still in this area when the Armistice with Turkey came into force at noon on Thursday, 31st October.

The Division concentrated around Sarafand (3 miles west of Lydda) by the 12th November, and on the 14th all units received notification that the Division would move back to Egypt. On the 19th the move began, and by the 1st December the 10th Division assembled at Cairo.

In January, 1919 demobilization began. On the 24th and 29th the advanced parties of three of the Indian battalions left for Suez for embarkation for India and the battalions followed on the 2nd, 4th, and 15th February. On the 25th, 18th Coy., 3/S. and M. was transferred to the 3rd (Lahore) Division. On the 6th March the artillery began to return the 18-pdrs. to Ordnance Stores. On the 8th two Indian battalions left to join the 75th Division ; on the 13th the greater part of the remaining artillery was transferred to the 7th (Meerut) Division ; on the 15th the 30th Brigade headquarters was disbanded, and on the same day two Indian battalions left to join the 75th Division. The Division had been thus weakened when, on the 17th March, unrest broke out in Egypt. Nevertheless small parties and columns were sent at once to Benha, Gamra, Giza, and Abu el Ella, and on the 26th demobilization was suspended. On the 20th April orders were received to reform the 10th Division—with 3 British and 9 Indian battalions—and this fresh reconstruction brings to an end the history of the Division. During the Great War the 10th (Irish) Division lost 9,363 killed, wounded, and missing.

---

* After this reconstruction of the Division all that remained of the original 10th (Irish) Division were the following units :

B (H.)/LVII [C (H.)/LXVIII—see Table and notes 9, 18, and 40] ;

C (H.)/LVII [C (H.)/LXVII—see Table and notes 9, 19, and 40] ;

D (H.)/LVII [C (H.)/CCLXIII—see Table and notes 9, 28, and 41] ;

66th Field Company, R.E. ; 10th Division Signal Company, and 25th Mobile Veterinary Section.

11TH (NORTHERN) DIVISION

G.O.C.

22 August, 1914	Major-General F. HAMMERSLEY.
23 August, 1915	Major-General E. A. FANSHAWE.
4 July, 1916	Lieut.-General SIR C. L. WOOLLCOMBE.
1 December, 1916	Br.-Gen. J. F. ERSKINE (acting).
5 December, 1916	Major-General A. B. RITCHIE (wounded, 9/5/17).
9 May, 1917	Br.-Gen. H. R. DAVIES (tempy.).
12 May, 1917	Major-General H. R. DAVIES (wounded, 13/9/18).
13 September, 1918	Br.-Gen. O. DE L'E. WINTER (acting).
13 October, 1918	Major-General H. R. DAVIES.

G.S.O. 1.

25 Aug., 1914...Major J. DUNCAN (acting).
13 Jan., 1915...Lt.-Col. N. MALCOLM.
29 Sept., 1915...Major J. DUNCAN (tempy.).
22 Oct., 1915...Lt.-Col. J. DUNCAN.
3 Feb., 1916...Captain J. F. S. D. COLERIDGE (acting).
10 Feb., 1916...Lt.-Col. T. N. S. M. HOWARD.
21 April, 1916...Lt.-Col. J. F. S. D. COLERIDGE.
31 Oct., 1917...Lt.-Col. A. CROOKENDEN.

A.-A. and Q.-M.-G.

22 Aug., 1914...Lt.-Col. G. DE W. VERNER.
13 Sept., 1914...Major W. F. L. GORDON (acting).
9 Oct., 1914...Colonel C. F. STEVENS.
23 Mar., 1915...Lt.-Col. A. E. DELAVOYE.
15 Feb., 1916...Lt.-Col. W. F. L. GORDON (sick, 23/10/18).
23 Oct., 1918...Lt.-Col. E. A. BRAY.

B.-G., R.A.

5 Oct., 1914...Br.-Gen. R. D. GUBBINS.
18 Mar., 1915...Br.-Gen. E. J. GRANET (wd., 13/8/15).
13 Aug., 1915...Lt.-Col. W. E. WINGFIELD* (acting).
23 Sept., 1915...Br.-Gen. J. L. PARKER.
12 Jan., 1916...Br.-Gen. G. S. DUFFUS.
28 Aug., 1916...Br.-Gen. J. W. F. LAMONT.
4 Nov., 1916...Lt.-Col. O. DE L'E. WINTER (acting).
4 Dec., 1916...Br.-Gen. J. W. F. LAMONT.
26 Dec., 1917...Br.-Gen. O. DE L'E. WINTER.
23 Sept., 1918...Br.-Gen. W. O. H. DODDS (from 5th Cdn. Div. Arty., tempy.).
13 Oct., 1918...Br.-Gen. O. DE L'E. WINTER.

C.R.E.

12 Oct., 1914...Lt.-Col. E. H. BLAND.
10 Aug., 1915...Lt.-Col. F. A. K. WHITE (sick, 17/12/15).
17 Dec., 1915...Major G. W. DENISON (acting).
4 Feb., 1916...Lt.-Col. F. A. K. WHITE.

---

* On 29/8/15, IX Corps reorganized the artillery at Suvla as Right Flank Artillery and Left Flank Artillery. B.-G., R.A., 11th Division, became B.-G., R.A., Right Flank Artillery, but with the same units under him. The change was mainly one of nomenclature (B.-G., R.A., 10th Division, was B.-G., R.A., Left Flank Artillery).

32nd BDE.

25 Aug., '14...Br.-Gen. H. HAGGARD
(wd., 7/8/15).
7 Aug., '15...Lt.-Col. J. T. R. WILSON
(acting).
23 Sept., '15...Br.-Gen. A. G. DALLAS.
7 Jan., '16...Br.-Gen. T. H. F. PRICE.
24 April, '18...Br.-Gen. W. P. S. FOORD.

33rd BDE.

26 Aug., '14...Br.-Gen. R. P. MAXWELL
(sick, 29/9/15).
29 Sept., '15...Major A. E. NORTON
(acting).
4 Oct., '15...Br.-Gen. G. B. HODSON
(wd., 14/12/15).
15 Dec., '15...Br.-Gen. J. HILL (tempy.).
22 Dec., '15...Br.-Gen. J. F. ERSKINE.
6 Mar., '17...Lt.-Col. D. MATHERS
(acting).
9 Mar., '17...Br.-Gen. H. R. DAVIES.
9 May, '17...Lt.-Col. D. MATHERS
(acting).
15 May, '17...Br.-Gen. A. C. DALY.
15 Sept., '17...Br.-Gen. F. G. SPRING.

34th BDE.

24 Aug., '14...Br.-Gen. Hon. C. LAMBTON.
13 Mar., '15...Br.-Gen. W. H. SITWELL.
18 Aug., '15...Lt.-Col. C. C. HANNAY (acting).
2 Oct., '15...Br.-Gen. J. HILL.
15 Dec., '15...Lt.-Col. B. A. WRIGHT (acting).
16 Dec., '15...Br.-Gen. J. F. ERSKINE (tempy.).
23 Dec., '15...Br.-Gen. J. HILL.
10 Feb., '17...Br.-Gen. S. H. PEDLEY.
22 Aug., '17...Br.-Gen. B. G. CLAY.

GENERAL NOTES

The following formations and Units also served with the 11th (Northern) Division :—

MOUNTED TROOPS :—1/2nd South-Western Mounted Brigade (R. 1st Devon., R.N. Devon., W. Som., with Sig. Trp., and Fd. Amb., under Br.-Gen. R. Hoare), was attached at Suvla from 9/10–15/11/15.

11th Div. Cavalry Squadron, was attached in England from 2/6/15—embarkation of the Division.

ARTILLERY :—LV Brigade, R.F.A.—from 10th Div. Arty.—was attached at Suvla from 30/8/15—Evacuation (C/LV was only attached from 28 and 29/10/15—Evacuation).

LVII (H.) Bde. (H.Q., A and B)—from 10th Div. Arty.—was attached at Suvla from 1/9–8/12/15.

CXVIII (H.) Brigade, R.F.A.—Bde. (458 H. and 459 H.) was formed at Woolwich on 16/2/15. Bde. went to France, disembkd. at le Havre on 11/3/15, and joined 1st Cdn. Div. on 14/3/15. On 12/8/15 A (H.)/LXXXI (H.) (from 17th Div. Arty.) joined CXVIII (H.), was numbered 460 (H.) on 25/9/15, and was renumbered 461 (H.) on 16/12/15. The 3 batteries were then lettered A (H.), B (H.), and C (H.). On 10/7/16 CXVIII (H.) left 1st Cdn. Div. and on 15/7/16 Bde. joined 11th Div. at Blangermont. On arrival in 11th Div., CXVIII (H.) was broken up : A (458) became D (H.)/LVIII ; B (459) became D (H.)/LIX ; and C (461) became D (H.)/LX.

IV Lowland (H.) Bde., R.F.A., T.F.—from 52nd Div. Arty.—was attached at Suvla from 20/8–19/12/15. (By 4/9/15 the strength of the brigade was only 5 offrs. and 151 o.r.)

501 (H.) Battery, see note 20.

IV Highland Mtn. Bde., R.G.A., T.F.—(H.Q., Argyll. Bty., and Ross and Cromarty Bty.)—from 51st Div. Arty.—was attached at Suvla from 7/8–12/8/15 ; the Mtn. Bde. was then transferred to the 10th Division.

10th Heavy Battery, R.G.A., was attached at Suvla from 14/8–17/12/15. 10th Heavy Battery disembkd. at Suvla on 9 and 10/8/15 and came into action on 14/8/15. (On 20/10/15 the daily expenditure of ammn. was reduced to 2 Lyddite and 4 Shrapnel per gun.) On 6 and 17/12/15, 10th Heavy Battery re-embkd. and returned to Mudros ; and on 3/1/16, 10th Heavy Battery reached Alexandria. (Also see General Notes, 10th Division.)

11th (Hull) Heavy Battery, R.G.A., was formed in 1914 for 11th Division. 11th Heavy Battery did not go abroad with 11th Div., but on 18/1/16 11th Heavy Battery moved from Woolwich to Denham, and on 19/1/16, 11th Heavy Battery joined XXXVIII Bde. On 8/2/16 11th Heavy Battery (armed with 5" B.L. Hows.) embkd. at Devonport and disembkd. at Mombasa on 14/3/16. On 31/1/18 11th Heavy Battery returned to England, and on 1/3/18 11th Heavy Battery was re-designated 545 Siege Battery.

91st Heavy Battery, R.G.A., was attached in England until 8/6/15. 91st Heavy Battery (4, 60-pdrs.) landed at Helles in July, 1915 and served there until 4/1/16 (Evacuation). 91st Heavy Battery reached Alexandria on 13/2/16, refitted, and then moved to el Qantara on 26/2/16. For the remainder of the Great War 91st Heavy Battery served with the E.E.F. in Egypt and Palestine.

MACHINE GUNS :—11th Div. Motor-Machine-Gun Battery, served in England with the Division from 9/6/15—embarkation of the Division.

OTHER UNITS :—21st Sanitary Section, served with 11th Division in Egypt. The Section went to France with the Division and arrived at Blangerval on 13/7/16. The Section left the Division on 9/12/16, and then took over a IV Corps Sanitary Area in the Fifth Army.

11th Division Motor Ambce. Workshop, served with the Division in England until the Division embarked for Gallipoli. The Workshop was absorbed by the Divisional Train.

By 21/2/18 the reorganization of the 11th Division on a 9-battalion basis had been completed ; and on 22/2/18 the pioneer battalion was reorganized on a 3-company basis.

11ᴛʜ (NORTHERN) DIVISION

ORDER OF BATTLE, 1914-1918

Dates	INFANTRY Brigades	Battalions and attached Units	Mounted Troops	ARTILLERY — Field Artillery Brigades	Batteries	Bde. Ammn. Colns.	Trench Mortar Btries. Medium	Heavy	Divnl. Ammn. Coln.	Engineers Field Cos.	Signal Service Divnl. Signal Coy.	Pioneers	M.G. Units	Field Ambulances	Mobile Vety. Secn.	Divnl. Emplnt. Coy.	Divnl. Train
1914 October (England)	32nd 33rd 34th	9/W. York, 6/Gr. How., 8/Duke's,[1] 6/Y. & L. 6/Linc., 6/Bord., 7/S. Staff., 9/Sher. For. 8/N.F., 9/L.F., 5/Dorset,[2] 11/Manch.	11th Div. Cyclist Coy.[3]	LVIII[4] LIX[4] LX[4] LXI (H.)[4]; 5	184, 185, 186 187, 188, 189 190, 191, 192 193 (H.), 194 (H.), 195 (H.)	LVIII B.A.C. LIX B.A.C. LX B.A.C. LXI (H.) B.A.C.	...	...	11th D.A.C.[6]	67th 68th 86th[7]	11th	6/E. York.[8] (P.)	...	33rd 34th 35th	22nd[9]	...	11th[10]
1915 August (Gallipoli)	32nd 33rd 34th	9/W. York, 6/Gr. How., 8/Duke's, 6/Y. & L. 6/Linc., 6/Bord., 7/S. Staff., 9/Sher. For. 8/N.F., 9/L.F., 5/Dorset, 11/Manch.	11th Div. Cyclist Coy.	LVIII[11] LIX[12] LX[13]	A, B, C, D[17]; 20 A, B, C, D[18]; 20 A, B, C, D[19]; 20	LVIII B.A.C. LIX B.A.C. LX B.A.C.	...	...	...[6]	67th 68th 80th	11th	6/E. York. (P.)	...	33rd 34th 35th	22nd	...	10th
1916 June (Egypt)	32nd 33rd 34th	9/W. York, 6/Gr. How., 8/Duke's, 6/Y. & L.; 32nd Bde. M.G. Coy.[14] 6/Linc., 6/Bord., 7/S. Staff., 9/Sher. For.; 33rd Bde. M.G. Coy.[14] 8/N.F., 9/L.F., 5/Dorset, 11/Manch.; 34th Bde. M.G. Coy.[14]	B. Sqdn., 1/Herts. Yeo.[15] 11th Div. Cyclist Coy.[16]	LVIII[17; 28] LIX[18; 27] LX[19; 28] CXXXIII[20]	A, B, C A, B, C A, B, C A,[17] B,[18] C[19]	LVIII B.A.C. LIX B.A.C. LX B.A.C. ...	...	...	...	67th 68th 86th	11th	6/E. York. (P.)	...	33rd 34th 35th	22nd	...	...
1917 June (France)	32nd 33rd 34th	9/W. York,[21] 6/Gr. How., 8/Duke's,[22] 6/Y. & L.; 32nd M.G. Coy.;[37] 32nd T.M. Bty.[23] 6/Linc., 6/Bord.,[24] 7/S. Staff., 9/Sher. For.; 33rd M.G. Coy.,[37] 33rd T.M. Bty.[23] 8/N.F., 9/L.F.,[25] 5/Dorset, 11/Manch.; 34th M.G. Coy.;[37] 34th T.M. Bty.[23]	...	LVIII[26] LIX[27]	A, B, C; D (H.) A, B, C; D (H.)	...[30]	X.11,[29] Y.11,[29] Z.11[29]	V.11[29]	11th D.A.C.[30]	67th 68th 86th	11th	6/E. York. (P.)	250th M.G. Coy.[31; 37]	33rd 34th 35th	22nd	213th[32]	11th[35]
1918 March (France)	32nd 33rd 34th	9/(York. Hsrs.) W. York,[31] 6/Gr. How.,[34] 6/Y. & L.; 32nd T.M. Bty. 6/Linc., 7/S. Staff., 9/Sher. For.; 33rd T.M. Bty. 8/N.F., 5/Dorset, 11/Manch.; 34th T.M. Bty.	...	LVIII LIX	A, B, C; D (H.) A, B, C; D (H.)	...	X.11,[35] Y.11[35]	...[36]	11th D.A.C.	67th 68th 86th	11th	6/E. York. (P.)	No. 11 Bn., M.G.C.[37]	33rd 34th 35th	22nd	213th	11th

1918 June (France)											
32nd......	9/(York. Hsrs.) W. York. & L.; 6/Y. & L.;	LVIII	...	X.11 Y.11	...	11th D.A.C.	67th 68th 86th	11th	6/E. York. (P.)	No. 11 Bn. M.G.C.	33rd 34th 35th
2/Gr. How.,38 32nd T.M. Bty.	LIX	A, B, C; D (H.)									22nd · 218th · 11th
33rd......	6/Linc., 7/S. Staff., 9/Sher.		A, B, C; D (H.)								
33rd T.M. Bty.											
34th......	8/N.F., 5/Dorset, 11/Manch.;										
34th T.M. Bty.											

NOTES

1 Bn. was transferred to 32nd Bde. (from 34th Bde.) on 18/1/15.

2 Bn. was transferred to 34th Bde. (from 33rd Bde.) on 18/1/15.

3 Cyclist Coy. was formed between 23/1–1/3/15.

4 Bties. were raised as 6-gun batteries and numbered. By Feb., 1915, all Bdes. were reorganized as 4-battery brigades, the batteries all became 4-gun batteries, and they were lettered A, B, C, D in each brigade.

5 Bde. remained in England when 11th Div. embkd. in July, 1915; and on 24/8/15 Bde. joined Guards Div. Arty. in France.

6 D.A.C. remained in England when 11th Div. embkd. in July, 1915.

7 Fd. Coy. joined on 7/2/15, from 21st Div.

8 Bn. was transferred from 32nd Bde. and became Pioneers on 18/1/15.

9 Joined on 16/4/15.

10 Train (formed of 112, 113, 114, and 115 Cos. A.S.C.) remained in England in 1915; the Train joined 28th Div. at Salonika on 1/4/16.

11 Bde. landed at Anzac on 9/8/15; on 16/8/15 Bde. was transferred to Left Flank Arty. at Suvla and then came under 10th Div. Bde. re-embkd. by 18/12/15 and reached Alexandria on 2/1/16.

12 A Bty. landed at C Beach, Suvla, on 7/8/15; the remdr. of Bde. disembkd. at Suvla on 9/8/15. Bde. re-embkd. between 9–19/12/15, and Bde. reached Alexandria between 22/12/15–2/1/16.

13 In Aug., 1915, Bde. remained in Egypt; it disembkd. at Suvla on 25/10/15 (under IX Corps). Bde. re-embkd. by 17/12/15, and reached Alexandria on 2/1/16.

14 Bde. M.G. Cos. were formed in Egypt: 32nd in March, 1916; 33rd by 23/3/16; and 34th by 1/3/16.

15 Sqdn. joined Div. on 4/4/16 at el Ferdan: embkd. at Alexandria with Div. on 27/8/16, and disembkd. at Marseille on 4/7/16. Sqdn. was transferred to VI Corps and was attached to 1/1/ Northants Yeo. (VI Corps Cav. Regt.) from 12/7/16. In 1917 Sqdn. returned to Egypt, and in 1918 B Sqdn. joined XXI Corps Cav. Regt. in Palestine.

16 Coy. came to France with 11th Div.; embkd. at Alexandria on 28/8/16, disembkd. at Marseille on 3/7/16. On 12/7/16 Cyclist Coy. was attached to VI Corps Cyclist Bn., left VI Corps on 19/1/17, and joined XVIII Corps Cyclist Bn. (11th, 60th, and 62nd Div. Cyclist Cos.).

17 D was transferred on 26/4/16 and became A (H.)/CXXXIII (n. 20).

18 D was transferred on 26/4/16 and became B (H.)/CXXXIII (n. 20).

19 D was transferred on 26/4/16 and became CXXXIII (H.) B.A.C. (On 22/6/16 CXXXIII (H.) B.A.C. became C (H.) CXXXIII—see note 20).

20 Bde. was formed at el Ferdan on 20/4/16 and known as The Howitzer Bde., R.F.A.; on 31/5/16 the title was changed to CXXXIII (H.) Bde. On 28/4/16 D/LVIII, D/LIX, and D/LX (18-pdr.) Bties. joined and became A (H.), B (H.), and B.A.C. On 22/6/16 the B.A.C. became C (H.). At first the Bde. was armed with 5" B.L. Hows. On 23/6/16 the 5" Hows. were exchanged for 18-pdr. Q.F. guns. On 29/8/16 C was broken up: R. Sec. joined B, and L. Sec. joined A/CXXXIII. On 15/11/16 501 (H.) joined CXXXIII. Between 27/11–4/12/16 CXXXIII was broken up: A made up A, B, and C/LVIII to 6, 18-pdrs. each; and B made up A, B, and C/LIX. 501 (H.) left CXXXIII on 27/11/16.

21 Bn. was reorganized between 10–13/10/17, and Bn. absorbed over 400 all ranks of 1/1/Yorkshire Hsrs. (1/York. Hsrs. had been training at No. 1 Training Camp, Etaples, since leaving XVII Corps Cav. Regt. on 28/8/17). Bn. then became 9/(Yorkshire Hussars) W. Yorkshire Regt.

23 32nd T.M. Bty. joined Bde. in France on 17/7/16, from Third Army T.M. School; and 33rd and 34th T.M. Bties. joined their Bdes. in France during July, 1917.

24 Bn. was disbanded and drafted between 2–9/2/18.

25 Bn. was disbanded and drafted between 3–21/2/18.

26 On 29/11/16 A/CXXXIII joined Bde. and was split up: Centre Sec. made up A, R. Sec. made up B, and L. Sec. made up C/LVIII to 6, 18-pdrs. each. On 24/1/17 R. Sec., D (H.)/LX joined and made up D (H.)/LVIII to 6, 4·5" Hows. (D (H.) had joined LVIII Bde. on 15/7/16 from CXVIII (H.) Bde.—see General Notes).

27 On 8 and 9/12/17 A, B, and C Bties. were made up to 6, 18-pdrs. each, by each Bty. absorbing 1 Sec. of B/CXXXIII (this Bty. had been attached to LIX since 27/11/17). On 25/1/17 L. Sec. D (H.)/LX joined and made up D (H.)/LIX to 6, 4·5" Hows. (D (H.) had joined LIX Bde. on 15/7/16 from CXVIII (H.) Bde.—see General Notes).

28 On 25/1/17 the Bde. was broken up: A and half C were transferred to XXXIV A.F.A. Bde.; B and half C went to LXXXIV A.F.A. Bde.; and D (H.) was split up between D (H.) LVIII and D (H.)/LIX, to make up each battery to 6, 4·5" Hows. D (H.) had joined LX Bde. on 15/7/16 from CXVIII (H.) Bde.—see General Notes.

29 The 3 Medium and 1 Heavy T.M. Bties. joined and were taken on the strength of the 11th Division on 9/8/16.

30 D.A.C. remained in England until July, 1916; on 4/7/16 D.A.C. disembkd. at le Havre, arrived at Blangerval on 7/7/16, and D.A.C. rejoined 11th Div. on 7/7/16.

31 Coy. left Grantham on 12/11/17, disembkd. at le Havre on 13/11/17, and joined 11th Div. on 13/11/17, at Noeux les Mines.

32 Coy. was formed in the Div. by 30/6/17.

33 Supply Sec. came from Egypt with 11th Div.; remdr. of the Train was formed in England and joined 11th Div. on 6/7/16 in France. The Cos. were numbered 479, 480, 481, and 482 Cos., A.S.C.

34 Bn. was reduced to T.C. on 14/5/18, and surplus of Bn. (21 offrs. and 640 o.r.) was absorbed on 16/5/18, at Mazingarbe, by 2/Gr. How. (See note 38). Bn. H.Q. and training cadre served with 66th Div., 19–30/6/18, and then went to U.K. with 25th Div.

35 Z was absorbed by X and Y on 3/2/18.

36 On the reorganization of the T.M. Bties., V left the Div. by 12/2/18.

37 Bn. was formed in the Div. on 28/2/18. It consisted of 32nd, 33rd, 34th, and 250th M.G. Cos.

38 Bn. was transferred from 21st Bde., 30th Div., and joined 32nd Bde., 11th Div., on 14/5/18 at Coupigny Huts. At Mazingarbe on 16/5/18 Bn. absorbed surplus of 6/Gr. How. (see note 34).

11TH (NORTHERN) DIVISION

FORMATION, BATTLES, AND ENGAGEMENTS

This New Army Division had no existence before the outbreak of the Great War.

A proclamation was issued on the 11th August, 1914 asking for an immediate addition of 100,000 men to the Regular Army (see Narrative 9th Division and Appendix I). Army Order No. 324 of the 21st August (amended by Army Order No. 382 of the 11th September) authorized the addition of six divisions (9th–14th) and Army Troops to the Regular Army. This augmentation formed the First New Army, and late in August, 1914 the 11th (Northern) Division began to assemble around Grantham.

On the 22nd August when the G.O.C. reached Grantham he found that only the A.-A. & Q.-M.-G. of the division had arrived. On the 27th the first batch of 1,000 infantry (with a small proportion of regular officers and non-commissioned-officers, from depôt staffs) reached Grantham. Other parties followed and by the 21st September the strength of the infantry had risen to 13,000. At first the infantry of the 11th Division consisted entirely of north country battalions ; later on, however, when the 6/East Yorkshire became the pioneer battalion its place was taken by a Wessex battalion—5/Dorsetshire.

At first there was the usual shortage of clothing, equipment, and arms, leading to some discomfort and to considerable delay in training for war. Nevertheless, on the 18th October Field-Marshal Earl Kitchener visited Grantham and inspected the infantry in Belton Park. Until the following April the Division remained scattered : infantry at Grantham, artillery at Leeds, Sheffield, Norwich, and Weedon ; engineers at Newark ; field ambulances at Sheffield ; train at Lichfield. Then on the 4th April the 11th Division began to move to its concentration area at Witley and Frensham, and final training was carried out and divisional operations undertaken.

On the 31st May H.M. the King inspected the 11th Division on Hankley Common, and on the 12th June orders were received that the Division was to be ready to leave at short notice for the Dardanelles. On the 30th June embarkation began at Liverpool, and the bulk of the Division sailed in the *Aquitania* and the *Empress of Britain*. On the 10th July the *Aquitania* with divisional headquarters and the 32nd Infantry Brigade reached Mudros. On the 23rd all headquarters and troops at Mudros left Lemnos and moved to Imbros, and the 11th Division completed concentration at Imbros on the 28th July.

At 8.30 p.m. on the 6th August the Division left Imbros for Suvla Bay ; the troops embarked in torpedo boat destroyers and motor lighters (about 500 in each vessel) each man carrying on him 220 rounds of ammunition and 2 days' iron rations. At 11.30 p.m. the flotilla anchored off Suvla, and shortly after m/n. 6th/7th August disembarkation began near Lala Baba.

During the Great War the 11th (Northern) Division served in Gallipoli and in Egypt, and on the Western Front (in France and Belgium), and was engaged in the following operations :

1915

BATTLES OF SUVLA

6–15 August	... ...	**The Landing at Suvla** [IX Corps].
7 August	... ...	**Capture of Karakol Dagh** (34th Bde.) [IX Corps].
21 August	... ...	**Battle of Scimitar Hill** [IX Corps].
21 August	... ...	**Attack on " W " Hills** [IX Corps].
Night, 19/20 Dec.	...	**Evacuation of Suvla** [IX Corps].

On the last night every gun, trench mortar, cart, and animal was withdrawn, and the 11th Division suffered no casualties to its personnel during the final evacuation of Suvla. On leaving Suvla the Division concentrated at Imbros.

1916

On the 12th January the Dardanelles Army was broken up, and on the 26th the 11th Division began embarking for Mudros, *en route* for Egypt. On the 2nd February the Division reached Alexandria, and completed concentration at Sidi Bishr by the 8th. On the 9th February the Division was posted to the XV Corps, and on the 19th the 11th Division took over A Section, Suez Canal Defences, with divisional headquarters at el Ferdan. Until June the Division remained in the Suez Canal Defences. On the 17th June instructions were received for the Division to embark for France. On the 20th June the advanced party left to embark at Alexandria, on the 25th the Division handed over A Section, Suez Canal Defences, to the 42nd Division, and on the 30th the advanced party reached St. Pol. Embarkation at Alexandria was completed on the 3rd July, and on the 7th divisional headquarters arrived at Flers (S.S.W. of St. Pol). The concentration around Flers was completed on the 15th July ; and by the 27th July the Division had taken over part of VI Corps front line (in the Third Army). During the remainder of the Great War the 11th Division took part in the following operations on the Western Front :

BATTLES OF THE SOMME
14 September ... ... Capture of the Wonder Work (32nd Bde.) [II Corps, Reserve Army].
15–22 September ... Battle of Flers-Courcelette [II Corps, Reserve Army].
26–28 September ... Battle of Thiepval Ridge [II Corps, Reserve Army].

1917

11–19 January ... ... Operations on the Ancre [IV Corps, Fifth Army].
9–14 June ... ... Battle of Messines [IX Corps, Second Army].

BATTLES OF YPRES.
16–18 August ... ... Battle of Langemarck [XVIII Corps, Fifth Army].
19 ; 22 ; and 27 August Fighting around St. Julien [XVIII Corps, Fifth Army].
26 Sept.–3 Oct. ... ... Battle of Polygon Wood [XVIII Corps, Fifth Army].
4 October ... ... Battle of Broodseinde [XVIII Corps, Fifth Army].
9 October ... ... Battle of Poelcappelle [XVIII Corps, Fifth Army].

1918

THE ADVANCE TO VICTORY
SECOND BATTLES OF ARRAS
30 August ... ... Battle of the Scarpe [XXII Corps, First Army].
2 and 3 September ... Battle of the Drocourt-Quéant Line [XXII Corps, First Army].

BATTLES OF THE HINDENBURG LINE
27 Sept.–1 Oct. ... ... Battle of the Canal du Nord [Canadian Corps, First Army].
8 and 9 October ... ... Battle of Cambrai [Canadian Corps, First Army].
9–12 October ... ... Pursuit to the Selle [Canadian Corps, First Army].

THE FINAL ADVANCE IN PICARDY
4 November... ... ... Battle of the Sambre [XXII Corps, First Army].
5–7 November ... ... Passage of the Grande Honnelle [XXII Corps, First Army].

On the 9th November the 11th Division established its outpost line beyond the Mons–Maubeuge road and the high ground to the east of Havay was occupied before 11 a.m. on the 11th November, when the Armistice brought hostilities to a close.

Between the 26th and 28th November the Division moved back behind the Schelde to Denain, Wallers, and Condé, and for the rest of the year educational training was undertaken and men were sent on technical courses. Demobilization began in January, 1919 and continued at an increasing pace ; on the 1st February the infantry of the division still numbered 8,239 all ranks, but by the 1st March this total had shrunk to 4,864. On the 19th February the outlying brigade at Condé moved in to Denain, and on the 17th March the G.O.C. left and took command of No. 1 Army Area. Gradually units were reduced to cadre strength, and in June the cadres began moving to England to be broken up. By the 28th June the infantry strength had dwindled to 228 all ranks and the war history of the Division then came to an end. During the Great War the 11th (Northern) Division lost 32,165 killed, wounded, and missing.

12TH (EASTERN) DIVISION

G.O.C.

24 August, 1914	Major-General J. SPENS.
15 March, 1915	Major-General F. D. V. WING (killed, 2/10/15).
2 October, 1915	Br.-Gen. W. K. McLEOD (acting).
3 October, 1915	Major-General A. B. SCOTT.
26 April, 1918	Major-General H. W. HIGGINSON.

G.S.O. 1.

21 Sept., 1914...Major J. K. COCHRANE (acting).
16 Jan., 1915...Lt.-Col. Hon. C. J. SACKVILLE-WEST.
5 Dec., 1915...Lt.-Col. C. J. C. GRANT.
15 Jan., 1917...Lt.-Col. C. J. B. HAY.
26 July, 1917...Lt.-Col. R. S. ALLEN (sick, 6/5/18).
6 May, 1918...Lt.-Col. W. R. PINWILL.
31 July, 1918...Major C. F. M. N. RYAN (acting).
3 Aug., 1918...Lt.-Col. J. D. BELGRAVE.

A.-A. & Q.-M.-G.

22 Aug., 1914...Major A. F. STEWART (acting).
12 Oct., 1914...Lt.-Col. H. P. HANCOX.
18 Oct., 1915...Lt.-Col. E. H. E. COLLEN.
5 Mar., 1918...Lt.-Col. F. R. BURNSIDE.

B.-G., R.A.

3 Oct., 1914...Br.-Gen. S. E. G. LAWLESS.
29 Mar., 1915...Br.-Gen. W. K. McLEOD.
30 Jan., 1916...Br.-Gen. E. H. WILLIS.
30 Sept., 1917...Br.-Gen. H. M. THOMAS.

C.R.E.

1 Oct., 1914...Lt.-Col. S. F. WILLIAMS.
22 July, 1916...Lt.-Col. W. BOVET (d. of w., 5/7/18).
5 July, 1918...Major J. D. GEMMILL (acting).
12 July, 1918...Lt.-Col. A. T. SHAKESPEAR.

35th BDE.

29 Aug., '14...Br.-Gen. C. H. VAN STRAUBENZEE (sick, 25/10/15).
25 Oct., '15...Lt.-Col. F. W. FOLEY (acting).
26 Oct., '15...Lt.-Col. G. D. JEFFREYS (acting).
2 Nov., '15...Br.-Gen. A. SOLLY-FLOOD.
8 Nov., '16...Lt.-Col. F. E. WALTER (acting).
12 Nov., '16...Lt.-Col. G. A. TRENT (acting).
16 Jan., '17...Lt.-Col. F. E. WALTER (acting).
28 Jan., '17...Br.-Gen. B. VINCENT (gassed, 9/8/18).
10 Aug., '18...Br.-Gen. A. T. BECKWITH (tempy.).
19 Sept., '18...Br.-Gen. B. VINCENT.

36th BDE.

24 Aug., '14...Br.-Gen. H. B. BORRADAILE.
10 Nov., '15...Br.-Gen. L. B. BOYD-MOSS.
28 Nov., '16...Br.-Gen. C. S. OWEN.

37th BDE.

26 Aug., '14...Br.-Gen. C. A. FOWLER.
5 Feb., '16...Lt.-Col. F. H. WARDEN (acting).
13 Feb., '16...Br.-Gen. A. B. E. CATOR.
4 Oct., '17...Lt.-Col. R. H. BALDWIN (acting).
9 Oct., '17...Br.-Gen. A. B. INCLEDON-WEBBER.

GENERAL NOTES

The following Units also belonged to, or served with, the 12th (Eastern) Division :—

ARTILLERY :—C (H.) Battery, R.F.A. (4, 4·5" Hows.), see note 16.

   12th Heavy Battery, exchanged its 4, 4·7" guns for 4, 60-pdrs. on 25/5/15, at Aldershot. On 31/5/15 the Heavy Battery embkd. at Southampton, disembkd. at le Havre on 1/6/15, and on 8/6/15 the Heavy Battery joined X Heavy Artillery Brigade, R.G.A. (Second Army) near Kemmel.

MACHINE GUNS :—9th Motor-Machine-Gun Battery, went to France with 12th Div. and disembkd. at le Havre on 30/5/15. Bty. left 12th Div. on 20/6/15 and joined II Anzac Corps at Blaringhem.

   198th Machine-Gun Company, was formed at Grantham. Coy. disembkd. at le Havre on 15/12/16 and joined 12th Div. on 20/12/16 at Liencourt. On 19/2/17 the Coy. left 12th Div. and joined 174th Bde., 58th Div., near Arras on 21/2/17.

INFANTRY :—3/4/Queen's, disembkd. at le Havre on 1/6/17, joined South African Bde., 9th Div., on 6/6/17 ; transferred to 12th Div., 23/7/17 ; and Bn. joined 62nd Bde., 21st Div., on 9/8/17. Bn. was broken up, 3–11/2/18.

   5/North'n. Bn. from Army Troops, First New Army, was converted into Pioneers, and joined 12th Div. in January 1915, as Pioneer Bn.

OTHER UNITS :—23rd Sanitary Section, went to France with 12th Div. and disembkd. at le Havre on 2/6/15. In April, 1917, 23rd Sanitary Section left 12th Div. and took over No. 7 Sanitary Area, Third Army.

   12th Div. Motor Amb. Workshop, landed at Rouen on 1/6/15 and joined 12th Div. on 7/6/15 near Pradelles. By 16/4/16 the Workshop was absorbed by 12th Div. Train.

On 27/2/18 the reorganization of the 12th Division on a 9-battalion basis was completed ; and on 1/3/18 the pioneer battalion (5/North'n.) was reorganized on a 3-company basis.

12TH (EASTERN) DIVISION

Dates	INFANTRY			ARTILLERY						Engineers		Pioneers	M.G. Units	Field Ambulances	Mobile Vety. Secn.	Divnl. Emplnt. Coy.	Divnl. Train
	Brigades	Battalions and attached Units	Mounted Troops	Field Artillery			Trench Mortar Btties.		Divnl. Ammn. Coln.	Field Cos.	Signal Service Divnl. Signal Coy.						
				Brigades	Batteries	Bde. Ammn. Colns.	Medium	Heavy									
1914 October (England)	35th ...... 36th 37th	7/Norf., 7/Suff., 9/Essex, 5/R. Berks. 8/R.F., 9/R.F., 7/R. Suss., 11/Middx. 6/Queen's, 6/Buffs, 7/E. Surr., 6/Q.O.R.W.K.	12th Div. Cyclist Coy.[1]	LXII[2] .... LXIII[2] .... LXIV[2] .... LXV (H.)[2] ...	196, 197, 198 199, 200, 201 202, 203, 204 205 (H.), 206 (H.), 207 (H.)	LXII B.A.C. LXIII B.A.C. LXIV B.A.C. LXV (H.) B.A.C.	...	...	12th D.A.C.	69th 70th 87th[3]	12th	5/North'n (P.)[3A]	...	36th 37th 38th	23rd[4]	...	12th[5]
1915 September (France)	35th 36th 37th	7/Norf., 7/Suff., 9/Essex, 5/R. Berks. 8/R.F., 9/R.F., 7/R. Suss., 11/Middx. 6/Queen's, 6/Buffs, 7/E. Surr., 6/Q.O.R.W.K.	A Sqdn., 1/K.E.H.[6] 12th Div. Cyclist Coy.[7]	LXII[2]; [8] ...... LXIII[2]; [9] ...... LXIV[2]; 10 ...... LXV (H.)[2]; 11	A, B, C, D A, B, C, D A, B, C, D A (H.), B (H.), D (H.)	LXII B.A.C. LXIII B.A.C. LXIV B.A.C. LXV (H.) B.A.C.	...	...	12th D.A.C.	69th 70th 87th	12th	5/North'n (P.)	...	36th 37th 38th	23rd	...	12th
1916 June (France)	35th ...... 36th 37th	7/Norf., 7/Suff., 9/Essex, 5/R. Berks.; 35th Bde. M.G. Coy.;[12] 35th T.M. Bty.[13] 8/R.F., 9/R.F., 7/R. Suss., 11/Middx.; 36th Bde. M.G. Coy.;[12] 36th T.M. Bty.[13] 6/Queen's, 6/Buffs, 7/E. Surr., 6/Q.O.R.W.K.; 37th Bde. M.G. Coy.;[12] 37th T.M. Bty.[13]	...	LXII[14] ...... LXIII[15] ...... LXIV[16] ...... LXV[17]	A, B, C; D (H.) A, B, C; D (H.) A, B, C A, B, C; D (H.)	...[20]	X.12[18] Y.12[18] Z.12[18]	V.12[19]	12th D.A.C.[20]	69th 70th 87th	12th	5/North'n (P.)	...	36th 37th 38th	23rd	...	12th
1917 June (France)	35th ...... 36th 37th	7/Norf., 7/Suff., 9/Essex, 5/R. Berks.,[21] 35th M.G. Coy.;[30] 35th T.M. Bty. 8/R.F.,[22] 9/R.F., 7/R. Suss., 11/Middx.;[23] 36th M.G. Coy.;[30] 36th T.M. Bty. 6/Queen's, 6/Buffs, 7/E. Surr.,[24] 6/Q.O.R.W.K.;[30] 37th M.G. Coy.;[30] 37th T.M. Bty.	...	LXII .... LXIII	A, B, C; D (H.) A, B, C; D (H.)	...	X.12 Y.12 Z.12[25]	V.12[26]	12th D.A.C.	69th 70th 87th	12th	5/North'n (P.)	235th M.G. Coy.[27]	36th 37th 38th	23rd	214th[28]	12th

		35th		LXII		X.12 Y.12	...26	12th D.A.C.	69th 70th 87th	12th	5/ North'n (P.)	No. 12 Bn. M.G.C. 30	36th 37th 38th	23rd	214th	12th
1918 March (France)		7/Norf., 7/Suff.,29 9/Essex; 35th T.M. Bty. 9/R.F., 7/R. Suss., 5/R. Berks.,21 36th T.M. Bty. 6/Queen's, 6/Buffs, 6/Q.O.R.W.K.; 37th T.M. Bty.	...	LXII .... A, B, C; D (H.) LXIII .... A, B, C; D (H.)	...	X.12 Y.12	...	12th D.A.C.	69th 70th 87th	12th	5/ North'n (P.)	No. 12 Bn. M.G.C.	36th 37th 38th	23rd	214th	12th
1918 July (France)		7/Norf., 9/Essex, 1/1/Camb.;31 35th T.M. Bty. 9/R.F., 7/R.Suss., 5/R.Berks.; 36th T.M. Bty. 6/Queen's, 6/Buffs, 6/Q.O.R.W.K.; 37th T.M. Bty.	...	LXII .... A, B, C; D (H.) LXIII .... A, B, C; D (H.)	...	X.12 Y.12	...	12th D.A.C.	69th 70th 87th	12th	5/ North'n (P.)	No. 12 Bn. M.G.C.	36th 37th 38th	23rd	214th	12th

NOTES

1 Formed in the division in 1914.

2 Batteries were raised as 6-gun batteries and numbered. By Feb., 1915, all brigades were reorganized as 4-battery brigades, the batteries all became 4-gun batteries, and they were lettered A, B, C, D in each brigade.

3 Joined Div. by Feb., 1915, from 22nd Div.

3A. Joined Div. in Jany., 1915 (see General Notes).

4 Joined Div. before embkn.; and landed at le Havre on 2/6/15.

5 The Cos. were numbered 116, 117, 118, 119 Cos., A.S.C.

6 Sqdn. joined Div. on 23/5/15 at Aldershot and disembkd. at le Havre on 1/6/15. Sqdn. left 12th Div. on 10/5/16, and on 1/6/16 joined 1/K.E.H. (IV Corps Cav. Regt.) at Valhuon.

7 Coy. left Div. and on 15/8/16 joined I Corps Cyclist Bn. at Verquin.

8 On 25/5/16 D Bty. left Bde. and became A/LXV, and A (H.)/LXV joined and became D (H.)/LXII.

9 On 25/5/16 D Bty. left Bde. and became B/LXV, and B (H.)/LXV joined and became D (H.)/LXIII.

10 On 25/5/16 D Bty. left Bde. and became C/LXV.

11 On 18/6/15 C (H.)/LXV was transferred to 27th Div. and became C (H.)/CXXIX on 6/9/15. On 25/5/16 LXV was reorganized: A (H.) and B (H.) left and became D (H.)/LXII and D (H.)/LXIII; and D/LXII, D/LXIII, and D/LXIV joined and became A, B, C/LXV. D (H.)/LXV remained D (H.)/LXV.

12 Bde. M.G. Cos. were formed as follows: 35th on 1/2/16 at St. Hilaire; 36th on 1/2/16 at Ham en Artois; and 37th by 4/2/16.

13 Light T.M. Bties. were formed as follows: 35th A (or 1) by 10/2/16, 35 B (or 2) by 30/3/16, and 35th T.M. Bty. by 25/6/16; 36th A (or 1) by 23/1/16, 36th B (or 2) by May, 1916, and 36th T.M. Bty. by 4/3/16, and 37th T.M. Bty. by 15/6/16.

14 Bde. was reorganized on 30/8/16: C was split up between A and B and made up each Bty. (A and B) to 6 guns; and C/LXV and half A/LXV joined and became C/LXII. On 7/1/17, 1 Sec., C (H)/LXII joined and made up D (H.)/LXII to 6 hows.

15 Bde. was reorganized on 30/8/16: half A/LXV and B/LXV joined and made up A, B, and C/LXIII to 6 guns each: D (H.)/LXIII was transferred and became D (H.)/LXIV; and D (H.)/LXV joined and became D (H.)/LXIII; at the same time Bde. H.Q./LXV joined and took over LXIII. On 7/1/17, 1 sec., C (H.)/LXIV joined and made up D (H.)/LXIII to 6 hows.

16 Bde. was reorganized between 30/8-1/9/16: C was broken up and L. Sec. joined A and R Sec. joined B, making up A and B to 6 guns each, and D (H.)/LXIII became D (H.)/LXIV. (Bty. joined Bde. on 11/10/16.) On 7/12/16 C (H.) joined LXIV. On 6/1/17, LXIV became an A.F.A. Bde., and D (H.)/LXIII to 6 hows. each; B/CLVIII (from 35th Div.) joined and made up C/LXIV, and 1 sec., D (H.)/CLVIII joined and made up D (H.)/LXIV to 6 hows.

17 On 30/8/16, LXV was broken up: Bde. H.Q. became Bde. H.Q./LXIII; R. Sec. A made up C/LXV to 6 guns, and L. Sec. A joined A/LXIII; R. Sec. B joined C/LXIII, and L. Sec. B joined B/LXIII; C/LXV (made up to 6 guns by R. Sec. A/LXV) became C/LXII; and D (H.)/LXV became D (H.)/LXIII.

18 X, Y, and Z were formed on 1/7/16.

19 V was formed on 31/7/16.

20 On 21/5/16 B.A.C.s were abolished and the D.A.C. was reorganized.

21 Bn. was transferred to 36th Bde. on 6/2/18.

22 Bn. was disbanded on 6/2/18.

23 Bn. was disbanded between 10-27/2/18.

24 Bn. was disbanded on 5/2/18.

25 Z was absorbed by X and Y on 16/2/18.

26 V was disbanded on 15/2/18. Personnel was absorbed by X and Y, and by 12th D.A.C.

27 Coy. disembkd. at le Havre on 13/7/17, and joined 12th Div. at Arras on 16/7/17. On 1/8/18 Coy. joined No. 12 Bn. M.G. Corps, and became D Coy.

28 Formed by 16/6/17.

29 Bn. was broken up on 19/5/18, and 11 offrs. and 408 o.r. were absorbed by 1/1/Camb. (see n. 31). Bn. H.Q. and training cadre served with 66th Div. from 18/8-20/9/18, and then went to L. of C. with 197th Bde.

30 Bn. consisted of 35th, 36th, 37th, and 235th M.G. Cos.; they became A, B, C, and D Cos. respectively.

31 Bn. joined 82nd Bde., 27th Div., in March, 1915, was transferred on 15/11/15 to VII Corps Troops, and on 29/2/16 to 118th Bde., 39th Div.; Bn. joined 35th Div., 12th Div., on 10/5/18 at Lealvillers. On 19/5/18, 1/1/Camb. absorbed 11 offrs. and 408 o.r., 7/Suff. (see n. 29).

12TH (EASTERN) DIVISION

FORMATION, BATTLES, AND ENGAGEMENTS

This New Army Division had no existence before the outbreak of the Great War.

A proclamation was issued on the 11th August 1914 asking for an immediate addition of 100,000 men to the Regular Army (see Narrative 9th Division, and Appendix I). Army Order No. 324 of the 24th August (amended by Army Order No. 382 of the 11th September) authorized the addition of six divisions (9th–14th) and Army Troops to the Regular Army. This augmentation formed the First New Army, and late in August, 1914 the 12th (Eastern) Division began to assemble around Colchester, with the artillery at Shorncliffe.

The 12th Division was chiefly recruited from the Eastern and Home Counties. After enlistment, drill and route marching began at once ; but only improvised wooden rifles were available to accustom the recruits in handling arms. As soon as battalions had recruited up to war establishment they moved to the infantry brigade centres and more advanced training was then undertaken. In November, 1914 the three infantry brigades concentrated near Hythe, and in February, 1915 the pioneer battalion joined the Division. Towards the end of February the training had advanced far enough for the whole Division to move and concentrate at Aldershot, to complete its intensive training for war and take part in divisional field manœuvres. In the early spring of 1915 no fewer than five divisions (10th–14th) of the six in the First New Army were concentrated at Aldershot for their final training.

On the 24th May Aldershot Training Centre issued orders to the 12th Division to embark for France between 29th May–1st June. On the 25th May the divisional advanced parties left, and on the 29th the Division began to entrain at Aldershot. The personnel went via Folkestone and Boulogne, and artillery, engineers, horses, and transport moved via Southampton and le Havre. By midnight 1st/2nd June the entrainment at Aldershot was completed. Meanwhile, on the 1st June, the units had begun to arrive to the southward of St. Omer and by the 4th all the units had reached the concentration area. On the 5th June the Division advanced and joined III Corps.

Throughout the remainder of the Great War the 12th Division served on the Western Front in France and Belgium and was engaged in the following operations :

1915

1–8 October...	**Battle of Loos** [XI Corps, First Army].	
13–19 October	**The Quarries (Hulluch)** [XI Corps, First Army].	

1916

2–18 March ... ... **Hohenzollern Craters** [I Corps, First Army].

BATTLES OF THE SOMME

2–8 July ... ... **Battle of Albert** [III Corps, Fourth Army, until 5/7 ; then X Corps, Reserve Army].

28 July–13 Aug. ... ... **Battle of Pozières Ridge** [II Corps, Reserve Army].

1–18 October ... ... **Battle of the Transloy Ridges** [XV Corps, Fourth Army].

1917

BATTLES OF ARRAS

9–12 April	**First Battle of the Scarpe** [VI Corps, Third Army].
28 and 29 April	**Battle of Arleux** [VI Corps, Third Army].
3 and 4 May	**Third Battle of the Scarpe** [VI Corps, Third Army].
12 May	**Attack on Devil's Trench** [VI Corps, Third Army].*

BATTLE OF CAMBRAI

20 and 21 November ...	**The Tank Attack** [III Corps, Third Army].
23–28 November... ...	**Capture of Bourlon Wood** [III Corps, Third Army].
30 Nov.–3 Dec.	**German Counter-Attacks** [III Corps, Third Army].

1918

FIRST BATTLES OF THE SOMME

25 March	**First Battle of Bapaume** [VII Corps, Third Army].**
28 March	**Battle of Arras** [V Corps, Third Army].
5 April	**Battle of the Ancre** [V Corps, Third Army].

THE ADVANCE TO VICTORY

8–11 August	**Battle of Amiens** [III Corps, Fourth Army].

SECOND BATTLES OF THE SOMME

22 and 23 August ...	**Battle of Albert** [III Corps, Fourth Army].

BATTLES OF THE HINDENBURG LINE

18 September	**Battle of Epéhy** [III Corps, Fourth Army].
29 and 30 September...	**Battle of the St. Quentin Canal** [III Corps, Fourth Army].
6–29 October	**THE FINAL ADVANCE IN ARTOIS AND FLANDERS** [VIII Corps, First Army].

On the 28th October the 36th Brigade established a post on the right bank of the Schelde to the east of Château l'Abbaye (N.W. of Condé), and this was the last active operation to be performed by the 12th Division in the Great War. On the 29th October the Division was relieved in the front line and it moved back to rest and train. On the 9th November the 12th Division was quartered in the area Nivelle-Landas-Rumegies, with divisional headquarters centrally placed at Sameon, and it was still in this area when the Armistice came into force two days later.

Between the 25th and 27th November the Division moved to the Auberchicourt area (east of Douai) and was employed on salvage work and training. On the 12th December the first party of coalminers left and thenceforward demobilization proceeded steadily. On the 3rd February 1919, H.R.H. the Prince of Wales arrived at divisional headquarters at Masny ; he spent the next two days with the Division and presented colours to the infantry service battalions. Demobilization proceeded with increasing speed and gradually the Division dwindled. On the 17th March the G.O.C. left, and on the 22nd March the 12th Division ceased to exist and the residue was thereafter designated 12th Division Brigade Group.***

During its war service in the Great War the 12th (Eastern) Division gained 6 Victoria Crosses and 3,053 other honours, and the Division lost 41,363 killed, wounded, and missing.

---

* From 20/6–25/10/1917, a period of eighteen weeks, the 12th Division held the line (east of Monchy) on an active front. (In VII Corps from 20/6–noon, 1/7 ; then in XVII Corps.)
** On arrival at Senlis in the morning of 25/3/18 the 12th Division came under VII Corps ; but between 8.20 p.m.–11.35 p.m. on the 25th the 12th Division was transferred to V Corps.
*** On 27/6/19 the 12th Division Brigade Group disappeared at Dunkirk.

13TH (WESTERN) DIVISION

G.O.C.

24 August, 1914	Major-General R. G. KEKEWICH (died, 5/11/14).
26 October, 1914	Major-General H. B. JEFFREYS.
15 March, 1915	Major-General F. C. SHAW (sick, 22/8/15).
22 August, 1915	Br.-Gen. J. H. DU B. TRAVERS (acting).
23 August, 1915	Major-General F. S. MAUDE.
10 July, 1916	Br.-Gen. W. DE S. CAYLEY (tempy.).
8 August, 1916	Major-General W. DE S. CAYLEY (to III (Tigris) Corps, 20/5/18 ; on leave to U.K. from 29/6/18).
20 May, 1918	Br.-Gen. J. W. O'DOWDA (acting).
[23 December, 1918...	Major-General Sir W. DE S. CAYLEY.]

G.S.O. 1.

24 Aug., 1914...Lt.-Col. M. EARLE
(acting).
19 Sept., 1914...Major D. M. WATT
(acting).
12 Nov., 1914...Lt.-Col. W. H. F. BASEVI.
11 Jan., 1915...Lt.-Col. W. GILLMAN.
9 Oct., 1915...Lt.-Col. R. J.T. HILDYARD
(sick, 10/7/16).
10 July, 1916...Major L. I. G.
MORGAN-OWEN (acting).
28 July, 1916...Lt.-Col. R. J. T. HILDYARD.
19 May, 1917...Major L. I. G.
MORGAN-OWEN (acting).
11 Sept., 1917...Lt.-Col. L. I. G.
MORGAN-OWEN.
24 Sept., 1918...Lt.-Col. C. KIRKPATRICK.
[18 Nov., 1918...Major L. V. BOND
(acting).]

A.-A. and Q.-M.-G.

23 Aug., 1914...Captain W. D. S.
BROWNRIGG (acting).
10 Oct., 1914...Colonel R. G. BURTON.
18 Nov., 1915...Lt.-Col. W. D. S.
BROWNRIGG.
5 July, 1918...Major A. R.
GODWIN-AUSTEN (acting).
5 Sept., 1918...Lt.-Col. W. D. S.
BROWNRIGG.
29 Sept., 1918...Major A. R.
GODWIN-AUSTEN (acting).
[15 Dec., 1918...Lt.-Col. A. R.
GODWIN-AUSTEN.]

B.-G., R.A.

12 Oct., 1914...Br.-Gen. A. B. HELYAR
(to B.-G., R.A., 10th Div.
on 11/10/15).
14 Dec., 1915...Br.-Gen. F. E. L. BARKER
(from B.-G., R.A., 10th Div. ;
sick, 2/6/16).*
2 June, 1916...Lt.-Col. R. A. VIGNE
(acting ; sick, 15/7/16).
15 July, 1916...Lt.-Col. W. P. L. DAVIES
(acting).
18 Nov., 1916...Br.-Gen. G. F. WHITE.
10 Dec., 1916...Lt.-Col. W. P. L. DAVIES
(acting).
17 Feb., 1917...Br.-Gen. W. P. L. DAVIES
(on leave to U.K., 28/6/18).
28 June, 1918...Lt.-Col. N. ST. C.
CAMPBELL (acting).
[23 Nov., 1918...Br.-Gen. W. P. L. DAVIES.]

C.R.E.

26 Oct., 1914...Lt.-Col. G. D. CLOSE
(wd., 8/8/15).
8 Aug., 1915...Major A. J. WOLFF
(acting).
21 Sept., 1915...Lt.-Col. A. J. WOLFF
(sick, 2/6/16).
3 June, 1916...Captain A. E. CONINGHAM
(acting ; sick, 23/8/16).
23 Aug., 1916...Captain W. H. ROBERTS
(acting).
By 28 Sept., 1916...Lt.-Col. W. H. ROBERTS.
29 Dec., 1916...Lt.-Col. W.
TYLDEN-PATTENSON.

---

* 10th Div. R.A. Hd. Qrs. became 13th Div. R.A. Hd. Qrs. on 14/12/15.   Br.-Gen. F. E. L. Barker was B.-G., R.A., 10th Div. from 29/11/15.

38th BDE.

5 Sept., '14...Br.-Gen. A. H. BALDWIN
(killed, 10/8/15).
11 Aug., '15...Br.-Gen. G. W. C.
KNATCHBULL (wd., 17/11/15).
17 Nov., '15...Lt.-Col. J. G. FAIRLIE
(acting).
19 Nov., '15...Br.-Gen. J. W. O'DOWDA
(sick, 7/11/16).
7 Nov., '16...Lt.-Col. B. MACNAGHTEN
(acting).
8 Nov., '16...Lt.-Col. A. R. HALL
(acting).
6 Dec., '16...Br.-Gen. J. W. O'DOWDA.
20 May, '18...Lt.-Col. F. H. CHARLTON
(acting).
[24 Dec., '18...Br.-Gen. J. W. O'DOWDA.]

39th BDE.

28 Aug., '14...Br.-Gen. W. DE S. CAYLEY.
10 July, '16...Lt.-Col. T. A. ANDRUS
(tempy.).
8 Aug., '16...Br.-Gen. T. A. ANDRUS.
17 June, '18...Lt.-Col. W. F. O. FAVIELL
(acting).
29 Sept., '18...Br.-Gen. T. A. ANDRUS.
[23 Jan., '19...Lt.-Col. R. P. Jordan
(acting).
9 Mar., '19...Col. D. SHUTTLEWORTH.
19 April, '19⎫ Br.-Gen. D.
–31 Aug., '19⎭   SHUTTLEWORTH.]

40th BDE.

5 Sept., '14...Br.-Gen. J. H. DU B. TRAVERS.
22 Aug., '15...Lt.-Col. A. HAY (acting).
24 Aug., '15...Br.-Gen. J. H. DU B. TRAVERS (sick, 20/9/15).
20 Sept., '15...Lt.-Col. A. HAY (acting).
5 Oct., '15...Br.-Gen. J. H. DU B. TRAVERS (sick, 17/10/15).
17 Oct., '15...Br.-Gen. A. C. LEWIN.
13 July, '18...Lt.-Col. C. E. KITCHIN (acting).
16 July, '18...Br.-Gen. A. C. LEWIN (to Dunsterforce, 30/7/18).
30 July, '18...Lt.-Col. C. E. KITCHIN (acting).
14 Sept., '18...Br.-Gen. A. C. LEWIN.

GENERAL NOTES

The following Units also served with 13th (Western) Division :—

MOUNTED TROOPS :—C Squadron, 33/Cavalry, from 5/3–30/3/16 ; C Sqdn. then rejoined its regiment at Shaikh Saad.

ARTILLERY :—13 Heavy Battery, R.G.A., was raised to form part of 13th Division and the Hy. Bty. at first was armed with 4·7″ guns. On 27/5/15 the Hy. Bty. returned its 4·7″ guns and drew 4, 60-pdrs. On 30/5/15 the Hy. Bty. received orders to embark for France as part of XVII Hy. Arty. Bde. Hy. Bty. embkd. on 2/6/15, disembkd. at le Havre on 3/6/15, was in action near Lacouture on 10/6/15, and by 30/6/15 the Hy. Bty. had fired 917 rounds. On 23/10/15 the Hy. Bty. left XVII Hy. Arty. Bde. and went to Marseille to embark with the 28th Div. for Salonika. The Hy. Bty. disembkd. at Salonika on 26/11/15. On 26/2/16 the Hy. Bty. joined XXXVII Hy. Arty. Bde., and the Hy. Bty. then served in Macedonia for the remainder of the War.

72 Heavy Battery, R.G.A (4, 4·7″ guns), was quartered at Peshawar in August, 1914. Hy. Bty. mobilized at Quetta on 9/12/15 and was re-armed with 4, 5″ B.L. Hows. Bty. embkd. at Karachi on 20/12/15, disembkd. at Basra on 26/12/15, reached Ali al Gharbi on 31/12/15, and Bty. was attached to 7th (Meerut) Div. until 2/5/16, when the Bty. was transferred to Corps Arty. On 24/8/16 Bty. joined 13th Div. ; and on 16/10/16 Bty. returned its 5″ how. equipment to Basra and by 1/11/16 it received 4·5″ how. equipment for 4 hows. On 23/11/16 Bty. was posted to LXVI Bde. (see note 22). On 17/6/17 Bty. left LXVI Bde. (on reorganization) and was transferred to 15th (Indian) Div. On 9/9/17 Bty. (4, 4·5″ hows.) joined VIII Bde., which had landed at Basra on 18/8/17 ; and, on 12/6/18, 72 Hy. Bty., R.G.A., became 428 (H.) Bty., R.F.A.

91 Heavy Battery, R.G.A. (4, 60-pdrs.), received orders on 7/6/15 to join 13th Div. and go to Gallipoli with the Division. On 11/7/15 the Hy. Bty. embkd., it landed at Helles on 24/7/15, and was attached to XX Hy. Arty. Group (Group Hd. Qrs. at Suvla). The Hy. Bty. remained in action at Helles until 4/1/16 ; it then re-embkd. and reached Alexandria on 13/2/16. On 26/2/16 the Hy. Bty. moved to el Qantara and joined No. 3 Section, Canal Defences. In 1917 the Hy. Bty. joined XCVI Bde., R.G.A. ; and for the remainder of the War the Hy. Bty. served in Egypt and Palestine.

2/104 Heavy Battery, R.G.A. (4, 60-pdrs.). 1 Section was attached to 13th Div. on 10/2/17 ; and the Battery was attached from 25/2–5/3/17. The Bty. was again attached on 25/10/17 ; and 1 Sec. left the Division on 28/11/17, and 2/104 (less 1 Sec.) on 5/12/17.

1 Sec., 157 Heavy Battery, R.G.A. (2, 60-pdrs.), was attached from 7/1–12/2/17.

159 Siege Battery, R.G.A. (4, 6″ hows.), was attached from 14/2–28/2/17.

177 Heavy Battery, R.G.A. (4, 60-pdrs.), was attached from 25/10/17–29/5/18.

384 Siege Battery, R.G.A. (4, 6″ hows.), was attached from 25/10/17–1/10/18.

387 Siege Battery, R.G.A. (4, 6″ hows.), was raised at Weymouth, 19/2–25/4/17, armed with 6″ hows. at Cosham on 18/6/17, and disembkd. at le Havre on 15/7/17. Bty. embarked at Taranto on 29/7/17, disembkd. at Basra on 18/8/17, reached Hinaidi on 3/10/17, and Bty. was attached to 13th Division from 25/10/17–24/3/18. Bty. went to Egypt, disembarked at Suez on 17/5/18, and served in Palestine for the remainder of the War.

26 (Jacob's) Mountain Battery, R.G.A. (6, 2·75″ guns). L. Sec. joined 13th Div. on 23/10/17 ; H.Q. and Centre Sec. joined Div. on 13/4/18 ; and R. Sec. joined Div. on 8/6/18. 26 Mtn. Bty. left 13th Div. on 10/8/18, en route for Persia.

92 A.-A. Sec. (2, 13-pdr., 6-cwt. guns), was attached from 6/5/17–2/1/18 ; and from 14/9–29/11/18.

" M " Sec., A.-A. (2, 2-pdr. pom-poms), was attached from 18/5–18/9/18.

" P " Sec., A.-A. (2, 2-pdr. pom-poms), was attached from 1/4–29/5/18 ; and from 10/6–8/11/18.

133, 135, 136, 137 Trench Howitzer Batteries (each 4, 2″ mortars), disembkd. at Basra on 9/11/16, received numbers on 5/12/16, and the first mortars arrived on 22/12/16. The 4 trench howitzer batteries were attached to the 13th Div. as follows :—**133,** from 23/1–2/2/17, and from 5–7/2/17 ; **135,** from 16–28/1/17, and from 6–7/2/17 ; **136,** from 18–28/1/17, and from 8–28/2/17 ; and **137,** from 18–28/1/17, and from 8–28/2/17.

INFANTRY :—2/7 Hants (from 134th Bde., 45th Div.) was attached to 40th Inf. Bde. from Sept. 1918—27/12/18.

8/Welsh, originally in 40th Inf. Bde., was converted into Divnl. Pioneer Bn. in January 1915.

5/Wilts. (from Army Troops) replaced 8/Welsh in 40th Inf. Bde.

OTHER UNITS :—24th Sanitary Section, served with the 13th Division in England and in July, 1915 the Section went to Egypt. For the remainder of the War the Section served on the L. of C. in Egypt and Palestine.

28th Sanitary Section, disembarked at Basra on 10/3/16, reached Shaikh Saad on 28/3/16 and joined 13th Division. The Section served in Mesopotamia with 13th Division for the remainder of the War.

13th Division Motor Ambce. Workshop, served in England with 13th Division. The Workshop remained in England when 13th Division embarked for Gallipoli in July, 1915.

13TH (WESTERN) DIVISION

Dates	INFANTRY — Brigades	Battalions and attached Units	Mounted Troops	ARTILLERY — Field Artillery: Brigades	Batteries	Bde. Ammn. Colns.	Trench Mortar Bties. Medium	Heavy	Divnl. Ammn. Coln.	Engineers Field Cos.	Signal Service Divnl. Signal Coy.	Pioneers	M.G. Units	Field Ambulances	Mobile Vety. Secn.	Divnl. Emplnt. Coy.	Divnl. Train
1914 October (England)	38th .... 39th 40th	6/K.O., 6/E. Lanc., 6/S. Lanc., 6/L.N.L. 9/R. War., 7/Glouc., 9/Worc., 7/N. Staff. 8/Ches., 8/R.W.F., 4/S.W.B., 5/Wilts.	13th Div. Cyclist Coy.[1]	LXVI[2] .... LXVII[2] .... LXVIII[2] .... LXIX (H.)[2]	208, 209, 210 211, 212, 213 214, 215, 216 217 (H.), 218 (H.), 219 (H.)	LXVI B.A.C. LXVII B.A.C. LXVIII B.A.C. LXIX (H.) B.A.C.	...	...	13th D.A.C.[3]	71st 72n1 88th[4]	13th	8/Welsh (P.)	...	39th 40th 41st	24th	...	13th[5]
1915 July (Gallipoli)	38th .... 39th 40th	6/K.O., 6/E. Lanc., 6/S. Lanc., 6/L.N.L. 9/R. War., 7/Glouc., 9/Worc., 7/N. Staff. 8/Ches., 8/R.W.F., 4/S.W.B., 5/Wilts.	13th Div. Cyclist Coy.	LXVI[2] ; [6] .... LXVII[2] ; [7] .... LXVIII[2] ; [8] .... LXIX (H.)[2] ; [9]	A, B, C, D A, B, C, D A, B, C, D A (H.), B (H.), C (H.), D (H.)	LXVI B.A.C. LXVII B.A.C. LXVIII B.A.C. LXIX (H.) B.A.C.	...	...	...	71st 72nd 88th	13th	8/Welsh (P.)	...	39th 40th 41st	24th	...	...
1916 February (Egypt)	38th .... 39th 40th	6/K.O., 6/E. Lanc., 6/S. Lanc., 6/L.N.L. 9/R. War., 7/Glouc., 9/Worc., 7/N. Staff. 8/Ches., 8/R.W.F., 4/S.W.B., 5/Wilts.	13th Div. Cyclist Coy.	LV[10] .... LVI[11] .... LXVI[12] .... LXIX (H.)[13]	A, B, C, D A, B, C, D A, B, C, D A (H.), B (H.), (C) (H.), D (H.)	LV B.A.C. LVI B.A.C. LXVI B.A.C. LXIX (H.) B.A.C.	...	...	...	71st 72nd 88th	13th	8/Welsh (P.)	...	39th 40th 41st	24th	...	...
1916 June (Mesopotamia)	38th .... 39th 40th	6/K.O., 6/E. Lanc., 6/S. Lanc., 6/L.N.L. 9/R. War., 7/Glouc., 9/Worc., 7/N. Staff. 8/Ches., 8/R.W.F., 4/S.W.B., 5/Wilts.	D Sqdn., 1/Herts. Yeo.[14] 13th Div. Cyclist Coy.	LV LXVI	A, B, C, D A, B, C, D A (H.)[15] ; [21] [LXIX H.]	LV B.A.C.[15] LXVI B.A.C.[15]	...	...	...	71st 72nd 88th	13th	8/Welsh (P.)	...	39th 40th 41st	24th	...	13th Div. Troops S. & T. Coln.[16] 10/Fd. Bakery[17] 31/Fd. Butchery[18]
1917 January (Mesopotamia)	38th 39th 40th	6/K.O., 6/E. Lanc., 6/S. Lanc., 6/L.N.L.; 38th M.G. Coy.;[19] 38th Bde. S. & T. Coy.[20] 9/R. War., 7/Glouc., 9/Worc., 7/N. Staff.; 39th M.G. Coy.;[19] 39th Bde. S. & T. Coy.[20] 8/Ches., 8/R.W.F., 4/S.W.B., 5/Wilts.; 40th M.G. Coy.;[19] 40th Bde. S. & T. Coy.[20]	13th Div. Cyclist Coy.	LV .... LXVI	A, B, C, D; A (H.)/ LXIX (H.)[21] A, B, C, D; 72 (H.)[22]	LV B.A.C. LXVI B.A.C.	••	...	...	71st 72nd 88th	13th	8/Welsh (P.)	...	39th 40th 41st	24th	...	13th Div. Troops S. & T. Coy. 10/Fd. Bakery 31/Fd. Butchery

		Battalions, etc.	Mounted Troops	Artillery (Brigades)	(Batteries)		Bde. Ammn. Cols.	Trench Mortar Btys.		Field Coys. R.E.	Signal	Pioneers	M.G. Units	Field Ambulances	Mob. Vet. Sec.		Divisional Train
1917 July (Mesopotamia)	38th	6/K.O., 6/E. Lanc., 6/S. Lanc, 6/L.N.L.; 38th M.G. Coy.; 38th Bde. S. & T. Coy.	D Sqdn. 1/Herts. Yeo.[23] 13th Div. Cyclist Coy.	LV[24] LXVI[25]	A, B, C; 60 (H.)[26]; A, B, C; 61 (H.)[27]	...	LV B.A.C. LXVI B.A.C.	...	...	71st 72nd 88th	13th	8/ Welsh (P.)	...	39th 40th 41st	24th	...	13th Div. Troops S. & T. Coy. 10/Fd. Bakery. 31/Fd. Butchery
	39th	9/R. War., 7/Glouc., 9/Worc., 7/N.Staff.; 39th Bde. S. & T. Coy.; 40th M.G. Coy.; 5/Wilts.; 40th Bde. S. & T. Coy.															
	40th	8/Ches., 8/R.W.F., 4/S.W.B., 5/Wilts.; 40th M.G. Coy.; 40th Bde. S. & T. Coy.															
1918 April (Mesopotamia)	38th	6/K.O., 6/E. Lanc., 6/S. Lanc, 6/L.N.L.; 38th M.G. Coy.; 38th T.M. Bty.;[28] 38th S.A.A. Sec.;[29] 38th S. & T. Coy.[34]	13th Div. Cyclist Coy.	LV LXVI	A, B, C; 60 (H.); A, B, C; 61 (H.)	...	LV B.A.C. LXVI B.A.C.	...	...	71st 72nd 88th	13th	8/ Welsh (P.)	273rd M.G. Coy.[30]	39th 40th 41st	24th	...	13th Div. Troops S. & T. Coy. 10/Fd. Bakery. 31/Fd. Butchery
	39th	9/R. War., 7/Glouc., 9/Worc., 7/N.Staff.; 39th M.G.Coy.; 39th T.M. Bty.;[28] 39th S.A.A. Sec.;[29] 39th S. & T. Coy.															
	40th	8/Ches., 8/R.W.F., 4/S.W.B., 5/Wilts.; 40th M.G. Coy.; 40th T.M. Bty.;[28] 40th S.A.A. Sec.;[29] 40th Bde. S. & T. Coy.[34]															
1918 August (Mesopotamia)	38th	6/K.O., 6/E. Lanc., 6/S. Lanc, 6/L.N.L.; 38th M.G. Coy.; 38th T.M. Bty.; 38th S.A.A. Sec.	13th Div. Cyclist Coy.	LV LXVI	A, B, C; 60 (H.); A, B, C; 61 (H.)	...	LV B.A.C. LXVI B.A.C.	X.13[32] X.13A[35]	...	71st 72nd[81] 88th	13th	8/ Welsh (P.)	273rd M.G. Coy.	39th 40th[51] 41st	24th	...	13th[34] 10/Fd. Bakery. 31/Fd. Butchery
	39th[31]	9/R. War.,[31] 7/Glouc.,[31] 9/ Worc.,[31] 7/N. Staff.;[31] 39th M.G. Coy.;[31] 39th T.M. Bty.;[31] 39th S.A.A. Sec.;[31] 39th Bde. S. & T. Coy.[31]															
	40th	8/Ches., 8/R.W.F., 4/S.W.B., 5/Wilts.; 40th M.G. Coy.; 40th T.M. Bty.; 40th S.A.A. Sec.															

NOTES

1 The Cyclist Coy. was formed late in 1914; it went to Gallipoli with the 13th Div.

2 Bties. were all raised on the 6-gun basis and numbered. By Feb., 1915, all Bdes. were reorganized as 4-battery Bdes., the Bties. all became 4-gun batteries, and Bties. were lettered A, B, C, D in each Bde. The batteries of LXIX (H.) were armed with 5″ B.L. howitzers.

3 The D.A.C. did not go overseas with the 13th Div.

4 Fd. Coy. joined Div. in England, in Jany., 1915, from 22nd Div.

5 The Train did not go overseas with the 13th Div.; supply details only accompanied 13th Div. overseas. The Train (120,121,122,123 Cos.) remained in England until 11/11/15, when it embkd. for Alexandria, joined 28th Div. as Divnl. Train on 16/11/15, and reached Salonika on 10/12/15. The Train served with 28th Div. for the rest of the War.

6 Bde. embkd. at Avonmouth on 15-17/6/15, reached Alexandria on 4/7/15, re-embkd. on 21/7/15, transhipped at Mudros, and Bde. H.Q., 4 Bties., and B.A.C. landed at Helles between 25-28/7/15. Bde. went into action under VIII Corps—part in Counter-Battery Group and part in Right Group. Bde. evacuated Helles between 1-7/1/16, concentrated with 13th Div. at Mudros until 12/1/16, and then sailed for Alexandria. Bde. disembkd. on 18/1/16 and reached Port Said on 29/1/16; Bde. was then 39 all ranks above and 35 horses and 6 guns below establishment.

7 Bde. embkd. at Avonmouth on 15/6/15, disembkd. at Alexandria on 29/6/15, and remained there until 9/10/15. Bde. then re-embkd., disembkd. at Salonika between 13-17/10/15, and joined 10th Div.

8 Bde. embkd. at Avonmouth on 18/6/15, disembkd. at Alexandria on 4/7/15, and remained there until 10/10/15. Bde. then re-embkd., disembkd. at Salonika between 13-15/10/15, and joined 10th Div.

9 Bde. embkd. at Avonmouth between 18-24/6/15, reached Alexandria on 6/7/15, and left there the B.A.C. and all horses and 1st Line wagons as well as 50 men from each unit; remainder of Bde. then sailed for Mudros and arrived on 9-11/7/15. Bde. H.Q. and 4 Bties. disembkd. at Anzac on 15-19/7/15 and went into action on 21 and 22/7/15: A and C with 1st Aus. Div. and B and D with A. and N.Z. Div. During Sept. and Oct. the ammn. expenditure only averaged 2¼ rounds per gun per day; and by the end of Nov. the effective strength of the Bde. was only 273 all ranks. Bde. evacuated Anzac on 19/12/15; A and B each abandoned 1 destroyed how.; and B, C, and D each destroyed all firing-battery wagons. On 31/12/15 the Bde. was reassembled at Alexandria.

10 Bde. was formed for 10th Div. Bde. embkd. on 7/7/15 with 10th Div., disembkd. at Alexandria on 19/7/15, reached Mudros on 28/8/15, served at Suvla from 30/8-19/12/15, and reached Alexandria on 3/1/16. Bde. was then allotted to 13th Div., and went with 13th Div. to Mesopotamia, embkg. on 17 and 18/2/16, and landing at Basra on 17/3/16.

11 Bde. was formed for 10th Div. Bde. embkd. on 8/7/15 with 10th Div., disembkd. at Alexandria on 20/7/15, reached Mudros on 13/8/15, served at Helles from 23/8/15-5/1/16, and reached Alexandria on 14/1/16. Bde. was then allotted to 13th Div. and went to Mesopotamia with 13th Div. Bde. embkd. at Port Said on 17/2/16, transhipped at Kowet on 4/3/16, and landed at Ashar on 7-10/8/16. On 2/7/16 Bde. was transferred to 7th (Meerut) Div. in Mesopotamia.

joined Bde. on 10/8/17. Bde. accompanied 7th (Meerut) Div. to Palestine early in 1918. On 1/4/18 the Bde. was transferred to 52nd (Lowland) Div. in Palestine; and in April, 1918, Bde. went to France with 52nd Div. Bde. then served with 52nd Div. for the remainder of the Great War.

12 Bde. sailed from Suez on 15/2/16, disembkd. at Basra on 2-6/3/16, and reached Shaikh Saad on 20/3/16.

13 Bde. embkd. at Alexandria on 14/2/16, cleared Suez on 18/2/16, and disembkd. at Basra on 7 and 9/3/16, and Bde. reached the front at Ora on 4/4/16. By 3/5/16 Bde. was broken up: A Bty. remained with 13th Div. (see n. 21); B Bty. joined 3rd (Lahore) Div., and eventually was posted to IV Bde.; C Bty. joined 14th (Indian) Div. and eventually was posted to XIII Bde.; and D Bty. joined 7th (Meerut) Div. and eventually was posted to IX Bde. Early in 1918 D Bty. accompanied 7th (Meerut) Div. to Palestine; and in Palestine on 1/4/18 D Bty. was transferred to 52nd (Lowland) Div. In April, 1918, D Bty. (in IX Bde.) went to France with 52nd Div. and served with 52nd Div. for the remainder of the Great War.

14 D Sqdn. left Alexandria on 27/3/16, embkd. at Suez on 28/3/16, and disembkd. at Basra on 16/3/16. Sqdn. joined 13th Div. at Shaikh Saad on 8/7/16 and served with 13th Div. until 20/11/16. Sqdn. was temporarily attached to Remount Depot at Amara until 31/12/16; then it joined 1 Sqdn., 10/Lcrs., 2 Sqdns., 32/Lcrs. and formed III (Tigris) Corps Cav. Regt.

15 On 24/8/16 S.A.A. secs. of B.A.C.s ceased to exist as units in Mesopotamia; and personnel and animals were transferred to Corps Ammn. Coln.

16 Formed in Mesopotamia. Before leaving Egypt in Feby., 1916 the Div. drew at Ismailia 1000 A.T. Carts (4 A.T. Carts = 1 G.S. Wagon; or 2 A.T. Carts = 1 G.S. Limbered Wagon).

17 Joined on 23/4/16, and then became a mobile unit. 10/Fd. Bakery was the first mobile British Fd. Bakery.

18 Joined on 23/4/16.

19 Bde. M.G. Cos. were formed as follows:—
38th—nucleus of coy. left Devonport on 18/9/18, disembkd. at Basra on 15/10/16, reached Amara on 24/10/16, amalgamated with provl. bde. m.g. coy., and formed 38th M.G. Coy.;
39th—nucleus of coy. arrived from England, reached Amara and on 25/10/16 amalgamated with provl. bde. m.g. coy., and formed 39th M.G. Coy. on 26/10/16;
40th—nucleus of Coy. left Grantham on 18/10/16, arrived Amara on 24/10/16, and amalgamated with provl. bde. m.g. coy. (formed on 23/5/16 with the m.g. secs. of the 4 bns.), and became 40th M.G. Coy.
Each M.G. Coy. had 16 Vickers light guns.

20 Formed by Jany., 1917.

21 A/LXIX (H.) was rearmed with 4·5″ hows. by 31/10/16; and on 23/11/16 A/LXIX (H.) joined LV. On 15/6/17 A/LXIX (H.) transferred from LV to 14th (Indian) Div., and its sec. of B.A.C. followed on 19/6/17. Bty. was eventually posted to XXX Bde., R.F.A.

22 72 (H.) Bty., R.G.A. (4, 4·5″ hows. and 1 sec. of B.A.C.), was attached to LXVI Bde. from 23/11/16-17/8/17 ; 72 (H.) and sec. of B.A.C. then joined 15th (Indian) Div.; 72 (H.) Bty. was eventually transferred to VIII Bde., with 3rd (Lahore) Div. (Also see General Notes.)

23 Sqdn. rejoined 13th Div. on 3/3/17 and served with Div. until 3/8/17. On 6/8/17 Sqdn. joined 15th (Indian) Div.

24 LV was reorganized in 3, 6-gun 18-pdr. bties. on 15/8/17: D was broken up, 1 sec. joined B and 1 sec. joined C. On 19/11/17 1 sec. of 388 Bty. arrived and made up A to 6, 18 pdrs. (also see n. 20).

25 LXVI was reorganized in 3, 6-gun 18-pdr. bties. on 15/6/17: D was broken up, 1 sec. joined A and 1 sec. joined B. On 19/11/17 1 sec. of 388 Bty. arrived and made up C to 6, 18-pdrs. (also see n. 27).

26 60 (H.)—6, 4·5″ hows. and 1 sec. of CXXXIV B.A.C. (from CXXXIV (H.), III Corps Arty.), joined LV on 19/6/17, from III (Tigris) Corps Arty. In Aug., 1914, 60 (H.) formed part of XLIV (H.) in 2nd Div. (I Corps, B.E.F.).

27 61 (H.)—6, 4·5″ hows.—from CXXXIV (H.), joined LXVI on 18/6/17 from III (Tigris) Corps Arty., and was followed on 19/6/17 by 1 sec. of CXXXIV B.A.C. In Aug., 1914, 61 (H.) formed part of VIII (H.) in 5th Div. (II Corps, B.E.F.).

28 Stokes mortars began to reach 13th Div. on 24/12/16; and Bde. T.M. Bties. formed as follows:—
38th—G Bty. was formed on 29/12/16, joined Div. on 18/1/17, and served with 39th Bde. until 7/10/17, when G was transferred to 38th Bde. It received its final organization on 1/2/18, and was redesignated 38th on 18/2/18;
39th—H Bty. was formed in Feb., 1917, for 36th Bde., 14th (Indian) Division; on 8/10/17 Bty. was transferred to 39th Bde. at Sadiya. Bty. received its final organization on 1/2/18, and was redesignated 39th on 18/2/18;
40th—I Bty. was formed by March, 1917, joined 40th Bde. on 23/9/17. Bty. received its final organization on 1/2/18, and was redesignated 40th on 18/2/18.

29 The Secs. were attached to Inf. Bdes. by March, 1918; and by 4/6/18 were manned by infantry personnel.

30 Formation of 13th Div. M.G. Coy. was authorized on 9/10/17, and formation of Coy. began 9-11/10/17. On 13/11/17 M.G. Coy. completed formation by taking over Secs. from 173rd, 195th, 225th, and 248th M.G. Cos. (which had landed at Basra on 8-9/11/17), and the 4 secs. were formed into a Coy. on 12-13/11/17. M.G. Coy. thus formed was numbered 273rd M.G. Coy.

31 On 1/7/18 39th Bde. Group received orders to join North Persia Force in Persia. 39th Bde. Group left 13th Div. between 10/7-19/8/18 and moved via Hamadan and Kasvin. On 24/8/18 Bde. H.Q. disembkd. at Baku (Russia) and attended a conference at Dunsterforce Hd. Qrs. (Also see General Notes on 39th Bde. on p. 41.)

32 Formation of Bty. was ordered on 25/6/18 ; 4, 6″ Newton Trench Mortars reached 13th Div. between 25/7/18 and X.13 was abolished on 24/11/18.

33 On 18/9/18 X.13A began to form. Between 10-13/10/18 X 13A was demobilized, and on 24/11/18 the Bty. was abolished.

34 On 1/8/18, 38th and 40th Bde. S. & T. Cos. were withdrawn from 38th and 40th Inf. Bdes. and, with 13th Div. Troops S. & T. Coy., were formed into 13th Div. Train. The 3 Cos. were numbered 1, 2, and 4 Cos.

39th INFANTRY BRIGADE, JULY, 1918–AUGUST, 1919

On 1/7/18, 39th Bde. (under Lt.-Col. W. F. O. Faviell, acting Brigadier) received orders to move to N. Persia (see note 31). The move began on 4/7/18. The Bde. was to move north via Khaniqin (25/7), Kermanshah (27/7), and Hamadan. The leading troops reached Hamadan on 29/7/18. On 1/8/18 troops were pushed on towards Kazvin and Enzeli. On 5/8/18, 7/N. Staff. reached Baku; and on 11/8/18 the rear troops of the Bde. reached Hamadan. By this time the Bde. was very scattered. On 12/8/18 Bde. Hd. Qrs. reached Kazvin, and small parties were daily leaving Kazvin for Baku. On 20/8/18, 9/R. War. arrived at Baku, and on the same day Bde. Hd. Qrs. left Kazvin and reached Kazian (near Enzeli) on 21/8/18. On 22/8/18, Bde. Hd. Qrs. embarked on Russian s.s. *Tuga*, disembarked at Baku on 24/8/18, and attended a conference at Dunsterforce Hd. Qrs. in Hotel Europe. (On 4/9/18, 9/Worc. (less No. 1 Coy., see below) reached Baku.) 39th Brigade took part in :—

DEFENCE OF BAKU (26/8–15/9/18)

39th Bde. held part of the defensive line, north and west of Baku: Digva–Binagadi–Mud Volcano.

The fighting at Baku was divided into 4 phases, viz. : (i) Turkish Attack on Mud Volcano (held by D Coy., 7/N. Staff.—Captain B. H. Sparrow) on 26/8/18 ; (ii) Turkish Attack on Binagadi Hill, 31/8/18 ; (iii) Turkish Attack on Digva, 1/9/18 ; and (iv) Turkish General Attack on Baku, 14/9/18.

On 26/8/18 the attack on Mud Volcano opened at 10.30 a.m., and at 1.30 p.m. Capt. Sparrow and the last of D Coy. were seen surrounded and engaged in hand to hand fighting. Only 6 unwounded men and a few early casualties got away, and the Company lost 3 offrs. and 80 o.r. killed, wounded, and missing. The Turks then moved against Binagadi Hill and the hill was hurriedly evacuated by the Armenian Bn. which held it. A Coy., 7/N. Staff., was hurried from Digva to Binagadi, and the Company arrived about 2.15 p.m., just in time to save the situation. A Company at once occupied the empty trenches and succeeded in surprising a party of 250 Turks who were moving up the western slope to occupy the hill. The Turks were driven back with heavy loss.

At 6 a.m. on 31/8/18 the Turks attacked Binagadi Hill in force, and at 8.30 a.m., after severe fighting, A Coy., 7/N. Staff., was ordered to withdraw to the Oil Derricks (south of the hill). In this defence the Coy. lost the commander and one other officer as well as 34 other ranks killed, wounded, and missing.

On 1/9/18 the Turks attacked Digva. The Armenians and Russians, near Digva, broke, and in covering their withdrawal 9/R. War. lost 4 offrs. and 67 o.r. either taken prisoner or missing. The fighting value of the local troops was negligible, and the responsibility for the defence of Baku really fell on the British force. On 14/9/18 the Turks launched a general attack against local troops who still occupied part of the Baku defences. The local troops broke at once and exposed the flanks of the British troops. Baku was evacuated, and the situation seemed so serious that all documents were destroyed. Eventually the Turks were held back; but owing to lack of reserves, the situation could not be restored and the British troops re-embarked. On 15/9/18 Bde. Hd. Qrs. reached Enzeli.

On 19/9/18, 9/Worc. moved to Resht ; on the same day Br.-Gen. Andrus returned from Ceylon and took over command of troops at Resht and Kazian, and on 29/9/18 Br.-Gen. Andrus resumed command of 39th Bde. On 29/9/18, 9/R. War. sailed from Enzeli to Krasnovodsk to join Maj.-Gen. W. Malleson's Force. On 1/10/18, 7/Glouc. was moving up from Bijar–Zenjan, and by the end of the month 7/Glouc. concentrated at Kazvin ; the other bns. were then at Enzeli, Resht, and Krasnovodsk. At noon on Thursday, 31st October, 1918, hostilities ceased with Turkey.

On 15/11/18, 7/Glouc. concentrated at Enzeli ; and on the same day, 39th Bde. Hd. Qrs. 7/Glouc. (less 1 Coy.), 9/Worc. (less 1 sec.), 7/N. Staff, 39th Bde. M.G. Coy. (less 1 sec. at Krasnovodsk), and 39th Bde. S. and T. Coy. embkd. at Enzeli and disembkd. at Baku on 17/11/18. The whole force at Baku was placed under B.-G.C., 39th Inf. Bde. On 30/11/18 the strength of the Bde. was 1,480 all ranks. On 9/12/18 the remaining Coy. of 7/Glouc. reached Baku, and on 12/12/18, 39th Bde. S.A.A. Sec. and part of 72/Fd. Coy. also arrived. At the end of the year the effective strength of the Bde. was 2,027 all ranks.

From 1/1/19 all troops in Baku came under the orders of G.H.Q., Constantinople, and on 16/3/19, 39th Bde., at Baku, was placed directly under 27th Div. at Tiflis. Demobilization proceeded slowly, and parties left for U.K. via Batum. On 7/4/19, 9/R. War. left Krasnovodsk and rejoined 39th Bde. at Baku on 10 and 12/4/19. On 13/6/19, 72nd Fd. Coy., R.E., left for Batum. On 14/6/19, 7/N. Staff. was disbanded, and the personnel left Baku and joined 7/R. Berks. at Tiflis. On 7/8/19, 9/R. War. left by train for Tiflis. On 13/8/19 orders were issued to evacuate Baku ; all animals, saddlery, and harness were to be sold. The move by train to Batum began on 15/8/19, and the evacuation of Baku was completed by 6 p.m., 24/8/19. 39th Bde. embarked at Batum for Constantinople on 29 and 30/8/19. 39th was demobilized on 31/8/19 at Constantinople.

9/R. War. reached Haidar Pasha (Constantinople) from Batum on 2/9/19, and moved to Tuzla (20 m. S.E. of Constantinople). On 24/9/19 the Bn. was disbanded and the personnel was transferred to 9/Worc.

7/Glouc. reached Haidar Pasha on 2/9/19. On 17/10/19 Bn. was absorbed by 8/O. and B.L.I.

9/Worc. On 13/8/19 No. 1 Coy. was sent by sea from Baku to Petrovsk and thence by rail to Novorossisk (on the Black Sea) to escort stores. No. 1 Coy. rejoined the Bn. at Haidar Pasha, where the Bn. arrived on 2/9/19. On 3/9/19 Bn. entrained for Tuzla. On 24/9/19 Bn. absorbed 9/R. War., and on 30/9/19, 9/Worc. absorbed 11/Worc. 9/Worc. was disbanded at Tuzla on 19/12/19.

7/N. Staff. See Brigade narrative above.

39th Bde. M.G. Coy. After arrival at Constantinople, the personnel was absorbed by 81st Bde. M.G. Coy.

39th Sanitary Section, reached Baku on 17/4/19 and joined 39th Bde. The Section left Baku on 20/8/19, embarked at Batum on 1/9/19, and landed at Haidar Pasha on 6/9/19. The Section went to Derije (near Ismid) and was disbanded there on 30/9/19.

13TH (WESTERN) DIVISION

FORMATION, BATTLES, AND ENGAGEMENTS

This New Army Division had no existence before the outbreak of the Great War.

A proclamation was issued on the 11th August, 1914 asking for an immediate addition of 100,000 men to the Regular Army (see Narrative 9th Division and Appendix I). Army Order No. 324 of the 21st August (amended by Army Order No. 382 of the 11th September) authorized the addition of six divisions (9th–14th) and Army Troops to the Regular Army. This augmentation formed the First New Army, and late in August, 1914 the 13th (Western) Division began to assemble.

The infantry brigades first assembled on Salisbury Plain. In September and October the 40th Brigade moved to Chisledon and Cirencester ; and in January, 1915 the 39th Brigade moved to Basingstoke. By the end of February the 13th Division concentrated for its final intensive training at Blackdown, near Farnborough ; equipment and arms were now practically complete and the artillery and engineers had joined the division. Divisional field manœuvres were undertaken.

On the 7th June, 1915 the Division received orders to prepare to move to the Mediterranean theatre of war. The motor bicycles and all mechanical transport (except 4 motor cars) were withdrawn ; and, except in the artillery, engineers, and signal company, first reinforcements were not to proceed with the Division. On the 10th June embarkation orders were received and the first transports sailed on the 13th. (Immediately before embarkation a third machine gun was issued to each infantry battalion). On the 16th June a message to the 13th Division was received from H.M. the King, and on the 18th divisional headquarters sailed from Avonmouth. Alexandria was reached on the 28th and headquarters landed at Mudros on the 4th July. Between the 6th–16th July the infantry of the Division crossed to Helles and relieved the 29th Division on the left of the line. The infantry returned to Mudros at the end of the month, and between 3rd–5th August the 13th Division landed at Anzac. Thereafter, and for the remainder of the Great War, the 13th (Western) Division served in Gallipoli, Egypt, and Mesopotamia, and was engaged in the following operations :

1915

BATTLES OF SUVLA

6–10 August	**Battle of Sari Bair** [Godley's Force].
7 August	**Russell's Top** (8/Ches. and 8/R.W.F.).
27 and 28 August ...	**Hill 60, Anzac** (4/S.W.B.) [Cox's Force].

13th Division was transferred from Anzac to Suvla, and between 28/8–5/9/15 the Division joined IX Corps on the Suvla Front. On 21/9/15 the Division took over No. 3 Section of IX Corps Front Line.

Night, 19/20 December   **Evacuation of Suvla** [IX Corps].

After the evacuation of Suvla the 13th Division concentrated at Mudros, and between 27–31/12/15 Divnl. Hd. Qrs. and the infantry of the Division (less 38th Inf. Bde.) moved from Mudros to Helles and took over the Left Section of VIII Corps Front Line.

1916

7 January	**Last Turkish Attacks at Helles** [VIII Corps].
Night, 8/9 January ...	**Evacuation of Helles** [VIII Corps].

After leaving Helles the 13th Division went to Mudros until 18/1/16 ; on this day the Division began to embark for Egypt, and by 31/1/16 the whole Division concentrated at Port Said. The Division then held posts on the Suez Canal. On 8/2/16 orders were received for the 13th Division to move to Mesopotamia, and on 12/2/16 the Suez Canal posts were handed over to the Ayrshire Yeomanry and Lanarkshire Yeomanry. On the same day the first troops of 13th Division left Port Said by rail for Suez, embarked at Suez on the 13th, sailed on the 14th, and disembarked at Basra on the 27th February. On the 2nd March the Division began to move by river up the Tigris, on the 13th March divisional headquarters reached Shaikh Saad, and by the 27th March the whole Division had arrived at Shaikh Saad (less 7/Glouc., of 39th Bde., segregated for fever at Basra ; 7/Glouc. rejoined 13th Division on 19/4/16). On 2/4/16, 13th Division took over a portion of Tigris Corps Front and became engaged in the third attempt to relieve Kut al Imara. From this time until the end of the Great War the 13th Division served in Mesopotamia and was engaged in the following operations :

THIRD ATTEMPT TO RELIEVE KUT AL IMARA

5 April	**Capture of Hanna and Fallahiya** [Tigris Corps].
9 April	**Second Attack on Sanniyat** [Tigris Corps].
17 and 18 April	**Bait 'Isa** [Tigris Corps].
22 April	**Third Attack on Sanniyat** [Tigris Corps].

1917

13 Dec., 1916–25 Feb., 1917 ... ... } BATTLE OF KUT AL IMARA [III Tigris Corps].

25 Jan.–5 Feb. ... ... Capture of the Hai Salient [III Tigris Corps].
9–16 Feb. ... ... Capture of the Dahra Bend [III Tigris Corps].

PURSUIT TO BAGHDAD

7–10 March ... ... Passage of the Diyala [III Tigris Corps].

11 March ... ... Occupation of Baghdad { (D Sqdn., 1/Herts. Yeo. and 6/K.O. entered the city at 10.30 a.m. ; and 2 cos., 4/S.W.B. and 5/Wilts. entered later.) [III Tigris Corps].

CONSOLIDATION OF THE BAGHDAD POSITION

27 and 28 March... ... Delli 'Abbas [Marshall's Column].
29 March ... ... Duqma [Marshall's Column].
9–15 April ... ... Nahr Kalis [Marshall's Column].
18 April ... ... Passage of the 'Adhaim (38th Brigade) [Marshall's Column].
30 April ... ... Shatt al 'Adhaim [Marshall's Column].
18–20 October ... ... Second Action of Jabal Hamrin [III Tigris Corps].
3–6 December ... ... Third Action of Jabal Hamrin [III Tigris Corps].

1918

29 April ... ... Tuz Khurmatli [III Tigris Corps].

After the fight on the 29th April the 13th Division halted at Tuz Khurmatli until the 5th May ; the Division then advanced northward past Tauq, reached Kirkuk on the 8th, and remained there until the 24th. On that day the Division began to retire southward through Taza Khurmatli, Tauq, and Tuz Khurmatli to Kifri, which was reached on the 28th May. Divisional headquarters now opened at Dawalib (2 m. east of Delli 'Abbas), and here they were destined to remain until after the conclusion of the War.

In July orders were received to send the 39th Infantry Brigade (with 72nd Field Company and 40th Field Ambulance) to join the North Persia Force ; and the Group left the 13th Division between 10th July and 19th August (see note 31 and General Notes).

Whilst it was around Dawalib the Division was employed in training, in the instruction of specialists, and in providing large working parties for the upkeep of roads. During July the average maximum shade temperature rose to 111·6°.

In October a column under Br.-Gen. A. C. Lewin* was pushed northwards. The column passed Tauq (20th), Taza Khurmatli (23rd), and entered Kirkuk on the 25th October. On the 28th Lewin's Column continued its northward advance and became engaged with a Turkish force which was in position covering the Altun Köpri bridge over the Little Zab, and at 7.30 a.m. on the 31st October the 12th Cavalry of Lewin's Column entered Altun Köpri. On the 1st November, however, the 13th Division received orders to cease hostilities at once ; the Armistice with Turkey had come into force at noon on the previous day—Thursday the 31st October.

On the 7th November Lewin's Column was abolished ; between 22nd and 30th November all the units rejoined 13th Division and headquarters of the column again became Headquarters 40th Infantry Brigade. On the 15th December all troops were withdrawn from forward areas, on the 16th I Tigris Corps took over Kirkuk and all

---

* Composition of LEWIN'S COLUMN :

Hd. Qrs., 40th Inf. Bde. and Bde. Signal Sec.,

Portion, B Flight, 30 Sqdn., R.A.F.,	No. 1 Pack Wireless Station,
12/Cav. (less 1 Sqdn.) and M.G. Sec.,	1 Sec., 71st Fd. Coy., R.E.,
A/LXVI (less 1 Sec.),	2 Bns. (8/R.W.F. and 4/S.W.B.), 40th Inf. Bde.,
1 Sec., 61/(H.)/LXVI,	H.Q. and 2 Sec., 40th M.G. Coy.,
Portion, LXVI B.A.C.,	Portion, 40th S.A.A. Sec.,
13/L.A.M. Bty.,	39th Fd. Ambce. (less 2 Secs.).

the posts to the north of that place, and by the 31st December the evacuation of the forward area was completed.

On the 1st January, 1919 the strength of British officers and other ranks with the 13th Division was 12,476. On the 11th January the Division began to move down the line of communications to 'Amara, and thereafter some units left on each day for 'Amara. Divisional headquarters started on the 31st January and reached 'Amara on the 2nd February. The final disbandment and disposal of the Division now proceeded rapidly. On the 11th February 6/E. Lanc. and 6/L.N.L. (of 38th Infantry Brigade) were selected to form part of the Army of Occupation in Mesopotamia, and on the 14th and 15th March they were posted to the 34th Indian Infantry Brigade. On the 4th March LV R.F.A. (less 60 How. Bty.) had also been selected for duty in the Army of Occupation.

By the beginning of March the strength of British officers and other ranks with the Division had dwindled to 5,034, and on the 11th orders were received for the Division to be reduced to cadre. The end came on the 17th March, and on that day the 13th Division, the only British Division to serve in Mesopotamia, ceased to exist. During the Great War the 13th Division lost 12,656 killed, wounded, and missing.*

---

* 7,822 of these casualties occurred in Mesopotamia.
In the Great War the 13th Division suffered 57,667 casualties from sickness (46,641 occurred in Mesopotamia).

14TH (LIGHT) DIVISION

G.O.C.

7 September, 1914	Major-General T. L. N. MORLAND.
17 October, 1914	Br.-Gen. F. A. FORTESCUE (acting).
22 October, 1914	Major-General V. A. COUPER.
30 December, 1914...	Br.-Gen. F. A. FORTESCUE (acting).
3 January, 1915	Major-General V. A. COUPER.
22 March, 1918	Major-General W. H. GREENLY.
27 March, 1918	Major-General Sir V. A. COUPER.
31 March, 1918	Major-General P. C. B. SKINNER.

G.S.O. 1.

7 Sept., 1914...Major W. J. T. GLASGOW (acting).
21 Sept., 1914...Captain E. J. L. THURLOW (acting).
22 Sept., 1914...Major K. M. DAVIE (acting).
22 Feb., 1915...Major C. C. ARMITAGE (acting).
24 Feb., 1915...Lt.-Col. H. ISACKE.
1 June, 1916...Lt.-Col. G. D. BRUCE.
19 Sept., 1917...Major E. R. MEADE-WALDO (acting).
8 Oct., 1917...Lt.-Col. A. G. BAYLEY.
14 May, 1918...Lt.-Col. R. S. FOLLETT.
19 Sept., 1918...Lt.-Col. T. E. L. HILL-WHITSON.

A.-A. and Q.-M.-G.

8 Sept., 1914...Captain L. J. COMYN (acting).
8 Oct., 1914...Colonel J. R. MATHEWES (sick, 8/2/15).
8 Feb., 1915...Captain L. J. COMYN (acting).
15 Feb., 1915...Colonel J. R. MATHEWES.
17 Mar., 1915...Major P. H. N. N. VYVYAN (acting).
19 Mar., 1915...Lt.-Col. H. H. F. TURNER.
13 Nov., 1915...Major C. PARSONS (acting).
25 Nov., 1915...Lt.-Col. C. L. C. HAMILTON.
24 Mar., 1917...Lt.-Col. P. E. LEWIS.
18 Mar., 1918...Lt.-Col. F. A. CORFIELD.

B.-G., R.A.

2 Oct., 1914...Br.-Gen. D. G. PRINSEP.
5 Sept., 1915...Br.-Gen. W. B. R. SANDYS.
4 Feb., 1917...Br.-Gen. E. HARDING-NEWMAN.

C.R.E.

15 Sept., 1914...Lt.-Col. H. PRENTICE.
12 July, 1915...Lt.-Col. A. F. SARGEANT (killed, 31/7/15).
31 July, 1915...Major J. P. MACKESY (acting).
4 Aug., 1915...Lt.-Col. T. A. H. BIGGE.
20 Dec., 1915...Lt.-Col. F. M. CLOSE (sick, 15/5/16).
15 May, 1916...Captain C. H. R. CHESNEY (acting).
20 May, 1916...Captain E. F. W. LEES (acting).
17 June, 1916...Lt.-Col. J. E. C. CRASTER.
2 June, 1917...Lt.-Col. D. S. COLLINS.

14TH (LIGHT) DIVISION

41st BDE.

23 Aug., '14...Br.-Gen. F. A. FORTESCUE.
6 May, '15...Br.-Gen. O. S. W. NUGENT.
12 Sept., '15...Lt.-Col. J. D. H.
                MAITLAND (acting).
28 Sept., '15...Br.-Gen. H. S. JEUDWINE.
20 Dec., '15...Br.-Gen. LORD BINNING.
23 April, '16...Br.-Gen. P. C. B. SKINNER.
31 Mar., '18...Lt.-Col. B. J. CURLING
                (acting).
3 April, '18...Br.-Gen. C. R. P. WINSER.
3 Sept., '18...Br.-Gen. W. F. SWENY.

42nd BDE.

24 Aug., '14...Br.-Gen. C. J. MARKHAM
                (sick, 16/8/15).
16 Aug., '15...Br.-Gen. F. A. DUDGEON.
9 Aug., '17...Br.-Gen. G. N. B. FORSTER
                (killed, 4/4/18).
5–7 April,'18...Br.-Gen. C. R. P. WINSER
                (of 41st Bde.—tempy.).
7 April, '18...Br.-Gen. H. T. DOBBIN.

43rd BDE.

24 Aug., '14...Br.-Gen. V. A. COUPER.
31 Oct., '14...Br.-Gen. G. COCKBURN (sick, 3/8/15).
3 Aug., '15...Lt.-Col. V. T. BAILEY (acting).
4 Aug., '15...Br.-Gen. P. R. WOOD.
1 Sept., '17...Br.-Gen. R. S. TEMPEST.
16 Sept., '18...Br.-Gen. G. E. PEREIRA.

GENERAL NOTES

The following Units also served with the 14th (Light) Division :—

ARTILLERY :—528 (H.) Bty., R.F.A. (4, 4·5″ Hows.), landed at le Havre on 16/10/16 and joined XLVIII Bde., R.F.A., on 21/10/16 (see notes 18, 28, 29, 30).

14th Heavy Battery (4, 4·7″ guns) was formed at Woolwich on 12/10/14 as 8th (New) Heavy Battery, R.G.A.—the first Heavy Battery of the New Army—but soon afterwards the designation of the battery was changed to 14th Heavy Battery, R.G.A. On 17/10/14 two 4·7″ guns (on converted 40-pdr. carriages) were received. On 9/2/15 the Heavy Battery joined 14th Div., and between 8–15/4/15 the Heavy Battery fired 50 rounds at practice camp on Salisbury Plain. At the end of April, 1915 the remaining two 4·7″ guns (on Mk. I carriages) arrived. 14th Heavy Battery went to France with 14th Div. and disembkd. at le Havre on 22/5/15. On 8/6/15, 14th Heavy Battery left 14th Div. and joined XVI. Heavy Artillery Bde. (9th, 14th, and Warwickshire Heavy Bties.).

MACHINE GUNS :—8th Motor-Machine-Gun Battery, joined the Div. in England, went to France with 14th Div. in May 1915, and served with 14th Div. until 5/11/16, when the Bty. was transferred to G.H.Q. Troops.

249th Machine-Gun Company, left Grantham on 16/7/17 and disembkd. at le Havre on 17/7/17. The Coy. joined Div. at Westoutre on 21/7/17, and served with 14th Div. until 1/10/17. The Coy. then left the Div., reached Marseille on 4/10/17, embkd. at Marseille on 15/10/17, arrived in Mesopotamia on 13/11/17, and joined 18th (Indian) Division on 5/2/18 (also see note 33).

OTHER UNITS :—25th Sanitary Section, joined 14th Div. in England, went to France with Div. in May 1915, and served with 14th Div. until 1/4/17, when the Section was transferred to a VII Corps Sanitary Area.

14th Division Motor Ambce. Workshop, went to France with Division in May 1915, and served with 14th Div. until April 1916, when the Workshop was absorbed by 14th Div. Train.

On 12/2/18 the reorganization of the 14th Division on a 9-battalion basis was completed ; and on 26/2/18 the pioneer battalion (11/King's) was reorganized on a 3-company basis.

14th DIVISION ARTILLERY
MARCH-SEPTEMBER, 1918

On 21/3/18 XLVI and XLVII lost all their guns and 20 offrs. and 239 o.r. were killed, wounded, and missing. B.-G., R.A., remained in action until 29/3/18 with 14th Div. Arty. Group (XCI R.F.A., CCXCVIII A.F.A., 130 Siege Bty., 137 and 138 Hy. Bties., and X and Y T.M. Bties.) covering Reynolds's Force. On 1/4/18 XLVI and XLVII (having refitted) were again in action on the Villers Bretonneux front under III Corps, and the Bdes. took part in the Battle of the Avre (4/4/18). XLVI and XLVII were withdrawn on 17/4/18. On 19/4/18 XLVI, XLVII, D.A.C., and No. 1 Coy., 14th Div. Train, moved to Berguette and came under XIII Corps, First Army. On 28 and 29/4/18 14th Div. Arty. relieved 50th Div. Arty. on the Hinges front and was attached to 3rd Div. (From 10/5–21/6/18 the B.-G., R.A. 14th Div., was in temporary command of 52nd Div. Arty., near Villers au Bois.) XLVII was relieved on 19/6/18 and returned to the line on 8/7/18, relieving XLVI. On 28/7/18 XLVI went into action again, under 46th Div. Arty. ; and on 26/8/18 XLVII came under 19th Div. Arty. On 6/9/18 H.Q., R.A. 14th Div., rejoined 14th Div. near Ypres. On 16/9/18 XLVI and XLVII were withdrawn from the line and on 19/9/18 XLVI and XLVII rejoined 14th Div.

14TH[1] (LIGHT) DIVISION

Dates	INFANTRY — Brigades	INFANTRY — Battalions and attached Units	Mounted Troops	ARTILLERY — Field Artillery — Brigades	Field Artillery — Batteries	Field Artillery — Bde. Ammn. Colns.	Trench Mortar Bties. — Medium	Trench Mortar Bties. — Heavy	Divnl. Ammn. Coln.	Engineers — Field Cos.	Signal Service — Divnl. Signal Coy.	Pioneers	M.G. Units	Field Ambulances	Mobile Vety. Secn.	Divnl. Emplnt. Coy.	Divnl. Train
1914 October (England)	41st[1] ... 42nd[1] ... 43rd[1] ...	7/K.R.R.C., 8/K.R.R.C., 7/R.B., 8/R.B. 5/O. & B.L.I., 5/K.S.L.I., 9/K.R.R.C., 9/R.B. 6/Som. L.I., 6/D.C.L.I., 6/K.O.Y.L.I., 10/D.L.I.	14th Div. Cyclist Coy.[2]	XLVI[3] ...... XLVII[3] ...... XLVIII[3] ...... XLIX (H.)[3] ...	148, 149, 150 151, 152, 153 154, 155, 156 157 (H.), 158 (H.), 159 (H.)	XLVI B.A.C. XLVII B.A.C. XLVIII B.A.C. XLIX (H.) B.A.C.	...	...	14th D.A.C.	61st 62nd 89th[4]	14th	11/King's[5] (P.)	...	42nd 43rd 44th	26th[6]	...	14th[7]
1915 September (France)	41st ...... 42nd 43rd	7/K.R.R.C., 8/K.R.R.C., 7/R.B., 8/R.B. 5/O. & B.L.I., 5/K.S.L.I., 9/K.R.R.C., 9/R.B. 6/Som. L.I., 6/D.C.L.I., 6/K.O.Y.L.I., 10/D.L.I.	D Sqdn., 1/D. of L.O. Yeo.[8] 14th Div. Cyclist Coy.[9]	XLVI[3; 10] ... XLVII[5; 11] ... XLVIII[5; 12] ... XLIX (H.)[5; 13]	A, B, C, D A, B, C, D A, B, C, D B (H.), C (H.), D (H.)	XLVI B.A.C. XLVII B.A.C. XLVIII B.A.C. XLIX (H.) B.A.C.	...	...	14th D.A.C.	61st 62nd 89th	14th	11/King's (P.)	...	42nd 43rd 44th	26th	...	14th
1916 June (France)	41st ...... 42nd 43rd	7/K.R.R.C., 8/K.R.R.C., 7/R.B., 8/R.B.; 41st Bde. M.G. Coy.;[14] 41st T.M. Bty.[15] 5/O. & B.L.I., 5/K.S.L.I., 9/K.R.R.C., 9/R.B.; 42nd Bde. M.G. Coy.;[14] 42nd T.M. Bty.[15] 6/Som. L.I., 6/D.C.L.I., 6/K.O.Y.L.I., 10/D.L.I.; 43rd Bde. M.G. Coy.;[14] 43rd T.M. Bty.[15]	...	XLVI[10; 16] ... XLVII[11; 17] ... XLVIII[12; 18; 30] ... XLIX[13; 19] ...	A, B, C; D (H.) ... A, B, C; D (H.) A, B, C; D (H.) A, B, C	...[22]	X.14[20] Y.14[20] Z.14[20]	V.14[21]	14th D.A.C.[22]	61st 62nd 89th	14th	11/King's (P.)	...	42nd 43rd 44th	26th	...	14th
1917 June (France)	41st ...... 42nd 43rd	7/K.R.R.C.,[23] 8/K.R.R.C., 7/R.B., 8/R.B.; 41st M.G. Coy.;[47] 41st T.M. Bty. 5/O. & B.L.I., 5/K.S.L.I., 240/K.R.R.C., 9/R.B.; 42nd M.G. Coy.;[47] 42nd T.M. Bty. 6/Som. L.I., 6/D.C.L.I.,[25] 6/K.O.Y.L.I.,[26] 10/D.L.I.,[27] 43rd M.G. Coy.;[47] 43rd T.M. Bty.	...	XLVI[28] ...... XLVII[29]	A, B, C; D (H.) A, B, C; D (H.)	...	X.14 Y.14 Z.14[31]	V.14[32]	14th D.A.C.	61st 62nd 89th	14th	11/King's (P.)	224th[33] M.G. Coy.	42nd 43rd 44th	26th	215th[34]	14th
1918 March (France)	41st ...... 42nd 43rd	8/K.R.R.C.,[35] 7/R.B.,[36] 8/R.B.,[37] 41st T.M. Bty.[38] 5/O. & B.L.I.,[39] 9/K.R.R.C.,[40] 42nd T.M. Bty.[38] 6/Som. L.I.,[42] 9/Sco. Rif.,[43] 7/K.R.R.C.;[23]; [44] 43rd T.M. Bty.[38]	...	XLVI ...... XLVII	A, B, C; D (H.) A, B, C; D (H.)	...	X.14[45] Y.14[45]	...[32]	14th D.A.C.[45]	61st 62nd 89th	14th	11/King's[46] (P.)	No. 14 Bn., M.G.C.[47]	42nd 43rd 44th	26th	215th[48]	14th

1918 August (France) After reconstitution.																
	14th	215th¹⁸	20th	42nd 43rd 44th	No. 14 Bn. M.G.C.⁶¹	15/ L.N.L.⁴⁶ (P.)	14th	61st 62nd 89th	14th D.A.C.⁶⁰	...	X.14⁶⁰ Y.14⁶⁰	...	...	XLVI⁵⁹ XLVII⁵⁹	...	18/Y. & L.⁴⁹ 22/D.L.I.,⁵⁰ 33/ Lond. (R.B.)⁵⁶ ; 41st T.M. Bty.⁵²	A, B, C ; D (H.) A, B, C ; D (H.)
41st																18/Y. & L.⁴⁹ 22/D.L.I.,⁵⁰ 33/ Lond. (R.B.)⁵⁶ ; 41st T.M. Bty.⁵²
42nd																6/(Wilts. Yeo.) Wilts. 5¹⁶/ Manch.,⁵⁴ 14/A. & S.H. ;⁵⁵ 42nd T.M. Bty.⁵²
43rd																12/Suff.⁵⁶ 20/Middx.,⁵⁷ 10/ H.L.I. ;⁵⁸ 43rd T.M. Bty.⁵²

NOTES

1 On formation the Division was numbered 8 and the 3 inf. bdes. were 23, 24, 25. By A.O. 382/1914 the 8th (Light) Division was renumbered 14, and the inf. bdes. were allotted the numbers, 41, 42, and 43.

2 Coy. was formed on 11/1/15.

3 Bties. were raised as 6-gun bties. and numbered. On 14/1/15 all Bdes. were reorganized as 4-battery bdes., the bties. all became 4-gun bties, and the bties. were lettered A, B, C, D in each bde. (Authy.—W.O. Letter, No. 20/Artillery/3818, A.G.6.)

4 On 16/1/15 a third Fd. Coy. was added to each division; and on 22/1/15 89th Fd. Coy. joined the Division, from 23rd Div.

5 Bn. originally formed part of Army Trps., First New Army; and on 11/1/15 Bn. became pioneer bn. of 14th Div.

6 Joined Div. at Aldershot in 1915.

7 Train consisted of 100, 101, 102, and 103 Cos. A.S.C. On 26/4/15 the Cos. were designated in the Train : H.Q. Coy., and Nos. 2, 3, and 4 Cos., 14th Div. Train.

8 Sqdn. joined Div. at Aldershot in 1915. Sqdn. left Div. on 10/5/16, and joined III Corps Cav. Regt. at Beaucourt on 11/5/16 (H.Q. and C and D Sqdns., C of I.O. Yeo. and C Sqdn., 1/Surrey Yeo.).

9 Left Div. and joined VI Corps Cyclist Bn. at Manin on 11/5/16.

10 On 24/5/16 D was transferred and became A/XLIX ; and C (H.)/XLIX joined and became D (H.)/XLVI.

11 On 24/5/16 D was transferred and became B/XLIX ; and B (H.)/XLIX joined and became D (H.)/XLVII.

12 On 24/5/16 D was transferred and became C/XLIX ; and D (H.)/XLIX joined and became D (H.)/XLVIII.

13 On 17/6/15 A (H.) was attached to 28th Div.; on 3/9/15 A (H.) was permanently transferred to 28th Div. and became A (H.)/CXXX(H.)—in 28th Div.—on 8/9/15. On 24/5/16 B (H.)/XLIX became D (H.)/XLVI, C (H.)/XLIX became D (H.)/XLVII, and D (H.)/XLIX became D (H.)/XLVIII. On the same day D/XLVI, D/XLVII, and D/XLVIII were transferred to XLIX and became A, B, and C/XLIX.

14 The M.G. Cos. were formed : 41st at Winnezeele on 15/2/16 ; 42nd by 24/2/16 ; and 43rd at Houtkerque on 16/2/16.

15 The T.M. Bties. were formed at Arras : 41st by 2/5/16 ; 42nd on 15/4/16 ; and 43rd by 24/4/16.

16 On 5/10/16 Bde. was reorganized : 1 sec., A/XLIX joined A ; 1 sec., A/XLIX joined B ; and 1 sec., C/XLIX joined C, making up A, B and C to 6, 18-pdrs. each.

17 On 6/10/16 Bde. was reorganized : 1 sec., B/XLIX joined A ; 1 sec., B/XLIX joined B ; and 1 sec., C/XLIX joined C, making up A, B, and C to 6, 18-pdrs. each.

18 On 5/10/16 Bde. was reorganized : C was broken up and 1 sec. joined A and 1 sec. joined B, making up A and B to 6, 18-pdrs. each. On 21/10/16 528 How. Bty. (4, 4·5″ hows.) joined Bde., and became C (H.)/XLVIII on 26/10/16. (Also see note 30.)

19 On 5 and 6/10/16 Bde. was broken up : A and 1 sec. C joined XLVI, and B and 1 sec. C joined XLVII—to complete the 18-pdr. bties. of XLVI and XLVII to 6 guns each.

20 The 3 T.M. Bties. were formed at Third Army School at Valbeurreux on 1 and 2/3/16. The bties. were each armed with 4, 2″ mortars. On 11/3/16 the 3 batteries joined the Division.

21 Heavy T.M. Bty. was formed at Wartlus on 18/7/16 and joined the Division on 28/7/16.

22 Between 21–30/5/16 the D.A.C. was reorganized, and the B.A.C.s were abolished.

23 On 2/2/18 Bn. was transferred to 43rd Bde.

24 On 3/2/18 Bn. was disbanded and drafted to 4/, 6/, 7/, and 8/K.S.L.I.

25 Between 6–20/2/18 Bn. was disbanded and drafted to 5/, 7/, and 10/D.C.L.I., and surplus went to 16/Entg. Bn.

26 On 12/2/18 Bn. left Div. and reported to III Corps Rft. Camp; and on 19/2/18 Bn. was used as nucleus of 16/Entg. Bn.

27 On 12/2/18 Bn. left Div.; on 19/2/18 part joined 16/Entg. Bn. and remdr. joined III Corps Rfts.

28 On 8/1/17, 1 Sec. C (H.)/XLVIII joined and made up D (H.)/XLVI to 6 hows.

29 On 8/1/17, 1 sec. C (H.)/XLVIII joined and made up D (H.)/XLVII to 6 hows.

30 On 7/1/17 XLVIII Bde. was reorganized and became XLVIII A.F.A. Bde. On 8/1/17, C (H.) was broken up to make up D (H.)/XLVI and D (H.)/XLVII to 6 hows. each. On 8/1/17, A/CLVIII (6, 18-pdrs.) joined from 35th Div. and became C/XLVIII; and on 16/2/17 1 Sec. D (H.)/CCXCIII joined from 58th Div. and made up D (H.)/XLVIII to 6 hows.

31 On 3/2/18, Z was broken up between X and Y.

32 On 19/1/18, V left Div. and went to Fifth Army Mortar School.

33 M.G. Coy. embkd. at Southampton on 12/11/17, reached Wizernes on 16/11/17, and joined Div. on 17/11/17 at Val d'Acquin. 224 M.G. Coy. took the place of 240 M.G. Coy. (see General Notes).

34 By 9/6/17 Coy. was formed as 215 Labour Coy. and later it became renamed 215 Emplnt. Coy.

35 Bn. left Div. on 10/6/18, was attached to 34th Div. on 27/6/18, and on same day Bn. was taken over by 39th Div. On 3/8/18. Bn. was disbanded.

36 On 27/4/18, Bn. was reduced to training cadre, and on 17/6/18 Bn. went to England with 41st Bde., 16th Div. At Pirbright on 17/6/18 Bn. was transferred to 43rd Bde. and became 33/Lond. (R.F.). On 19/6/18, Bn. was transferred back to 41st Bde. and Bn. was renamed 33/Lond. (R.B.).

37 Bn. left Div. on 16/6/18. On 27/6/18, Bn. was attached to 34th Div., and on same day Bn. was taken over by 39th Div. On 3/8/18, Bn. was disbanded.

38 Bde. T.M. Bties. were broken up by 14/4/18, and men were used as rfts.

39 Bn. left Div. on 16/6/18 and joined 49th Bde., 16th Div., at Boulogne on 18/6/18. Bn. went to England, reformed with 18/Glouc., became 18/Glouc., and joined 49th Bde., 16th Div., on 20/6/18.

40 Bn. left Div. on 16/6/18, was attached to 34th Div.. and on 27/6/18 Bn. joined 38th Div. On 3/8/18 Bn. was disbanded.

41 Bn. left Div. on 16/6/18, was attached to 34th Div., and on 27/6/18 Bn. joined 39th Div. On 3/8/18. Bn. was disbanded.

42 Bn. left Div. on 16/6/18 and joined 49th Bde., 16th Div., at Boulogne, on 18/6/18. Bn. went to England, absorbed 13/D.C.L.I. on 20/6/18, and then 6/Som. L.I. joined 49th Bde., 16th Div.

43 Bn. joined 43rd Bde. on 5/2/18 from 27th Bde., 9th Div. On 23/4/18 Bn. left 14th Div., joined S.A. Inf. Bde., 9th Div. On 23/4/18, and on 12/9/18 Bn. was transferred to 28th Bde., 9th Div.

44 Bn. left Div. on 16/6/18, and joined 49th Bde., 16th Div., at Boulogne on 18/6/18. Bn. went to England, reformed with 34/Lond. and became 34/Lond. (K.R.R.C.). Bn. joined 49th Bde., 16th Div., on 27/6/18.

45 The 2 medium T.M. Bties. and S.A.A. Sec. of D.A.C. were broken up on 25/4/18, and men used for rfts. (See note 60.)

46 Reorganized as an inf. bn. on 15/4/18 and attached to 43rd Bde. Bn. was reduced to training cadre on 27/4/18. Bn. embkd. at Boulogne with 43rd Bde. and reached England on 17/6/18. Bn. was made up by drafts, and on 19/6/18 Bn. was redesignated 15/L.N.L. (P.). On 5/7/18 Bn. returned to France as Pioneer Bn. of 14th Div.

47 M.G. Bn. was formed in March, 1918; it consisted of 41st, 42nd, 43rd, and 224th M.G. Cos. M.G. Bn. was disbanded on 11/4/18, and personnel went to Abbeville for drafting.

48 Emplnt. Coy. was reformed in England in June, 1918, and the reformed Coy. returned to France in July, 1918, with 14th Div.

[TURN OVER

The following Units and Training Cadres served with the 14th Division between April-June, 1918 :—

Unit	From	Served with 14th Div.		Transferred to	Notes
		From	To		
2/4/Som. L.I. ...	232nd Bde., 75th Div....	7/6	– 16/6/18	Pioneers, 34th Div.	Formerly in 135th Bde., 45th Div.
6/R. Innis. Fus. ...	31st Bde., 10th Div. ...	7/6	– 16/6/18	103rd Bde., 34th Div. (19–28/6/18)	To 151st Bde., 50th Div., on 16/7/18.
5/R. Ir. Fus. ...	31st Bde., 10th Div. ...	3/6	– 16/6/18	198th Bde., 66th Div. (23/7/18)	To 48th Bde, 16th Div., on 29/8/18.
5/Conn. Rang. ...	29th Bde., 10th Div. ...	7/6	– 16/6/18	199th Bde., 66th Div. (25/8/18)	—
6/Leins. ...	29th Bde., 10th Div. ...	7/6	– 16/6/18	34th Div. (19–28/6/18)	To 198th Bde., 66th Div. on 20/7/18. Bn. was disbanded on 12/9/18.
156th Fd. Coy., R.E.	16th Div. ...	15/5	– 16/6/18	16th Div. (13/8/18)	
157th Fd. Coy., R.E.	16th Div. ...	15/5	– 31/5/18	16th Div.	
11/Entg. Bn. ...	...	24/4	– 30/4/18.		
13/Entg. Bn. ...	...	19/4	– 16/6/18.		
14/Entg. Bn. ...	...	19/4	– 24/4/18.		
63 Labour Coy.	...	6/5	– 16/6/18.		
79 Labour Coy.	...	6/5	– 16/6/18.		
159 Labour Coy.	...	17/5	– 16/6/18.		
712 Labour Coy.	...	8/5	– 16/6/18.		
725 Labour Coy.	...	6/5	– 16/6/18.		
733 Labour Coy.	...	17/5	– 16/6/18.		

Portuguese :—

Unit	From	Served with 14th Div.		Transferred to	Notes
		From	To		
1st Div. H.Q. ...	...	17/5	– 16/6/18.		
1st Inf. Bde. (H.Q. and 21/, 22/, 28/, and 34/Bns.)		17/5	– 16/6/18.		
2nd Inf. Bde. (H.Q. and 12/, 24/, 25/, and 35/Bns.)		13/4	– 16/6/18.		
3rd Inf. Bde. (H.Q. and 9/, 14/, and 15/Bns.)		12/5	– 16/6/18.		14/Bn. was also attached, 1–10/5/18.
2 Batteries (personnel) ...	...	17/5	– 12/6/18.		
2nd and 3rd Fd. Cos. ...	...	30/4	– 16/6/18.		
2nd and 4th Cos., S. and M. ...	...	17/5	– 16/6/18.		
2 Pioneer Cos. ...	...	24/4	– 16/6/18.		
1 Labour Coy. ...	...	30/4	– 16/6/18.		
2nd M.G. Coy. ...	...	17/5	– 16/6/18.		
3rd M.G. Coy....	...	17/5	– 16/6/18.		

NOTES—contd.

RECONSTITUTED DIVISION.

49 Bn. formed at Margate on 11/6/18; joined 41st Bde. at Pirbright on 18/6/18 and absorbed training cadre of 2/7/W. York. (formerly 62nd Div.) on 19/6/18. Bn. landed at Boulogne on 3/7/18.

50 Bn. formed at Brookwood on 19/6/18, absorbed training cadre of 2/7/Duke's (formerly 62nd Div.), and joined 41st Bde. Bn. landed at Boulogne on 3/7/18.

51 Bn. was formed at Clacton-on-Sea on 7/6/18, reached Pirbright on 18/6/18, absorbed training cadre of 7/R.B. on 18/6/18 (see n. 36), and joined 43rd Bde. On 19/6/18 Bn. was transferred to 41st Bde. and its designation altered from 33/Lond. (R.F.) to 33/Lond. (R.B.). Bn. landed at Boulogne on 3/7/18.

52 Bde. T.M. Bties. were reformed in England in June, 1918; and went to France with Bdes. in July, 1918.

53 Bn. (formerly in 58th Bde., 19th Div.) reduced to training cadre, joined 14th Div. at Boulogne on 16/6/18. Bn. reached Brookwood on 17/6/18, absorbed 9/Dorset on 18/6/18, joined 42nd Bde. on 19/6/18, and previous designation 6/(Wilts. Yeo.) Wilts. was confirmed on 20/6/18. Bn. landed at Boulogne on 4/7/18.

54 Bn. (formerly in 90th Bde., 30th Div.) reduced to training cadre, joined 14th Div. at Boulogne on 16/6/18, and reached Cowshot on 16/6/18. Bn. joined 42nd Bde. on 21/6/18, and absorbed 29/Manch. Bn. landed at Boulogne on 4/7/18.

55 Bn. (formerly in 120th Bde., 40th Div.) reduced to training cadre, joined 14th Div. at Boulogne on 16/6/18, reached Cowshot on 17/6/18, absorbed 17/A. & S.H., and joined 42nd Bde. on 21/6/18. Bn. landed at le Havre on 3/7/18.

56 Bn. (formerly in 121st Bde., 40th Div.) reduced to training cadre, joined 14th Div. at Boulogne on 16/6/18, and reached Pirbright on 17/6/18. Bn. absorbed 16/Suff. (P.), joined 43rd Bde. on 19/6/18, and landed at Boulogne on 5/7/18.

57 Bn. (formerly in 121st Bde., 40th Div.) reduced to training cadre, joined 14th Div. at Boulogne on 16/6/18, reached Brookwood on 17/6/18, and joined 43rd Bde. On 20/6/18 Bn. absorbed 34/Middx. Bn. landed at Boulogne on 5/7/18.

58 10/H.L.I. and 11/H.L.I. went to France in 1915 in 28th Bde., 9th Div. Bns. joined 48th Bde., 15th Div., on 14/5/16, amalgamated on 16/5/16, and became 10/11/H.L.I.; Bn. was transferred to 120th Bde., 40th Div. and joined on 16/2/18. On 16/6/18 Bn., reduced to training cadre, joined 14th Div. at Boulogne, reached Brookwood on 17/6/18, joined 42nd Bde. on 17/6/18, transferred to 43rd Bde. on 19/6/18, absorbed 22/H.L.I., and Bn. became 10/H.L.I. on 21/6/18. Bn. landed at Boulogne on 5/7/18.

59 Divnl. Arty. was detached from the Div. on 27/3/18 (when 14th Div. withdrew to refit) and returned to the Div. on 6-19/9/18. (See General Notes.)

60 X and Y (6" Newton mortars) were formed at Deepcut on 17/6/18, went to France with 14th Div., and landed at Boulogne on 5/7/18. S.A.A. Sec. of D.A.C. was reformed in England and returned to France on 1/7/18 with 14th Div. (See note 45.)

61 Bn. was formed at Grantham on 14/6/18, and Cos. were lettered A, B, C, and D. Bn. went to France 3-5/7/18 with 14th Div.; it was the first complete M.G. Bn. to leave England.

14TH (LIGHT) DIVISION

FORMATION, BATTLES, AND ENGAGEMENTS

This New Army Division had no existence before the outbreak of the Great War.

A proclamation was issued on the 11th August 1914 asking for an immediate addition of 100,000 men to the Regular Army (see Narrative 9th Division, and Appendix 1). Army Order No. 324 of the 21st August, 1914 authorized the addition of six divisions (8th–13th) and Army Troops to the Regular Army. This augmentation formed the First New Army, and early in September, 1914 the 8th (Light) Division, the senior division of the First New Army, began to assemble at Aldershot. The three infantry brigades of the Division were numbered : 23rd, 24th, and 25th.

It was, however, soon ascertained that the additional regular battalions released from the overseas garrisons would suffice to form another regular division.* In consequence of this, Army Order No. 382 of the 11th September, 1914 directed that henceforward the number of the Light Division would be 14, and its infantry brigades would be renumbered 41, 42, and 43. On Monday the 14th September, 1914 this new numbering came into force ; and, instead of being the senior division, the Light Division became the junior division of the First New Army.

On the 26th September, whilst it was still at Aldershot, H.M. the King inspected the 14th (Light) Division on Queen's Parade. Late in November, 1914 the Division moved out to billets in the Guildford and Godalming district, and on Friday the 22nd January, 1915 the Division was inspected on Hankley Common by Field-Marshal Earl Kitchener. The Division remained in billets around Guildford until the 18th February, and the troops then returned to Stanhope Lines, Aldershot. Divisional field manœuvres and the final training for war were now undertaken.

On the 11th May a warning was received from the War Office that the 14th Division would proceed overseas on the 14th ; this date, however, was altered to the 18th May, and on the 18th entrainment began. The Division then crossed from Southampton to le Havre, and by the 25th May it completed its concentration around Watten (north-west of St. Omer). For the remainder of the Great War the 14th Division served on the Western Front in France and Belgium and was engaged in the following operations :

1915

30 and 31 July	**Hooge (German Liquid Fire Attack)** [VI Corps, Second Army].
25 September	**Second Attack on Bellewaarde** [VI Corps, Second Army].

1916

BATTLES OF THE SOMME

13–30 August	**Battle of Delville Wood** [XV Corps, Fourth Army].
15 and 16 September ...	**Battle of Flers-Courcelette** [XV Corps, Fourth Army].

1917

14 March–5 April ...	**German Retreat to the Hindenburg Line** [VII Corps, Third Army].

BATTLES OF ARRAS

9–12 April	**First Battle of the Scarpe** [VII Corps, Third Army].
3 and 4 May	**Third Battle of the Scarpe** [VII Corps, Third Army].

BATTLES OF YPRES

18 August	**Battle of Langemarck** [II Corps, Fifth Army].
22–26 August**	**Fighting on the Menin Road** [II Corps, Fifth Army].
12 October	**First Battle of Passchendaele** [X Corps, Second Army].

* 8th (Regular) Division (23rd, 24th, and 25th Brigades) was formed between 19th September and 2nd October, 1914. The 12 battalions came from India (3), S. Africa (1), Aden (1), Egypt (3), Malta (3), and Bermuda (1). The 8th Division disembarked at le Havre on the 6th and 7th November, 1914 and served on the Western Front for the remainder of the Great War (see Part 1).

** 41st Inf. Bde. until 28/8/17.

E

1918

FIRST BATTLES OF THE SOMME

21–23 March ... ... **Battle of St. Quentin** [III Corps, Fifth Army].
4 April ... ... **Battle of the Avre** [XIX Corps, Fourth Army].

Between 21st March and 5th April the 14th Division had 5,781 casualties, and by the 6th April the last unit of the Division had been withdrawn from the Line (except the Artillery, see General Notes). The Division was then moved back between Lillers and Aire and was employed on the construction of the Army Line. On the 26th April the infantry was reduced to training staffs. Various units were attached (see General Notes), and during May the Division and attached units worked on the Lillers–Steenbecque–Morbecque Line. On the 11th June the Division was informed that it would proceed to England and then be made up to strength. Before leaving for England some reorganization of units took place (see Notes and General Notes). On the 16th June the Division entrained at Aire, on the 17th the Division and its new units crossed from Boulogne to Folkestone, reached Brookwood the same day, and the units were then completed with troops of Category B. Brigades and battalions were reorganized (see Table and Notes), and in July (between the 2nd and 6th) the reconstituted 14th Division crossed back to France and assembled around Wierre Effroy (N.E. of Boulogne) in the Second Army area. On the 29th August the 14th Division took over the left divisional sector of II Corps front line in the Second Army (north-east of Ypres) and before the end of the Great War the reconstituted Division took part in the following operations :

THE ADVANCE TO VICTORY

THE FINAL ADVANCE IN FLANDERS

28 Sept.–2 Oct. ... ... **Battle of Ypres** [XIX Corps, until 10 a.m., 2/10/18 ; then XV Corps, Second Army].
14–19 October ... ... **Battle of Courtrai** [XV Corps, Second Army].

The 14th Division remained in the line and gradually advanced towards the Schelde. On the 4th November divisional headquarters opened at Tourcoing, and on the 5th the 41st Brigade crossed the Schelde (near Helchin) and constructed three footbridges across the river. Pushing on, the Division reached a line between Chemin Vert and Celles by 10.30 a.m. on the 9th November. XV Corps was then ordered to stand fast, and the 29th Division (X Corps) from the north and 59th Division (XI Corps) from the south joined hands in front of XV Corps and XV was then withdrawn into Army Reserve, with the 14th Division in billets astride the Schelde from Helchin to Herseaux (east of Tourcoing). When the Armistice with Germany came into force at 11 a.m. on the 11th November the 14th Division still occupied the same position.

At first the Division was employed on filling in craters, repairing roads, etc., and in carrying on training and education. Demobilization began in December and the first party left on the 11th. Before the end of the month the Division lost 843 men. In January, 1919 demobilization continued at a steadily increasing rate, on the 28th January 12 officers and 465 other ranks left for England, and on the 24th March the 14th Division ceased to exist.* During the Great War the 14th (Light) Division lost 37,100 killed, wounded, and missing.

---

* Cadres left for England on 4th June, equipment guards left by 27th June, and the divisional office at Herseaux closed at 9.30 a.m. on Sunday the 29th June, 1919.

15TH (SCOTTISH) DIVISION

G.O.C.

14 September, 1914	Major-General A. WALLACE.
12 December, 1914...	Br.-Gen. M. G. WILKINSON (acting).
15 December, 1914...	Major-General C. J. MACKENZIE.
15 March, 1915	Br.-Gen. F. E. WALLERSTEIN (acting).
22 March, 1915	Major-General F. W. N. McCRACKEN.
17 June, 1917	Major-General H. F. THUILLIER.
11 October, 1917	Major-General H. L. REED, V.C. (sick, 4/7/18).
4 July, 1918	Br.-Gen. E. B. MACNAGHTEN (acting).
9 July, 1918	Major-General H. L. REED, V.C.

G.S.O. 1.

17 Sept., 1914...Major E. J. HENDERSON (acting).
3 Mar., 1915...Lt.-Col. J. T. BURNETT-STUART.
22 Nov., 1915...Major E. G. WACE (acting).
25 Nov., 1915...Lt.-Col. H. H. S. KNOX.
14 May, 1917...Lt.-Col. H. F. BAILLIE.
10 July, 1918...Lt.-Col. W. H. DIGGLE.

A.-A. and Q.-M.-G.

19 Sept., 1914...Captain H. W. SNOW (acting).
16 Oct., 1914...Colonel H. M. JOHNSTON.
18 Nov., 1914...Captain H. W. SNOW (acting).
8 April, 1915...Lt.-Col. E. F. TAYLOR.
29 Aug., 1916...Lt.-Col. C. R. BERKELEY.
25 Oct., 1918...Lt.-Col. C. D. HORSLEY.

B.-G., R.A.

3 Oct., 1914...Br.-Gen. E. A. LAMBART.
25 Aug., 1915...Br.-Gen. E. W. ALEXANDER, V.C.
24 April, 1916...Br.-Gen. E. B. MACNAGHTEN (sick, 13/9/16).
13 Sept., 1916...Br.-Gen. D. FASSON (tempy.).
21 Sept., 1916...Br.-Gen. E. B. MACNAGHTEN.
29 June, 1918...Lt.-Col. C. ST. M. INGHAM (acting).
15 July, 1918...Br.-Gen. E. B. MACNAGHTEN.
8 Oct., 1918...Br.-Gen. C. ST. M. INGHAM.

C.R.E.

15 Oct., 1914...Lt.-Col. G. S. CARTWRIGHT.
7 Mar., 1916...Major S. MILDRED (acting).
9 Mar., 1916...Lt.-Col. R. S. WALKER.
26 Oct., 1917...Lt.-Col. J. M. ARTHUR.

E*

44th BDE.

14 Sept., '14...Br.-Gen. M. G. WILKINSON.
18 April, '16...Br.-Gen. F. J. MARSHALL.
12 Nov., '17...Br.-Gen. E. HILLIAM.
19 May, '18...Br.-Gen. N. A. THOMSON.
20 June, '18...Lt.-Col. R. A. BULLOCH
(acting).
5 July, '18...Br.-Gen. N. A. THOMSON.
14 Aug., '18...Lt.-Col. R. A. BULLOCH
(acting).
10 Sept., '18...Br.-Gen. N. A. THOMSON.

45th BDE.

15 Sept., '14...Br.-Gen. F. E.
WALLERSTEIN
(invalided, 11/10/15).
12 Oct., '15...Br.-Gen. E. W. B. GREEN.
13 April, '16...Br.-Gen. W. H. L.
ALLGOOD.
22 May, '18...Br.-Gen. N. A.
ORR-EWING.
30 Sept., '18...Lt.-Col. N. MACLEOD
(acting).
21 Oct., '18...Br.-Gen. N. A. ORR-EWING.

46th BDE.

14 Sept., '14...Br.-Gen. E. J. COOPER.
30 Nov., '14...Lt.-Col. G. DE W. VERNER (acting).
9 Dec., '14...Br.-Gen. A. G. DUFF (injured, 22/7/15).
22 July, '15...Lt.-Col. A. V. USSHER (acting).
29 July, '15...Br.-Gen. T. G. MATHESON.
18 Mar., '17...Br.-Gen. E. A. FAGAN (gassed, 19/7/17).
19 July, '17...Br.-Gen. F. J. MARSHALL (tempy.).
23 July, '17...Lt.-Col. K. J. BUCHANAN (acting).
2 Aug., '17...Br.-Gen. D. R. SLADEN.
11 Feb., '18...Br.-Gen. A. F. LUMSDEN (killed, 24/6/18).
24 June, '18...Lt.-Col. A. C. L. STANLEY CLARKE (acting).
28 June, '18...Br.-Gen. V. M. FORTUNE.

GENERAL NOTES

The following Units also belonged to, or served with, the 15th (Scottish) Division :—

ARTILLERY :—532 (H.) Bty., R.F.A. (4, 4·5″ Hows.), see note 22.

    15th Heavy Battery (4, 60-pdrs.), was raised for the 15th (Scottish) Division ; but the Heavy Battery went to Gallipoli, and on 10/8/15 was attached to the 10th (Irish) Division at Suvla (see General Notes, 10th Division).

TRENCH MORTARS :—3rd T.M. Battery (Medium), ⎫ served with the Division in September
            63rd T.M. Battery (2″), ⎭   and October, 1915.

MACHINE GUNS :—11th Motor-Machine-Gun Battery, joined the Division on 23/6/15 at Chiseldon Camp, and served with the Division until 22/7/16. The Battery was then transferred to I Corps.

INFANTRY :—4/Suff., landed at le Havre on 9/11/14 and joined 8th (Jullundur) Bde., 3rd (Lahore) Div., on 4/12/14. Bn. left Jullundur Bde. on 10/11/15 and was attached to 137th Bde., 46th Div., until 15/11/15, when Bn. was transferred to 46th Bde., 15th Div. Bn. left 46th Bde. on 27/2/16 and joined 98th Bde., 33rd Div.

    4/B.W., see note 40.

    4/Sea. H., landed at le Havre on 6/11/14 and joined 19th (Dehra Dun) Bde., 7th (Meerut) Div., on 18/12/14. Bn. left Dehra Dun Bde. on 6/11/15 and was attached to 137th Bde., 46th Div., until 15/11/15, when Bn. was transferred to 46th Bde., 15th Div. Bn. left 46th Bde. on 6/1/16 and joined 154th Bde., 51st Div., on 7/1/16.

OTHER UNITS :—32nd Sanitary Section, went to France with the 15th Division and served with the Division until 29/3/17, when the Section was transferred to a XIX Corps Sanitary Area.

    15th Division Motor Ambce. Workshop, went to France with the 15th Division and served with the Division until 9/4/16, when the Workshop was absorbed by the 15th Div. Train.

———————————

On 21/2/18 the reorganization of the 15th Division on a 9-battalion basis was completed ; and by 11/3/18 the pioneer battalion was reorganized on a 3-company basis.

15TH (SCOTTISH) DIVISION

Dates	INFANTRY			ARTILLERY						Engineers	Signal Service	Pioneers	M.G. Units	Field Ambulances	Mobile Vety. Secn.	Divnl. Emplnt. Coy.	Divnl. Train
	Brigades	Battalions and attached Units	Mounted Troops	Field Artillery		Bde. Ammn. Colns.	Trench Mortar Bties.		Divnl. Ammn. Coln.	Field Cos.	Divnl. Signal Coy.						
				Brigades	Batteries		Medium	Heavy									
1914 October (England)	44th	9/B.W., 8/Sea. H., 9/Gord. H.,[1] 10/Gord. H.	15th Div. Cyclist Coy.[2]	LXX[3]	220, 221, 222	LXX B.A.C.	...	...	15th D.A.C.	73rd[4]	15th	...	...	...	27th	...	15th[5]
	45th	13/R. Scots, 7/R.S.F., 6/Cam. H., 11/A. & S.H.		LXXI[3]	223, 224, 225	LXXI B.A.C.				74th[4]							
	46th	7/K.O.S.B., 8/K.O.S.B., 10/ Sco. Rif., 12/H.L.I.		LXXII[3]	226, 227, 228	LXXII B.A.C.				91st[4]							
				LXXIII (H.)[3]	229 (H.), 230 (H.), 231 (H.)	LXXIII (H.) B.A.C.											
1915 September (France)	44th	9/B.W., 8/Sea. H., 10/Gord. H.,[6] 7/Cam. H.[7]	B Sqdn., Westld. and Cumbld. Yeo.[10] 15th Div. Cyclist Coy.[11]	LXX[3; 12]	A, B, C, D	LXX B.A.C.	...	...	15th D.A.C.	73rd	15th	9/ Gord. H.[1] (P.)	...	45th[16]	27th	...	15th
	45th	13/R. Scots, 7/R.S.F.,[8] 6/ Cam. H., 11/A. & S.H.		LXXI[3; 13]	A, B, C, D	LXXI B.A.C.				74th				48th[18]			
	46th	7/K.O.S.B.,[9] 8/K.O.S.B.,[9] 10/Sco. Rif., 12/H.L.I.		LXXII[3; 14]	A, B, C, D	LXXII B.A.C.				91st				47th[15]			
				LXXIII (H.)[3; 15]	B (H.), C (H.), D (H.)	LXXIII (H.) B.A.C.											
1916 June (France)	44th	9/B.W., 8/Sea. H., 8/10/Gord. H.,[6] 7/Cam. H.; 44th Bde. M.G. Coy.;[17] 44th T.M. Bty.[18]	...	LXX[20]	A, B, C; D (H.)	...[26]	X.15[24] Y.15[24] Z.15[24]	V.15[25]	15th D.A.C.[26]	73rd	15th	9/ Gord. H. (P.)	...	45th	27th	...	15th
	45th	13/R. Scots, 6/7/R.S.F.,[8] 6/ Cam. H., 11/A. & S.H.; 45th Bde. M.G. Coy.;[17] 45th T.M. Bty.[18]		LXXI[21]	A, B, C; D (H.)					74th				46th			
	46th	7/8/K.O.S.B.,[9] 10/Sco. Rif., 10/11/H.L.I.,[19] 12/H.L.I.;[17] 46th Bde. M.G. Coy.;[17] 46th T.M. Bty.[18]		LXXII[22]	A, B, C; D (H.)					91st				47th			
				LXXIII[23]	A, B, C												
1917 June (France)	44th	9/B.W.,[27] 8/Sea. H., 8/10/Gord. H., 7/Cam. H.; 44th M.G. Coy.; 44th T.M. Bty.	...	LXX	A, B, C; D (H.)	...	X.15 Y.15 Z.15[31]	V.15[32]	15th D.A.C.	73rd	15th	9/ Gord. H. (P.)	225th[33] M.G. Coy.	45th	27th	216th[34]	15th
	45th	13/R. Scots, 6/7/R.S.F.,[28] 6/ Cam. H., 11/A. & S.H.; 45th M.G. Coy.; 45th T.M. Bty.		LXXI	A, B, C; D (H.)					74th				46th			
	46th	7/8/K.O.S.B., 10/Sco. Rif., 10/11/H.L.I.,[29] 12/H.L.I.;[30] 46th M.G. Coy.; 46th T.M. Bty.								91st				47th			
1918 March (France)	44th	8/Sea. H., 8/10/Gord. H.,[35] 7/Cam. H.;[36] 44th T.M. Bty.	...	LXX	A, B, C; D (H.)	...	X.15 Y.15	...	15th D.A.C.	73rd	15th	9/ Gord. H. (P.)	No. 15 Bn., M.G.C.[39]	45th	27th	216th	15th
	45th	13/R. Scots, 6/Cam. H., 11/A. & S.H.;[37] 45th T.M. Bty.		LXXI	A, B, C; D (H.)					74th				46th			
	46th	7/8/K.O.S.B.,[37],[38] 10/Sco. Rif., 9/B.W.;[27],[38] 46th T.M. Bty.								91st				47th			

1918 June (France)		...	LXX .... LXXI	...	X.15 Y.15	...	15th D.A.C.	73rd 74th 91st	15th	9/ Gord. H. (P.)	No. 15 Bn., M.G.C.	27th 45th 46th 47th	216th	15th
44th	4/5/B.W.,[40] 8/Sea. H., 1/5/Gord. H.,[41] 44th T.M. Bty.		A, B, C; D (H.)											
45th	13/R. Scots, 6/Cam. H., 1/8/A. & S.H.,[42] 45th T.M. Bty.		A, B, C; D (H.)											
46th	1/9/R. Scots,[43] 7/8/K.O.S.B., 10/Sco. Rif.; 46th T.M. Bty.													

NOTES

1 On 12/1/15 Bn. (in 44th Bde.) was selected as Pioneer Bn. of 15th Div.

2 Cyclist Coy. was formed on 23/12/14.

3 Bties. were raised as 6-gun batteries and numbered. By Feb., 1915, all brigades were reorganized as 4-battery brigades; the batteries all became 4-gun batteries, and the batteries were lettered A, B, C, D in each brigade.

4 73rd and 74th Fd. Cos. were formed at Aldershot in Sept., 1914. 91st Fd. Coy. joined 15th Div. in Jany., 1915, at Bordon, from 24th Div.

5 The Cos. were numbered 138, 139, 140, and 141 Cos., A.S.C.

6 10/Gord. H. amalgamated with 8/Gord. H. (from 26th Bde., 9th Div.) on 11/5/16, and became 8/10/Gord. H. (The surplus formed 11/Entg. Bn.).

7 Bn. (from Third Hundred Thousand) joined 44th Bde. on 13/1/15.

8 7/R.S.F. amalgamated with 6/R.S.F. (from 27th Bde., 9th Div.) on 13/5/16 and became 6/7 R.S.F.

9 7 and 8/K.O.S.B. amalgamated at Bethune on 28/5/16 and became 7/8/K.O.S.B.

10 Sqdn. joined 15th Div. at Marlborough on 23/8/15. In May, 1916, the Sqdn. left 15th Div. and joined XI Corps Cav. Regt. on 15/5/16.

11 Coy. was transferred on 21/8/16 to I Corps Cyclist Bn.

12 On 7/6/16 D Bty. left Bde. and became B/LXXIII; and B (H.)/LXXIII joined and became D (H.)/LXX.

13 On 7/6/16 D Bty. left Bde. and became C/LXXIII; and C (H.)/LXXIII joined and became D (H.)/LXXI.

14 On 7/6/16 D Bty. left Bde. and became D/LXXIII; and D (H.)/LXXIII joined and became D (H.)/LXXII.

15 Bde. disembkd. at le Havre on 0/7/15 with A (H.), B (H.), C (H.), and D (H.), each Bty. armed with 4, 4·5″ Hows. On 7/8/15 A (H.) left LXXIII and Bty. became C (H.)/CXXX (H.), in the 28th Div., on 8/9/15. On 7/8/16 LXXIII was reorganized: B (H.)/LXX, C (H.), and D (H.) left Bde. and became D (H.)/LXX, D (H.)/LXXI, and D (H.)/LXXII: on the same day D/LXX, D/LXXI, and D/LXXII joined and became B, C, and D/LXXIII. In July, 1916, B, C, and D Bties. were redesignated A, B, and C.

16 The 3 Fd. Ambces. joined 15th Div. at Marlborough on 23/8/15.

17 The 3 M.G. Cos. were formed on 9/2/16; 46th joined 46th Bde. on 11/2/16, and 44th and 45th joined 44th and 45th Bdes. on 12/2/16.

18 The 3 T.M. Bties. were formed in the Bdes. as follows: 44th—A. 44 and B. 44 by 11/2/16, later became 44/1 and 44/2, and 44th T.M. Bty. was formed by 25/8/16; 45th—A. 45 and B. 45 formed in Feb., 1916, later became 45/1 and 45/2, and 45th T.M. Bty. was formed by 17/8/16; 46th—A. 46 and B. 46 formed by 5/2/16 and 23/2/16, later became 46/1 and 46/2, and 46th T.M. Bty. was formed by 20/6/16.

19 10/H.L.I. and 11/H.L.I. were raised as part of 28th Bde., 9th Div., and served with it until 6/5/16; the 2 Bns. were attached to S. African Inf. Bde. (in 9th Div.) from 6-14/5/16, and on 14/5/16 the 2 Bns. were transferred to 46th Bde., 15th Div. On 16/5/16 10/H.L.I. and 11/H.L.I. amalgamated and became 10/11/H.L.I.

20 Bde. was reorganized 1-3/12/16: C was split up between A and B and made up A and B to 6 guns each; C/LXXIII joined and became C/LXX. On 22/1/17 532 (H.)/LXXIII joined and made up D (H.) to 6 hows.

21 Bde. was reorganized 1-3/12/16: C was split up between A and B and made up A and B to 6 guns each; B/LXXIII joined and became C/LXXXI. On 22/1/17 1 sec., 532 (H.)/LXXII joined and made up D (H.) to 6 hows.

22 532 (H.)—4, 4·5″ hows.—disembkd. at le Havre on 11/11/16 and joined LXXII on 10/11/16. Bde. was reorganized on 1 and 2/12/16: C was split up between A and B and made up A and B to 6 guns each. On 20/1/17 LXXII became an A.F.A. Bde., and B/CCLII (from 50th Div.) joined and became C/LXXII. On 22/1/17 532 (H.) left LXXII and was broken up to make up D (H.)/LXX and D (H.)/LXXI to 6 hows. each. 1 Sec. howitzers joined and made up D (H.)/LXXII to 6 howitzers by 20/1/17.

23 Bde. was reorganized and then broken up 1-3/12/16: A was split up between B and C to make up B and C to 6 guns each; and B/LXXIII joined LXXI and became C/LXX, and C/LXXIII joined LXX and became C/LXX.

24 The 3 Medium T.M. Bties. joined by June, 1916.

25 The Heavy T.M. Bty. joined by Nov. 1916.

26 On 22/5/16 B.A.C.s were abolished and the D.A.C. was reorganized.

27 Bn. was transferred to 46th Bde. on 7/2/18.

28 Bn. was transferred to 59th Div. on 21/2/18 as Pioneer Bn. On 7-10/5/18 Bn. was reduced to T.C. and attached to 176th Bde., 16th Div. On 18/6/18 Bn. joined 47th Bde., 16th Div., at Boulogne and went to England. On 20/6/18 Bn. joined 18/Sco. Rif. at Deal; and on 2/7/18 18/Sco. Rif. joined 48th Bde., 16th Div.

29 On 1/2/18 Bn. was transferred to 119th Bde., 40th Div., and on 16/2/18 to 120th Bde. On 6/5/18 Bn. was reduced to T.C.; on 31/5/18 Bn. joined 34th Div.; on 10/6/18 Bn. was transferred to 14th Div. at Boulogne, reached Bookwood on 17/6/18 and joined 42nd Bde., transferred to 43rd Bde. on 19/6/18. Bn. absorbed 22/H.L.I. and became 10/H.L.I. on 21/6/18. Bn. landed at Boulogne on 5/7/18.

30 On 3/2/18 Bn. was transferred to 106th Bde., 35th Div.

31 On 9/2/18 Z was broken up between X and Y.

32 V left the division on 9/2/18.

33 Coy. formed at Grantham; embkd. at Southampton on 11/7/17, disembkd. at le Havre on 12/7/17, left le Havre on 18/7/17, and joined 15th Div. at Brandhoek on 19/7/17.

34 Divnl. Emplmt. Coy. (1 offr., 106 o.r.) joined on 22/5/17; became 216th Divnl. Emplmt. Coy. by 30/8/17.

[TURN OVER]

NOTES—continued.

35 Bn. was reduced to T.C. on 6/6/18 ; T.C. was transferred to 118th Bde., 39th Div., on 9/6/18 ; surplus remained in 44th Bde., and on 7 and 8/6/18 was absorbed by 1/5 Gord. H. (see note 41).

36 Bn. reduced to T.C. on 10/6/18, part of remdr. joined 6/Cam. H. (45th Bde.) on 11/6/18, and surplus was transferred to Base. T.C. left 15th Div. on 10/6/18, joined 118th Bde., 39th Div., on 11/6/18 ; left 39th Div. on 28/7/18, joined X1X Corps Rft. Camp on 30/7/18 ; left Rft. Camp on 13/8/18, and rejoined 39th Div. On 14/8/18 the Bn. was disbanded.

37 Bn. reduced to T.C. on 9/6/18, and surplus joined 1/8/A. and S.H. On 11/8/18 T.C. was transferred to 118th Bde., 39th Div. ; T.C. became X Corps Rft. Bn. on 30/7/18, and was disbanded on 26/8/18, when all (except C.O. and 1 W.O.) joined 1/8/A. and S.H.

38 Bn. reduced to T.C. on 19/5/18 (surplus of 42 offrs. and 672 o.r. had been absorbed on 16/5/18 by 4/5/B.W. in 118th Bde., 39th Div., see note 40). T.C. left 15th Div. on 19/5/18, joined 118th Bde., 39th Div., on 21/5/18, left 39th Div. on 17/6/18, and joined 48th Bde., 16th Div., at Boulogne ; T.C. reached England on 18/6/18. On 19/6/18 9/B.W. was reformed from 15/B.W., and on 2/7/18 9/B.W. joined 47th Bde., 16th Div. ; and on 28/7/18 9/B.W. landed at le Havre.

39 Bn. was formed on 17/3/18. Bn. consisted of 44th, 45th, 46th, and 225th M.G. Cos.

40

4/B.W. landed at le Havre on 26/2/15, joined 21st (Bareilly) Bde., 7th (Meerut) Div., on 4/3/15 ; Bn. was transferred to 139th Bde., 46th Div., on 6/11/15 ; to 44th Bde., 15th Div., on 14/11/15 ; to 154th Bde., 51st Div., on 6/1/16 ; to 118th Bde., 39th Div., on 29/2/16 ; and on 15/3/16 Bn. amalgamated with 5/B.W. and became 4/5/B.W. (37 offrs. and 1051 o.r.).

5/B.W. landed at le Havre on 2/11/14, joined 24th Bde., 8th Div., at Neuf Berquin on 13/11/14, became Pioneer Bn., 8th Div., on 18/10/15 ; Bn. was transferred to 154th Bde., 51st Div., on 6/1/16 ; to 118th Bde., 39th Div., on 29/2/16 ; and on 15/3/16 Bn. amalgamated with 4/B.W. (see above).

4/5/B.W. was reformed on 6/5/18 (19 offrs. and 350 o.r.). On 14/5/18 Bn. left 118th Bde., 39th Div., and joined 46th Bde., 15th Div., on 15/5/18. On 16/5/18 Bn. absorbed 42 offrs. and 672 o.r. of 9/B.W. (see note 38) ; and on 3/6/18 Bn. was transferred from 46th Bde. to 44th Bde.

41 Bn. served in 153rd Bde., 51st Div., until 2/2/18, then in 183rd Bde., 61st Div., until 1/6/18, when Bn. was transferred to 44th Bde., 15th Div.

42 Bn. served in 152nd Bde., 51st Div., until 7/2/18, then in 183rd Bde., 61st Div., until 1/6/18, when Bn. was transferred to 45th Bde., 15th Div. Bn. absorbed surplus of 11/A. and S.H. on 9/6/18.

43 Bn. served in 154th Bde., 51st Div., until 6/2/18, then in 183rd Bde., 61st Div., until 1/6/18, when Bn. was transferred to 46th Bde., 15th Div. Bn. joined 46th Bde. on 2/6/18.

15TH (SCOTTISH) DIVISION

FORMATION, BATTLES, AND ENGAGEMENTS

This New Army Division had no existence before the outbreak of the Great War.

On the 6th August 1914 Parliament sanctioned an increase of 500,000 all ranks to the Regular Army. The first hundred thousand men raised for this purpose were used to form the First New Army. The formation of the divisions of the Second New Army from the second augmentation of a hundred thousand men was authorized by Army Order No. 382 of the 11th September 1914 (see Appendix I). Six more divisions (15th–20th) and Army Troops were now added to the Regular Army, and during September 1914 the 15th (Scottish) Division, the senior division of the Second New Army, began to assemble at Aldershot.

Whilst it was at Aldershot H.M. the King inspected the Division on the 26th September. This was the first time the Division paraded as a formed unit and, with the exception of the staff, the Division paraded in plain clothes. The Division remained at Aldershot until the 18th–22nd November when it moved to Salisbury Plain.

On the 22nd January 1915 the Division paraded in most inclement weather for another inspection, this time by Field-Marshal Earl Kitchener and M. Millerand (French Minister of War). On this occasion all ranks paraded in uniform, and sufficient obsolete drill rifles were available to arm the front ranks of battalions ; but many essentials were still lacking.

Horses arrived soon after the assembly of the Division. At first, however, not much use could be made of them as only a headstall was available for each animal ; some time elapsed before harness and saddlery reached the Division. In the artillery in the early days the only equipment was an improvised gun made from a log of wood mounted on the Bordon funeral gun-carriage ; somewhat later the artillery armament was doubled by annexing a 9-pdr. brass muzzle-loading gun from the Ordnance Officers' Mess. Later on the divisional artillery received some early 15-pdr. B.L. equipments and some French 90 mm. B.L.s ; neither equipment was more than 20 years out of date. Modern Q.F. field guns and 4·5″ howitzers only arrived much later, and it was nearing mid-June, 1915 before gun-sights were received. Nevertheless on the 21st June it was a division ready to take the field which paraded for the second time before H.M. the King on Sidbury Hill.

On the 3rd July the Division received the warning that it was to move to France ; entrainment began on the 7th, and by the 13th July the Division completed its concentration around Tilques (near St. Omer). On the 15th July the Division began moving south towards Bethune, and on the 17th July the Division joined IV Corps, First Army. For the remainder of the Great War the 15th Division served on the Western Front in France and Belgium and was engaged in the following operations :—

1915

25 and 26 September ...   **Battle of Loos** [IV Corps, First Army].

1916

27 and 29 April ...   ...   **German Gas Attacks, Hulluch Front** [I Corps, First Army].
11 May...   ...   .   **The Kink** [I Corps, First Army].

BATTLES OF THE SOMME

8 Aug.–3 Sept.   ...   ...   **Battle of Pozières Ridge** [III Corps, Fourth Army].
15–18 September   ...   **Battle of Flers-Courcelette** [III Corps, Fourth Army].
15 September   ...   ...   **Capture of Martinpuich.**
9–18 October   ...   ...   **Battle of the Transloy Ridges** [III Corps, Fourth Army].

1917

BATTLES OF ARRAS

9–11 April	**First Battle of the Scarpe** [VI Corps, Third Army].
23 and 24 April	**Second Battle of the Scarpe** [VI Corps, Third Army].
23 April	**Capture of Guémappe.**

BATTLES OF YPRES

31 July–2 Aug.	**Battle of Pilckem Ridge** [XIX Corps, Fifth Army].
17 and 18 August ...	**Battle of Langemarck** (46th Bde.) [XIX Corps, Fifth Army].
22 August	**Fighting for Zevenkote** [XIX Corps, Fifth Army].

1918

21 March–5 April ...	**FIRST BATTLES OF THE SOMME** [XVII Corps, Third Army].
24 and 25 March... ...	**Battle of Bapaume** [XVII Corps, Third Army].
28 March	**Battle of Arras** [XVII Corps, Third Army].

THE ADVANCE TO VICTORY

BATTLES OF THE MARNE

23 July–2 August ...	**Battle of the Soissonais and of the Ourcq*** [XX (French) Corps, Tenth (French) Army].
28 July	**Attack on Buzancy.**
2 Oct.–11 Nov.	**THE FINAL ADVANCE IN ARTOIS AND FLANDERS** [I Corps, Fifth Army].

The 15th Division started its final advance from the vicinity of Loos and Hulluch, where it had received its baptism of fire in 1915. Pressing forward, the Division crossed the Haute Deule Canal on the 15th October and reached the line of the Schelde on the 21st October. On the 8th November the Division crossed the Schelde to the south of Antoing, and advancing eastwards the 15th Division reached the line of the Dendre to the south of Ath by 11 a.m. on the 11th November. The Armistice then came into force and hostilities ceased.

On the 12th November the Division was informed that it would be transferred to III Corps, Second Army, and it would take part in the Advance to the Rhine. On the 21st this arrangement was cancelled, and III Corps was transferred to the Fifth Army on the 22nd. On the 7th December H.M. the King, accompanied by T.R.H. The Prince of Wales and Prince Albert, passed through the divisional area, and all the units of the 15th Division were formed up on each side of the road. On the 10th December the first batch of men (coalminers) left for demobilization. On the 15th December the Division began to move into its new area around Nivelles, and divisional headquarters opened at Braine le Château on the 16th December.

In 1919 demobilization proceeded gradually and the Division slowly dwindled. On the 25th March the G.O.C. left, on the 26th the " G " office was closed down, and on the 2nd April headquarters moved to Clabecq. During the next two months cadres and equipment guards of the various units left the Division and returned to Scotland ; and on the 27th June the 15th (Scottish) Division finally passed out of existence. During the Great War the 15th Division lost 45,542 killed, wounded, and missing.

---

* In this Battle British, French, and American artilleries co-operated.

16TH (IRISH) DIVISION

G.O.C.

23 September, 1914	Lieutenant-General Sir L. W. PARSONS.
22 January, 1915	Br.-Gen. R. D. LONGE (acting).
25 January, 1915	Lieutenant-General Sir L. W. PARSONS.
28 March, 1915	Colonel R. S. H. MOODY (acting).
6 April, 1915	Lieutenant-General Sir L. W. PARSONS.
5 December, 1915...	Major-General W. B. HICKIE (sick, 10/2/18).
10 February, 1918	Br.-Gen. F. W. RAMSAY (acting).
23 February, 1918	Major-General Sir C. P. A. HULL.
4 May, 1918	Br.-Gen. F. W. RAMSAY (acting).
10 May, 1918	Major-General A. B. RITCHIE.

G.S.O. 1.

18 Sept., 1914...Captain B. E. CROCKETT (acting).

11 Jan., 1915...Lt.-Col. G. A. S. CAPE.

4 July, 1915...Major L. C. JACKSON (acting).

12 Oct., 1915...Lt.-Col. L. C. JACKSON.

A.-A. and Q.-M.-G.

15 Sept., 1914...Major G. A. C. WEBB (acting).

10 Oct., 1914...Colonel T. JERMYN.

3 Nov., 1914...Lt.-Col. D. T. HAMMOND.

30 Oct., 1915...Lt.-Col. G. A. C. WEBB.

12 April, 1918...Lt.-Col. W. B. RENNIE.

B.-G., R.A.

25 Oct., 1914...Br.-Gen. C. E. GOULBURN. (Left 16th Div. on 28/7/15, and became B.-G., R.A., Guards Div., in France, on 30/8/15.)

23 Sept., 1915...Br.-Gen. E. J. DUFFUS.

3 Nov., 1916...Lt.-Col. H. M. THOMAS (acting).

4 Nov., 1916...Br.-Gen. C. E. C. G. CHARLTON (sick, 1/9/17).

1 Sept., 1917...Lt.-Col. H. M. THOMAS (acting).

8 Sept., 1917...Br.-Gen. C. E. C. G. CHARLTON.

C.R.E.

23 Oct., 1914...Lt.-Col. J. E. VANRENEN. (Left 16th Div. on 13/8/15, and became C.R.E., Guards Div., in France, on 26/8/15.)

16 Aug., 1915...Lt.-Col. W. L. PALMER.

7 Oct., 1916...Lt.-Col. R. F. A. BUTTERWORTH.

22 July, 1918...Major E. I. SCOTT (acting).

26 July, 1918...Lt.-Col. F. SUMMERS.

47th BDE.

15 Sept., '14...Br.-Gen. P. J. MILES.
20 Jan., '16...Br.-Gen. G. E. PEREIRA.
23 Nov., '17...Br.-Gen. H. G. GREGORIE.
13 April, '18...Br.-Gen. B. C. DENT.

48th BDE.

18 Sept., '14...Br.-Gen. K. J. BUCHANAN.
17 Jan., '16...Lt.-Col. Sir F. W. SHAW,
Bart. (acting).
23 Jan., '16...Br.-Gen. F. W. RAMSAY.
4 May, '18...Lt.-Col. K. C. WELDON
(acting).
10 May, '18...Br.-Gen. F. W. RAMSAY.
13 June, '18...Lt.-Col. G. DRAGE (acting).
15 June, '18...Lt.-Col. F. E. ASHTON
(acting).
20 June, '18...Br.-Gen. R. N. BRAY.

49th BDE.

15 Sept., '14...Br.-Gen. R. D. LONGE.
7 Feb., '16...Br.-Gen. P. LEVESON-GOWER.
5 May, '18...Br.-Gen. H. E. P. NASH.

GENERAL NOTES

The following Units also served with the 16th (Irish) Division :—

ARTILLERY :—54th (E. Anglian) Div. Arty. (I, II, III (H.), and IV Bdes.), was attached from 24–31/12/15.

56th (1st London) Div. Arty. (I, II, III London Bdes.), was attached from 1/1–25/2/16 : I Bde., 1/1–25/2/16 ; and II and III Bdes., 1–8/1/16, and 18–25/2/16.

16th Heavy Battery (4, 60-pdrs.), was raised for the 16th Div., but the Heavy Battery went to France independently. On 10/7/15 the Heavy Battery disembkd. at le Havre, left le Havre on 11/7/15, and joined XXI Heavy Artillery Bde., R.G.A., on 15/7/15.

INFANTRY :—11/R. Ir. F., see note 70.

10/R. Dub. F., left Dublin on 5/8/16 and went to Pirbright. Bn. disembkd. at le Havre on 19/8/16 and joined 190th Bde., 63rd (R.N.) Div., on 21/8/16. On 23/6/17 Bn. was transferred to 48th Bde., 16th Div. ; Bn. absorbed surplus personnel of 8/ and 9/R.D.F. on 24/10/17, and left for VII Corps Rft. Depôt on 13/2/18. On 15/2/18 Bn. was disbanded and the personnel joined 19/Entg. Bn.

19/Entrenching Bn., was formed in Feb., 1918, from personnel of 7/Leins. and 10/R.D.F. On 22/3/18 Bn. was attached to 24th Div., and on 4/4/18 Bn. was transferred to 16th Div. On 5/5/18, 19/Entg. Bn. was disbanded : personnel joined 2/R.M.F., the transport was distributed in the 16th Div. and the surplus went to Abbeville.

OTHER UNITS :—81st Sanitary Section, left Chelsea and disembkd. at le Havre on 19/12/15, with 16th Div. Section remained with 16th Div. until April, 1917 when the Section was transferred to a Sanitary Area in IX Corps, Second Army.

16th Division Motor Ambce. Workshop, mobilized at Grove Park, disembkd. at Rouen on 23/6/15, and joined 3rd (Lahore) Div. on 3/7/15 as Lahore Div. Motor Ambce. Workshop. On 25/12/15 the Workshop was transferred to 16th Div. and became 16th Div. Motor Ambce. Workshop. By 9/4/16 the Workshop was absorbed by 16th Div. Train.

On 14/2/18 the reorganization of the 16th Division on a 9-battalion basis was completed ; and on 8/3/18 the pioneer battalion (11/Hants.) was reorganized on a 3-company basis.

16th DIVISION ARTILLERY, APRIL–SEPTEMBER, 1918

After the 3rd April (when the 16th Division was withdrawn from the battle-front) the 16th Division Artillery was left in the line covering 14th Div. (XIX Corps), north of Villers Bretonneux, and 16th Div. Artillery was engaged in the Battle of the Avre on 4/4/18. On 7/4, 16th Div. Arty. was relieved and withdrew to Vers, and on 12/4 it was placed under 51st Div. Arty. to cover 61st Div. near St. Venant. CLXXVII, CLXXX, and 16th D.A.C. were engaged in the Battle of Hazebrouck (12–15/4) and in the Battle of Bethune (18/4) in XI Corps, First Army. On 3/5/18 H.Q., 16th Div. Arty., relieved H.Q., 51st Div. Arty., and on 29/5 H.Q., 61st Div. Arty., relieved H.Q., 16th Div. Arty. ; but CLXXVII, CLXXX, and 16th D.A.C. remained in action on the St. Venant front, covering 61st Div., until 22/6/18, when the two brigades and D.A.C. were relieved by the 66th Div. Arty. On 24/6, 16th Div. Arty. was withdrawn into First Army Reserve. On 17/7, 16th Div. Arty. was transferred to Cdn. Corps and went into action on 18/7 to cover 1st Cdn. Div. On 30/7, 16th Div. Arty. was transferred to XVII Corps and on 2/8 the brigades were covering 57th and 58th Divs. On 23/8 Cdn. Corps relieved XVII Corps, and on 26 and 27/8 the brigades co-operated in an attack by the Cdn. Corps astride the Scarpe (Battle of the Scarpe) ; and CLXXVII was engaged on 2 and 3/9 in the Battle of the Drocourt–Quéant Line. On 28/8/18 H.Q., 16th Div. Arty., rejoined 16th Div. ; and on 7/9/18 CLXXVII, CLXXX, and 16th D.A.C. rejoined 16th Division, and the brigades came into action covering their own division.

Dates	Brigades	Battalions and attached Units	Mounted Troops	Artillery — Field Artillery: Brigades	Batteries	Bde. Ammn. Colns.	Trench Mortar Bties. Medium	Heavy	Divnl. Ammn. Coln.	Engineers Field Cos.	Signal Service Divnl. Signal Coy.	Pioneers	M.G. Units	Field Ambulances	Mobile Vety. Secn.	Divnl. Emplnt. Coy.	Divnl. Train
1914 October (Ireland)	47th	6/R. Irish Regt.,[1] 6/Conn. Rang., 7/Leins, 8/R.M.F., 8/R.D.F., 9/R.D.F.	16th Div. Cyclist Coy.,[3]	LXXIV[4]	232, 233, 234	LXXIV B.A.C.	...	...	16th D.A.C.	75th	16th	11/Hants.,[6] (P.)	...	48th	47th	...	16th[7]
	48th	7/R. Ir. Rif.,[2] 9/R.M.F., 8/R.D.F., 9/R.D.F.		LXXV[4]	235, 236, 237	LXXV B.A.C.				76th				49th			
	49th	7/R. Innis. F., 8/R. Innis. F., 7/R. Ir. F., 8/R. Ir. F.		LXXVI[4]	238, 239, 240	LXXVI B.A.C.				95th[5]				50th			
				LXXVII (H.)[4]	241 (H.), 242 (H.), 243 (H.)	LXXVII (H.) B.A.C.											
1915 July (Ireland)	47th	6/R. Irish Regt., 6/Conn. Rang., 7/Leins, 8/R.M.F., 8/R.D.F., 9/R.D.F.	C Sqdn., S. Irish Horse[17]	LXXIV[4]; 9	A, B, C, D	LXXIV B.A.C.	...	...	16th D.A.C.[12]	75th[15]	16th[15]	11/Hants. (P.)	...	48th[16]	47th	...	16th
	48th	7/R. Ir. Rif., 9/R.M.F., 8/R.D.F., 9/R.D.F.		LXXV[4]; 10	A, B, C, D	LXXV B.A.C.				76th[13]				49th[16]			
	49th	7/R. Innis. F., 8/R. Innis. F., 7/R. Ir. F., 8/R. Ir. F.	16th Div. Cyclist Coy.[18]	LXXVI[4]; 10, LXXVII (H.)[4] 4; 11; 24	A, B, C, D / A (H.), B (H.), C (H.), D (H.)	LXXVI B.A.C. / LXXVII (H.) B.A.C.				95th[14]				50th[16]			
1916 June (France)	47th	6/R. Irish Regt., 6/Conn. Rang., 7/Leins, 8/R.M.F.,[19] 47th Bde. M.G. Coy.,[20] 47th T.M. Bty.[21]	17 & 18 ...	LXXVII 11; 24; 43	A, B, C; D (H.)	...[50]	X.16[28] Y.16[28] Z.16[28]	V.16[29]	16th D.A.C.[30]	155th[31]	16th[32]	11/Hants. (P.)	...	111th[33]	47th	...	16th
	48th	7/R. Ir. Rif.,[22; 36] 1/R.M.F.,[19] 8/R.D.F., 9/R.D.F.;[39] 48th Bde. M.G. Coy.,[20] 48th T.M. Bty.[21]	...	CLXXVII[25 ...]	A, B, C; D (H.)					156th[31]				112th[33]			
	49th	7/R. Innis. F., 8/R. Innis. F., 7/R. Ir. F.,[23] 8/R. Ir. F.,[23] 49th Bde. M.G. Coy.,[20] 49th T.M. Bty.[21]		CLXXX[26 ...]	A, B, C; D (H.)					157th[31]				113th[33]			
				CLXXXII 27; 46	A, B, C; D (H.)												
1917 June (France)	47th	6/R. Irish Regt.,[34] 6/Conn. Rang., 7/Leins,[35] 1/R.M.F.; 56 47th M.G. Coy.;[55] 47th T.M. Bty.	...	CLXXVII[44]	A, B, C; D (H.)	...	X.16 Y.16 Z.16[47]	V.16[48]	16th D.A.C.	155th	16th	11/Hants. (P.)	260th M.G. Coy.[49]	111th	47th	217th[50]	16th
	48th	7/R. Ir. Rif.,[37] 2/R.D.F.,[38] 8/R.D.F.,[39] 9/R.D.F.;[39] 48th M.G. Coy.;[55] 48th T.M. Bty.		CLXXX[45]	A, B, C; D (H.)					156th				112th			
	49th	2/R. Irish Regt.,[40] 7/R. Innis. F.,[41] 8/R. Innis. F.,[41] 7/8/R. Ir. F.,[41; 23; 42] 49th M.G. Coy.;[55] 49th T.M. Bty.								157th				113th			

[TURN OVER

Component (heading)	1918 March (France)	1918 August (France) — After reconstitution
	16th	16th
	217th	217th[78]
	47th	47th
	111th 112th 113th	111th 112th 113th
	11/Hants.(P.)	11/Hants.(P.)
	No. 16 Bn., M.G.C.[63]	No. 16 Bn., M.G.C.[77]
	16th	16th
	155th 156th 157th	155th 156th[76] 157th
	16th D.A.C.	16th D.A.C.[74];[75]
	X.1661 Y.1661	X.1675 Y.1675
	...	...
	...	...
	CLXXVII CLXXX	CLXXVII[74] CLXXX
	...	...
	A, B, C; D (H.) / A, B, C; D (H.)	A, B, C; D (H.) / A, B, C; D (H.)
47th.....	6/Conn. Rang.,[51] 2/Leins.,[52] 1/R.M.F.,[55] 47th T.M. Bty.[54]	14/Leic.,[64] 18/Welsh,[65] 9/B.W.,[66] 47th T.M. Bty.[67]
48th.....	2/R.M.F.,[55] 1/R.D.F.,[56] 2/R.D.F.;[57] 48th T.M. Bty.[54]	22/N.F.,[68] 18/Sco. Rif.,[69] 5/R. Ir. F.,[70] 48th T.M. Bty.[67]
49th.....	2/R. Irish Regt.,[58] 7/(S. Ir. Horse) R. Irish Regt.,[59] F.;[60] 49th T.M. Bty.[54]	6/Som. L.I.,[71] 18/Glouc.,[72] 34/Lond. (K.R.R.C.);[73] 49th T.M. Bty.[67]

NOTES

1 On 5/3/15 the Bn. absorbed a Coy. of the Guernsey Militia (7 offrs. and 238 o.r.).

2 On 5/3/15 the Bn. absorbed a Coy. of the Jersey Militia (6 offrs. and 224 o.r.).

3 The Cyclist Coy. was formed at the Old Barracks, Fermoy, on 11/12/14.

4 Bties. were raised as 6-gun bties. and numbered. On 23/1/15 all Bdes. were reorganized as 4-battery bdes., the bties. all became 4-gun bties., and in each bde. the bties. were lettered A, B, C, D. (Authy.—W.O. Letter, No. 20/Artillery/3818, A.G.6).

5. Fd. Coy. (6 offrs., 290 o.r., and 22 horses) joined Div. in Ireland on 30/1/1915, from 26th Div.

6 Bn. was raised after the outbreak of War, allotted to Second New Army as an Army Troops Bn., and attached to 16th Div. by 20/9/14. On 3/12/14, 11/Hants. was converted into Pioneer Bn. of 16th Div.

7 Train consisted of 142, 143, 144, and 145 Cos., A.S.C.

8 Bn. was disbanded on 30/5/16. (3 offrs. and 146 o.r. joined 1/R.M.F., 7 offrs. and 140 o.r. joined 2/R.M.F., and 12 offrs. and 200 o.r. joined 8/R.M.F.)

9 Bde. left 16th Div. in Ireland in July, 1915, and went to Salisbury Plain. Bde. landed at le Havre on 29/8/15, and joined Guards Div. on 30/8/15.

10 Bdes. left 16th Div. in Ireland in July, 1915, and went to Salisbury Plain. Bdes. landed at le Havre on 3/9/15, and joined Guards Div. on 4/9/15.

11 Bde. left Fermoy on 30/7/15, and reached Salisbury Plain on 4/8/15. Bde. went to Aldershot in Aug., 1915, received 4·5" hows. on 30/8/15, and Bde. went to Bordon on 4/12/15 and took part in gun-practice from 5-9/1/16.

12 D.A.C. left 16th Div. in Ireland in July, 1915, and went to Salisbury Plain. D.A.C. landed at le Havre on 28/8/15, and joined Guards Div. on 3/9/15.

13 Fd. Cos. left 16th Div. in Ireland on 13 and 15/8/15, and went to Salisbury Plain. Fd. Cos. landed at le Havre on 23 and 24/8/15, and joined Guards Div. on 25 and 26/8/15.

14 Fd. Coy. left 16th Div. in Ireland on 17/8/15, and went to Salisbury Plain. Fd. Coy. landed at le Havre on 25/8/15, and joined 7th Div. on 30/8/15.

15 Signal Coy. left 16th Div. in Ireland on 9/8/15, and went to Southampton. Sig. Coy. landed at le Havre on 16/8/15, and joined Guards Div. on 18/8/15.

16 The 3 Fd. Ambces. left 16th Div. in Ireland in June, 1915, went to Salisbury Plain, and joined 37th Div. The 3 Fd. Ambces. landed at le Havre on 29/7, 31/7, and 1/8/15.

17 Sqdn. joined 16th Div. at Aldershot, and went to France with the Div. in Dec., 1915. On 17/5/16 Sqdn. left 16th Div. and joined I Corps Cav. Regt.

18 Coy. was disbanded on 1/6/16; and the personnel was drafted to the Bns. in the 16th Div.

19 Bn. (21 offrs. and 446 o.r.) was absorbed by 1/R.M.F. on 23/11/16.

20 M.G. Cos. disembkd. at le Havre on 26/4/16 and joined Bdes.: 47th and 48th on 28/4/16; and 49th on 29/4/16.

21 T.M. Bties. were formed in Bdes.:
47th—47/1 and 47/2 were formed on 21/3/16 and became 47th T.M. Bty. by 16/6/16;
48th—48/1 and 48/2 were formed by 23/3/16 and became 48th T.M. Bty. by 24/6/16;
49th—49/1 and 49/2 were formed by 29/3/16 and became 49th T.M. Bty. by 16/6/16.

22 Bn. served with 29th Div. from 12/1/15-25/4/16; Bn. was then transferred to L. of C.; and Bn. joined 48th Bde. on 28/5/16.

23 Bns. were amalgamated on 15/10/16 and became 7/8/R. Ir. R.

24 Bde. disembkd. at le Havre on 17 and 18/2/16 and joined 16th Div. On 2/6/16 LXXVII (H.) Bde. was reorganized: A (H.), B (H.), and D (H.) were transferred and became D (H.)/CLXXX, D (H.)/CLXXXII, and D (H.)/CLXXVII; at the same time C (H.)/LXXVII was redesignated D (H.)/LXXVII, and D/CLXXVII, D/CLXXX, and D/CLXXXII joined and became A, B, and C/LXXVII.

25 Bde. concentrated in Jany., 1916, with 10th Div. Arty. at Bordon, disembkd. at le Havre on 18/2/16, and joined 10th Div. on 22/2/16. On 2/8/16 Bde. was reorganized : D Bty. was transferred and became A/LXXVII and D (H.)/LXXVII joined and became D (H.)/CLXXVII.

26 Bde. concentrated in Jany., 1916, with 16th Div. Arty. at Bordon, disembkd. at le Havre on 17/2/16, and joined 16th Div. on 22/2/16. On 2/8/16 Bde. was reorganized : D Bty. was transferred and became B/LXXVII and A (H.)/LXXVII joined and became D (H.)/CLXXX.

27 Bde. concentrated in Jany., 1916, with 16th Div. Arty. at Bordon, disembkd. at le Havre on 19/2/16, and joined 16th Div. on 22/2/16. On 2/8/16 Bde. was reorganized ; D Bty. was transferred and became C/LXXVII and B (H.)/LXXVII joined and became D (H.)/CLXXXII.

28 The Medium T.M. Bties. joined by June, 1916.

29 The Heavy T.M. Bty. joined by 5/9/16.

30 D.A.C. concentrated in Jany., 1916, with 16th Div. Arty. at Bordon; disembkd. at le Havre on 19/2/16, and joined 16th Div. on 22/2/16. On 28 and 29/5/16 D.A.C. was reorganized and the B.A.C.s were abolished.

31 The 3 Fd. Cos. joined the Div. in Ireland in Aug., 1915.

32 Sig. Coy. joined the Div. at Aldershot in Sept., 1915.

33 The 3 Fd. Ambces. joined the Div. at Aldershot in Sept., 1915.

34 Bn. was disbanded on 9/2/18 : part went to 2/R. Ir. Regt. and part to 7/(S. Ir. Horse) R. Ir. Regt.

35 Bn. was disbanded on 14/2/18 : part joined 2/Leins. and remdr. went to 19/Entg. Bn.

36 On 22/11/16 Bn. was transferred from 48th to 47th Bde.

37 On 23/8/17 Bn. was transferred from 48th to 49th Bde. On 14/10/17 Bn. was transferred to 108th Bde., 36th Div., and joined on 15/10/17; Bn. (17 offrs. and 515 o.r.) was then absorbed by 2/R. Ir. Rif.

NOTES—continued.

38 Bn. joined from 10th Bde., 4th Div., on 16/11/16; and on 10/2/18 Bn. absorbed 10 offrs. and 200 o.r. from 8/9/R.D.F. (note 39).

39 Bns. were amalgamated on 24/10/17 and surplus joined 10/R.D.F. On 10/2/18, 8/9/R.D.F. was disbanded: 10 offrs. and 200 o.r. joined 1/R.D.F., 10 offrs. and 200 o.r. joined 2/R.D.F., and on 19/2/18 the remdr. formed 20/Entg. Bn.

40 Bn. served in 8th Bde., 3rd Div., until 24/10/14, in 4th Div., until 22/5/16, in 22nd Bde., 7th Div., until 14/10/16, and Bn. then joined 49th Bde., 16th Div.

41 Bns. were amalgamated on 28/8/17 and became 7/8/R. Innis. F.

42 Bn. was disbanded on 10/2/18: 12 offrs. and 240 o.r. joined 1/R. Ir. F., 11 offrs. and 220 o.r. joined 9/R. Ir. F. (108th Bde., 36th Div.), and the remdr. (4 offrs. and 130 o.r.) was drafted.

43 On 25/8/16 Bde. was reorganized: A was broken up and 1 Sec. joined B and 1 Sec. joined C, making up B and C to 6, 18-pdrs. each; C then became A. D (H.)/CLXXXII joined and became C (H.)/LXXVII. On 22/2/17, LXXVII became an A.F.A. Bde.; D (H.) left LXXVII and was broken up to make up D (H.)/CLXXVII and D (H.)/CLXXX to 6 hows. each. C (H.)/LXXVII became D (H.)/LXXVII and was made up to 6 hows. by 1 sec. C (H.)/CLXXII; and A/CLXXII joined and became C/LXXVII. LXXVII B.A.C. was formed from parts of 16th D.A.C. and 36th D.A.C.

44 On 27/8/16 Bde. was reorganized: 1 sec. A/CLXXXII joined and made up A/CLXXVII to 6, 18-pdrs., 1 sec. B/CLXXXII made up B/CLXXVII, and 1 sec. B/CLXXXII made up C/CLXXVII to 6 guns each. On 22/2/17, 1 sec. D (H.)/LXXVII joined and made up D (H.)/CLXXVII to 6 hows.

45 On 27/8/16 Bde. was reorganized: H.Q./CLXXXII joined and became H.Q./CLXXX, 1 sec. A/CLXXXII joined and made up A/CLXXX to 6, 18-pdrs., 1 sec. C/CLXXXII made up B/CLXXX, and 1 sec. C/CLXXXII made up C/CLXXX to 6 guns each. On 22/2/17, 1 sec. D (H.)/LXXVII joined and made up D (H.)/CLXXX to 6 hows.

46 On 27/8/16 CLXXXII was broken up (see notes 43, 44, and 45).

47 In Feb., 1918, the Medium T.M. Bties. were reorganized in 2, 6-mortar bties., and by 27/2/18 Z was broken up between X and Y.

48 V Heavy T.M. Bty. left the Division in February, 1918.

49 Coy. disembkd. at le Havre on 15/1/18, and joined Div. on 18/1/18.

50 Coy. was formed by 30/6/17.

51 Bn. reduced to T.C. on 13/4/18, and remdr. joined 2/Leins. T.C. joined 34th Div. on 17/6/18; 117th Bde., 39th Div., on 27/6/18; and on 3/8/18 the T.C. was disbanded.

52 Bn. joined from 73rd Bde., 24th Div., on 2/2/18; on 14/2/18 Bn. absorbed 3 offrs. and 225 o.r. of 7/Leins., and on 13/4/18 Bn. absorbed 5 offrs. and 281 o.r. of 6/Conn. Raug. On 23/4/18 Bn. was transferred to 88th Bde., 29th Div.

53 On 19/4/18 Bn. absorbed surplus personnel of 2/R.M.F.; and on 20/4/18 Bn. was transferred to 172nd Bde., 57th Div.

54 Bde. T.M. Bties. were broken up and personnel absorbed: 47th after 25/4/18; 48th by 13/4/18; and 49th by 4/4/18.

55 Joined on 3/2/18 from 3rd Bde., 1st Div. Bn. was reduced to T.C. on 19/4/18, and surplus joined 1/R.M.F. (note 53). On 31/5/18 Bn. was transferred to 94th Bde., 31st Div. Bn. was reformed on 6/6/18 and absorbed 6/R.M.F. On 16/6/18 Bn. was transferred to L. of C.; and on 15/7/18 Bn. joined 150th Bde., 50th Div.

56 Joined on 19/10/17 from 86th Bde., 29th Div. Bn. absorbed 10 offrs. and 200 o.r. from 8/9/R.D.F. on 10/2/18; and on 14/4/18, 1/ and 2/R.D.F. amalgamated. On 19/4/18 1/2/R.D.F. was reformed; the comp. bn. became 1/R.D.F.; 2/R.D.F. absorbed surplus personnel of 2/R.D.F. and on 20/4/18, 1/R.D.F. joined 86th Bde., 29th Div.

57 On 19 and 20/4/18 Bn. was reduced to T.C. (see note 56). On 1/6/18 Bn. joined 94th Bde., 31st Div., and on 6/6/18 Bn. was reformed and absorbed 7/R.D.F. On 16/6/18 Bn. was transferred to L. of C., and on 15/7/18 Bn. joined 149th Bde., 50th Div.

58 Bn. absorbed on 9/2/18, 7 offrs. and 296 o.r. of 6/R. Ir. Regt., on 18/4/18, 108 o.r. of 7/R. Ir. Regt., and on 22/4/18 the surplus personnel of 7/8/R. Innis. F. On 23/4/18 Bn. was transferred to 188th Bde., 63rd (R.N.) Div.

59 Bn. was formed in France in Sept., 1917, from S. Irish Horse and T.C. Bn. joined 49th Bde. on 14/10/17. On 18/4/18 Bn. was reduced to T.C., and on 17/6/18 Bn. joined 102nd Bde., 34th Div. On 26/6/18 T.C. Bn. left 34th Div., moved to Widdebroucq, and reformed by absorbing: 85 o.r. R. Irish Regt., 250 o.r. R.M.F., and 500 o.r. R.D.F. Offrs., to complete W.E., joined between 26-30/6/18. On 4/7/18, 7/(S. Irish Horse) R. Irish Regt. joined 21st Bde., 30th Div.

60 On 22/4/18 Bn. was reduced to T.C. and surplus personnel joined 2/R. Ir. Regt. On 17/6/18 T.C. Bn. was transferred to 102nd Bde., 34th Div. Bn. left 34th Div. on 26/6/18, joined G.H.Q. Troops and reformed—absorbing 18 offrs. and 857 o.r. 8/R.B. On 3/7/18, 7/8/R. Innis. F. joined 89th Bde., 30th Div.

61 X and Y were broken up on 20/4/18, and the personnel was absorbed.

62 Bn. was reduced to T.C. on 22/4/18 and attached 47th Bde.; surplus personnel went to the Base on 2/5/18. T.C. Bn. accompanied 16th Div. to Aldershot on 18/6/18. Bn. went to Lowestoft on 20/6/18, reformed by absorbing 13/Bord., and on 3/7/18, 11/Hants. (P.) returned to Aldershot. On 1/8/18, 11/Hants. embkd. at Folkestone and disembkd. at Boulogne.

63 Bn. was formed by 9/8/18; it consisted of 47th, 48th, 49th, and 208th M.G. Cos. On 8/5/18 the M.G. Bn. left for Camiers, personnel was reposted to inf. bns., and the transport went to Abbeville.

RECONSTITUTED DIVISION

64 T.C. of 2/4/Leic. (from 59th Div.) joined 16th Div. at Boulogne on 18/6/18, amalgamated at Aldeburgh with 14/Leic. and became 14/Leic. On 26/6/18 Bn. rejoined 16th Div. at Aldershot.

65 T.C. of 18/Welsh (from 40th Div.) joined 16th Div. at Boulogne on 18/6/18, amalgamated at N. Walsham with 25/Welsh, and became 18/Welsh. On 7/7/18 Bn. rejoined 16th Div. at Aldershot.

66 T.C. of 9/B.W. (from 39th Div.) joined 16th Div. at Boulogne on 18/6/18, amalgamated on 19/6/18 at Deal with 15/B.W., and became 9/B.W. On 2/7/18 Bn. rejoined 10th Div. at Aldershot.

67 Bde. T.M. Bties. were reformed in July, 1918, in England.

68 T.C. of 22/N.F. (from 34th Div.) joined 16th Div. at Boulogne on 18/6/18, amalgamated at Margate with 38/N.F., and became 22/N.F. On 2/7/18 Bn. rejoined 16th Div. at Aldershot.

69 T.C. of 8/7/R.S.F. (from 59th Div.) joined 16th Div. at Boulogne on 18/6/18, amalgamated on 20/6/18 at Deal with 18/Sco. Rif., and became 18/Sco. Rif. On 2/7/18 Bn. rejoined 16th Div. at Aldershot.

70 T.C. of 7/R.D.F. (from 31st Div.) joined 16th Div. at Samer on 10/6/18, amalgamated at Greatham (Durham) with 11/R. Ir. F., and became 11/R. Ir. F. On 28/6/18 Bn. rejoined 16th Div. at Aldershot. On 24/8/18, 5/R. Ir. F. (from 66th Div.—Bn. had been previously in 31st Bde., 10th Div.) joined 16th Div. in France and absorbed 11/R. Ir. F. on 29/8/18.

71 T.C. of 6/Som. L.I. (from 14th Div.) joined 16th Div. at Boulogne on 18/6/18, amalgamated at Cromer with 13/D.C.L.I., and became 6/Som. L.I. On 4/7/18 Bn. rejoined 16th Div. at Aldershot.

72 T.C. of 5/O. and B.L.I. (from 14th Div.) joined 16th Div. at Boulogne on 18/6/18, amalgamated at Clacton with 18/Glouc., and became 18/Glouc. On 2/7/18 Bn. joined 16th Div. at Aldershot.

73 T.C. of 7/K.R.R.C. (from 14th Div.) joined 16th Div. at Boulogne on 18/6/18, amalgamated at Clacton with 34/Lond., and became 34/Lond. (K.R.R.C.). On 27/6/18 Bn. joined 16th Div. at Aldershot.

74 Rejoined 16th Div. on 7/9/18. (H.Q., R.A., 16th Div. Arty., rejoined on 28/8/18).

75 Formed in England and joined Div. at Aldershot on 24/6/18; No. 3 Sec., 16th D.A.C. (1 offr. and 161 o.r.) also joined on 24/6/18.

76 Fd. Coy. rejoined 16th Div. on 13/8/18.

77 M.G. Bn. was formed at Grantham on 18/6/18, embkd. at Southampton on 15/7/18, disembkd. at le Havre on 16/7/18, left le Havre on 18/7/18, and joined 16th Div. on 2/8/18 at Samer.

78 Coy. reformed in England and disembkd. at Boulogne on 31/7/18.

The following Units and Training Cadres served with the 16th Division between April-June, 1918 :—

Unit.	From	Served with 16th Div. From	Served with 16th Div. To	Transferred to	Notes.
2/10/King's (T.C.)	55th Div.	27/4	– 17/6/18	34th Div.	see note 64.
4/Lincoln. (T.C.)	59th Div.	3/6	– 17/6/18	34th Div.	see note 69.
2/4/Leic. (T.C.)	59th Div.	18/6/18	– ...	...	see note 72.
6/7/R.S.F. (T.C.)	59th Div.	18/6/18	– ...	...	
5/O. & B.L.I. (T.C.)	14th Div.	18/6/18	– ...	...	
2/5/Sher. For. (T.C.)	59th Div.	3/6	– 17/6/18	34th Div.	
20/Middx. (T.C.)	40th Div.	31/5	– 16/6/18	14th Div.	
7/K.R.R.C. (T.C.)	14th Div.	18/6/18	– ...	...	see note 73.
5/N. Staff. (T.C.)	59th Div.	3/6	– 17/6/18	34th Div.	
11/R. Irish F.	...	28/6	– 29/8/18	...	see note 70.
6/R.M.F. (T.C.)	31st Div.	10/6	– 17/6/18	34th Div.	
7/R.D.F. (T.C.)	31st Div.	10/6/18	– ...	...	see note 70.
10/R.D.F.	63rd Div.	23/6/17	– 13/2/18	...	see General Notes.

Portuguese :—

Unit.	From	Served with 16th Div. From	Served with 16th Div. To	Transferred to	Notes.
1st Inf. Bde. (H.Q. and 21/, 22/, 28/, and 34/ Bns.)		14/4	– 16/5/18	14th Div.	
2 Batteries (personnel)		26/4	– 16/5/18	14th Div.	
1 Coy., Engineers		14/4	– 16/5/18	14th Div.	
2 Pioneer Cos.		23/4	– 16/5/18	14th Div.	

F

16TH (IRISH) DIVISION

FORMATION, BATTLES, AND ENGAGEMENTS

This New Army Division had no existence before the outbreak of the Great War.

Army Order No. 382 of the 11th September 1914 authorized the further addition of six divisions (15th–20th) and Army Troops to the Regular Army (see Appendix I). This augmentation formed the Second New Army, and during September 1914 the 16th (Irish) Division began to assemble in Ireland.

Divisional headquarters formed in Dublin, and the infantry brigades at Fermoy, Buttevant, and Tipperary. The artillery was at Cahir, Fermoy, and Kilkenny; the engineers at Moore Park, Kilworth; the army troops battalion (which became the divisional pioneer battalion) at Mullingar. On the 8th October divisional headquarters moved to Mallow. On the 9th March 1915 the pioneer battalion went to Kilworth, on the 19th June the 48th Brigade moved from Buttevant to Mallow, and on the 21st June divisional headquarters was transferred to Fermoy.

Meanwhile the training of the Division had progressed slowly, hampered by lack of equipment and *matériel* and by other difficulties. In the artillery it was some time before the batteries were able to obtain even 15 horses each for training purposes; and up to February 1915 the howitzer brigade had only managed to collect an old 12-pdr. B.L. gun to use for drill. Thus the Division gradually fell behind the time-table. In August it was decided to transfer three of the artillery brigades (18-pdrs.), the D.A.C., two of the field companies, and the divisional signal company to the Guards Division which was then forming in France. At the same time the third field company was sent to France to join the 7th Division. The three field ambulances had already been transferred to the 37th Division, and they reached France by the beginning of August. (See Table and Notes.)

It was September 1915 before the remainder of the 16th Division left Ireland and moved to Aldershot for its final intensive training. At last on the 10th December the Division was notified that embarkation would begin on the 17th. Even then the Division left for France without the divisional artillery, 49th Infantry Brigade, motor-machine-gun battery, one section signal company, one field ambulance, and one company of the Train. The 16th Division began disembarkation at le Havre on the 18th, and by the 22nd December had completed its concentration south of Bethune in the area of IV Corps, First Army. On the 22nd February 1916 the new divisional artillery joined the Division in France (see notes 24–27) and on the 24th February the 49th Brigade arrived. The Division was now complete. For the remainder of the Great War the 16th Division served on the Western Front in France and Belgium and was engaged in the following operations :—

1916

27 and 29 April ... ... **German Gas Attacks, Hulluch Front** [I Corps, First Army].

BATTLES OF THE SOMME

3–6 September ... ... **Battle of Guillemont** (On 3/9, 47th Bde.; on 4/9, 47th and 48th Bdes.; and on 5/9, 16th Div.) [XIV Corps, Fourth Army].

9 September ... ... **Battle of Ginchy** [XIV Corps, Fourth Army].

1917

7–9 June ... ... **Battle of Messines** [IX Corps, Second Army].
7 June ... ... **Capture of Wytschaete.**

BATTLES OF YPRES

31 July–2 Aug. ... ... **Battle of Pilckem Ridge** [In Reserve, XIX Corps, Fifth Army].
16–18 August ... ... **Battle of Langemarck** [XIX Corps, Fifth Army].

20 November ... ... **Attack north of Bullecourt** [VI Corps, Third Army].

1918

21 March–3 April ... **FIRST BATTLES OF THE SOMME** [VII Corps until 25/3 ; then XIX Corps, Fifth Army, until 2/4 ; then XIX Corps, Fourth Army].

21–23 March ... ... **Battle of St. Quentin** [VII Corps, Fifth Army].

26 and 27 March ... **Battle of Rosières** [XIX Corps, Fifth Army].

Between the 21st March and 3rd April the 16th Division had 7,149 casualties. Except the artillery (see General Notes) and the machine guns, which were left to cover the 14th Division, the 16th Division was relieved by the 3rd April, and on the 4th April the Division concentrated in the Hallencourt West Area. On the 10th the Division was transferred to XIII Corps, First Army, and the work of reorganizing and refitting began. On the 14th April the three infantry brigades were formed into a composite infantry brigade (under Br.-Gen. F. W. Ramsay) and moved to Thérouanne, and on the 16th this brigade began work on the G.H.Q. Line at Isbergues, in front of Aire. On the same day the Division was reorganized in four battalions and six training staffs. Work on the G.H.Q. Line continued until the 14th May, when the Division moved to Samer (south-east of Boulogne) and was employed in training American troops (4th and 80th American Divisions). On the 14th June the Division was informed that it would be moved to England to be reconstituted, and on the 18th June the 16th Division proceeded to Aldershot and began reconstitution (see Notes, and the Table in General Notes). The reconstituted division returned to France on the 27th July, and on the 2nd August the 16th Division was concentrated in the Samer area in First Army Reserve. On the 18th August the Division moved forward and on the 22nd took over the centre sector of the front held by I Corps, Fifth Army ; the divisional artillery rejoined between the 28th August and 7th September. The 16th Division was then complete and before the Armistice it took part in the following operations :—

THE ADVANCE TO VICTORY

2 Oct.–11 Nov. ... ... **THE FINAL ADVANCE IN ARTOIS AND FLANDERS** [I Corps, Fifth Army].

Starting its advance from near Vermelles the 16th Division crossed the Schelde on the 9th November and occupied Guéronde (north of Antoing). When the Armistice brought hostilities to a close at 11 a.m. on the 11th November, the Division was halted on the Schelde and the engineers were repairing and strengthening the bridges.

Until the end of November the Division remained billeted to the west of Seclin. The month was spent in training—military, educational, and recreational, and on the 11th December the first party (coal miners) left for demobilization. In January 1919 the Division dwindled further as demobilization went on. The Division was still in the same billets when H.R.H. the Prince of Wales stayed with it from the 1st to the 3rd February and inspected the units. By the 30th March the dwindling division was drawn in around railhead at Templeuve, and nearly all the units had been reduced to cadre. On the 29th May all cadres were further reduced by 75 per cent., and at the end of the month the Division was broken up in France. Its history had come to an end. During the Great War the 16th Division lost 28,398 killed, wounded, and missing.

F*

17TH (NORTHERN) DIVISION

G.O.C.

18 September, 1914	... ...	Major-General W. R. KENYON-SLANEY.
25 January, 1915 ...	... ...	Major-General T. D. PILCHER.
13 July, 1916	... ...	Major-General P. R. ROBERTSON.

G.S.O. 1.

21 Oct., 1914...Major L. H. THORNTON
(acting).
19 Jan., 1915...Lt.-Col. T. R. C. HUDSON
(sick, 20/9/15).
20 Sept., 1915...Lt.-Col. A. H. MARINDIN.
8 May, 1916...Lt.-Col. R. J. COLLINS.
19 May, 1917...Lt.-Col. E. M. BIRCH.

A.-A. and Q.-M.-G.

25 Aug., 1914...Captain E. C. PACKE
(acting).
9 Oct., 1914...Colonel F. C. MUSPRATT.
26 June, 1916...Lt.-Col. W. N. NICHOLSON.
15 April, 1918...Lt.-Col. A. E. J. WILSON.

B.-G., R.A.

13 Oct., 1914...Br.-Gen. A. B. PURVIS.
8 April, 1915...Br.-Gen. H. K. JACKSON.
4 Jan., 1916...Br.-Gen. L. M. PHILPOTTS
(tempy.).
10 Jan., 1916...Br.-Gen. R. G. OUSELEY
(wd., 21/7/16).
1 Aug., 1916...Lt.-Col. G. A. CARDEW
(acting).
9 Aug., 1916...Br.-Gen. A. S. BUCKLE
(sick, 16/8 ; died 18/8/1916).
21 Aug., 1916...Br.-Gen. P. WHEATLEY.

C.R.E.

26 Oct., 1914...Colonel H. R. GALE.
3 Jan., 1916...Major P. G. H. HOGG
(acting).
28 Jan., 1916...Lt.-Col. C. M. CARPENTER.
8 April, 1918...Lt.-Col. F. A. FERGUSON.

50th BDE.

11 Sept., '14...Br.-Gen. C. T. REAY.
6 May, '15...Br.-Gen. F. L. BANON.
26 Feb., '16...Br.-Gen. W. J. T. GLASGOW.
3 Dec., '16...Br.-Gen. C. YATMAN.
17 April, '18...Lt.-Col. G. E. WANNELL
(acting).
20 April, '18...Br.-Gen. G. GWYN-THOMAS.
8 Sept., '18...Lt.-Col. F. E. METCALFE
(acting).
9 Sept., '18...Br.-Gen A. R. C. SANDERS
(killed, 20/9/18).
23 Sept., '18...Br.-Gen. J. F. R. HOPE.

51st BDE.

3 Sept., '14...Br.-Gen. W. B. CAPPER.
1 Oct., '14...Br.-Gen. W. S. KAYS.
10 June, '15...Br.-Gen. R. B. FELL.
6 July, '16...Br.-Gen. G. F. TROTTER.
1 June, '17...Br.-Gen. C. E. BOND
(sick, 14/10/17)
14 Oct., '17...Lt.-Col. F. E. METCALFE
(acting).
16 Nov., '17...Br.-Gen. C. E. BOND.
30 May, '18...Br.-Gen. R. M. DUDGEON.

52nd BDE.

14 Sept., '14...Br.-Gen. H. C. SURTEES.
18 Mar., '16...Br.-Gen. J. L. J. CLARKE.
20 Nov., '16...Br.-Gen. G. D. GOODMAN.
20 Mar., '17...Lt.-Col. T. S. H. WADE (acting).
23 Mar., '17...Br.-Gen. J. L. J. CLARKE.
1 June, '17...Br.-Gen. A. J. F. EDEN (injured, 5/4 ;
evacuated, 11/4/18).
11 April, '18...Lt.-Col. G. E. WANNELL (acting).
14 April, '18...Br.-Gen. W. ALLASON.

GENERAL NOTES

The following Units also served with the 17th (Northern) Division :—

ARTILLERY :—17th Heavy Battery (4, 60-pdrs.), was raised for the 17th Div., but the Heavy Battery went abroad independently. The Heavy Battery left Charlton Park in Oct. 1915, disembkd. at le Havre on 8/10/15, arrived at Villers Bretonneux (in XII Corps Area) on 9/10/15, and joined XXIX Heavy Artillery Brigade, R.G.A.

INFANTRY :—3/4/Q.O.R.W. Kent, from 202nd Bde., 67th Div., disembkd. at le Havre on 1/6/17, joined S. African Bde., 9th Div., on 6/6/17, was attached to 101st Bde., 34th Div., on 15/6/17, to 103rd Bde., 34th Div., on 18/6/17, and on 22/6/17 Bn. joined 51st Bde., 17th Div. From 12/7–3/8/17 Bn. was employed as Pioneers. On 3/8/17 Bn. was transferred to 52nd Bde., 17th Div. 3/4/Q.O.R.W. Kent was disbanded between 5–20/2/18, and drafts were sent to 6/, 7/, and 8/Q.O.R.W. Kent ; the surplus joined 7/Entg. Bn.

MACHINE-GUN UNIT :—No. 12 Motor-Machine-Gun Battery, left Bisley and joined 17th Div. at Flowerdown Camp, Winchester, on 10/7/15. The M.-M.-G. Battery disembkd. at le Havre on 13/7/15. On 7/5/16 the Battery was transferred to X Corps and joined on 10/5/16.

OTHER UNITS :—34th Sanitary Section, went to France with 17th Div. and disembkd. at le Havre on 16/7/15. On 10/3/17 the Section was transferred to a XIII Corps Sanitary Area.

17th Division Motor Ambce. Workshop, left Grove Park on 15/6/15, went to France with 17th Div., and reached Rouen on 14/7/15. The Workshop rejoined 17th Div. at Boeschepe on 25/7/15. On 2/4/16 the Workshop was absorbed by 17th Div. Supply Column.

On 23/2/18 the reorganization of the 17th Division on a 9-battalion basis was completed ; and on 27/2/18 the pioneer battalion (7/Y. and L.) was reorganized on a 3-company basis.

Dates	INFANTRY Brigades	Battalions and attached Units	Mounted Troops	ARTILLERY Field Artillery Brigades	Batteries	Bde. Ammn. Colns.	Trench Mortar Bties. Medium	Heavy	Divnl. Ammn. Coln.	Engineers Field Cos.	Signal Service Divnl. Signal Coy.	Pioneers	M.G. Units	Field Ambulances	Mobile Vety. Secn.	Divnl. Emplnt. Coy.	Divnl. Train
1914 October (England)	50th 51st 52nd	10/W. York., 7/E. York.,7/Gr. How., 7/Y. & L.,[1] 8/S. Staff., 10/Sher. For. 7/Linc., 9/N.F., 10/L.F., 9/Duke's, 12/Manch.	17th Div. Cyclist Coy.[2]	LXXVIII[3] LXXIX[3] LXXX[3] LXXXI (H.)[3]	244, 245, 246 247, 248, 249 250, 251, 252 253 (H.), 254 (H.), 255 (H.)	LXXVIII B.A.C. LXXIX B.A.C. LXXX B.A.C. LXXXI (H.) B.A.C.	...	...	17th D.A.C.	77th 78th 93rd[4]	17th	...	...	51st[4A] 52nd[4A] 53rd[4A]	...	...	17th[5]
1915 September (France)	50th 51st 52nd	10/W. York., 7/E. York., 7/ Gr. How., 6/Dorset.[6] 7/Linc., 7/Bord., 8/S. Staff., 10/Sher. For. 9/N.F., 10/L.F., 9/Duke's, 12/ Manch.	A Sqdn., York. Dgns.[7] 17th Div. Cyclist Coy.[8]	LXXVIII[3];[9] LXXIX[3];[10] LXXX[3];[11] LXXXI 3;[12]	A, B, C, D A, B, C, D A, B, C, D B (H.), C (H.), D (H.)	LXXVIII B.A.C. LXXIX B.A.C. LXXX B.A.C. LXXXI B.A.C.	...	...	17th D.A.C.	77th 78th 93rd	17th	7/ Y. & L.[1] (P.)	...	51st 52nd 53rd	29th[13]	...	17th
1916 June (France)	50th 51st 52nd	10/W. York., 7/E. York., 7/ Gr. How., 6/Dorset.; 50th Bde. M.G. Coy.;[14] 50th T.M. Bty.[15] 7/Linc., 7/Bord., 8/S. Staff., 10/Sher. For.; 51st Bde. M.G. Coy.;[14] 51st T.M. Bty.[15] 9/N.F., 10/L.F., 9/Duke's, 12/Manch.; 52nd Bde. M.G. Coy.;[14] 52nd T.M. Bty.[15]	...	LXXVIII[9];[16] LXXIX[10],[17] LXXX[11],[18] LXXXI[12],[19]	A, B, C; D (H.) A, B, C; D (H.) A, B, C; D (H.) A, B, C	...[21]	X.17[20] Y.17[20] Z.17[20]	V.17[20]	17th D.A.C.[21]	77th 78th 93rd	17th	7/ Y. & L. (P.)	...	51st 52nd 53rd	29th	...	17th
1917 June (France)	50th 51st 52nd	10/W. York., 7/E. York., 7/ Gr. How.,[22] 6/Dorset.; 50th M.G. Coy.;[31] 50th T.M. Bty. 7/Linc., 7/Bord.,[23] 8/S. Staff.[24] 10/Sher. For.; 51st M.G. Coy.;[31] 51st T.M. Bty. 9/N.F.[25] 10/L.F., 9/Duke's, 12/Manch.;[26] 52nd M.G. Coy.;[31] 52nd T.M. Bty.	...	LXXVIII[16] LXXIX[17]	A, B, C; D (H.) A, B, C; D (H.)	...	X.17 Y.17 Z.17[27]	V.17[28]	17th D.A.C.	77th 78th 93rd	17th	7/ Y. & L. (P.)	236th M.G. Coy.[29]	51st 52nd 53rd	20th	218th[30]	17th

1918 March (France)		...	LXXVIII ...... LXXIX	...	X.17 Y.17	...	17th D.A.C.	77th 78th 93rd	17th	7/ Y. & L. (P.)	No. 17 Bn. M.G.C.,51	51st 52nd 53rd	29th	218th	17th
50th	10/W. York., 7/E. York., 6/ Dorset.; 50th T.M. Bty.		A, B, C; D (H.)												
51st	7/Linc., 7/(Westld. & Cumbld. Yeo.) Bord.,[23] 10/Sher. For.; 51st T.M. Bty.		A, B, C; D (H.)												
52nd	10/L.F., 9/Duke's, 12/(D. of L. Own Yeo.) Manch.,[26] 52nd T.M. Bty.														

NOTES

1 In March, 1915, the Bn. (of 50th Bde.) was converted into the divnl. pioneer bn.

2 The Cyclist Coy. was formed in the Div. on 23/1/15.

3 Bties. were raised as 6-gun bties., and numbered. In Jany., 1915, all Bdes. were reorganized as 4-battery bdes., the bties. all became 4-gun bties., and in each bde. the bties. were lettered A, B, C, D.

4 Fd. Coy. was transferred from 25th Div., at Branksome, and on 20/1/15 joined 17th Div.

4A The three Fd. Ambces. joined the Div. at Southampton on 12–14/7/15, during embarkation.

5 Train consisted of 146, 147, 148, and 149 Cos., A.S.C.

6 Bn. (from Army Troops) joined Bde. in March, 1915, to replace 7/Y. and L. (P.).

7 Sqdn. joined Div. in England in June, 1915, and disembkd. at le Havre on 16/7/15. On 10/5/16 Sqdn. left Div. and joined II Corps Cav. Regt.

8 On 24/5/16 Cyclist Coy. left Div. and joined II Corps Cyclist Bn. on 25/5/16.

9 On 20/5/16, D was transferred and became A/LXXXI, and B (H.)/LXXXI joined and became D (H.)/LXXVIII.

10 On 20/5/16, D was transferred and became B/LXXXI, and C (H.)/LXXXI joined and became D (H.)/LXXIX.

11 On 20/5/16, D was transferred and became C/LXXXI, and D (H.)/LXXXI joined and became D (H.)/LXXX.

12 On 12/8/16 A (H.)/LXXXI (H.) and a sec. of LXXXI (H.) B.A.C. left and joined CXVIII Bde. with 1st Cdn. Div. On 20/5/16, LXXXI was reorganized : B (H.), C (H.), and D (H.) were transferred and became D (H.)/LXXVIII, D (H.)/LXXIX, and D (H.)/LXXX ; and D/LXXVIII, D/LXXIX, and D/LXXX, joined and became A, B, and C/LXXXI.

13 Sec. joined Div. in England, and disembkd. at le Havre on 16/7/15.

14 The three Bde. M.G. Cos. disembkd. at le Havre on 9/2/16, and joined 17th Div. at Reninghelst on 12/2/16.

15 T.M. Bties. were formed in Bdes. :
50th—50/1 by 29/4/16, 50/2 by 8/6/16, and they became 50th T.M. Bty. by 25/6/16 ;
51st—51/1 by 11/5/16, 51/2 by 7/6/16, and they became 51st T.M. Bty. by 3/7/16 ;
52nd—52/1 by 31/8/16, 52/2 on 20/5/16, and they became 52nd T.M. Bty. by 15/8/16.

16 On 1/9/16, A and right sec. of B/LXXX joined and were split up to complete A, B, and C/LXXVIII to 6, 18-pdrs. each. On 22/1/17, 1 sec. of D (H.)/LXXXI joined and made up D (H.)/LXXVIII to 6 hows.

17 On 31/8/16 left sec. of B and C/LXXX joined and were split up to complete A, B, and C/LXXIX to 6, 18-pdrs. each. On 10/1/17, 1 sec. of D (H.)/LXXXI to 6 hows.

18 On 31/8/16, LXXX was broken up : A and right sec. of B were transferred to LXXVIII to complete A, B, and C/ LXXVIII to six 18-pdrs. each ; left sec. of B and C were transferred to LXXIX to complete A, B, and C/LXXIX to six 18-pdrs. each ; and D (H.) was transferred and became again D (H.)/LXXXI.

19 Between 2–4/9/16 D (H.) rejoined from LXXX and became again D (H.)/LXXXI ; and C/LXXXI was split up to complete A and B/LXXXI to six 18-pdrs. each. Between 10–27/1/17, LXXXI was broken up : on 19/1/17 A/LXXXI was transferred and became A/CXLVII A.F.A. Bde., and B/LXXXI became C/LXXVI A.F.A. Bde. ; D (H.)/LXXXI left on 10 and 11/1/17 and was split up, 1 sec. joined D (H.)/ LXXVIII to complete the bty. to 6 hows., and 1 sec. made up D (H.)/LXXIX to 6 hows.

20 The Medium and Heavy T.M. Bties. were formed and joined by 22/8/16.

21 Between 9–11/5/16 B.A.C.s were abolished and the D.A.C. was reorganized.

22 Bn. was disbanded on 10/2/18, and 34 offrs. and 700 o.r. were drafted to 6/, 12/, and 13/Gr. How.

23 On 22/9/17 Bn. absorbed 21 offrs. and 239 o.r. of Westld. and Cumbld. Yeo., and the designation was then changed to 7/(Westld. and Cumbld. Yeo.) Bn., Border Regt.

24 On 10 and 12/2/18 Bn. sent drafts to 2/6 and 7/S. Staff. ; on 23/2/18, 8/S. Staff. was disbanded, and the surplus joined 7/Entg. Bn.

25 On 3/8/17 Bn. was transferred to 104th Bde., 34th Div.

26 On 24/9/17 Bn. absorbed 7 offrs. and 125 o.r. of 1/D. of L. Own Yeo., and the designation was then changed to 12/(D. of L. Own Yeo.) Bn., Manchester Regt.

27 On 28/2/18 Z was broken up and distributed between X and Y.

28 On 28/2/18 V was transferred to V H.T.M. Bty., V Corps.

29 Coy. disembkd. at le Havre on 17/7/17, and joined the Div. on the same day.

30 Coy. formed by 9/6/17.

31 Bn. was formed on 24/2/18 ; it consisted of 50th, 51st, 52nd, and 236th M.G. Cos.

17TH (NORTHERN) DIVISION

FORMATION, BATTLES, AND ENGAGEMENTS

This New Army Division had no existence before the outbreak of the Great War.

Army Order No. 382 of the 11th September 1914 authorized the further addition of six divisions (15th–20th) and Army Troops to the Regular Army (see Appendix I). This augmentation formed the Second New Army, and during September 1914 the 17th (Northern) Division began to assemble around Wareham.

By the end of September 1914 all the surplus stores of arms, equipment, and uniform had been issued, and for some time no uniforms were available for the rank and file of the 17th Division. Even blankets were scarce in the improvised billets and later on in the crowded camps. For months the infantry had only a few old drill-pattern rifles ; and machine guns had to be represented by home-made dummy guns. In October a varied assortment of peace-time uniforms arrived ; the infantry then paraded in red coats, combined with civilian head-dresses and overcoats. At the same time a supply of tents was issued to the Division, and the men were placed under canvas until the unsettled November weather compelled the abandonment of tents ; the units were then moved into recently erected huts. Before the end of 1914 the infantry received a large supply of Lee-Enfield magazine rifles and a generous supply of ammunition ; elementary musketry instruction became possible. Then, in March 1915 a limited issue of service rifles and new leather equipment was made to the infantry.

In the Artillery most of the officers had everything to learn, and it was soon found that 20 per cent. of the recruits, who had been accepted in the rush, were unfit for military service and had to be replaced, also very few of the recruits had ever ridden or had any previous experience with horses. At the outset the only available artillery *matériel* was a few limbers and wagons, together with some ancient and obsolete guns and two old French 90-mm. guns, dating from the war of 1870—pieces which were more suitable for museums than for a training centre. Even so the guns were without sights, and naturally no dial sights, directors, range tables, or telephones were available. But ingenuity, assisted by the local carpenters, provided rough and ready imitations of the missing stores, and allowed the recruits to be given some training during the early months. The first horses for the artillery arrived in February 1915, the 18-pdrs. were issued in April, and the first howitzers reached Swanage in the middle of May.

During this time the artillery had been in empty houses in Swanage and the infantry brigades had shifted their quarters more than once. Originally the three infantry brigades were around Wareham ; but in October 1914 the brigades were at Wareham (50th), West Lulworth (51st), and Bovington Camp, Wool (52nd). In December the 51st moved to Wool, and the 52nd to Wimborne. In March 1915 the 51st returned to West Lulworth, and the 52nd moved back to Wool. These stations were maintained until May. Between the 27th May and the 1st June the Division marched to Winchester, Romsey, Hursley, Pitt Corner, and Flowerdown, and final intensive training for the field was undertaken.

On the 5th July the Division was informed that it would be retained in England for some time and be employed on Home Defence. At midnight this arrangement was cancelled and the 17th Division was ordered to embark for France between the 12th and 15th July. On the 6th the advanced party left, and on the same day the Division completed its mobilization—but the three field ambulances only joined the Division at Southampton during embarkation. On the 12th July embarkation began. By the 17th the Division concentrated to the southward of St. Omer, and on the 19th July it moved forward and came under V Corps, Second Army. For the remainder of the Great War the 17th Division served on the Western Front in France and Belgium and was engaged in the following operations :—

1915

9 August	**Hooge** [V Corps, Second Army].

1916

14 Feb. ; and 2 March	**The Bluff** [V Corps, Second Army].

BATTLES OF THE SOMME

1–10 July	**Battle of Albert** [XV Corps, Fourth Army].
2 July	**Capture of Fricourt.**
1–12 August	**Battle of Delville Wood** [XV Corps, Fourth Army].

1917

BATTLES OF ARRAS

12–14 April	**First Battle of the Scarpe** [VI Corps, Third Army].
23 and 24 April	**Second Battle of the Scarpe** [VI Corps, Third Army].
13–16 May	**Capture and Defence of Roeux** [XVII Corps, Third Army].

BATTLES OF YPRES

12 October	**First Battle of Passchendaele** [XIV Corps, Fifth Army].
8–10 November	**Second Battle of Passchendaele** [XIX Corps, Fifth Army].

1918

FIRST BATTLES OF THE SOMME

21–23 March	**Battle of St. Quentin** [V Corps, Third Army].
24 and 25 March... ...	**First Battle of Bapaume** [V Corps, Third Army].

THE ADVANCE TO VICTORY
SECOND BATTLES OF THE SOMME

21–23 August	**Battle of Albert** [V Corps, Third Army].
31 Aug.–3 Sept.	**Second Battle of Bapaume** [V Corps, Third Army].

BATTLES OF THE HINDENBURG LINE

18 September	**Battle of Epéhy** [V Corps, Third Army].
8 and 9 October	**Battle of Cambrai** [V Corps, Third Army].
9–12 October	**Pursuit to the Selle** [V Corps, Third Army].

THE FINAL ADVANCE IN PICARDY

17–23 October	**Battle of the Selle** [V Corps, Third Army].
4 November...	**Battle of the Sambre** [V Corps, Third Army].

The advance was continued steadily. On the 8th November the leading troops of the Division crossed the Avesnes–Maubeuge road and on the 9th Beaufort was occupied. When hostilities ceased at 11 a.m. on the 11th November the leading brigade (52nd) of the 17th Division had established outposts along the line of the R. Solre (south-east of Maubeuge).

On the 12th and 13th the Division was drawn back to the Inchy–Troisvilles–Bertry–Esnes area (west of Le Cateau), and the rest of the month of November was spent in reorganization, salvage work, and recreational training. On the 6th December the 17th Division began to move back behind Amiens ; the move was completed by the 15th, and the Division then settled down in billets in the Hallencourt area (south-east of Abbeville). Recreation and education were the principal activities, and a demobilization scheme was prepared.

Demobilization began in January 1919. In the first two months of the year the Division lost 6,006 all ranks, and during March the principal duty of the weakened division was to provide guards for the numerous supply trains which traversed the Third Army area. Gradually the Division disappeared. Battalions were reduced to no more than 50 all ranks, merely sufficient to act as equipment guards. Demobilization was completed in May, and at the end of the month the Division ceased to exist. During the Great War the 17th Division lost 40,258 killed, wounded, and missing.

18TH (EASTERN) DIVISION

G.O.C.

14 September, 1914 ... ... Lieut.-General Sir L. W. PARSONS
(transferred to 16th Div. on 22/9/14).
2 October, 1914 ... ... Major-General F. I. MAXSE.
15 January, 1917 ... ... Major-General R. P. LEE.

G.S.O. 1.

15 Sept., 1914...Major A. BRYANT (acting).
3 Mar., 1915...Lt.-Col. T. H. SHOUBRIDGE.
15 Dec., 1915...Major A. BRYANT (tempy.).
28 Jan., 1916...Lt.-Col. A. BRYANT.
2 Sept., 1916...Lt.-Col. W. D. WRIGHT, V.C.
12 July, 1918...Lt.-Col. G. BLEWITT.

A.-A. and Q.-M.-G.

21 Sept., 1914...Captain A. D. M. BROWNE (acting).
9 Oct., 1914...Colonel S. D. GORDON.
7 May, 1915...Lt.-Col. E. V. D. RIDDELL.
4 Nov., 1916...Lt.-Col. H. J. PACK-BERESFORD.
17 April, 1917...Major R. H. L. CUTBILL (acting).
2 May, 1917...Lt.-Col. H. L. ALEXANDER (tempy.).
7 May, 1917...Lt.-Col. R. H. L. CUTBILL.

B.-G., R.A.

28 Oct., 1914...Br.-Gen. F. G. STONE.
23 Aug., 1915...Br.-Gen. C. C. VAN STRAUBENZEE.
4 June, 1916...Br.-Gen. S. F. METCALFE.
6 July, 1917...Br.-Gen. W. EVANS.
7 Aug., 1918...Lt.-Col. A. THORP (acting).
11 Aug., 1918...Br.-Gen. T. O. SEAGRAM.

C.R.E.

18 Oct., 1914...Lt.-Col. T. C. SKINNER.
1 Sept., 1915...Lt.-Col. H. G. JOLY DE LOTBINIÈRE.
19 Jan., 1917...Lt.-Col. H.M. HENDERSON (killed, 10/3/17).
10 Mar., 1917...Major W. M. HAYMAN (acting).
19 Mar., 1917...Lt.-Col. C. B. O. SYMONS.

53rd BDE.

16 Sept., '14...Br.-Gen. F. B. W. RICHARDSON.
21 April, '15...Br.-Gen. W. B. HICKIE.
28 Nov., '15...Br.-Gen. H. J. M. MACANDREW.
27 April, '16...Lt.-Col. H. G. DE L. FERGUSON (acting).
3 May, '16...Br.-Gen. H. W. HIGGINSON.
24 April, '18...Br.-Gen. M. G. H. BARKER.

54th BDE.

16 Sept., '14...Br.-Gen. H. B. SCAIFE.
13 Mar., '15...Br.-Gen. W. C. G. HENEKER (wd., 10/12/15).
10 Dec., '15...Col. G. E. RIPLEY (acting).
13 Dec., '15...Lt.-Col. C. C. CARR (acting).
15 Dec., '15...Lt.-Col. T. H. SHOUBRIDGE (tempy.).
23 Jan., '16...Br.-Gen. T. H. SHOUBRIDGE.
6 April, '17...Br.-Gen. C. CUNLIFFE-OWEN.
22 Oct., '17...Br.-Gen. L. W. DE V. SADLEIR-JACKSON (wd., 22/8/18).
22 Aug., '18...Lt.-Col. A. E. PERCIVAL (acting).
24 Aug., '18...Br.-Gen. J. A. TYLER (tempy.).
24 Sept., '18...Lt.-Col. R. TURNER (acting).
12 Oct., '18...Br.-Gen. O. C. BORRETT (gassed, 24/10/18).
24 Oct., '18...Lt.-Col. R. TURNER (acting).
25 Oct., '18...Lt.-Col. K. C. WELDON (acting).
6 Nov., '18...Br.-Gen. O. C. BORRETT.
[19 Nov., '18...Br.-Gen. L. W. DE V. SADLEIR-JACKSON.]

55th BDE.

19 Sept., '14...Br.-Gen. J. H. POETT.
8 June, '15...Br.-Gen. A. MARTYN.
22 Oct., '15...Lt.-Col. W. F. ELMSLIE (acting).
26 Oct., '15...Br.-Gen. T. D. JACKSON.
9 Oct., '16...Br.-Gen. F. B. NUGENT.
18 Oct., '16...Br.-Gen. G. D. PRICE.
9 Nov., '17...Br.-Gen. E. A. WOOD (sick, 24/10/18).
24 Oct., '18...Lt.-Col. A. P. B. IRWIN (acting).
[19 Nov., '18...Br.-Gen. O. C. BORRETT.]

GENERAL NOTES

The following Units also served with the 18th (Eastern) Division :—

ARTILLERY :—18th Heavy Battery (4, 60-pdrs.), was raised for the 18th Division, but the Heavy Battery did not accompany the 18th Division to France in July, 1915. The Heavy Battery left Woolwich in November, embarked at Devonport on 17/10/15, disembarked at Alexandria on 1/11/15, re-embarked at Alexandria on 23/11/15, and disembarked at Salonika on 28/11/15. For the remainder of the Great War the 18th Heavy Battery served in Macedonia.

INFANTRY :—10/R.F., was attached to the 18th Division on formation and served in England with the Division until 24/2/15; 10/R.F. then joined 111th Bde., 37th Division, went to France with the 37th Div. in July 1915, and for the remainder of the Great War the Bn. served in the 37th Div. on the Western Front.

6/Lond. and 7/Lond. (174th Bde., 58th Div.) were attached to 18th Division on 4/4/18 and served with the 18th Div. in the Battle of the Avre (First Battles of the Somme, 1918).

MACHINE-GUN UNITS :—No. 15 Motor-Machine-Gun Battery, was formed at Bisley on 29/5/15, joined 18th Div. on 22/7/15, went to France with the Division, and disembarked at le Havre on 25/7/15. The Battery served on the Western Front with the 18th Division until 4/5/16, the Battery was then transferred to XV Corps.

265th and 278th Machine-Gun Companies, see note 34.

OTHER UNITS :—35th Sanitary Section, joined 18th Div. in England, went to France with the Division, and disembarked at le Havre on 28/7/15. The Sanitary Section served with the 18th Division until 24/3/17, when it left the Division and took over No. 1 Sanitary Area in the Fifth Army.

18th Division Motor Ambce. Workshop, was formed for the 14th Div. at Grove Park on 14/4/15. The Workshop moved to Hungerford on 6/5/15 and was transferred to the 10th (Irish) Div., but on 3/6/15 the Workshop was transferred to the 18th Div. On 23/7/15 the Workshop moved to Avonmouth, embkd. on 24/7/15, and disembkd. at Rouen on 26/7/15. The Workshop joined the 18th Div. at Flesselles on 1/8/15. By 16/4/16 the Workshop was absorbed by the Divnl. Supply Column.

On 11/2/18 the reorganization of the 18th Division on a 9-battalion basis was completed; and on 4/3/18 the pioneer battalion (8/R. Suss.) was reorganized on a 3-company basis.

18TH (EASTERN) DIVISION

Dates	INFANTRY Brigades	Battalions and attached Units	Mounted Troops	ARTILLERY — Field Artillery Brigades	Field Artillery Batteries	Bde. Ammn. Colns.	Trench Mortar Bties. Medium	Trench Mortar Bties. Heavy	Divnl. Ammn. Coln.	Engineers Field Cos.	Signal Service Divnl. Signal Coy.	Pioneers	M.G. Units	Field Ambulances	Mobile Vety. Secn.	Divnl. Emplnt. Coy.	Divnl. Train.
1914 October (England)	53rd	8/Norf., 8/Suff., 10/Essex, 6/R. Berks.	18th Div. Cyclist Coy.[2]	LXXXII[3]	256, 257, 258	LXXXII B.A.C.	...	...	18th D.A.C.	79th	18th	...	...	54th[5]	30th	...	18th[6]
	54th	11/R.F., 8/R. Suss.,[1] 6/North'n, 12/Middx.		LXXXIII[3]	259, 260, 261	LXXXIII B.A.C.				80th				55th[5]			
	55th	7/Queen's, 7/Buffs, 8/E. Surr., 7/Q.O.R.W.K.		LXXXIV[3]	262, 263, 264	LXXXIV B.A.C.				92nd[4]				56th[5]			
				LXXXV (H.)[3]	265 (H.), 266 (H.), 267 (H.)	LXXXV (H.) B.A.C.											
1915 September (France)	53rd	8/Norf., 8/Suff., 10/Essex, 6/R. Berks.	C Sqdn., Westmid. and Cumbld. Yeo.[8] 18th Div. Cyclist Coy.[9]	LXXXII[5; 10]	A, B, C, D	LXXXII B.A.C.	...	...	18th D.A.C.	79th	18th	8/R. Suss.[1] (P.)	...	54th	30th	...	18th
	54th	11/R.F.,[7] 6/North'n, 12/Middx.		LXXXIII[5; 11]	A, B, C, D	LXXXIII B.A.C.				80th				55th			
	55th	7/Queen's, 7/Buffs, 8/E. Surr., 7/Q.O.R.W.K.		LXXXIV[5; 12]	A, B, C, D	LXXXIV B.A.C.				92nd				56th			
				LXXXV (H.)[5; 13]	A (H.), B (H.), C (H.), D (H.)	LXXXV (H.) B.A.C.											
1916 June (France)	53rd	8/Norf., 8/Suff., 10/Essex, 6/R. Berks.; 53rd Bde. M.G. Coy.;[14] 53rd T.M. Bty.[15]	...	LXXXII ......[10; 16]	A, B, C; D (H.)	...[23]	X.18[20], V.18[20], Z.18[20]	V.18[21], W.18[22]	18th D.A.C.[23]	79th	18th	8/R. Suss. (P.)	...	54th	30th	...	18th
	54th	11/R.F., 7/Bedf., 6/North'n, 12/Middx.;[14] 54th Bde. M.G. Coy.;[14] 54th T.M. Bty.[15]		LXXXIII......[11; 17]	A, B, C; D (H.)					80th				55th			
	55th	7/Queen's, 7/Buffs, 8/E. Surr.; 55th Bde. M.G. Coy.;[14] 55th T.M. Bty.[15]		LXXXIV......[12; 18]	A, B, C; D (H.)					92nd				56th			
				LXXXV[15; 19]	A, B, C												
1917 June (France)	53rd	8/Norf.,[24] 8/Suff.,[25] 10/Essex, 6/R. Berks.,[26] 53rd M.G. Coy.;[34] 53rd T.M. Bty.	...	LXXXII[16]	A, B, C; D (H.)	...	X.18, Y.18, Z.18[29]	V.18[30]	18th D.A.C.	79th	18th	8/R. Suss. (P.)	...	54th	30th	210th[31]	18th
	54th	11/R.F., 7/Bedf., 6/North'n, 12/Middx.;[27] 54th M.G. Coy.;[34] 54th T.M. Bty.		LXXXIII[17]	A, B, C; D (H.)					80th				55th			
	55th	7/Queen's, 7/Buffs, 8/E. Surr., 7/Q.O.R.W.K.,[28] 55th M.G. Coy.;[34] 55th T.M. Bty.								92nd				56th			
1918 March (France)	53rd	10/Essex, 8/R. Berks.,[32] 7/Q.O.R.W.K.,[28] 53rd T.M. Bty.	...	LXXXII......[ ]	A, B, C; D (H.)	...	X.18, Y.18	...	18th D.A.C.	79th	18th	8/R. Suss. (P.)	No. 18 Bn., M.G.C.[34]	54th	30th	210th	18th
	54th	11/R.F., 7/Bedf.,[33] 6/North'n,; 54th T.M. Bty.		LXXXIII......[ ]	A, B, C; D (H.)					80th				55th			
	55th	7/Queen's, 7/Buffs, 8/E. Surr.; 55th T.M. Bty.								92nd				56th			

	LXXXII LXXXIII	...	X.18 Y.18	...	18th D.A.C.	79th 80th 92nd	18th	8/ R. Suss. (P.)	No. 18 Bn., M.G.C.	54th 55th 56th	30th	219th	18th
53rd	A, B, C; D (H.) A, B, C; D (H.)	10/Essex, 8/R. Berks., 7/ Q.O.R.W.K.; 53rd T.M. Bty.											
54th		11/R.F. 2/Bedf.,36 6/North'n.; 54th T.M. Bty.											
55th		7/Queen's, 7/Buffs, 8/E. Surr.; 55th T.M. Bty.											

1918 June (France)

G

NOTES

1 On 4/2/15 Bn. (of 54th Bde.) was converted into the divnl. pioneer bn. (Authy.—W.O. Letter, No. 20/Infantry/640, A.G.1., d/d. 23/1/15).

2 The Cyclist Coy. was formed on Tuesday, 8/12/14.

3 Bties. were raised as 6-gun bties. and numbered. On 26/2/15 the divnl. artillery was reorganized: Bdes. became 4-battery bdes.; the bties. all became 4-gun bties.; and in each Bde. the bties. were lettered A, B, C, D (Authy.—W.O. Letter, No. 20/Artillery/3818, A.G.6, d/d.6/1/15).

4 In Jany., 1915, the Fd. Coy. joined 18th Div., from 24th Div.

5 The three Fd. Ambces. joined on 18/6/15.

6 Train consisted of 150, 151, 152, and 153 Cos., A.S.C.

7 Bn. (from Army Troops) joined Bde. on 25/2/15, to replace 8/R. Suss. (P.)—see note 1.

8 Sqdn. joined Div. in England on 15/6/15. On 10/5/16 the Sqdn. left the Div. and joined XI Corps Cav. Regt. on 15/5/16.

9 On 21/5/16 Cyclist Coy. left the Div., and joined XIII Corps Cyclist Bn. on 22/5/16.

10 On 24/5/16 D Bty. left Bde. and became A/LXXXV; and C (H.)/LXXXV joined and became D (H.)/LXXXII.

11 On 24/5/16 D Bty. left Bde. and became B/LXXXV; and D (H.)/LXXXV joined and became D (H.)/LXXXIII.

12 On 24/5/16 D Bty. left Bde. and became C/LXXXV; and A (H.) LXXXV joined and became D (H.)/LXXXIV.

13 On 8/2/16 B (H.) left, joined IV W. Lanc. (H.) Bde. [later CCLXXVIII] in the 55th Div.. and became C (H.). On 23/5/16 C (H.)/CCLXXVII became D (H.)/CCLXXVII. On 24/5/16 LXXXVIII was reorganized: A (H.), C (H.), and D (H.) left the Bde. and became respectively A (H.)/LXXXIV, D (H.)/LXXXII, and D (H.)/LXXXIII; and D/LXXXVIII, and D/LXXXIV joined LXXXV and became A, B, and C/LXXXV.

14 The three Bde. M.G. Cos. landed at le Havre on 9/2/16 and joined the Div. at Ritemont on 13/2/16.

15 T.M. Bties. were formed in Bdes.:
53rd—63/1 and 53/2 by 28/4/16, and they became 53rd T.M. Bty. by 17/6/16;
54th—54/1 and 54/2 by 6/4/16, and they became 54th T.M. Bty. by 1/6/16;
55th—55/1 and 55/2 between 22-29/4/16, and they became 55th T.M. Bty. by 17/6/16.

16 On 3/12/16 the 18-pdr. Bties. were completed to 6 guns each: R. Sec., A/LXXXV joined and made up A; L. Sec., A/LXXXV made up C; and R. Sec., C/LXXXV made up B. On 9/2/17 R. Sec., D (H.)/LXXXIV joined and made up D (H.)/LXXXII to 6 hows.

17 On 3/12/16 the 18-pdr. Bties. were completed to 6 guns each: L. Sec., C/LXXXV joined and made up A; R. Sec., B/LXXXV made up B; and L. Sec., B/LXXXV made up C. On 9/2/17 L. Sec., D (H.)/LXXXIV joined and made up D (H.)/LXXXIII to 6 hows.

18 On 3/12/16 C was broken up to complete A and B/ LXXXIV to six 18-pdrs. each. On 25/1/17 Bde. became an A.F.A. Bde.: D (H.)/LXXXIV was broken up and R. Sec. joined LXXXII on 9/2/17 and made up D (H.)/LXXXII to 6 hows.; and on the same day L. Sec. completed D (H.)/ LXXXIII. On 8/2/17, LXXXIV A.F.A. Bde. was completed by B and 1/2 C/LX (from 11th Div.) which became C/LXXXIV, and D (H.) and L. Sec., C (H.)/CCLX (from 51st Div.) joined and became D (H.)/LXXXIV.

19 On 3/12/16 LXXXV was broken up to complete the 18-pdr. Bties. of LXXXII and LXXXIII to six guns each; for this purpose A and R Sec. C were transferred to LXXXII, and B and L. Sec. C were transferred to LXXXIII (see notes 16 and 17). Sections were transferred complete—personnel, horses, guns, and wagons.

20 The three Medium T.M. Bties. were formed and joined the Div. by 19/6/16.

21 V was formed on 28/4/16; the H.T.M. Bty. was at Fourth Army T.M. School from 28/4–4/5/16, joined Div. on 6/5/16, and opened fire near Billon Wood on 27/6/16.

22 W was formed on 21/5/16, and the H.T.M. Bty. was broken up by 28/11/16. W never received any mortars.

23 On 17/5/16 the B.A.C.s were abolished and the D.A.C. was reorganized; B.A.C.s then formed sections of the reconstituted D.A.C.

24 On 6/2/18 Bn. was disbanded and drafted to 7/Norf. (12th Div.), 9/Norf. (6th Div.), and 18/Entg. Bn.

25 On 7/2/18 Bn. was disbanded and drafted to 2/Suff. (3rd Div.), 4/Suff. (P.) (58th Div.), 7/Suff. (12th Div.), and 18/Entg. Bn.

26 On 6/2/18 Bn. was disbanded and drafted to 1/R. Berks. (2nd Div.), 2/R. Berks. (8th Div.), and 5/R. Berks. (12th Div.).

27 On 11/2/18 Bn. was disbanded; the surplus joined 18/Entg. Bn.

28 On 9/2/18 Bn. was transferred to 53rd Bde.

29 Between 4–19/2/18 the Medium (4-mortar) T.M. Bties. were reorganized: Z was broken up and distributed between X and Y, to make up X and Y to 6 mortars each.

30 V left the Div. by 19/2/18 and became II Corps H.T.M. Bty.

31 Coy. (1 offr. and 90 o.r.) joined the Div. on 3/6/17.

32 On 2/2/18 Bn. was transferred from 1st Bde., 1st Div., and joined 53rd Bde. on 3/2/18.

33 On 25/5/18 Bn. was reduced to T.C., and remainder was absorbed by 2/Bedf. On 26/5/18 T.C. left 18th Div., joined 89th Bde., 30th Div., on 15/6/18, was transferred to 197th Bde., 66th Div., on 19/6/18, and on 31/7/18 the T.C. was absorbed by 2/Bedf. (54th Bde.—note 35).

34 Bn. was formed on 16/2/18, and it then consisted of 53rd, 54th, and 55th M.G. Cos. On 30/3/18, 278th M.G. Coy. disembkd. at le Havre, joined Div. on 9/4/18, and became D Coy. in No. 18 M.G. Bn. On 30/3/18, 265th M.G. Coy. landed at le Havre; 265th M.G. Coy. joined Div. on 17/4/18, and was then broken up to reinforce the four Cos. of No. 18 M.G. Bn.

35 Bn. went to Belgium with 7th Div. in Oct., 1914, and served in 21st Bde., 7th Div., until 19/12/15, when Bn. (with 21st Bde.) was transferred to 30th Div. Bn. then served in 89th Bde. and 90th Bde., 30th Div., until 22/5/18, when Bn. was transferred to and joined 54th Bde., 18th Div.

18TH (EASTERN) DIVISION

FORMATION, BATTLES, AND ENGAGEMENTS

This New Army Division had no existence before the outbreak of the Great War.

Army Order No. 382 of the 11th September 1914 authorized the further addition of six divisions (15th–20th) and Army Troops to the Regular Army (see Appendix I). This augmentation formed the Second New Army, and during September 1914 the 18th (Eastern) Division began to assemble around Colchester.

In the earliest days of the formation of the Division, trains brought large bodies of recruits who knew no word of command and were accompanied by no officers or non-commissioned-officers. In consequence the detrainment of a party was apt to resemble the arrival of a football excursion crowd. The officer who met one of these trains could only tell the mob to follow him, and then lead the men to the particular encampment which was to accommodate them. The food was sufficient, but coarse ; there were no canteens, the tents were crowded, the nights were chilly, there were never enough blankets to go round. Nevertheless in those tedious early days all ranks made the best of everything. At first the men had to march and drill in the civilian suits and boots which they wore on joining ; any men whose boots became soleless had to do slow marching on grass. After some time blue uniforms and forage caps arrived, and later on sufficient khaki uniforms were received to allow at least one suit to be issued to each platoon. But the training was progressive and never slackened ; and in April 1915 the Division, in full marching order, covered 62 miles in 48 hours.

It was weeks after the infantry had received rifles before any guns were issued to the divisional artillery. At first the only armament was limited to one improvised wooden gun per battery, and up to November 1914 no battery had more than a score of horses. Nevertheless the difficulties and deficiencies were overcome.

Between the 4th–12th May the Division moved to Salisbury Plain and divisional headquarters opened at Codford. On the 24th June the 18th Division was inspected by H.M. the King ; and in July the Division was informed that it was to be prepared to embark for the Western Front. On the 24th July the move to France began, headquarters started on the 25th, and on the 30th July the Division completed its concentration near Flesselles (south of Doullens) in the Third Army area. The Division was placed under X Corps. For the remainder of the Great War the 18th Division served on the Western Front in France and Belgium and was engaged in the following operations :—

1915

1916

BATTLES OF THE SOMME

1–8 July	**Battle of Albert** [XIII Corps, Fourth Army].
14–17 July	**Battle of Bazentin Ridge** [XIII Corps, Fourth Army].
14 July	**Capture of Trônes Wood** (54th Bde.).
19–21 July	**Battle of Delville Wood** (53rd Bde., under 9th Div.) [XIII Corps, Fourth Army].
26–28 September ...	**Battle of Thiepval Ridge** [II Corps, Reserve Army].
1–5 Oct. ; and 17 Oct.–11 Nov. ... ...}	**Battle of the Ancre Heights** [II Corps, Reserve Army—became Fifth Army on 30/10].
30 Sept.–5 Oct.	**Capture of the Schwaben Redoubt** (55th Bde.).
21 October	**Capture of Regina Trench.**
13–18 November... ...	**Battle of the Ancre** [II Corps, Fifth Army].

1917

16 Jan.–13 March	...	**Operations on the Ancre** [II Corps, Fifth Army].
17 and 18 February	...	**Miraumont.**
10 March	...	**Capture of Irles** (53rd Bde.).
14–20 March ...	...	**German Retreat to the Hindenburg Line** [II Corps, Fifth Army].

BATTLES OF ARRAS

3 and 4 May ...	...	**Third Battle of the Scarpe** [VII Corps, Third Army].

BATTLES OF YPRES

31 July	...	**Battle of Pilckem Ridge** [II Corps, Fifth Army].
10 August	...	**Inverness Copse** [II Corps, Fifth Army].
16 and 17 August	...	**Battle of Langemarck** (53rd Bde., with 56th Div.) [II Corps, Fifth Army].
12 October	...	**First Battle of Passchendaele** [XVIII Corps, Fifth Army].
22 October	...	**Capture of Poelcappelle** [XVIII Corps, Fifth Army].
5–10 November ...	...	**Second Battle of Passchendaele** [XIX Corps, Fifth Army].

1918

FIRST BATTLES OF THE SOMME

21–23 March ...	...	**Battle of St. Quentin** [III Corps, Fifth Army].
4 April	...	**Battle of the Avre** [XIX Corps, Fourth Army].
24 and 25 April ...	...	**Villers Bretonneux** [III Corps, Fourth Army].

THE ADVANCE TO VICTORY

8 and 9 August ...	...	**Battle of Amiens** [III Corps, Fourth Army].

SECOND BATTLES OF THE SOMME

21–23 August ...	...	**Battle of Albert** [III Corps, Fourth Army].
23 August	...	**Capture of Usna and Tara Hills.**
27 August	...	**Capture of Trônes Wood** (53rd Bde.).
31 Aug.–3 Sept. ...	...	**Second Battle of Bapaume** [III Corps, Fourth Army].

BATTLES OF THE HINDENBURG LINE

18 September ...	...	**Battle of Epéhy** [III Corps, Fourth Army].
29 Sept.–1 Oct. ...	...	**Battle of the St. Quentin Canal** [III Corps, until noon, 1/10 ; then XIII Corps, Fourth Army].

THE FINAL ADVANCE IN PICARDY

20–26 October ...	...	**Battle of the Selle** [XIII Corps, Fourth Army].
4 November... ...	...	**Battle of the Sambre** [XIII Corps, Fourth Army].

On the 6th November the advanced troops of the 18th Division made good the line of the railway (along the south-eastern side of the Forest of Mormal) near Sassegnies, and pushed out patrols to the left bank of the River Sambre. The 18th Division was then drawn back into XIII Corps Reserve ; and, when the Armistice brought hostilities to a close, the Division was billeted in villages around Le Cateau. Here the Division remained until the end of the year ; all ranks were given educational and recreational training and were employed on salvage work. On the 4th December, H.M. The King accompanied by H.R.H. The Prince of Wales passed through the 18th Division area. Demobilization began on the 10th December and coal-miners and pivotal men left during the month.

During January 1919 demobilization proceeded at an increasing pace ; and at midnight 19th/20th March 1919 the 18th Division ceased to exist. During its war service the Division gained 11 Victoria Crosses and (approximately) 4,382 other honours. In this same period the 18th Division lost 46,503 killed, wounded, and missing. The Roll of Honour, deposited in St. James's Church at Colchester, contains the names of 13,727 officers, non-commissioned-officers, and men.

G*

19TH (WESTERN) DIVISION

G.O.C.

25 September, 1914	... ...	Major-General C. G. M. FASKEN.
13 December, 1915...	... ...	Major-General G. T. M. BRIDGES.
6 April, 1917	... ...	Br.-Gen. W. P. MONKHOUSE (acting).
7 April, 1917	... ...	Major-General Hon. A. R. MONTAGU-STUART-WORTLEY (tempy.).
24 May, 1917	... ...	Major-General C. D. SHUTE (tempy.).
19 June, 1917	... ...	Major-General G. T. M. BRIDGES (wounded, 20/9/17).
20 September, 1917	... ...	Br.-Gen. W. P. MONKHOUSE (acting).
22 September, 1917	... ...	Major-General G. D. JEFFREYS.

G.S.O. 1.

22 Sept., 1914...Major W. S. BANKS (acting).
28 Jan., 1915...Lt.-Col. A. S. BUCKLE.
13 Jan., 1916...Lt.-Col. R. M. JOHNSON.
26 Mar., 1917...Lt.-Col. E. HEWLETT.
28 Oct., 1917...Lt.-Col. H. F. MONTGOMERY.

A.-A. and Q.-M.-G.

11 Oct., 1914...Lt.-Col. P. W. DRAKE-BROCKMAN.
29 April, 1915...Lt.-Col. P. M. DAVIES.
15 Jan., 1917...Lt.-Col. J. L. BUXTON.
6 Sept., 1917...Lt.-Col. A. M. COLLARD (tempy.).
10 Sept., 1917...Lt.-Col. G. E. HAWES.

B.-G., R.A.

30 Oct., 1914...Br.-Gen. W. H. SUART.
3 June, 1915...Br.-Gen. C. E. LAWRIE.
25 Dec., 1915...Br.-Gen. R. FITZMAURICE.
18 July, 1916...Br.-Gen. W. P. MONKHOUSE.
11 Sept., 1918...Lt.-Col. E. J. R. PEEL (tempy.).
15 Sept., 1918...Br.-Gen. E. J. R. PEEL.

C.R.E.

28 Oct., 1914...Major P. G. GRANT.
10 Mar., 1915...Lt.-Col. C. W. DAVY.
26 Mar., 1916...Lt.-Col. S. LLOYD OWEN.
24 Dec., 1916...Lt.-Col. P. E. HODGSON.
8 Nov., 1918...Lt.-Col. A. N. LAWFORD.

56th BDE.

18 Sept., '14...Br.-Gen. B. G. LEWIS
(sick, 17/12/15).
17 Dec., '15...Lt.-Col. C. S. SHEPHERD
(acting).
19 Dec., '15...Lt.-Col. C. R. P. WINSER
(acting).
22 Dec., '15...Br.-Gen. C. A. C.
VAN STRAUBENZEE.
6 June, '16...Lt.-Col. T. FITZJOHN
(acting).
11 June, '16...Lt.-Col. C. R. P. WINSER
(acting).
13 June, '16...Br.-Gen. F. G. M. ROWLEY.
20 Nov., '16...Br.-Gen. W. LONG
(killed, 28/1/17).
28 Jan., '17...Col. C. V. TROWER (acting).
1 Feb., '17...Br.-Gen. E. CRAIG-BROWN.
5 Sept., '17...Lt.-Col. T. FITZJOHN
(acting).
6 Sept., '17...Lt.-Col. C. R. P. WINSER
(acting).
6 Sept., '17...Br.-Gen. F. G. WILLAN
(sick, 7/4/18).
7 April, '18...Br.-Gen. R. M. HEATH.

57th BDE.

14 Sept., '14...Br.-Gen. L. T. C. TWYFORD.
16 June, '16...Br.-Gen. C. C. ONSLOW
(sick, 20/7/16).
20 July, '16...Lt.-Col. W. LONG (acting).
22 July, '16...Br.-Gen. G. D. JEFFREYS.
1 Jan., '17...Br.-Gen. C. R. BALLARD.
6 April, '17...Br.-Gen. T. A. CUBITT.
24 May, '18...Br.-Gen. A. J. F. EDEN
(wounded, 10/8/18).
10 Aug., '18...Lt.-Col. R. B. UMFREVILLE
(acting) ; (sick, 19/8/18).
19 Aug., '18...Lt.-Col. P. R. WHALLEY
(acting).
30 Aug., '18...Br.-Gen. A. J. F. EDEN.

58th BDE.

15 Sept., '14...Br.-Gen. C. T. BECKER.
8 July, '15...Br.-Gen. D. M. STUART.
19 Jan., '16...Br.-Gen. G. D. JEFFREYS (wounded, 14/4/16).
14 April, '16...Lt.-Col. R. A. BERNERS (acting).
29 April, '16...Br.-Gen. A. J. W. DOWELL.
10 Jan., '17...Br.-Gen. A. E. GLASGOW.

GENERAL NOTES

The following Units also served with the 19th (Western) Division :—

ARTILLERY :—515 (H.) Bty., R.F.A. (4, 4·5″ Hows.), see note 18.

19th Heavy Battery (4, 60-pdrs.), was raised for the 19th Division but went to France independently. The Heavy Battery landed at le Havre on 15/7/15 and joined XXI Bde., R.G.A., on 20/7/15.

INFANTRY :—1/4/King's, disembarked at le Havre on 6/3/15, joined 9th (Sirhind) Bde., 3rd (Lahore) Div., at Robecq on 9/3/15 ; Bn. left Lahore Div. on 10/11/15 and joined 137th Bde., 46th Div. On 3/12/15 the Bn. was transferred to 56th Bde., 19th Div., and on 19/12/15 to 58th Bde., 19th Div. On 25/2/16 the Bn. was transferred from 19th Div. to 98th Bde., 33rd Div., and served in 33rd Div. until the end of the Great War.

MACHINE-GUN UNIT :—No. 13 Motor-Machine-Gun Battery, joined 19th Division at Bulford on 14/7/15, disembarked at le Havre on 17/7/15, and served with 19th Div. until 7/3/16. On 7/3/16 the Battery was transferred to 33rd Div., and on 9/5/16 the Bty. left 33rd Div. and joined VIII Corps.

OTHER UNITS :—36th Sanitary Section, joined 19th Div. at Salisbury, went to France with 19th Div., and disembkd. at le Havre on 20/7/15. The Section served with 19th Div. until 9/3/17 ; the Section was then transferred to V Corps, and on 9/5/17 the Section was transferred to Third Army.

19th Division Motor Ambce. Workshop, left Marlborough on 16/7/15 and embarked at Avonmouth. The Workshop disembarked at Rouen on 18/7/15, left Rouen on 22/7/15, and joined 19th Div. at Busnes on 26/7/15. On 6/4/16 the Workshop was absorbed by the Divnl. Supply Column.

———————————

On 22/2/18 the reorganization of the 19th Division on a 9-battalion basis was completed ; and on 9/3/18 the pioneer battalion (5/S.W.B.) was reorganized on a 3-company basis.

19TH (WESTERN)[1] DIVISION

Dates	INFANTRY Brigades	INFANTRY Battalions and attached Units	Mounted Troops	ARTILLERY Field Artillery Brigades	ARTILLERY Field Artillery Batteries	Bde. Ammn. Colns.	Trench Mortar Bties. Medium	Trench Mortar Bties. Heavy	Divnl. Ammn. Coln.	Engineers Field Cos.	Signal Service Divnl. Signal Coy.	Pioneers	M.G. Units	Field Ambulances	Mobile Vety. Secn.	Divnl. Emplnt. Coy.	Divnl. Train
1914 October (England)	56th 57th 58th	7/K.O., 7/E. Lanc., 7/S. Lanc., 7/L.N.L. 10/R. War., 8/Glouc., 10/Worc., 8/N. Staff. 9/Ches., 9/R.W.F., 5/S.W.B.,[2] 9/Welsh.	19th Div. Cyclist Coy.[3]	LXXXVI[4] LXXXVII[4] LXXXVIII[4] LXXXIX (H.)[4]	268, 269, 270 271, 272, 273 274, 275, 276 277 (H.), 278 (H.), 279 (H.)	LXXXVI B.A.C. LXXXVII B.A.C. LXXXVIII B.A.C. LXXXIX (H.) B.A.C.	...		19th D.A.C.	81st[5] 82nd[5] 94th[6]	19th[7]	...	...	57th 58th 59th	31st	...	19th[8]
1915 September (France)	56th 57th 58th	7/K.O., 7/E. Lanc., 7/S. Lanc., 7/L.N.L. 10/R. War., 8/Glouc., 10/Worc., 8/N. Staff. 9/Ches., 9/R.W.F., 9/Welsh, 6/Wilts.[9]	C Sqdn., 1/York. Dgns.[10] 19th Div. Cyclist Coy.[11]	LXXXVI[4];[12] LXXXVII[4];[13] LXXXVIII[4];[14] LXXXIX (H.)[4];[15]	A, B, C; D A, B, C; D A, B, C; D A (H.), C (H.), D (H.)	LXXXVI B.A.C. LXXXVII B.A.C. LXXXVIII B.A.C. LXXXIX (H.) B.A.C.	...		19th D.A.C.	81st 82nd 94th	19th	5/ S.W.B.[2] (P.)	...	57th 58th 59th	31st	...	19th
1916 June (France)	56th 57th 58th	7/K.O., 7/E. Lanc., 7/S. Lanc., 7/L.N.L.; 56th Bde. M.G. Coy.;[16] 56th T.M. Bty.[17] 10/R. War., 8/Glouc., 10/Worc., 8/N. Staff.; 57th Bde. M.G. Coy.;[16] 57th T.M. Bty.[17] 9/Ches., 9/R.W.F., 9/Welsh, 6/Wilts.; 58th Bde. M.G. Coy.;[16] 58th T.M. Bty.[17]	...	LXXXVI[12];[18] LXXXVII[13];[19] LXXXVIII[14];[20] LXXXIX[15];[21]	A, B, C; D (H.) A, B, C; D (H.) A, B, C; D (H.) A, B, C	...[23]	X.19[22] Y.19[22] Z.19[22]	W.19[22]	19th D.A.C.[23]	81st 82nd 94th	19th	5/ S.W.B. (P.)	...	57th 58th 59th	31st	...	19th
1917 June (France)	56th 57th 58th	7/K.O.,[24] 7/E. Lanc., 7/S. Lanc.,[25] 7/L.N.L.,[26] 56th M.G. Coy.;[27] 56th T.M. Bty.[31] 10/R. War., 8/Glouc., 10/Worc., 8/N. Staff.;[28] 57th M.G. Coy.; 57th T.M. Bty. 9/Ches.,[29] 9/R.W.F., 9/Welsh,[30] 58th M.G. Coy.; 58th T.M. Bty.	...	LXXXVII[19] LXXXVIII[20]	A, B, C; D (H.) A, B, C; D (H.)	...	X.19[32] Y.19[32] Z.19[32]	W.19[33]	19th D.A.C.	81st 82nd 94th	19th	5/ S.W.B. (P.)	246th M.G. Coy.[34]	57th 58th 59th	31st	220th[35]	19th
1918 March (France)	56th 57th 58th	9/Ches.,[29] 1/4/K.S.L.I.,[36] 8/N. Staff.;[28] 56th T.M. Bty.[31] 10/R. War., 8/Glouc., 10/Worc.,;[37] 57th T.M. Bty. 9/R.W.F., 9/Welsh, 6/(Wilts. Yeo.) Wilts.;[30];[38] 58th T.M. Bty.	...	LXXXVII[19] LXXXVIII[20]	A, B, C; D (H.) A, B, C; D (H.)	...	X.19 Y.19		19th D.A.C.	81st 82nd 94th	19th	5/ S.W.B. (P.)	No. 19 Bn., M.G.C.[39]	57th 58th 59th	31st	220th	19th

1918 July (France)	19th	20th	31st	57th 58th 59th	No. 19 Bn. M.G.C.	5/ S.W.B. (P.)	19th	81st 82nd 94th	19th D.A.C.	...	X.19 Y.19	...	LXXXVII LXXXVIII	...	19th
56th	9/Ches., 1/4/K.S.L.I., 8/N. Staff., 56th T.M. Bty.												LXXXVII ...		A, B, C; D (H.)
57th	10/R. War., 8/Glouc., 3/ Worc.; 37, 40 57th T.M. Bty.												LXXXVIII ...		A, B, C; D (H.)
58th	9/R.W.F., 9/Welsh, 2/ Wilts.,38 41 58th T.M. Bty.														

NOTES

1 The Official Title of the Division—19th (Western) Division—was brought into use from 21/11/14.

2 Bn. (of 58th Bde.) became provisional pioneer Bn. of the Div. on 29/12/14; the conversion was finally approved on 10/1/15.

3 Cyclist Coy. began to form on 19/11/14 (A.O. 13 of 10/11/14.)

4 Bties. were raised as 6-gun bties. and numbered. In Feb., 1915, the divnl. artillery was reorganized: Bdes. became 4-battery bdes.; the Bties. all became 4-gun. bties.; and in each Bde. the Bties. were lettered A, B, C, D.

5 The two Fd. Cos. joined from Bulford on 28 and 29/9/14.

6 94th Fd. Coy. (from 25th Div.)—6 offrs., 247 o.r., and 31 horses—joined at Andover on 26/1/15.

7 2, 3, and 4 Secs. joined their respective Inf. Bdes. on 14/6/15.

8 The Train (25 offrs., 600 o.r., and 80 horses) arrived at Windmill Hill on 3/11/14. The Train consisted of 154, 155, 156, and 157 Cos., A.S.C.

9 Bn. (from Army Troops) replaced 5/S.W.B. (P.) in 58th Bde. on 29/12/14.

10 Sqdn. joined Div. at Bulford on 26/6/15, and disembkd. at le Havre on 20/7/15. Sqdn. left Div. on 21/4/16, was attached to 3rd Cav. Div. from 21/4–9/5/16, and on 9/5/16 Sqdn. joined II Corps Cav. Regt.

11 Coy. left Div. on 21/4/16, was attached to 3rd Cav. Div. from 21/4–7/5/16, and on 8/5/16 Coy. joined III Corps Cyclist Bn.

12 On 25/5/16 D Bty. left Bde. and became A/LXXXIX; and A (H.)/LXXXIX joined Bde. and became D (H.)/LXXXVI.

13 On 25/5/16 D Bty. left Bde. and became B/LXXXIX; and C (H.)/LXXXIX joined Bde. and became B (H.)/LXXXVII.

14 On 25/5/16 D Bty. left Bde. and became C/LXXXIX; and D(H.)/LXXXIX joined Bde. and became D(H.)/LXXXVIII.

15 On 7/8/15 B (H.) left Bde. and was attached to XXXI (28th Div.) until 8/9/15; Bty. then became B (H.)/CXXX (H.) (28th Div.) until 25/7/16, then D (H.)/CXLVI (28th Div.) until 10/8/17, when Bty. became D (H.)/III (28th Div.). On 25/5/16 LXXXIX (H.) was reorganized: A (H.), C (H.), and D (H.) left Bde. and became D (H.)/LXXXVI, D (H.)/LXXXVII, D (H.)/LXXXVIII; and D/LXXXVII, and D/LXXXVII, and D/LXXXVIII joined Bde. and became A, B, and C/LXXXIX.

16 A provisional 56th M.G. Coy. existed between Sept.-Dec., 1915. On 9/2/16 the 56th, 57th, and 58th M.G. Cos. disembkd. at le Havre and joined the Div. on 14/2/16.

17 T.M. Bties. were formed in Bdes.:
56th—56/1 by 11/4/16 and 56/2 by 20/5/16, and they became 56th T.M. Bty. by 17/6/16;
57th—57 A and 57 B by 6/2/16, became 57/1 and 57/2 by 17/3/16; and they became 57th T.M. Bty. by 15/6/16;
58th—58 A by 13/2/16, became 58/1 by 17/3/16, 58/2 appeared by 28/5/16; and 58/1 and 2 became 58th T.M. Bty. by 15/6/16.

18 On 9/9/16 C was broken up: R. Sec. made up A, and L. Sec. made up B to 6 guns each. On 12/11/16, 516 (H.) joined Bde. and became C (H.). On 23/1/17 LXXXVI became an A.F.A. Bde.; B/CCLX (1 Lowland)—18-pdrs.—joined from 51st Div. and made up D (H.) to 6 hows. On 28/1/17 C (H.)/LXXXVI and was broken up: R. Sec. made up D (H.)/LXXXVII, and L. Sec. made up D (H.)/LXXXVIII to 6 hows.

19 On 8 and 9/9/16 the 18-pdr. Bties. were made up to 6 guns each: L. Sec., B/LXXXIX made up A; R. Sec., B/LXXXIX made up B; and R. Sec., A/LXXXIX made up C to 6 guns each. On 28/1/17 R. Sec., C (H.)/LXXXVI joined and made up D (H.) to 6 hows.

20 Bde. was reorganized on 8/9/16 in 6-gun 18-pdr. bties.: A was split up; C/LXXXIX joined and with 1 sec., A/LXXXVIII became A/LXXXVIII; 1 sec., A/LXXXVIII completed B/LXXXVIII to 6 guns; and L. Sec., A/LXXXIX joined and made up C/LXXXVIII to 6 guns. On 28/1/17 L. Sec., C (H.)/LXXXVI joined and made up D (H.) to 6 hows.

21 On 8 and 9/9/16 the Bde. was broken up: R. Sec., A and R. and L. Secs., B were transferred to LXXXVII and made up the three 18-pdr. bties. to 6 guns each (note 19); and L. Sec., A made up C/LXXXVIII to 6 guns, and C/LXXXIX and 1 sec., A/LXXXVIII became A/LXXXVIII (see note 20).

22 Medium and Heavy T.M. Bties. were formed by May, 1916.

23 On 18/5/16 B.A.C.s were abolished and the D.A.C. was reorganized.

24 Bn. was disbanded between 6–22/2/18. Drafts joined 1/4 and 1/5/K.O. in 56th Div., and remdr. joined 6/Engl. Bn.

25 Bn. was disbanded on 6/2/18, and drafted to 1/E. Lanc. (34th Div.) and 2/E. Lanc. (8th Div.).

26 Bn. was disbanded on 22/2/18; 23 offrs. and 640 o.r. joined 6/E:ntg. Bn., and the remdr. went to the Base.

27 Bn. was disbanded on 10/2/18, and drafted to 1/L.N.L. (1st Div.) and 2/5/L.N.L. (Pioneers, 57th Div.).

28 On 7/2/18 Bn. was transferred to 56th Bde.

29 On 7/2/18 Bn. was transferred to 56th Bde.

30 On 3/9/17, 1/R. Wilts. Yeo. left XV Corps and joined No. 3 Inf. Base Depot, Rouen; and on 26/9/17. 1/R. Wilts. Yeo. (14 offrs. and 232 o.r.) joined 58th Bde. and amalgamated with 6/Wilts. Bn. was then designated 6/(Wilts. Yeo.) Wilts.

31 The original 58th T.M. Bty. was broken up on 5/2/18; and the 58th T.M. Bty. was reconstructed by 6/3/18.

32 The 3 Medium T.M. Bties. were reorganized on 18/2/18 in 2 T.M. Bties. of 6" Newton T.M.s each: Z was disbanded; the personnel of X and Y joined Y; and X was reformed from W 19 (note 33).

33 W was disbanded on 18/2/18, and the personnel of W reformed X 19.

34 Coy. disembkd. at le Havre on 16/7/17, and joined the Div. at Bailleul on 19/7/17.

35 The Coy. was formed by 14/7/17.

36 Bn. sailed for India on 30/10/14 with 44th (Home Counties) Div. (T.F.). Bn. served in Burma from 10/12/14, and in Singapore from 10/2/15 (with part in Hong Kong from 5/4/15). Bn. left Hong Kong on 13/4/17 and Singapore on 14/4/17. Bn. was in Ceylon from 19/4–3/5/17, at Cape Town from 30/5–29/6/17, and Bn. reached le Havre on 29/7/17. Bn. joined 190th Bde., 63rd (R.N.) Div. on 18/8/17, and on 4/2/18 Bn. was transferred to 58th Bde., 19th Div.

37 Bn. was reduced to T.C. on 22/8/18 and the surplus was absorbed by 3/Worc. T.C., 10/Worc., left 10th Div. on 22/6/18 and joined 74th Bde., 25th Div. On 28/8/18 Bn. was transferred and joined 121st Bde., 40th Div., on 29/6/18. On 10/7/18 T.C. 10/Worc. was absorbed by 17/Worc. (Pioneers) in 40th Div.

38 Bn. was reduced to T.C. on 13/5/18 and the surplus—20 offrs. and 509 o.r.—was absorbed by 2/Wilts. T.C., 6/Wilts., left 19th Div. on 13/5/18, joined 21st Bde., 30th Div., on 16/5/18, was transferred on 19/5/18 to 90th Bde., 30th Div., left 30th Div. on 16/6/18, joined 42nd Bde., 14th Div., at Boulogne on 10/6/18, and went to England. Bn. absorbed 9/Dorset. on 18/6/18, rejoined 42nd Bde. on 19/6/18, and served with 42nd Bde., 14th Div., until the end of the Great War.

39 Bn. was formed on 14/2/18, and consisted of 56tb, 57tb, 58th, and 246th M.G. Cos.

40 Bn. (in Aug., 1914, was in 7th Bde., 3rd Div.) and joined 57th Bde. on 22/8/18 from 74th Bde., 25th Div., and absorbed surplus of 10/Worc.

41 Bn. (in Oct., 1914, was in 21st Bde., 7th Div.) and joined 58th Bde. on 13/5/18 from 21st Bde., 30th Div., and absorbed surplus of 6/Wilts.

19TH (WESTERN) DIVISION

FORMATION, BATTLES, AND ENGAGEMENTS

This New Army Division had no existence before the outbreak of the Great War.

Army Order No. 382 of the 11th September 1914 authorized the further addition of six divisions (15th–20th) and Army Troops to the Regular Army (see Appendix I). This augmentation formed the Second New Army, and during September 1914 the 19th (Western) Division began to assemble near Bulford.

At first the infantry brigades were camped at Tidworth, Ludgershall, and Grately. In December the brigades went into comfortable billets at Andover and Whitchurch, Basingstoke, and Weston-super-Mare. The early discomforts and difficulties were similar to those which were experienced by all the divisions of the New Armies, consequently a few D.P. rifles were received with enthusiasm.

By March 1915 the Division was clothed in khaki and a great advance had been made in training. During March the Division concentrated around Tidworth to begin its final intensive preparation for the field, and regimental training was completed by mid-May. On the 7th June the 19th Division first operated together as a complete division, and between the 12th and 18th June the 19th Division Artillery carried out its first gun-practice. On Wednesday, the 23rd June, the 19th Division was inspected by H.M. The King ; and, at the end of the parade, His Majesty said to the General-Officer-Commanding : " Your Division is as good as anything I have seen in the New Army."

On the 11th July the advanced party of the 19th Division left for France, on the 16th the Division began to move, and by the 21st July it had crossed to France and completed its concentration near St. Omer. For the remainder of the Great War the 19th Division served on the Western Front in France and Belgium and was engaged in the following operations :—

1915

25 Sept.–2 Oct.	**Battle of Loos** [Indian Corps, First Army].
25 September	**Action of Piètre.**

1916

BATTLES OF THE SOMME

1–9 July	**Battle of Albert** [III Corps, Fourth Army].
2–4 July	**Capture of la Boisselle.**
20–22 July	**Fighting for High Wood** [III Corps, Fourth Army].
23–31 July	**Battle of Pozières Ridge** [III Corps, Fourth Army].
22 Oct.–11 Nov.	**Battle of the Ancre Heights** [II Corps, Reserve Army, until 30/10 ; then Fifth Army].
13–18 November... ...	**Battle of the Ancre** [II Corps, Fifth Army].

1917

7–14 June ... ...   **Battle of Messines** [IX Corps, Second Army].

BATTLES OF YPRES

20–25 September ...   **Battle of Menin Road Ridge** [IX Corps, Second Army].
26 Sept.–3 Oct. ... ...   **Battle of Polygon Wood** [IX Corps, Second Army].
 4 October ... ...   **Battle of Broodseinde** [IX Corps, Second Army].
 9 October ... ...   **Battle of Poelcappelle** [IX Corps, Second Army].
12 October ... ...   **First Battle of Passchendaele** [IX Corps, Second Army].
26 Oct.–10 Nov. ... ...   **Second Battle of Passchendaele** [IX Corps, Second Army].

1918

FIRST BATTLES OF THE SOMME

21–23 March ... ...   **Battle of St. Quentin** [V Corps until 3 p.m., 21/3 ; then IV Corps, Third Army].
24 and 25 March... ...   **Battle of Bapaume** [IV Corps, Third Army].

BATTLES OF THE LYS

10 and 11 April ... ...   **Battle of Messines** [IX Corps, Second Army].
13–15 April ... ...   **Battle of Bailleul** [IX Corps, Second Army].
17 and 18 April ... ...   **First Battle of Kemmel Ridge** [IX Corps, Second Army].

29 May–6 June ... ...   **Battle of the Aisne** [IX Corps, Fifth (French) Army].

THE ADVANCE TO VICTORY

THE FINAL ADVANCE IN PICARDY

18–23 October ... ...   **Battle of the Selle** [XVII Corps, Third Army].
 4 November ... ...   **Battle of the Sambre** [XVII Corps, Third Army].
 5–7 November ... ...   **Passage of the Grande Honnelle** [XVII Corps, Third Army].

The pursuit continued. The 19th Division advanced through Malplaquet on the 8th November and secured the Bois de la Lanière (west of the Maubeuge–Mons road) on the 9th November. After this the advance of the Division came to an end ; the 24th and the 11th Divisions, on either side, joined hands and the 19th Division then passed into XVII Corps Reserve. On the 10th the Division was drawn back into billets to the west of Bavai, and it was in the same position when the Armistice brought hostilities to a close at 11 a.m. on the 11th November.

On the 14th and 15th November the Division moved back to the Rieux area (north-east of Cambrai), and on 24th, 25th, and 26th November it moved farther back to billets in the Beauquesne–Candas area, with headquarters at Naours (south of Doullens). All miners left for demobilization at the end of December ; and during January and February 1919 demobilization went on at an increasing rate. Finally at midnight 18th/19th March the 19th Division ceased to exist and the last cadres all returned to England between the 21st and 27th June 1919. During the Great War the 19th Division lost **39,381** killed, wounded, and missing.

20TH (LIGHT) DIVISION

G.O.C.

15 September, 1914	Major-General Sir E. O. F. HAMILTON.
19 October, 1914	Br.-General R. H. DAVIES.
26 October, 1914	Major-General R. H. DAVIES.
20 February, 1915	Br.-Gen. J. HOTHAM (acting).
20 March, 1915	Major-General R. H. DAVIES.
8 March, 1916	Major-General W. DOUGLAS SMITH.
19 March, 1917	Major-General T. G. MATHESON.
9 August, 1917	Major-General W. DOUGLAS SMITH.
3 April, 1918	Major-General G. G. S. CAREY.

G.S.O.1.

23 Sept., 1914...Major E. MARTIN (acting).
9 Oct., 1914...Major H. C. MACTIER (acting).
23 Nov., 1914...Captain G. H. BARNETT (acting).
4 Feb., 1915...Major W. R. N. MADOCKS.
10 Mar., 1915...Lt.-Col.W.R.N.MADOCKS (sick, 6/1/17).
6 Jan., 1917...Major F. S. G. PIGGOTT (acting).
9 Jan., 1917...Lt.-Col. J. McD. HASKARD.
25 July, 1918...Lt.-Col. M. O. CLARKE.
19 Sept., 1918...Lt.-Col. F. W. GOSSET (tempy.).
3 Oct., 1918...Lt.-Col. A. W. STERICKER.

A.-A. and Q.-M.-G.

23 Sept., 1914...Captain G. H. BARNETT (acting).
20 Oct., 1914...Colonel R. H. TWIGG.
14 Dec., 1914...Lt.-Col. F. R. P. KANE.
18 Mar., 1915...Lt.-Col. F. C. DUNDAS.
5 April, 1917...Lt.-Col. H. G. B. MILLER.

B.-G., R.A.

3 Nov., 1914...Br.-Gen. J. HOTHAM.
24 Oct., 1916...Lt.-Col. F. A. WILSON (acting).
13 Nov., 1916...Br.-Gen. W. B. BROWELL.
10 Aug., 1917...Br.-Gen. H. W. A. CHRISTIE.

C.R.E.

Nov., 1914...Colonel E. R. KENYON.
17 Feb., 1916...Lt.-Col. A. ROLLAND.
18 July, 1917...Lt.-Col. E. M. NEWELL.

59th BDE.

14 Sept., '14...Br.-Gen. G. F. LESLIE.
6 July, '15...Br.-Gen. C. D. SHUTE.
14 Oct., '16...Br.-Gen. R. C.
                        BROWNE-CLAYTON.
26 Aug., '17...Br.-Gen. H. H. G. HYSLOP.
3 April, '18...Br.-Gen. R. M. OVENS.
8 June, '18...Br.-Gen. A. C. BAYLAY.

60th BDE.

12 Sept., '14...Br.-Gen. A. E. W.
                        COLVILLE.
8 July, '15...Br.-Gen. J. W. G. ROY.
5 May, '16...Br.-Gen. Hon. L. J. P.
                        BUTLER.
24 Oct., '17...Br.-Gen. F. J. DUNCAN.
5 June, '18...Br.-Gen. W. R. H. DANN.

61st BDE.

18 Sept., '14...Br.-Gen. O'D. C. GRATTAN.
6 July, '15...Br.-Gen. C. ROSS.
13 Nov., '15...Br.-Gen. W. F. SWENY (wounded, 2/6/16).
3 June, '16...Lt.-Col. C. J. HOBKIRK (acting).
19 July, '16...Br.-Gen. W. F. SWENY (sick, 24/7/16).
27 July, '16...Br.-Gen. W. E. BANBURY.
12 Mar., '18...Br.-Gen. J. K. COCHRANE.

GENERAL NOTES

The following Units also served with the 20th (Light) Division :—

ARTILLERY :—20th Heavy Battery (4, 60-pdrs.), was raised for the 20th Div., but went to France independently. The Heavy Battery disembkd. at le Havre on 7/8/15 and joined X Corps on 9/8/15 ; after several attachments, the Heavy Battery left Marseille on 28/11/15, disembkd. at Salonika on 5/12/15, and joined XXXVII Hy. Bde., No. 2 Group, XII Corps Artillery on 24/2/16. The Heavy Battery served in Macedonia for the remainder of the Great War.

MACHINE-GUN UNIT :—No. 14 Motor-Machine-Gun Battery, was formed and joined the 20th Div. by 26/1/15, disembkd. at le Havre on 21/7/15, and served with the 20th Div. until 22/4/16. On 11/5/16 the Bty. joined I Anzac Corps.

OTHER UNITS :—33rd Sanitary Section, joined 20th Div. at Salisbury, went to France with the 20th Div., and disembkd. at le Havre on 24/7/15. On 24/4/17 Sanitary Sections were transferred to Army Troops, and 33rd Sany. Sec. took over a Fourth Army Sanitary Area.

20th Division Motor Ambce. Workshop, mobilized at Grove Park from 16–21/6/15, joined 20th Div. at Salisbury on 22/6/15, went to France with 20th Div., and disembkd. at Rouen on 22/7/15 ; the Workshop left Rouen on 25/7/15, and rejoined 20th Div. at Lumbres on 26/7/15. On 31/3/16 the Workshop was abolished and the personnel and vehicles were transferred to 20th Div. Supply Coln.

On 20/2/18 the reorganization of the 20th Division on a 9-battalion basis was completed ; and on 24/2/18 the pioneer battalion (11/D.L.I.) was reorganized on a 3-company basis.

20TH (LIGHT) DIVISION

Dates	Infantry — Brigades	Infantry — Battalions and attached Units	Mounted Troops	Artillery — Field Artillery — Brigades	Artillery — Field Artillery — Batteries	Artillery — Bde. Ammn. Colns.	Artillery — Trench Mortar Bties. Medium	Artillery — Trench Mortar Bties. Heavy	Artillery — Divnl. Ammn. Coln.	Engineers — Field Cos.	Signal Service — Divnl. Signal Coy.	Pioneers	M.G. Units	Field Ambulances	Mobile Vety. Secn.	Divnl. Emplnt. Coy.	Divnl. Train
1914 October (England)	59th ... 60th ... 61st ...	10/K.R.R.C., 11/K.R.R.C., 10/R.B., 11/R.B. 6/O. & B.L.I., 6/K.S.L.I., 12/K.R.R.C., 12/R.B. 7/Som. L.I., 7/D.C.L.I., 7/K.O.Y.L.I., 11/D.L.I.[1]	20th Div. Cyclist Coy.[2]	XC[5] .... XCI[5] .... XCII (H.)[5] ... XCIII[5]	280, 281, 282 283, 284, 285 286 (H.), 287 (H.), 288 (H.) 289, 290, 291	XC B.A.C. XCI B.A.C. XCII (H.) B.A.C. XCIII B.A.C.	...	...	20th D.A.C.	83rd 84th 96th[4]	20th	...	...	60th 61st 62nd	32nd[5]	...	20th[5]
1915 September (France)	59th ... 60th ... 61st ...	10/K.R.R.C., 11/K.R.R.C., 10/R.B., 11/R.B. 6/O. & B.L.I., 6/K.S.L.I., 12/K.R.R.C., 12/R.B. 12/King's,[7] 7/Som. L.I., 7/D.C.L.I., 7/K.O.Y.L.I.	H.Q. D Sqdn.[8] and M.G. Sec., 1/Westmld. and Cumbld. Yeo., 20th Div. Cyclist Coy.[9]	XC; [10] .... XCI; [11] .... XCII (H.)[3]; [12] XCIII[3]; [13] ...	A, B, C, D A, B, C, D A (H.),[12] B (H.), C (H.), D (H.) A, B, C, D	XC B.A.C. XCI B.A.C. XCII (H.) B.A.C. XCIII B.A.C.	...	...	20th D.A.C.	83rd 84th 96th	20th	11/D.L.I. (P.)	...	60th 61st 62nd	32nd	...	20th
1916 June (France)	59th ... 60th ... 61st ...	10/K.R.R.C., 11/K.R.R.C., 10/R.B., 11/R.B.; 59th Bde. M.G. Coy.;[14] 59th T.M. Bty.[15] 6/O. & B.L.I., 6/K.S.L.I., 12/K.R.R.C., 12/R.B.; 60th Bde. M.G. Coy.;[14] 60th T.M. Bty.[15] 12/King's, 7/Som. L.I., 7/D.C.L.I., 7/K.O.Y.L.I.; 61st Bde. M.G. Coy.;[14] 61st T.M. Bty.[15]	...	XC10; [16] ..... XCI11; [17] ... XCII12; [18] ... XCIII13; [19] ...	A, B, C; D (H.) A, B, C; D (H.) A, B, C A, B, C; D (H.)	...[21]	X.20[20] Y.20[20] Z.20[20]	V.20[20]	20th D.A.C.[21]	83rd 84th 96th	20th	11/D.L.I. (P.)	...	60th 61st 62nd	32nd	...	20th
1917 June (France)	59th ... 60th ... 61st ...	10/K.R.R.C.,[22] 11/K.R.R.C., 10/R.B.,[23] 11/R.B.; 59th M.G. Coy.;[31] 59th T.M. Bty. 6/O. & B.L.I.,[24] 6/K.S.L.I., 12/K.R.R.C., 12/R.B.; 60th M.G. Coy.;[31] 60th T.M. Bty. 12/King's, 7/Som. L.I., 7/D.C.L.I., 7/K.O.Y.L.I.;[25] 61st M.G. Coy.;[31] 61st T.M. Bty.	...	XCI7 .... XCII8	A, B, C; D (H.) A, B, C; D (H.)	...	X.20 Y.20 Z.20[26]	V.20[27]	20th D.A.C.	83rd 84th 96th	20th	11/D.L.I. (P.)	217th[28] M.G. Coy.	60th 61st 62nd	32nd	221st[29]	20th

Brigades	Battalions (and Bde. T.M. Bty.)	Mounted Troops	Artillery Bdes.	Batteries	B.A.C.	D.A.C.	T.M. Bties.	Field Coys. R.E.	Signal Coy.	Pioneers	M.G. Units	Field Ambs.	Mob. Vet. Sec.	Empl. Coy.	Train
59th	2/Sco. Rif.,[30] 11/K.R.R.C., 11/R.B.; 59th T.M. Bty.	...	XCI	A, B, C; D (H.)	...	20th D.A.C.	X.20 / Y.20	83rd, 84th, 96th	20th	11/ D.L.I. (P.)	No. 20 Bn.,[31] M.G.C.	60th, 61st, 62nd	32nd	221st	20th
60th	6/K.S.L.I.; 12/K.R.R.C., 12/R.B.; 60th T.M. Bty.		XCII	A, B, C; D (H.)											
61st	12/King's, 7/Som. L.I., 7/D.C.L.I.; 61st T.M. Bty.														

1918 March (France)

NOTES

1. On 6/1/15 Bn. (of 61st Bde.) was converted into the divnl. pioneer battalion.

2. On 22/12/14 the Cyclist Coy. began to form at Pirbright.

3. Bties. were raised as 6-gun batteries and numbered. On 15/1/15 the designation of the batteries was revised: Bties. were lettered in each Bde.—A, B, C, and D—the Bdes. all became 4-battery bdes., and the Bties. all became 4-gun batteries. (Authy.—W.O. Letter, No. 20/Artillery/3818, A.G.6, d/d. 6/1/15).

4. On 1/2/15 the Fd. Coy. (strength—7 offrs., 282 o.r., and 17 horses) joined 20th Div., at Woking, from 26th Div.

5. Joined Div. in England, and in July, 1915, went to France with the Div.

6. Train consisted of 158, 159, 160, and 161 Cos., A.S.C.

7. Bn. was an Army Troops Bn., Second New Army, and in Sept., 1914, Bn. was attached to 20th Div. In Jany., 1915, Bn. took the place of 11/D.L.I. (converted into Pioneer Bn.—see note 1).

8. Joined Div. at Lark Hill before 24/6/15, went to France with Div., and disembkd. at le Havre on 24/7/15. Div. Cav. left Div. on 29/4/16, was attached to 2nd Cav. Div. from 30/4—14/5/16, and joined XI Corps Cav. Regt. on 15/5/16.

9. Coy. disembkd. at le Havre on 22/7/15, served with Div. until 17/5/16, when Coy. was transferred to XIV Corps; and on 26/5/16 Coy. was absorbed in the newly-formed XIV Corps Cyclist Bn.

10. On 11/5/16 D Bty. left Bde. and became A/XCII; and B (H.)/XCII joined Bde. and became D (H.)/XC.

11. On 12/5/16 C (H.)/XCII joined Bde. and became B/XCII; and C (H.)/XCII joined Bde. and became D (H.)/XCI.

12. On 9/8/15 A (H.) was transferred to 27th Div., joined on 10/8/15, and became B (H.)/CXXIX (H.) on 6/9/15. On 25/7/16 B (H.)/CXXIX was transferred to I, and became D (H.)/I (in 27th Div.). On 11 and 12/5/16 XCII was reorganized: B (H.), C (H.), and D (H.) left and became D (H.)/XC, D (H.)/XCI, and D (H.)/XCIII; and D (H.)/XCIII joined Bde. and became A, B, and C/XCII.

13. On 11/5/16 D Bty. left Bde. and became C/XCII; and D (H.)/XCII joined Bde. and became D (H.)/XCIII.

14. Bde. M.G. Cos. joined as follows: 59th left Grantham on 23/2/16, disembkd. at le Havre on 25/2/16, and joined Div. on 3/3/16; 60th left Grantham on 23/2/16 and on 1/3/16 disembkd. at le Havre on 25/2 and on 2/3/16; and joined Div. on 3/3/16; 61st disembkd. at le Havre on 25/2/16, and joined Div. on 3/3/16.

15. T.M. Bties. were formed in the Bdes. :
59th—59/1 by 10/4/16, 59/2 by 25/4/16 by 16/7/16;
59th T.M. Bty. by 16/7/16;
60th—60/1 by 18/4/16, and 60th T.M. Bty. by 12/7/16;
61st—61/1 and 61/2 by 4/5/16, and they became 61st T.M. Bty. by 12/6/16.

16. On 30/8/16 B was split up, L. Sec. joined A, and R. Sec. joined C, making up A and C to 6, 18-pdrs. each; C was then transferred and became B/XCI, A became C/XCII, and D (H.) became D (H.)/XCII. XC Bde. then ceased to exist.

17. On 30 and 31/8/16 B was broken up and made up A and C to 6 guns each; C/XC joined XCI and became B/XCI. On 8/1/17, 1 Sec. D (H.)/XCIII joined and made up D (H.)/XCI to 6 hows.

18. On 30 and 31/8/16 C was split up, L. Sec. joined B, and R. Sec. joined A, making up B and A to 6, 18-pdrs. each; A/XC joined XCII and became C/XCII; and D (H.)/XC became D (H.)/XCII. On 8/1/17, 1 Sec. D (H.)/XCIII joined and made up D (H.)/XCII to 6 hows.

19. Between 22-31/8/16 A was broken up and made up B and C to 6, 18-pdrs. each; C/XCII then became A/XCIII. On 8/1/17 Bde. became an A.F.A. Bde.; D (H.) was broken up, 1 sec. joined D (H.)/XCI and 1 sec. joined D (H.)/XCII, making up each Bty. to 6 hows. On 16/1/17 B/CLXVI joined from 33rd Div. and became C/XCIII. (This A.F.A. Bde. never had a D (H.) Bty.).

20. The Medium and Heavy T.M. Bties. were formed by 24/5/16.

21. Between 12-15/5/16 the B.A.C.s were abolished and the D.A.C. was reorganized.

22. Bn. was disbanded on 5/2/18. (Drafts of 36 offrs. and 743 o.r. went to 1/, 11/, 12/, 13/, 16/, and 17/K.R.R.C., and the surplus joined 14/Entg. Bn.).

23. Bn. was disbanded between 4-14/2/18. (Drafts of 36 offrs. and 744 o.r. went to 3/, 11/, 12/, and 13/R.B.; and the surplus went to XXII Corps Rft. Camp on 14/2/18, and on 21/2/18 surplus joined 14/Entg. Bn.).

24. Bn. was disbanded between 2-9/2/18. (Drafts of 36 offrs. and 700 o.r. went to 2/, 2/4, and 5/O. and B.I.I.; and the surplus joined 14/Entg. Bn.).

25. Bn. was disbanded between 16-20/2/18; and Bn. then constituted 14/Entrenching Bn.

26. On 2/2/18 Z was broken up and distributed between X and Y.

27. On 2/2/18 V was broken up, and the personnel was transferred to XXII Corps H.T.M. Bty.

28. Coy. disembkd. at le Havre on 17/3/17, and joined Div. at Carnoy on 23/3/17.

29. Coy. was formed in the Div. by 30/6/17.

30. Bn. served in 23rd Bde., 8th Div., from Oct., 1914, until Feb., 1918; and on 3/2/18 Bn. was transferred to and joined 59th Bde., 20th Div.

31. Bn. was formed on 15/3/18, and consisted of 59th, 60th, 61st, and 217th M.G. Cos.

20TH (LIGHT) DIVISION

FORMATION, BATTLES, AND ENGAGEMENTS

This New Army Division had no existence before the outbreak of the Great War.

Army Order No. 382 of the 11th September 1914 authorized the further addition of six divisions (15th–20th) and Army Troops to the Regular Army (see Appendix I). This augmentation formed the Second New Army, and during September, 1914 the 20th (Light) Division, the junior division of the Second New Army, began to assemble in the Aldershot area.

At first the infantry brigades formed at Blackdown, Deepcut, and Cowshott Camp ; and all units encountered the usual difficulties which were eventually overcome by goodwill and keenness. The divisional artillery was started by sending to Deepcut two officers and two drafts of nearly 2,000 men each. The available artillery accommodation, which had been built for two brigades with a total peace-time strength of 700, was strained to its utmost : rooms originally intended for 20 men had now to accommodate about 50. By December, in the Artillery, the men were clothed partly in full dress blue uniforms, partly in canvas suits, and partly in shoddy thin blue suits. By this time a few horses had also arrived, and the available saddlery was made up of civilian-pattern snaffles, regulation bridles, hunting saddles, and colonial saddles. Each artillery brigade also possessed enough harness for one six-horse team, and each brigade also had 4 guns (2 French 90 m/m. and 2, 15-pdrs.) but no sights. In February 1915 twelve old 18-pdr. Q.F.s arrived from India and each 18-pdr. battery received one gun, henceforward proudly known as " our battery's gun."

Later on in February 1915 the Division moved to Witley, Godalming, and Guildford ; but part of the divisional artillery had to go by train as there was not enough harness to move all the vehicles. The issue of khaki now began, additional horses and harness arrived, and the divisional ammunition column was completed with mules.

In April 1915 the Division marched to Salisbury Plain, covering the 63 miles in four days. On arrival the artillery drew its remaining harness, and modern 18-pdr. Q.F. equipments were received ; but it was somewhat later before the 4·5″ howitzer equipments were issued. From the outset the 4·5″ howitzers were equipped with No. 7 dial sights, whereas until July 1916 there were only No. 1 dial sights for the division's 18-pdrs. In June all the batteries went to gun-practice. The training for war was now nearing its final stage.

On the 24th June H.M. The King inspected the 20th Division on Knighton Down. Embarkation for France began on the 20th July and by the afternoon of the 26th July the Division completed its concentration in the area to the west of St. Omer. For the remainder of the Great War the 20th Division served on the Western Front in France and Belgium and was engaged in the following operations :—

1915

25 September ... ... **Attack towards Fromelles** [III Corps, First Army].

1916

2–13 June ... ... **Battle of Mount Sorrel** [XIV Corps, Second Army].

BATTLES OF THE SOMME

21 Aug.–3 Sept. ... ... **Battle of Delville Wood** [XIV Corps, Fourth Army].
3–5 September ... ... **Battle of Guillemont** [XIV Corps, Fourth Army].
16–20 September ... **Battle of Flers-Courcelette** [XIV Corps, Fourth Army].
27 September ... ... **Battle of Morval** [XIV Corps, Fourth Army].
1–8 October... ... ... **Battle of the Transloy Ridges** [XIV Corps, Fourth Army].

1917

14 March–5 April	...	**German Retreat to the Hindenburg Line** [XIV Corps, until 2 p.m., 25/3 ; then XV Corps, Fourth Army].
26 May–16 June ...	...	**Actions on the Hindenburg Line** [IV Corps, Fifth Army, until 10 a.m., 31/5 ; then Third Army].

BATTLES OF YPRES

16–18 August	... ...	**Battle of Langemarck** [XIV Corps, Fifth Army].
20–25 September	...	**Battle of Menin Road Ridge** [XIV Corps, Fifth Army].
26–28 September	...	**Battle of Polygon Wood** [XIV Corps, Fifth Army].

BATTLE OF CAMBRAI

20 and 21 November ...		**The Tank Attack** [III Corps, Third Army].
23–28 November...	...	**Capture of Bourlon Wood** [III Corps, Third Army].
30 Nov.–2 Dec.	...	**German Counter-Attacks** [III Corps, Third Army].

1918

22 March–2 April	...	**FIRST BATTLES OF THE SOMME.**
22 and 23 March...	...	**Battle of St. Quentin** [XVIII Corps, Fifth Army].
24 and 25 March...	...	**Actions at the Somme Crossings** [XVIII Corps, Fifth Army].
26 and 27 March...	...	**Battle of Rosières** [XVIII Corps, Fifth Army].

THE ADVANCE TO VICTORY

2–6 October...	... ...	**The Final Advance in Artois** [VIII Corps, Fifth Army].

At 6 p.m. on the 6th October the 12th Division relieved the 20th Division in the front line and the 20th Division spent the remainder of the month training in the Monchy Breton area. On the 31st October the 20th Division moved to the Cambrai area and was transferred to XVII Corps, Third Army. On the 1st November the divisional artillery (XCI and XCII Brigades) went into action to support the 19th Division ; and on the 10th November the 60th Infantry Bde. relieved two brigades of 24th Division (VI Corps, Third Army), and the 60th Brigade remained in the front line on the Maubeuge–Mons road until the Armistice brought hostilities to a close at 11 a.m. on the 11th November. At this time 20th Division headquarters and the 61st Brigade had reached Feignies, midway between Bavai and Maubeuge ; and at 4 p.m. on the 11th the 20th Division relieved the 24th in the front line.

On the 23rd November the 20th Division began to move back through Cambrai to the Toutencourt–Marieux area, and by the 2nd December the move was completed. The remainder of December was spent in training, education, recreation, and in preparing for demobilization.

On the 7th January 1919 the first party (6 officers and 74 other ranks) left the Division for demobilization ; by the end of the month the Division had lost 85 more officers, and 2,702 more men from this cause, and during February an additional 74 officers and 2,691 other ranks left to be demobilized. Thus the Division shrank. On the 11th April the command of the skeleton of the division devolved on a lieutenant-colonel. On the 28th May the cadre of divisional headquarters left for England and the war story of the 20th (Light) Division came to an end. During the Great War the 20th Division lost 35,470 killed, wounded, and missing.

H*

21ST DIVISION

G.O.C.

16 September, 1914	Lieut.-General Sir E. T. H. HUTTON.
11 April, 1915	Major-General G. T. FORESTIER-WALKER.
18 November, 1915	Major-General C. W. JACOB
	(wounded, 4/3/16).
4 March, 1916	Br.-Gen. G. M. GLOSTER (acting).
1 April, 1916	Major-General C. W. JACOB.
22 May, 1916	Major-General D. G. M. CAMPBELL.

G.S.O. 1.

19 Sept., 1914...Captain L. W. G. BUTLER
(acting).
29 Mar., 1915...Lt.-Col. F. CUNLIFFE
OWEN.
18 June, 1915...Lt.-Col. T. F. FREMANTLE
(tempy.).
21 June, 1915...Lt.-Col. F. CUNLIFFE
OWEN.
5 July, 1915...Major D. FORSTER
(acting).
16 Aug., 1915...Lt.-Col. F. E. LL. DANIELL
(killed, 4/3/16).
4 Mar., 1916...Major D. FORSTER
(acting).
7 Mar., 1916...Lt.-Col. A. T. PALEY.
17 Oct., 1917...Lt.-Col. H. E. FRANKLYN.

A.-A. and Q.-M.-G.

18 Sept., 1914...Major H. W. W. WOOD
(acting).
13 Oct., 1914...Colonel R. H. D. THRING.
12 Oct., 1915...Lt.-Col. F. H. DANSEY.
21 Nov., 1915...Major H. J.
PACK-BERESFORD (acting).
28 Nov., 1915...Lt.-Col. G. J.
ACLAND-TROYTE.

B.-G., R.A.

9 Nov., 1914...Br.-Gen. C. H.
ALEXANDER.
6 Oct., 1915...Br.-Gen. R. A. C.
WELLESLEY.
12 May, 1917...Br.-Gen. F. POTTS
(tempy.).
13 May, 1917...Br.-Gen. H. W. NEWCOME.
30 Oct., 1918...Lt.-Col. H. A. BOYD
(acting).
10 Nov., 1918...Br.-Gen. W. B. BROWELL.

C.R.E.

13 Oct., 1914...Colonel H. F. CHESNEY
(sick, 1/6/15).
1 June, 1915...Major C. COFFIN (acting).
9 June, 1915...Lt.-Col. C. COFFIN.
9 Jan., 1917...Major H. J. COUCHMAN
(acting).
16 Jan., 1917...Lt.-Col. G. H. ADDISON.
19 July, 1918...Lt.-Col. G. MASTER.

62nd BDE.

18 Sept., '14...Br.-Gen. T. G. L. H.
ARMSTRONG.
4 Sept., '15...Br.-Gen. E. B. WILKINSON.
11 June, '16...Lt.-Col. H. B. WARWICK
(acting).
13 June, '16...Br.-Gen. C. G. RAWLING
(killed, 28/10/17).
28 Oct., '17...Captain G. M. SHARPE
(acting).
1 Nov., '17...Br.-Gen. G. H. GATER.

63rd BDE.

18 Sept., '14...Br.-Gen. G. J. FITZ M.
SOADY (sick, 26/6/15).
26 June, '15...Col. A. L. LINDESAY(acting).
31 Aug., '15...Br.-Gen. N. T. NICKALLS
(killed, 26/9/15).
27 Sept., '15...Lt.-Col. E. R. HILL
(tempy.).
7 Oct., '15...Br.-Gen. E. R. HILL.
(Bde. was transferred and joined 37th
Div. on 8/7/16.)

64th BDE.

18 Sept., '14...Br.-Gen. H. S. FITZGERALD.
30 July, '15...Lt.-Col. R. A. SMITH
(acting).
18 Aug., '15...Br.-Gen. G. M. GLOSTER.
5 Mar., '16...Lt.-Col. J. L. J. CLARKE
(acting).
18 Mar., '16...Lt.-Col. C. COFFIN (acting).
31 Mar., '16...Br.-Gen. G. M. GLOSTER.
13 June, '16...Br.-Gen. H. R. HEADLAM.
28 July, '18...Br.-Gen. A. J. McCULLOCH
(wounded, 24/8/18).
24 Aug., '18...Lt.-Col. C. E. R.
HOLROYD-SMYTH (acting).
28 Aug., '18...Br.-Gen. C. V. EDWARDS.

110th BDE.

(Bde. joined from 37th Div. on 7/7/16.)

[9 June, '16]..Br.-Gen. W. F. HESSEY.
20 June, '17...Lt.-Col. W. N. STEWART
(acting).
22 July, '17...Br.-Gen. LORD LOCH
(sick, 4/1/18).
4 Jan., '18...Lt.-Col. W. N. STEWART
(acting).
4 Jan., '18...Br.-Gen. D. E. CAYLEY.
16 Mar., '18...Br.-Gen. H. R. CUMMING.

GENERAL NOTES

The following Units also served with the 21st Division :—

ARTILLERY :—533 (H.) Bty., R.F.A. (4, 4·5″ hows.), landed at le Havre on 6/10/16 and joined XCVI Bde. on 22/10/16 (see note 28).

21st Heavy Battery (4, 60-pdrs.), was raised for the 21st Div., but the Heavy Battery went to France independently. The Heavy Battery went to France with XXII Heavy Artillery Bde. and disembkd. at le Havre on 21/8/15. The Heavy Battery served on the Western Front for the remainder of the Great War.

W Medium Trench Mortar Bty., served with the 21st Division from May–August, 1916.

INFANTRY :—3/4/Queen's, served in England from Oct., 1914–May, 1917, with 200th Bde., 67th Div. On 1/6/17 Bn. disembkd. at le Havre, joined S. African Bde., 9th Div., on 6/6/17, was transferred to 12th Div. on 23/7/17, and on 9/8/17 Bn. joined 62nd Bde., 21st Div. By 11/2/18 the Bn. was disbanded ; a draft of 10 offrs. and 184 o.r. left on 3/2/18 to join 7/Queen's (55th Bde., 18th Div.), the transport was sent to the 8th Div., and on 11/2/18 Bn. Hd. Qrs. was disbanded and the Bn. ceased to exist.

2/S. Lanc., served with 7th Bde., 3rd Div., from August, 1914–October, 1915. On 18/10/15 the Bn. was transferred (with 7th Bde.) to 25th Div., and Bn. was posted to 75th Bde., 25th Div., on 26/10/15. On 21/6/18 Bn. joined 64th Bde., 21st Div., and Bn. served with 64th Bde. until 30/6/18 when the Bn. left to join 89th Bde., 30th Div.

OTHER UNITS :—38th Sanitary Section, joined 21st Div. in England, went to France with the Div., and disembkd. at le Havre on 12/9/15. The Sanitary Section was transferred on 1/4/17 from 21st Div. to Army Troops, Third Army.

21st Division Motor Ambce. Workshop, left Avonmouth on 8/9/15 and disembkd. at Rouen. The Workshop joined 21st Div. in France by 13/9/15. The Workshop was abolished by April 1916, and the personnel and vehicles were transferred to 21st Div. Supply Column.

On 13/2/18 the reorganization of the 21st Division on a 9-battalion basis was completed ; and on 22/2/18 the pioneer battalion (14/N.F.) was reorganized on a 3-company basis.

The following composite Forces were formed by the 21st Division during the German Offensive in March, 1918 :—

(i) **Br.-Gen. H. R. Headlam's Force** (composite Bns. from 62nd, 64th, and 110th Bdes., and a composite M.G. Coy.—1,500 with 8 Vickers Machine Guns) served with 35th Div. from 1 p.m., 25/3, and then under 3rd Aus. Div. from 6 p.m., 28/3–31/3/18, when the Force rejoined 21st Div. ;

(ii) **Br.-Gen. H. R. Cumming's Force** (elements of 62nd, 64th, and 110th Bdes.) served with 35th Div. from 4 p.m., 24/3, and then under 3rd Aus. Div. from 12.10 a.m., 27/3–28/3/18, when the Force rejoined 21st Div. ;

(iii) **Lt.-Col. A. J. McCulloch's Force** (composite Bn., organized from parties of 62nd, 64th, and 110th Bdes., and 14/N.F., Pioneers) served with 35th Div. from 5 a.m., 26/3–30/3/18, when the Force rejoined 21st Div. ;

(iv) **Br.-Gen. G. H. Gater's Force** (composite Bns. from 62nd, 64th, and 110th Bdes., with 66 Lewis Guns of 4th Tank Bde.) was formed on 28/3, and served with 3rd Aus. Div. on 29 and 30/3/18 ; the Force then rejoined 21st Div.

During the **Battle of the Aisne, 1918,** the 21st Division, on 31/5/18, formed an **Independent Brigade** under **Br.-Gen. G. H. Gater.** This Brigade consisted of composite Bns. from 62nd, 64th, and 110th Bdes.—1,200 rifles—with 1 Comp. Fd. Coy., 1 Pioneer Coy., 63rd Fd. Ambce., and No. 2 Coy., Divnl. Train. On 1/6/18 Gater's Bde. moved forward and on 2/6/18 the Bde. occupied the line south of the Marne between Dormans and Verneuil under the Fifth (French) Army. On 19/6/18 Gater's Bde. rejoined 21st Division in the Abbeville area (south of the Somme).

| Dates | INFANTRY | | | ARTILLERY | | | | | | Engineers | Signal Service | Pioneers | M.G. Units | Field Ambulances | Mobile Vety. Secn. | Divnl. Emplnt. Coy. | Divnl. Train |
	Brigades	Battalions and attached Units	Mounted Troops	Field Artillery — Brigades	Batteries	Bde. Ammn. Colns.	Trench Mortar Bties. Medium	Heavy	Divnl. Ammn. Coln.	Field Cos.	Divnl. Signal Coy.						
1914 October (England)	62nd ...... 63rd 64th	12/N.F., 13/N.F., 8/E. York., 10/Gr. How. 14/Linc.,¹ 8/Linc,12/W. York., 10/Y & L. 9/K.O.Y.L.I., 10/K.O.Y.L.I., 14/D.L.I., 15/D.L.I.	21st Div. Cyclist Coy.²	XCIV³ .... XCV³ .... XCVI³ .... XCVII (H.)³	A, B, C, D A, B, C, D A, B, C, D A (H.), B (H.), C (H.), D (H.)	XCIV B.A.C. XCV B.A.C. XCVI B.A.C. XCVII (H.) B.A.C.	...	...	21st D.A.C.	85th⁴ 86th⁵	21st	...	...	63rd 64th 65th	33rd⁶	...	21st⁷
1915 September (France)	62nd ...... 63rd 64th	12/N.F., 13/N.F., 8/E. York.,⁸ 10/Gr. How. 8/Linc., 8/Som. L.I.,⁹ 12/W. York.,¹⁰ 10/Y. & L. 9/K.O.Y.L.I., 10/K.O.Y.L.I.,¹¹ 14/D.L.I., 15/D.L.I.	A Sqdn., S. Irish Horse¹² 21st Div. Cyclist Coy.¹³	XCIV¹⁴......... XCV¹⁵ .... XCVI¹⁶ .... XCVII (H.)¹⁷	A, B, C, D A, B, C, D A, B, C, D A (H.), B (H.), C (H.), D (H.)	XCIV B.A.C. XCV B.A.C. XCVI B.A.C. XCVII (H.) B.A.C.	...	...	21st D.A.C.	97th¹⁸ 98th¹⁸ 126th¹⁹	21st	14/ N.F.¹ (P.)	...	63rd 64th 65th	33rd	...	21st
1916 June (France)	62nd ...... 63rd²⁰ ... 64th	12/N.F., 13/N.F., 1/Linc.,²¹ 10/Gr. How.; 62nd Bde. M.G. Coy.,²² 62nd T.M. Bty.²³ 8/Linc., 8/Som. L.I., 4/Middx.,²⁴ 10/Y. & L.; 63rd Bde. M.G. Coy.;²² 63rd T.M. Bty. ²³ 1/E. York.,²⁵ 9/K.O.Y.L.I., 10/K.O.Y.L.I., 15/D.L.I.; 64th Bde. M.G. Coy.;²² 64th T.M. Bty.²³	...	XCIV¹⁴; ²⁶ ... XCV¹⁵; ²⁷ ... XCVI¹⁶; ²⁸ ... XCVII¹⁷; ²⁹	A, B, C; D (H.) A, B, C; D (H.) A, B, C; D (H.) A, B, C	...³¹	X.21³⁰ Y.21³⁰ Z.21³⁰	V.21³⁰	21st D.A.C.³¹	97th 98th 126th	21st	14/ N.F. (P.)	...	63rd 64th 65th	33rd	...	21st
1917 June (France)	62nd ...... 64th ...... 110th³² ...	12/N.F.,³³ 13/N.F.,³³ 1/Linc., 10/Gr. How.;³⁴ 62nd M.G. Coy.;³⁵ 62nd T.M. Bty. 1/E. York., 9/K.O.Y.L.I., 10/ K.O.Y.L.I.,³⁵ 15/D.L.I.; 64th M.G. Coy.;³⁵ 64th T.M. Bty. 6/Leic., 7/Leic., 8/Leic.,³⁵ 9/Leic.;³⁵ 110th M.G. Coy.;³⁵ 110th T.M. Bty.	...	XCIV²⁶ .... XCV²⁷	A, B, C; D (H.) A, B, C; D (H.)	...	X.21 Y.21 Z.21³⁷	V.21³⁸	21st D.A.C.	97th 98th 126th	21st	14/ N.F. (P.)	237th M.G. Coy.³⁹	63rd 64th 65th	33rd	222nd⁴⁰	21st
1918 March (France)	62nd ...... 64th ...... 110th ...	12/13/N.F.,³³ 1/Linc.,⁴¹ 62nd T.M. Bty. 1/E. York., 9/K.O.Y.L.I., 15/ D.L.I.; 64th T.M. Bty. 6/Leic., 7/Leic., 8/Leic.;⁴² 110th T.M. Bty.	...	XCIV .... XCV	A, B, C; D (H.) A, B, C; D (H.)	...	X.21 Y.21	...	21st D.A.C.	97th 98th 126th	21st	14/ N.F. (P.)	No. 21 Bn.., M.G.C.⁴³	63rd 64th 65th	33rd	222nd	21st

1918 July (France)				XCIV XCV	...	X.21 Y.21	...	21st D.A.C.	97th 98th 126th	21st	14/ N.F. (P.)	No. 21 Bn. M.G.C.	63rd 64th 65th	33rd	222nd	21st
62nd......	12/13/N.F.; 62nd T.M. Bty.			A, B, C; D (H.)												
64th......	1/E. York, 9/K.O.Y.L.I., 15/D.L.I.; 64th T.M. Bty.			A, B, C, D (H.)												
110th......	6/Leic., 7/Leic., 1/Wilts.; 44 110th T.M. Bty.															

NOTES

1 In Jany., 1915, Bn. (of 63rd Bde.) was converted into the divnl. pioneer battalion.

2 Coy. was formed in Feb., 1915, and billeted in Aston Clinton.

3 In Jany., 1915, the Bdes. were organized as 4-battery brigades; the Btles. were 4-gun batteries, and were lettered—A, B, C, D—in each brigade.

4 In Jany., 1915, the Coy. was transferred to 10th (Irish) Div.

5 On 7/2/15 the Coy. was transferred to 11th (Northern) Div.

6 Joined Div. in England in 1915.

7 Train consisted of 182, 183, 184, and 185 Cos., A.S.C.

8 On 15/11/15 Bn. left the Div. and joined 8th Bde., 3rd Div. on 16/11/15. On 17/2/18 Bn. amalgamated with 12/W. York. (9th Bde.) and formed 10/Entg. Bn.

9 Early in 1915 Bn. joined 63rd Bde. and took the place of 14/N.F. (converted into Divnl. Pioneer Bn.—see note 1).

10 On 15/11/15 Bn. left the Div. and joined 9th Bde., 3rd Div., on 16/11/15. On 17/2/18 Bn. amalgamated with 8/E. York. (8th Bde.) and formed 10/Entg. Bn.

11 Bn. left 8th Bde., 3rd Div., and joined 18th Bde., 6th Div., on 28/11/15. The Bn. was disbanded on 1/2/18.

12 The Sqdn. joined Div. in England and disembkd. at le Havre on 12/9/15. On 9/5/16 the Sqdn. left 21st Div. and joined XV Corps Cav. Regt. on 11/5/16.

13 Coy. disembkd. at le Havre on 10/9/15. On 10/5/16 the Coy. left 21st Div. and joined XV Corps Cyclist Bn. on 11/5/16.

14 On 20/5/16 B/XCIV left and became B/XCVII; D/XCIV became B/XCIV'; and B(H.)/XCVII joined and became D(H.)/XCIV.

15 On 20/5/16 A/XCV left and became A/XCVII; D/XCV became A/XCV; and A(H.)/XCVII joined and became D (H.)/XCV.

16 On 15/5/16 C/XCVI left and became C/XCVII; D/XCVI became C/XCVI; and C (H.)/XCVII joined and became D (H.)/XCVI.

17 On Sunday, 5/12/15, D (H.)/CXXXXI. left and joined 2nd Cdn. Div. and became A (H.)/CXXXXI. Between 15-20/5/16 the Bde. was reorganized : A (H.), B (H.), and C (H.) left and became D (H.)/XCV, D (H.)/XCIV, and D (H.)/XCVI.; and A/XCV, B/XCIV, and C/XCVI joined and became A, B, and C/XCVII.

18 On 30/1/15, 97th and 98th Fd. Cos. joined at Cheshan from 30th Div., to replace 85th and 88th Fd. Cos. (notes 4 and 5).

19 126th Fd. Coy. joined the Div. at Chesham in March, 1915.

20 63rd Bde. was transferred complete and joined 37th Div. on 8/7/16.

21 Bn. left 9th Bde., 3rd Div., on 13/11/15 and joined 62nd Bde. on 14/11/15.

22 M.G. Cos. joined as follows:—
62nd left Grantham on 23/2/16, disembkd. at le Havre on 2/3/16, and joined Div. at Armentières on 4/3/16;
63rd disembkd. at le Havre on 2/3/16, and joined Div. at Armentières on 4/3/16;
64th left Grantham on 24/2/16, disembkd. at le Havre on 25/2/16, and joined Div. at Armentières on 4/3/16.

23 T.M. Btles. were formed as follows :—
62nd—62/1 by 20/3/16, 62/2 by 28/3/16, and they became 62nd T.M. Bty. by 16/6/16;
63rd—63/1 on 17/3/16, 63/2 on 28/3/16, and they became 63rd T.M. Bty. by 16/6/16;
64th—64/1 on 17/3/16, 64/2 on 28/3/16, and they became 64th T.M. Bty. by 19/6/16.

24 Bn. left 8th Bde., 3rd Div., and joined 63rd Bde. on 14/11/15.

25 Bn. left 18th Bde., 6th Div., on 26/11/15 and joined 64th Bde. on 27/11/15.

26 On 28 and 29/8/16 XCIV was reorganized : B and 1 sec. C joined from XCVII; and 1 sec. B joined A, 1 sec. B joined B and 1 sec. C joined C, making up A, B, & C/XCIV to 6, 18-pdrs. each. On 13/1/17, 1 sec. A (H.)/XCVI joined and made up D (H.)/XCIV to 6 hows.

27 On 28 and 29/8/16 XCV was reorganized : A and 1 sec. C joined from XCVII, and A/XCV was broken up; A/XCVII and 1 sec. A/XCV joined Div., and 1 sec. C/XCV joined B/XCV, and 1 sec. C/XCVII joined C/XCV, thus making up the 18-pdr. batteries to 6, 18-pdrs. each. On 13/1/17, 1 sec. A (H.)/XCVI joined and made up D (H.)/XCV to 6 hows.

28 On 29/8/16 A was split up and R. Sec. made up C and L. Sec. made up B to 6, 18-pdrs. each. On 22/10/16 533 (H.) Bty. joined the Bde. and was redesignated A (H.)/XCVI. On 13/1/17 XCVI was split up : 1 Sec. A (H.) joined D (H.)/XCIV, and 1 Sec. A (H.) joined D (H.)/XCV; B/XCVI became A/XXXVIII A.F.A. Bde.; C/XCVI became C/CVIII A.F.A. Bde., and 1 Sec. D (H.)/XCVI made up D (H.)/XXXVIII A.F.A. Bde., and 1 Sec. D (H.)/XCVI made up D (H.)/CVIII A.F.A. Bde. to 6 hows. each.

29 Between 28—31/8/16 XCVII was broken up : A/XCVII became A/XCV: 1 Sec. B made up A/XCIV, and 1 Sec. B made up B/XCIV; 1 Sec. C made up C/XCIV, and 1 Sec. C made up C/XCV.

30 The T.M. Btles. served with the Div.—
MEDIUM—X (late 42nd T.M. Bty.) and Z (late 51st T.M. Bty.) from 1/3/16, and Y (late 45th T.M. Bty.) from 13/3/16;
HEAVY—V from 1/6/16.

31 On 11/5/16 B.A.C.s were abolished and the D.A.C. was reorganized in 2 Echelons (A and B). A Echelon was organized in 3 Sections (1, 2, and 3), and each section had 3 offrs., 168 o.r., 213 horses, and 33 vehicles. B Echelon had 4 offrs., 256 o.r., 331 horses, and 47 G.S. Wagons.

32 110th Bde. was transferred complete from 37th Div. and joined 21st Div. on 7/7/18.

33 On 10/8/17 the 2 Bns. were amalgamated and became 12/13/N.F.

34 On 10/2/18 Bn. was disbanded; drafts were sent to 30th Div. (104) and to 50th Div. (281), and on 13/2/18 the surplus went to VII Corps Rft. Camp.

35 Between 8–13/2/18 Bn. was disbanded; drafts were sent to 31st Div. (52) and to 32nd Div. (420), and the surplus went to VII Corps Rft. Camp.

36 Between 8–13/2/18 Bn. was disbanded; drafts were sent to 6/Leic. (68), 7/Leic. (258), 8/Leic. (251); and to 11/Leic. (P.), in 6th Div. (169); and the surplus went to VII Corps Rft. Camp.

37 In Feb., 1918, Z was broken up between X and Y.

38 In Feb., 1918, V H.T.M. Bty. left 21st Div.

39 Coy. left Grantham on 13/7/17, disembkd. at le Havre on 14/7/17, and joined Div. on 17/7/17 at Moyenneville.

40 Coy. was formed by 30/8/17.

41 Bn. left 25th Bde., 8th Div., on 3/2/18 and joined 62nd Bde. on 4/2/18.

42 Bn. was reduced to T.C. on 28/6/18 and surplus (13 offrs. and 809 o.r.) joined 7/Leic. On 29/8/18 T.C. 8/Leic. left Div., moved to Boulogne, and on 30/6/18 joined 7th Bde., 25th Div. T.C. went to England with 25th Div. On 7/7/18 T.C. 8/Leic. left 25th Div. and became 14/Duke's at Clacton-on-Sea.

43 Bn. was formed by 24/2/18 and consisted of 62nd, 64th, 110th, and 237th M.G. Cos.

44 Bn. left 7th Bde., 25th Div., on 20/6/18 and joined 110th Bde. on 21/6/18.

21st DIVISION

FORMATION, BATTLES, AND ENGAGEMENTS

This New Army Division had no existence before the outbreak of the Great War.

On the 6th August 1914 Parliament sanctioned an increase of 500,000 all ranks to the Regular Army. The First and Second New Armies (9th–20th Divisions) were formed from the first two hundred thousand men raised for this purpose. The formation of the divisions of the Third New Army, from the third augmentation of a hundred thousand men, was authorized by Army Order No. 388 of the 13th September, 1914 (see Appendix I). Six more divisions (21st–26th) and Army Troops were now added to the Regular Army, and during September 1914 the 21st Division, the senior division of the Third New Army, began to assemble in the neighbourhood of Tring.

The 21st Division was collected in billets and then went into camp at Halton Park. Mud and rain, however, brought about a return to billets before the end of November 1914, and the Division was then quartered in Tring, Aylesbury, Leighton Buzzard, High Wycombe, and Maidenhead ; the artillery was in High Wycombe and Berkhamsted ; the engineers were at Chesham, and the Train was at Dunstable.

In May 1915 the infantry was concentrated in hutments at Halton, the artillery was at Aston Clinton (with one brigade at Berkhamsted), and the engineers were at Wendover. Towards the end of June service rifles were received and the general course of musketry began. In July the artillery and engineers moved to the Aldershot area ; and on the 9th August, the musketry being completed, the infantry began moving from Halton to Witley Camp. On the 12th August, whilst the infantry and signal company were on the march, the columns were inspected by Field-Marshal Earl Kitchener. Towards the end of August the artillery went to Larkhill for gun-practice, and shortly afterwards the 21st Division received orders that it was to move to France. The first advanced party left on the 2nd September, the troops began to entrain on the 7th, and by the 13th September the Division was concentrated in the Tilques area (west of St. Omer). For the remainder of the Great War the 21st Division served on the Western Front in France and Belgium and was engaged in the following operations :—

1915

25 and 26 September ... **Battle of Loos** [XI Corps, First Army].

1916

BATTLES OF THE SOMME

1–3 ; and 11–13 July... **Battle of Albert** [XV Corps, Fourth Army].
14–17 July ... ... **Battle of Bazentin Ridge** [XV Corps, Fourth Army].
17–22 September ... **Battle of Flers-Courcelette** [XV Corps, Fourth Army].
25–28 September ... **Battle of Morval** [XV Corps, Fourth Army].
26 September ... ... **Capture of Gueudecourt.**
1 October ... ... **Battle of the Transloy Ridges** [XV Corps, Fourth Army].

1917

29 March–5 April ... **German Retreat to the Hindenburg Line** [VII Corps, Third Army].
BATTLES OF ARRAS
9–14 April ... ... **First Battle of the Scarpe** [VII Corps, Third Army].
3 and 4 May ... ... **Third Battle of the Scarpe** [VII Corps, Third Army].

31 May–16 June ... ... **Actions on the Hindenburg Line** [VII Corps, Third Army].
BATTLES OF YPRES
29 Sept.–3 Oct. ... ... **Battle of Polygon Wood** [X Corps, Second Army].
4 October ... ... **Battle of Broodseinde** [X Corps, Second Army].
26 Oct.–10 Nov. ... ... **Second Battle of Passchendaele** [X Corps, Second Army].
BATTLE OF CAMBRAI
2 and 3 December ... **German Counter-Attacks** [VII Corps, Third Army].

1918

FIRST BATTLES OF THE SOMME

21–23 March	**Battle of St. Quentin** [VII Corps, Fifth Army].
24 March	**First Battle of Bapaume** [VII Corps, Fifth Army, until 4 a.m., 25/3 ; then Third Army].*

BATTLES OF THE LYS**

10 and 11 April	**Battle of Messines** (62nd Bde., under 9th Div.) [IX Corps, Second Army].
13–15 April	**Battle of Bailleul** (62nd Bde., under 9th Div.) [XXII Corps, Second Army].
17–19 April	**First Battle of Kemmel Ridge** [XXII Corps, Second Army].
25 and 26 April	**Second Battle of Kemmel Ridge** [XXII Corps, Second Army].
29 April	**Battle of the Scherpenberg** [XXII Corps, Second Army].
27–30 May	**Battle of the Aisne** [IX Corps, Sixth (French) Army, until 29/5 ; then Fifth (French) Army].***

THE ADVANCE TO VICTORY
SECOND BATTLES OF THE SOMME

21–23 August	**Battle of Albert** [V Corps, Third Army].
31 Aug.–2 Sept.	**Second Battle of Bapaume** [V Corps, Third Army].

BATTLES OF THE HINDENBURG LINE

18 September	**Battle of Epéhy** [V Corps, Third Army].
29 Sept.–2 Oct.	**Battle of St. Quentin Canal** [V Corps, Third Army].
8 October	**Battle of Cambrai** [V Corps, Third Army].

THE FINAL ADVANCE IN PICARDY

23–25 October	**Battle of the Selle** [V Corps, Third Army].

During the night of the 26th/27th October the Division was relieved in the front line. On the 29th, after some reorganization, the 21st Division took over the Left Sector of the V Corps front until the 3rd November. On the 5th November the Division once more went into the front line and took part in the Second Phase of the V Corps operations : the 21st Division attacked and captured Berlaimont (5th), forced the crossing of the Sambre, near Aulnoye (6th), pushed on towards the Maubeuge–Avesnes road, and reached Eclaibes (7th). The Division was then relieved in the front line ; it retired to Berlaimont in the Sambre valley to rest and reorganize. The Division was still halted around Berlaimont when the Armistice brought hostilities to a close at 11 a.m. on the 11th November.

On the 12th November the leading troops of the Division moved to Beaufort (east of the Maubeuge–Avesnes road), and the rest of the month was employed in training and recreation. Between the 12th–20th December the Division moved back to the south of the Somme (west of Amiens), and spent the remainder of the month in education, recreation, and demobilization.

Between the 12th and 29th January 1919 over 200 men a day went home for demobilization ; and in February 2,723 all ranks and 976 horses left. During March 763 all ranks and 1,173 animals were demobilized, and 16 officers and 790 other ranks were drafted to various units in the Army of Occupation. On the 1st April the remainder of the Division was collected around Longpré, on the 6th the first cadre of a unit left the Division to entrain for the Base, on the 29th the command of the Division devolved on a lieutenant-colonel, and on the 19th May the 21st Division ceased to exist in France. During the Great War the 21st Division lost 55,581 killed, wounded, and missing.

---

* See General Notes for Headlam's, Cumming's, McCulloch's, and Gater's Forces.

** During the Battles of the Lys the following formations were attached to and served with the 21st Division: 39th Div. Comp. Bde. (5,000, under Br.-Gen. A. B. Hubback), 10/4–1/5/18 ; 146th Bde. (49th Div.), 10–19/4/18 ; 21st Bde. (30th Div.), 20/4–2/5/18 ; 89th Bde. (30th Div.), 25/4–2/5/18 ; and 58th Bde. (19th Div.), 28–30/4/18.

*** See General Notes for Gater's Independent Brigade.

22ND DIVISION

G.O.C.

17 September, 1914 ... ... Major-General R. A. MONTGOMERY.
17 June, 1915 ... ... Major-General Hon. F. GORDON
(sick, 7/5/17).
7 May, 1917 ... ... Br.-Gen. J. DUNCAN (tempy.).
24 June, 1917 ... ... Major-General J. DUNCAN.

G.S.O. 1.

18 Sept., 1914...Colonel H. W. G. GRAHAM.
3 Mar., 1915...Captain W. J. MAXWELL
SCOTT (acting).
12 April, 1915...Lt.-Col. H. E. GOGARTY
(sick, 25/10/15).
25 Oct., 1915...Lt.-Col. W. J. MAXWELL
SCOTT.
3 Aug., 1917...Major K. M. LAIRD
(tempy.).
13 Aug., 1917...Lt.-Col. T. G.
GAYER-ANDERSON.

A.-A. and Q.-M.-G.

17 Sept., 1914...Colonel C. W. MUIR.
24 Oct., 1915...Lt.-Col. A. F. STEWART.
11 Dec., 1916...Lt.-Col. H. C. W. H.
WORTHAM.

B.-G., R.A.

31 Oct., 1914...Br.-Gen. J. W. HAWKINS.
29 June, 1915...Br.-Gen. A. W. GAY.
19 Jan., 1916...Colonel G. H. BITTLESTON
(acting).
16 Feb., 1916...Br.-Gen. S. D. BROWNE.
6 Sept., 1916...Lt.-Col. A. G. ARBUTHNOT
(acting).
9 Sept., 1916...Br.-Gen. H. H. BOND
(Acting B.-G., R.A.,
XII Corps on 27/9/17).
27 Sept., 1917...Lt.-Col. C. MacI. RITCHIE
(acting).
5 Nov., 1917...Br.-Gen. H. H. BOND.
3 July, 1918...Br.-Gen. H. E. CAREY.

C.R.E.

17 Oct., 1914...Colonel J. A. TANNER.
7 Oct., 1915...Major H. L. G. BELL
(acting).
11 Oct., 1915...Lt.-Col. D. M.F. HOYSTED
(sick, 12/5/17).
12 May, 1917...Major H. L. G. BELL
(acting).
4 July, 1917...Lt.-Col. P. G. FRY.

65th BDE.

23 Sept., '14...Br.-Gen. F. W. J.
                 CAULFEILD.
 8 June, '15...Br.-Gen. L. N. HERBERT.
19 Oct., '16...Lt.-Col. W. J. LAMBERT
                 (acting).
28 Oct., '16...Colonel W. L. ROCKE
                 (acting).
18 Nov., '16...Br.-Gen. G. E. BAYLEY.
23 April, '18...Lt.-Col. B. J. MAJENDIE
                 (tempy.).
29 May, '18...Br.-Gen. B. J. MAJENDIE.

66th BDE.

30 Sept., '14...Br.-Gen. C. P. RIDLEY.
 5 July, '15...Br.-Gen. H. O. D. HICKMAN
                (sick, 6/11/16).
 6 Nov., '16...Lt.-Col. J. D. B. ERSKINE
                (acting).
15 Nov., '16...Br.-Gen. F. S.
              MONTAGUE-BATES.

67th BDE.

19 Sept., '14...Br.-Gen. R. B. WILLIAMS.
16 June, '15...Br.-Gen. E. S. HEARD.
23 Oct., '15...Br.-Gen. A. MARTYN (sick, 17/12/15).
17 Dec., '15...Lt.-Col. H. F. COOKE (tempy.).
17 Jan., '16...Br.-Gen. H. F. COOKE.
 3 Sept., '17...Br.-Gen. A. D. MACPHERSON.

GENERAL NOTES

The following Units also served with the 22nd Division :—

ARTILLERY :—22nd Heavy Battery, R.G.A. (4, 60-pdrs.), was raised for the 22nd Division, but the Heavy Battery went abroad independently. The Heavy Battery mobilized at Woolwich on 20/8/15, embkd. at Southampton on 31/8/15, disembkd. at le Havre on 1/9/15, and on 5/9/15 the Heavy Battery joined XXII Hy. Arty. Bde. For the remainder of the Great War the 22nd Heavy Battery served on the Western Front.

INFANTRY :—10/Hants. (from 82nd Bde., 27th Div.) joined 22nd Div. on 15/1/19. After the 22nd Div. had been broken up 10/Hants. joined 85th Bde., 28th Div.

2/Q.V.O. Rajput L.I. (from 51st Ind. Inf. Bde., 17th Ind. Div., in Mesopotamia) joined 22nd Div. on 20/1/19. Bn. left 22nd Div. on 1/2/19 for 27th Div. ; and later on Bn. joined 84th Bde., 28th Div.

1/10/Jats (from 55th Ind. Inf. Bde., 18th Ind. Div., in Mesopotamia) joined 22nd Div. on 21/1/19. Bn. left 22nd Div. on 31/1/19 and moved to Uchantar. Bn. embkd. at Salonika on 17/2/19, disembkd. at Batum on 21/2/19, joined 80th Bde., 27th Div., and on 29/8/19 Bn. was transferred to 84th Bde., 28th Div.

95/Russell's Inf. (from 56th Ind. Inf. Bde., attached to 15th Ind. Div., in Mesopotamia) joined 22nd Div. on 22/1/19. Bn. left 22nd Div. on 19/2/19 for the Base, and Bn. then joined 83rd Bde., 28th Div.

OTHER UNITS :—39th Sanitary Section, went to France with the 22nd Div. in September 1915, embkd. at Marseille on 30/10/15, and went to Macedonia with the Div. 39th Sanitary Section served with the 22nd Div. in Macedonia for the remainder of the Great War.

22nd Division Motor Ambce. Workshop, went to France with the 22nd Div. in September 1915. The Workshop was left behind in France when the 22nd Div. went to Macedonia in October 1915.

On 2/7/18 the reorganization of the 22nd Division on a 9-battalion basis was completed. The Pioneer Bn. (9/Border) remained a 4-company organization.

22ND DIVISION

Dates	INFANTRY — Brigades	INFANTRY — Battalions and attached Units	Mounted Troops	ARTILLERY — Field Artillery — Brigades	ARTILLERY — Field Artillery — Batteries	ARTILLERY — Field Artillery — Bde. Ammn. Colns.	Trench Mortar Bties. — Medium	Trench Mortar Bties. — Heavy	Divnl. Ammn. Coln.	Engineers — Field Cos.	Signal Service — Divnl. Signal Coy.	Pioneers	M.G. Units	Field Ambulances	Mobile Vety. Secn.	Divnl. Emplnt. Coy.	Divnl. Train
1914 October (England)	65th	9/K.O., 14/King's, 12/L.F.	22nd Div. Cyclist Coy.[2]	XCVIII[3]	A, B, C, D	XCVIII B.A.C.	...		22nd D.A.C.	87th[4] 88th[5]	22nd	9/Bord.[6] (P.)	...	66th 67th 68th	34th[7]	...	22nd[8]
	66th	9/E. Lanc.,[1] 9/S. Lanc., 8/		XCIX[3]	A, B, C, D	XCIX B.A.C.											
	67th	12/Ches., K.S.L.I., 13/Manch. 11/R.W.F., 7/S.W.B., 11/Welsh		C[3] CI (H.)[3]	A, B, C, D A (H.), B (H.), C (H.), D (H.)	C B.A.C. CI B.A.C.											
1915 September (France)	65th	9/K.O., 14/King's, 12/L.F.	D Sqdn.[9] 1/Lothians and Border Horse. 22nd Div. Cyclist Coy.	XCVIII	A, B, C, D	XCVIII B.A.C.	...		22nd D.A.C.	99th[10] 100th[10] 127th[11]	22nd	9/Bord. (P.)	...	66th 67th 68th	34th	...	22nd[12]
	66th	12/Ches., 9/S. Lanc., 8/ K.S.L.I., 13/Manch.		XCIX	A, B, C, D	XCIX B.A.C.											
	67th	11/R.W.F., 7/S.W.B., 11/Welsh		C CI (H.)	A, B, C, D A (H.), B (H.), C (H.), D (H.)	C B.A.C. CI B.A.C.											
1916 July (Macedonia)	65th	9/K.O., 14/King's, 12/L.F., 9/E. Lanc.; 65th Bde. M.G. Coy.;[13] 65th T.M. Bty.;[14] 65th S.A.A. Sec. Ammn. Coln.[15]	D Sqdn.[16] 1/Lothians and Border Horse. 22nd Div. Cyclist Coy.[17]	XCVIII[18]	A, B, C; D (H.)	XCVIII B.A.C.	...		22nd D.A.C.[22]	99th 100th 127th	22nd	9/Bord. (P.)	...	66th 67th 68th	34th	...	22nd[23]
	66th	12/Ches., 9/S. Lanc., 8/K.S.L.I., 13/Manch.; 66th Bde. M.G. Coy.;[13] 66th T.M. Bty.;[14] 66th S.A.A. Sec. Ammn. Coln.[15]		XCIX[19]	A, B; C; D (H.)	XCIX B.A.C.											
	67th	11/R.W.F., 7/S.W.B., 11/Welsh; 67th Bde. M.G. Coy.;[13] 67th T.M. Bty.;[14] 67th S.A.A. Sec. Ammn. Coln.[15]		C[20] CI[21]	A, B; C; D (H.)	C B.A.C. CI B.A.C.											
1917 July (Macedonia)	65th	9/K.O., 14/King's,[24] 12/L.F.,[25] 9/E. Lanc.; 65th M.G. Coy.; 65th S.A.A. Sec. Ammn. Coln.	...	XCVIII[28]	A, B; D (H.)	XCVIII B.A.C.	...		...[22]	99th 100th 127th	22nd	9/Bord. (P.)	...	66th 67th 68th	34th	816th[32]	22nd[33]
	66th	12/Ches., 9/S. Lanc., 8/ K.S.L.I., 13/Manch.;[26] 66th M.G. Coy.; 66th T.M. Bty.; 66th S.A.A. Sec. Ammn. Coln.		XCIX[29]	A, B; D (H.)	XCIX B.A.C.											
	67th	11/R.W.F., 7/S.W.B.,[27] 11/Welsh; 67th M.G. Coy.; 67th T.M. Bty.; 67th S.A.A. Sec. Ammn. Coln.		C[30] CI[31]	A, B, C; D (H.)[30] A, B; D (H.)	C B.A.C. CI B.A.C.											

1918 August (Macedonia)

		Batteries	Artillery Bde.	B.A.C.
65th	9/K.O., 8/S.W.B.,[27] 9/E. Lanc.; 65th M.G. Coy.; 65th T.M. Bty.; 65th S.A.A. Sec. Ammn. Coln.	A, B ; D (H.)	XCVIII......	XCVIII B.A.C.
66th	12/Ches., 9/S. Lanc., 8/K.S.L.I.; 66th M.G. Coy.; 66th T.M. Bty.; 66th S.A.A. Sec. Ammn. Coln.	A, B, C	XCIX	XCIX B.A.C.
			C0......	C B.A.C.
67th	11/R.W.F., 7/S.W.B., 11/Welsh; 67th M.G. Coy.; 67th T.M. Bty.; 67th S.A.A. Sec. Ammn. Coln.	A; B; D (H.)	CI	CI B.A.C.

(Column headings at head of table: 22nd · 816th · 34th · ... · 9/ Bord. (P.) · 22nd · 99th, 100th, 127th · ... · ... · ... · XCVIII B.A.C., XCIX B.A.C. · ...)

NOTES

1 Bn. (from Army Troops) joined 66th Bde. in Feb., 1915, to replace 9/Bord., and the latter became Divnl. Pioneer Bn. (see note 6).

2 Cyclist Coy. was formed in the Div. in Feb., 1915.

3 In Jany., 1915, the Bdes. were organized as 4-battery brigades, the Bties., were 4-gun batteries, and were lettered—A, B, C, D—in each Brigade.

4 In Feby., 1915, 87th Fd. Coy. was transferred to 12th Div.

5 In Jany., 1915, 88th Fd. Coy. was transferred to 13th Div.

6 Bn. left 66th Bde. in Febry., 1915, and was converted into the Pioneer Bn. Bn. was replaced in 66th Bde. by 12/Ches. (see note 1).

7 Joined Div. in England, and in Sept., 1915, went to France with the Div.

8 Train consisted of 186, 187, 188, and 189 Cos., A.S.C.

9 Joined Div. in England, and in Sept., 1915, the Sqdn. went to France with the Div.

10 In Febry., 1915, 99th and 100th Fd. Cos. joined from 31st Div., to replace 87th and 88th Fd. Cos. (see notes 4 and 5).

11 127th Fd. Coy. joined before June, 1915.

12 Train went to France with 22nd Div. in Sept., 1915; in Oct., 1915, when the Div. embkd. for Salonika, the Train remained in France and was attached to the 18th Div. on 5 and 6/11/15. On 7/11/15 the Train joined 30th Div. at Ailly le Haut Clocher, and served in France with the 30th Div. for the remainder of the Great War.

13 The 3 Bde. M.G. Cos. embkd. at Devonport on 5/7/16, disembkd. at Salonika on 14/7/16, joined the Division on 14/7/16, and were posted to the Inf. Bdes.

14 The Bde. T.M. Bties. joined as follows :—65th on 3/11/16 ; 66th on 5/11/16 ; and 67th (formed on 11/10/16) joined on 4/11/16.

15 S.A.A. Secs. were attached to Inf. Bdes. by 17/8/16.

16 Sqdn. left the Div. on 29/11/16 ; was attached to 8th Mtd. Bde. from 30/11/16—12/1/17 ; was then employed with 60th and 26th Divs., and on escorts and police duties until 11/5/17. Sqdn. then joined XII Corps Cav. Regt. (on its formation).

17 Coy. left the Div. on 11/12/16, joined XII Corps H.Q. on 12/12/16 ; and on 22/12/16 formed XII Corps Cyclist Bn., together with 26th Div. Cyclist Coy.

18 On 21/7/16 D left and became A/CI ; and A (H.)/CI joined and became D (H.)/XCVIII.

19 On 21/7/16 D left and became B/CI ; and B (H.)/CI joined and became D (H.)/XCIX.

20 On 21/7/16 C left and became C/CI ; D/C became C/C ; and C (H.)/CI joined and became D (H.)/C.

21 On 21/7/16, CI was reorganized : A (H.), B (H.), and C (H.) left and became D (H.)/XCVIII, D (H.)/XCIX, and D (H.)/C ; and D/XCVIII, D/XCIX, and C/C joined CI and became A, B, and C/CI. D (H.)/CI remained as before.

22 In Jany., 1917, the 22nd D.A.C. was abolished, and on 22/1/17 22nd D.A.C. became A Sec. in the newly formed XII Corps A.C.

23 Train (consisting of 108, 109, 110, and 111 Cos., A.S.C.) was raised as 10th Div. Train ; but when the 10th Div. went to Gallipoli in July, 1915, the Train remained in England. Eventually, allotted to the 22nd Div., the Train embkd. on the *Winifredian*, disembkd. at Salonika on 29/11/15, and joined 22nd Div. on 2 and 3/12/15. On 30/10/16 the Train was reorganized in Pack and Wheel Echelons, and 844, 845, 846, and 847 Pack Cos. joined.

24 Bn. left Div. on 11/6/18, arrived Forges les Eaux on 26/6/18, was under L. of C. (France) until 23/7/18, when Bn. joined 66th Div. On 13/8/18 Bn. was absorbed by 18/King's (Lanc. Hsrs.) in 197th Bde., 66th Div., and on 10/9/18, 18/King's was transferred to 199th Bde., 66th Div.

25 Bn. left Div. on 2/7/18, arrived Forges les Eaux on 16/7/18, was under L. of C. (France) until 22/7/18, when Bn. joined 66th Div. On 13/8/18 Bn. was absorbed by 6/L.F. in 199th Bde., 66th Div., and on 22/9/18, 6/L.F. was transferred to 198th Bde., 66th Div.

26 Bn. left Div. on 28/6/18, arrived Abancourt on 11/7/18, was under L. of C. (France) until 21/7/18, when Bn. joined 66th Div. On 13/8/18 Bn. was absorbed by 9/Manch. in 199th Bde., 66th Div.

27 On 30/6/18 Bn. was transferred to 65th Bde. (from 67th Bde.).

28 On 5/1/17 A Bty. was broken up : L. Sec. made up C to 6 guns, and R. Sec. made up B ; C Bty. then became A Bty.

29 On 5/1/17 A Bty. was broken up : L. Sec. made up C to 6 guns, and R. Sec. made up B ; C Bty. then became A Bty.

30 In Jany., 1917, C Bde. underwent no reorganization. (At the time C Bde. was being considered for conversion to Mountain Arty.) On 12/6/17 D (H.) was transferred and became D (H.)/CXIV in 26th Div. (On 10/10/17 the How. Bty. became D (H.)/LVII.) C Bde. remained three 4-gun 18-pdr. Bties.

31 On 5/1/17 A Bty. was broken up : L. Sec. made up C to 6 guns, and R. Sec. made up B ; C Bty. then became A Bty.

32 Formed by 10/10/17.

33 On 7/8/17 the Train was reorganized : 845, 846, & 847 (Pack) Cos. were broken up, and the personnel was distributed between 108, 109, 110, and 111 (Wheel) Cos. and 844 (Pack) Coy.

22ND DIVISION

FORMATION, BATTLES, AND ENGAGEMENTS

This New Army Division had no existence before the outbreak of the Great War.

Army Order No. 388 of the 13th September 1914 authorized the addition of six divisions (21st–26th) and Army Troops to the Regular Army (see Appendix I). This augmentation formed the Third New Army, and during September 1914 the 22nd Division began to assemble at Eastbourne and Seaford, with the divisional artillery at Lewes.

The units of the 22nd Division were faced with the difficulties which invariably confront all hastily raised formations. There was a serious shortage of trained officers and non-commissioned-officers to act as instructors, a complete lack of arms, and no clothing or equipment. Local purchase of articles, including clothing, was permitted ; and in this way one battalion in the 67th Brigade procured khaki uniforms and boots for its men, and so forestalled the other battalions of the Brigade by many months. Even if the shade of the clothing was slightly more brown, yet in the early days it was a great advantage to have a strong-wearing and soldierly uniform.

In October the troops moved out to camps at Seaford and remained under canvas until December. Heavy, persistent rains and high winds then necessitated a return to billets in Eastbourne. When the troops left the sodden, wind-swept camps the men were soaked to the skin, dressed in nondescript clothing, carrying blankets of every hue, and without proper equipment, and each battalion with only about sixty old drill-pattern rifles. An eye witness not inaptly described the columns as resembling a nomad tribe on the move. But the spirit of the troops was excellent and the men behaved as if they were schoolboys out for a picnic on a bright summer's day.

Until April 1915 the troops remained in billets in Eastbourne ; then the battalions went to Maidstone for a fortnight's course of entrenching, before moving into huts at Seaford. Whilst the Division was at Seaford the transport and animals arrived. On the 1st June the Division began to move to Aldershot. Arms and equipment were now completed, musketry and gun-practice were undertaken, and the final intensive training for the field was carried out.

On the 3rd September the Division began to move to France, and by the 9th September it had effected its concentration around Flesselles (north of Amiens). On the 18th September the Division took over from the French a sector of the front line astride the Amiens–St. Quentin road. The 22nd Division served on the Western Front in France until the end of October 1915 ; and it then embarked for the Macedonian Front, on which it served for the remainder of the Great War.

1915

On the 20th October, whilst it was still in front of Amiens, the Division was informed that it would be withdrawn from the front line and moved to another theatre of war, and on the 23rd October command of the 22nd Division's sector of the front line passed to the 6th (French) Division. On the 25th the Division began entraining at Longueau for Marseille, and embarkation for the Macedonian theatre started on the 27th October and continued until the 2nd November (the embarkation of the divisional artillery only began on the 19th November). The transports proceeded direct to Salonika and during November the Division completed its disembarkation at that base. (The last artillery brigade, however, only landed at Salonika on the 13th Dec.). Whilst it was in Macedonia the 22nd Division took part in the following operations :—

8–13 December ... ... **Retreat from Serbia** (Advd. D.H.Q., 65th Inf. Bde., 9/Bord. (P.), 68th Fd. Ambce.).

1916

10–18 August	**Horseshoe Hill (S.W. of Dojran)** [XII Corps].
13 and 14 September ...	**Machukovo** [XII Corps].

1917

24 and 25 April ; and ⎱ **Battle of Dojran** [XII Corps].
  8 and 9 May ... ... ⎰

1918

18 and 19 September... **Battle of Dojran** [XII Corps].

On the 21st September the enemy evacuated the main line in front of the 22nd Division, and on the 22nd September the Division advanced and occupied the line between Lake Dojran and P Ridge. On the 23rd the Division continued advancing, and on the 24th the 65th Brigade, the leading troops of the 22nd Division, reached Zeus Junction (3 miles north of Lake Dojran). Pressing forward, by the 26th September the advanced guard of the Division was under Pt. 1472 (Signal Allemand) in the angle between the Bulgaria–Greece and Bulgaria–Serbia frontiers. No further advance was made before noon on the 30th September, and the Armistice with Bulgaria then brought hostilities to a close in the Macedonian theatre of war.

On the 11th October the Division began to move back to Güvezne, and the march was continued to Stavros, which was reached between 18th–20th October. The infantry then embarked in destroyers at Stavros to proceed to Dede Agach, but the artillery, field ambulances, train, and all wheeled transport moved by road. On the arrival of the destroyers at Dede Agach it was too rough to put the infantry ashore in the available lighters, in consequence the destroyers returned to Stavros and the infantry disembarked. On the 27th October the infantry re-embarked and on the 28th made a successful landing at Dede Agach. On the 29th the Division advanced to the Maritsa and reached Makri (on the Adrianople road) ; but the Armistice with Turkey came into force at noon on the 31st October and further operations had to be abandoned.

During November the 22nd Division moved to Kavalla (16th) and then to Stavros (21st) ; here the Division remained until the 5th January 1919 when it began to move to the Sarigöl–Yanesh area, and on the 13th January divisional headquarters opened at Chugunsi. Demobilization now began. On the 27th February three battalions (9/K.O., 9/E. Lanc., 9/S. Lanc.) left to join the 28th Division, and by the end of the month the divisional artillery was reduced to cadre. On the 12th March divisional headquarters moved to Yanesh, and between 28th and 31st March the three infantry brigades were disbanded. The war history of the Division was concluded. During the Great War the 22nd Division lost 7,728 killed, wounded, and missing.

23RD DIVISION

G.O.C.

18 September, 1914	... ...	Major-General J. M. BABINGTON.
15 October, 1918	... ...	Br.-Gen. J. BYRON (acting).
20 October, 1918	... ...	Br.-Gen. H. GORDON (acting).
21 October, 1918	... ...	Major-General H. F. THUILLIER.

G.S.O. 1.

18 Sept., 1914...Major H. J.
BARTHOLOMEW (acting).
17 Feb., 1915...Captain H. J. N. DAVIS
(acting).
27 Feb., 1915...Major C. F. WATSON
(acting).
27 Mar., 1915...Colonel F. ST. D. SKINNER.
1 April, 1915...Lt.-Col. D. J. M. FASSON.
24 June, 1915...Lt.-Col. A. BLAIR.
13 Feb., 1916...Lt.-Col. C. F. WATSON.
23 Jan., 1917...Lt.-Col. C. EVANS.
28 Mar., 1918...Lt.-Col. H. R.
SANDILANDS.

A.-A. and Q.-M.-G.

12 Oct., 1914...Colonel E. W. S. K.
MACONCHY.
23 June, 1915...Captain H. N. YOUNG
(acting).
24 June, 1915...Lt.-Col. R. O. BURNE.
7 Mar., 1916...Lt.-Col. H. B. DES V.
WILKINSON (sick, 28/5/17).
28 May, 1917...Lt.-Col. E. F. FALKNER.

B.-G., R.A.

6 Nov., 1914...Col. F. B. ELMSLIE
(tempy.).
18 Nov., 1914...Br.-Gen. F. B. ELMSLIE.
24 June, 1915...Br.-Gen. D. J. M. FASSON.
15 Jan., 1917...Lt.-Col. W. A. NICHOLSON.
(acting).
18 Jan., 1917...Br.-Gen. Sir D.
ARBUTHNOT, Bt. (sick, 20/5/17).
20 May, 1917...Lt.-Col. G. BADHAM-
-THORNHILL (acting).
19 June, 1917...Br.-Gen. Sir D.
ARBUTHNOT, Bt.
28 July, 1918...Br.-Gen. J. BYRON.

C.R.E.

2 Nov., 1914...Colonel A. C. FOLEY.
9 June, 1915...Lt.-Col. P. J. J.
RADCLIFFE.
30 Sept., 1915...Lt.-Col. A. G. BREMNER.
6 Feb., 1917...Lt.-Col. E. H. ROOKE
(to XIV Corps, 28/10/18).
28 Oct., 1918...Major R. A. TURNER
(acting).
[13 Nov., 1918...Lt.-Col. E. H. ROOKE.]

68th BDE.

29 Sept., '14...Br.-Gen. G. H. OVENS.
19 Nov., '14...Br.-Gen. B. J. C. DORAN.
18 Feb., '15...Maj.-Gen. B. J. C. DORAN.
26 May, '15...Colonel G. A. ASHBY
(acting).
3 June, '15...Br.-Gen. E. PEARCE
SEROCOLD (sick, 1/2/16).
1 Feb., '16...Colonel D. S. STEWART
(acting).
8 Feb., '16...Br.-Gen. H. PAGE-CROFT.
18 Aug., '16...Br.-Gen. G. N. COLVILE.
27 Feb., '17...Maj.-Gen. Hon. A. R.
MONTAGU-STUART-WORTLEY.
31 Mar., '17...Br.-Gen. G. N. COLVILE.
27 Sept., '17...Lt.-Col. M. G. H. BARKER
(acting).
14 Oct., '17...Br.-Gen. C. D. V.
CARY-BARNARD.

69th BDE.

29 Sept., '14...Br.-Gen. F. S. DERHAM.
8 Mar., '16...Br.-Gen. T. S. LAMBERT.
25 May, '18...Lt.-Col. R. S. HART
(acting).
26 May, '18...Br.-Gen. A. B. BEAUMAN.

70th BDE.

25 Sept., '14...Br.-Gen. Sir D. A. KINLOCH, Bt.
11 Sept., '15...Br.-Gen. L. F. PHILIPS [sick, 5/11/15].*

(On 18/10/15 the Bde. was transferred for attachment to 8th Div.)

24th BDE.

(On 18/10/15 the Bde. was transferred, from the 8th Div., for attachment to 23rd Div.)

[1 Aug., '15]..Br.-Gen. R. S. OXLEY.
11 July, '16...Br.-Gen. A. J. F. EDEN.

(On 15/7/16 the Bde. left 23rd Div. and returned to 8th Div.)

70th BDE.

(On 16/7/16 the Bde. left 8th Div. and rejoined 23rd Div. on 17/7/16.)

[8 Nov., '15]*Br.-Gen. H. GORDON.
20 Oct., '18...Lt.-Col. S. L. WHATFORD.
22 Oct., '18...Br.-Gen. H. GORDON.

---

* Between 5/11/15 and 8/11/15 Lt.-Col. J. O. Travers acted as Brigade Commander.

GENERAL NOTES

The following Units also served with the 23rd Division :—

ARTILLERY :—23rd Heavy Battery, R.G.A. (4, 60-pdrs.), was raised for the 23rd Div., but the Hy. Bty. went to France independently. 23rd Heavy Battery disembkd. at le Havre on 15/9/15, and joined No. 1 Group, H.A.R. (I Corps) on 17/9/15 ; on 11/11/15 the Heavy Battery joined XXII H.A. Bde. For the remainder of the Great War the Heavy Battery served on the Western Front.

ENGINEERS :—2 Sections, 180th Tunnelling Company, R.E., were attached to the 23rd Division from 3–28/10/15.

INFANTRY :—

8/Leic., 9/Leic.,
{ Army Troops Battalions, Third New Army, were attached to the 23rd Division from 3/10/14–Thursday, 8/4/15. The two Bns. were then transferred to Southern Command and the two Bns. moved to Perham Down and joined 110th Bde., 37th Div. (On 7/7/16, 110th Bde. was transferred to 21st Division.)

9/S. Staff., Army Troops Battalion, Third New Army, was attached to the 23rd Division from 3/10/14. In April 1915 the Battalion was converted into the divisional pioneer battalion of the 23rd Division (note 17).

OTHER UNITS :—40th Sanitary Section, joined the 23rd Division on 20/8/15 at Bordon, went to France with the Div., and disembkd. at le Havre on 28/8/15. On 10/4/17 the Sanitary Section was transferred to X Corps, and the Section took over VIIA Sanitary Area in the Second Army.

23rd Division Motor Ambce. Workshop, reached Rouen on 26/8/15, left Rouen on 29/8/15, and reported to 23rd Div. at Tilques on 30/8/15. In April 1916 the Workshop was abolished and the personnel and vehicles were transferred to 23rd Div. Supply Column.

On 14/9/18 the reorganization of the 23rd Division on a 9-battalion basis was completed ; and on 11/5/18 the pioneer battalion (9/S. Staff.) was reorganized on a 3-company basis.

23RD DIVISION

Dates	Brigades	Battalions and attached Units	Mounted Troops	Brigades	Batteries	Bde. Ammn. Colns.	T.M. Bties. Medium	T.M. Bties. Heavy	Divnl. Ammn. Coln.	Field Cos.	Divnl. Signal Coy.	Pioneers	M.G. Units	Field Ambulances	Mobile Vety. Secn.	Divnl. Emplnt. Coy.	Divnl. Train
1914 October (England)	68th ...... 69th 70th	10/N.F., 11/N.F., 12/D.L.I., 13/D.L.I. 11/W. York., 8/Gr. How., 9/Gr. How., 10/Duke's. 11/Sher. For., 8/K.O.Y.L.I., 8/Y. & L., 9/Y. & L.	23rd Div. Cyclist Coy.[1]	CII[2] .... CIII[2] .... CIV[2] .... CV (H.)[2]	A, B, C, D A, B, C, D A, B, C, D A (H.), B (H.), C (H.), D (H.)	CII B.A.C. CIII B.A.C. CIV B.A.C. CV (H.) B.A.C.	...	...	23rd D.A.C.	89th[3] 90th[4]	23rd[5]	...	...	60th 70th 71st	35th[6]	...	23rd[7]
1915 September (France)	68th ...... 69th ...... 70th[8]	10/N.F., 11/N.F., 12/D.L.I., 13/D.L.I. 11/W. York., 8/Gr. How., 9/Gr. How., 10/Duke's. 11/Sher. For., 8/K.O.Y.L.I., 8/Y. & L., 9/Y. & L.	H.Q., M.G. Sec., and C Sqdn.,[9] 1/D. of L. Own Yeo. 23rd Div. Cyclist Coy.[10]	CII[11] .... CIII[11] .... CIV[13] .... CV (H.)[14]	A, B, C, D A, B, C, D A, B, C, D A (H.), B (H.), C (H.), D (H.)	CII B.A.C. CIII B.A.C. CIV B.A.C. CV (H.) B.A.C.	...	...	23rd D.A.C.	101st[15] 102nd[16] 128th[18]	23rd	9/S. Staff.[17] (P.)	...	60th 70th 71st	35th	...	23rd
1916 June (France)	24th[18] ... 68th 69th	1/Worc., 2/E. Lanc., 1/Sher. For., 2/Northn.; 24th Bde. M.G. Coy.;[19] 24th T.M. Bty.[20] 10/N.F., 11/N.F., 12/D.L.I., 13/D.L.I.; 68th Bde. M.G. Coy.;[19] 68th T.M. Bty.[20] 11/W. York., 8/Gr. How., 9/Gr. How., 10/Duke's; 69th Bde. M.G. Coy.;[19] 69th T.M. Bty.[20]	...	CII[11]; [21] ...... CIII[12]; [22] ...... CIV[15]; [23] ...... CV[14]; [24]	A, B, C; D (H.) A, B, C; D (H.) A, B, C; D (H.) A, B, C; D (H.)	...[27]	X.23[25] Y.23[25] Z.23[25]	V.23[26]	23rd D.A.C.[27]	101st 102nd 128th	23rd	9/S. Staff. (P.)	...	60th 70th 71st	35th	...	23rd
1917 June (France)	68th ...... 69th ...... 70th[28] ...	10/N.F., 11/N.F., 12/D.L.I., 13/D.L.I.; 68th M.G. Coy.;[38] 68th T.M. Bty. 11/W. York., 8/Gr. How., 9/Gr. How., 10/Duke's; 69th M.G. Coy.;[38] 69th T.M. Bty. 11/Sher. For., 8/K.O.Y.L.I., 9/Y. & L.; 70th M.G. Coy.;[29];[38] 70th T.M. Bty.[30]	...	CII[21] .... CIII[22]	A, B, C; D (H.) A, B, C; D (H.)		X.23 Y.23 Z.23[31]	V.23[32]	23rd D.A.C.	101st 102nd 128th	23rd	9/S. Staff. (P.)	194th M.G. Coy.[33]	60th 70th 71st	35th	223rd[34]	23rd

Date	Inf. Bde.	Battalions	Arty. Bde.	Batteries	Med. T.M.	H.T.M.	D.A.C.	Field Coys.	Signal	Pioneers	M.G.	Field Ambs.	Mob. Vet.	Empl. Coy.	Train
1918 April (Italy)	68th	10/N.F., 11/N.F., 12/D.L.I., 13/D.L.I.;35 68th T.M. Bty.	CII	A, B, C; D (H.)	X.2231 Y.2231	...32	23rd D.A.C.	101st 102nd 128th	23rd	9/S. Staff. (P.)	23rd Bn., M.G.C.38	69th 70th 71st	35th	223rd	23rd
	69th	11/W. York., 8/Gr. How., 9/Gr. How.,36 10/Duke's; 69th T.M. Bty.	CIII	A, B, C; D (H.)											
	70th	11/Sher. For.,37 8/K.O.Y.L.I., 8/Y. & L., 9/Y. & L.; 70th T.M. Bty.													
1918 October (Italy)	68th	10/N.F., 11/N.F., 12/D.L.I.; 68th T.M. Bty.	CII	A, B, C; D (H.)	X.23 Y.23	...	23rd D.A.C.	101st 102nd 128th	23rd	9/S. Staff. (P.)	23rd Bn., M.G.C.	69th 70th 71st	35th	223rd	23rd
	69th	11/W. York., 8/Gr. How., 10/Duke's; 69th T.M. Bty.	CIII	A, B, C; D (H.)											
	70th	8/K.O.Y.L.I., 8/Y. & L.; 70th T.M. Bty.													

NOTES

1 Coy. began to form on 15/1/15 in Marlborough Lines, Aldershot.

2 In Jany., 1915, the Bdes. were organized as 4-battery brigades; the Bties. were 4-gun batteries, and were lettered—A, B, C, D—in each brigade.

3 On 22/1/15 the Fd. Coy. was transferred to 14th (Light) Div.

4 In Jany., 1915, the Fd. Coy. was transferred to 9th (Scottish) Div.

5 From 9/8/15 the Bde. Secs. were attached to the Inf. Bdes.

6 The Sec. joined the Div. on 20/6/15 at Bordon.

7 Train formed on 16/1/15, consisted of 100, 101, 102, and 103 Cos., A.S.C.

8 On 18/10/15 the Bde. was transferred to the 8th Div. for attachment, in exchange for 24th Bde. (note 18).

9 Joined the Div. on 27/6/15 at Bordon, went to France with the Div., and disembkd. at le Havre on 28/8/15; left the Div. on 20/4/16, attached to 1st Cav. Div. from 20/4–4/5/16, and joined III Corps Cav. Regt. on 14/5/16.

10 Coy. left the Div. on 20/4/16, attached to 1st Cav. Div. from 20/4—9/5/16, and joined IV Corps Cyclist Bn. on 10/5/16.

11 On 19/5/16 D Bty. left CII and became A/CV; and A (H.)/CV joined CII and became D (H.)/CII.

12 On 20/5/16 D Bty. left CIII and became B/CV; and B (H.)/CV joined CIII and became D (H.)/CIII.

13 On 19/5/16 D Bty. left CIV and became C/CV; and C (H.)/CV joined CIV and became D (H.)/CIV.

14 On 19 and 20/5/16 CV was reorganized : A (H.), B (H.), and C (H.) left CV and became D (H.)/CII, D (H.)/CIII, and D (H.)/CIV; D/CII, D/CIII, and D/CIV joined CV and became A, B, and C/CV; and D (H.)/CV remained D (H.)/CV.

15 On 1/2/15, 101st and 102nd Fd. Cos. joined at Aldershot from 32nd Div., to replace 89th and 90th Fd. Cos. (notes 3 and 4).

16 128th Fd. Coy. joined Div. at Shorncliffe by 9/4/15.

17 Bn. (originally an Army Troops Bn., Third New Army) was attached to 23rd Div. from Oct., 1914. The Bn. was converted into 23rd Div. Pioneer Bn. by 21/4/15.

18 On 18/10/15 the Bde. left 8th Div. and joined 23rd Div., for attachment, in exchange for 70th Bde. (note 8). On 16/7/16, 24th Bde. left the 23rd Div. and returned to the 8th Div.

19 M.G. Cos. were formed and joined Bdes. as follows :—
24th—formed in the Bde. by 17/2/16;
68th—formed at Grantham on 13/12/15, disembkd. le Havre on 25/2/16, and joined Bde. on 4/3/16;
69th—left Grantham on 24/2/16, disembkd. le Havre on 2/3/16, and joined Bde. on 4/3/16.

20 T.M. Bties. were formed in the Bdes. as follows :—
24th—24/1 (A/24 until 29/3/16) by 12/2/16, 24/2 by 15/4/16, and they became 24th T.M. Bty. by 13/6/16;
68th—A/68 by 8/3/16, 68/1 by 16/3/16, and 68th T.M. Bty. by 16/5/16;
69th—69/1 (A/69 until 16/3/16) by 5/2/16, 69/2 by 24/4/16, and they became 69th T.M. Bty. by 23/6/16.

21 On 3/9/16, 1 sec. A/CV made up A, 1 sec. A/CV made up B, and 1 sec. C/CV made up C/CII to 6, 18-pdrs. each. On 18/1/17, L. sec. C (H.)/CIV joined and made up D (H.)/CII to 6 hows.

22 Between 1–3/9/16, 1 sec. B/CV made up B, 1 sec. B/CV made up C, and 1 sec. C/CV made up A/CIII to 6, 18-pdrs. each. On 18/1/17, R. sec. C (H.)/CIV joined and made up D (H.)/CIII to 6 hows.

23 On 3/9/16 C was split up to make up A and B to 6, 18-pdrs. each ; and D (H.)/CIV joined and became C (H.)/CIV. On 18/1/17 C (H.) was broken up and made up D (H.)/CII and 1 sec. made up D (H.)/CIII to 6 hows. each. CIV became an A.F.A. Bde. on 18/1/17; on 21/1/17 B/CCXXXVIII joined (from 47th Div.) and became C/CIV, and by 9/4/17 D (H.) had been made up to 6 hows.

24 Bde. was broken up between 1–3/9/16 : A and 1 sec. C were transferred to CII, and B and 1 sec. C to CIII, to make up the 18-pdr. Bties. of CII and CIII to 6 guns each ; and D (H.)/CV became C (H.)/CIV.

25 Medium T.M. Bties. were formed as follows :—
X—raised as 12th T.M. Bty. in 1915 was attached to 23rd Div. in Jany., 1916, and it became X. 23 in the middle of March, 1916;
Y—raised as 21st T.M. Bty. in 1915 was attached to 23rd Div. in Jany., 1916, and became Y. 23 on 15/3/16;
Z—was formed in the 23rd Div. in March, 1916.

26 V was formed in the 23rd Div. in March, 1916.

27 Between 15–19/6/16 B.A.C.s were abolished and the D.A.C. was reorganized.

28 On 16/7/16 the Bde. left 8th Div. and rejoined 23rd Div. on 17/7/16 (see note 8).

29 Coy. was formed at Grantham and disembkd. at le Havre on 2/3/16. Coy. joined 70th Bde. on 5/3/16 at Fleurbaix, whilst Bde. was serving with 8th Div. (notes 8 and 28).

30 70/1 (A/70 until 18/3/16) was formed by 25/1/16, 70/2 by 14/4/16, and they became 70th T.M. Bty. by 18/6/16. (70th Bde. was then serving with 8th Div.—notes 8 and 29).

31 Medium T.M. Bties. were rearmed in Feb., 1918, with 4, 6" Newton T.M.s each ; and on 8/3/18 Z was broken up and distributed between X and Y, making each up to 6 T.M.s ; the reorganization was completed by 18/3/18.

32 V was abolished on 29/10/17 and the H.T.M. Bty. completed its disbandment on 2/11/17.

33 Formed at Grantham ; the Coy. disembkd. at le Havre on 13/12/16 and joined 23rd Div. on 16/12/16 near Vlamertinghe.

34 Coy. was formed by 30/6/17.

35 On 14/9/18 Bn. left Div. in Italy and on 18 and 19/9/18 Bn. joined 74th Bde., 25th Div., in France.

36 On 13/9/18 Bn. left Div. in Italy and on 17/9/18 Bn. joined 74th Bde., 25th Div., in France.

37 On 13/9/18 Bn. left Div. in Italy and on 18/9/18 Bn. joined 74th Bde., 25th Div., in France.

38 Bn. was. formed in Italy on 1/4/18 and consisted of 68th, 69th, 70th, and 194th M.G. Cos.; the Cos. were designated in the Bn. by letters—A, B, C, D.

23RD DIVISION

FORMATION, BATTLES, AND ENGAGEMENTS

This New Army Division had no existence before the outbreak of the Great War.

Army Order No. 388 of the 13th September 1914 authorized the addition of six divisions (21st–26th) and Army Troops to the Regular Army (see Appendix I). This augmentation formed the Third New Army, and during September 1914 the 23rd Division began to assemble near Frensham (in the Aldershot area).

Many difficulties had to be overcome in the early days. At first there was a great shortage of officers ; and no trained clerks joined with divisional headquarters, consequently orders had to be issued verbally to adjutants until clerks, typewriters, and stationery could be collected. Trained cooks also were non-existent and the messing of the troops was undertaken by a catering firm. The civilian clothing, in which the men joined, was in rags by the time that emergency blue clothing was issued in the middle of October, and 20,000 suits of underclothing and pairs of boots had to be purchased in Yorkshire. During October 100 old Lee-Metford rifles were issued to each battalion for drill, in November 8 L.M.E. service rifles and 400 sets of old buff equipment arrived for each battalion, and in December old pattern water-bottles and white haversacks were received.

In November 1914 the divisional artillery began to form at Mytchett Camp. At first each brigade was commanded by a second-lieutenant, and it was fortunate that at this time the commands were merely nominal. The first armament received was the 90 m/m. French gun. The 18-pdrs. and 4·5″ howitzers were not issued to the Division until the middle of 1915.

At the beginning of December 1914 the weather broke and the Division was moved into Aldershot, with part of the artillery at Ewshott. On the 22nd January 1915, in heavy rain, the Division was inspected on the Queen's Parade by Field-Marshal Earl Kitchener, accompanied by the French Minister of War (M. Millerand) ; on this occasion the troops paraded in blue serge uniforms and civilian greatcoats, and the infantry had D.P. rifles. On the 10th February the battalion allowance of wire and sandbags was doubled, and stress was laid on the troops being taught to entrench and to construct obstacles at night. At the end of this month the Division moved to the Shorncliffe area, and here the Division remained until the end of May when it moved to Bordon and Bramshott. The final intensive preparation then began. On the 16th August the Division was inspected on Hankley Common by H.M. the King, and the order to embark for France was received on the 20th. On the 21st the first advanced party left, on the 23rd the Division began entraining, on the 26th the first units arrived in the concentration area, and on the 29th August the Division completed concentration around Tilques (north-west of St. Omer). The 23rd Division served on the Western Front in France and Belgium until November 1917, when it entrained for the Italian Front, on which it served for the remainder of the Great War. From 1915 to 1918 the 23rd Division was engaged in the following operations :—

1915

1916

BATTLES OF THE SOMME

4–11 July	**Battle of Albert** [III Corps, Fourth Army].	
10 July	**Capture of Contalmaison.***	
26 July–8 Aug.	**Battle of Pozières Ridge** [III Corps, Fourth Army].	
19–22 Sept.	**Battle of Flers-Courcelette** [III Corps, Fourth Army].	
25–28 Sept.	**Battle of Morval** [III Corps, Fourth Army].	
1–9 Oct.	**Battle of the Transloy Ridges** [III Corps, Fourth Army].	
7 October	**Capture of Le Sars.**	

* After the 23rd Division had captured Contalmaison the Commander-in-Chief asked the Divisional Commander what he would like. General Babington replied : " Give me back my 70th Brigade." Within a week the 70th Brigade returned to the 23rd Division (see Table, and notes 8, 18, and 28).

1917

7–14 June ... ... **Battle of Messines** [X Corps, Second Army].

BATTLES OF YPRES

20–24 September ... **Battle of Menin Road Ridge** [X Corps, Second Army].
28 Sept.–2 Oct. ... ... **Battle of Polygon Wood** [X Corps, Second Army].
12 October ... ... **First Battle of Passchendaele** [X Corps, Second Army].

At 10.30 a.m. on the 23rd October the 23rd Division handed over the front line, on the 28th it received warning that it was to be ready to entrain for an unknown destination, on the 31st October the C.-in-C. inspected the Division at Leulinghem, and, in a speech at the conclusion of the parade, the C.-in-C. informed all ranks that the 23rd Division was to move to the Italian Front. The Divisional Supply Column entrained on the 30th October and the infantry began entrainment on the 6th November. On the 16th November the 23rd Division completed detrainment and concentration between Mantua and Marcaria ; and on arrival the Division joined XIV Corps. On the 19th November the Division moved forward, and on the 4th December took over the front line on the Montello (behind the River Piave) from the 70th (Italian) Division.

1918

The 23rd Division held the front line until the 18th February, took over the Montello sector again on the 26th February and held it until the 14th March, when the Division was relieved by the 51st (Italian) Division. The 23rd Division moved westward, and on the 23rd March took over the right sector of the line on the Asiago Plateau from the 11th (Italian) Division. The 23rd Division held this part of the front until the 23rd April ; and, after resting, took over the right sector again on the 19th May. The Division then took part in :—

BATTLE OF THE PIAVE

15 and 16 June ... ... **The Fighting on the Asiago Plateau** [XIV Corps, Sixth (Italian) Army].

On the 23rd July the Division handed over its front line sector to the 48th Division ; and on the 19th August the 23rd Division took over the left sector of XIV Corps front on the Asiago Plateau. On the 27th September the 23rd Division handed over this sector to the 20th (Italian) Division, and on the 23rd October the 23rd Division took over the left divisional sector of the XIV Corps Front on the Piave. The Division then took part in the final operations :—

26th Oct.–4 Nov. ... **BATTLE OF VITTORIO VENETO** [XIV Corps, Tenth (Italian) Army].
Night 26/27–28 Oct. ... **Passage of the Piave.**
29th October ... ... **Passage of the Monticano.**

On the 2nd November the 23rd Division came into XIV Corps Reserve, and at 3 p.m. on the 4th November, when the Armistice with Austria brought hostilities to a close in the Italian theatre of war, the Division was halted midway between the Rivers Livenza and Meduna, to the east of Sacile.

On the 8th November the Division began to march back, on the 10th it recrossed the Piave, and on the 11th dismounted units entrained at Treviso and went into a billeting area to the west of Vicenza, with divisional headquarters at Arzignano ; the artillery and transport marched to this new area. On the 27th November H.M. the King of Italy reviewed the XIV Corps at Castelgomberto Aerodrome, the 23rd Division being represented by the 68th Infantry Brigade and by detachments from the remainder of the Division. During December the troops were employed at lectures, recreation, and in preparing for demobilization.

In January and February 1919 demobilization proceeded at an increasing rate. On the 13th February orders were issued that the Army of Occupation in Italy would be a mixed brigade of all arms. By March the 23rd Division was reduced to cadre strength, and it then passed out of existence. During the Great War the 23rd Division lost 23,574 killed, wounded, and missing.

24TH DIVISION

G.O.C.

19 September, 1914	Major-General Sir J. G. RAMSAY.
3 October, 1915	Major-General J. E. CAPPER.
12 May, 1917	Br.-Gen. H. C. SHEPPARD (acting).
18 May, 1917	Major-General L. J. BOLS.
12 September, 1917	Br.-Gen. E. S. HOARE NAIRNE (acting).
15 September, 1917	Major-General A. C. DALY.

G.S.O. 1.

17 Sept., 1914...Lt.-Col. C. F. HEYWORTH-SAVAGE (tempy.).

11 Jan., 1915...Major Sir W. A. I. KAY, Bt. (acting).

16 May, 1915...Lt.-Col. C. G. STEWART.

23 Feb., 1916...Lt.-Col. Sir W. A. I. KAY.

9 Nov., 1916...Captain H.　[Bt. BOYD-ROCHFORT (acting).

1 Dec., 1916...Lt.-Col. Sir W. A. I. KAY,

5 Oct., 1917...Lt.-Col. H. C.　[Bt. MAITLAND-MAKGILL-CRICHTON.

31 Jan., 1918...Lt.-Col. J. H. MACKENZIE.

26 Aug., 1918...Major C. G. LING (acting).

27 Aug., 1918...Lt.-Col. C. M. LONGMORE.

A.-A. and Q.-M.-G.

7 Oct., 1914...Captain J. H. LLOYD (acting).

10 Oct., 1914...Colonel H. T. KENNY.

28 Sept., 1915...Lt.-Col. J. F. I. H. DOYLE.

24 Dec., 1917...Lt.-Col. E. V. D. RIDDELL.

14 April, 1918...Lt.-Col. Hon. R. H. COLLINS.

B.-G., R.A.

9 Nov., 1914...Br.-Gen. Sir G. V. THOMAS, Bt.

26 Oct., 1915...Br.-Gen. L. M. PHILPOTTS (killed, 8/9/16).

8 Sept., 1916...Lt.-Col. D. R. COATES (acting).

11 Sept., 1916...Br.-Gen. H. C. SHEPPARD.

5 Sept., 1917...Br.-Gen. E. S. HOARE NAIRNE.

22 Mar., 1918...Lt.-Col. D. W. L. SPILLER (acting).

24 Mar., 1918...Lt.-Col. W. STIRLING (acting).

27 Mar., 1918...Br.-Gen. E. S. HOARE NAIRNE.*

26 Oct., 1918...Br.-Gen. H. G. LLOYD.

C.R.E.

14 Oct., 1914...Lt.-Col. H. E. G. CLAYTON.

25 July, 1915...Lt.-Col. A. J. CRAVEN.

12 Feb., 1917...Major C. N. RIVERS-MOORE (acting).

4 Mar., 1917...Lt.-Col. A. J. CRAVEN.

2 April, 1917...Major F. P. HEATH (acting).

4 April, 1917...Lt.-Col. T. T. BEHRENS.

24 Aug., 1917...Major J. H. PRIOR (acting).

4 Sept., 1917...Lt.-Col. A. D. WALKER (killed, 26/3/18).

26 Mar., 1918...Major J. H. PRIOR (tempy.).

1 April, 1918...Lt.-Col. J. H. PRIOR.

---

* Br.-Gen. E. S. Hoare Nairne acted from 22–24 March, 1918, as B.-G., R.A., of the 50th (Northumbrian) Division ; and on 25 and 26 March, 1918, as B.-G., R.A., of the 8th Division.

71st BDE.

17 Sept., '14...Br.-Gen. B. St. J. BARTER.
28 Aug., '15...Colonel M. T. SHEWEN
(tempy.).
31 Aug., '15...Br.-Gen. M. T. SHEWEN.

(On 11/10/15 71st Bde. was transferred to 6th Div.)

17th BDE.

(On 14/10/15 17th Bde. left 6th Div. and joined 24th Div.)

[23 Sept., '15]..Br.-Gen. J. W. V. CARROLL
(sick, 16/1/17).
16 Jan., '17...Lt.-Col. A. M. TRINGHAM
(acting).
18 Jan., '17...Lt.-Col. R. PIGOT (acting).
12 Feb., '17...Br.-Gen. P. V. P. STONE.
1 Feb., '18...Lt.-Col. A. M. TRINGHAM
(acting).
4 Mar., '18...Br.-Gen. P. V. P. STONE.
7 June, '18...Br.-Gen. G. THORPE.

72nd BDE.

19 Sept., '14...Br.-Gen. B. R. MITFORD.
14 Mar., '17...Br.-Gen. W. F. SWENY.
13 Dec., '17...Br.-Gen. R. W. MORGAN.

73rd BDE.

19 Sept., '14...Br.-Gen. W. A. OSWALD.
26 Sept., '15...Br.-Gen. R. G. JELF
(sick, 9/11/16).
9 Nov., '16...Lt.-Col. Sir W. A. I. KAY,
Bt. (acting).
1 Dec., '16...Lt.-Col. L. W. LUCAS
(acting).
19 Dec., '16...Br.-Gen. W. J. DUGAN.
15 July, '18...Br.-Gen. R. J. COLLINS.

GENERAL NOTES

The following Units also served with the 24th Division :—

ARTILLERY :—522 (H.) Bty., R.F.A. (4, 4·5″ hows.), disembkd. at le Havre on 4/10/16 and joined CVIII on 8/10/16 (see note 26).

24th (New) Heavy Bty., R.G.A.* (4, 60-pdrs.), was raised for the 24th Div. and served with the Div. at Mytchett Camp from 12/6–27/8/15. 24th (New) Heavy Battery was redesignated 130th Heavy Battery, and on 9/10/15 joined XXXV Heavy Artillery Brigade (on formation) at Charlton. 130th Heavy Battery embkd. at Southampton on 7/2/16, disembkd. at Alexandria on 20/2/16 ; returned to France in April 1916, disembkd. at Marseille on 14/4/16, and joined XXI H.A.G. on 12/5/16.

13th Division Ammn. Coln., was attached in England from 3/7–6/8/15.

INFANTRY :—

11/R. Warwick., was attached in England from before March 1915 to 9/4/15. Bn. then joined 112th Bde., 37th Div., and served with 37th Div. until Bn. was disbanded in Feb., 1918.

13/R.F., was attached in England from before March 1915 to 9/4/15. Bn. then joined 111th Bde., 37th Div., and served with 37th Div. until Bn. was disbanded in Feb., 1918.

12/Sher. For., was attached in England from before March, 1915. In April 1915, Bn. was converted into Divnl. Pioneer Bn. (note 18).

1/2/London, joined 24th Div. in France on 14/10/15, with 17th Inf. Bde. (note 19). On 9/2/16 Bn. left Div. and joined 169th Bde., 56th Div., on 10/2/16.

MACHINE GUNS :—No. 3 Motor-Machine-Gun Battery, served with the Div. from 30/10–23/11/15, and the Bty. was then transferred to 3rd Div.

OTHER UNITS :—13th Division Train, was attached in England from 3/7–20/8/15. On 16/11/15 the Train became 28th Div. Train.

41st Sanitary Section, joined Div. at Blackdown on Friday, 20/8/15 and disembkd. at le Havre on 2/9/15. The Section left the Div. on 5/4/17 and took over No. 6 Sanitary Area, First Army.

24th Division Motor Ambce. Workshop, joined Div. in England, disembkd. at Rouen on 31/8/15, rejoined Div. on 7/9/15, and in April 1916 the Workshop was transferred to and absorbed by 24th Div. Supply Column.

On 13/2/18 the reorganization of the 24th Division on a 9-battalion basis was completed ; and on 4/3/18 the pioneer battalion (12/Sher. For.) was reorganized on a 3-company basis.

---

* 24th Heavy Battery, R.G.A. (4, 60-pdrs.) was serving with the 6th Division at the outbreak of the Great War ; and in September 1914 24th Heavy Battery went to France with the 6th Division.

24TH DIVISION

Dates	INFANTRY Brigades	Battalions and attached Units	Mounted Troops	ARTILLERY — Field Artillery Brigades	Batteries	Bde. Ammn. Colns.	Trench Mortar Bties. Medium	Heavy	Divnl. Ammn. Coln.	Engineers Field Cos.	Signal Service Divnl. Signal Coy.	Pioneers	M.G. Units	Field Ambulances	Mobile Vety. Secn.	Divnl. Emplnt. Coy.	Divnl. Train
1914 October (England)	71st ...... 72nd...... 73rd	9/Norf., 9/Suff., 8/Bedf., 11/Essex. 8/Queen's, 8/Buffs, 9/E. Surr., 8/R.W.K. 12/R.F., 9/R. Suss., 7/Northn., 13/Middx.	24th Div. Cyclist Coy.[1]	CVI[2] .... CVII[2] .... CVIII[2] .... CIX (H.)[2]	A, B, C, D; A, B, C, D; A, B, C, D; A (H.), B (H.), C (H.), D (H.)	CVI B.A.C. CVII B.A.C. CVIII B.A.C. CIX (H.) B.A.C.	...	...	24th D.A.C.	91st[3] 92nd[4]	24th	...	...	72nd 73rd 74th	36th[5]	...	24th[6]
1915 September (France)	71st ...... 72nd...... 73rd	9/Norf., 9/Suff., 8/Bedf., 11/Essex. 8/Queen's, 8/Buffs,[8] 9/E. Surr., 8/R.W.K. 12/R.F.,[9] 9/R. Suss., 7/Northn., 13/Middx.	A Sqdn.[10] 1/R. Glasgow Yeo. 24th Div. Cyclist Coy.[11]	CVI[2]........ CVII[13] .... CVIII[14] .... CIX (H.)[15]	A, B, C, D; A, B, C, D; A, B, C, D; A (H.), B (H.), C (H.), D (H.)	CVI B.A.C. CVII B.A.C. CVIII B.A.C. CIX (H.) B.A.C.	...	...	24th D.A.C.	103rd[16] 104th[18] 129th[17]	24th	12/ Sher. For.[18] (P.)	...	72nd 73rd 74th	36th	...	24th
1916 June (France)	17th[19] ...... 72nd...... 73rd	8/Buffs,[8] 1/R.F., 12/R.F.,[9] 3/R.B.; 17th Bde. M.G. Coy.;[20] 17th T.M. Bty.[21] 8/Queen's, 9/E. Surr., 8/ R.W.K., 1/N. Staff.;[22] 72nd Bde. M.G. Coy.;[20] 72nd T.M. Bty.[21] 9/R. Suss., 7/Northn., 13/ Middx., 2/Leins.;[23] 73rd Bde. M.G. Coy.;[20] 73rd T.M. Bty.[21]	...	CVI[2 ; 24] .... CVII[13 ; 25] .... CVIII[14 ; 26] .. CIX[15 ; 27]	A, B, C; D (H.) A, B, C; D (H.) A, B, C; D (H.) A, B, C	...[30]	X.24[28] Y.24[28] Z.24[28]	V.24[29]	24th D.A.C.[50]	103rd 104th 129th	24th	12/ Sher. For. (P.)	...	72nd 73rd 74th	36th	...	24th
1917 June (France)	17th ...... 72nd...... 73rd	8/Buffs,[31] 1/R.F., 12/R.F.,[32] 3/R.B.; 17th M.G. Coy.;[39] 17th T.M. Bty. 8/Queen's,[33] 9/E. Surr., 8/ R.W.K., 1/N. Staff.; 72nd M.G. Coy.;[39] 72nd T.M. Bty. 9/R. Suss., 7/Northn., 13/ Middx., 2/Leins.;[34] 73rd M.G. Coy.;[39] 73rd T.M. Bty.	...	CVI[24]...... CVII[25]	A, B, C; D (H.) A, B, C; D (H.)	...	X.24 Y.24 Z.24[35]	V.24[36]	24th D.A.C.	103rd 104th 129th	24th	12/ Sher. For. (P.)	191st M.G. Coy.[37]	72nd 73rd 74th	36th	224th[38]	24th

130

1918 March (France)			
	24th		
	22nd		
	36th		
	72nd 73rd 74th		
	No. 24 Bn.. M.G.C.39		
	12/ Sher. For. (P.)		
	24th		
	103rd 104th 129th		
	24th D.A.C.		
	...		
	X.24 Y.24		
	...		
	CVI	A, B, C; D (H.)	
	CVII	A, B, C; D (H.) ...	
	...		
17th	8/Queen's,33 1/R.F., 3/R.B.; 17th T.M. Bty.		
72nd	9/E. Surr.; 8/R.W.K.; 1/N. Staff.; 72nd T.M. Bty.		
73rd	9/R. Suss.; 7/Northn., 13/ Middx.; 73rd T.M. Bty.		

L

NOTES

1 Coy. was formed by 15/2/15 and concentrated at Henfield on 17/2/15.

2 In Jany., 1915, the Bdes. were organized as 4-battery brigades; the Bties. were 4-gun batteries, and were lettered—A, B, C, D in each Brigade.

3 In Jany., 1915, 91st Fd. Coy. was transferred to 15th Div. at Bordon.

4 In Jany., 1915, 92nd Fd. Coy. was transferred to 18th Div.

5 Joined Div. at Blackdown on 25/6/15.

6 Train consisted of 194, 195, 196, and 197 Cos., A.S.C.

7 On 11/10/15 the Bde. was transferred to the 6th Div., in exchange for 17th Bde. (see note 19).

8 On 18/10/15 Bn. was transferred from 72nd Bde. to 17th Bde.

9 On 18/10/15 Bn. was transferred from 73rd Bde. to 17th Bde.

10 Sqdn. joined Div. at Blackdown on 30/6/15. Sqdn. disembkd. at le Havre on 1/9/15, left Div. on 29/4/16, was attached to 2nd Cav. Div. from 30/4–14/5/16, and on 21/5/16 Sqdn. joined V Corps Cav. Regt.

11 Coy. disembkd. at le Havre on 31/8/15, left Div. on 29/4/16, was attached to 2nd Cav. Div. from 30/4–17/5/16, and on 18/5/16 Coy. joined V Corps Cyclist Bn.

12 On 13/5/16 D Bty. left and became A/CIX; and A (H.)/CIX joined CVI and became D (H.)/CVI.

13 On 13/5/16 D Bty. left and became B/CIX; and D (H.)/CIX joined CVII and became D (H.)/CVII.

14 On 13/5/16 D Bty. left and became C/CIX; and B (H.)/CIX joined CVIII and became D (H.)/CVIII.

15 On 3/12/15, 2nd Cdn. Div., on 7/12/15. On 13/5/16 CIX was reorganized: A (H.), B (H.), and D (H.)/CIX became D (H.)/CVI, D (H.)/CVIII, and D (H.)/CVII; and D/CVI D/CVII, and D/CVIII joined CIX and became A, B, C/CIX.

16 In Feb., 1915, 103rd and 104th Fd. Cos. joined from 33rd Div., to replace 91st and 92nd Fd. Cos. (see notes 3 and 4).

17 129th Fd. Coy. joined before 7/4/15.

18 Bn. (from Army Troops) was attached to Div. before March, 1915; and by 7/4/15 Bn. was converted into 24th Div. Pioneer Bn.

19 On 14/10/15, 17th Bde. (1/R.F., 1/N. Staff., 2/Leins. 3/R.B., and 2/Lond.) was transferred from 6th Div. and joined 24th Div., to replace 71st Bde. (see note 7). 2/Lond. left 17th Bde. on 9/2/16 (see General Notes).

20 M.G. Cos. were formed and joined Bdes. as follows :—17th—formed in the Bde. on 17/1/16, at Poperinghe; 72nd—formed at Grantham; disembkd. at le Havre on 11/8/16, and joined Bde. at Ouderdom on 14/8/16; 73rd—mobilized at Grantham on 22/2/16; disembkd. at le Havre on 11/3/16, and joined Bde. at Ouderdom on 14/3/16.

21 T.M. Bties. were formed in the Bdes. :—17th—17/1 by 22/3/16, 17/2 by April, 1916, and they became 17th T.M. Bty. by 28/7/16; 72nd—72/1 joined Div. on 11/3/16, 72/2 was formed on 10/4/16, and they became 72nd T.M. Bty. on 19/7/16; 73rd—73/1 by 17/3/16, 73/2 by 24/5/16, and they became 73rd T.M. Bty. on 15/6/16.

22 On 18/10/15 Bn. was transferred from 17th Bde. to 72nd Bde.

23 On 18/10/15 Bn. was transferred from 17th Bde. to 73rd Bde.

24 On 3/10/16 A & R. Sec. B/CIX joined CVI: R. Sec. A/CIX made up A, L. Sec. A/CIX made up B, and R. Sec. B/CIX made up C/CVI to 6, 18-pdrs. each. On 27/1/17, 1 sec. C (H.)/CVIII joined and made up D (H.)/CVI to 6 hows.

25 On 3/10/16 L. Sec. B & C/CIX joined CVII: L. Sec. B/CIX made up A, R. Sec. C/CIX made up B, and L. Sec. C/CIX made up C/CVII to 6, 18-pdrs. each. On 27/1/17, 1 sec. C (H.)/CVIII joined and made up D (H.)/CVII to 6 hows.

26 On 3/10/16 A Bty. was broken up : R. Sec. A made up C and L. Sec. A made up B to 6, 18-pdrs. each. On 8/10/16, 522 (H.) Bty.—4, 4·5" H.—joined Bde. from England and became A (H.); on 18/10/16, C Bty. was redesignated A and A (H.) became C (H.)/CVIII. On 27/1/17 CVIII became an A.F.A. Bde.: C (H.) left and was broken up to make up D (H.)/CVI and D (H.)/CVII to 6 hows. each : C/XCVI (6, 18-pdrs.) joined from 21st Div. and became C/CVIII; and 1 sec. D (H.)/XCVI also joined and made up D (H.)/CVIII to 6 hows.

27 On 3/10/16 CIX was broken up : A Bty. and R. Sec. B were transferred to CVI, and L. Sec. B and C Bty. to CVII, they were then allotted by secs. to make up the 18-pdr. Bties. of CVI and CVII to 6 guns each (notes 24 and 25).

28 The 3 Medium T.M. Bties. were formed by 30/4/16.

29 V joined by 30/7/16.

30 B.A.C.s were abolished and the D.A.C. was reorganized on 13/5/16.

31 Between 8–13/2/18 Bn. was drafted to 1/Buffs (6th Div.), 6/Buffs (12th Div.), and VII Corps Rft. Camp. On 13/2/18 Bn. was disbanded.

32 Between 2–13/2/18 10/R.F. (17th Bde.), 11/R.F. (18th Div.), and VII Corps Rft. Camp. On 13/2/18 Bn. was disbanded.

33 On 7/2/18 Bn. was transferred to 17th Bde.

34 On 1/2/18 Bn. left 24th Div. and joined 47th Bde., 16th Div., on 2/2/18.

35 In Febry., 1918, Z was absorbed by X and Y Medium T.M. Bties.

36 In Febry., 1918, V H.T.M. Bty. was transferred to Corps Troops.

37 Coy. disembkd. at le Havre on 13/12/16 and joined Div.

38 Coy. joined Div. on 24/5/17.

39 Bn. was formed on 5/3/18, and consisted of 17th, 72nd, 73rd, and 191st M.G. Cos.

24TH DIVISION

FORMATION, BATTLES, AND ENGAGEMENTS

This New Army Division had no existence before the outbreak of the Great War.

Army Order No. 388 of the 13th September 1914 authorized the addition of six divisions (21st–26th) and Army Troops to the Regular Army (see Appendix I). This augmentation formed the Third New Army, and during September 1914 the 24th Division began to assemble in and around Shoreham.

The difficulties which the First and Second New Armies had to overcome in training were accentuated in the case of the divisions of the Third New Army; equipment and uniforms were scarcer and took longer to provide, trained instructors were fewer, because the pool of retired officers was nearly exhausted after the needs of the First and Second New Armies had been met, and any wounded officers who rejoined for duty were posted to divisions which were ready to take the field.

In 1914 only the supply of untrained personnel seemed inexhaustible. So it was with the 24th Division. The battalions speedily reached a strength of a thousand men, all of whom, officers and men, had everything to learn; no battalion had more than two retired regular officers, including the commanding officer. At first accommodation was extemporized; churches, cinemas, and halls had to be used. The Division was then placed under canvas, but the weather broke and the troops were then billeted until huts could be built. Arms, uniform, and equipment were slow in arriving: it was March 1915 before makeshift drab clothing could be issued, and service rifles only became available between May and July.

Between the 19th and 23rd June the 24th Division, accompanied by its divisional artillery and engineers, marched in three groups from the Shoreham district to the Aldershot Training Centre, and the final war training then began and gun-practice was carried out. On Thursday, the 19th August, Field-Marshal Earl Kitchener inspected the Division on Chobham Ridges, and between 11 a.m. and noon on the next day H.M. the King visited the 24th Division on Chobham Common. On the 21st the Division received orders to be ready to embark for France, on the 28th August the troops began to entrain, and on the 4th September the Division completed its concentration between St. Pol and Etaples, to the north of the Canche.

For the remainder of the Great War the 24th Division served on the Western Front in France and Belgium and was engaged in the following operations :—

1915

25 and 26 September   **Battle of Loos** [XI Corps, First Army].

1916

30 April ... ...   **Wulverghem** (German Gas Attack) [V Corps, Second Army].

BATTLES OF THE SOMME

11–22 Aug.; and ⎫
31 Aug.–2 Sept.   ⎬   **Battle of Delville Wood** [XIII Corps, until m/n., 16/17; then
　　　　　　　　　⎭　　　　XIV Corps; and from 31/8, XV Corps, Fourth Army].

3–5 September ... ...   **Battle of Guillemont** [XV Corps, Fourth Army].

1917

BATTLES OF ARRAS

9–14 April ... ...   **Battle of Vimy Ridge** [I Corps, First Army].

7–14 June   ... ...   **Battle of Messines** [X Corps, Second Army].

31 July–13 Sept.   ...   **BATTLES OF YPRES**
31 July–2 Aug. ... ...   **Battle of Pilckem Ridge** [II Corps, Fifth Army].
16–18 August   ... ...   **Battle of Langemarck** [II Corps, Fifth Army].

BATTLE OF CAMBRAI

30 Nov.–3 Dec. ... ...   **The German Counter-Attacks** [VII Corps, Third Army].

1918

FIRST BATTLES OF THE SOMME

21–23 March   ... ...   **Battle of St. Quentin** [XIX Corps, Fifth Army].
24 and 25 March   ...   **Actions at the Somme Crossings** [XIX Corps, Fifth Army].
26 and 27 March   ...   **Battle of Rosières** [XIX Corps, Fifth Army].
4 April   ... ...   **Battle of the Avre** [XIX Corps, Fourth Army].

THE ADVANCE TO VICTORY
BATTLES OF THE HINDENBURG LINE

8 and 9 October ... ...   **Battle of Cambrai** [XVII Corps, Third Army].

9–12 October   ... ...   **Pursuit to the Selle** [XVII Corps, Third Army].

THE FINAL ADVANCE IN PICARDY

4 November   ... ...   **Battle of the Sambre** [XVII Corps, Third Army].
5–7 November ... ...   **Passage of the Grande Honnelle** [XVII Corps, Third Army].

The Division continued to advance ; by 6 p.m. on the 10th November the divisional outpost line had been established 1½ miles to the east of the Maubeuge–Mons road, and this line was still held at 11 a.m. on the 11th November when the Armistice brought hostilities to a close. At 4 p.m. on the 11th the G.O.C. of the 24th Division handed over command of his part of the front to the G.O.C. of the 20th Division. Between the 17th–19th the 24th Division moved back and billeted between Denain and Douai, and between the 25–27th November it moved northwards to an area between St. Amand and Orchies. On the 18th December the Division shifted its quarters again and moved to Tournai. During the time which had elasped since the Armistice the Division had been employed on salvage work, recreational training, and education.

In January 1919 demobilization went on at an increasing pace. On the 11th January the daily rate was increased to 86. During the next two months demobilization proceeded rapidly and by the 26th March the Division was reduced to a brigade group of cadres. The war history of the Division was concluded. During the Great War the 24th Division lost 35,362 killed, wounded, and missing.

L*

25TH DIVISION

G.O.C.

18 September, 1914	Major-General F. VENTRIS.
27 May, 1915	Major-General B. J. C. DORAN.
4 June, 1916	Major-General E. G. T. BAINBRIDGE.
4 August, 1918	Major-General J. R. E. CHARLES.

G.S.O. 1.

19 Sept., 1914...Colonel F. G. BLAIR.
10 Jan., 1915...Major E. M. BIRCH
(acting).
26 May, 1915...Lt.-Col. D. M. WATT.
18 May, 1916...Lt.-Col. E. M. BIRCH.
8 Jan., 1917...Major H. S. ADAIR
(acting).
12 Jan., 1917...Lt.-Col. O. H. L.
NICHOLSON.
28 Nov., 1917...Captain E. K. B. FURZE
(acting).
16 Dec., 1917...Lt.-Col. R. T. LEE.
5 Aug., 1918...Lt.-Col. D. F. ANDERSON.

A.-A. and Q.-M.-G.

19 Sept., 1914...Captain H. A. STANSFIELD
(acting).
12 Oct., 1914...Colonel A. W. S. WINGATE.
11 April, 1916...Lt.-Col. R. F. LEGGE.
8 Mar., 1918...Lt.-Col. F. ST. J.
TYRWHITT.
3 May, 1918...Lt.-Col. Hon. E. P. J.
STOURTON.

B.-G., R.A.

10 Nov., 1914...Br.-Gen. H. A. BETHELL.
16 June, 1916...Br.-Gen. B. R. KIRWAN.
13 Oct., 1916...Lt.-Col. E. R. H. J.
CLOETÉ (acting).
27 Oct., 1916...Br.-Gen. K. J.
KINCAID-SMITH.

C.R.E.

17 Nov., 1914...Lt.-Col. C. R. DOBBS.
30 Aug., 1916...Lt.-Col. R. J. DONE.

74th Bde.

18 Sept., '14...Br.-Gen. A. J. W. ALLEN.
7 Feb., '16...Br.-Gen. G. N. GOING.
10 May, '16...Lt.-Col. J. D. CROSBIE
(acting).
16 May, '16...Br.-Gen. G. A. ARMYTAGE
(sick, 17/10/16).
17 Oct., '16...Br.-Gen. H. K. BETHELL.
31 Mar., '18...Br.-Gen. H. M.
CRAIGIE-HALKETT.

75th BDE.

19 Sept., '14...Br.-Gen. J. A. H.
WOODWARD.
8 Feb., '16...Br.-Gen. H. F. JENKINS
(sick, 9/7/16).
9 July, '16...Lt.-Col. G. S. ST. AUBYN
(acting).
10 July, '16...Br.-Gen. E. ST. G. PRATT.
27 Nov., '16...Br.-Gen. H. B. D. BAIRD.
9 Feb., '18...Br.-Gen. H. T. DOBBIN.
8 April, '18...Lt.-Col. J. B. ALLSOPP
(acting).
9 April, '18...Br.-Gen. C. C. HANNAY
(sick, 22/5/18).
22 May, '18...Lt.-Col. A. M. TRINGHAM
(acting).
27 May, '18...Br.-Gen. A. A. KENNEDY.
30 June, '18...Lt.-Col. G. P. LUND (acting).
5 July, '18...Br.-Gen. A. G. PRITCHARD.
31 Aug., '18...Br.-Gen. M. N. TURNER.
(On 9/9/18, 75th Bde. was renumbered
236th Bde. and left 25th Div.)

76th BDE.

20 Sept., '14...Br.-Gen. H. J. ARCHDALE.
21 July, '15...Br.-Gen. E. ST. G. PRATT.
(On 15/10/15 76th Bde. was transferred
to 3rd Div.)

75th BDE.

(75th Bde. was reformed on 17/9/18.)
17 Sept., '18...Br.-Gen. M. E. RICHARDSON
(sick, 30/9/18).
30 Sept., '18...Lt.-Col. H. N. YOUNG
(acting).
1 Oct., '18...Br.-Gen. C. W. FRIZELL.

7th BDE.

(On 18/10/15 7th Bde. left 3rd Div. and
joined 25th Div.
[23 July, '15]..Br.-Gen. C. GOSLING
(wd., 1/5/16).
1 May, '16...Lt.-Col. J. D. CROSBIE
(acting).
8 May, '16...Br.-Gen. C. E. HEATHCOTE.
30 Aug., '16...Br.-Gen. C. C. ONSLOW.
9 Aug., '17...Lt.-Col. A. C. JOHNSTON
(acting).
29 Aug., '17...Br.-Gen. C. J. GRIFFIN
(wd., 29/5/18).
29 May, '18...Br.-Gen. H. R. HEADLAM
(tempy.).
31 May, '18...Br.-Gen. C. J. HICKIE.

GENERAL NOTES

The following Units also served with the 25th Division :—

ARTILLERY :—507 (H.) Bty., R.F.A. (4, 4·5″ hows.), disembkd. at le Havre on 9/11/16. Bty. was attached to 7th Div. from 11/11–5/12/16, and on 5/12/16 the Bty. joined CXIII Bde., 25th Div. (see note 26).

25 Heavy Battery, R.G.A. (4, 60-pdrs.), was raised for the 25th Division, but the Heavy Battery went abroad independently. On 9/10/15 the Heavy Battery joined XXXV Heavy Artillery Bde. (on formation) at Charlton. In Jany., 1916, 25th Heavy Battery went out to Egypt with XXXV Heavy Artillery Bde. and disembkd. at Alexandria on 22/1/16. In April 1916, XXXV Heavy Artillery Bde. returned to France, disembkd. at Marseille on 14/4/16, and 25th Heavy Battery left XXXV Heavy Artillery Bde. and joined I H.A.G. on 18 and 19/4/16.

INFANTRY :—6/Ches., Bn. joined on 28/5/18 from 118th Bde., 39th Div., and on 17/6/18 6/Ches. absorbed 16 offrs. and 492 o.r. of 11/Ches. (75th Bde.). On 20/6/18 6/Ches. formed No. 3 Bn. in 25th Div. Comp. Bde. ; and, with the Bde., the Bn. was transferred to 50th Div. on 22/6/18. On 8/7/18 6/Ches. joined 21st Bde., 30th Div.

MACHINE GUNS :—100th Bn., M.G.C., was attached to the 25th Div. from 2–15/10/18.

OTHER UNITS :—42nd Sanitary Sec., went to France with the 25th Div., and disembkd. at le Havre on 28/9/15. On 18/4/17 the Sanitary Section left 25th Div. and took over a Second Army Sanitary Area.

25th Division Motor Ambce. Workshop, joined 25th Div. in England, disembkd. at Rouen on 25–28/9/15, and rejoined 25th Div. on 1/10/15. On 7/4/16 the Workshop was absorbed by the Divnl. Supply Column.

On 16/2/18 the reorganization of the 25th Division on a 9-battalion basis was completed ; and on 28/2/18 the pioneer battalion (6/S.W.B.) was reorganized on a 3-company basis.

25th (DIV.) COMPOSITE BRIGADE

A Composite Brigade was formed in the 25th Div. on 20 and 21/6/18, composed as under :—

No. 1 Bn.	{ 11/L.F., 4/S. Staff. ;
No. 2 Bn.	{ 8/Bord., 9/L.N.L. ;
No. 3 Bn.	6/Ches.

On 22/6/18 the Composite Brigade* was transferred to the 50th Div. and served with the 50th Div. until 7/7/18. The Comp. Bde. was then broken up at Huppy. (Also see notes 39, 42, 44, 46, and General Notes.)

25th DIVISION ARTILLERY (MAY—OCTOBER, 1918)

On 26/5/18 CX was placed under 8th Div. (IX Corps) and CXII under 21st Div. (IX Corps). The Brigades took part in the Battle of the Aisne. On 27/5/18 CX formed a Composite Battery, and on 31/5/18 CXII came under 8th Div. The Composite Battery rejoined 25th Div. on 4/6/18, and CXII rejoined on 21/6/18.

On 30/6/18 the 25th Div. moved to England and the 25th Div. Arty. was then transferred to the Third Army. On 7/7/18, 25th Div. Arty. was attached to IV Corps, and on 28/7/18 it was transferred to III Corps, Fourth Army. On 31/7/18 25th Div. Arty. went into the line covering 58th Div., and from 4/8/18–30/8/18 it covered 12th Div. and took part in the Battle of Amiens (8–11/8/18) and the Battle of Albert (21–23/8/18). On 30/8/18 the 25th Div. Arty. was transferred to cover 47th Div. (III Corps) and took part in the Second Battle of Bapaume (31/8–3/9/18). On 6/9/18, 25th Div. Arty. was transferred in the line to cover 58th Div., it was drawn back into reserve on 8/9/18 and attached to 74th Div., and on 12/9/18 to 12th Div. On 14/9/18 CX was transferred to cover 18th Div. and CXII to cover 12th Div. (III Corps), and CX and CXII took part in the Battle of Epéhy (18/9/18). On 25/9/18, 25th Div. Arty. was attached to the Australian Corps and took part in the Battle of St. Quentin Canal (29/9–2/10/18). On 4/10/18 25th Div. Arty. rejoined 25th Division in the line near Lieramont.

---

* The following Units accompanied the Composite Brigade :—106 Fd. Coy., Wireless Sec. and 1 Cable Sec. (25th Div. Sig. Coy.), 75th Bde. Sig. Sec., Composite Light T.M. Bty., and 75th Fd. Ambce.

25TH DIVISION

Dates	INFANTRY Brigades	INFANTRY Battalions and attached Units	Mounted Troops	ARTILLERY Field Artillery Brigades	ARTILLERY Field Artillery Batteries	Bde. Ammn. Coins.	Trench Mortar Bties. Medium	Trench Mortar Bties. Heavy	Divnl. Ammn. Coln.	Engineers Field Cos.	Signal Service Divnl. Signal Coy.	Pioneers	M.G. Units	Field Ambulances	Mobile Vety. Secn.	Divnl. Emplnt. Coy.	Divnl. Train
1914 October (England)	74th ...... 75th 76th	11/L.F., 13/Ches., 8/L.N.L., 9/L.N.L. 10/Ches., 11/Ches., 8/Bord., 8/S. Lanc. 8/K.O., 13/King's,5 10/ R.W.F., 7/K.S.L.I.	25th Div. Cyclist Coy.1	CX2 .... CXI2 .... CXII2 .... CXIII (H.)2 ...	A, B, C, D A, B, C, D A, B, C, D A (H.), B (H.), C (H.), D (H.)	CX B.A.C. CXI B.A.C. CXII B.A.C. CXIII (H.) B.A.C.	...	...	25th D.A.C.	93rd3 94th4	25th	6/ S.W.B.5 (P.)	...	75th 76th 77th	37th	...	25th6
1915 September (France)	74th ...... 75th 76th9	11/L.F., 13/Ches., 8/L.N.L., 9/L.N.L. 10/Ches.,8 11/Ches., 8/Bord., 8/S. Lanc. 8/K.O., 13/King's,5 10/R.W.F., 7/K.S.L.I.	H.Q., M.G. Sec., and B Sqdn.,10 1/ Lothians and Border Horse. 25th Div. Cyclist Coy.11	CX12 .... CXI12 .... CXII14 ...... CXIII (H.)15 ...	A, B, C, D A, B, C, D A, B, C, D A (H.), B (H.), C (H.), D (H.)	CX B.A.C. CXI B.A.C. CXII B.A.C. CXIII (H.) B.A.C.	...	...	25th D.A.C.	105th16 106th16 130th17	25th	6/ S.W.B. (P.)	...	75th 76th 77th	37th	...	25th
1916 June (France)	7th18 ...... 74th 75th	10/Ches.,8 3/Worc., 8/L.N.L.,7 1/Wilts.; 7th Bde. M.G. Coy.;19 7th T.M. Bty.20 11/L.F., 13/Ches., 9/L.N.L., 2/R. Ir. Rif.;21 74th Bde. M.G. Coy.;19 74th T.M. Bty.20 11/Ches., 8/Bord.,2/S. Lanc.,22 8/S. Lanc.; 75th Bde. M.G. Coy.;19 75th T.M. Bty.20	...	CX12; 23 ...... CXI13; 24 ..... CXII14; 25 .... CXIII15; 26 ...	A, B, C, D A, B, C; D (H.) A, B, C; D (H.) A, B, C	...28	X.2527 Y.2527 Z.2527	W.2527	25th D.A.C.28	105th 106th 130th	25th	6/ S.W.B. (P.)	...	75th 76th 77th	37th	...	25th
1917 June (France)	7th ...... 74th 75th	10/Ches., 3/Worc.,29 8/ L.N.L.,30 1/Wilts.; 7th M.G. Coy.;49 7th T.M. Bty. 11/L.F., 13/Ches.,31 9/L.N.L., 2/R. Ir. Rif.;32 74th M.G. Coy.;49 74th T.M. Bty. 11/Ches., 8/Bord., 2/S. Lanc., 8/S. Lanc.;33 75th M.G. Coy.;49 75th T.M. Bty.	...	CX23 .... CXII25	A, B, C; D (H.) A, B, C; D (H.)	...	X.25 Y.25 Z.2534	W.2535	25th D.A.C.	105th 106th 130th	25th	6/ S.W.B. (P.)	195th M.G. Coy.36	75th 76th 77th	37th	225th37	25th
1918 March (France)	7th ...... 74th 75th	10/Ches.,38 4/S. Staff.,39 1/ Wilts.,40 7th T.M. Bty.41 11/L.F.,42 3/Worc.,29;43 9/ L.N.L.,44 74th T.M. Bty.41 11/Ches.,45 8/Bord.,46 2/S. Lanc.,47 75th T.M. Bty.41	...	CX .... CXII	A, B, C; D (H.) A, B, C; D (H.)	...	X.25 Y.25	...	25th D.A.C.	105th 106th 130th	25th	6/ S.W.B. (P.)48	No. 25 Bn.49 M.G.C.	75th 76th 77th	37th	225th	25th

138

After reconstitution

Infantry Brigades and their units

Period	7th Bde.	74th Bde.	75th Bde.	Bde. T.M. Bty.
1918 July (England)	7th.... 8/Leic.,[50] 10/Ches.,[38] [51] 13/E. Surr.[52]	74th.... 13/Gr. How.,[53] 2/7/L.F.,[54] 21/Middx.,[55]	75th[56] 17/King's,[57] 6/Gr. How.,[58] 11/R. Suss.[59]	
1918 September (France)	7th.... 9/Devon.,[62] 20/Manch.,[63] 21/Manch.,[64]	74th.... 9/Gr. How.,[65] 11/Sher. For.,[66] 13/D.L.I.,[67]	75th[68] 1/8/R. War.,[69] 1/5/Glouc.,[70] 1/8/Worc.,[71]	7th T.M., 74th T.M., 75th T.M. Bty.[72]

Divisional Troops

Period	Artillery		T.M.	D.A.C.	Fd. Coys. R.E.		Pioneers	M.G.	Fd. Ambces.	Mob. Vet.	Emp. Coy.	Train
1918 July (England)	CX* .... A, B, C; D (H.)	CXII* .... A, B, C; D (H.)	X.25* Y.25*	25th D.A.C.	105th* 106th* 130th*	25th*	11/ S. Lanc. (P.)[60]	No. 25 Bn.,* M.G.C.	75th* 76th* 77th*	37th*	225th[61]	25th*
1918 September (France)	CX .... A, B, C; D (H.)	CXII .... A, B, C; D (H.)	X.25 Y.25	25th D.A.C.	105th 106th 130th	25th	11/ S. Lanc. (P.)[60]	No. 25 Bn. M.G.C.	75th 76th 77th	37th	225th[61]	25th

*These units did not accompany 25th Div. to England on 30/6/18. On 16 & 17 Sept. these units rejoined 25th Div. at St. Riquier (east of Abbeville) except 25th Div. Arty. (rejoined on 4/10/18) ; 130th Fd. Coy., 76th, and 77th Fd. Ambces. (on 29/9) ; 11/S. Lanc. P. (on 13/10) ; and No. 25 Bn., M.G.C. (on 19/10/18).

NOTES

1 Cyclist Coy. was formed in Febry., 1915.

2 In Jany., 1915, the Bdes. were organized as 4-battery brigades; the Btics. were 4-gun batteries, and were lettered —A, B, C, D—in each Brigade.

3 On 28/1/15, 93rd Fd. Coy. was transferred to 17th Div.

4 On 26/1/15, 94th Fd. Coy. was transferred to 19th Div.

5 Bn. left 76th Bde. in Febry., 1915, and was converted into the Pioneer Bn. Bn. was replaced in 76th Bde. by 13/King's (from Army Troops).

6 Train consisted of 198, 199, 200, and 201 Cos., A.S.C.

7 On 26/10/15 Bn. was transferred from 74th Bde. to 7th Bde. (25th Div.).

8 On 26/10/15 Bn. was transferred from 75th Bde. to 7th Bde. (25th Div.).

9 On 15/10/15, 76th Bde. was transferred from 25th Div. to 3rd Div. in exchange for 7th Bde. (see note 18).

10 Joined Div. in England, embkd. for le Havre on 27/9/15, and served with 25th Div. until 10/5/16, when the Cav. left and joined V Corps Cav. Regt. on 11/5/16.

11 Embkd. for le Havre on 25/9/15, and served with the Div. until 9/5/16, when the Cyclist Coy. was transferred to XVII Corps Cyclist Bn.

12 On 31/5/16 D Bty. left and became A/CXIII ; and A (H.)/CXIII joined CX and became D (H.)/CX.

13 On 31/5/16 D Bty. left and became B/CXIII ; and C (H.)/CXIII joined CXI and became D (H.)/CXI.

14 On 31/5/16 D Bty. left and became C/CXIII ; and D (H.)/CXIII joined CXII and became C/CXIII ; and D/CXII joined CXI and became D (H.)/CXI.

15 On 17/12/15 B (H.) left CXIII and became B (H.)/CXXXI, with 2nd Cdn. Div. On 31/5/16 CXIII was reorganized : A (H.), C (H.), and D (H.)/CXIII left and became D (H.)/CX, D (H.)/CXI, and D (H.)/CXII ; and D/CX, D/CXI, and D/CXII joined CXIII and became A, B, and C/CXIII.

16 In Feb., 1915, 105th and 106th Fd. Cos. joined from 34th Div., to replace 93rd and 94th Fd. Cos. (see notes 3 and 4).

17 130th Fd. Coy. joined before June, 1915.

18 On 18/10/15, 7th Bde. (3/Worc., 2/S. Lanc., 1/Wilts., 2/R. Ir. Rif.) was transferred from 3rd Div. and joined 25th Div., to replace 76th Bde. (note 9).

19 M.G. Cos. were formed and joined Bdes. as follows :—
7th—formed in the Bde. on 12/1/16 at Ploegsteert ;
74th—left Grantham on 10/3/16, disembkd. at le Havre on 11/3/16, and joined 74th Bde. on 17/3/16 at Chelers ;
75th—formed at Grantham on 19/12/15, disembkd. at le Havre on 11/3/16, and joined 75th Bde. on 15/3/16 at Grossart.

20 T.M. Btlies. were formed in the Bdes. :—
7th—7/1 by 9/3/16, 7/2 by 16/4/16, and they became 7th T.M. Bty. by 17/6/16 ;
74th—74/1 joined on 23/3/16, 74/2 joined on 22/4/16, and they became 74th T.M. Bty. by 14/6/16 ;
75th—75/1 joined on 23/3/16, 75/2 was formed on 29/4/16, and they became 75th T.M. Bty. by 16/6/16.

21 On 26/10/15 Bn. was transferred from 7th Bde. to 74th Bde. (25th Div.).

22 On 26/10/15 Bn. was transferred from 7th Bde. to 75th Bde. (25th Div.).

23 On 26 and 27/11/16 C was broken up to make up A and B to 6, 18-pdrs. each ; and A/CXI and L Sec. C/CXI joined, merged together, and became C/CX (6, 18-pdrs.). On 14/2/17 R. Sec. C (H.)/CXIII joined and made up D(H.)/CX to 6 hows.

24 On 27/11/16 Bde. was broken up ; L. Sec. C made up A to 6, 18-pdrs. and the Bty. then became C/CX ; B and R. Sec. C were transferred to CXII to make up the 3, 18-pdr. Btles. of CXII to 6 guns each ; and on 28/11/16 D (H) joined CXIII and became C (H.)/CXIII.

25 On 26 and 27/11/16 B and R. Sec. C/CXI joined and were split up in 3 sections to make up A, B, and C/CXII to 6, 18-pdrs. each. On 14/2/17 L. Sec. C (H.)/CXII joined and made up D (H.)/CXII to 6 hows.

26 On 26 and 27/11/16 C Bty. was broken up to complete A and B to 6, 18-pdrs. each ; on 28/11/16 D (H.)/CXI joined and became C (H.)/CXIII ; and on 5/12/16 507 (H.) was transferred from 7th Div. Arty. and became D (H.)/CXIII (see General Notes). On 14/2/17 CXIII became an A.F.A. Bde. ; C (H.) left, was broken up, and R. Sec. made up D (H.)/CX and L. Sec. made up D (H.)/CXII to 6 hows. each ; and on 22/2/17 B/CLXXII (6, 18-pdrs.) joined from 36th Div. and became C/CXIII ; and 1 sec. C (H.)/CLXXII joined and made up D (H.)/CXIII to 6 hows.

27 The 3 Medium T.M. Btles. were formed and joined the Div. by 19/4/16 ; and W Hvy. T.M. Bty. by 17/6/16.

28 On 26/5/16 B.A.C.s were abolished and the D.A.C. was reorganized.

29 On 10/11/17 Bn. was transferred to 74th Bde.

30 Between 10–16/2/18 Bn. was disbanded and drafted : 21 offrs. and 480 o.r. went to 2/4 and 1/5/L.N.L. (170th Bde., 57th Div.), and the remdr. was absorbed by No. 5 Entg. Bn.

31 On 6/2/18 Bn. was disbanded, and personnel was absorbed by No. 5 Entg. Bn.

32 On 13/11/17 Bn. left 25th Div. and joined 108th Bde., 36th Div., on 14/11/17.

33 On 6/2/18 Bn. was disbanded and surplus was absorbed by No. 5 Entg. Bn. on 13/2/18.

34 On 4/3/18 Z was broken up and distributed between X and Y.

35 On 4/3/18 W was broken up ; part of the personnel went to X and Y, and remdr. joined V H.T.M. Bty. IV Corps.

36 Coy. left Grantham on 12/12/16, disembkd. at le Havre on 18/12/16, and joined Div. on 16/12/16 at Meteren.

37 Coy. joined Div. (from Boulogne) on 21/5/17.

NOTES—contd.

38 On 21/8/18 Bn. was reduced to T.C. and surplus (10 ofrs. and 353 o.r.) went to 9/Ches. (56th Bde., 19th Div.). Bn. T.C. went to England with Div.

39 Bn. disembkd. at le Havre on 11/10/17. On 21/8/18 Bn. joined No. 1 Bn. Comp. Bde.; on 22/8/18 Bn. was transferred with Comp. Bde. to 50th Div. Bn. was reduced to T.C. on 11/7/18, transferred to 39th Div. on 15/8/18, and on 9/11/18 Bn. was demobilized.

40 Bn. left Div. on 20/6/18 and joined 110th Bde., 21st Div., on 21/6/18.

41 On 18/6/18 Bde. T.M. Bties. were broken up and the personnel was used to form a Light T.M. Bty. for the Comp. Bde.

42 On 21/8/18 Bn. joined No. 1 Bn., Comp. Bde., and on 22/8/18 Bn. was transferred with Comp. Bde. to 50th Div. On 12/8/18 Bn. completed disbandment in France.

43 On 22/6/18 Bn. joined No. 1 Bn., Comp. Bde., and on 21/8/18 Bn. was transferred to 57th Bde., 19th Div.

44 On 21/8/18 Bn. joined No. 2 Bn., Comp. Bde., and on 22/8/18 Bn. was transferred with Comp. Bde. to 50th Div. Between 5–12/8/18 Bn. was disbanded in France.

45 On 17/6/18 Bn. was reduced to T.C. and surplus (16 ofrs. and 492 o.r.) was absorbed by 6/Ches. (see General Notes). On 19/6/18 T.C. left 25th Div. and joined 39th Div. on 23/6/18.

46 On 21/8/18 Bn. joined No. 2 Bn., Comp. Bde., and on 22/8/18 Bn. was transferred with Comp. Bde. to 50th Div. In July, 1918, Bn. was broken up in France.

47 On 20/8/18 Bn. left 25th Div., and joined 64th Bde., 21st Div., on 21/8/18; and on 30/8/18 Bn. was transferred to 89th Bde., 30th Div.

48 On 20/6/18 Bn. was transferred (temporarily) to 50th Div. On 1/7/18 Bn. left 50th Div. and joined 30th Div. (as Pioneer Bn.) on 2/7/18.

49 Bn. was formed on 1/3/18 and consisted of 7th, 74th, 75th, and 105th M.G. Cos. Bn. left Div. on 29/6/18: was transferred to Third Army on 23/7/18, and allotted to 59th Div. Joined 59th Div. on 20/7/18, and served with 59th Div. until 2/10/18, Bn. was then transferred to XI Corps Reserve, and was attached to 66th Div. from 5–18/10/18. On 19/10/18 M.G. Bn. rejoined 25th Div.

50 Bn. (in 110th Bde., 21st Div.) was reduced to T.C. on 28/6/18. T.C. left 21st Div. on 29/6/18, joined 7th Bde. at Boulogne on 30/6/18. On 7/7/18 Bn. left 25th Div. and became 14/Duke's at Clacton-on-Sea.

51 On 30/6/18 Bn. went to England in 7th Bde., and on 7/7/18 Bn. left 25th Div. and became 15/S.W.B. On 16/7/18 Bn. moved to N. Walsham.

52 Bn. (in 119th Bde., 40th Div.) was reduced to T.C. on 5/5/18. T.C. left 40th Div. on 3/6/18, served with 34th Div. 3–17/6/18, with 39th Div. 17–30/6/18, and joined 7th Bde. at Boulogne on 30/6/18. In England, T.C. left 25th Div. on 16/7/18 and moved to Lowestoft.

53 Bn. (in 121st Bde., 40th Div.) was reduced to T.C. on 6/5/18. T.C. left 40th Div. on 3/6/18, served with 34th Div. 3–17/6/18, with 39th Div. 17–29/6/18, and joined 74th Bde. at Boulogne on 30/6/18. Bn. reformed in England; and on 9/9/18 joined 236th Bde. (late 75th Bde., note 56), and went to N. Russia with 236th Bde. in Oct., 1918.

54 Bn. (in 197th Bde., 66th Div.) was reduced to T.C. on 25/4/18. On 30/6/18 T.C. joined 74th Bde. at Boulogne. On 3/7/18, in England, Bn. became 24/L.F.; and later on Bn. was broken up in England and used for drafts.

55 Bn. (in 118th Bde., 40th Div.) was reduced to T.C. on 5/5/18. T.C. left 40th Div. on 3/6/18, served with 34th Div. 3–17/6/18, with 39th Div. 17–29/6/18, and joined 74th Bde. at Boulogne on 30/6/18. On 16/7/18, in England, T.C. left 25th Div. and moved to Cromer.

56 On 9/9/18, 75th Bde. was renumbered 236th Bde. and left 25th Div. 236th Bde. was reformed in England (Bde. H.Q., 17/King's, 6/Gr. How., 18/Gr. How., 11/R. Suss., 236th T.M. Bty., 236th Sig. Sec.). On 15/10/18 Bde. embkd. at Dundee for service in N. Russia, and H.Q. and 6/ and 13/Gr. How. disembkd. at Murmansk on 27/11/18.

57 Bn. (in 89th Bde., 30th Div.) was reduced to T.C. on 14/5/18. T.C. left 30th Div. on 19/6/18, served with 66th Div. 19–30/6/18, joined 75th Bde. at Boulogne on 30/6/18. Bn. reformed in England, and on 9/9/18 joined 236th Bde. (late 75th Bde., note 56). In Oct., 1918, Bn. went to N. Russia with 236th Bde.

58 Bn. (in 32nd Bde., 11th Div.) was reduced to T.C. on 14/5/18. T.C. left 11th Div. on 19/6/18, served with 66th Div. 10–30/6/18, joined 75th Bde. at Boulogne on 30/6/18. Bn. reformed in England, and on 9/9/18 joined 236th Bde. (late 75th Bde., note 56). In Oct., 1918, Bn. went to N. Russia with 236th Bde.

59 Bn. (in 116th Bde., 39th Div.) was reduced to T.C. on 23/5/18. T.C. left 39th Div. on 30/6/18 and joined 75th Bde. at Boulogne on 30/6/18. Bn. returned to England, reformed, and on 9/9/18 joined 236th Bde. (late 75th Bde., note 56) for service in N. Russia.

60 Bn. (formerly Pioneers, 30th Div.) was reduced to T.C. on 15/5/18. T.C. left 30th Div. on 19/6/18, served with 66th Div. 19–30/6/18, joined 25th Div. at Boulogne, and went to England with 25th Div. Bn. reformed in England, and returned to France on 7 and 8/10/18. On 11/10/18 at Roisel Bn. came again under orders of the 25th Div., and on 13/10/18 Bn. concentrated with 25th Div. at Prémont, and became Pioneer Bn., 25th Div.

61 On 30/6/18 Coy. went from Boulogne to England with 25th Div.; and on 15/9/18 Coy. returned to Boulogne with 25th Div. H.Q. and Bde. H.Q. of 7th and 74th Bdes.

RECONSTITUTED DIVISION

62 Left 20th Bde., 7th Div. (in Italy) on 13/9/18, and joined 7th Bde. on 16/9/18 at Canchy.

63 Left 22nd Bde., 7th Div. (in Italy) on 13/9/18, and joined 7th Bde. on 16/9/18 at Canchy.

64 Left 91st Bde., 7th Div. (in Italy) on 13/9/18, and joined 7th Bde. on 16/9/18 at Canchy.

65 Left 69th Bde., 23rd Div. (in Italy) on 13/9/18, and joined 74th Bde. on 17/9/18 at St. Riquier.

66 Left 70th Bde., 23rd Div. (in Italy) on 13/9/18, and joined 74th Bde. on 18/9/18 at St. Riquier.

67 Left 68th Bde., 23rd Div. (in Italy) on 14/9/18, and joined 74th Bde. on 18 and 19/9/18 at St. Riquier.

68 75th Bde. was reformed on 17/9/18 at Gapennes (north of St. Riquier).

69 Left 143rd Bde., 48th Div. (in Italy) on 11/9/18, and joined 75th Bde. on 19/9/18.

70 Left 145th Bde., 48th Div. (in Italy) on 11/9/18, and joined 75th Bde. on 17/9/18.

71 Left 144th Bde., 48th Div. (in Italy) on 12/9/18, and joined 75th Bde. on 17 and 18/9/18.

72 Bde. Light T.M. Bties. began reforming on 13/10/18.

25TH DIVISION

FORMATION, BATTLES, AND ENGAGEMENTS

This New Army Division had no existence before the outbreak of the Great War.

Army Order No. 388 of the 13th September 1914 authorized the addition of six divisions (21st–26th) and Army Troops to the Regular Army (see Appendix I). This augmentation formed the Third New Army, and during September 1914 the 25th Division began to assemble in camps at Codford St. Peter and Fisherton de la Mere (to the west of Salisbury).

During the first months the units of the 25th Division were confronted with the usual difficulties which result from a shortage of regular officers and trained instructors and a total lack of arms and equipment. In some of the battalions it was possible to issue about half the men with red coats, and these men paraded in red coats, drab trousers, and every type of civilian headgear ; the remainder were dressed entirely in civilian suits. Naturally a considerable time elapsed before any rifles or equipment were issued to the Division.

In the middle of October the weather broke and the condition of the camps became indescribable. Roads leading to the camps were impassable, and as the men had no change of clothing all training had to be suspended. On the 4th November the Division learned that it was to move into billets in the Bournemouth area and this welcome change was completed by the middle of the month.

Even as late as February 1915 battalions had only received drill-pattern rifles and the men were only half-equipped. At the beginning of May the Division left Bournemouth and marched to Romsey, and it was encamped there for 3 weeks. At the end of May the Division marched to Aldershot and its final training began. Equipment was soon completed and transport arrived, but it was August before service rifles were received.

On the 12th August Field-Marshal Earl Kitchener inspected the Division and early in September H.M. the King saw the 25th Division as it was returning from a tactical exercise. Shortly afterwards the Division was informed that it was to proceed overseas. Entrainment began on the 25th, and on the 30th September the Division completed its concentration around Nieppe. For the remainder of the Great War the 25th Division served on the Western Front in France and Belgium and was engaged in the following operations :—

1915

1916

| 21 May | ... ... | German Attack on Vimy Ridge [XVII Corps, Third Army]. |

BATTLES OF THE SOMME

3–13 July	Battle of Albert [X Corps, Reserve Army].
14–16 July	Battle of Bazentin Ridge [X Corps, Reserve Army].
18 Aug.–3 Sept.	Battle of Pozières Ridge [II Corps, Reserve Army].
3 September	Fighting for Mouquet Farm.
1–22 October	Battle of the Ancre Heights [II Corps, Reserve Army].
9 October	Capture of Stuff Redoubt.
21 October	Capture of Regina Trench.

1917

| 7–14 June ... ... | Battle of Messines [II Anzac Corps, Second Army]. |

BATTLES OF YPRES

| 31 July–2 Aug. ... ... | Battle of Pilckem Ridge [II Corps, Fifth Army]. |
| 10 August ... ... | Capture of Westhoek [II Corps, Fifth Army]. |

1918

FIRST BATTLES OF THE SOMME

21–23 March	**Battle of St. Quentin** [IV Corps, Third Army].
24 and 25 March ...	**Battle of Bapaume** [IV Corps, Third Army].

BATTLES OF THE LYS

9–11 April ... ... **Battle of Estaires** (74th Bde.) [XV Corps, First Army].

10 and 11 April ... ... **Battle of Messines** (less 74th Bde.) [IX Corps, Second Army].

11 April ... ... **Loss of Hill 63** (7th Bde.) [IX Corps, Second Army].

13–15 April ... ... **Battle of Bailleul** [IX Corps, Second Army].

17–19 April ... ... **First Battle of Kemmel Ridge** (Inf. Bdes. under 34th Div.) [IX Corps, Second Army].

25 and 26 April ... ... **Second Battle of Kemmel Ridge** [II (Fr.) Cav. Corps on 25/4 ; and on 26/4 XXII Corps, Second Army].

29 April ... ... **Battle of the Scherpenberg** [XXII Corps, Second Army].

27 May–6 June ... ... **Battle of the Aisne** [IX Corps, Sixth (French) Army, until 29/5 ; then Fifth (French) Army].

On the 26th June 25th Div. Hd. Qrs. opened at Royon in X Corps area, and orders were received that Divnl. Hd. Qrs., three Inf. Bde. Hd. Qrs., 12 motor cyclists (25th Div. Sig. Coy.), and the Divnl. Employment Coy. would proceed to England, together with the training cadres of 10/Ches. and of ten other battalions. On the 30th June the 25th Div. (detailed above) embarked at Boulogne, and the training cadres of nine infantry battalions and one pioneer battalion joined on board (see Table). The 25th Div. disembarked at Folkestone at 3.30 p.m., entrained at once, and Mytchett Camp (Aldershot) was reached during the evening of the 30th June. During July the training cadres moved into the Eastern Command to absorb men (see Table and Notes), and the 75th Bde. returned to Mytchett Camp on the 25th and 26th August. On the 9th September the 75th Bde. became the 236th Bde. ; and the 236th Bde. left the 25th Division for Service in N. Russia (see Table and note 56). On the 14th September, 25th Div. Hd. Qrs. and the Divnl. Employment Coy. moved from Aldershot to Folkestone, the 7th and 74th Bde. Hd. Qrs. joining en route at Waterloo Station. On the 15th the 25th Div. disembarked at Boulogne and reached St. Riquier (near Abbeville) on the 16th. Units which had been left behind in France rejoined the Division on the 16th and 17th, and between the 16th and 19th September nine battalions (from the 7th, 23rd, and 48th Divisions in Italy) joined the 25th Div. at St. Riquier. The 7th, 74th, and 75th Bdes. were then reformed (see Table and notes 62–71). The 25th Div. moved to Henencourt on the 27th September, came under XIII Corps (Fourth Army) on the 28th, moved to Montauban on the 29th September, and on the 1st October the Division reached Combles. On the 3rd October the Division took over part of the front line south of Gouy, and thereafter was engaged as follows :—

THE ADVANCE TO VICTORY
BATTLES OF THE HINDENBURG LINE

4 and 5 October ... ... **Battle of the Beaurevoir Line** [XIII Corps, Fourth Army].

8 and 9 October ... ... **Battle of Cambrai** [XIII Corps, Fourth Army].

9–11 October ... ... **Pursuit to the Selle** [XIII Corps, Fourth Army].

THE FINAL ADVANCE IN PICARDY

17–25 October ... ... **Battle of the Selle** [XIII Corps, Fourth Army].

4 November ... ... **Battle of the Sambre** [XIII Corps, Fourth Army].

4 November ... ... **Passage of the Sambre-Oise Canal at Landrecies.**

The 25th Division continued to advance and by the evening of the 7th November it had crossed the Grande Helpe and established a line just east of St. Hilaire (north-west of Avesnes). The Division was then relieved in the front line and it drew back behind the Sambre at Landrecies. The 25th Division was still resting in the area Landrecies—Preux—Bousies when the Armistice brought hostilities to a close at 11 a.m. on the 11th November.

On the 13th November the Division marched back to Le Cateau and was employed on salvage work until the 29th and 30th November ; it then moved back to billets in the villages east of Cambrai. On the 4th December H.M. the King passed through the area occupied by the Division and the units lined the roads near the villages in which they were billeted. The month was passed in salvage work and lectures. In January 1919 salvage work continued and demobilization began. Gradually the Division dwindled ; by the 28th March it was reduced to cadre strength and its war history then came to an end. During the Great War the 25th Division lost 48,289 killed, wounded, and missing.

26TH DIVISION

G.O.C.

18 September, 1914	Major-General E. C. W. MACKENZIE-KENNEDY (to XII Corps, 4/1/17 ; Sick, 14/1/17).
4 January, 1917	Br.-Gen. A. W. GAY (tempy.).
10 March, 1917	Major-General A. W. GAY (sick, 7/7/17).
7 July, 1917	Br.-Gen. A. J. POOLE (acting).
2 August, 1917	Major-General A. W. GAY.
27 September, 1917	Br.-Gen. H. D. WHITE-THOMSON (acting).
4 November, 1917	Major-General A. W. GAY.

G.S.O. 1.

19 Sept., 1914...Captain R. F. GROSS (acting).
23 Feb., 1915...Major C. E. CORKRAN (tempy.).
26 Feb., 1915...Lt.-Col. C. E. CORKRAN.
12 Mar., 1915...Captain B. P. LEFROY (acting).
15 June, 1915...Major R. W. HARE (tempy.).
28 June, 1915...Lt.-Col. R. W. HARE (sick, 14/12/15).
14 Dec., 1915...Major G. W. HASLEHURST (acting).
20 Dec., 1915...Lt.-Col. B. J. CURLING (sick, 24/7/16).
24 July, 1916...Lt.-Col. V. ASSER (acting).
10 Aug., 1916...Major G. W. HASLEHURST (tempy.).
19 Aug., 1916...Lt.-Col. G. W. HASLEHURST (sick, 12/10/16).
12 Oct., 1916...Major W. C. GARSIA (acting).
27 Oct., 1916...Lt.-Col. P. L. HANBURY.
31 July, 1917...Major A. G. LEECH (acting).
22 Sept., 1917...Lt.-Col. P. L. HANBURY.
31 Dec., 1917...Major E. S. W. TIDSWELL (acting).
13 Jan., 1918...Lt.-Col. E. S. W. TIDSWELL.

A.-A. and Q.-M.-G.

3 Oct., 1914...Major C. S. H. WAYMOUTH (acting).
10 Oct., 1914...Colonel G. W. MAXWELL.
19 Mar., 1915...Major E. J. BUCKLEY (tempy.).
9 April, 1915...Lt.-Col. E. J. BUCKLEY.
30 May, 1915...Lt.-Col. D'O. B. DAWSON.
30 June, 1916...Lt.-Col. F. G. L. THURLOW (sick, 26/8/16).
26 Aug., 1916...Captain R. M. B. NEEDHAM (acting).
1 Sept., 1916...Lt.-Col. F. G. L. THURLOW.
26 Nov., 1916...Major R. M. B. NEEDHAM (acting).
29 Dec., 1916...Lt.-Col. F. G. L. THURLOW.
10 Dec., 1917...Major R. M. B. NEEDHAM (acting).
26 Jan., 1918...Lt.-Col. F. G. L. THURLOW.
17 Mar., 1918...Lt.-Col. F. J. G. AGG.

B.-G., R.A.

17 Nov., 1914...Br.-Gen. E. M. FLINT.
5 Oct., 1915...Br.-Gen. F. T. RAVENHILL (sick, 5/6/16).
6 June, 1916...Lt.-Col. C. H. FORD (acting).
18 June, 1916...Br.-Gen. T. BRUCE.
18 July, 1916...Lt.-Col. C. H. FORD (acting).
17 Aug., 1916...Br.-Gen. T. BRUCE (Acting B.-G., R.A., XII Corps, 22/6/17).
22 June, 1917...Lt.-Col. F. W. MACKENZIE (acting).
10 Aug., 1917...Lt.-Col. C. MAC I. RITCHIE (acting).
26 Aug., 1917...Br.-Gen. T. BRUCE.
8 July, 1918...Lt.-Col. G. H. GORDON (acting).
23 Aug., 1918...Br.-Gen. T. BRUCE.

C.R.E.

3 Nov., 1914...Lt.-Col. W. T. DIGBY.
4 Oct., 1915...Lt.-Col. C. G. W. HUNTER (Acting C.E., XII Corps, 3/7/16).
3 July, 1916...Major W. R. IZAT (acting).
26 July, 1916...Lt.-Col. C. G. W. HUNTER (Acting C.E., XII Corps, 1/12/17).
1 Dec., 1917...Major H. L. G. BELL (acting).
9 Jan., 1918...Lt.-Col. G. B. PEARS.
28 April, 1918...Major R. G. PRICHARD (acting).
3 May, 1918...Lt.-Col. G. B. PEARS.

77th BDE.

25 Sept., '14...Br.-Gen. H. P. SHEKLETON.
25 Oct., '14...Br.-Gen. Sir H. H.
STEWART, Bart.
29 Oct., '15...Br.-Gen. G. L. HIBBERT
(sick, 25/8/16).
25 Aug., '16...Lt.-Col. H. A. THOMPSON
(acting).
27 Aug., '16...Br.-Gen. F. S. MONTAGUE-
BATES (tempy.).
20 Sept., '16...Br.-Gen. G. L. HIBBERT.
6 Feb., '17...Lt.-Col. R.
FALCONAR-STEWART (acting).
8 Feb., '17...Br.-Gen. W. A. BLAKE.
19 July, '17...Lt.-Col. G. H. F. WINGATE
(acting).
7 Sept., '17...Br.-Gen. W. A. BLAKE.

78th BDE.

25 Sept., '14...Br.-Gen. E. A. D'A.
THOMAS.
26 Apr, '16...Br.-Gen. J. DUNCAN.
13 Jan., '17...Colonel W. L. ROCKE
(acting).
22 Feb., '17...Br.-Gen. J. DUNCAN.
7 May, '17...Lt.-Col. T. N. S. M.
HOWARD (tempy.).
22 May, '17...Br.-Gen. T. N. S. M.
HOWARD.
11 Sept., '17...Lt.-Col. G. H. F. WINGATE
(acting).
5 Nov., '17...Br.-Gen. T. N. S. M.
HOWARD.
11 April, '18...Br.-Gen. G. H. F. WINGATE.

79th BDE.

17 Sept., '14...Br.-Gen. J. FISHER.
8 Sept., '15...Br.-Gen. A. J. POOLE.
24 Nov., '16...Colonel W. L. ROCKE (acting).
30 Dec., '16...Br.-Gen. A. J. POOLE.
7 July, '17...Lt.-Col. F. C. NISBET (acting).
2 Aug., '17...Br.-Gen. A. J. POOLE.

GENERAL NOTES

The following Units also served with the 26th Division :—

MOUNTED TROOPS :—1/Lothians and Border Horse from 22/9–5/10/18.

ARTILLERY :—XXXI Bde., R.F.A. (69, 100, and D (H.) Bties.)—of the 28th Division Artillery—was attached to the 26th Division Artillery from 17/6–24/8/17. XXXI Bde. then returned to the 28th Division.

    131st Heavy Battery, R.G.A. (4, 60-pdrs.), was raised and formed at Lewisham on 22/1/15 for the 26th Division*, but the Heavy Battery went abroad independently. 131st Heavy Battery disembkd. at le Havre on 9/3/16, arrived Doullens on 12/3/16, and joined XXIII Heavy Artillery Bde. at Etrée Wamin (8 miles S.S.E. of St. Pol).

    IV Highland Mountain Brigade (Argyllshire, Ross and Cromarty, and Buteshire Mountain Bties.—2·75″ guns), from 23-25/8/18.

OTHER UNITS :—43rd Sanitary Section, joined the Division in England on 19/8/15, went to France with the Division, and disembarked at le Havre on 22/9/15. The Sanitary Section accompanied the Division to Salonika in December 1915, and served in Macedonia with the 26th Division for the remainder of the Great War.

    26th Division Motor Ambce. Workshop, was raised for the 26th Division. The personnel travelled from Southampton to Rouen (19–20/9/15), and the vehicles went from Avonmouth to Rouen (18–22/9/15). The Workshop left Rouen on 23/9/15, and joined 26th Division on 24/9/15. In November 1915, when the 26th Division went to Macedonia, the Workshop remained in France.

On 4/7/18 the reorganization of the 26th Division on a 9-battalion basis was completed. The Pioneer Bn. (8/O. & B.L.I.) remained a 4-company organization.

---

* 26th Heavy Battery, R.G.A. (4, 60-pdrs.) was serving with the 1st Division at the outbreak of the Great War ; and in August 1914, 26th Heavy Battery went to France with the 1st Division.

ORDER OF BATTLE, 1914-1918

Dates	INFANTRY Brigades	Battalions and attached Units	Mounted Troops	ARTILLERY — Field Artillery Brigades	Batteries	Bde. Ammn. Colns.	Trench Mortar Bttes. Medium	Heavy	Divnl. Ammn. Coln.	Engineers Field Cos.	Divnl. Signal Coy.	Pioneers	M.G. Units	Field Ambulances	Mobile Vety. Secn.	Divnl. Emplt. Coy.	Divnl. Train
1914 October (England)	77th ...... 78th 79th	8/R.S.F., 11/Sco. Rif., 10/B.W., 12/A. & S.H. 9/Glouc., 11/Worc., 7/O. & B.L.I., 7/R. Berks. 10/Devon., 8/D.C.L.I., 12/Hants., 7/Wilts.	26th Div. Cyclist Coy.1	CXIV3 ...... CXV3 ...... CXVI3 ...... CXVII (H.)3,2	A, B, C, D A, B, C, D A, B, C, D A (H.), B (H.), C (H.), D (H.)	CXIV B.A.C. CXV B.A.C. CXVI B.A.C. CXVII (H.) B.A.C.	...	...	26th D.A.C.	95th3 96th4	26th	8/O. & B.L.I.5 (P.)	...	78th6 79th6 80th6	38th7	...	26th8
1915 September (France)	77th ...... 78th 79th	8/R.S.F., 11/Sco. Rif., 10/B.W., 12/A. & S.H. 9/Glouc., 11/Worc., 7/O. & B.L.I., 7/R. Berks. 10/Devon., 8/D.C.L.I., 12/Hants., 7/Wilts.	A Sqdn.,9 1/Lothians and Border Horse. 26th Div. Cyclist Coy.	CXIV ...... CXV ...... CXVI ...... CXVII (H.)	A, B, C, D A, B, C, D A, B, C, D A (H.), B (H.), C (H.), D (H.)	CXIV B.A.C. CXV B.A.C. CXVI B.A.C. CXVII (H.) B.A.C.	...	...	26th D.A.C.	107th10 108th10 131st11	26th	8/O. & B.L.I. (P.)	...	78th 79th 80th	38th	...	26th12
1916 July (Macedonia)	77th ...... 78th 79th	8/R.S.F., 11/Sco. Rif., 10/B.W., 12/A. & S.H.; 77th Bde. M.G. Coy.;13 77th T.M. Bty.;14 77th S.A.A. Sec. Ammn. Coln.15 9/Glouc., 11/Worc., 7/O. & B.L.I., 7/R. Berks.; 78th Bde. M.G. Coy.;15 78th T.M. Bty.;14 78th S.A.A. Sec. Ammn. Coln.15 10/Devon., 8/D.C.L.I., 12/Hants., 7/Wilts.; 79th Bde. M.G. Coy.;13 79th T.M. Bty.;14 79th S.A.A. Sec. Ammn. Coln.15	A Sqdn.,16 1/Lothians and Border Horse. 26th Div. Cyclist Coy.17	CXIV18 ...... CXV19 ...... CXVI20 ...... CXVII21	A, B, C A, B, C; D (H.) A, B, C; D (H.) A, B, C; D (H.)	CXIV B.A.C. CXV B.A.C. CXVI B.A.C. CXVII B.A.C.	...	...	26th D.A.C.22	107th 108th 131st	26th	8/O. & B.L.I. (P.)	...	78th 79th 80th	38th	...	26th23
1917 July (Macedonia)	77th ...... 78th 79th	8/R.S.F., 11/Sco. Rif., 10/B.W.,24 12/A. & S.H.; 77th M.G. Coy.; 77th T.M. Bty.; 77th S.A.A. Sec. Ammn. Coln. 9/Glouc.,25 11/Worc., 7/O. & B.L.I., 7/R. Berks.; 78th M.G. Coy.; 78th T.M. Bty.; 78th S.A.A. Sec. Ammn. Coln. 10/Devon., 8/D.C.L.I., 12/Hants., 7/Wilts.;26 79th M.G. Coy.; 79th T.M. Bty.; 79th S.A.A. Sec. Ammn. Coln.	...	CXIV27 ...... CXV28 ...... CXVI29 ...... CXVII30	A, B, C A, B; D (H.) A, B; D (H.) A, B; D (H.)	CXIV B.A.C. CXV B.A.C. CXVI B.A.C. CXVII B.A.C.	...	...	...22	107th 108th 131st	26th	8/O. & B.L.I. (P.)	...	78th 79th 80th	38th	817th51	26th52

	77th	LVII33 CXIV CXV CXVI	...	LVII B.A.C. / CXIV B.A.C. / CXV B.A.C. / CXVI B.A.C.	...	...	107th 108th 131st	26th	8/O. & B.L.I. (P.)	...	78th 79th 80th	38th	817th	26th
1918 August (Macedonia)														
77th	8/R.S.F., 11/Sco. Rif., 12/A. & S.H.; 77th M.G. Coy.; 77th T.M. Bty.; 77th S.A.A. Sec. Ammn. Coln.	A; B; D (H.)27; 33		LVII B.A.C.										
78th	11/Worc., 7/O. & B.L.I., 7/R. Berks.; 78th M.G. Coy.; 78th T.M. Bty.; 78th S.A.A. Sec. Ammn. Coln.	A, B, C		CXIV B.A.C.										
79th	10/Devon., 8/D.C.L.I., 12/Hants.; 79th M.G. Coy.; 79th T.M. Bty.; 79th S.A.A. Sec. Ammn. Coln.	A; B; D (H.)		CXV B.A.C.										
		A; B; D (H.)		CXVI B.A.C.										

NOTES

1 The Cyclist Coy. was formed on 4/1/15, and it was billeted in Westbury.

2 In Janry., 1915, the Bdes. were organized as 4-battery brigades; the Bties. were 4-gun batteries, and were lettered—A, B, C, D—in each Brigade.

3 On 29/1/15 96th Fd. Coy. left 26th Div. at Warminster, went to Ireland and joined 16th Div. on 30/1/15 at Moore Park; and on 30/8/15 the Fd. Coy. joined 7th Div. in France.

4 On 1/2/15 99th Fd. Coy. left 26th Div. at Warminster and joined 20th Div. at Woking.

5 Bn. (from Army Troops, Third New Army) was attached to Div. from Nov., 1914; and on 25/1/15 Bn. was constituted Divnl. Pioneer Bn.

6 On 25/8/15 the 3 Fd. Ambces. (each 10 offrs. and 220 o.r. strong) joined the Div.

7 The Sec. joined on 18/7/15.

8 Train consisted of 202, 203, 204, and 205 Cos., A.S.C.

9 Sqdn. (6 offrs., 129 o.r.) joined Div. on 30/7/15 at Sutton Veny.

10 On 30/1/15, 107th and 108th Fd. Cos. joined from 35th Div., to replace 95th and 96th Fd. Cos. (see notes 3 and 4).

11 131st Fd. Coy. joined by 25/4/15.

12 Train went to France with 26th Div. in Sept., 1915, In Nov., 1915, when the Div. embkd. for Salonika, the Train remained in France, and on 20/11/15 joined 32nd Div. (on arrival of Div. in France). Train served with 32nd Div. for the remainder of the Great War.

13 The 3 Bde. M.G. Cos. left Grantham on 4/7/16, embkd. at Devonport on 5/7/16, disembkd. at Salonika on 14/7/16, and joined Inf. Bdes. as follows :—
77th on 24/7/16;
78th on 22/7/16; and
79th on 15/7/16.

14 The Bde. T.M. Bties. joined as follows :—
77th on 3/11/16;
78th by 12/11/16; and
79th on 3/11/16.

15 On 23/3/16 S.A.A. Secs. were numbered 77th, 78th, and 79th; and by 27/7/16 S.A.A. Secs. were attached to the Inf. Bdes.

16 Sqdn. left the Div. on 29/11/16, was attached to 8th Mtd. Bde. from 30/11/16—14/1/17, was then attached to Divisions to furnish Guards, Escorts, etc., and on 11/5/17 Sqdn. joined XII Corps Cav. Regt. (on formation).

17 Coy. left the Div. on 16/12/16; and, with 22nd Div. Cyclist Coy., formed XII Corps Cyclist Bn. on 22/12/16.

18 On 20/7/16 A was transferred and became A/CXVII; and D/CXIV was redesignated and became A/CXIV.

19 On 20/7/16 D was transferred and became B/CXVII; and B (H.)/CXVII joined and became D (H.)/CXV.

20 On 20/7/16 D was transferred and became C/CXVII; and C (H.)/CXVII joined and became D (H.)/CXVI.

21 On 17/5/16 A (H.)/CXVII (H.) was transferred to the 10th Div. and on 10/5/16 A (H.) joined LVII (H.)—in 10th Div.—and became A (H.)/LVII (H.). On 20/7/16 B (H.) was transferred and became D (H.)/CXV, C (H.) was transferred and became D (H.)/CXVI, and D (H.)/CXVII remained in the Brigade as D (H.)/CXVI. On the same day A/CXIV, D/CXV, and D/CXVI joined and became A, B, and C/CXVI.

22 D.A.C. moved to Marseille on 21/11/15, embkd.on 29/1/16, disembkd. at Salonika on 8/2/16, remained at Salonika until 25/7/16, then marched and rejoined 26th Div. on 31/7/16. On 22/1/17 the 26th D.A.C. ceased to exist; it was absorbed by the newly formed XII Corps A.C. and became B Sec., XII Corps A.C.

23 Train (consisting of 112, 113, 114, and 115 Cos., A.S.C.) was raised as 11th Div. Train; but when 11th Div. embkd. for Gallipoli in July, 1915, the Train remained in England. Eventually allotted to the 26th Div., the Train reached Salonika between 27/12/15 (112 Coy.)—31/3/16 (remdr. of Train—delayed en route and halted at Alexandria from 24/2—28/3/16). On 1/4/16 the Train joined 26th Div. In Oct., 1916, the Train was reorganized in Pack and Wheel Echelons, and 848, 849, 850, and 851 Pack Cos. joined the Train.

24 Bn. left the Div. on 30/6/18, arrived at Abancourt on 14/7/18, and joined 197th Bde., 66th Div., on 21/7/18. On 20/9/18 Bn. (in 197th Bde.) was transferred to L. of C., and on 15/10/18 Bn. was disbanded and drafted.

25 Bn. left the Div. on 4/7/18, moved via Itea and Taranto and reached Serqueux on 17/7/18, was attached to 50th Div. until 21/7/18, joined 108th Bde., 66th Div., on 22/7/18, and on 22/9/18 Bn. became Pioneer Bn., 66th Div.

26 Bn. left the Div. on 16/6/18, arrived Serqueux on 1/7/18, left Serqueux on 15/7/18, and joined 150th Bde., 50th Div., on the same day at Martin Eglise.

27 On 12/0/17, D (H.)/C from 22nd Div. became D (H.)/CXIV; and on 19/10/17, D (H.) was transferred to LVII (n. 33). In Dec, 1917, the Bde. underwent no reorganization.

28 On 27/12/16 C Bty. was broken up : 1 sec. joined A and 1 sec. joined B, making up A and B Bties. to 6, 18-pdrs.

29 On 28/12/16 C Bty. was broken up : A Bty. absorbed R. Sec. of C, and B Bty. absorbed L. Sec. of C, making up A and B Bties. to 6, 18-pdrs. each.

30 Between 26-30/12/16 A Bty. was broken up : and R. Sec. of A joined B, and L. Sec. of A joined C, making up B and C to 6, 18-pdrs. each ; C was then redesignated A. On 3/6/17 Bde. left 26th Div. and was attached to 60th Div. Bde. reorganized in 3, 4-gun 18-pdr. Bties. (A, B, and C) and 1, 4-gun How. Bty. (D). Bde. embkd. at Salonika, disembkd. at Alexandria on 5/7/17, reached el Ferdan on 6/7/17, and reorganized : C was broken up to complete A and B to 6, 18-pdrs. each, and D (H.) was redesignated C (H.). On 9/8/17 CXVII joined 74th Div. at Deir el Balah, and Bde. served with 74th Div. for the remainder of the War.

31 Formed in Oct., 1917.

32 Between 28-30/7/17 the Train was reorganized : 849, 850, and 851 (Pack) Cos. were broken up and the personnel was absorbed by 113, 114, and 115 (Wheel) Cos. respectively. The Train then comprised 4 Wheel Cos. (112-116) and 1 Pack Coy. (848).

33 LVII (H.) was raised in 1914 for 10th (Irish) Div., and served with the 10th Div. until 28/8/17. (Between 20-23/7/16 LVII (H.) became LVII.) LVII was transferred to XII Corps on 28/8/17 in Macedonia, and in September, 1917, LVII was transferred to and joined 26th Division. D (H.) was transferred and became C (H.)/CCLXIII in 10th (Irish) Div. in Palestine on 11/10/17. On 19/10/17, D (H.)/CXIV was transferred and became D (H.)/LVII.

M

26TH DIVISION

This New Army Division had no existence before the outbreak of the Great War.

Army Order No. 388 of the 13th September 1914 authorized the addition of six divisions (21st–26th) and Army Troops to the Regular Army (see Appendix I). This augmentation formed the Third New Army, and during September 1914 the 26th Division, the junior division of the Third New Army, began to assemble at Codford St. Mary, Sherrington, Stockton, and Wylye (to the west of Salisbury).

Khaki uniform was unobtainable when the units were raised, and at first the men had to be clothed in any makeshift uniforms which the old clothing contractors could supply. No badges were available, and for identification the battalions in each brigade wore patches of buff, blue, white, or green. Later on it became possible to issue the troops with blue clothing and some uniformity was then secured. More time, however, elapsed before any drill-pattern rifles, accoutrements, or equipment were available. Nevertheless, as long as fine weather lasted, "barrack-square" training proceeded vigorously; but the rain began towards the end of October and soon turned the ground into a sea of soft, sticky, ankle-deep slime; all useful work was then brought to a standstill. The men had no change of clothing or boots, there were no floor-boards to the tents, and the sixteen occupants of a bell tent lay side by side on a floor of mud. It was a welcome relief when, in November, the troops were ordered to move into billets, even though this move caused the wide dispersion of the Division. The units were billeted: Divisional Headquarters at Greenhill, Sutton Veny; 77th Brigade in Bristol; 78th Brigade in Cheltenham, Worcester, Oxford, and Reading; and 79th Brigade in Bath, Marlborough, Hungerford, and Basingstoke. The engineers were quartered at Warminster and Sutton Veny. Drill-pattern rifles were now received and training was carried on as strenuously as possible.

Khaki uniform and equipment were issued between February and April 1915, and in March the transport joined the units. Between the 26th April and the 8th May the units left billets and concentrated in huts between Sutton Veny and Longbridge Deverill (near Warminster). Brigade training was begun, and the drill-pattern rifles were gradually replaced by Mark III Lee-Enfield rifles. In July divisional training started and the final preparation for the field was undertaken. After this was concluded, all officers and men were given three days' 'farewell leave' prior to mobilization. On the 10th September mobilization was completed, and the Division received orders that it would move to France between the 18th and 21st September. On the 12th September the first advanced party left, the Division began moving on the 18th and on the 23rd September the 26th Division completed its concentration around Guignemicourt (west of Amiens).

Starting from the 28th September, brigades and units were attached to divisions in the line for training and work, and for part of the time the divisional artillery covered the 22nd Division (on the right of the British line) and the 5th Division. Until early in November 1915 the 26th Division served on the Western Front in France; the Division then embarked for the Macedonian Front, on which it served for the remainder of the Great War.

1915

On the 31st October the Division was ordered to be ready to embark at Marseille during November, and on the 1st November the Division learned that it was to move to the Macedonian Theatre. On the 2nd November the Division concentrated at Flesselles, entrainment started on the 9th and embarkation on the 11th November; on the 23rd the Division began to arrive at Salonika. On the 26th December units moved from Lembet (north of Salonika) to Happy Valley Camp.

1916

On the 22nd January the *Norseman*, with the divisional train on board, was torpedoed in the Gulf of Salonika; but the vessel was beached and all the personnel (and 500 mules —out of 1,000) were saved. By the 8th February the 26th Division had completed its concentration at Happy Valley. The 26th Division then served in the following operations in Macedonia:—

10–18 August ... ... **Horseshoe Hill (S.W. of Dojran)** [XII Corps].

1917

24 and 25 April ; and   **Battle of Dojran** [XII Corps].
8 and 9 May

1918

18 and 19 September   **Battle of Dojran** [XII Corps].
22–noon, 30th Sept. ...   **Pursuit to the Strumica Valley** [XVI Corps].

In the pursuit the leading troops of the Division moved through Valandova and crossed the Serbia–Bulgaria boundary on the 25th September. On the 26th Strumica was occupied and the bridge over the River Strumica was secured. At noon on the 30th September when the Armistice brought hostilities with Bulgaria to a close the 26th Division was occupying a line from Gradošor to Hamzali, with divisional headquarters at Dragomir (4½ miles E.N.E. of Strumica).

On the 6th October the Division began to advance on Radomir (S.W. of Sofia), and on the 18th reached Kocerinovo. The plan was now changed and the Division was directed to move towards Adrianople. On the 19th Dupnica was reached ; the infantry brigades then moved by rail from Radomir to Mustafa Pasha (west of Adrianople). The 77th Brigade reached Mustafa Pasha on the 21st and advanced divisional headquarters detrained on the 24th. Until the 30th the three infantry brigades remained ready to seize Adrianople if the opportunity arose, but at noon on the 31st October the Armistice with Turkey brought to a close all further operations in this Theatre of War.

On the 2nd November the 26th Division was transferred from XVI Corps to the Army of the Danube (General Berthelot) and received orders to move to Tirnovo, but at 3 p.m. on the 4th November the Armistice with Austria came into force. On the 8th the Division began to move to Levski. On the 11th November, however, the destination was altered to Ruščuk (on the Danube), and the Division concentrated there by the 17th. On the 28th November a contingent was sent to represent the Division in the official entry into Bucharest on the 1st December. During December the Division also despatched detachments into the Dobruja. On the 15th December the 26th Division was transferred from the Army of the Danube to the Army of Occupation of Bulgaria (General Chrétien). On the 31st December divisional headquarters left Ruščuk and opened at Varna on the 1st January 1919, and the Brigade Groups were then located : 77th at Ruščuk, 78th at Dobrič, and 79th around Silistria.

In February demobilization began and proceeded rapidly. By the 3rd March the Division only numbered 6,500 all ranks and most of the outlying detachments in the Dobruja had been reduced or withdrawn. Italian troops arrived in April and gradually relieved the Division ; and between the 19th–22nd April a Composite Brigade (under Br.-Gen. W. A. Blake) left the Division for Egypt. The end had now come and at Varna on the 10th May 1919 the Division ceased to exist. During the Great War the 26th Division lost 8,022 killed, wounded, and missing.

APPENDICES
1; 2, 3, 4, 5,
6, 7, 8, & 9

AUGMENTATION OF THE ARMY, 1914.

RAISING THE FIRST THREE NEW ARMIES.

On the 6th August 1914 Parliament sanctioned an increase of 500,000 men for the Regular Army, and on the 11th August a proclamation (see p. 2) called on 100,000 men to enlist immediately for 3 years or for the duration of the War.

Army Order 311, issued on the 16th August, dealt with this augmentation of the Army ; but this Army Order was cancelled, and on the 21st August Army Order 324 was substituted for it. The latter Order stated that H.M. the King approved the addition to the Army of six divisions (8th–13th) and Army Troops.

Army Order 324 was itself amended on the 11th September by Army Order 382, which directed that the 8th (Light) Division was to become the 14th (Light) Division ;* the first augmentation of the Army would then consist of the 9th–14th Divisions and Army Troops. Army Order 382 also authorized an addition to the Army of another six divisions (15th–20th) and Army Troops. But recruits were pouring in** and on the 13th September Army Order 388 gave formal approval for the addition to the Regular Army of yet another six divisions (21st–26th) and Army Troops.

The composition of each of the new divisions, the nomenclature of the new formations and units allotted to each of the divisions, as well as the particular battalions which were to be raised as Army Troops, were given in appendices to Army Orders 324, 382, and 388.

Army Order 324 directed that the new battalions were to become additional battalions of the Regiments of Infantry of the Line, and the battalions would be given numbers following consecutively on the existing battalions of their regiments, distinguished by the word " Service " in brackets after the number. Analogous arrangements (without the addition of the word " Service ") were made for the numbering of the Field Artillery Brigades, Field Companies R.E., and Field Ambulances R.A.M.C.

Army Order 324 also gave instructions that, under the administration of the Home Commands, all recruits were to be clothed and equipped at depôts—if sufficient clothing and equipment existed (see Narratives in this Part). Subsequently recruits would be collected at the training centres at which the new brigades and divisions were to be formed under the divisional generals.

Finally, Army Order 389 (issued on the 14th September) stated that the several additions to the Army would be organized and known as follows :—

9th to 14th Divisions and Army Troops... ... ... First New Army.

15th to 20th Divisions and Army Troops ... ... Second New Army.

21st to 26th Divisions and Army Troops ... ... Third New Army.

The eighteen divisions, formed from the men who enlisted in August and September 1914, served and fought in six different theatres of war, and in this volume are recorded the battles and engagements in which these divisions took part.

---

* The formation, from troops of overseas garrisons, of the 8th (Regular) Division—23rd, 24th, and 25th Infantry Brigades—between 19th September and 2nd October, 1914, was the reason for the renumbering of the 8th (Light) Division and its infantry brigades. The 8th Division disembarked in France early in November, 1914, and served in France for the remainder of the Great War (see Part I).

** 500,000 men were raised by the 15th September, 1914.

WAR ESTABLISHMENT OF 14th (Light) DIVISION (England, 1915), and 10th (Irish)

<table>
<tr><td>

Appendix 2.

14th (LIGHT) DIVISION (England, 1915).
Authority—W. E. of New Armies, d/d. 1/4/1915.

</td><td>

Appendix 3.

14th (LIGHT) DIVISION (France, 1918).
Authority—W. E. Part VII, d/d. 31/10/1918.

</td></tr>
<tr><td>

Divnl. H.Q.

Infantry :
   3 Brigades
   (12 Inf. Battalions, with 4 machine guns each).

Mounted Troops :
   1 Cavalry Squadron ;
   1 Cyclist Company.

Artillery :
   H.Q., Divnl. Artillery ;
   3 Field Artillery Brigades (12 batteries—
     18-pdr. Q.F.) and 3 B.A.C.s ;
   1 Field Artillery (How.) Brigade (4 batteries—
     4·5″ How.) and 1 (How.) B.A.C. ;
   1 Heavy Battery (4, 60-pdr. B.L.) and Hy.
     Bty. A.C.
   1 Divnl. Ammn. Coln.

Engineers :
   H.Q., Divnl. Engineers ;
   3 Field Companies.

Signal Service :
   1 Signal Company.

Pioneers :
   1 Pioneer Battalion
   (4 machine guns).

   3 Field Ambulances.
   1 Sanitary Section.
   1 Mobile Veterinary Section.
   1 Motor Ambulance Workshop.
   1 Divnl. Train.

</td><td>

Divnl. H.Q.

Infantry :
   3 Brigades
   (9 Inf. Battalions, with 36 Lewis guns each);
   3 Light Trench-Mortar Batteries
   (8, 3″ Stokes mortars each).

Artillery :
   H.Q., Divnl. Artillery ;
   2 Field Artillery Brigades
     (8 batteries—6, 18-pdr. Q.F. and 2, 4·5″
     How.) ;
   2 Medium Trench-Mortar Batteries
     (6, 2″ mortars each) ;
   1 Divnl. Ammn. Coln.

Engineers :
   H.Q., Divnl. Engineers ;
   3 Field Companies.

Signal Service :
   1 Signal Company.

Pioneers :
   1 Pioneer Battalion
   (12 Lewis guns).

Machine-Gun Unit :
   1 Machine-Gun Battalion
   (4 Companies, with 16 Vickers M.G.s each).

   3 Field Ambulances.
   1 Mobile Veterinary Section.
   1 Divnl. Employment Company.
   1 Divnl. Train.

</td></tr>
</table>

	WAR ESTABLISHMENT, APRIL, 1915.		WAR ESTABLISHMENT, OCTOBER, 1918 (FRANCE).	
All Ranks	19,614		16,035	
Horses and Mules	5,818		3,838	
Guns	68		48	
18-pdr. Q.F.		48		36
4·5″ How.		16		12
60-pdr. B.L.		4		
Trench Mortars			36	
Stokes				24
Medium				12
Heavy				
Machine Guns	52		400	
Vickers		52		64
Lewis				336
Carts and Vehicles	958		870	
Cycles	538		341	
Motor Cycles	19		44	
Motor Cars	11		11	
Motor Lorries	4		3	
Motor Ambulance Cars	21		21	

* In mid-September, 1918, the 3 Infantry Brigades were reorganized on a 3-battalion basis.

14th (Light) DIVISION (France, 1918), 23rd DIVISION (Italy, 1918), DIVISION (Palestine, 1918).

Appendix 4. 23rd DIVISION (Italy, 1918). Authority—W. E. Part XX, d/d. 9/8/1918.	Appendix 5. 10th (IRISH) DIVISION (Palestine, 1918). Authority—W. E. Part XI (Egypt), d/d. 11/11/1918.
Divnl. H.Q.	**Divnl. H.Q.**
Infantry : 3 Brigades (12 Inf. Battalions,* with 16 Lewis guns each) ; 3 Light Trench-Mortar Batteries (8, 3″ Stokes mortars each).	**Infantry :** 3 Brigades (12 Inf. Battalions—3 British and 9 Indian—with 16 Lewis guns each) ; 3 Light Trench-Mortar Batteries (8, 3″ Stokes mortars each).
Artillery : H.Q., Divnl. Artillery ; 2 Field Artillery Brigades (8 batteries—6, 18-pdr. Q.F. and 2, 4·5″ How.) ; 2 Medium Trench-Mortar Batteries (4, 2″ mortars each) ; 2 Mobile Trench-Mortar Sections** (2, 6″ mortars each) ; 1 Divnl. Ammn. Coln.	**Artillery :** H.Q., Divnl. Artillery ; 3 Field Artillery Brigades (9 batteries—6, 18-pdr. Q.F. and 3, 4·5″ How.) ; 1 Divnl. Ammn. Coln.
Engineers : H.Q., Divnl. Engineers ; 3 Field Companies.	**Engineers :** H.Q., Divnl. Engineers ; 2 Field Companies ; 1 Field Company, Sappers and Miners.
Signal Service : 1 Signal Company.	**Signal Service :** 1 Signal Company.
Pioneers : 1 Pioneer Battalion (8, Lewis guns).	**Pioneers :** 1 Indian Pioneer Battalion.
Machine-Gun Unit : 1 Machine-Gun Battalion (4 Companies, with 16 Vickers M.G.s each).	**Machine-Gun Unit :** 1 Machine-Gun Battalion (3 Companies, with 16 Vickers M.G.s each).
3 Field Ambulances. 1 Mobile Veterinary Section. 1 Divnl. Employment Company. 1 Divnl. Train.	3 Combined Field Ambulances. 1 Sanitary Section. 1 Mobile Veterinary Section. 1 Divnl. Train.

WAR ESTABLISHMENT, AUGUST, 1918 (ITALY).		**WAR ESTABLISHMENT, NOVEMBER, 1918 (PALESTINE).**		
16,003*		19,929		All Ranks.
4,105		6,052***		Horses and Mules.
48		48		Guns.
	36		36	18-pdr. Q.F.
	12		12	4·5″ How.
				60-pdr. B.L.
36**		24		Trench Mortars.
	24		24	Stokes.
	8			Medium.
	4**			Heavy.
264		240		Machine Guns.
	64		48	Vickers.
	200		192	Lewis.
818		720		Carts and Vehicles.
672		270		Cycles.
24		29		Motor Cycles.
11		9		Motor Cars.
3		4		Motor Lorries.
21		21		Motor Ambulance Cars.

** The Mobile T.M. Sections (6″ Mortars) never joined.   *** Includes 117 camels and 52 donkeys.

Appendix 6.	Appendix 7.
11th (NORTHERN) DIVISION (Gallipoli, 1915).	**26th DIVISION (Macedonia, 1915).**
Authority—W. E. adapted from W.E. d/d. 9/5/15.	Authority—Special Establishments, Salonika. 3, d/d. 1/11/15.

Divnl. H.Q.	Divnl. H.Q.
Infantry :	**Infantry :**
3 Brigades (12 Inf. Battalions, with 4 Vickers M.G.s each).	3 Brigades (12 Inf. Battalions, with 4 Vickers M.G.s each) ; 3 Small Arm Ammn. Sections.
Mounted Troops :	**Mounted Troops :**
1 Cavalry Squadron ; 1 Cyclist Company.	1 Cavalry Squadron ; 1 Cyclist Company.
Artillery :	**Artillery :**
H.Q., Divnl. Artillery ; 3 Field Artillery Brigades (12 batteries—4, 18-pdr. Q.F. each) ; 3 Brigade Ammn. Colns. ; 1 Field Artillery (How.) Brigade (4 batteries—4, 4·5″ How. each) ; 1 (How.) Brigade Ammn. Coln ; 1 Divnl. Ammn. Coln.	H.Q., Divnl. Artillery ; 3 Field Artillery Brigades (12 batteries—4, 18-pdr. Q.F. each) ; 3 Brigade Ammn. Colns. ; 1 Field Artillery (How.) Brigade (4 batteries—4, 4·5″ How. each) ; 1 (How.) Brigade Ammn. Coln. ; 1 Divnl. Ammn. Coln.
Engineers :	**Engineers :**
H.Q., Divnl. Engineers ; 3 Field Companies.	H.Q., Divnl. Engineers ; 3 Field Companies.
Signal Service :	**Signal Service :**
1 Signal Company.	1 Signal Company.
	Pioneers :
	1 Pioneer Battalion (4 Vickers M.G.s).
3 Field Ambulances. 1 Motor Ambulance Workshop. 1 Mobile Veterinary Section. 1 Divnl. Train.	3 Field Ambulances. 1 Sanitary Section. 1 Mobile Veterinary Section. 1 Divnl. Train.

WAR ESTABLISHMENT, AUGUST, 1915 (GALLIPOLI).		**WAR ESTABLISHMENT, NOVEMBER, 1915 (MACEDONIA).**	
All Ranks	18,317		21,766
Horses and Mules	5,423		8,844
Guns	64		64
18-pdr. Q.F.	48		48
4·5″ How.	16		16
60-pdr. B.L.			
Trench Mortars			
Stokes			
Medium			
Heavy			
Machine Guns	48		52
Vickers	48		52
Lewis			
Carts and Vehicles	1,058		1,070
Cycles	426		202
Motor Cycles	25		15
Motor Cars	12		1
Motor Lorries	3		
Motor Ambulance Cars	21		

Note.—For the composition of the 11th (Northern) Division in August 1915, on arrival at Suvla (Gallipoli), see Table, p. 22.

* On 4/7/1918 the 26th Division was red

Appendix 8.	**Appendix 9.**
26th DIVISION (Macedonia, 1918).	**13th (WESTERN) DIVISION (Mesopotamia, 1918).**
Authority—W. E. Part XII (Salonika), d/d. 11/11/1918.	Authority—W. E. for formations and units, Mesopotamia, d/d. 1918.
Divnl. H.Q.	Divnl. H.Q.
Infantry : 3 Brigades (12 Inf. Battalions,* with 16 Lewis guns each) ; 3 Machine-Gun Companies (24 Vickers M.G.s each) ; 3 Light Trench Mortar Batteries (8, 3″ Stokes Mortars each) ; 3 Small Arm Ammn. Sections.	**Infantry :** 3 Brigades (12 Inf. Battalions, with 16 Lewis guns each) ; 3 Machine-Gun Companies (16 Vickers M.G.s each) ; 3 Light Trench Mortar Batteries (8, 3″ Stokes Mortars each) ; 3 Small Arm Ammn. Sections.
	Mounted Troops : 1 Cyclist Company.
Artillery : H.Q., Divnl. Artillery ; 3 Field Artillery Brigades (9 batteries—6, 18-pdr. Q.F. (6-gun) and 3 (4-gun) 4·5″ How.) ; 3 Brigade Ammn. Colns.	**Artillery :** H.Q., Divnl. Artillery ; 2 Field Artillery Brigades (8 batteries—6, 18-pdr. Q.F. and 2, 4·5″ How.) ; 2 Brigade Ammn. Colns. ; 2 Medium Trench Mortar Batteries (4, 6″ Newton Trench Mortars each).
Engineers : H.Q., Divnl. Engineers ; 3 Field Companies.	**Engineers :** H.Q., Divnl. Engineers ; 3 Field Companies.
Signal Service : 1 Signal Company.	**Signal Service :** 1 Signal Company.
Pioneers : 1 Pioneer Battalion (16 Lewis guns).	**Pioneers :** 1 Pioneer Battalion (16 Lewis guns).
	Machine-Gun Unit : 1 Machine-Gun Company (16 Vickers M.G.s).
3 Field Ambulances. 1 Sanitary Section. 1 Mobile Veterinary Section. 1 Divnl. Employment Company. 1 Divnl. Train.	3 Field Ambulances. 1 Sanitary Section. 1 Mobile Veterinary Section. 1 Divnl. Train. 1 Field Bakery. 1 Field Butchery.

WAR ESTABLISHMENT, NOVEMBER, 1918 (MACEDONIA).		**WAR ESTABLISHMENT, AUGUST, 1918 (MESOPOTAMIA)****		
20,314		19,996		All Ranks.
7,463		6,652		Horses and Mules.
48		48		Guns.
	36		36	18-pdr. Q.F.
	12		12	4·5″ How.
				60-pdr. B.L.
24		32		Trench Mortars.
	24		24	Stokes.
			8	Medium.
				Heavy.
280		272		Machine Guns.
	72		64	Vickers.
	208		208	Lewis.
665		1,069		Carts and Vehicles.
18		125		Cycles.
16		22		Motor Cycles.
13		13		Motor Cars.
1		1		Motor Lorries.
		21		Motor Ambulance Cars.

uced to a 9-battalion basis (pp. 145 ; and 147).   ** The totals are approximately correct.

INDEX OF FORMATIONS

BRIGADES AND DIVISIONS

Infantry Brigades—*Continued.*

48th, 62 ; 64 ; 65 ; 68.
49th, 62 ; 64 ; 65 ; 68.
50th, 72 ; 74 ; 75 ; 76.
51st, 72 ; 74 ; 75 ; 76.
52nd, 72 ; 74 ; 75 ; 76 ; 77.
53rd, 80 ; 82 ; 83 ; 84 ; 85 .
54th, 80 ; 82 ; 83 ; 84.
55th, 80 ; 82 ; 83 ; 84.
56th, 88 ; 90 ; 91 ; 92.
57th, 88 ; 90 ; 91 ; 92.
58th, 88 ; 90 ; 91 ; 92 ; 109 fn.**
59th, 96 ; 98 ; 99 ; 100.
60th, 96 ; 98 ; 99 ; 100 ; 101.
61st, 96 ; 98 ; 99 ; 100 ; 101.
62nd, 104 ; 106 ; 107 ; 109.
63rd, 104 ; 106 ; 107.
64th, 104 ; 106 ; 107.
65th, 112 ; 114 ; 115 ; 116 ; 117.
66th, 112 ; 114 ; 115 ; 117.
67th, 112 ; 114 ; 115 ; 116 ; 117.
68th, 120 ; 122 ; 123 ; 125.
69th, 120 ; 122 ; 123.
70th, 120 ; 122; 123 ; 124 fn.*
71st, 128 ; 130 ; 131.
72nd, 128 ; 130 ; 131.
73rd, 128 ; 130 ; 131.
74th, 136 ; 138 ; 139 ; 142.
75th, 136 ; 138 ; 139 ; 140, notes 56 & 68 ; 142.
76th, 136 ; 138 ; 139.
77th, 144 ; 146 ; 147 ; 148 ; 149.
78th, 144 ; 146 ; 147 ; 148 ; 149.
79th, 144 ; 146 ; 147 ; 148 ; 149.
89th, 109 fn.**
110th, 104 ; 106 ; 107.
146th, 109 fn.**
236th, 140, note 56.
Blake's Composite Brigade, 149.
Gater's Independent Brigade, 105 ; 109 fn.***
South African, 4 ; 5 ; 6 ; 7 ; 8 ; 9.
12th Division Brigade Group, 33.
25th Division Composite Brigade, 137 ; 142.
39th Division Composite Brigade, 109 fn.**

Mounted Brigades—

1/2nd South-Western, 21.

DIVISIONS

8th, 51 fn. ; 153 fn.*
8th (Light), 9 fn. ; 51 ; 153.
9th (Scottish), 3—9 ; 153.
10th (Irish), 11—18 ; 153 ; 157.

Divisions—*Continued.*

11th (Northern), 19—25 ; 153 ; 158.
12th (Eastern), 27—33 ; 153.
13th (Western), 9 fn. ; 35—44 ; 153 ; 159.
14th (Light), 9 fn. ; 45—52 ; 153 ; 156.
15th (Scottish), 53—60 ; 153.
16th (Irish), 61—69 ; 153.
17th (Northern), 71—77 ; 153.
18th (Eastern), 79—85 ; 153.
19th (Western), 87—93 ; 153.
20th (Light), 95—101 ; 153.
21st, 103—109 ; 153.
22nd, 111—117 ; 153.
23rd, 119—125 ; 153 ; 157.
24th, 127—133 ; 153.
25th, 135—142 ; 153.
26th, 143—149 ; 153 ; 158 ; 159.

ADDITIONAL UNITS

Heavy Batteries, R.G.A.—

9th, 5.
10th, 13 ; 21. ˙
11th, 21.
12th, 29.
13th, 37.
14th, 47.
15th, 13 ; 55.
16th, 63.
17th, 73.
18th, 81.
19th, 89.
20th, 97.
21st, 105.
22nd, 113.
23rd, 121.
24th, 129 fn.
24th (New), 129.
25th, 137.
26th, 145 fn.
72nd, 37.
91st, 21 ; 37.
2/104th, 37.
130th [24th (New)], 129
131st, 145.
157th, 37.
177th, 37.

Siege Batteries, R.G.A.—

159th, 37.
384th, 37.
387th, 37.

Printed under the authority of His Majesty's Stationery Office
by Waterlow & Sons Limited, London and Dunstable

S.O. Code No. 70-307-3-1.

HISTORY OF THE GREAT WAR

BASED ON OFFICIAL DOCUMENTS

BY DIRECTION OF THE HISTORICAL SECTION OF THE COMMITTEE OF IMPERIAL DEFENCE

ORDER OF BATTLE
OF DIVISIONS

• PART 3b •

New Army Divisions (30-41)
and 63rd (R.N.) Division

Compiled by
MAJOR A. F. BECKE
R.F.A. (Retired), Hon. M.A. (Oxon.)

The Naval & Military Press Ltd

Reproduced by kind permission of the Central Library,
Royal Military Academy, Sandhurst

Published by

The Naval & Military Press Ltd

Unit 10, Ridgewood Industrial Park,

Uckfield, East Sussex,

TN22 5QE England

Tel: +44 (0) 1825 749494

Fax: +44 (0) 1825 765701

www.naval–military-press.com

www.military-genealogy.com

© The Naval & Military Press Ltd 2007

ORDER OF BATTLE OF DIVISIONS

Part 1   The Regular British Divisions

Part 2a The Territorial Force Mounted Divisions and
The 1st-Line Territorial Force Divisions (42-56)

Part 2b The 2nd-Line Territorial Force Divisions (57th-69th),
with The Home-Service Divisions (71st-73rd)
and 74th and 75th Divisions

Part 3   New Army Divisions (9-26 and 30-41)
and 63rd (R.N.) Division

Part 4   The Army Council, G.H.Q.s, Armies, and Corps 1914–1918

*In reprinting in facsimile from the original, any imperfections are inevitably reproduced
and the quality may fall short of modern type and cartographic standards.*

Printed and bound by Antony Rowe Ltd, Eastbourne

PREFACE

This Part concludes the Orders of Battle of the ninety British Divisions which were in existence during the Great War of 1914-1918.

Orders of Battle for the fifteen regular British divisions were given in Part 1 of this series. Parts 2-A and 2-B contained the Orders of Battle of five mounted divisions, fourteen 1st-line and fourteen 2nd-line Territorial Force divisions, as well as three home-service divisions (71st-73rd), and the 74th and 75th Divisions (formed in Egypt). Part 3-A gave the Orders of Battle of the eighteen New Army divisions (9th–26th), which formed the First, Second, and Third New Armies.

The present Part (3-B) contains the Orders of Battle of nineteen divisions: twelve New Army divisions (30th–41st), which formed the new Fourth and Fifth New Armies, the 63rd (Royal Naval) Division, and in Appendices 1 A–1 F the Orders of Battle of the six divisions (30th–35th) which formed the original Fourth New Army and were broken up with it in April 1915 (Appendix II).

The series will be concluded with a volume dealing with G.H.Q.s, Armies, and Corps.

The nineteen divisions in this Part were all war-time formations, not a single one was in existence at the outbreak of the Great War. During the War thirteen of these divisions served and fought on the Western Front, in Gallipoli, in Egypt, in Macedonia, and in Italy.

Of the twelve divisions (30th–41st) of the new Fourth and Fifth New Armies only two had a distinguishing territorial title, in addition to the number allotted to the division. The other ten New Army divisions, as well as the six divisions of the original Fourth New Army (Appendices 1 A–1 F), received numbers alone, like regular divisions of the original B.E.F. The Royal Naval Division did not have a number (63rd) allotted to it until July 1916; it then retained its original designation as a sub-title.

No unit or formation of the divisions included in this Part kept a war diary before embarkation orders arrived. In only a few cases have divisional routine orders been preserved. The absence of official records has made uphill-work of the reconstruction of the troubles and difficulties experienced by these new formations in the early days of their existence. It is necessary, however, to stress once more the shortage of clothing, equipment, and arms, and the lack of sufficient trained instructors, which nearly every unit had to face from the day of its formation. In some cases the deficiencies were not made up until a short time before the final preparation began for active service abroad. For trained instructors the divisions of the Fourth and Fifth New Armies had to rely chiefly on officers and n.c.o.'s who had been wounded in the earlier fighting and had since recovered sufficiently to report for duty. Considering the general unpreparedness of the country for participation in a great war, it is remarkable that all the twelve New Army divisions (30th–41st) were able to leave England between July 1915 and June 1916.

In the Royal Naval Division the lack of trained instructors was naturally not so marked, nor could the men be regarded as recruits. It is well-known that this division embarked in September and October 1914 to take part in the Antwerp Operations, and also participated in the whole of the Gallipoli Campaign. Nevertheless in October 1914 the unsuitability for field operations of the clothing of the naval ratings, and the late issue to them of up-to-date rifles, together with their deficiencies of essential equipment (water-bottles, haversacks, etc.), as well as the entire lack of machine guns and artillery, and the insufficient means of inter-communication, in the Division, must all be remembered when considering the participation of this Division in the Antwerp operations.

As far as they exist, routine orders, divisional histories, regimental histories, and private accounts have been used in the compilation of each divisional narrative to bring out the difficulties which each division had to face and surmount in its early training before embarkation. From embarkation onwards the war diaries provide the principal source of information.

As this is the concluding part of this series of divisional orders of battle, it seems appropriate to point out that, at the moment, divisional histories exist for only forty-one of the ninety divisions; for the nineteen divisions contained in this Part only seven divisional histories have appeared. It seems unlikely that this number of divisional histories will be increased in the near future; some divisions—home-service ones for instance—will probably never have their histories written. The need, therefore, is apparent for some short but comprehensive account of the divisions, which will give at least the commanders and staffs, the changing organization of formations and units, and the engagements in which the divisions took part. In this way the essential and important details will be placed on record and made available for reference; the share of each division in the long struggle and the final triumph can also be appreciated.

The divisional field artillery of the Fourth and Fifth New Armies at first consisted of four 4-battery brigades, three being 18-pdr. brigades and the other a 4.5-inch howitzer brigade; each battery was a 4-gun or 4-howitzer battery. On arrival in France the organization of these divisional artilleries conformed to that of the first three New Armies which had preceded them overseas—actually this organization was the seventh different field artillery establishment to appear on the Western Front. But during 1916 a uniform divisional artillery establishment was secured for the Western Front—by the introduction of mixed brigades of 18-pdrs. and 4.5-inch howitzers. The 6-gun 18-pdr. battery was adopted as soon as possible, and in January 1917 4.5-inch howitzer batteries were also increased to 6 pieces each. At the same time divisional artilleries were reduced to two (mixed) field artillery brigades, that is from sixty-four pieces (1916) to forty-eight. From January 1917 until the end of the Great War all the British divisions serving on the Western Front had identical artillery establishments.

The Royal Naval Division on coming to France, in 1916, received its divisional artillery—transferred from the 63rd (2nd Northumbrian) Division (a 2nd-line Territorial Force Home Service division which had just been broken up). Thereafter this divisional artillery conformed to the organization of a divisional artillery on the Western Front.

The numerous and sometimes complicated reorganizations of the field artillery brigades and batteries are given in the notes to the various tables.

As in previous parts of this series, the lists of Commanders and Staff Officers do not show temporary changes due to absences on short leave, at short courses, or at schools of instruction.

In the Divisional Tables each considerable change in composition is shown. In any case the organization of the division is given for each year, and at one or more important periods in its history.

In the lists of Battles and Engagements occasional deviations have been made from the *Report of the Battles Nomenclature Committee* (published in 1921), in order to include actions of which a division has reason to be proud. In every case, after the battle in which a division fought, the Corps and Army in which the division served at the time is given in square brackets. If a division did not happen to be engaged during a whole year in some specific action, then only the year is shown, but this signifies that the division was on active service in the field during this period.

ii

In the lists, the words "Action" and "Affair" have been omitted and only the date and name of these engagements are given.* The periods when the divisional artillery, engineers, and pioneers were left in the line, after the relief of a division, are not shown.

Neither the attachments of Army field artillery brigades** to a division, nor the attachment of R.G.A. brigades, are shown in the General Notes to the Tables. All other attachments are given either in the Tables or in the General Notes. In order that the Tables shall be as clear as possible, the numerous notes are printed on the page following each Table.

The battle casualties of the division, as recorded in its war diaries, are given at the conclusion of each divisional narrative. To Mr. H. A. Cordery my grateful thanks are due for his labours in extracting these figures.

Appendix 1 gives the formation and story of the (original) Fourth New Army; and *Appendices 1A–1F* give the orders of battle of the six divisions which composed this New Army.

Appendix 2 is a table showing the numbering of the Divisions and Infantry Brigades of the original Fourth and Fifth New Armies, and the renumbering which came into force as a result of the breaking-up of the original Fourth New Army in April 1915.

Appendix 3 consists of two tables :

   3A gives the Divisions already in existence in Great Britain and Ireland in August 1914, and those which were raised during 1914–1918 ;

   3B shows where the ninety divisions, furnished by Great Britain and Ireland, served during the Great War. No fewer than sixty-nine of the ninety divisions served in one or more of the six principal theatres of operations.

Appendix 4 gives the Order of Battle of the (temporary) Composite Division, formed in Gallipoli in May 1915.

Appendix 5 is Marshal Foch's message to the people of Northern Ireland, issued in November 1928.

Corrigenda to Parts 1, 2-A, 2-B, and 3-A are also issued with this Part.

Each divisional story was submitted for comment to the General Officer who commanded the division at the end of the Great War ; in addition, copies were sent to any officer who had served for a long period with the division. I am very grateful to all the divisional commanders and other officers who have assisted in checking and correcting these tables and for providing additional information. I am glad to record my gratitude for the considerable assistance which I have received both from the War Office Library and from "R" (Records), War Office. Without the help of the latter I should have been unable to recover many of the dates.

I am also greatly indebted to the Staff of the Historical Section (Military Branch) for the skilled help which they have given me on all occasions. In particular, my most grateful thanks are due to Mr. S. Woolgar for the continuous and valuable assistance which he has given me during the compilation of this Part.

Any corrections or amendments to these Tables should be sent to the Secretary, Historical Section, Committee of Imperial Defence, Richmond Terrace, Whitehall, S.W.1.

A.F.B.

December, 1939.

---

*The Action of Tieghem, 31st October, 1918, would appear as " 31 October, Tieghem."
**Formed in France early in 1917, after the final reorganization of the divisional artilleries.

iii

CONTENTS

iv

LIST OF ABREVIATIONS

NOTE.—For the period of the Great War the titles of regiments have been taken from the 1914-1918 Army Lists.

A.

(A.-A.)...	(Anti-Aircraft).
A.-A.& Q.-M.-G.	Assistant-Adjutant & Quarter-Master-General.
A.C.C.	Army Cyclist Corps (Home Service).
A. & S.H.	Argyll & Sutherland Highlanders.
A.F.A. Bde. ...	Army Field Artillery Brigade.
A.H.Q.	Army Head-Quarters.
Amb. or Ambce.	Ambulance.
Ammn. Coln. ...	Ammunition Column.
Ammn. Park ...	Ammunition Park.
Anzac	Australian & New Zealand Army Corps.
A.R.O.	Army Routine Order.
Arty.	Artillery.
A.S.C.	Army Service Corps.
A.T.	Army Troops.
A.T. Carts ...	Army Transport Carts.
Aus.	Australian.
Aux.	Auxiliary.

B.

B.A.C.	Brigade Ammunition Column.
Bde.	Brigade.
Bedf.	Bedfordshire Regiment.
Bedf. Yeo. ...	Bedfordshire Yeomanry.
B.E.F.	British Expeditionary Force.
Berks.	Berkshire.
B.F.T.	British Forces in Turkey.
B.-G., R.A. ...	Brigadier-General, Commanding Royal Artillery.
B.-G., R.H.A. ...	Brigadier-General, Commanding Royal Horse Artillery.
B.L.	Breech-loader.
B.L.C.	B.L. Converted.
Bn.	Battalion.
Bord.	Border Regiment.
Br.-Gen.	Brigadier-General.
Bty.	Battery.
Bucks.	Buckinghamshire.
Buffs	Buffs (East Kent Regiment).
B.W.	Black Watch (Royal Highlanders).
B.W.I.	British West Indies Regiment

C.

Camb.	Cambridgeshire Regiment.
Cam. H.	Cameron Highlanders.
Cav.	Cavalry.
C.B.	Cavalry Brigade.
C.C.S.	Casualty Clearing Station.
cd.	command.
C.D.M.T. Coy ...	Cavalry Divisional Mechanical Transport Company.
Cdn.	Canadian.
C.F.A.	Combined Field Ambulance.
C.G.	Coldstream Guards.
Ches.	Cheshire Regiment.
C.I.	Central India.
Col.-Cdt.	Colonel-Commandant.
Comp.	Composite.
Conn. Rang. ...	Connaught Rangers.
Co.	County.
Coy.	Company.
Cos.	Companies.
C.R.E.	Commanding Royal Engineers.
C.R.H.A.	Commanding Royal Horse Artillery.

D.

d.	died.
D.A.	Divisional Artillery.
D.A.C.	Divisional Ammunition Column.
D.C.L.I.	Duke of Cornwall's Light Infantry.
D.E. Coy.	Divisional Employment Company.
Detnt.	Detachment.
Devon.	Devonshire Regiment.
D.G.	Dragoon Guards.
Dgns.	Dragoons.
Disembkd.... ...	Disembarked.
Disembkn.... ...	Disembarkation.
Div.	Division.
Divnl.	Divisional.
D.L.I.	Durham Light Infantry.
D.M.C.	Desert Mounted Corps.
D. of L. Own Yeo.	Duke of Lancaster's Own Yeomanry.
d. of w.	died of wounds.
Dorset.	Dorsetshire Regiment.
D.P.	Drill-pattern.
Duke's	Duke of Wellington's (West Riding Regiment).

E.

E.	East; or Eastern.
E.E.F....	Egyptian Expeditionary Force.
E. Lanc.	East Lancashire Regiment.
Embkd.	Embarked.
Emplnt. or Emplynt.	Employment.
Eng.	Engineers.
Entg. Bn.	Entrenching Battalion.
Essex	Essex Regiment.
E. Surr.	East Surrey Regiment.
evacd.	evacuated.
E. York	East Yorkshire Regiment.

F.

Fd.	Field.

G.

(G.)	(Graduated Battalion).
Garr. Gd.	Garrison Guard Battalion.
G. B. or Garr. Bn.	Garrison Battalion.
Gds.	Guards.
G.G.	Grenadier Guards.
G.H.Q.	General Head-Quarters.
Glam.	Glamorganshire.
Glouc.	Gloucestershire Regiment.
G.O.C....	General Officer Commanding.
Gord. H.	Gordon Highlanders.
Gr. How.	Green Howards (Alexandra, Princess of Wales's Own Yorkshire Regiment).
G.S.O.1.	General Staff Officer (1st Grade).

H.

(H.)	(Howitzer).
H.A.C.	Honourable Artillery Company.
H.A.G.	Heavy Artillery Group.
Hants.	Hampshire Regiment.
H.A.R....	Heavy Artillery Reserve.
H.B.	Heavy Battery.

vi

H.—continued.		
H.D. Trps.	...	Home Defence Troops.
Hereford.	...	Herefordshire.
Herts.	...	Hertfordshire Regiment.
H.L.I.	...	Highland Light Infantry.
Home Cties.	...	Home Counties.
Househd.	...	Household.
How. Bde.	...	Howitzer Brigade.
How. Bty.	...	Howitzer Battery.
H.Q.	...	Head-Quarters.
Hsrs.	...	Hussars.
H.T.	...	Horse Transport.
H.T.M.B.	...	Heavy Trench Mortar Battery.
Hy. Bde.	...	Heavy Brigade.
H.B., or Hy. Bty.		Heavy Battery.
Hy. Bty. A.C.	...	Heavy Battery Ammunition Column.

I.

I.G.	...	Irish Guards.
Ind.	...	Indian.
Inf.	...	Infantry.
Ir.	...	Irish.
It.	...	Italian.

K.

k. or kd.	...	Killed.
K.E. Horse		King Edward's Horse.
K.G.O.		King George's Own.
King's		King's (Liverpool Regiment).
K.O.	...	King's Own (Royal Lancaster Regiment).
K.O.S.B.	...	King's Own Scottish Borderers.
K.O.Y.L.I.	...	King's Own (Yorkshire Light Infantry).
K.R.R.C.	...	King's Royal Rifle Corps.
K.S.L.I.	...	King's (Shropshire Light Infantry).

L.

Lcrs.	...	Lancers.
Leic.	...	Leicestershire Regiment.
Leic. Yeo.	...	Leicestershire Yeomanry.
Leins.	...	Leinster Regiment.
L.F.	...	Lancashire Fusiliers.
L.G.	...	Life Guards.
L.I.	...	Light Infantry.
Linc.	...	Lincolnshire Regiment.
L.N.L.	...	Loyal North Lancashire Regiment.
L. of C.	...	Line of Communications.
Lond.	...	London Regiment.
L.R.B.	...	London Rifle Brigade.
L.S.	...	London Scottish.
L.Sec.	...	Left Section.

M.

Manch.	...	Manchester Regiment.
Mar.	...	Marine.
Med.	...	Medium.
M.E.F.	...	Mediterranean Expeditionary Force [Gallipoli].
M.G.C.	...	Machine-Gun Corps.
M.G. Coy.	...	Machine-Gun Company.
M.G. Sec.	...	Machine-Gun Section.
M.G. Sqdn.	...	Machine-Gun Squadron.
M.I.	...	Mounted Infantry.
Middx.	...	Middlesex Regiment.
Midld.	...	Midland.
Mk.	...	Mark.
M.M.G.	...	Motor Machine Gun.
Mobn.	...	Mobilization.
Mob. Vety. Sec.		Mobile Veterinary Section.
Mon. or Monmth.		Monmouthshire Regiment.

M—continued.		
Montgom.	...	Montgomeryshire.
M.T.	...	Mechanical Transport.
Mtd.	...	Mounted.
Mtn.	...	Mountain.

N.

N.	...	North ; or Northern.
Newfdld.	...	Newfoundland.
N.F.	...	Northumberland Fusiliers.
N. Irish H.	...	North Irish Horse.
N.M. Fd. Coy.		North Midland Field Company.
Norf.	...	Norfolk Regiment.
Northants. Yeo.		Northamptonshire Yeomanry.
Northbn.	...	Northumbrian.
Northd.	...	Northumberland.
Northn.	...	Northamptonshire Regiment.
N. Som.	...	North Somerset.
N. Staff.	...	North Staffordshire Regiment.
N.S.W.	...	New South Wales.
N.Z. & A.	...	New Zealand and Australian.

O.

O. & B.L.I.	...	Oxfordshire & Buckinghamshire Light Infantry.
Offrs.	...	Officers.
O.R.	...	Other ranks.

P.

(P.)	...	(Pioneers).
P.E.	...	Peace Establishment.
Pemb.	...	Pembrokeshire.
P.P.C.L.I.	...	Princess Patricia's Canadian Light Infantry.
P.O. Rif.	...	Post Office Rifles.
Provl.	...	Provisional.
P.W.O.	...	Prince of Wales's Own.

Q.

Q.O.O. Hsrs.	...	Queen's Own Oxfordshire Hussars.
Q.O.R.R. Staff. Yeo.	}	Queen's Own Royal Regiment, Staffordshire Yeomanry.
Q.O.R.W.K.	...	Queen's Own (Royal West Kent Regiment).
Queen's	...	Queen's (Royal West Surrey Regiment).
Q.V. Rif.	...	Queen Victoria's Rifles.
Q.W. Rif.	...	Queen's Westminster Rifles.

R.

R.	...	Royal.
R.A.F.	...	Royal Air Force.
R.A.S.C.	...	Royal Army Service Corps.
R.B.	...	Rifle Brigade.
R. Berks.	...	Royal Berkshire Regiment.
R. Cdn. H.A.	...	Royal Canadian Horse Artillery.
R.D.F.	...	Royal Dublin Fusiliers.
R.E.	...	Royal Engineers.
Regt.	...	Regiment.
R.F.	...	Royal Fusiliers.
R.F.A.	...	Royal Field Artillery.
Rfts.	...	Reinforcements.
R.G.A.	...	Royal Garrison Artillery.
R. Guern. L.I.		Royal Guernsey Light Infantry.
R.H.A.	...	Royal Horse Artillery.
R.H.G.	...	Royal Horse Guards.
Rid.	...	Riding.
R. Innis. F.	...	Royal Inniskilling Fusiliers.
R. Ir. F.	...	Royal Irish Fusiliers.
R. Irish Regt.	...	Royal Irish Regiment.
R. Ir. Rif.	...	Royal Irish Rifles.
R.M.A.	...	Royal Marine Artillery.
R.M.F.	...	Royal Munster Fusiliers.
R.M.L.I.	...	Royal Marine Light Infantry.

R.—*continued.*		
R.N.A.C.D.	...	Royal Naval Armoured Car Division.
R.N.D.	... ...	Royal Naval Division.
R. Scots	... ..	Royal Scots (Lothian Regiment).
R. Sec.	... ...	Right Section.
R.S.F.	... ...	Royal Scots Fusiliers.
R. Suss.	... ...	Royal Sussex Regiment.
R.W.	... ..	Royal Warrant.
R. War.	... ...	Royal Warwickshire Regiment.
R.W.F.	... ..	Royal Welsh Fusiliers.
R.W.K.	... ..	Queen's Own (Royal West Kent Regiment).

S.

S.	... ...	South ; or Southern.
S.A. or S. Afr.		South African.
S.A.A. Sec.	...	Small-Arm-Ammunition Section.
S.B.	... ...	Siege Battery.
S.B.A.C.	... ...	Siege Battery Ammunition Column.
Sco. Rif.	... ...	The Cameronians (Scottish Rifles).
Sea. H.	... ...	Seaforth Highlanders.
Sec. or Secn.	...	Section.
S.G.	... ...	Scots Guards.
Sher. For.	...	Sherwood Foresters (Nottinghamshire & Derbyshire Regiment).
Sig.	... .	Signal.
S. Irish H.	..	South Irish Horse.
S. Lanc.	... ...	South Lancashire Regiment.
S. & M.	... ...	Sappers and Miners.
S.M. Fd. Coy.	...	South Midland Field Company.
Som. L.I.	... ...	Somerset Light Infantry.
Sqdn.	... ...	Squadron.

S—*continued.*

S. Staff.	... ...	South Staffordshire Regiment.
Suff.	... ...	Suffolk Regiment.
S.W.B.	... ...	South Wales Borderers.

T.

T.A.	... ...	Territorial Army.
T.C.	... ...	Training Cadre.
T. & S. Coln.	...	Transport & Supply Column.
Tempy.	... ...	Temporary.
T.F.	... ...	Territorial Force.
T.M. Bty.	... ...	Trench Mortar Battery.
Trp.	... ...	Troop.

U.

U.K.	... ...	United Kingdom.

V.

Vety.	... ...	Veterinary.

W.

W.	... ...	West ; or Western.
w. or wd.	... ...	wounded.
War.	... ...	Warwickshire.
W.E.	... ...	War Establishment.
Welsh	... ...	Welsh Regiment.
W.G.	... ...	Welsh Guards.
Westld. & Cumbld. Yeo }		Westmorland and Cumberland Yeomanry.
Wilts.	... ...	Wiltshire Regiment.
Worc.	... ...	Worcestershire Regiment.
W. Rid.	... ...	West Riding.
W. York.	... ...	West Yorkshire Regiment.

Y.

Y. & L.	... ...	York & Lancaster Regiment.
Yeo.	... ...	Yeomanry.

*Quand un peuple entier est armé et veut défendre
sa liberté. il est invincible.*

Bonaparte (1797).

*Une réunion d'hommes ne fait pas des soldats ;
l'exercise. l'instruction, et l'addresse leur en donnent
le véritable caractère.*

Napoléon (1806).

30TH DIVISION

G.O.C.

4 May 1915	... ...	Major-General W. FRY.
13 May 1916	... ...	Br.-Gen. HON. C. J. SACKVILLE-WEST (acting).
17 May 1916	... ...	Major-General J. S. M. SHEA.
30 April 1917	... ...	Major-General W. DE L. WILLIAMS.

G.S.O.1.

5 May 1915...Captain G. F. TORREY (acting).
10 May 1915...Major S. W. KING (acting).
23 May 1915...Major S. W. KING.
.5 June 1915...Lt.-Col. S. W. KING.
8 Nov. 1915...Lt.-Col. W. H. F. WEBER.
27 April 1917...Lt.-Col. H. R. BLORE.
21 June 1918...Lt.-Col. P. NEAME, V.C.
[15 Nov., 1918...Lt.-Col. W. M. BECKWITH].

A.-A. & Q.-M.-G.

11 May 1915...Captain F. H. HARVEY (acting).
21 May 1915...Captain A. E. STANLEY CLARKE (acting).
14 June 1915...Lt.-Col. M. F. HALFORD.
31 Aug. 1915...Captain A. E. STANLEY CLARKE (acting).
6 Sept. 1915...Major F. A. CORFIELD (acting).
13 Sept. 1915...Major L. HUME-SPRY.
24 Sept. 1915...Lt.Col. L. HUME-SPRY.
9 April 1916...Lt.-Col. A. G. PRATT.
8 Feb. 1917...Major F. A. CORFIELD (acting).
11 Feb. 1917...Lt.-Col. A. E. STANLEY CLARKE.

B.-G., R.A.

12 Feb. 1915...Br.-Gen. A. J. ABDY.
7 Nov. 1915...Br.-Gen. F. A. G. Y. ELTON.
9 April 1916...Br.-Gen. G. H. A. WHITE (sick, 31/5/17).
31 May 1917...Lt.-Col. HON. G. F. STANLEY (acting).
12 June 1917...Br.-Gen. E. H. STEVENSON (tempy.).
1 Sept. 1917...Br.-Gen. G. H. A. WHITE.
25 Feb. 1918...Lt.-Col. W. W. JELF (acting).
24 Mar. 1918...Br.-Gen. G. H. A. WHITE.
24 May 1918...Br.-Gen. H. A. KAY.
31 July 1918...Lt.-Col. G. MASTERS (acting).
3 Aug. 1918...Br.-Gen. F. W. MACKENZIE (sick, 18/8/18).
13 Aug. 1918...Lt.-Col. G. MASTERS (acting).
11 Sept. 1918...Br.-Gen. F. F. LAMBARDE.

C.R.E.

9 Feb. 1915...Lt.-Col. A. E. PANET.
23 Jan. 1917...Lt.-Col. G. W. DENISON.
10 Sept. 1918...Lt.-Col. P. F. STORY.

89th BDE.
(originally 110th Bde.)

10 Dec. '14...Br.-Gen. Hon. F. C. STANLEY,
16 June '17...Br.-Gen. W. W. NORMAN.
9 Sept. '17...Br.-Gen. W. W. SEYMOUR.
25 Sept. '17...Br.-Gen. Hon. F. C. STANLEY.
11 April '18...Lt.-Col. G. ROLLO (acting).
12 April '18...Br.-Gen. R. A. M. CURRIE.
27 Aug. '18...Lt.-Col. R. A. IRVINE (acting).
15 Sept. '18...Br.-Gen. R. A. M. CURRIE.

90th BDE.
(originally 111th Bde.)

30 Dec. '14...Br.-Gen. H. C. E. WESTROPP.
3 Sept. '15...Br.-Gen. C. J. STEAVENSON (sick, 20/8/16).
20 Aug. '16...Lt.-Col. H. J. GRISEWOOD (acting).
28 Aug. '16...Lt.-Col. R. K. WALSH (acting).
2 Sept. '16...Br.-Gen. C. J. STEAVENSON (sick, 21/9/16).
21 Sept. '16...Lt.-Col. R. K. WALSH (acting).
23 Sept. '16...Lt.-Col. J. H. LLOYD (acting).
13 Oct. '16...Br.-Gen. J. H. LLOYD.
13 Nov. '17...Br.-Gen. G. A. STEVENS.
21 Feb. '18...Lt.-Col. H. S. POYNTZ (acting).
26 Mar. '18...Br.-Gen. G. A. STEVENS.
11 Aug. '18...Lt.-Col. R. J. L. OGILBY (acting).
18 Aug. '18...Br.-Gen. G. A. STEVENS.

91st BDE.
(originally 126th Bde.)

1 Jan. '15...Br.-Gen. F. J. KEMPSTER.

(Bde. transferred to 7th Div. on 19/12/15).

21st BDE.

(On 19 & 20/12/15 Bde. joined from 7th Div.).
[3 Dec. '15]...Br.-Gen. Hon. C. J. SACKVILLE-WEST (wd., 30/7/16).
30 July '16...Lt.-Col. W. H. YOUNG (acting).
5 Aug. '16...Br.-Gen. R. W. MORGAN.
5 Mar. '17...Lt.-Col. R. M. T. GILLSON (acting).
9 Mar. '17...Br.-Gen. J. PONSONBY (sick, 17/3/17).
17 Mar. '17...Lt.-Col. R. M. T. GILLSON (acting).
20 Mar. '17...Br.-Gen. G. D. GOODMAN.
6 Nov. '17...Lt.-Col. C. V. EDWARDS (acting).
6 Dec. '17...Br.-Gen. G. D. GOODMAN.

GENERAL NOTES

The following Units also served with the 30th Division :—

ARTILLERY :—**514 (H.) Battery, R.F.A.** (4, 4.5″ Hows.), see note 32.

11 (Hull) Heavy Battery, R.G.A., was raised in 1914 for the 11th (Northern) Division, but from June 1915 the Heavy Battery was attached to the 30th Division. On 14/3/16 11 Heavy Battery (5″ B.L. Hows.) disembkd. at Mombasa, returned to England on 31/1/18, and on 1·3/18 was redesignated 545 Siege Battery.

125 Heavy Battery, R.G.A. (4, 60-pdrs.) was raised for the 30th Div. The Hy. Bty. disembkd. at le Havre on 29/4/16, joined XV Corps Hy. Arty. on 3/5/16, and XXIII Hy. Arty. Group on 20/5/16.

INFANTRY :—**T.C., 2/5/Lincoln.**, joined 21st Bde. (from 177th Bde., 59th Div.) on 29/5/18, transferred to 90th Bde. on 15/6/18, transferred to 66th Div. on 19/6/18, and was absorbed by 5/Linc. (138th Bde., 46th Div.) on 31/7/18.

T.C., 7/Bedford., joined 21st Bde. (from 54th Bde., 18th Div.) on 26/5/18, transferred to 89th Bde. on 15/6/18, transferred to 66th Div. on 19/6/18, and was absorbed by 2/Bedf. (54th Bde., 18th Div.) on 31/7/18.

T.C., 6/Green Howards, joined 21st Bde. (from 32nd Bde., 11th Div.) on 18/5/18, transferred to 90th Bde. on 15/6/18, transferred to 66th Div. on 19/6/18 ; joined 75th Bde., 25th Div., on 30/6/18 ; and (in England) joined 236th Bde. on 9/9/18, for service in N. Russia.

T.C., 7/Sher. For., joined 21st Bde. (from 178th Bde., 59th Div.) on 29/5/18, transferred to 90th Bde. on 15/6/18, transferred to 66th Div. on 19/6/18, and to 39th Div. on 15/8/18.

T.C., 6/Wilts., joined 21st Bde. (from 58th Bde., 19th Div.) on 16/5/18, transferred to 90th Bde. on 19/5/18, transferred to 42nd Bde., 14th Div., on 15/6/18, and joined on 16/6/18.

5/R. Irish F., (formerly in 31st Bde., 10th Div.), joined 21st Bde. (from 14th Div.) on 17/6/18, transferred to 198th Bde., 66th Div., on 23/7/18, and joined 48th Bde., 16th Div., on 29/8/18.

14/A. & S. H., joined 90th Bde. (from 120th Bde., 40th Div.) on 8/4/18. Bn. was reduced to T.C. on 14/5/18, surplus went to Base and T.C. joined 21st Bde. on 15/5/18 ; T.C. rejoined 90th Bde. on 19/5/18, was transferred to 42nd Bde., 14th Div., on 15/6/18, and joined on 16/6/18.

MACHINE-GUN UNIT :—**19th Motor-Machine-Gun Battery** joined Div. on 10/2/16, and Bty. was transferred to 18th Div. on 6/6/16.

OTHER UNITS :—**70th Sanitary Section** joined Div. in England, and disembarked at le Havre on 10/11/15. On 2/4/17 the Section left the Div. and took over No. 9 Sanitary Area, VII Corps.

30th Div. Motor Ambce. Workshop arrived at Rouen on 9/11/15, left Rouen on 13/11/15, and joined Div. at Ailly le Haut Clocher on 14/11/15. By 7/4/16 the Workshop ceased to be a separate unit and it was merged in 30th Div. A.S.C. workshops.

On 20/2/18 the reorganization of the 30th Division on a 9-battalion basis was completed ; and on 8/3/18 the pioneer battalion (11/S. Lanc.) was reorganized on a 3-company basis.

21st Composite Bde. (21st Bde. H.Q., 2/Bedf. (with 2 Cos. 2/Wilts.), 2/Gr. How., 16/Manch. (with 2 Cos. 17/Manch.), and 202nd Fd. Coy., R.E.), under Br.-Gen. G. D. Goodman, was formed on 19/4/18 and served for the remainder of the Battles of the Lys under the 21st Div., XXII Corps, Second Army. On 27/4/18 the 21st Comp. Bde. was withdrawn from the line, returned to the 30th Div., and was broken up on 1/5/18. 89th Bde. and 21st Bde., with fighting personnel of 90th Bde., were then formed into one Brigade—30th Composite Bde.—and placed under the command of the Brigadier of the 89th Bde. (see below).

30th Composite Bde., under Br.-Gen. R. A. M. Currie, was formed on 2/5/18 and was composed as follows :—

17/King's (with all available fighting men of 18/ and 19/King's),

2/Bedf. (with all available fighting men of 2/Wilts.),

2/Gr. How. (with all available fighting men of 16/ and 17/Manch.),

together with 202nd Fd. Coy. R.E., C. Coy., No. 30 Bn. M.G.C., and No. 4 Coy. 30th Div. Train.

On 2/5/18 the 30th Comp. Bde. was attached to 49th Div., XXII Corps, Second Army ; and from the night of 5/6/5—9/5/18 the Composite Bde. (under 33rd Division) held part of the XXII Corps Front Line, south of Ypres. On 11/5/18 the Composite Bde. left XXII Corps ; the 30th Composite Bde. was then broken up and the units returned to their own formations.

30TH DIVISION [1]

Dates	INFANTRY — Brigades	INFANTRY — Battalions and attached Units	INFANTRY — Mounted Troops	ARTILLERY — Field Artillery Brigades	ARTILLERY — Field Artillery Batteries	ARTILLERY — Bde. Ammn. Colns.	ARTILLERY — Trench Mortar Bties. Medium	ARTILLERY — Trench Mortar Bties. Heavy	ARTILLERY — Divnl. Ammn. Coln.	Engineers — Field Cos.	Signal Service — Divnl. Signal Coy.	Pioneers	M.G. Units	Field Ambulances	Mobile Vety. Sec.	Divnl. Emplnt. Coy.	Divnl. Train
1915 May (England)	89th[3] ...... 90th ...... 91st[3]	17/King's,[4] 18/King's,[4] 19/ King's,[4] 20/King's[4] / 16/Manch.,[4] 17/Manch.,[4] 18/ Manch.,[4] 19/Manch.[4] / 20/Manch.,[5] 21/Manch.,[4] 22/ Manch.,[4] 24/Manch.[6]	D Sqdn.,[7] 1/Lanc. Hsrs., 30th Div. Cyclist Coy.[8]	CXLVIII[9] ...... CXLIX[9] ...... CL[9] ...... CLI (H.)[9]	A, B, C, D / A, B, C, D / A, B, C, D / A (H.), B (H), C (H.), D (H.)	CXLVIII B.A.C. CXLIX B.A.C. CL B.A.C. CLI (H.) B.A.C.	...	...	30th D.A.C.[10]	200th[11] 201st[11] 202nd[11]	30th[12]	11/S. Lanc.[13] (P.)	...	96th[14] 97th[14] 98th[14]	40th	...	30th[16]
1915 December (France)	89th ...... 90th ...... 91st[19]	17/King's,[17] 18/ King's, 20/King's / 16/Manch., 17/Manch., 18/Manch.,[18] 19/Manch. / 20/Manch., 21/Manch., 22/Manch., 24/Manch.	D Sqdn.,[19] 1/Lanc. Hsrs., 30th Div. Cyclist Coy.[20]	CXLVIII[21] ...... CXLIX[21] ...... CL[21] ...... CLI (H.)[21]	A, B, C, D / A, B, C, D / A (H.), B (H.), C (H.), D (H.)	CXLVIII B.A.C. CXLIX B.A.C. CL B.A.C. CLI (H.) B.A.C.	...	...	30th D.A.C.	200th 201st 202nd	30th	11/S. Lanc. (P.)	...	96th 97th 98th	40th	...	30th
1916 June (France)	21st[23] ...... 89th 90th	18 King's,[23] 2/Gr. How.,[24] 2/ Wilts., 19/Manch.;[25] 21st T.M. Bde. M.G. Coy.;[26] 21st T.M. Bty.[27] / 20/ King's, 19/King's, Bde. M.G. Coy.;[29] 89th T.M. Bty.[30] / 2/R.S.F.,[31] 16/Manch., 18/Manch.; 90th Bde. M.G. Coy.;[32] 90th T.M. Bty.[33]	...	CXLVIII[35] ...... CXLIX[35] ...... CL[36] ...... CLI[36]	A, B, C; D (H.) / A, B, C; D (H.) / A, B, C; D (H.) / A, B, C	...	X.30[40] Y.30[40] Z.30[40]	V.30[40]	30th D.A.C.[38]	200th 201st 202nd	30th	11/S. Lanc. (P.)	...	96th 97th 98th	40th	...	30th
1917 June (France)	21st ...... 89th 90th	18/King's,[37] 2/Gr. How., 2/ Wilts., 19/Manch.; 21st T.M. M.G. Coy.; 21st T.M. Bty. / 17/King's, 19/King's, 2/Bedf.; 89th M.G. Coy.; 89th T.M. Bty. / 2/R.S.F., 16/Manch., 18/Manch.; 90th M.G. Coy.; 90th T.M. Bty.	...	CXLVIII ...... CXLIX	A, B, C; D (H.) / A, B, C; D (H.)	...	X.30 Y.30 Z.30	V.30[44]	30th D.A.C.	200th 201st 202nd	30th	11/S. Lanc. (P.)	226th[44] M.G. Coy.	96th 97th 98th	40th	227th[44]	30th

	Bde	Battalions	Artillery Bde	Batteries		T.M. Btys.		D.A.C.	Fd. Coys. R.E.	Signal	Pioneers	M.G.	M.G. Coys.			Train
1918 March (France)	21st	2/Gr. How., 2/Wilts., 17/Manch.; 21st T.M. Bty.	CXLVIII	A, B, C; D (H.)	...	X.30 Y.30	...	30th D.A.C.	200th 201st 202nd	30th	11/S. Lanc. (P.)	No. 30 Bn. M.G.C.	96th 97th 98th	40th	227th	30th
	89th	17/King's, 18/(Lanc. Hsrs.), 19/King's; 89th T.M. Bty.	CXLIX	A, B, C; D (H.)												
	90th	2/Bedf., 2/R.S.F., 16/Manch.; 90th T.M. Bty.														
1918 July (France) *After Reconstitution*	21st	7/R. Ir. Regt., 1/8/Ches.; 21st T.M.	CXLVIII	A, B, C; D (H.)	...	X.30 Y.30	...	30th D.A.C.	200th 201st 202nd	30th	6/S.W.B. (P.)	No. 30 Bn. M.G.C.	96th 97th 98th	40th	227th	30th
	89th	2/S. Lanc., 7/8/R. Innis. F.; 89th T.M. Bty.	CXLIX	A, B, C; D (H.)												
	90th	2/14/Lond., 2/15/Lond., 2/17/Lond., 2/18/Lond.; 90th T.M. Bty.														

NOTES

1 Raised as 37th Div. on 27/4/15; became 30th Div. on 27/4/15. 89th and 90th Bdes. were raised as 110th and 111th Bdes. (in original 37th Div.—note 1), and they were renumbered on 27/4/15; at the same time 112th Bde. was transferred to 35th (formerly 42nd) Div. and then renumbered 104th; and, to take its place, 126th Bde. from 35th (formerly 42nd) Div. joined 30th Div. and became 91st Bde.

2 The battalions were designated: 1st, 2nd, 3rd, 4th City of Liverpool.

3 The battalions were designated: 1st, 2nd, 3rd, 4th City of Manchester.

4 The battalions were designated: 5th, 6th, 7th City of Manchester.

5 The battalion was designated: Oldham Bn.

6 Sqdn. joined Div. at Netheravon on 29/10/15.

7 Coy. was formed Div. at Grantham by 4/9/15.

8 The four Bdes. were each designated: County Palatine. The Bdes. were raised as 4-battery brigades; in each brigade the batteries were lettered—A, B, C, D—and each battery was a 4-gun battery. By 13/8/15 the four Bdes. had joined the Div. at Grantham.

9 The D.A.C. was designated: County Palatine.

10 Each Fd. Coy. was designated: County Palatine.

11 The Signal Coy. was designated: County Palatine; the Coy. joined the Div. at Grantham on 19/6/15.

12 The Pioneer Bn. was designated: St. Helen's Bn.; by 14/5/15 the Bn. joined the 30th Div. at Grantham.

13 The 3 Fd. Ambces. were raised for the original 32nd Div. (APP. 1 C); in June 1915 they joined the (new) 32nd Div.; and on 2/11/15 the 3 Fd. Ambces. were transferred to the 30th Div., at Larkhill, to replace 111th, 112th, 113th Fd. Ambces. which in Sept. 1915 had been transferred to the 16th Div.

14 The original Train (213, 214, 215, 216 Cos., A.S.C.) joined at Grantham on 2/6/15, but remained in England until Feb. 1916, then went to France, and on 13/2/16 became 56th Div. Train. In Nov. 1915 on arrival of the 30th Div. in France, the 30th Div. Train took over the 22nd Div. Train on 7/11/15—186, 187, 188, 189 Cos., A.S.C.

15 Bde. was transferred to 7th Div.; Bde. left on 19/12/15 and joined 7th Div., on 20/12/15. (24/Manch. became Divnl. Pioneer Bn. in 7th Div. on 22/5/16.)

16 On 25/12/15 Bn. was transferred to 21st Bde. (note 25).

17 On 21/12/15 Bn. was transferred to 21st Bde. (note 25).

18 Sqdn. disembkd. at le Havre on 10/11/15; Sqdn. was attached to 2nd Ind. Cav. Div. from 13-26/4/16; Sqdn. left 30th Div. on 11/5/16 and joined VIII Corps Cav. Regt. on 11/5/16.

19 Coy. disembkd. at le Havre on 8/11/15; Coy. was attached to 2nd Ind. Cav. Div. from 13-26/4/16; Coy. left 30th Div. on 21/5/16 and joined XIII Corps Cyclist Bn. on 22/5/16.

20 On 21/5/16 D Bty. left and became A/CLI; and A (H.)/CLI joined and became D (H.)/CXLVIII.

21 On 21/5/16 D Bty. left and became B/CLI; and B (H.)/CLI joined and became D (H.)/CXLIX.

22 On 21/5/16 D Bty. left and became C/CLI; and D (H.)/CLI joined and became D (H.)/CL.

23 On 8/2/16 C (H.), joined III Highland (H.) Bde. and a section of the B.A.C. left CLI (H.), joined III Highland (H.) Bde. in 51st Div., and became R (H.). On 17/5/16 R (H.) was transferred to 7th Div.; Bde. left on 19/12/15 ...

24 On 8/2/16 C (H.), and a section of the B.A.C. left CLI (H.), joined III Highland (H.) Bde. in 51st Div., and became R (H.). On 17/5/16 R (H.) was reorganized: A (H.), B (H.), and D (H.)/CXLVIII, D (H.)/CXLIX, and D/CL. On 21/5/16 CLI was reorganized: A (H.), B (H.), and D (H.)/CL; and D/CXLVIII, D/CXLIX, and D/CLI.

25 21st Bde. (2/Bedf., 2/Gr. How., 2/R.S.F., 2/Wilts.) was transferred from 7th Div. to replace 91st Bde. (note 16), and 21st Bde. joined 30th Div. on 19 & 20/12/15.

NOTES—continued

[29] Bde. M.G. Cos. were formed as follows: 21st—formed, 1–8/3/16, in the Bde.; 89th—disembkd. at le Havre on 11/2/16 and joined Bde. at Sailly Laurette on 13/3/16; 90th—disembkd. at le Havre on 11/3/16 and joined Bde. at Bray on 13/3/16;

[30] T.M. Btts. were formed in the Bdes. as follows: 21st—21/1 and 21/2 by 27/3/16, and they became 21st T.M. Bty. by 5/7/16; 89th—89/1 by 15/3/16, 89/2 by 12/4/16, and they became 89th T.M. Bty. by 16/6/16; 90th—90/1 and 90/2 by 28/4/16, and they became 90th T.M. Bty. by 16/6/16.

[31] Bn. joined Bde. on 20/12/15 from 21st Bde. (note 25).

[32] Bn. joined Bde. on 20/12/15 from 21st Bde. (note 25).

[33] On 25 & 26/8/16 the Bde. was reorganized: C was split up, and 1 sec. made up B to 6 18-pdrs. each; A/CLI joined Bde. and became C/CXLVIII. On 2/1/17 1 sec. D (H.)/CL, joined D (H.)/CXLVIII and made up the Bty. to 6 hows.

[34] Between 26/8–2/9/16 the Bde. was reorganized B was split up, and 1 sec. made up A and 1 sec. made up C to 6 18-pdrs. each; B/CLI joined Bde. and became B/CXLIX. On 2/1/17 1 sec. D (H.)/CL, joined D (H.)/CXLIX and made up the Bty. to 6 hows.

[35] Between 26/8–2/9/16 the Bde. was reorganized: A was split up, and 1 sec. made up B and 1 sec. made up C to 6 18-pdrs. each; C/CL, then became A/CL; 514 (H.) Bty. (disembkd. at le Havre on 6/11/16) joined Div. on 10/11/16, and became C (H.)/CL. Between 1–5/1/17 the Bde. reorganized: on 2/1/17 D (H.) was broken up, and 1 sec. joined D (H.)/CXLVIII and 1 sec. joined D (H.)/CXLIX, making up each How. Bty. to 6 hows.; and C (H.)/CL, was then designated D (H.)/CL; A/CXLVII (H.)/CL, joined (from 49th Div.) and became C/CL; 1 sec. D (H.)/CCXLVII joined and made up D (H.)/CL, to 6 hows.; CL then became an A.F.A. Bde.

[36] On 26/8/16 the Bde. was broken up: R. Sec. C made up A and L. Sec. C made up B to 6 18-pdrs. each; A/CLI then became C/CXLVIII and B/CLI became B/CXLIX.

[37] The 3 T.M. Btts. joined the 28th Bde. by 16/4/16.

[38] The 3 T.M. Btts. joined the Div. by 7/10/16.

[39] The Heavy T.M. Bty. joined the Div. by 16/4/16.

[40] On 16/5/16 the D.A.C. was reorganized and the B.A.C.s were abolished. (G.H.Q. letters, O.B.818, of 28/4, 6/5, and 22/5/16.)

[41] On 24/9/17 Bn. absorbed 16 offrs. & 290 o.r. of 1/Lanc. Hsrs.; on 11/2/19 Bn. was transferred to 89th Bde.

[42] On 6/2/18 Bn. was disbanded: 13 offrs. & 290 o.r. went to 16/Manch, 15 offrs. & 282 o.r. to 17/Manch, and remdr. to 17/Entg. Bn.

[43] On 6/2/18 Bn. was disbanded and used as rfts. for 17/, 18/, and 19/King's.

[44] On 11/2/18 Bn. was transferred to 90th Bde.

[45] On 11/2/18 Bn. was transferred to 21st Bde.

[46] On 20/2/18 Bn. was disbanded, and then formed C and D Cos. of 17/Entg. Bn.

[47] Between 28/1–11/2/18 the 3 Medium T.M. Btts. were reorganized in 2 Batteries—X and Y.

[48] Heavy T.M. Bty. left the Div. between 4–11/2/18.

[49] M.G. Coy. disembkd. at le Havre on 12/7/17, and joined the Div. on 19/7/17.

[50] Coy. joined the Div. on 24/5/17.

[51] On 14/5/18 Bn. was transferred to 32nd Bde., 11th Div.

[52] On 13/5/18 Bn. was transferred to 58th Bde., 19th Div.

[53] On 15/5/18 Bn. was reduced to T.C., surplus (1 offr. & 155 o.r.) went to the Base, and the T.C. joined 90th Bde. on 16/5/18. On 19/6/18 the T.C. was transferred to 66th Div.

[54] The 3 Bns. T.M. Btts. were broken up by 21/4/18; they were reformed by 10/7/18.

[55] On 14/5/18 Bn. was reduced to T.C., surplus (4 offrs. & 218 o.r.) went to the Base. On 19/6/18 the T.C. was transferred to 66th Div.

[56] On 14/5/18 Bn. was reduced to T.C., surplus (273 o.r.) went to the Base. On 19/6/18 T.C. was transferred to 66th Div., joined 197th Bde. on 8/8/18, absorbed 14/King's (from 22nd Div.) on 13/8/18, and on 19/9/18 Bn. was transferred to 199th Bde., 66th Div.

[57] On 14/5/18 Bn. was reduced to T.C., surplus (1 offr. & 223 o.r.) went to the Base. On 19/6/18 the T.C. was transferred to 66th Div.

[58] On 22/5/18 Bn. was transferred to 54th Bde., 18th Div.

[59] On 7/4/18 Bn. was transferred to 120th Div., 40th Div.; on 25/4/18 Bn. was transferred to S. African Bde., 9th Div., and joined on 26/4/18; on 15/9/18 Bn. was transferred to 28th Bde., 9th Div.

[60] On 13/5/18 Bn. was reduced to T.C., surplus went to the Base; on 15/5/18 T.C. was transferred to 21st Bde., returned to 90th Bde. on 15/5/18; and on 15/6/18 T.C. was transferred to 42nd Bde., 14th Div., and joined on 16/6/18.

[61] On 15/5/18 Bn. was reduced to T.C. and was transferred to the 66th Div. on 19/6/18. On 30/6/18 Bn. was transferred to the 25th Div., and on 13/10/18 Bn. became Pioneer Bn., 25th Div.

[62] Bn. was formed on 1/3/18 and consisted of 21st, 89th, 90th, and 226th M.G. Cos. On 13/5/18 Bn. was reduced to T.C.; 13 offrs. & 540 o.r. joined 31st Bn., M.G.C., and on 14/5/18 the remdr. went to M.G.C. Base Depot for disposal as rfts.

RECONSTITUTED DIVISION

[63] Bn. served in 49th Bde., 16th Div., from 14/10/17–18/4/18; the Bn. was then reduced to T.C.; the T.C. of Bn. served with 34th Div. from 17–26/6/18. The Bn. was then reformed by absorbing 85 o.r. R. Ir. Regt., 250 o.r. R.M.F., and 500 o.r. R.D.F. Offrs. to complete W.E. joined between 26–30/6/18. On 4/7/18 Bn. joined 21st Bde.

[64] Bn. served in 118th Bde., 39th Div., until 28/5/18. On 20/6/18 Bn. formed No. 3 Bn. in 25th Div. Comp. Bde., and on 21/6/18 the Comp. Bde. was transferred to 50th Comp. Div. On 8/7/18 Bn. joined 21st Bde.

[65] Bn. left 181st Bde., 60th Div. (in Palestine) on 26/5/18 and joined 21st Bde. on 8/7/18.

[66] Bn. served in 7th Bde., 3rd Div., from Aug. 1914–Oct. 1915. From 26/10/15–20/6/18 Bn. was in 75th Bde., 25th Div.: from 21–30/6/18 Bn. was in 64th Bde., 21st Div.; and on 1/7/18 Bn. joined 89th Bde.

[67] The two Bns. served in 49th Bde., 16th Div., from formation; the two Bns. amalgamated on 23/8/17; reduced to T.C. on 22/4/18; served with 34th Div. 17–26/6/18. On 26/6/18 Bn. was reformed, and joined 89th Bde. on 3/7/18.

[68] Bn. left 180th Bde., 60th Div. (in Palestine) on 27/5/18 and joined 89th Bde. on 30/6/18.

[69] The three Bns. left 179th Bde., 60th Div. (in Palestine) on 30/5/18 and joined 90th Bde. on 1/7/18 (2/14) and on 2/7/18 (2/15 & 2/16).

[70] Bn. served as Pioneer Bn. in 25th Div. from Feb. 1915–20/6/18, then with 50th Div. from 20/6–1/7/18, and joined 30th Div. as Pioneer Bn. on 2/7/18.

[71] On 21/5/18 Bn. was formed in XIX Corps (from 221, 262, 264, 271, & 272 M.G. Cos. from Egypt) and designated "A" Bn., M.G. Corps. On 29/6/18 "A" Bn. joined 30th Div. and was re-designated No. 30 Bn.

30TH DIVISION

FORMATION, BATTLES, AND ENGAGEMENTS

This New Army Division had no existence before the outbreak of the Great War.

On the 6th August 1914 Parliament sanctioned an increase of 500,000 all ranks to the Regular Army, and the First, Second, and Third New Armies (9th—26th Divisions) were formed from the first three hundred thousand men raised in this way.

On the 10th December 1914 the formation of the Fifth New Army (37th—42nd Divisions) was authorized ; this brought into existence the 37th Division and its infantry brigades (110th, 111th, and 112th). In April 1915 the original Fourth New Army of six divisions (30th—35th) was broken up, so that it could be used for replacing casualties in the eighteen divisions (9th—26th) of the first three New Armies (see Appendix 1). The original Fifth New Army (37th—42nd Divisions) then became the Fourth New Army, and its six divisions were renumbered (30th—35th). In this way, on the 27th April 1915, the 37th Division became the 30th Division ; at the same time its 110th and 111th Infantry Brigades were renumbered 89th and 90th. The 112th Infantry Brigade was transferred to the (renumbered) 35th Division and then became the 104th Brigade ; its place in the 30th Division was taken by the 126th Brigade from the original 42nd (later 35th) Division, and on arrival this Brigade received the number 91st (see Appendix 2).

The Earl of Derby was mainly responsible for raising the units which formed the 30th (originally 37th) Division ; and he gave permission for the 30th Division to adopt, as its divisional sign, the crest of the Stanleys—On a torse gold and azure beaded gules, a golden eagle standing upon a nest gold containing an infant swaddled gules. In the divisional sign, however, the torse and nest were replaced by a cap of maintenance, and the sign was worked in silver on a black cloth ground.

In the 89th Brigade the sub-titles of the battalions were 1st, 2nd, 3rd, and 4th City of Liverpool (17/, 18/, 19/, and 20/ King's) ; in the 90th Brigade the sub-titles were 1st, 2nd, 3rd, and 4th City of Manchester (16/, 17/, 18/, and 19/ Manchester). In the 91st Brigade were the 5th, 6th, and 7th City of Manchester (20/, 21/, and 22/ Manchester) ; in addition, the 8th City of Manchester (23/Manchester) had been posted originally to the 91st Brigade, as its fourth battalion. 23/Manchester, however, was composed entirely of men between the heights of 5ft. and 5ft. 8in. and it was usually known as ' the Bantams,' and before May 1915 this battalion was transferred from the 30th Division to the 104th Brigade, 35th Division ; its place in the 91st Brigade was then taken by 24/Manchester (whose sub-title, Oldham, commemorated the town in which it had been raised).

The four artillery brigades (CXLVIII, CXLIX, CL, and CLI), as well as the D.A.C., were all recruited in Lancashire and were designated " County Palatine." In addition, the three field companies and the signal company each bore " County Palatine " as its sub-title, to denote where it was recruited ; but the pioneer battalion (11/S. Lanc.), which had been raised at St. Helen's in September 1914, bore the sub-title of St. Helen's.

Towards the end of April 1915 the 30th Division began to assemble at Grantham : the infantry joined by the end of April, the pioneer battalion reported by the middle of May, and the Train arrived at the beginning of June. The delay occasioned to training by the lack of modern arms and equipment can be realized by the announcement which was made on the 19th July, in Divisional Routine Order No. 191, that a gun-carriage was now available—for funerals. By the middle of August the Divisional Artillery reached Grantham ; and on the 14th September the 30th Division left Grantham and moved to Larkhill (Salisbury Plain) to undergo its final intensive preparation for the field. In the middle of October the Divisional Artillery began gun-practice on the West Down ranges, and at 1 a.m. on the 31st October orders were received that the first advance party would leave for France on the 1st November. On the 4th November the Division was inspected by Lord Derby, and he read to the Division a message from H.M. the King. Entrainment began on the 6th. The Division crossed from Southampton to le Havre and from Folkestone to Boulogne ; and on the 12th November concentration was completed to the north of the Somme at Ailly le Haut Clocher (N.N.W. of Amiens). For the remainder of the Great War the 30th Division served on the Western Front in France and Belgium and was engaged in the following operations :—

1915

1916

BATTLES OF THE SOMME

1–5 ; & 7–13 July ...	**Battle of Albert** [XIII Corps, Fourth Army].
1 July	**Capture of Montauban.**
7–13 July	**Fighting in Trônes Wood.**
10–18 October	**Battle of the Transloy Ridges** [XV Corps, Fourth Army].

1917

14 March–5 April ...	**German Retreat to the Hindenburg Line** [VII Corps, Third Army].

BATTLES OF ARRAS

9–13 April	**First Battle of the Scarpe** [VII Corps, Third Army].
23 & 24 April	**Second Battle of the Scarpe** [VII Corps, Third Army].

BATTLES OF YPRES

31 July–2 August ...	**Battle of Pilckem Ridge** [II Corps, Fifth Army].

1918

FIRST BATTLES OF THE SOMME

21–23 March	**Battle of St. Quentin** [XVIII Corps, Fifth Army].
24 & 25 March	**Actions at the Somme Crossings** [XVIII Corps, Fifth Army].
26 & 27 March	**Battle of Rosières** [XVIII Corps, Fifth Army].

BATTLES OF THE LYS

17–19 April	**First Battle of Kemmel Ridge** (89th Bde.) [IX Corps, Second Army].
25 & 26 April	**Second Battle of Kemmel Ridge** (89th & 21st Comp.* Bdes.) [XXII Corps, Second Army].
29 April	**Battle of the Scherpenberg** (89th & 21st Comp.* Bdes.) [XXII Corps, Second Army].

THE ADVANCE TO VICTORY**
THE FINAL ADVANCE IN FLANDERS

1 September	**Capture of Neuve Église** (89th Bde.) [X Corps, Second Army].
2 September	**Capture of Wulverghem** (21st Bde.) [X Corps, Second Army].
28 Sept.–2 Oct.	**Battle of Ypres** [X Corps, Second Army].
14–19 Oct.	**Battle of Courtrai** [X Corps, Second Army].

The advance continued, and on the 21st October the 30th Division reached the Schelde at Helchin; then on the night of the 27th/28th October the 30th Division moved northwards and took over a divisional front at Avelghem. On the 9th November the 89th Brigade forced the passage of the Schelde; the Division at once advanced through Anserœuil and reached Renaix that night. On the 10th the line was pushed forward and the 30th Division occupied Ellezelles, confronting the German rearguards which held a line through Flobecq. On the 11th November the 7/Dragoon Guards (7th Cav. Bde., 3rd Cav. Div.) passed through the infantry; and by 11 a.m., when the Armistice brought hostilities to a close, the 7/D.G. and the leading infantry of the 89th Brigade had reached a line from Ghoy—la Livarde (N.W. of Lessines).

On the 14th November the 29th Division took over the 30th Division front, and the 30th Division then moved back to billets to the south of Renaix. On the 15th the Division began to move back again and by the 17th it went into billets between Courtrai and Mouscron. On the 28th November the Division began to move farther back to the Blaringhem area; the move was completed by the 4th December and divisional headquarters then opened at Renescure. On the 27th December the Division was detailed for duty at the Base Ports; on the 30th the move began to Dunkirk, Calais, Boulogne, and Etaples, during January 1919 the units reached their allotted stations, and on the 18th January divisional headquarters opened at la Capelle (E. of Boulogne). On the 12th February the Division was divided between Boulogne and Etaples; but meanwhile demobilization had been proceeding, and in the middle of May the first unit left for England and other units were disbanded in France. Even so it was not until the 1st September 1919 that the Division ceased to exist. During the Great War the 30th Division lost 35,182 killed, wounded, and missing.

---

*See General Notes.
**For the reconstitution of the 30th Division between 13/5—8/7/18 see Table and notes 47—67.

31ST DIVISION

G.O.C.

26 July 1915	Major-General E. A. FANSHAWE.
16 August 1915	Br.-Gen. E. H. MOLESWORTH (acting).
24 August 1915	Major-General R. WANLESS O'GOWAN.
21 March 1918	Major-General R. J. BRIDGFORD.
6 May 1918	Major-General J. CAMPBELL.

G.S.O.1.

11 June 1915...Major H. R. CUMMING (acting).
24 Aug. 1915...Lt.-Col. H. R. CUMMING.
2 April 1916...Lt.-Col. J. S. J. PERCY.
4 Sept. 1916...Lt.-Col. W. B. SPENDER.

A.-A. & Q.-M.-G.

14 June 1915...Lt.-Col. J. H. A. ANNESLEY.
1 Jan. 1917...Lt.-Col. W. H. ANNESLEY.

B.-G., R.A.

7 May 1915...Br.-Gen. S. E. G. LAWLESS.
16 Nov. 1915...Br.-Gen. J. A. TYLER.

31st Div. Artillery (H.Q., CLV., CLXI, CLXIV (H.), CLXVIII, & D.A.C.) remained in England, when the 31st Div. went to Egypt, and joined 32nd Div. in France between 30/12/15—8/1/16.

On 8/12/15 H.Q., CLXV, CLXIX, CLXX, CLXXI (H.), and D.A.C. (formerly 32nd Div. Artillery) joined 31st Div., and embarked at Devonport to proceed to Egypt with 31st Div.

[15 Nov. 1915]...Br.-Gen. E. P. LAMBERT.

C.R.E.

25 July 1915...Lt.-Col. H. E. G. CLAYTON.
6 April 1916...Lt.-Col. J. P. MACKESY.
6 Mar. 1918...Lt.-Col. E. E. F. HOMER (wd., 26/8/18).
26 Mar. 1918...Major R. A. S. MANSEL (acting).
9 April 1918...Lt.-Col. F. L. N. GILES.

92nd BDE.

(originally 113th Bde.)

31 Dec.	'14...Br.-Gen. Sir. H. G. Dixon.
2 July	'15...Br.-Gen. A. Parker.
10 June	'16...Br.-Gen. O. de L. Williams.

93rd BDE.

(originally 114th Bde.)

17 Dec.	'14...Br.-Gen. E. H. Molesworth.
8 Oct.	'15...Br.-Gen. H. B. Kirk (sick, 4/5/16 ; died, 12/5/16).
5 May	'16...Lt.-Col. H. Bowes (acting).
17 May	'16...Br.-Gen. J. D. Ingles (sick, 27/3/18).
27 March	'18...Lt.-Col. C. H. Gurney (acting).
27 March	'18...Lt.-Col. R. D. Temple (acting).
5 April	'18...Br.-Gen. S. C. Taylor (wd., 1/10/18 ; died 11/10/18).
1 Oct.	'18...Lt.-Col. A. V. Nutt (acting).
1 Oct.	'18...Lt.-Col. A. W. Rickman (acting).
4 Oct.	'18...Br.-Gen. G. B. F. Smyth.

94th BDE.

(originally 115th Bde.)

28 Dec.	'14...Br.-Gen. H. Bowles.
22 Sept.	'15...Br.-Gen. G. T. C. Carter-Campbell (sick, 23/5/16).
23 May	'16...Lt.-Col. A. W. Rickman (acting).
15 June	'16...Br.-Gen. H. C. Rees.
2 July	'16...Br.-Gen. G. T. C. Carter-Campbell.
30 Jan. '18	
17 Feb. '18	Lt.-Col. G. B. Waudhope (acting).

Between 11—17/2/18 the 94th Bde. was broken up.

4th GUARDS BDE.

Bde. was formed on 8/2/18 ; and at noon on 8/2/18 the 4th Gds. Bde. joined 31st Div.

8 Feb.	'18...Br.-Gen. Lord Ardee (gassed, 27/3/18).
27 Mar.	'18...Lt.-Col. Hon. H. R. L. G. Alexander (acting).
4 April	'18...Br.-Gen. Hon. L. J. P. Butler (gassed, 24/4/18).
24 April	'18...Lt.-Col. Hon. H. R. L. G. Alexander (acting).
27 April	'18...Lt.-Col. R. B. J. Crawfurd (acting).
7 May	'18...Br.-Gen. Hon. L. J. P. Butler.

On 20/5/18 the Bde. was transferred to G.H.Q. Reserve. (4th Gds. Bde. rejoined Guards Div. at Maubeuge on 17/11/18.)

94th (YEOMANRY) BDE.

The 94th Bde. was reformed on 30/5/18 and joined 31st Div. on 31/5/18. (94th Bde was reconstituted on 21/6/18).*

1 June	'18...Br.-Gen. A. Symons (sick, 3/11/18).
3 Nov.	'18...Lt.-Col. J. Sherwood-Kelly, V.C. (acting).
[12 Nov.	'18...Br.-Gen. Hon. L. J. P. Butler].

*See General Notes ; also Table and Notes 56—60.

GENERAL NOTES

The following Units also served with the 31st Division :—

ARTILLERY :—517(H.) Battery, R.F.A. (4, 4.5″ Hows.) disembkd, at le Havre on 11/11/16 and joined CLXIX Bde.* on 20/11/16 (see note 29).

124 (2nd Hull) Heavy Battery, R.G.A. (4,60-pdrs.) was raised for the 31st Division but went abroad independently. On 29/4/16 the Heavy Battery disembkd. at le Havre and joined XIII H.A. Bde. on 1/5/16.

OTHER UNITS :—71st Sanitary Section joined Div. on 10/11/15 at Fovant; went abroad with Div. to Egypt and then to France, disembkg. at Marseille on 8/3/16. Sanitary Sec. was transferred from 31st Div. to XIII Corps between 4—11/3/17.

31st Div. Motor Ambce. Workshop went abroad with 31st Div. to Egypt in Dec. 1915; Workshop was transferred (with 31st Div. Train) to 52nd Div. in Egypt by 21/4/16. Workshop served with 52nd Div. until June 1917, and the Workshop was then absorbed in 52nd Div. Supply Column.

On 17/2/18 the reorganization of the 31st Division on a 9-battalion basis was completed; and on 3/3/18 the pioneer battalion (12/K.O.Y.L.I.) was reorganized on a 3-Company basis.

OTHER NOTES :—12/K.O.Y.L.I. (P.) was attached to Fifth Army Troops on 1/7/17, for work on Light Railways. The Bn. was administered by: XVIII Corps, 1/7—22/8/17; XIX Corps on 7/9/17; V Corps, 8—27/9/17; and II ANZAC Corps, 28/9—19/11/17. The Bn. was attached to 50th Div. from 20—29/11/17, and on 30/11/17 the Bn. rejoined 31st Div.

92nd Composite Bde. On 16/4/18 31st Div. was in XV Corps Reserve near Hondeghem. At this time the 31st Div. was very weak, owing to heavy casualties, and it was decided to reorganize the Div. in two Bdes. as a temporary measure. The 4th Gds. Bde. would form one Bde., and the other Bde. would be formed by an amalgamation of the 92nd and 93rd Bdes., to be called 92nd Composite Bde., placed under the B.-G. Cdg. 92nd Inf. Bde. (Br.-Gen. O. de L. Williams). The 92nd Comp. Bde. was to consist of the following units :—
92nd Comp. Bn. (10/ and 11/E. York.), 93rd Comp. Bn.(15/W.York. and 18/D.L.I.), and 94th Comp. Bn. (11/E. Lanc. and 13/Y. & L.).
The 92nd Comp. Bde. was formed on 16/4/18; and it was broken up and ceased to exist at 11.30 p.m. on 18/4/18. The 92nd and 93rd Inf. Bdes. were then reformed as before.

94th Infantry Bde. On 30/5/18 the 94th Bde. was reformed at first with (1) 2/L.N.L., (2) T.C., 2/R.M.F., and (3) T.C., 2/R.D.F.
(1) 2/L.N.L. Bn. (formerly in 234th Bde., 75th Div.) was ordered to France in May 1918, from L. of C. at Gaza; Bn. left Egypt on 18/5/18, disembkd. at Marseille on 27/5/18, and joined 94th Bde. on 4/6/18. On 22/6/18 Bn. was transferred to and joined 103rd Bde., 34th Div. and on 28/6/18 Bn. was transferred to 101st Bde., 34th Div. (2) T.C., 2/R.M.F. Bn. (formerly in 48th Bde., 16th Div.) joined 94th Bde. on 31/5/18. On 6/6/18 2/R.M.F. was reformed by absorbing 6/R.M.F.** (formerly in 30th Bde., 10th Div.); and on 16/6/18 2/R.M.F. was transferred to L. of C. On 15/7/18 2/R.M.F. joined 150th Bde., 50th Div.
(3) T.C., 2/R.D.F. Bn. (formerly in 48th Bde., 16th Div.) joined 94th Bde. on 1/6/18. On 6/6/18 2/R.D.F. was reformed by absorbing 7/R.D.F.*** (formerly in 30th Bde., 10th Div.), and on 16/6/18 2/R.D.F. was transferred to L. of C. On 15/7/18 2/R.D.F. joined 149th Bde., 50th Div.
On 21/6/18 the 94th Bde. was finally reconstituted and became 94th (Yeomanry) Bde. (see Table and notes 56—60).

---

* CLXIX Bde., which was broken up in January 1917 (see note 29) must not be confused with CLXIX A.F.A. Bde. (376, 377, 378, & 379 Batteries). CLXIX A.F.A. Bde. left England on 14/5/17 and disembkd. at le Havre on 15/5/17.

** 6/R.M.F. (formerly in 30th Bde., 10th Div.) left 10th Div. in Palestine on 30/4/18, disembkd. at Marseille 1/6/18, and joined 94th Bde. on 5/6/18. On 7/6/18 Bn. was reduced to T.C.; surplus absorbed by 2/R.M.F. T.C., 6/R.M.F. joined 16th Div. on 10/6/18, 34th Div. on 17/6/18, and 39th Div. on 27/6/18. T.C., 6/R.M.F. was disbanded on 3/8/18.

*** 7/R.D.F. (formerly in 30th Bde., 10th Div.) left 10th Div. in Palestine on 30/4/18, disembkd. at Marseille 1/6/18, and joined 94th Bde. on 5/6/18. On 6/6/18 Bn. was reduced to T.C. and surplus was absorbed by 2/R.D.F. T.C., 7/R.D.F. joined 16th Div. on 10/6/18, was absorbed by 11/R. Ir. F. on 19/6/18; 11/R. Ir. F. joined 16th Div. at Aldershot on 28/6/18. On 29/8/18, in France, 5/R. Ir. F. absorbed 11/R. Ir. F., and was posted to 48th Bde., 16th Div.

31st DIVISION [1]

Date	INFANTRY		Mounted Troops	ARTILLERY					Divnl. Ammn. Coln.	Engineers	Signal Service	Pioneers	M.G. Units	Field Ambulances	Mobile Vety. Sec.	Divnl. Emplt. Coy.	Divnl. Train
	Brigades	Battalions and attached Units		Field Artillery		Bde. Ammn. Colns.	Trench Mortar Bties.			Field Cos.	Divnl. Signal Coy.						
				Brigades	Batteries		Medium	Heavy									
1915 May (England)	92nd [2];[3]	10/E. York, 11/E. York, 12/E. York., 13/E. York.	H.Q., M.G. Sec. & B Sqdn., 1/Lanc. Hrs. 31st Div. Cyclist Coy.[7]	CLV[2];[8]	A, B, C, D	CLV B.A.C.[8]	...	...	31st D.A.C.[1];[3]	210th[18] 211th[18] 223rd[18]	31st[11] Divnl. Signal Coy.	12/ K.O.Y. L.I. (P.)	...	93rd[12] 94th[13] 95th[14]	41st	...	31st[14]
	93rd[4];[5]	15/W. York, 18/W. York., 18/D.L.I.		CLXI[2];[9]	A, B, C, D	CLXI B.A.C.[9]											
	94th[3];[6]	11/E. Lanc., 12/Y. & L., 13/Y. & L., 14/Y. & L.		CLXIV (H.)[9];[9]	A (H.), B (H.), D (H.), C	CLXIV (H.) B.A.C.[9]											
				CLXVIII[9];[9]	A, B, C, D	CLXVIII B.A.C.[9]											
1916 April (France)	92nd	10/E. York., 11/E. York, 12/E. York., 13/E. York., 92/1/T.M. Bty.[15] 92/2/T.M. Bty.[16]	H.Q., M.G. Sec., & B Sqdn.[15] 1/Lanc. Hrs. 31st Div. Cyclist Coy.[16]	CLXV[1];[21]	A, B, C, D	CLXV B.A.C.[20]	X.31[23] Y.31[19] Z.31[19]	...	31st D.A.C.[20]	210th 211th 223rd	31st	12/ K.O.Y. L.I. (P.)	...	93rd 94th 95th	41st	...	31st[14]
	93rd	15/W. York., 18/W. York., 18/D.L.I.; 93/1/T.M. Bty.[16] 93/2/T.M. Bty.[16]		CLXIX[20];[21]	A, B, C, D	CLXIX B.A.C.[20]											
	94th	11/E. Lanc., 12/Y. & L., 13/Y. & L.; 94/1/T.M. Bty.[17]	31st Div. Cyclist Coy.[16]	CLXX[20];[21]	A, B, C, D	CLXX B.A.C.[20]											
		94/1/T.M. Bty.[17]		CLXXI (H.)[20];[24]	A (H.), B (H.), D (H.), C	CLXXI (H.) B.A.C.[20]											
1916 June (France)	92nd	10/E. York., 11/E. York., 12/E. York., 92nd Bde. M.G. Coy.[25] 92nd T.M. Bty.[27]	...	CLXV[28];[25]	A, B, C; D (H.)	[26]	X.31 Y.31 Z.31	V.31[22]	31st D.A.C.[30]	210th 211th 223rd	31st	12/ K.O.Y. L.I. (P.)	...	93rd 94th 95th	41st	...	31st
	93rd	15/W. York., 16/W. York., 18/W. York., 18/D.L.I.; 93rd Bde. M.G. Coy.[25] 93rd T.M. Bty.[25]		CLXIX[25];[25]	A, B, C; D (H.)												
	94th	11/E. Lanc., 12/Y. & L., 13/Y. & L., 14/Y. & L.; 94th Bde. M.G. Coy.[25] 94th T.M. Bty.[25]		CLXX[28];[25]	A, B, C; D (H.)												
				CLXXI[25];[25]	A, B, C; D (H.)												
1917 June (France)	92nd	10/E. York., 11/E. York., 12/E. York.[39] 13/E. York.[39] 92nd M.G. Coy.[40] 92nd T.M. Bty.	...	CLXV	A, B, C; D (H.)	...	X.31 Y.31 Z.31[40]	V.31[27]	31st D.A.C.	210th 211th 223rd	31st	12/ K.O.Y. L.I. (P.)	243rd M.G. Coy.[42]	93rd 94th 95th	41st	228th[40]	31st
	93rd[39]	15/W. York.[37] 16/W. York.[37] 18/W. York.[38] 18/D.L.I.[38] 93rd M.G. Coy.[43] 93rd T.M. Bty.		CLXX	A, B, C; D (H.)												
	94th[39]	11/E. Lanc.[39] 12/Y. & L.[41] 13/Y. & L.[43] 14/Y. & L.[44] 94th M.G. Coy.[44] 94th T.M. Bty.[45]															

1918 March (France)	4th Gds.[8]	4/G.G.,[10] 3/C.G.,[11] 2/Ir. G.,[12] 4th Gds. T.M. Bty.[14]	CLXV ....[32] CLXX ....[32]	A, B, C; D (H.) A, B, C; D (H.)	...	...	X.31 Y.31	31st D.A.C.	210th 211th 223rd	31st	12/ K.O.Y.L.I. (P.)	No. 31 Bn.[38] M.G.C.	93rd 94th 95th	41st	228th	31st
	92nd	10/E. York, 11/E. York, 11/E. Lanc.,[?] 92nd T.M. Bty.														
	93rd	15/W. York, 18/D.L.I.,[?] 23rd T.M. Bty.														
1918 June (France)	92nd	10/E. York, 11/E. Lanc.,[?] 92nd T.M. Bty.	CLXV ....[32] CLXX ....[32]	A, B, C; D (H.) A, B, C; D (H.)	...	...	X.31 Y.31	31st D.A.C.	210th 211th 223rd	31st	12/ K.O.Y.L.I. (P.)	No. 31 Bn. M.G.C.	93rd 94th 95th	41st	228th	31st
	93rd	15/W. York, 13/Y. & L.,[?] 93rd T.M. Bty.														
	94th (Yeo.)[?]	12(Norf. Yeo. Bn.) Norf.,[?] 12 (Ayr. & Lanark. Yeo. Bn.) R.S.F.,[?] 24 (Denbigh. Yeo. Bn.) R.W.F.,[?] 94th T.M. Bty.[?]														

NOTES

[1] Raised as 38th Div. ; became 31st Div. on 27/4/15.

[2] Raised as 113th, 114th, & 115th Bdes. (in 38th Div.) ; became 92nd, 93rd, & 94th Bdes. in 31st Div. (see note 1) on 27/4/15.

[3] The battalions were designated : 1st, 2nd, 3rd, & 4th Hull.

[4] The battalions were designated : 1st Leeds, 1st Bradford, 2nd Bradford, and 1st County of Durham.

[5] The battalions were designated : Accrington, Sheffield, 1st Barnsley, and 2nd Barnsley.

[6] Joined at Netheravon on 27/11/15.

[7] Formed by 13/8/15.

[8] The four Bdes. were designated : West Yorkshire, Yorkshire, Huddersfield, and Rotherham ; and the D.A.C. was designated Hull. The Bdes. were raised as 4-battery brigades ; in each brigade the batteries were lettered— A, B, C, D—and each battery was a 4-gun battery. By 5/8/15 the four Bdes. had joined the Div. at Ripon.

[9] Before the embkn. of the 31st Div., the 31st Div. Artillery (H.Q., 4 Bdes. & B.A.C.s, and D.A.C.) left the 31st Div. on 2/12/15 and moved to Larkhill. Between 30/12/15–3/1/16 this Div. Arty. (H.Q., 4 Bdes. & B.A.C.s, and D.A.C.) joined 32nd Div. in France and became 32nd Div. Arty.

[10] Each Fd. Coy. was designated : Leeds.

[11] The Signal Coy. was designated : Leeds.

[12] The Pioneer Bn. was designated : Miners.

[13] The 3 Fd. Ambces. joined at Rolleston Down, Larkhill on 27/11/15 ; they had been raised for the original 31st Div. (App. 1B).

[14] In Aug. 1915 the Train consisted of 217, 218, 219, & 220 Cos., A.S.C., and this Train accompanied 31st Div. to Egypt. When the 31st Div. moved to France in March 1916 the Train remained in Egypt, joined 52nd Div. between 1–10/3/16, and became 52nd Div. Train. In March 1916 32nd Div. Train (221, 222, and 223 Cos., A.S.C.) moved to France, was completed with 279 Coy., A.S.C. (formerly R.N. Div. Supply Coln.) ; and H.Q. and 221, 222, 223, & 279 Cos. joined 31st Div. at Hallencourt on 14 & 15/3/16 and became 31st Div. Train.

[15] 92/1 & 92/2 were formed by 11/4/16.

[16] 93/1 & 93/2 joined on 12/4/16.

[17] 94/1 & 94/2 were formed by 12/4/16.

[18] Sqdn. was attached Secunderabad Cav. Bde., 2nd Indian Cav. Div., from 27/3–10/4/16 ; left 31st Div. on 9/5/16 and joined VIII Corps Cav. Regt. on 9/5/16.

[31] Coy. left 31st Div. on 9/5/16 and joined VIII Corps Cyclist Bn.

[32] H.Q.R.A., the four Bdes. (CLXV, CLXIX, CLXX, CLXXI) with the four B.A.C.s, and the D.A.C. were raised between April–June 1915 for the 32nd Div. On 8/12/15 32nd Div. Arty. left the 32nd Div. at Heytesbury, embkd. at Devonport, and became 31st Div. Arty. from that date.

[33] On 22/5/16 D Bty. left and became A/CLXV; and A (H.)/CLXXI joined and became D (H.)/CLXV.

[34] On 22/5/16 D Bty. left and became B/CLXXI; and B (H.)/CLXXI joined and became D (H.)/CLXIX.

[35] On 22/5/16 D Bty. left and became C/CLXXI; and C (H.)/CLXXI joined and became D (H.)/CLXX.

[36] On 22/5/16 CLXXI was reorganized : A (H.), B (H.), & C (H.) left and became D (H.)/CLXV, D (H.)/CLXIX, and D (H.)/CLXX, respectively ; and A (H.), B, and C/CLXXI, and D (H.)/CLXXI remained D (H.)/CLXXI.

[37] X, Y, & Z were formed on 31/3/16.

[38] The three Bdes. M.G. Cos. left Grantham on 15/5/16, assembled at le Havre 17/5/16, left le Havre on 19/5/16 and joined the Inf. Bdes. as follows : 92nd and 93rd on 20/5/16 and 94th on 21/5/16.

NOTES—continued

³¹ Bde. Light T.M. Bties. were formed as follows: 92nd—92/1 & 92/2 became 92nd T.M. Bty. by 12/6/16; 93rd—93/1 & 93/2 became 93rd T.M. Bty. by 12/6/16; 94th—94/1 & 94/2 became 94th T.M. Bty. by 14/6/16.

³² At noon on 30/8/16 B/CLXV joined, and 1 sec. A made up A/CLXV, 1/2 B/CLXXI joined, and 1 sec. A made up B/CLXV, and 1 sec. B made up of C/CLXV to 6, 18-pdrs. each. On 26/1/17 R. Sec. D (H.) joined from CLXIX and made up D (H.)/CLXV to 6 hows.

³³ At noon on 30/8/16 Bde. was reorganized: C was split up, and 1 sec. made up A and 1 sec. made up B to 6 18-pdrs. each, and 1 sec. made up D (H.)/CLXIX joined and became C (H.)/CLXIX. On 20/11/16 517 (H.)—see General Notes—joined CLXIX. Between 24–31/1/17 CLXIX was broken up: on 29/1/17 A became C/XXIII A.F.A. Bde. at noon on 28/1/17 B was redesignated C/XIV A.F.A. Bde. and joined XIV on 13/2/17; C (H.) was broken up—1 sec. made up D (H.)/XIV A.F.A. Bde. to 6 hows. on 13/2/17, and 1 sec. made up D (H.)/XXIII A.F.A. Bde. to 6 hows. on 24/1/17; D (H.) was broken up on 24/1/17 and R. Sec. made up D (H.)/CLXV and L. Sec. made up D (H.)/CLXIX to 6 hows, each; and 517 (H.) was also broken up—1 sec. made up D (H.)/CLV A.F.A. Bde. to 6 hows. on 25/1/17, and 1 sec. made up D (H.)/CCCXI A.F.A. Bde. to 6 hows. on 25/1/17.

³⁴ On 29 & 30/8/16 Bde. was reorganized: C/CLXXI (formerly D/CLXX) and 1/2 B/CLXXI joined, and C made up A and B/CLXX and 1/2 B/CLXXI made up C/CLXX to 6 18-pdrs. each. On 24/1/17 L. Sec. D (H.)/CLXIX joined, became Centre Sec. D (H.)/CLXX, and made up D (H.)/CLXX to 6 hows.

³⁵ Between 27–30/8/16 CLXXI Bde. was broken up: A & ½ B joined CLXV and C & ½ B joined CLXX, and the six sections were used to make up A, B, & C/CLXV and A, B, & C/CLXX to 6 18-pdrs. each; and D (H.)/CLXXI became C (H.)/CLXIX on 1/9/16.

³⁶ On 4/6/16 V arrived from the T.M. School.

³⁷ On 22/5/16 the D.A.C. was reorganized and the B.A.C.s were abolished.

³⁸ Bn. was disbanded on 8/2/18; 33 offrs. & 733 o.r. were drafted to 6/, 7/, 10/, & 11/E. York, and the remdr. joined No. 4 Entg. Bn.

³⁹ Bn. was disbanded on 8/2/18 and drafted; remdr. joined No. 4 Entg. Bn.

⁴⁰ 17/W. York. (from 106th Bde., 35th Div.) joined 31st Div. on 5/12/17, and amalgamated with 15/W. York. (in 93rd Bde.) on 7/12/17.

⁴¹ Bn. was disbanded on 10/2/18; 3 offrs. & 132 o.r. joined 15/W. York. and remdr. (12 offrs. & 583 o.r.) joined No. 3 Entg. Bn.

⁴² Bn. was disbanded on 5/2/18; 33 offrs. & 720 o.r. were drafted to nine W. York. Bns., and remdr. joined No. 3 Entg. Bn.

⁴³ 94th Inf. Bde. was broken up between 11–16/2/18, and it ceased to exist on 17/2/18.

⁴⁴ Bn. was transferred to and joined 92nd. Bde. on 11/2/18.

⁴⁵ Bn. was disbanded between 11–17/2/18; 13 offrs. & 280 o.r. were drafted to 7/Y. & L., 15 offrs. & 300 o.r. to 13/Y. & L., and the remdr. went to No. 4 Entg. Bn.

⁴⁶ Bn. was attached to 4th Gds. Bde. from 12–17/2/18 and on 17/2/18 Bn. was transferred to and joined 93rd Bde.

⁴³ Bn. was disbanded on 16/2/18; 5 offrs. & 100 o.r. were drafted to 1/4/Y. & L., 5 offrs. & L., and the remdr. went to No. 4 Entg. Bn.

⁴⁴ M.G. Coy. was attached to 4th Gds. Bde. from 11/2–3/3/18. On formation of No. 31 M.G. Bn., the Coy. joined M.G. Bn. as C Coy.

⁴⁵ T.M. Bty. was attached to 4th Gds. Bde. from 12/2/18. On 19/3/18 T.M. Bty. handed over Stokes Mortars (complete) to 4th Gds. T.M. Bty., and 94th T.M. Bty. then disappeared.

⁴⁶ The Medium T.M. Bties. were reorganized between 15–22/2/18: Z was broken up: matériel divided between X & Y; personnel went to X.

⁴⁷ V Heavy T.M. Bty. was broken up by 15/2/18.

⁴⁸ M.-G. Coy. disembkd. at le Havre on 15/7/17, left le Havre on 17/7/17, and joined Div. at Mt. St. Eloi on 18/7/17.

⁴⁹ Formed by 9/6/17.

⁵⁰ On 8/2/18 4th Gds. Bde. was formed in the Guards Div., and at noon on 8/2/18 4th Gds. Bde. joined 31st Div. 4th Gds. Bde. served with 31st Div. until 20/5/18 when the Bde. was transferred to G.H.Q. Reserve. 4th Gds. Bde. rejoined the Guards Div. at Maubeuge on 17/11/18; the 3 Bns. then returned to their original Bdes., and 4th Gds. Bde. H.Q. and T.M. Bty. were disbanded.

⁵¹ Bn. (from 3rd Gds. Bde.) joined 4th Gds. Bde. on 8/2/18; Bn. rejoined 3rd Gds. Bde. on 17/11/18.

⁵² Bn. (from 1st Gds. Bde.) joined 4th Gds. Bde. on 8/2/18; Bn. rejoined 1st Gds. Bde. on 17/11/18.

⁵³ Bn. (from 2nd Gds. Bde.) joined 4th Gds. Bde. on 8/2/18; Bn. rejoined 2nd Gds. Bde. on 17/11/18.

⁵⁴ T.M. Bty. formed on 18/3/18, took over Stokes Mortars (complete) from 94th T.M. Bty. on 19/3/18. 4th Gds. T.M. Bty. was disbanded on 17/11/18.

⁵⁵ Bn. was formed at le Comte on 3/3/18; it consisted of 92nd, 93rd, 94th, and 243rd M.G. Cos.

⁵⁶ On 30/5/18 94th Bde. was reformed, principally from T.C. Bns. (see General Notes). On 21/6/18 the Bde. was reconstituted with 3 Bns. from the 74th (Yeomanry) Division—the Broken Spur Division—and 94th Bde. was then redesignated 94th (Yeomanry) Bde.

⁵⁷ 1/Norf. Yeo. (3rd Dismtd. Bde.) was reorganized and designated 12/Norf. in Feb. 1917. Joined 74th Div. at Deir el Balah with 230th (3rd Dismtd.) Bde. on 12/4/17. Bn. left 230th Bde., 74th Div. (in France) on 21/6/18 and joined 94th Bde.

⁵⁸ 1/Ayr. Yeo. and 1/Lanark. Yeo. (2nd Dismtd. Bde.) amalgamated on 4/1/17, and designated 12/R.S.F. in Feb. 1917. Joined 74th Div. at el 'Arish with 229th (2nd Dismtd.) Bde. on 9/3/17. Bn. left 229th Bde., 74th Div. (in France) on 21/6/18 and joined 94th Bde.

⁵⁹ 1/Denbigh. Yeo. (4th Dismtd. Bde.) reorganized on 23/12/16, and was designated 24/R.W.F. in Feb. 1917. Joined 74th Div. at Khan Yunis with 231st (4th Dismtd.) Bde. on 4/4/17. Bn. left 231st Bde., 74th Div. (in France) on 21/6/18 and joined 94th Bde.

⁶⁰ T.M. Bty. was formed from personnel of Bns. of 94th Bde. on 7/6/18, but was broken up on 19/6/18 and the personnel rejoined their units. On 29/6/18 the 94th T.M. Bty. was reformed with personnel from 12/Norf., 12/R.S.F., and 24/R.W.F.

31ST DIVISION

FORMATION, BATTLES, AND ENGAGEMENTS

This New Army Division had no existence before the outbreak of the Great War.

On the 10th December 1914 the formation of the Fifth New Army (37th–42nd Divisions) was authorized; this brought into existence the 38th Division and its infantry brigades (113th, 114th, and 115th). In April 1915 the original Fourth New Army of six divisions (30th–35th) was broken up, so that it could be used for replacing casualties in the eighteen divisions (9th–26th) of the first three New Armies (see Appendix 1). The original Fifth New Army (37th–42nd Divisions) then became the Fourth New Army, and its six divisions were renumbered (30th–35th). In this way, on the 27th April 1915, the 38th Division became the 31st Division; at the same time its three infantry brigades (113th. 114th. and 115th) were renumbered 92nd, 93rd, and 94th (see Appendix 2).

In the 92nd Brigade the sub-titles of the battalions were 1st, 2nd, 3rd, and 4th Hull (10/, 11/, 12/, and 13/East Yorkshire); in the 93rd Brigade the sub-titles were 1st Leeds (15/West Yorkshire), 1st and 2nd Bradford (16/ and 18/West Yorkshire), and 1st County of Durham (18/Durham Light Infantry); and in the 94th Brigade they were Accrington (11/East Lancashire), Sheffield (12/York & Lancaster), and 1st and 2nd Barnsley (13/ & 14/York & Lancaster). The artillery brigades were designated West Yorkshire (CLV), Yorkshire (CLXI), Huddersfield (CLXIV), and Rotherham (CLXVIII), and the D.A.C. came from Hull. The field companies and signal company were designated Leeds, and the pioneer battalion had the sub-title Miners. Many of the units retained their local character until the end of the Great War.

In most units, until early in 1915, the men were billeted in their own homes and the preliminary training had to be carried on in the various home towns. Individuals with any previous military training were rare, and rarer still were any men who had any experience of active service. The rapid development of nearly all the units, as efficient military fighting machines, was delayed and made far more difficult in these important early months by the almost complete absence of trained instructors, and the lack of equipment and modern types of weapons.

During November 1914 one of the battalions was moved from its home town and placed in huts, so that it might be available to strengthen the Humber Defences. Unfortunately, for the comfort of the men, the huts were in a very unfinished state, indeed, many had no doors or windows; also sixty men had to be crowded into every hut, although each building had been designed to hold only thirty. In December when the C.O. of this same battalion was asked to report on the efficiency of the rifles which had been issued to his men, he felt compelled to send the perfectly truthful answer: ' Rifles will certainly go off, doubtful which end.'

Another unit (18/D.L.I.) had an exceptional experience in England. It was raised and equipped by the Earl of Durham and a committee of gentlemen of the County of Durham, and Lord Durham placed Cockpen Hall at its disposal. By early in October 1914 the battalion had recruited up to full strength. The men came from Durham, South Shields, Sunderland, Hartlepool, and Darlington, and the minimum height was 5ft. 9in. On the 16th November the C.O. was ordered to send two companies to Hartlepool to assist in coast defence duty, and he was able to select men for this detachment from those who had already fired a course on an open range. On the 15th December 1914 the officer in command of the Tyne and Tees defences was warned that on the following day enemy warships might raid the East Coast. The 18/D.L.I. detachment manned its trenches and was in position on the morning of the 16th December, when the *Derfflinger*, *Von der Tann*, and *Blücher* loomed up out of the mist and opened fire on the place. The German ships fired some 1,500 shells, and caused casualties of 119 killed and over 300 wounded; among these were included the losses of the 18/D.L.I. detachment—6 killed and 10 wounded. The 18/D.L.I. therefore, holds the proud record of being the first New Army battalion to come under enemy fire.

Towards the end of May and during June 1915 local training came to an end and the units allotted to the 31st Division began to assemble at South Camp, Ripon. Brigade training was started in earnest, and in August musketry was undertaken. In September the Division moved from Ripon to Fovant and the final intensive preparation for war took place on Salisbury Plain.

On the 29th November the Division was informed that it would begin embarking for France on the 6th December; and advance parties left for Southampton (30th Nov.) and Folkestone (1st Dec.). At 10.15 a.m. on the 2nd December, however, the Division was warned that it would not move to France, but it would go to Egypt, accompanied by the 32nd Division Artillery. On the same day the original advance parties were recalled; and the 31st Division Artillery left the 31st Division and a month later joined the 32nd Division in France; and on embarkation the 32nd Division Artillery joined the 31st Division (see Table). Owing to an injury received in France H.M. the King was unable to inspect the 31st Division before embarkation, but on the 6th December His Majesty's farewell message was received by the Division.

On the 7th December embarkation began at Devonport, and on Christmas Eve divisional headquarters reached Port Said.

1915

1916

By the 23rd January 1916 the last unit (CLXXI Brigade, R.F.A.) had disembarked in Egypt. Meanwhile the Division had been taking over No. 3 Section, Suez Canal Defences, and on the 23rd January divisional headquarters moved from Port Said to Qantara (headquarters of No. 3 Section).

On the 26th Feb. orders were received for the 31st Div. to embark for France and an embarkation table was enclosed. On the 27th Feb. the advance parties and divisional cavalry left Qantara for Port Said. On the 1st March divisional headquarters closed at Qantara and embarked the same day at Port Said. On the 6th March the first units of the 31st Division began disembarking at Marseille and on the 16th March disembarkation was completed. The 31st Division then concentrated south of the Somme around Hallencourt (S.E. of Abbeville), in the VIII Corps area.

For the remainder of the Great War the 31st Division served on the Western Front in France and Belgium and was engaged in the following operations :—

BATTLES OF THE SOMME

1 July	**Battle of Albert** [VIII Corps, Fourth Army].
1 July	**Attack on Serre.**
13–18 November	**Battle of the Ancre** (XIII Corps, Fifth Army].

1917

22 Feb.–12 March ...	**Operations on the Ancre** [V Corps, Fifth Army].

BATTLES OF ARRAS

3 & 4 May	**Third Battle of the Scarpe** [XIII Corps, First Army].
28 June	**Capture of Oppy Wood** [XIII Corps, First Army].

1918

FIRST BATTLES OF THE SOMME

23 March ... ... Battle of St. Quentin [VI Corps, Third Army].
24 & 25 March ... ... Battle of Bapaume [VI Corps, Third Army].
28 March ... ... First Battle of Arras [VI Corps, Third Army].

BATTLES OF THE LYS

11 April ... ... Battle of Estaires [XV Corps, First Army].
12–14 April ... ... Battle of Hazebrouck [XV Corps, First Army, until noon 12/4 ; then XV Corps, Second Army].
12–14 April ... ... Defence of Nieppe Forest (4th Gds. Bde.) [XV Corps].

28 June ... ... La Becque [under XI Corps, First Army].

THE ADVANCE TO VICTORY

13 August ... ... Capture of Vieux Berquin [XV Corps, Second Army].

THE FINAL ADVANCE IN FLANDERS

28 Sept.–2 Oct. ... ... Battle of Ypres [XV Corps, Second Army].
31 October ... ... Tieghem [II Corps, Second Army].

On the 3rd November the 31st Division was withdrawn into Second Army Reserve and billeted around Halluin (S. of Menin). On the 5th November the Division was informed that it was to be transferred to XIX Corps and it was to take over part of the line near Avelghem (W. of the Schelde) on the night of the 6th/7th. On the 9th November the Schelde was bridged and a crossing was effected. The Division then pushed forward and by 11 a.m. on the 11th November, when the Armistice brought hostilities to a close, divisional headquarters had been opened at Renaix, the leading infantry brigade (92nd) had reached Everbecq, and cyclists had pushed on as far as the Dendre and found the river bank clear of the enemy.

On the 13th November the 31st Division began to move back and by the 30th it was located around Arques and Blendecques, to the southward of St. Omer. On the 11th December demobilization (chiefly of coalminers) began, and by the end of the year 5 officers and 1691 men had left the Division for England.

In January 1919 demobilization proceeded at a steadily increasing rate, and by the end of the month 110 officers and 4931 other ranks had left the Division. Demobilization of the animals also began in January. In February 113 officers and 3634 other ranks left, and during March the Division was reduced to cadre. On the 13th May cadres of units began entraining at Wizernes to move to England (via Dunkirk), and on the 20th May 1919 the Division ceased to exist. During the Great War the 31st Division lost 30,091 killed, wounded, and missing.

32ND DIVISION

G.O.C.

29 June 1915	Major-General W. H. RYCROFT.
22 November 1916	Major-General R. W. R. BARNES (sick, 9/1/17).
9 January 1917	Br.-Gen. J. A. TYLER (acting).
16 January 1917	Major-General R. W. R. BARNES (sick, 29/1/17).
29 January 1917	Br.-Gen. J. A. TYLER (acting).
19 February 1917	Major-General C. D. SHUTE.
24 May 1917	Major-General Hon. A. R. MONTAGU-STUART-WORTLEY (tempy.).
20 June 1917	Major-General C. D. SHUTE.
27 April 1918	Br.-Gen. J. A. TYLER (acting).
27 April 1918	Major-General J. CAMPBELL.
6 May 1918	Br.-Gen. F. W. LUMSDEN, V.C. (acting).
7 May 1918	Major-General R. J. BRIDGFORD.
31 May 1918	Major-General T. S. LAMBERT.

G.S.O.1.

30 June 1915...Major F. W. GOSSET (acting).
24 Aug. 1915...Lt.-Col. F. W. GOSSET.
28 Apr. 1916...Major A. C. GIRDWOOD (acting).
2 May 1916...Lt.-Col. E. G. WACE.
28 Nov. 1916...Lt.-Col. A. E. McNAMARA.
2 Sept. 1918...Lt.-Col. E. FitzG. DILLON.

A.-A. & Q.-M.-G.

27 June 1915...Lt.-Col. G. E. PIGOTT (sick, 28/11/16).
28 Nov. 1916...Major Hon. E. P. J. STOURTON (acting).
5 Jan. 1917...Lt.-Col. C. O. V. GRAY.
11 Nov. 1917...Lt.-Col. J. P. B. ROBINSON (sick, 27/11/17).
27 Nov. 1917...Captain G. H. TEALL (acting).
17 Jan. 1918...Lt.-Col. J. P. B. ROBINSON.

B.-G., R.A.

3 June 1915...Major K. H. GREGORY (acting).
6 June 1915...Br.-Gen. H. H. BUTLER.
15 Nov. 1915...Br.-Gen. E. P. LAMBERT.
32nd Div. Artillery (H.Q., CLXV, CLXIX, CLXX, CLXXI (H.), & D.A.C.) was transferred to 31st Div. from 2/12/15, and embarked for Egypt with 31st Div. in Dec. 1915.

Between 30/12/15—3/1/16 H.Q., CLV, CLXI, CLXIV (H.), CLXVIII, & D.A.C. (formerly 31st Div. Artillery) joined 32nd Div. in France.

[16 Nov. 1915]...Br.-Gen. J. A. TYLER.
29 Jan. 1917...Lt.-Col. R. FITZMAURICE (acting).
19 Feb. 1917...Br.-Gen. J. A. TYLER.
24 Aug. 1918...Lt.-Col. Lord WYNFORD (acting ; wd. 24/8/18).
25 Aug. 1918...Lt.-Col. C. R. B. CARRINGTON (acting).
24 Sept. 1918...Br.-Gen. J. A. TYLER.
2 Oct. 1918...Lt.-Col. C. R. B. CARRINGTON (acting).
6 Oct. 1918...Br.-Gen. J. A. TYLER.

C.R.E.

Formation ...Colonel DUNCAN CAMPBELL.
21 Aug. 1915...Lt.-Col. J. LANG (tempy.).
3 Sept. 1915...Lt.-Col. E. P. BROOKER.
9 July 1916...Lt.-Col. M. L. PEARS (tempy.).
10 July 1916...Lt.-Col. A. A. CROOKSHANK.
11 Jan. 1917...Major R. F. MAINGUY (acting).
26 Jan. 1917...Lt.-Col. R. H. THOMAS.
1 July 1917...Lt.-Col. G. C. POLLARD.

95th BDE.
(originally 116th Bde.)

22 Dec. '14...Br.-Gen. J. T. EVATT.
17 Aug. '15...Br.-Gen. C. R. BALLARD.

On 26/12/15 the Bde. Staff and 4 battalions of the 95th Bde. were exchanged for the Bde. Staff of the 14th Bde. (5th Div.) and 4 battalions of the 5th Division. At noon on 12/1/16 the 14th Inf. Bde., 5th Div., was redesignated 95th Bde.

96th BDE.
(originally 122nd Bde.)

21 Dec. '14...Br.-Gen. J. G. HUNTER.
20 May '15...Br.-Gen. W. THUILLIER.
28 Aug. '15...Br.-Gen. C. YATMAN.
24 Nov. '16...Lt.-Col. A. E. GLASGOW
(acting).
4 Dec. '16...Br.-Gen. L. F. ASHBURNER.
20 Aug. '17...Br.-Gen. A. C. GIRDWOOD.

14th BDE.

On 26/12/15 the 14th Brigade Staff and 4 battalions from the 5th Division were exchanged for the Bde. Staff and the 4 battalions of the 95th Bde., 32nd Div. On 7/1/16 the 95th Inf. Bde., 32nd Div., was redesignated 14th Bde.

[10 Sept. '15]...Br.-Gen. C. W. COMPTON.
24 Nov. '16...Br.-Gen. W. W. SEYMOUR
(sick, 12/4/17).
12 April '17...Br.-Gen. F. W. LUMSDEN
(V.C., 8/6/17*; killed, 4/6/18).
4 June '18...Lt.-Col. V. B. RAMSDEN
(acting).
10 June '18...Br.-Gen. L. P. EVANS, V.C.

97th BDE.
(originally 117th Bde.)

5 Jan. '15...Br.-Gen. F. HACKET-THOMPSON.
1 Sept. '15...Br.-Gen. J. B. JARDINE (sick, 21/2/17).
22 Feb. '17...Lt.-Col. C. R. I. BROOKE (acting).
8 Mar. '17...Br.-Gen. C. A. BLACKLOCK.
17 Mar. '18...Br.-Gen. J. R. M. MINSHULL-FORD (sick, 1/10/18).
1 Oct. '18...Br.-Gen. J. A. TYLER (tempy.).
6 Oct. '18...Br.-Gen G. A. ARMYTAGE.

---

*The V.C. was awarded for his gallantry at Francilly on 8/4/17 (Gazette of 8/6/17).

GENERAL NOTES

The following Units also served with the 32nd Division :—

MOUNTED TROOPS :—B. Sqdn., North Irish Horse, from 21/5—19/6,16.

ARTILLERY :—

H.Q., R.A., 53rd (Welsh) Div.,
I Welsh (How.) Bde.
    (2 Bties. 4, 4.5″ H. each),

II Welsh Bde.
    (3 Bties. 4, 18-pdrs. each),

Cheshire Bde.
    (3 Bties. 4, 18-pdrs. each),

IV Welsh Bde.
    (3 Bties. 4, 18-pdrs. each),

53rd (Welsh) D.A.C.

In Oct. 1915 the Bties. had been re-armed with 4.5″ Hows. and 18-pdr. Q.F.s. On 20/11/15 the Bdes. began embkg. for France and disembkd. at le Havre between 21–25/11/15, and concentrated in the 32nd Div. area around Pont Remy (on the Somme) between 22–26/11/15. The 53rd Div. Artillery remained attached to the 32nd Div. until 27/12/15. On 1/2/16 the 53rd Div. Arty., with a party (1 offr. and 34 o.r.) from 53rd D.A.C., began entraining at Pont Remy for Marseille, disembkd. at Alexandria on 11/2/16, and completed concentration in Egypt with the 53rd (Welsh) Div. on 22/2/16. (53rd D.A.C. with 54th D.A.C. became 55th D.A.C. in France on 29/1/16).

536 (H.) Bty., R.F.A. (4, 4.5″ Hows.) disembkd. at le Havre on 6/10/16 and joined CLV on 10/10/16 (note 36).

133 Heavy Battery, R.G.A. (4, 4.7″) was attached to the 32nd Div. The Hy. Bty. disembkd. at le Havre on 27/5/16, and joined XLVIII H.A.G. on 29/5/16.

PIONEERS :—12/L.N.L. (P.), from 60th Div., served with 32nd Div. (as Pioneer Bn.) from 16/11/16—5/1/17. Bn. embkd. at Marseille on 12/1/17, disembkd. at Salonika on 28/1/17, and rejoined 60th Div. (as Pioneer Bn.) at Snevce on 13/2/17.

Other Units :—72nd Sanitary Section left Chelsea on 10/11/15, moved to Codford, and joined 32nd Div.; Section disembkd. at le Havre on 25/11/15. On 17/4/17 Section was transferred to a IV Corps Sanitary Area.

32nd Div. Motor Ambce Workshop was raised for 26th Div. and went to France with 26th Div. in Sept. 1915. Workshop left 26th Div. on 13/11/15 and moved to Doullens. Workshop joined 32nd Div. on 20/11/15 and title of unit was changed to 32nd Div. M.A.W. On 6/4/16 the Workshop was disbanded, and the personnel was transferred to and absorbed by 32nd Div. Supply Coln.

On 22/2/18 the reorganization of the 32nd Division on a 9-battalion basis was completed ; and on 22/2/18 the pioneer battalion (16/H.L.I.) was reorganized on a 3-company basis.

32ND DIVISION [1]

ORDER OF BATTLE, 1915-1918

Dates	INFANTRY — Brigades	Battalions and attached Units	Mounted Troops	ARTILLERY — Field Artillery: Brigades	Batteries	Bde. Ammn. Colns.	Trench Mortar Btles. — Medium	Heavy	Divnl. Ammn. Coln.	Engineers — Field Cos.	Signal Service — Divnl. Signal Coy.	Pioneers	M.G. Units	Field Ambulances	Mobile Vety. Sec.	Divnl. Emplnt. Coy.	Divnl. Train
1915 May (England)	95th [2], [3]	14/R. War., 15/R. War, 16/ R. War., 12/Glouc.	B Sqdn. [4] S. Ir. Horse.	CLXV [5], [6]	A, B, C, D	CLXV B.A.C. [6]	...	...	32nd D.A.C. [10]	206th [11] 218th [11] 219th [12]	32nd [13]	17/ N.F. (P.) [12]	...	96th [14] 97th [14] 98th [14]	42nd [16]	...	32nd [44]
	96th [4], [4]	16/N.F., 15/L.F., 16/L.F., 19/L.F.		CLXIX [8], [9]	A, B, C, D	CLXIX B.A.C. [9]											
	97th [3], [3]	11/Bord., 15/H.L.I., 16/ H.L.I., 17/H.L.I.	32nd Div. Cyclist Coy. [7]	CLXX [9], [9]	A, B, C, D	CLXX B.A.C. [9]											
				CLXXI (H.) [9]	A (H.), B (H.), C (H.), D (H.)	CLXXI (H.) B.A.C. [9]											
1915 December (France)	95th [17]	14/R. War., [17] 15/R. War. [17] 16/R. War., 12/Glouc. [19]	B Sqdn. [20] S. Ir. Horse.	CLV [23], [23]	A, B, C, D	CLV B.A.C. [23]	...	...	32nd D.A.C. [31]	206th 218th 219th	32nd	17/ N.F. (P.)	...	90th [37] 91st [37] 92nd [37]	42nd	...	32nd [44]
	96th	16/N.F., 15/L.F., 16/L.F., 19/L.F. [19]	32nd Div. Cyclist Coy. [21]	CLXI [23], [24]	A, B, C, D	CLXI B.A.C. [25]											
	97th	11/Bord., 15/H.L.I., 16/ H.L.I., 17/H.L.I.		CLXIV (H.) [25], [26]	A (H.), B (H.), C (H.), D (H.)	CLXIV (H.) [25] B.A.C.											
				CLXVIII [27], [28]	A, B, C, D	CLXVIII B.A.C. [28]											
1916 June (France)	14th [33]	5/6/R. Scots, [30] 1/Dorset, [30] 2/Manch., [31] 15/H.L.I.; [32] 14th Bde. M.G. Coy.; [33] 14th T.M. Bty. [30]	...	CLV [33], [34]	A, B, C; D (H.)	... [42]	X.32 [40] Y.32 [40] Z.32 [40]	V.32 [41] W.32 [41]	32nd D.A.C. [43]	206th 218th 219th	32nd	17/ N.F. (P.) [34]	...	90th 91st 92nd	42nd	...	32nd [44]
	96th	16/N.F., 15/L.F., 16/L.F., 2/R. Innis. F. [34] 96th Bde. M.G. Coy.; [35] 96th T.M. Bty. [34]		CLXI [34], [37]	A, B, C; D (H.)												
	97th	11/Bord., 2/K.O.Y.L.I., [36] 16/ H.L.I., 17/H.L.I.; [38] 97th Bde. M.G. Coy.; [38] 97th T.M. Bty. [34]		CLXIV [35], [38]	A, B, C; D (H.)												
				CLXVIII [35], [39]	A, B, C												
1917 June (France)	14th	5/6/R. Scots, 1/Dorset., 2/ Manch., [44] 15/H.L.I.; 14th M.G. Coy.; [43] 14th T.M. Bty.	...	CLXI [47]	A, B, C; D (H.)	...	X.32 [46] Y.32 [46] Z.32 [46]	V.32 [41]	32nd D.A.C.	206th 218th 219th	32nd	... [45]	219th [49] M.G. Coy.	90th 91st 92nd	42nd	229th [53]	32nd
	96th	16/N.F., [44] 15/L.F., 16/L.F., 2/R. Innis. F.; [47] 96th M.G. Coy.; [48] 96th T.M. Bty.		CLXVIII [48]	A, B, C; D (H.)												
	97th	11/Bord., 2/K.O.Y.L.I., 16/ H.L.I., [49] 17/H.L.I.; [50] 97th M.G. Coy.; [51] 97th T.M. Bty.															

Period	Brigade	Battalions	Artillery Bdes.		Med. T.M. Btys.		D.A.C.	Field Cos. R.E.	Signal Coy.	Pioneers	M.G.C.	Field Ambulances	Mobile Vet. Sec.	Emp. Coy.	Train
1918 March (France)	14th	5/6 R. Scots, 1/Dorset, 15/H.L.I.; 14th T.M. Bty.	CLXI ...... A, B, C; D (H.)	...	X.32	...	32nd D.A.C.	206th	32nd	16/H.L.I. (P.)	No. 32 Bn. M.G.C.	90th	42nd	229th	32nd
	96th	15/L.F., 16/L.F., 2/Manch.; 96th T.M. Bty.	CLXVIII ...... A, B, C; D (H.)		Y.32			218th				91st			
	97th	11.Bord., 2/K.O.Y.L.I., 10/A. & S.H.; 97th T.M. Bty.						219th				92nd			
1918 May (France)	14th	5/6 R. Scots, 1/Dorset, 15/H.L.I.; 14th T.M. Bty.	CLXI ...... A, B, C; D (H.)	...	X.32	...	32nd D.A.C.	206th	32nd	16/H.L.I. (P.)	No. 32 Bn. M.G.C.	90th	42nd	229th	32nd
	96th	15/L.F., 16/L.F., 2/Manch.; 96th T.M. Bty.	CLXVIII ...... A, B, C; D (H.)		Y.32			218th				91st			
	97th	1/5/Bord., 2/K.O.Y.L.I., 10/A. & S.H.; 97th T.M. Bty.						219th				92nd			

NOTES

[1] Raised as 39th Div.; became 32nd Div. on 27/4/15. 95th & 97th Bdes. were raised as 116th & 117th Bdes. (in original 39th Div.), they were renumbered on 27/4/15; at the same time 118th Bde. was transferred to 33rd (formerly 40th) Div. and then renumbered 98th; and, to take its place, 122nd Bde. from 34th (formerly 41st) Div. joined 32nd Div. and became 96th Bde.

[2] The battalions were designated: 1st, 2nd, & 3rd Birmingham, and Bristol.

[3] The battalions were designated: Newcastle, and 1st, 2nd, & 3rd Salford.

[4] The battalions were designated: Lonsdale, and 1st, 2nd, & 3rd Glasgow.

[5] Joined Div. in England; disembkd. at le Havre on 25/11/15.

[6] Formed at Wensley on 10/8/15; reached Codford on 24/8/15; disembkd. at le Havre on 22/11/15.

[7] The Divnl. Artillery was designated: 2nd County Palatine. The Bdes. were raised as 4-battery brigades; in each brigade the batteries were lettered—A, B, C, D—and each battery was a 4-gun battery. The 4 Bdes. were raised by the Earl of Derby between 29/4-21/5/15 at Lytham and St. Annes on Sea.

On 14/11/15 32nd Div. Arty. was informed it would remain in England on departure of 32nd Div. to France, and the Arty. was to follow in Dec. 1915. On 2/12/15 orders arrived for the transfer of the 32nd Div. Arty. (H.Q., 4 Bdes. & B.A.C.s, and D.A.C.) to the 31st Div.; the Arty. then joined 31st Divn. on embkn. for Egypt in Dec. 1915, and the Arty. thereafter served with the 31st Div. (in Egypt & France).

[8] Formed at Heytesbury on 10/9/15, and in Dec. 1915 was transferred to the 31st Div. (see note 9).

[9] The 3 Field Cos. were designated: Glasgow; they joined the Div. in England, and disembkd. at le Havre between 23-25/11/15.

[10] The Signal Coy. was designated: Reading; it joined the Div. in England, and disembkd. at le Havre between 21-23/11/15.

[11] The Bn. was designated on 11/1/15 : N.E.R. Pioneers; it joined the Div. in England, and disembkd. at le Havre on 21/11/15.

[12] The 3 Fd. Ambces. were raised for the original 32nd Div.; in June 1915 they joined the new 32nd Div. (originally 39th Div.—note 1), and on 2/11/15 were transferred to the 30th Div., with which they served for the rest of the War.

[13] Joined Div. in England, and disembkd. at le Havre on 25/11/15.

[14] The Train (221, 222, 223, & 224 Cos., A.S.C.) joined the Div. in England and served until Nov. 1915 with the 32nd Div.; but on the embkn. of the 32nd Div. for France the Train remained in England. In March 1916 32nd Div. Train (H.Q., 221, 222, & 223 Cos., A.S.C.) moved to France; the Train was completed with 279 Coy., A.S.C. (formerly R.N. Div. Supply Coln.), joined 31st Div. at Hallencourt on 14 & 15/3/16, and became 31st Div. Train.

[15] On 26/12/15 the Bde. Staff and 4 Bns. of the 95th Bde. were transferred in exchange for the Bde Staff of the 14th Bde. and 4 Bns. of the 5th Div. At noon on 12/1/16 the reconstituted 14th Bde., 5th Div., was designated 95th Bde.

[16] Bn. was transferred to 14th Bde., 32nd Div., on 5/1/16; on 29/7/16 Bn. was transferred from 14th Bde. to G.H.Q. Troops; and on 7/8/16 Bn. became Pioneer Bn. of the 49th Div.

[17] Bn. was transferred to 14th Bde., 32nd Div., on 3/1/16.

[18] Sqdn. left Div. on 14/5/16 and joined XV Corps Cav. Regt.

NOTES—continued

Coy. left Div. on 31/5/16, joined X Corps Cyclist Bn., and became A Coy.

H.Q., R.A., the four Bdes. (CLV, CLXI, CLXIV (H.), CLXVIII) with the four B.A.C.s and the D.A.C. were raised for the 31st Div., but left the 31st Div. in England on 2/12/15 and moved to Larkhill. Between 30/12/15–3/1/16 this Divnl. Arty. (H.Q., 4 Bdes., 4 B.A.C.s & D.A.C.) joined 32nd Div. in France and became 32nd Div. Arty.

On 26/5/16 D Bty. left and became A/CLXIV; and A (H.)/CLXIV joined and became D (H.)/CLV.

On 26/5/16 D Bty. left and became B/CLXIV; and B (H.)/CLXIV joined and became D (H.)/CLXI.

On 16/2/16 D (H.) was transferred to 49th Div., joined IV W. Rid. (H.) Bde., and became D (H.)/IV W. Rid. (H.) Bde. On 26/5/16 A (H.) & B (H.) left CLXIV and became D (H.)/CLV and D/CLXI, and D/CLXVIII joined and became A, B, & C/CLXIV.

On 26.5/16 D Bty. left and became C/CLXIV.

The 3 Fd. Ambces. were raised for the original 30th Div. (App. 1A). In November 1915 the 3 Fd. Ambces. joined the 32nd Div. (formerly 39th Div.—note 1A) in England; and the 3 Fd. Ambces. disembkd. at le Havre between 21–23/11/15.

Between 24–31/12/15 the Bde. Staff of the 14th Bde., 5th Div., and 4 Bns. of the 5th Div. were transferred in exchange for the Bde. Staff and the 4 Bns. of the 95th Bde., 32nd Div. (note 17). On 7/1/16 the reconstituted 95th Bde. in the 32nd Div. was designated 14th Bde.

1/5/R. Scots served in Gallipoli, Egypt, and France with 88th Bde., 29th Div., until 24/4/16, when the Bn. was transferred to L. of C., France. 1/6/R. Scots served in Egypt with Western Frontier Force from 21/11/15–27/2/16; left Egypt 8/5/16, disembkd. at Marseille 16/5/16, amalgamated with 1/5/R. Scots on 15/6/16, and Bn. was designated 5/6/R. Scots. On 29/7/16 5/6/R. Scots joined 14th Bde. at Bethune.

On 31/12/15 Bn. was transferred from 15th Bde., 5th Div., to 95th Bde. (later 14th Bde.), 32nd Div.

On 30/12/15 Bn. was transferred from 14th Bde., 5th Div., to 95th Bde. (later 14th Bde.), 32nd Div.

Bde. M.G. Coy. were formed:
14th—by Feb. 1916;
96th and 97th—left Grantham on 10/3/16; disembkd. at le Havre on 11/3/16, and the M.G. Cos. joined 96th and 97th Bdes. on 15/3/16.

Bde. Light T.M. Btries. were formed:
14th—14/1 & 14/2 by 26/3/16, they became 14th T.M. Bty. on 16/6/16;

96th—96/1 by 15/3/16, 96/2 by 22/4/16, they became 96th T.M. Bty. by 21/6/16;
97th—97/1 by 15/4/16, 97/2 joined on 8/4/16, they became 97th T.M. Bty. on 17/6/16.

Bn. joined 14th Bde., 5th Div. (from Third Army Troops) on 18/11/15; and on 24/12/15 Bn. was transferred to 96th Bde., 32nd Div.

On 28/12/15 Bn. was transferred from 13th Bde., 5th Div., to the 97th Bde., 32nd Div.

On 15–17/9/16 the Bde. was reorganized: A was split up between B & C to make up B & C to 6 18-pdrs. each, and C then became A. On 10/10/16 536 (H.) Bty. joined from England and became C (H.)/CLV. On 20/1/17 CLV became an A.F.A. Bde.; C (H.) was split up and 1 sec. made up D (H.)/CLXI and 1 sec. made up D (H.)/CLXVIII to 6 hows. each; on 25/1/17 1 sec. 517 (H.)/CLXIX joined from CLXIX Bde. (31st Div.) and made up D (H.)/CLV to 6 hows.; and on 10/2/17 A/CCCVIII joined from 61st Div. and became C/CLV.

On 17/9/16 the Bde. was reorganized: A was made up to 6 18-pdrs. by 1 sec. A/CLXIV, B was made up by 1 sec. A/CLXIV, and C by 1 sec. C/CLXVIII. On 20/1/17 1 sec. C (H.)/CLV joined and made up D (H.)/CLXI to 6 hows.

On 17/9/16 the Bde. was broken up: A was transferred to CLXI to make up A & B/CLXI to 6 18-pdrs. each; B with 1 sec. C/CLXVIII became C/CLXVIII; C with 1 sec. A/CLXVIII became A/CLXVIII; and D (H.) became D (H.)/CLXVIII.

On 15–17/9/16 the Bde. was reorganized: C/CLXIV and 1 sec. A/CLXVIII became A/CLXVIII; B was made up to 6 18-pdrs. by 1 sec. A/CLXVIII; B/CLXIV and 1 sec. C/CLXVIII became C/CLXVIII; and 1 sec. C/CLXVIII made up C/CLXI to 6 18-pdrs. On 17/9/16 D (H.)/CLXIV joined and became D (H.)/CLXVIII; and on 20/1/17 1 sec. C (H.)/CLV joined and made up D (H.)/CLXVIII to 6 hows.

Formed by May 1916.

Formed by June 1916. On 28/12/16 W was broken up.

On 26/5/16 the D.A.C. was reorganized and the B.A.C.s were abolished.

On 19/10/16 Pioneer Bn. left Div. and joined G.H.Q. Rly. Construction Troops until 31/8/17; Bn. rejoined Div. at Ghyvelde on 2/9/17, served with Div. until 15/11/17, and then became again G.H.Q. Rly. Constrn. Troops. On 31/5/18 Bn. was posted tempy. to 52nd Div. as Pioneer Bn., and on 30/6/18 Bn. was posted permanently to 52nd Div.

The Train (202, 203, 204, 205 Cos., A.S.C.) went to France with 26th Div., disembkg. at le Havre on 19–21/9/15. When 26th Div. left France in Nov. 1915 for Macedonia, the Train remained in France; on 20/11/15 the Train joined 32nd Div. near Ailly le Haut Clocher, and on 25/11/15 was designated 32nd Div. Train.

On 6/2/18 Bn. was transferred to 96th Bde.

On 7/2/18 Bn. was disbanded; A Coy. went to 1/4/N.F., B Coy. to 1/5/N.F., C Coy. to 1/6/N.F. in 50th Div.; D Coy. to 1/7/N.F. in 42nd Div.; and remdr. to 13/Entg. Bn.

Bn. left 32nd Div. on 31/1/18 and joined 109th Bde., 36th Div., on 3/2/18.

On 22/2/18 Bn. became Divnl. Pioneer Bn.

On 11/2/18 Bn. was disbanded: larger portion was drafted, and surplus went to 13/Entg. Bn.

On 12/2/18 the 6" Medium T.M. Btles. were reorganized: V (Heavy) ceased to exist and became X; old X was broken up to complete V (new X) and new Y; new Y was made up of old Y, Z, and part of old X. Old Z ceased to exist and was merged in new Y. New X and Y had 6, 6" Medium T.M.s each.

On 12/2/18 V Heavy T.M. Bty. ceased to exist and became X Medium T.M. Bty. (note 50).

Coy. disembkd. at le Havre 16/3/17 and joined Div. at Nesle on 25/3/17.

Formed by 4/6/17.

Bn. left 26th Bde., 9th Div., on 15/2/18 and joined 97th Bde. on 17/2/18.

Bn. formed on 21/2/18; it consisted of 14th, 96th, 97th, and 219th M.G. Cos.

On 7/5/18 1/5/Bord. was transferred from Pioneer Bn., 66th Div., to 97th Bde., 32nd Div. 1/5/Bord. had served on L. of C., France, from 26/10/14; with 50th Div. (149th and 151st Bdes.) from 5/5/15–12/2/18; and with 66th Div. (Pioneer Bn.) from 13/2–7/5/18.

11/Bord. (97th Bde.) was reduced to T.C. on 10/5/18, and the remdr. (10 offrs. & 123 o.r.) was then absorbed by 1/5/Bord. (in 97th Bde.). The T.C., 11/Bord. was transferred to the 66th Div. and served with the 66th Div. from 13/5–31/7/18. The T.C., 11/Bord. was then absorbed by 1/5/Bord. (in 97th Bde.).

32ND DIVISION

FORMATION, BATTLES, & ENGAGEMENTS.

This New Army Division had no existence before the outbreak of the Great War.

On the 10th December 1914 the formation of the Fifth New Army (37th–42nd Divisions) was authorized; this brought into existence the 39th Division and its infantry brigades (116th, 117th, and 118th). In April 1915 the original Fourth New Army of six divisions (30th–35th) was broken up, so that it could be used for replacing casualties in the eighteen divisions (9th–26th) of the first three New Armies (see Appendix 1). The original Fifth New Army (37th–42nd Divisions) then became the Fourth New Army, and its six divisions were renumbered (30th–35th). In this way, on the 27th April 1915, the 39th Division became the 32nd Division; at the same time the 116th and 117th Brigades were renumbered 95th and 97th. The 118th Brigade was transferred to the (renumbered) 33rd Division and then became the 98th Brigade; its place in the 32nd Division was taken by the 122nd Brigade from the original 41st (later 34th) Division, and on arrival this Brigade received the number 96th (see Appendix 2.)

In the 95th Brigade the sub-titles of the battalions were 1st, 2nd, and 3rd Birmingham (14/, 15/, and 16/R. Warwickshire) and Bristol (12/Glouc.); in the 96th Brigade the sub-titles were Newcastle (16/N.F.) and 1st, 2nd, and 3rd Salford (15/, 16/, and 19/L.F.); and in the 97th Brigade they were Lonsdale (11/Border) and 1st, 2nd, and 3rd Glasgow (15/, 16/, and 17/H.L.I.). Some really expeditious work was accomplished: 15/H.L.I. was raised in 16 hours on Sunday the 13th September 1914; and 17/N.F. (later the pioneer battalion, raised at Hull and designated N.E.R. Pioneers) was completely equipped in 80 days after the first recruit had been enlisted. In April and May 1915 the Earl of Derby raised the four artillery brigades in Lytham (2) and St. Annes (2), and the divisional artillery received the designation of 2nd County Palatine. The field companies came from Glasgow and the signal company from Reading.

At first the men were billeted at home. Until uniforms were available various devices were used to distinguish the recruits of the different units, e.g., one battalion had a piece of red cord round the right shoulder, another had an armlet on the left arm, etc. In some cases, whilst waiting for khaki, dull bluish-grey uniforms were provided for the men.

As soon as possible the Glasgow battalions (15/, 16/, & 17/H.L.I.) were sent to Gailes on the Ayrshire coast and the men were placed under canvas until huts could be constructed. Another battalion (11/Border) was encamped at Blackhall; but the November rains turned the place into a sea of mud and prevented the carpenters from working on the huts; consequently, until Christmas, the men had to be quartered in the Grand Stand, in the stabling, and in various temporary shelters on the racecourse. When the fine weather broke 11/Border received 1,000 great-coats and 1,000 blankets from the Earl of Lonsdale, and by March 1915 the battalion reached full strength—1,350 (this included the depot company of 250).

In May 1915 the infantry brigades were moved into Shropshire. Unfortunately, the ground at Prees Heath was found to be unsuitable for brigade training and in the latter half of June the three brigades moved to Yorkshire; two were then quartered at Wensley, but the other brigade was at Richmond (10 miles away). Brigade training now started in earnest, and from this time begins the real history of the 32nd Division.

At the end of July the battalions started a weekly musketry course at Strensall, although in many cases worn and defective rifles had to be used. Until this course of musketry opened, several units had only been able to carry out perfunctory shooting on miniature ranges with .22″ ammunition. In August the 32nd Division moved to Codford (Salisbury Plain), and began early in September the final stages of training for the field.

On the 11th November orders were received for the move of the Division to France and the first advance party left on the 12th. On the 14th the Division was informed that its Divisional Artillery would remain in England and be replaced by the 31st Division Artillery (see Table and notes 9 & 22). On the 19th, the day on which the Division began to entrain for the ports of embarkation, a farewell message was received from H.M. the King. The Division crossed to France and on the 26th November completed its concentration around Ailly le Haut Clocher, to the north of the Somme (see General Notes, under Artillery). Throughout the remainder of the Great War the 32nd Division served on the Western Front in France and Belgium and was engaged in the following operations :—

1915
1916

BATTLES OF THE SOMME

1–3 July	**Battle of Albert** [X Corps, Fourth Army].
14 and 15 July	**Battle of Bazentin Ridge** [X Corps, Reserve Army].
23 Oct.–11 Nov.	**Battle of the Ancre Heights** [In reserve, II Corps, Reserve Army].
17–19 Nov.	**Battle of the Ancre** [V Corps, Fifth Army].

1917

11 Jan.–15 Feb. ...	**Operations on the Ancre** [V Corps, Fifth Army].
14 March–5 April ...	**German Retreat to the Hindenburg Line** [IV Corps, Fourth Army].
20 June–7 Oct.	**Operations on the Flanders Coast** [XV Corps, Fourth Army].
10 and 11 July	**Defence of Nieuport** [XV Corps, Fourth Army].

1918

FIRST BATTLES OF THE SOMME

28 March	**First Battle of Arras** (97th Bde., attached 31st Div.) [VI Corps, Third Army].
3 April	**Capture of Ayette** (14th & 96th Bdes.) [VI Corps, Third Army].
5 April	**Battle of the Ancre** [VI Corps, Third Army].

THE ADVANCE TO VICTORY

10 and 11 August ...	**Battle of Amiens** [Cdn. Corps, Fourth Army].

SECOND BATTLES OF THE SOMME

21–23 August	**Battle of Albert** [Aus. Corps, Fourth Army].
31 Aug.–3 Sept.	**Second Battle of Bapaume** [Aus. Corps, Fourth Army].

BATTLES OF THE HINDENBURG LINE

29 Sept.–2 Oct.	**Battle of the St. Quentin Canal** [IX Corps, Fourth Army].
3 and 4 October ...	**Battle of the Beaurevoir Line** [IX Corps, Fourth Army].

THE FINAL ADVANCE IN PICARDY

4 November	**Battle of the Sambre** [IX Corps, Fourth Army].
4 November	**Passage of the Sambre—Oise Canal.**

The advance eastward continued; le Grand Fayt was occupied on the 6th, Avesnes was captured on the 8th, and at 11 a.m. on the 11th November, when the Armistice brought hostilities to a close, the 32nd Division occupied Avesnes, covered by an outpost line through Semeries (3 miles to the east of Avesnes).

On the 13th November the Division was informed that it would take part in the advance to the Rhine, and on the 15th it concentrated to the south-east of Avesnes. The advance began on the 19th November; but on the 15th December the Division halted on the Meuse between Dinant and Namur, to act as part of the reserve to the Army in Germany. Divisional headquarters were at Bioul.

From the 22nd to the 25th January 1919 H.R.H. the Prince of Wales stayed with the 32nd Division and visited the units. On the 28th the Division began entraining for Bonn, and on the 3rd February it took over the southern sector of the Cologne bridgehead. On the 15th March the history of the 32nd Division came to an end when it was renamed The Lancashire Division. During the Great War the 32nd Division lost 34,226 killed, wounded, and missing.

NOTE.—Between 25/2–19/3/19 16/H.L.I.(P.), 15/H.L.I., 10/A. & S.H., 5/6/R.S., 2/Manch., 2/K.O.Y.L.I., and 1/Dorset., left the Division; the battalions were replaced by 12/L.N.L.(P.), 13/King's, 53/Manch., 51/King's, 51/Manch., 52/Manch., and 52/King's.

33RD DIVISION

G.O.C.

1 July 1915	Br.-Gen. R. G. GORDON-GILMOUR (acting).
9 July 1915	Major-General F. S. MAUDE.
20 August 1915	Br.-Gen. R. G. GORDON-GILMOUR (acting).
25 August 1915	Br.-Gen. R. H. TWIGG (acting).
27 August 1915	Major-General G. H. THESIGER.
7 September 1915	Br.-Gen. R. H. TWIGG (acting).
16 September 1915	Major-General H. J. S. LANDON.
28 September 1916	Major-General R. J. PINNEY (injured, 2/9/17).
2 September 1917	Br.-Gen. P. R. WOOD (tempy.).
12 September 1917	Major-General P. R. WOOD.
28 November 1917	Major-General R. J. PINNEY.

G.S.O.1.

1 July 1915...Major W. H. TRAILL (acting).
19 July 1915...Lt.-Col. A. SYMONS.
25 Sept. 1916...Lt.-Col. D. FORSTER (wd., 5/9/17).
5 Sept. 1917...Major H. D. DENISON-PENDER (acting).
9 Sept. 1917...Lt.-Col. W. J. MAXWELL SCOTT.
24 Dec. 1917...Lt.-Col. E. C. GEPP.
1 June 1918...Lt.-Col. M. O. CLARKE.
24 July 1918...Lt.-Col. E. A. OSBORNE.

A.-A. & Q.-M.-G.

1 July 1915...Lt.-Col. R. S. STEWART.
30 Aug. 1915...Major C. F. ALLEYNE (acting).
18 Sept. 1915...Lt.-Col. H. B. DES V. WILKINSON (sick, 16/12/15).
16 Dec. 1915...Major C. F. ALLEYNE (acting).
25 Dec. 1915...Lt.-Col. P. R. C. COMMINGS.
30 Oct. 1917...Lt.-Col. E. C. PACKE.
8 Feb. 1918...Lt.-Col. J. G. RAMSAY.

B.-G., R.A.

9 July 1915...Br.-Gen. W. H. SUART.
12 Nov. 1915...Br.-Gen. C. F. BLANE.
21 Mar. 1917...Br.-Gen. C. G. STEWART.
29 July 1918...Br.-Gen. G. H. W. NICHOLSON.

C.R.E.

3 Aug. 1915...Lt.-Col. F. E. G. SKEY (sick, 8/4/16).
3 April 1916...Captain W. GARFORTH (acting).
24 April 1916...Lt.-Col. F. M. WESTROPP.
30 Oct. 1916...Lt.-Col. G. F. EVANS.
[22 Nov. 1918...Lt.-Col. H. L. BINGAY].

98th BDE.
(originally 118th Bde.)

22 Sept. '14...Br.-Gen. R. G. GORDON-GILMOUR.
16 Nov. '15...Br.-Gen. E. P. STRICKLAND.
11 June '16...Lt.-Col. H. C. COPEMAN (acting).
12 June '16...Br.-Gen. F. M. CARLETON.
28 Aug. '16...Br.-Gen. C. R. G. MAYNE (tempy.).
1 Sept. '16...Br.-Gen. J. D. HERIOT-MAITLAND.
8 Nov. '18...Br.-Gen. L. J. WYATT.

99th BDE.
(originally 120th Bde.)

19 Dec. '14...Br.-Gen. R. O. KELLETT.

(On 25/11/15 the Bde. was transferred to the 2nd Division).

19th BDE.

(On 25/11/15 the Bde. joined from the 2nd Division).

[14 June '15]...Br.-Gen. P. R. ROBERTSON.
13 July '16...Br.-Gen. C. R. G. MAYNE.
28 Aug. '16...Lt.-Col. J. G. CHAPLIN (acting).
31 Aug. '16...Br.-Gen. C. R. G. MAYNE.
8 Mar. '18...Lt.-Col. ST. B. R. SLADEN (acting ; killed, 12/3/18).
12 Mar. '18...Lt.-Col. H. STORR (acting ; wd., 13/3/18).
13 Mar. '18...Lt.-Col. H. B. SPENS (acting).
25 Mar. '18...Br.-Gen. C. R. G. MAYNE.

100th BDE.
(originally 119th Bde.)

19 Dec. '14...Br.-Gen. R. H. TWIGG.
5 Feb. '16...Lt.-Col. O. DE L. WILLIAMS (acting).
19 Feb. '16...Br.-Gen. A. W. F. BAIRD.

GENERAL NOTES

The following also served with the 33rd Division :—

ARTILLERY :—

H.Q., R.A., 54th (East Anglian) Div.,
I E. Anglian Bde.
   (3 Bties. 4, 18-pdrs. each),

II E. Anglian Bde.
   (3 Bties. 4, 18-pdrs. each),

III E. Anglian (How.) Bde.
   (2 Bties. 4, 4.5″ H. each),

IV E. Anglian Bde.
   (3 Bties. 4, 18-pdrs. each),

54th (E. Anglian) D.A.C.

Before leaving England the Bties. were rearmed with 18-pdrs. and 4.5″ Hows. On 8/11/15 33rd Division was informed that the 54th (E. Anglian) Div. Arty. would move to France with the 33rd Division and be attached until relieved in France by the 33rd Div. Artillery. On 17/11/15 the 54th Div. Arty. began to embark at Southampton and on 21/11/15 it had concentrated around Blaringhem with the 33rd Div. 54th (E. Anglian) Div. Arty. left 33rd Div. on 12/12/15. 54th Div. Arty. began to move to Marseille on 11/1/16, began embkn. on 30/1/16, and completed disembkn. at Alexandria on 14/2/16. 54th Div. Arty. rejoined 54th Div. at Mena Camp (Cairo) between 8–15/2/16. (On 29/1/16 54th D.A.C. took over equipt. and horses from 53rd D.A.C. and became 55th D.A.C.; 1 offr. & 34 o.r. from 54th D.A.C. accompanied 54th Div. Artillery to Egypt.)

126 (Camberwell) Heavy Battery (4, 60-pdrs) was raised in 1915, in Camberwell, at the same time as the 33rd Div. Artillery. The Heavy Battery disembkd. at le Havre on 29/4/16, and joined XXII H.A. Group on 2/5/16.

INFANTRY :—1/6/Scottish Rifles, joined 23rd Bde., 8th Div., from U.K. on 24/3/15, was transferred to 154th Bde., 51st Div., on 2/6/15, and was transferred to 51st Div. Troops on 12/1/16 and trained as Pioneers. On 21/2/16 Bn. was transferred to 33rd Div., and on 25/2/16 Bn. was posted to and joined 100th Bde. (see note 32).

MACHINE-GUN UNIT :—19th Motor-Machine-Gun Battery joined the Div. in England on 9/11/15. The Battery went to France independently and disembkd. at le Havre on 6/2/16.

OTHER UNITS :—73rd Sanitary Section joined the Div. in England, went to France with the Div., and disembkd. at le Havre on 18/11/15. The Sany. Sec. was transferred on 81/8/17 to XV Corps.

33rd Div. Motor Ambce. Workshop joined the Div. in England, went to France with the Div., and disembkd. at le Havre on 18/11/15 (vehicles disembkd. at Rouen on 19/11/15). On 24/11/15 the Workshop reached Busnes and rejoined 33rd Div. On 31/3/16 the Workshop was absorbed by 33rd Div. Supply Column.

On 15/2/18 the reorganization of the 33rd Division on a 9-battalion basis was completed; and on 22/2/18 the pioneer battalion (18/Middx.) was reorganized on a 3-company basis.

Dates	INFANTRY			ARTILLERY						Engineers			M.G. Units	Field Ambulances	Mobile Vety. Sec.	Divnl. Emplnt. Coy.	Divnl. Train
	Brigades	Battalions and attached Units	Mounted Troops	Field Artillery		Bde. Ammn. Colns.	Trench Mortar Btles.		Divnl. Ammn. Coln.	Field Cos.	Divnl. Signal Coy.	Pioneers					
				Brigades	Batteries		Medium	Heavy									
1915 May (England)	98th[2];[3] ... 99th[3];[4] ... 100th[3];[5] ...	18/R.F., 19/R.F., 20/R.F., 21/R.F. 17/R.F., 22/R.F., 23/R.F., 24/R.F. 13/Essex, 16/Middx., 17/Middx., 16/K.R.R.C.[7]	F Sqdn.,[6,8] N. Ir. Horse. 33rd Div. Cyclist Coy.[7]	CLVI[9] .... CLXII[9] .... CLXVI .... CLXVII (H.)[9]	A, B, C, D A, B, C, D A, B, C, D A (H.), B (H.), C (H.), D (H.)	CLVI B.A.C. CLXII B.A.C. CLXVI B.A.C. CLXVII (H.) B.A.C.	...	...	33rd D.A.C.[9]	212th[9] 222nd[9] 226th[9]	33rd[10]	18/ Middx.[11] (P.)	...	99th[12] 100th[12] 101st[12]	43rd[13]	...	33rd[14]
1915 November (France)	98th ...... 99th[15] 100th	18/R.F.,[18] 19/R.F.,[16] 20/ R.F.,[17] 21/R.F.[18] 22/R.F., 23/R.F., 24/R.F. 13/Essex,[16] 16/Middx.,[17] 17/Middx.,[16] 16/K.R.R.C.	B Sqdn.[16] N. Ir. Horse. 33rd Div. Cyclist Coy.[16]	CLVI[16] .... CLXII[16] .... CLXVI[17] .... CLXVII (H.)[16]	A, B, C, D A, B, C, D A, B, C, D A (H.), B (H.), C (H.), D (H.)	CLVI B.A.C. CLXII B.A.C. CLXVI B.A.C. CLXVII (H.) B.A.C.	.:	...	33rd D.A.C.	212th 222nd 226th[19]	33rd[19]	18/ Middx. (P.)	...	99th 100th[19] 101st	43rd	...	33rd[19];[20]
1916 June (France)	19th[21] ...... 98th 100th	20/R.F.,[17] 2/R.W.F.,[22] 1/Sco. Rif., 5/6/Sco. Rif.,[23] 19th Bde. M.G. Coy.,[24] 19th T.M. Bty.[24] 4/King's,[25] 1/4/Suff.,[26] 1/ Middx.,[27] 2/A. & S. H.,[28] 98th Bde. M.G. Coy.,[29] 98th T.M. Bty.[30] 1/Queen's,[28] 2/Worc.,[29] 16/ K.R.R.C., 1/9/H.L.I.,[31] 100th Bde. M.G. Coy.,[32] 100th T.M. Bty.[33]	...	CLVI[34];[43] CLXII[34];[44] CLXVI[44];[45] CLXVII[44];[46]	A, B, C; D (H.) A, B, C; D (H.) A, B, C; D (H.) A, B, C	...[48]	X.33[34] Y.33[44] Z.33[44]	V.33[47]	33rd D.A.C.[48]	11th[49] 212th 222nd	33rd[21]	18/ Middx. (P.)	...	19th[51] 99th 101st	43rd	...	33rd[51]
1917 June (France)	19th ...... 98th 100th	20/R.F.,[52] 2/R.W.F.,[53] 1/Sco. Rif., 5/6/Sco. Rif.; 19th M.G. Coy.;[54] 19th T.M. Bty. 4/King's, 1/4/Suff.,[55] 1/Middx., 2/A. & S.H.; 98th M.G. Coy.;[56] 98th T.M. Bty. 1/Queen's,[56] 2/Worc., 16/ K.R.R.C., 1/9/H.L.I.; 100th M.G. Coy.;[56] 100th T.M. Bty.	...	CLVI......... CLXII	A, B, C; D (H.) A, B, C; D (H.)	...	X.33[64] Y.33[64] Z.33[64]	V.33[64]	33rd D.A.C.	11th 212th 222nd	33rd	18/ Middx. (P.)	248th M.G. Coy.[64]	19th 99th 101st	43rd	230th[47]	33rd[64]

1918 March (France)				...	...	X.33rd Y.33rd	"	33rd D.A.C.	11th 212th 222nd	33rd	18/ Middx. (P.)	No. 33 Bn.** M.G.C.	19th 99th 101st	43rd	230th	33rd
19th	1/Queen's,** 1/Sco. Rif., 5/8/ Sco. Rif.; 19th T.M. Bty.	CLVI.........	...	A, B, C; D (H.)												
98th	4/King's, 1/Middx., 2/A. & S.H.; 98th T.M. Bty.	CLXII.........		A, B, C; D (H.)												
100th	2/Worc., 16/K.R.R.C., 1/9/ H.L.I.; 100th T.M. Bty.															

NOTES

¹ Raised as 40th Div.; became 33rd Division on 27/4/15.

² 99th & 100th Bdes. were raised as 120th & 119th Bdes. (in original 40th Div.), they were renumbered on 27/4/15; at the same time 121st Bde. was transferred to the newly-formed 39th Div., and renumbered 116th; and the 118th Bde. from the 32nd (formerly 39th) Div. joined 33rd Div. and became 98th & 99th Bdes. 33rd Div. concentrated at Clipstone Camp by 1/7/15, & 100th Bde. arrived between 4–13/7/15.

³ The battalions were designated: 1st, 2nd, 3rd, 4th Public Schools.

⁴ The battalions were designated: Empire, Kensington, and 1st & 2nd Sportsman.

⁵ The battalions were designated: West Ham, Public Schools, 1st Football, and Church Lads Bde.

⁶ Joined Div. in England and disembkd. at le Havre on 18/11/15.

⁷ Coy. was formed 20–26/7/15, and disembkd. at le Havre on 16 & 17/11/15.

⁸ The Divnl. Artillery was designated: Camberwell. The Bdes. were raised as 4-battery brigades; in each brigade the batteries were lettered—A, B, C, D—and each battery was a 4-gun battery. The 4 Bdes. and D.A.C. were raised in Camberwell between 14/1–1/6/15. The Divnl. Artillery reached Bulford 5–10/8/15; embkd. at Southampton on 12–13/12/15 and completed its concentration at Aire and Thiennes at 2.30 p.m., 16/12/15.

⁹ The 3 Fd. Cos. were designated: Tottenham. 212th and 222nd joined at Clipstone Camp on 14/7/15, and 226th at Bulford on 31/7/15. The 3 Fd. Cos. disembkd. at le Havre on 17 & 18/11/15.

¹⁰ The Sig. Coy. was designated: Tottenham; it joined at Bulford on 31/7/15.

¹¹ The Pioneer Bn. was designated: 1st Public Works. The Bn. arrived at Clipstone Camp on 13/7/15; it disembkd. at le Havre on 15/11/15.

¹² The 3 Fd. Ambces. (raised for the original 33rd Div.—App. 1D) joined the Div. in England and disembkd. at le Havre 15–18/11/15.

¹³ Joined Div. at Bulford on 16/9/15; disembkd. at le Havre on 18/11/15.

¹⁴ Train (225, 226, 227, 228 Cos., A.S.C.) joined at Clipstone Camp on 7/7/15. In Nov. 1915 Train remained in England when 33rd Div. went to France. On 24/3/16 Train disembkd. in France, joined the 29th Div. on 20/3/16, and Train served with 29th Div. for the remdr. of the War.

¹⁵ On 27/11/15 Bn. was transferred to 19th Inf. Bde.; and on 26/2/16 Bn. was transferred to G.H.Q. Troops, and was drafted.

¹⁶ On 27/2/16 Bn. was transferred to G.H.Q. Troops and was drafted.

¹⁷ On 27/11/15 Bn. was transferred to 19th Inf. Bde.

¹⁸ On 28/2/16 Bn. was transferred to G.H.Q. Troops and was drafted.

¹⁹ On 25/11/15 99th Coy. (17/, 22/, 23/, & 24/R.N.F.) with No. 3 Sec. Divnl. Sig. Coy., 100th Fd. Ambce., and No. 3 Coy. Divnl. Train (172 Coy.) were transferred to 2nd Div.

²⁰ On 22/12/15 Bn. was transferred to and joined 6th Bde., 2nd Div. Bn. was disbanded on 10/2/18.

²¹ On 25/2/16 Bn. was transferred to G.H.Q. Troops; and on 25/4/16 Bn. joined 86th Bde., 29th Div. Bn. was disbanded on 11/2/18.

²² On 8/12/15 Bn. was transferred to 6th Bde., 2nd Div. Bn. was disbanded on 10/2/18.

²³ On 25/5/16 the designation of the Sqdn. was changed from F to B. On 19/4/16 Sqdn. left the Div. and was attached to 1st Cav. Div. (20/4–12/5/16); 49th Div. (16–20/5/16); and 33rd Div. (21/5–19/6/16). On 21/6/16 Sqdn. joined X Corps Cav. Regt.

²⁴ On 19/4/16 Coy. left the Div. and was attached to 1st Cav. Div. (20/4–9/5/16). On 10/5/16 Coy. joined XI Corps Cyclist Bn.

²⁵ On 19/5/16 D Bty. left and became A/CLXVII; and A (H.)/CLXVII joined and became D (H.)/CLVI.

²⁶ On 19/5/16 D Bty. left and became B/CLXVII; and C (H.)/CLXVII joined and became B (H.)/CLXII.

²⁷ On 16/5/16 D Bty. left and became C/CLXVII; and D (H.)/CLXVII joined and became D (H.)/CLXVI.

²⁸ On 14/2/16 B (H.) Bty. and 1 subsec. CLXVII B.A.C. left CLXVII (H.) and joined 1/IV London (H.) Bde. in 56th Div. Between 16–20/5/16 CLXVII was reorganised: A (H.), C (H.), and D (H.) left and became D (H.)/CLVI, D (H.)/CLXII, and D (H.)/CLXVI; and D/CLVI, D/CLXII, and D/CLXVI joined and became A, B, and C/CLXVII.

²⁹ On 2/12/15 the Fd. Coy. was transferred to the 2nd Div.

³⁰ Train (170, 171, 172, 173 Cos., A.S.C.), formerly 1/London (56th) Divl. Train, joined 28th Div. on 21/12/14 at Winchester as 28th Div. Train. The Train embkd. for France on 15/1/15. On 13/11/15 the Train (170–173 Cos.) was transferred, in France, from 28th Div. and became 33rd Div. Train.

³¹ On 25/11/15 19th Inf. Bde. (2/R.W.F., 1/Sco. Rif., 1/Middx., 2/A. & S.H., & 5/Sco. Rif.) with Sec. 2nd Div. Signal Coy., 19th Fd. Ambce., and No. 2 Coy., 2nd Div. Train (8 Coy., A.S.C.) were transferred from 2nd Div. and joined 33rd Div.

³² On 29/5/16 1/6/Sco. Rif. (see General Notes) was transferred from 100th Bde. to 19th Bde. and amalgamated with 1/5/Sco. Rif. in 19th Bde. (n.31); surplus went to G.H.Q. Troops. The joint Bn. was designated 5/6 Sco. Rif.

³³ Bde. M.G. Cos. joined Bdes. as follows:
19th—formed in the Bde. on 24/2/16;
98th—disembkd. at le Havre on 26/4/16, and joined Bde. on 28/4/16;
100th—left Grantham 25/4/16, disembkd. at le Havre 26/4/16, and joined Bde. on 28/4/16.

³⁴ Bde. Light T.M. Btles. were formed:
19th—19/1 (A/19 until 23/3/16) by 26/1/16, 19/2 (B/19 until 23/3/16) by 15/3/16, and they became 19th T.M. Bty. by 24/6/16;
98th—98/1 (A/98 until 26/3/16) by 27/1/16, 98/2 by 23/4/16, and they became 98th T.M. Bty. by 30/6/16;
100th—100th T.M. Bty. was formed by 13/6/16.

NOTES—*continued*

" Bn. disembkd. at le Havre 6/3/15, served with Lahore Div. 9/3-10/11/15, with 48th Div. 10/11-3/12/15, and with 19th Div. 3/12/15-25/2/16; then Bn. was transferred to 98th Bde., and Bn. joined 98th Bde. at Annequin on 27/2/16.

" Bn. disembkd. at le Havre 9/11/14, served with Lahore Div. 4/12/14-10/11/15, with 46th Div. 10-15/11/15, with 15th Div. 15/11/15-27/2/16; then Bn. was transferred to 98th Bde., and joined 98th Bde. on 28/2/16.

" On 27/11/15 Bn. joined 98th Bde. from 19th Bde.

" On 27/11/15 Bn. joined 98th Bde. from 19th Bde.

" On 15/12/15 Bn. joined 100th Bde. from 5th Bde., 2nd Div.

" On 20/12/15 Bn. joined 100th Bde. from 5th Bde., 2nd Div.

" Bn. served with 5th Bde., 2nd Div., 23/11/14-30/1/16; with G.H.Q. Troops 30/1-29/5/16; and Bn. then joined 100th Bde.

" On 12/9/16 A and ½ B/CLXVII joined and made up A, B, and C/CLVI to 6 18-pdrs. each. On 14/1/17 R. Sec. D (H.)/CLXVI joined and made up D (H.)/CLVI to 6 hows.

" On 12/9/16 ½ B and C/CLXVII joined: C/CLXVII and ½ A/CLXII made A/CLXII; ½ A/CLXVII and B/CLXII made B/CLXII; and ½ B/CLXVII and C/CLXII made C/CLXII—each battery was then a 6-gun battery. On 14/1/17 L. Sec. D (H.)/CLXVI joined and made up D (H.)/CLXII to 6 hows.

" On 12/9/16 C Bty. was broken up to make up A and B to 6, 18-pdrs. each. On 14/1/17 CLXVI was broken up: A was transferred and became A/XXVI A.F.A. Bde.; B was transferred and became C/XCIII A.F.A. Bde. on 16/1/17; and D (H.) was split up: R. Sec. joined D (H.)/CLVI and L. Sec. joined D (H.)/CLXII, making the 2 batteries up to 6 hows. each.

" By noon 12/9/16 CLXVII was broken up: A and ½ B joined CLVI, and ½ B and C joined CLXII, to make up the 18-pdr. batteries of CLVI and CLXII to 6 18-pdrs. each (notes 42, 43).

" Medium T.M. Btics. were formed by 4/5/16.

" Heavy T.M. Bty. was formed on 29/5/16.

" On 22/5/16 the four B.A.C.s were absorbed in the D.A.C.; and the D.A.C. was reformed in H.Q. and 4 Sections.

" On 2/12/15 the Pd. Coy. was transferred from 2nd Div.

" Between 2-15/2/18 Bn. was disbanded: 19 offrs & 520 o.r. were posted to other Bns., and the surplus went to VIII Corps Rft. Camp.

" On 4/2/18 Bn. was transferred to 115th Bde., 38th (Welsh) Div., and joined on 6/2/18.

" On 14/2/18 Bn. was transferred as Pioneers to 58th Div., and joined on 15/2/18.

" On 5/2/18 Bn. was transferred from 100th Bde. to 19th Bde.

" Between 1-21/2/18 the Medium T.M. Btics. were reorganized: Z was abolished and absorbed by X & Y; each then became a T.M. Bty. with 6, 6" Newton T.M.s

" Between 1-21/2/18 V was abolished and the personnel was absorbed by X and Y.

" On 17/7/17 M.G. Coy. disembkd. at le Havre and joined the Div. on 21/7/17.

" Coy. joined the Div. by 1/6/17; on 12/6/17 Coy. was allotted the number 230th.

" Tmin consisted of 8, 170, 171, and 173 Cos., A.S.C. (notes 19, 30, and 31).

" Bn. formed 9-19/2/18; it consisted of 19th, 98th, 100th, and 248th M.G. Cos.

33RD DIVISION

FORMATION, BATTLES, AND ENGAGEMENTS

This New Army Division had no existence before the outbreak of the Great War.

On the 10th December 1914 the formation of the Fifth New Army (37th–42nd Divisions) was authorized; this brought into existence the 40th Division and its infantry brigades (119th, 120th, and 121st). In April 1915 the original Fourth New Army of six divisions (80th–85th) was broken up, so that it could be used for replacing casualties in the eighteen divisions (9th–26th) of the first three New Armies (see Appendix 1). The original Fifth New Army (37th–42nd Divisions) then became the Fourth New Army, and its six divisions were renumbered (80th–35th). In this way, on the 27th April 1915, the 40th Division became the 33rd Division; at the same time the 120th Brigade was renumbered 99th and the 119th Brigade became the 100th. The 121st Brigade was transferred to the newly-formed 39th Division and was then renumbered 116th; its place in the 33rd Division was taken by the 118th Brigade from the original 89th (later 82nd) Division, and on arrival this Brigade received the number 98th (see Appendix 2).

In the 98th Brigade the four battalions (18/, 19/, 20/, & 21/Royal Fusiliers) were designated the 1st, 2nd, 3rd, and 4th Public Schools; in the 99th Brigade the sub-titles of the battalions were Empire (17/R.F.), Kensington (22/R.F.), and 1st and 2nd Sportsman (23/ & 24/R.F.); and in the 100th Brigade the sub-titles were West Ham (13/Essex), Public Schools (16/Middlesex), 1st Football (17/Middlesex), and Church Lads Brigade (16/K.R.R.C.). The Field Companies and the Signal Company were designated Tottenham, and the pioneer battalion (18/Middlesex) had the sub-title of 1st Public Works.

Early in January 1915 the War Office authorized the Mayor of Camberwell to raise an artillery brigade (CLVI). The local response was so prompt and effective that in March further authority was given to raise another brigade (CLXII), and this second brigade was recruited up to strength by the middle of May. The War Office was then informed that a mass of would-be recruits still existed in the Camberwell neighbourhood and from these men the whole of the artillery could be raised for the 83rd Division. Authority was given at once to recruit the two remaining brigades (CLXVI and CLXVII), the heavy battery (126th), and the divisional ammunition column. These additional units were raised without any difficulty or delay; and thus it came about that the personnel of the 83rd Division Artillery was provided by the men of Camberwell and Dulwich. At first, whilst the brigades were at Dulwich, only three 15-pdrs. and dummy loaders were available; but in July, four 18-pdrs. arrived, and on the 26th July the first 4.5″ howitzer reached CLXVII (H.) Brigade.

Meanwhile on the 1st July the 83rd Division began to assemble at Clipstone Camp (Notts.), and by the 18th all the infantry concentrated there. On the 8rd August the Division started to move to Bulford, Perham Down, and Tidworth. Between the 5th–10th the divisional artillery arrived; and on the 10th August the concentration of the Division on Salisbury Plain was completed. The Division now began its final intensive preparation for the field.

On the 4th November the Division was ordered to prepare to move to France; the artillery and the train, however, would not accompany it. The divisional artillery was to follow later and rejoin in France (see note 8), and the Division was to take with it the 54th (East Anglian) Division Artillery (see General Notes).

On the 8th November H.M. the Queen inspected the Division on Figheldean Down, and H.M. the King also sent a message. On the 9th the Division received orders to move and on the 12th entrainment began. On the 16th the first units began to arrive in the concentration area, and on the 21st November the Division and its attached artillery completed concentration around Morbecque. For the remainder of the Great War the 33rd Division served on the Western Front in France and Belgium and was engaged in the following operations :—

1915

1916

BATTLES OF THE SOMME

12 and 13 July	Battle of Albert [Corps Reserve, XV Corps, Fourth Army].
14–17 July	Battle of Bazentin Ridge [XV Corps, Fourth Army].
18–21 July	Attacks on High Wood [XV Corps, Fourth Army].
25 Oct.–7 Nov.	Capture of Dewdrop and Boritska Trenches [XIV Corps, Fourth Army].

1917

BATTLES OF ARRAS

14 April	First Battle of the Scarpe (19th Bde. under 21st Div.) [VII Corps, Third Army].
23 and 24 April	Second Battle of the Scarpe [VII Corps, Third Army].
20–30 May	Actions on the Hindenburg Line [VII Corps, Third Army].
18–28 Aug.	Operations on the Flanders Coast (Nieuport Sector) [XV Corps, Fourth Army].

BATTLES OF YPRES

24 and 25 Sept.	Battle of Menin Road Ridge [X Corps, Second Army].
26 and 27 Sept.	Battle of Polygon Wood [X Corps, Second Army].

1918

BATTLES OF THE LYS

11 April	Battle of Messines (100th Bde., in reserve to 25th Div.) [IX Corps, Second Army].
12–15 April	Battle of Hazebrouck [IX Corps, Second Army].
13–15 April	Battle of Bailleul (100th Bde., under 25th Div.) [IX Corps, Second Army].
14 April	Defence of Neuve Eglise (100th Bde.).
17–19 April	First Battle of Kemmel Ridge [IX Corps, Second Army].
8 May	Fighting for and recapture of Ridge Wood (with Comp. Bde., 30th Div., attached) [XXII Corps, Second Army].

1918

(continued)

THE ADVANCE TO VICTORY
BATTLES OF THE HINDENBURG LINE

18 September ... ... **Battle of Epéhy** [V Corps, Third Army].

29 Sept.–2 Oct. ... ... **Battle of the St. Quentin Canal** [V Corps, Third Army].

3–5 Oct. ... ... **Battle of the Beaurevoir Line** [V Corps, Third Army].

9 October ... ... **Battle of Cambrai** [V Corps, Third Army].

9–12 October ... ... **Pursuit to the Selle** [V Corps, Third Army].

THE FINAL ADVANCE IN PICARDY

23–25 October ... ... **Battle of the Selle** [V Corps, Third Army].

On the 26th October the attack was continued and the Division captured the village of Englefontaine. During the night of the 26th/27th the Division was relieved in the front line by the 38th (Welsh) Division, and the 33rd Division then concentrated around Troisvilles. On the 5th November the Division advanced through the Forest of Mormal heading for the Sambre; during the afternoon the leading battalions crossed the river and established bridgeheads along the line of the St. Quentin—Maubeuge railway. On the 6th Leval was captured, and by 9 p.m. on the 7th November the advanced troops were on a line to the west of the Avesnes—Maubeuge road; the Division was then again relieved in the front line by the 38th Division, and drew back into the Sambre Valley near Leval. On the 11th November it was still in the same position when the Armistice brought hostilities to a close.

On the 12th the Division concentrated around Berlaimont, on the 15th November it moved back to Montigny (S.W. of le Cateau); and on the 4th December H.M. the King passed through the divisional area. On the 6th December the Division began to march back to the Hornoy area (W. of Amiens and S. of the Somme) and the move was completed by the 17th.

In 1919 demobilization proceeded rapidly, and divisional headquarters moved to the coast at Quiberville (13th January), then to Varengeville (31st January), and lastly to Etretat in the le Havre area (28th February). Gradually units dwindled to cadre, and on the 15th May the first cadres embarked for England. On the 18th June divisional headquarters was reduced to Equipment Guard and on the 30th June the war history of the 33rd Division came to an end. During the Great War the 33rd Division lost 37,404 killed, wounded, and missing.

34TH DIVISION

G.O.C.

5 July 1915 ... ... Major-General E. C. INGOUVILLE-WILLIAMS
(killed, 22/7/16).
23 July 1916 ... ... Br.-Gen. R. W. R. BARNES (acting).
25 July 1916 ... ... Major-General C. L. NICHOLSON.

G.S.O.1.

28 June 1915...Major P. B. O'CONNOR
(acting).
25 Sept. 1915...Lt.-Col. N. J. G.
CAMERON.
24 Nov. 1915...Major P. B. O'CONNOR
(acting).
29 Dec. 1915...Lt.-Col. H. ST. C.
WILKINS.
9 Feb. 1916...Lt.-Col. R. H. MANGLES.
20 Feb. 1917...Lt.-Col. H. E. R. R.
BRAINE.
29 Dec. 1917...Lt.-Col. SIR T. A. A. M.
CUNINGHAME, Bt.
30 April 1918...Lt.-Col. J. G. DOONER
(killed, 31/7/18).
31 July 1918...Lt.-Col. R. M. TYLER
(tempy.).
10 Aug. 1918...Lt.-Col. B. C. BATTYE.

A.-A. & Q.-M.-G.

15 June 1915...Major R. F. LOCK
(acting).
3 Aug. 1915...Lt.-Col. G. R. H. NUGENT
(sick, 13/11/15).
13 Nov. 1915...Major R. F. LOCK
(acting).
22 Nov. 1915...Lt.-Col. G. R. H.
NUGENT.
16 Mar. 1916...Lt.-Col. O. K. CHANCE
(sick, 9/5/17).
9 May 1917...Lt.-Col. R. M. TYLER.
22 Sept. 1918...Major H. D. PARKIN
(acting).
21 Oct. 1918...Lt.-Col. H. W. GRUBB.
[16 Dec. 1918...Lt.-Col. H. D. PARKIN].

B.-G., R.A.

6 July 1915...Br.-Gen. F. B. ELMSLIE.
16 Nov. 1915...Br.-Gen. A. D. KIRBY.
19 Feb. 1917...Br.-Gen. W. J. K.
RETTIE.
12 May 1917...Br.-Gen. E. C. W. D.
WALTHALL.

C.R.E.

17 Mar. 1915...Colonel A. C.
MACDONNELL.
9 Feb. 1917...Lt.-Col. A. C. DOBSON.

101st BDE.
(new formation)

19 June '15...Br.-Gen. H. G. FITTON*
    (wd., 18/1/16 ; died, 20/1/16).
18 Jan. '16...Colonel C. W. SOMERSET
    (acting).
28 Jan. '16...Br.-Gen. R. C. GORE
    (killed, 14/4/18).
14 April '18...Lt.-Col. A. STEPHENSON
    (acting).
23 April '18...Br.-Gen. W. J. WOODCOCK.

102nd BDE.
(originally 123rd Bde.)

28 Dec. '14...Br.-Gen. T. P. B. TERNAN.
(On 6/7/16 102nd Bde. was attached to
    37th Division).

111th BDE.**

(On 6/7/16 111th Bde., from 37th Div.,
    was attached to 34th Division).
[9 April '15]...Br.-Gen. R. W. R.
    BARNES.
(On 22/8/16 111th Bde. rejoined 37th
    Division).

102nd BDE.

(On 22/8/16 102nd Bde. rejoined 34th
    Division).
[28 Dec. '14]...Br.-Gen. T. P. B.
    TERNAN.
22 April '17...Br.-Gen. N. A. THOMSON.
21 May '18...Br.-Gen. E. HILLIAM.

103rd BDE.
(originally 124th Bde.)

17 Dec. '14...Br.-Gen. W. A. COLLINGS.
22 May '15...Br.-Gen. W. E. O'LEARY.
27 Sept. '15...Br.-Gen. H. H. L. MALCOLM (sick, 5/11/15).
24 Nov. '15...Lt.-Col. N. J. G. CAMERON (acting).
26 Dec. '15...Br.-Gen. N. J. G. CAMERON (wd., 1/7/16).
 1 July '16...Lt.-Col. G. R. V. STEWARD (acting).
 4 July '16...Br.-Gen. H. E. TREVOR.
(On 6/7/16 103rd Bde. was attached to 37th Division).

112th BDE.**

(On 6/7/16 112th Bde., from 37th Div., was attached to 34th
    Division.)
[14 Sept. '15]...Br.-Gen. P. M. ROBINSON.
(On 22/8/16 112th Bde. rejoined 37th Division).

103rd BDE.

(On 22/8/16 103rd Bde. rejoined 34th Division).
[4 July '16]...Br.-Gen. H. E. TREVOR (sick, 18/4/17).
18 April '17...Lt.-Col. M. E. RICHARDSON (acting).
25 April '17...Br.-Gen. C. J. GRIFFIN.
10 Aug. '17...Br.-Gen. H. E. TREVOR (gassed, 21/10/17).
21 Oct. '17...Lt.-Col. E. M. MOULTON-BARRETT (acting).
25 Oct. '17...Lt.-Col. R. D. TEMPLE (acting).
20 Nov. '17...Br.-Gen. J. G. CHAPLIN.
31 Aug. '18...Br.-Gen. R. I. RAWSON.

---

* Prior to taking command of the 101st Inf. Bde., Br.-Gen. H. G. Fitton had been Brigade Commander, Tyne Garrison, from 18/11/1914–18/6/1915.

** For the composition of the 111th and 112th Inf. Bdes. see General Notes (opposite).

GENERAL NOTES

The following also served with the 34th Division :—

111th Inf. Bde.(Br.-Gen. R. W. R. Barnes—10/R.F., 13/R.F., 13/K.R.R.C., 13/R.B., 111th M.G. Coy., 111th T.M. Bty.); 112th Inf. Bde. (Br.-Gen. P. M. Robinson—11/R. War., 6/Bedf., 8/E. Lanc., 10/L.N.L., 112th M.G. Coy., 112th T.M. Bty.); and 9/N. Staff. (P),

from 37th Division were attached from 6/7—22/8/16 to the 34th Division, in exchange for

102nd Inf. Bde. (Br.-Gen. T. P. B. Ternan), 103rd Inf. Bde. (Br.-Gen. H. E. Trevor), and 18/N.F.(P.)

ARTILLERY :—516 (H.) Battery, R.F.A. (4, 4.5″ Hows.) disembkd. at le Havre on 4/10/16, arrived Bailleul on 7/10/16, and joined CLXXV Bde. (see Note 24). 130 Heavy Battery, R.G.A. (4, 60-pdrs.) was raised for the 34th Division, but the Heavy Battery went abroad independently. The Hy. Bty. embkd. on 7/2/16, disembkd. at Alexandria on 20/2/16, and joined XXXV Hy. Arty. Group. The Hy. Bty. returned to France on 14/4/16 and joined XXI Hy. Arty. Group on 12/5/16.

OTHER UNITS :—74th Sanitary Section joined the Division in England, went to France with the Division, and disembkd. at le Havre on 11/1/16. Sanitary Section left the Division on 31/3/17, and took over a Sanitary Area in XVII Corps, Third Army.

34th Div. Motor Ambce. Workshop went to France with the Division and disembkd. at Rouen on 10/1/16. The Workshop rejoined the Division on 14/1/16 at Renescure. On 31/3/16 the Workshop was disbanded, and the personnel and vehicles joined 34th Div. Supply Column.

On 27/2/18 the reorganization of the 34th Division on a 9-battalion basis was completed ; and between 27/2–2/3/18 the pioneer battalion (18/N.F.) was reorganized on a 8-company basis.

34th Division Artillery, May–July 1918. In May 1918 the infantry of the 34th Division was reduced to cadre (notes 39-49); but the 34th Division Artillery (see Table) went into the line between 8–16/5/18 and was under B.-G., R.A., 5th Division. Relieved between 1–3/7/18 the 34th D.A. then occupied the East Poperinghe (or Blue) Line from 6–11/7/18 ; and on 22/7/18 the 34th D.A. moved into action to cover the 34th Division, holding the line Tigny—Hartennes.

34TH DIVISION ¹

Dates	INFANTRY			ARTILLERY						Engineers		Pioneers	M.G. Units	Field Ambulances	Mobile Vety. Sec.	Divnl. Emplnt. Coy.	Divnl. Train
	Brigades	Battalions and attached Units	Mounted Troops	Field Artillery			Trench Mortar Btties.		Divnl. Ammn. Coln.	Field Cos.	Signal Service Divnl. Signal Coy.						
				Brigades	Batteries	Bde. Ammn. Colns.	Medium	Heavy									
1915 May (England)	101st²,³ .... 102nd³,⁴ 103rd³,⁵	15/R.S., 16/R.S., 10/Linc., 11/Suff. 20/N.F., 21/N.F., 22/N.F., 23/N.F. 24/N.F., 25/N.F., 26/N.F., 27/N.F.	E Sqdn.,⁶ N. Ir. Horse 34th Div. Cyclist Coy.⁷	CLII⁸ .... CLX⁸ .... CLXXV⁸ .... CLXXVI (H.)⁹	A, B, C, D A, B, C, D A, B, C, D A (H.), B (H.), C (H.), D (H.)	CLII B.A.C. CLX B.A.C. CLXXV B.A.C. CLXXVI (H.) B.A.C.	...	...	34th D.A.C.⁸	207th⁹ 208th⁹ 209th⁹	34th⁹	18/ N.F.¹⁰ (P.)	...	102nd¹¹ 103rd¹¹ 104th¹¹	44th¹²	...	34th¹³
1916 January (France)	101st ...... 102nd 103rd	15/R.S., 16/R.S., 10/Linc., 11/Suff. 20/N.F., 21/N.F., 22/N.F., 23/N.F. 24/N.F., 25/N.F., 26/N.F., 27/N.F.	E Sqdn.,¹⁴ N. Ir. Horse 34th Div. Cyclist Coy.¹⁵	CLII¹⁶ .... CLX¹⁷ .... CLXXV¹⁸ .... CLXXVI (H.)¹⁹	A, B, C, D A, B, C, D A, B, C, D A (H.), B (H.), C (H.), D (H.)	CLII B.A.C. CLX B.A.C. CLXXV B.A.C. CLXXVI (H.) B.A.C.	...	...	34th D.A.C.	207th 208th 209th	34th	18/ N.F. (P.)	...	102nd 103rd 104th	44th	...	34th
1916 May (France)	101st ...... 102nd 103rd	15/R.S., 16/R.S., 10/Linc., 11/Suff.; 101st Bde. M.G. Coy.,²⁰ 101st T.M. Bty.²¹ 20/N.F., 21/N.F., 22/N.F., 23/N.F.; 102nd Bde. M.G. Coy.,²² 102nd T.M. Bty.²³ 24/N.F., 25/N.F., 26/N.F., 27/N.F.; 103rd Bde. M.G. Coy.,²⁴ 103rd T.M. Bty.²⁵	...	CLII¹⁶,²⁶ CLX¹⁷,²⁶ CLXXV¹⁸,²⁶ CLXXVI¹⁹,²⁶	A, B, C; D (H.) A, B, C; D (H.) A, B, C; D (H.) A, B, C	...²⁸	X.34²⁹ Y.34³⁰ Z.34³¹	V.34³²	34th D.A.C.³³	207th 208th 209th	34th	18/ N.F. (P.)	...	102nd 103rd 104th	44th	...	34th
1917 June (France)	101st ...... 102nd 103rd	15/R.S., 16/R.S., 10/Linc.,³⁴ 11/Suff.; 101st M.G. Coy.,³⁵ 101st T.M. Bty. 20/N.F., 21/N.F.,³⁶ 22/N.F., 23/N.F.; 102nd M.G. Coy.,³⁷ 102nd T.M. Bty. 24/N.F.,³⁸ 25/N.F.,³⁸ 26/N.F.,³⁸ 27/N.F.,³⁸ 103rd M.G. Coy.,³⁹ 103rd T.M. Bty.	...	CLII³⁸ .... CLX³³	A, B, C; D (H.) A, B, C; D (H.)	...	X.34 Y.34 Z.34³⁵	V.34³⁶	34th D.A.C.	207th 208th 209th	34th	18/ N.F. (P.)	240th M.G. Coy.³⁷	102nd 103rd 104th	44th	231st³⁴	34th

44

Order of Battle

	Infantry Brigade & Battalions	Field Art. Bde.	Batteries	Med. T.M.			D.A.C.	Field Coys. R.E.	Signal	Pioneers	M.G.	Field Ambulances	Mobile Vet. Sec.	Div. Emp. Coy.	Train
1918 March (France)	101st ... 15/R.S.,[31] 16/R.S.,[31] 11/Suff.,[31] 101st T.M. Bty.[31]	CLII	A, B, C; D (H.)	X.34[35]	...	...	34th D.A.C.	207th	34th	18/N.F.[34] (P.)	No. 34 Bn. M.G.C.	102nd	44th	231st	34th
	102nd ... 22/N.F.,[31] 23/N.F.,[31] 25/N.F.,[31] 102nd T.M. Bty.[31]	CLX	A, B, C; D (H.)	Y.34[35]				208th				103rd			
	103rd ... 9/(North'd Hus.) N.F.,[31] 10/Linc.,[31] 1/E. Lanc.;[31] 103rd T.M. Bty.[31]							209th				104th			
1918 July (France) *After Reconstitution*	101st ... 2/4/Queen's,[33] 1/4/R. Suss.,[33] 2/L.N.L.;[33] 101st T.M. Bty.	CLII	A, B, C; D (H.)	X.34	...	...	34th D.A.C.	207th	34th	2/4/Som. L.I.[34] (P.)	No. 34 Bn. M.G.C.	102nd	44th	231st	34th
	102nd ... 1/4/Ches.,[33] 1/7/Ches.,[33] 1/1/Hereford,[33] 102nd T.M. Bty.	CLX	A, B, C; D (H.)	Y.34				208th				103rd			
	103rd ... 1/5/K.O.S.B.,[33] 1/8/Sco. Rif.,[33] 1/5/A. & S.H.;[33] 103rd T.M. Bty.							209th				104th			

NOTES

1 Raised as 41st Div. on 27/4/15; became 34th Div. on 27/4/15. 102nd & 103rd Bdes. were raised on 27/4/15; 123rd & 124th Bdes. and renumbered on 27/4/15; the 102nd Bde. was transferred to 32nd Div. and renumbered 96th; its place was taken by the 101st Bde., formed in June 1915.

2 The battalions were designated: 1st & 2nd Edinburgh, Grimsby, and Cambridge.

3 The battalions were designated: 1st, 2nd, 3rd, 4th Tyneside Scottish.

4 The battalions were designated: 1st, 2nd, 3rd, 4th Tyneside Irish.

5 Sqdn. joined Div. in England and disembkd. at le Havre on 12/1/16.

6 Coy. was formed in Sept. 1915 on Salisbury Plain; Coy. disembkd. at le Havre on 11/1/16.

7 The Artillery Bdes. were designated: Nottingham, Wearside, Staffordshire, Leicestershire, and the D.A.C. was designated Nottingham. The Bdes. were raised as 4-battery brigades; in each brigade the batteries were lettered—A, B, C, D—and each battery was a 4-gun battery.

8 The 3 Fd. Coes. & Signal Coy. were designated: Norfolk, and in Feb. 1915 were raised as 38th (Norfolk) Div., R.E. On 10/5/15 the numerical designation was changed, from 38th to 34th, and the R.E. became 34th (Norfolk) Div., R.E. On 23/7/15 the R.E. moved to Kirkby Malzeard and joined 34th Div.; the R.E. disembkd. at le Havre between 8-12/1/16.

9 Bn. joined Div. at Kirkby Malzeard in June 1915; Bn. disembkd. at le Havre on 8/11/16. The Bn. was designated: 1st Tyneside Pioneers.

10 Raised for the original 34th Div. (App. 1E) the 3 Fd. Ambces. joined the new 34th Div. (note 1) between 8-10/11/15; the 3 Fd. Ambces. disembkd. at le Havre between 9-12/11/16.

11 Joined Div. in England; disembkd. at le Havre on 11/1/16.

12 Train (229, 230, 231, 232 Cos., A.S.C.) joined Div. at Kirkby Malzeard in June 1915; disembkd. at le Havre between 8-12/1/16.

13 Sqdn. was attached to 2nd Cav. Div. from 19-30/4/16; on 10/5/16 Sqdn. left 34th Div. and joined VII Corps Cav. Regt.

14 Coy. was attached to 2nd Cav. Div. from 19/4-1/5/16; on 11/5/16 Coy. left 34th Div. and joined III Corps Cyclist Bn. on 12/5/16.

15 At 11 a.m. on 22/5/16 A Bty. left and became A/CLXXVI; D/CLII then became A/CLII; and C (H.)/CLXXVI joined and became D (H.)/CLII.

16 At 11 a.m. on 22/5/16 B Bty. left and became B/CLX; and A (H.)/CLXXVI joined and became D (H.)/CLX.

17 At 11 a.m. on 22/5/16 C Bty. left and became C/CLXXVI; D/CLX then became C/CLX; and A (H.)/CLXXVI joined and became D (H.)/CLX.

18 On 4/2/16 B (H.) Bty. and 1 subsec. CLXXVI (H.) B.A.C. left CLXXVI (H.) Bde. and joined I/VIII London (H.) Bde. in 47th Div. At 11 a.m. on 22/5/16 A (H.), C (H.), and D (H.) left CLXXVI and became D (H.)/CLX, L. Sec. B made up B/CLX, and L. Sec. C made up C/CLX to 6 guns each. On 24/11/16 1 sec. C (H.)/CLXXV joined and became A, B, and C/CLXXVI.

19 101st M.G. Coy. was formed at Grantham on 21/2/16, left Grantham on 24/4/16, disembkd. at le Havre on 26/4/16, and joined Bde. on 27/4/16; 102nd M.G. Coy. left Grantham on 25/4/16, disembkd. at le Havre on 26/4/16, and joined Bde. on 27/4/16; 103rd M.G. Coy. left Grantham on 24/4/16, disembkd. at le Havre on 25/4/16, and joined Bde. on 27/4/16.

20 Bde. Light T.M. Btes. were formed:
101st—101/1 (A/101 until 10/3/16) by 18/2/16, 101/2 by 10/4/16, and they became 101st T.M. Bty. by 6/7/16;
102nd—102/1 (A/102 until 12/3/16) by 16/2/16, 102/2 by 1/6/16, and they became 102nd T.M. Bty. by 17/6/16;
103rd—103/1 (A/103 until 12/3/16) by 17/2/16, 103/2 by 6/5/16, and they became 103rd T.M. Bty. by 20/6/16.

21 By noon on 28/8/16 the 18-pdr. Btes. were made up to 6 guns each: A was made up by R. Sec. C/CLII and became A/CLXXVI; B was made up by L. Sec. C/CLII; and A/CLXXVI joined CLII and became A/CLII. On 24/11/16 1 sec. C (H.)/CLXXV joined and made up D (H.)/CLII to 6 hows.

22 By noon on 28/8/16 the 18-pdr. Btes. were made up to 6 guns each: B and L. Sec. C joined from CLXXVI and R. Sec. B made up A/CLX, L. Sec. B made up B/CLX, and L. Sec. C made up C/CLX to 6 guns each. On 24/11/16 1 sec. C (H.)/CLXXV joined and made up D (H.)/CLX to 6 hows.

NOTES—continued

At noon on 28/8/16 B Bty. was broken up and R. Sec. made up A and L. Sec. made up C to 6 guns each; C then became B. On 7/10/16 516 (H.) Bty. joined and became C (H.)/CLXXV. On 24/11/16 C (H.) was broken up and 1 sec. made up D (H.)/CLII and 1 sec. made up D (H.)/CLX to 6 hows. each. CLXXV became an A.F.A. Bde. on 26/1/17; D (H.) was made up to 6 hows.; and between 26-28/2/17 A (6, 18-pdrs.)/CLXXXVII joined from 57th Div. and became C/CLXXV. On 21/11/17 CLXXV A.F.A. Bde. left France for Italy, detraining in Italy on 24/11/17; on 23-31/3/18 CLXXV left Italy and detrained in France on 30/3-5/4/18.

At noon on 28/8/16 the Bde. was broken up: R. Sec. C Bty. made up A to 6 guns, A was then transferred to CLII and became A/CLII; B and L Sec. C/CLXXVI joined CLX, and R. Sec. B made up A, L. Sec. B made up B, and L. Sec. C made up C/CLX to 6 guns each.

Joined by 18/6/16.

Joined by 16/8/16.

At 11 a.m. on 18/5/16 the B.A.C.s were abolished and the D.A.C. was reorganized.

On 3/2/18 Bn. was transferred to 103rd Bde.

On 3/2/18 Bn. was disbanded.

On 3/2/18 Bn. was disbanded.

On 10/8/17 24/ and 27/N.F. were amalgamated; and on 26/2/18 24/27/N.F. was disbanded—28 offrs. & 551 o.r. were drafted between 6-10/2/18, and surplus went to VI Corps Rft. Camp.

On 3/2/18 Bn. was transferred to 102nd Bde.

On 27/2/18 Bn. was disbanded; 6 offrs. & 419 o.r. were drafted between 3-8/2/18, and surplus went to VI Corps Rft. Camp and to No. 9 Entg. Bn.

On 6/3/18 the three 4-mortar Medium T.M. Btles. were reorganized in two 6-mortar batteries; Z was broken up and absorbed by X and Y.

On 6/3/18 V H.T.M. Bty. was transferred to VI Corps.

Coy. was formed at Grantham on 24/2/17, left Grantham on 14/7/17, disembkd. at le Havre on 15/7/17, and joined Div. at Beauvincourt on 18/7/17.

Joined Div. ca 25/5/17.

On 16/5/18 Bn. was reduced to T.C. and surplus (7 offrs. & 581 o.r.) left for the Base; on 17/8/18 T.C. was transferred to 116th Bde., 39th Div.; on 14/8/18 Bn. was disbanded and personnel joined 13/R.S. (45th Bde., 15th Div.).

On 16/5/18 Bn. was reduced to T.C. and surplus (3 offrs. & 328 o.r.) left for the Base; on 17/6/18 T.C. was transferred to 116th Bde., 39th Div.; on 14/8/18 Bn. was disbanded and personnel joined 1/9/R.S. (46th Bde., 15th Div.).

On 16/5/18 Bn. was transferred to 103rd Bde., and on 26/5/18 Bn. was transferred to 183rd Bde., 61st Div.

Bde. L.T.M. Btles. were broken up between 12-16/5/18 and the personnel rejoined Bns. The Bde. L.T.M. Btles. were reformed: 101st on 2/7/18; 102nd on 10/7/18; and 103rd on 1/7/18.

On 17/5/18 Bn. was reduced to T.C. and surplus (6 offrs. & 463 o.r.) left for the Base; on 17/6/18 T.C. left for transfer to 16th Div., joined 16th Div. at Boulogne, absorbed 38/N.F. in England, and on 2/7/18 22/N.F. rejoined 16th Div. and was posted to 48th Bde.

On 17/5/18 Bn. was reduced to T.C. and surplus (4 offrs. & 407 o.r.) left for the Base; on 17/6/18 T.C. was transferred to 116th Bde., 39th Div.; on 16/8/18 T.C. was transferred to 198th Bde., 66th Div., and on 20/9/18 T.C. left 66th Div. for L. of C. with 197th Bde.

On 15 & 16/5/18 surplus was transferred to the Base. On 17/6/18 T.C. was transferred to 39th Div.; on 16/8/18 T.C. was transferred to 66th Div., and on 20/9/18 T.C. left 66th Div. for L. of C. with 197th Bde.

On 3/8/17 9/N.F. joined Bde. from 52nd Bde., 17th Div.; on 25/9/17 Bn. absorbed 2/1/North'd. Hsrs. and unit was designated 9/(N.H.) N.F. On 26/5/18 Bn. was transferred to 183rd Bde., 61st Div. (2/1/North'd. Hsrs. went to France, 19/3/17; served with XIX Corps Cav. Regt., 26/3-28/8/17; and then joined Inf. Base Depot at Etaples.)

On 16/5/18 Bn. was transferred to 101st Bde. and reduced to T.C. on 18/5/18; T.C. was transferred back to 103rd Bde. on 11/6/18; T.C. was transferred to 116th Bde., 39th Div., on 17/6/18; and 20/9/18 T.C. left the 66th Div. for L. of C. with 197th Bde.

On 1/2/18 Bn. joined Bde. from 11th Bde., 4th Div.; and on 26/5/18 Bn. was transferred to 183rd Bde., 61st Div.

Pioneer Bn. was reduced to T.C. on 18/5/18 and surplus left for the Base; on 17/6/18 T.C. was transferred to 116th Bde., 39th Div.; and on 16/8/18 T.C. joined 66th Div. On 20/9/18 T.C. left 66th Div. for L. of C. with 197th Bde.

Bn. formed on 28/2/18; it consisted of 101st, 102nd, 103rd, and 240th M.G. Coe.

RECONSTITUTED DIVISION

Bn. left 160th Bde., 53rd Div. (Palestine) on 31/5/18, embkd. at Alexandria on 1/6/18, disembkd. at Taranto on 21/8/18, arrived at Proven on 29/6/18, and joined 101st Bde. on 30/6/18.

Bn. left 160th Bde., 53rd Div. (Palestine) on 30/5/18, embkd. at Alexandria on 17/6/18, disembkd. at Taranto on 21/6/18, arrived at Proven on 29/6/18, and joined 101st Bde.

On 22/6/18 Bn. joined 103rd Bde. from 94th Bde., 31st Div. (see General Notes, 31st Div.), and on 28/6/18 Bn. was transferred to 101st Bde.

Bn. left 159th Bde., 53rd Div. (Palestine) on 31/5/18 (1/4/Ches.) and on 1/6/18 (1/7/Ches.), they embkd. at Alexandria on 17/6/18, disembkd. at Taranto on 22/6/18, arrived at Proven on 30/6/18, and joined 102nd Bde. on 1/7/18.

Bn. left 158th Bde., 53rd Div. (Palestine) on 1/6/18, embkd. at Alexandria on 17/6/18, disembkd. at Taranto on 22/6/18, arrived at Proven on 30/6/18, and joined 102nd Bde. on 1/7/18.

On 28/6/18 Bn. was transferred from 155th Bde., 52nd Div., and joined 103rd Bde.

On 28/6/18 Bn. was transferred from 156th Bde., 52nd Div., and joined 103rd Bde.

On 28/6/18 Bn. was transferred from 157th Bde., 52nd Div., and joined 103rd Bde.

Bn. disembkd. in India in Jan. 1915 with 2/1 S.-W. (13th) Bde., 2nd Wessex (45th) Div. In Sept. 1917 Bn. left 136th Bde., 45th Div., and landed at Suez on 25/9/17 Bn. joined 232nd Bde., 75th Div., on 16/10/17 near Deir el Balah; on 2/5/18 Bn. left 232nd Bde., disembkd. at Port Said on 23/5/18, disembkd. at Marseille on 1/6/18, reached Berguette on 7/6/18, joined 34th Div. on 19/6/18 at Berthen; and on 5/7/18 Bn. became Pioneer Bn. of 34th Div. at Proven, and was then reorganized in 3 Companies.

The following Units and Training Cadres served with the 34th Division in June 1918 :

Unit	From	Served with 34th Div. From	To	Transferred to	Notes
2/10/King's (T.C.)	16th Div.	17/6 –	27/8/18	39th Div.	Bn. was reformed between 26–30/6/18 and joined 21st Bde., 30th Div., on 4/7/18.
4/Linc. (T.C.)	16th Div.	17/6 –	27/8/18	39th Div.	
7/R. Ir. Regt. (T.C.)	49th Bde., 16th Div.	17/6 –	26/6/18	L. of C.	
18/Gr. How. (T.C.)	121st Bde., 40th Div.	3/6 –	17/6/18	39th Div.	Joined 151st Bde., 50th Div., on 16/7/18.
6/R. Innis. F.	14th Div.	19/6 –	27/6/18	L. of C.	
7/8/R. Innis. F. (T.C.)	49th Bde., 16th Div.	17/6 –	26/6/18	L. of C.	Bn. was reformed on 26/6/18 and joined 89th Bde., 30th Div., on 3/7/18.
18/E. Surr. (T.C.)	119th Bde., 40th Div.	3/6 –	17/6/18	39th Div.	
2/5/Sher. For. (T.C.)	49th Bde., 16th Div.	17/6 –	28/6/18	39th Div.	
21/Middx. (T.C.)	119th Bde., 40th Div.	3/6 –	17/6/18	39th Div.	
8/K.R.R.C. (T.C.)	41st Bde., 14th Div.	27/6/18		39th Div.	
9/K.R.R.C. (T.C.)	42nd Bde., 14th Div.	19/6 –	27/6/18	39th Div.	
5/N. Staff. (T.C.)	16th Div.	17/6 –	27/6/18	39th Div.	
10/11/H.L.I. (T.C.)	120th Bde., 40th Div.	3/6 –	16/6/18	14th Div.	
14/H.L.I. (T.C.)	120th Bde., 40th Div.	8/6 –	17/6/18	39th Div.	
5/Conn. Rang.	14th Div.	19/6 –	27/6/18	L. of C.	Bn. joined 197th Bde., 66th Div., on 22/7/18, and was transferred to 199th Bde. on 25/8/18.
6/Conn. Rang. (T.C.)	47th Bde., 16th Div.	17/6 –	27/6/18	39th Div.	
8/R.B. (T.C.)	41st Bde., 14th Div.	27/6/18		39th Div.	
9/R.B. (T.C.)	42nd Bde., 14th Div.	19/6 –	27/6/18	39th Div.	
6/Leins.	14th Div.	18/6 –	27/6/18	L. of C.	Bn. joined 198th Bde., 66th Div., on 20/7/18, and on 12/9/18 Bn. was disbanded.
6/R.M.F. (T.C.)	16th Div.	17/6 –	27/6/18	39th Div.	

47

34TH DIVISION

FORMATION, BATTLES, & ENGAGEMENTS

This New Army Division had no existence before the outbreak of the Great War.

On the 10th December 1914 the formation of the Fifth New Army (37th–42nd Divisions) was authorized; this brought into existence the 41st Division and its infantry brigades (122nd, 123rd, and 124th). In April 1915 the original Fourth New Army of six divisions (30th–35th) was broken up, so that it could be used for replacing casualties in the eighteen divisions (9th–26th) of the first three New Armies (see Appendix 1). The original Fifth New Army (37th–42nd Divisions) then became the Fourth New Army, and its six divisions were renumbered (30th–35th). In this way, on the 27th April 1915, the 41st Division became the 34th Division; at the same time its 123rd and 124th Brigades were renumbered 102nd and 103rd. The 122nd Brigade was transferred to the (renumbered) 32nd Division and then became the 96th Brigade; it was replaced in the 34th Division by a newly-formed brigade which received the number 101st (see Appendix 2).

The units were raised as follows: in the 101st Bde., 15/Royal Scots in Edinburgh and Manchester, 16/Royal Scots in Edinburgh, 10/Lincolnshire in Grimsby, and 11/Suffolk in Cambridge; all the battalions of the 102nd Bde. (Tyneside Scottish) and the 103rd Bde. (Tyneside Irish) were raised in Newcastle. In the Artillery, CLII came from Nottingham, CLX from Sunderland, CLXXV from Staffordshire, and CLXXVI (H.) from Leicestershire. The pioneer battalion (18/N.F.—designated 1st Tyneside Pioneers) was raised in Newcastle by the Newcastle and Gateshead Chamber of Commerce.

Early in February 1915 the War Office authorized the Lord Mayor of Norwich to raise the 38th (Norfolk) Divisional Royal Engineers—207th, 208th, and 209th Field Companies and 38th Signal Company. At first the recruits were billeted in private houses in Norwich, and the trade-testing of the men for sapper ratings was carried out at the City Corporation Works, under the direction of the City Engineer. On the 10th May notification was received from the War Office that the numerical designation was changed from 38th to 34th; in consequence of this the title became the 34th (Norfolk) Divisional Royal Engineers, and at the same time the signal company was renumbered 34th. On the 23rd July R.E. headquarters and all the four units moved to Kirkby Malzeard and on arrival came under G.O.C. 34th Division.

In June and July the 101st Brigade concentrated at Fountains Abbey, but the 102nd and 103rd Brigades remained at their training camps at Alnwick and Woolsington; the pioneer battalion and other divisional troops were at Kirkby Malzeard (6 miles from Ripon). On the 15th June the D.-A.-A. & Q.-M.-G. reached Ripon, took over two houses and began collecting clerks and furniture. Whilst divisional headquarters was still at Ripon the D.-A.-A. & Q.-M.-G. received a telegram announcing the arrival on the next day of 300 mules for the Division. The D.-A.-A. & Q.-M.-G. assisted by the G.S.O.3 and six mounted military policemen detrained the mules; but hardly had the station-yard been filled by this crowd of squealing, kicking mules when another trainload of mules pulled into the platform—this latter consignment was for the 34th Division. It then transpired that the first trainload of mules, which had just been detrained by the zealous D.-A.-A. & Q.-M.-G. and his assistants, was intended for the 31st Division.

Between the 28th–31st August the Division moved to Salisbury Plain; and divisional headquarters opened at Cholderton but moved on the 30th September to Sutton Veny. Final intensive training was undertaken and proceeded progressively until the end of the year. On the 3rd January 1916 embarkation orders for France were received, entrainment began on the 7th, and on the 15th January the Division completed its concentration around la Crosse (east of St. Omer). For the remainder of the Great War the 34th Division served on the Western Front in France and Belgium and was engaged in the following operations :—

1916
BATTLES OF THE SOMME

1–3; & 10–13 July ...	**Battle of Albert*** [III Corps, Fourth Army].
2 July	**Capture of Scots and Sausage Redoubts.**
14–17 July	**Battle of Bazentin Ridge*** [III Corps, Fourth Army].
31 July–15 August ...	**Battle of Pozières Ridge*** [III Corps, Fourth Army].
15 September	**Battle of Flers-Courcelette** (103rd Inf. Bde. & 18/N.F. (P.),** attached to 15th Div.) [III Corps, Fourth Army].

1917
BATTLES OF ARRAS

9–14 April	**First Battle of the Scarpe** [XVII Corps, Third Army].
23 & 24 April	**Second Battle of the Scarpe** (103rd Inf. Bde.*** attached to 51st Div.) [XVII Corps, Third Army].
28 & 29 April	**Battle of Arleux** [XVII Corps, Third Army].
26 August	**Hargicourt** [III Corps, Third Army].
13–23 October	**BATTLES OF YPRES** [XIV Corps, Fifth Army].

1918
FIRST BATTLES OF THE SOMME

21–23 March	**Battle of St. Quentin** [VI Corps, Third Army].

BATTLES OF THE LYS

9–11 April	**Battle of Estaires** [XV Corps, First Army].
12–15 April	**Battle of Bailleul** [XV Corps, First Army, until 6 p.m. 12/4; then IX Corps, Second Army].
17–19 April	**First Battle of Kemmel Ridge** [IX Corps, Second Army].

---

* 111th and 112th Inf. Bdes., and 9/N. Staff. (P.) (37th Div.) were attached to the 34th Div. at this time (see General Notes).
** 103rd Inf. Bde., 18/N.F. (P.), and No. 4 Coy., Divnl. Train, were attached to the 15th Div. from 27/8–18/9/16; they rejoined 34th Div. at Estaires on 22 and 23/9/16.
*** 103rd Inf. Bde. was attached to 51st Div. from 22-10 a.m. 25/4/17.

1918

(continued).

The 34th Division handed over its front-line sector at 6 a.m. 21st April, concentrated behind Poperinghe, and was reorganized; it was then employed on digging the Abeele, Poperinghe, and Watou lines. On the 13th May the infantry of the Division moved back to the Lumbres area, was reduced to cadre, and was employed in training American troops. On the 13th June the Division was informed that it would be reconstituted as a first-line division; on the 18th divisional headquarters moved to Samer, and between 19th June–1st July the Division was reconstituted (see Table). After reconstitution the Division was engaged in the following operations :—

THE ADVANCE TO VICTORY

THE BATTLES OF THE MARNE

22 July–3 August ...	**Battle of the Soissonais & of the Ourcq** [XXX (Fr.) Corps, Tenth (Fr.) Army].
1 August	**Capture of Beugneux Ridge.**

THE FINAL ADVANCE IN FLANDERS

28 & 29 September ...	**Battle of Ypres** [X Corps, Second Army].
14–19 October	**Battle of Courtrai** [X Corps, Second Army].
25 October	**Ooteghem** [X Corps, Second Army].
31 October	**Tieghem** [II Corps, Second Army].

On the 1st November the Division was withdrawn into Corps Reserve, concentrated east of Courtrai, and was occupied in refitting and training until the Armistice brought hostilities to a close at 11 a.m. on the 11th November.

On the 14th November the Division began to move forward and by the 18th it was halted west of the Dendre with its head at Lessines. On the 17th November a divisional order announced that the 34th Division was to form part of the force which would advance into Germany; meanwhile, until the end of November the units continued to carry out light training. Between the 12th–19th December the division advanced and billeted in an area south-west of Namur, and on the 22nd December miners and pivotal men left for demobilization.

On the 17th January 1919 the Division began entraining for the Rhine, and on the 29th January the 34th Division completed taking over the right of the X Corps sector of the Cologne Bridgehead. During March the infantry of the Division was reconstituted. On the 15th March 1919 the Division was renamed Eastern Division and the war history of the 34th Division came to an end. During the Great War the 34th Division lost 41,188 killed, wounded, and missing.

35TH DIVISION

G.O.C.

1 July 1915	Br.-Gen. J. G. HUNTER (tempy.).
5 July 1915	Major-General R. J. PINNEY.
17 September 1916	Br.-Gen. H. O'DONNELL (acting).
28 September 1916	Major-General H. J. S. LANDON.
9 July 1917	Major-General G. McK. FRANKS.
27 March 1918	Br.-Gen. A. H. MARINDIN (tempy.).
7 April 1918	Major-General A. H. MARINDIN.

G.S.O.1.

3 July 1915...Major R. A. STEEL (acting).
17 July 1915...Major E. F. CALTHROP (acting).
25 Aug. 1915...Lt.-Col. R. N. GREATHED.
17 Jan. 1916...Major V. C. CLIMO (acting).
17 Jan. 1916...Lt.Col. C. R. NEWMAN.
5 Sept. 1917...Lt.-Col. H. W. B. THORP.
5 Nov. 1918...Lt.-Col. N. H. C. SHERBROOKE.

A.-A. & Q.-M.-G.

21 June 1915...Major N. E. B. BELLAIRS (acting).
23 June 1915...Lt.-Col. A. W. HASTED.
6 Dec. 1916...Lt.-Col. C. T. M. HARE.
23 Aug. 1917...Captain J. McM. MILLING (acting).
4 Sept. 1917...Lt.Col. H. M. FARMAR.
6 Sept. 1918...Lt.-Col. L. M. JONES.

B.-G., R.A.

30 June 1915...Br.-Gen. A. B. PURVIS.
29 Aug. 1915...Br.-Gen. W. C. STAVELEY (sick, 20/10/17).
20 Oct. 1917...Br.-Gen. F. A. WILSON (tempy.).
1 Nov. 1917...Br.-Gen. W. EVANS (tempy.).
8 Nov. 1917...Br.-Gen. W. R. N. MADOCKS.
15 Mar. 1918...Lt.-Col. H. M. DAVSON (acting).
28 Mar. 1918...Br.-Gen. W. R. N. MADOCKS.

C.R.E.

16 July 1915...Major W. H. D. CAPLE (acting).
26 July 1915...Lt.-Col. G. O. BIGGE (sick, 2/8/15).
4 Aug. 1915...Major W. H. D. CAPLE (acting).
19 Aug. 1915...Lt.-Col. H. W. RUSHTON.
23 Sept. 1917...Lt.-Col. J. W. SKIPWITH.
23 Feb. 1918...Major J. W. LL. DAVIES (acting).
26 Mar. 1918...Lt.-Col. J. W. SKIPWITH.
30 Mar. 1918...Major J. W. LL. DAVIES (acting).
24 April 1918...Lt.-Col. J. W. SKIPWITH.

104th BDE.
(originally 112th Bde.)

2 Jan. '15...Br.-Gen. G. M. MACKENZIE.
14 April '16...Br.-Gen. J. W.
SANDILANDS.

105th BDE.
(originally 125th Bde.)

28 Dec. '14...Br.-Gen. W. THUILLIER.
20 May '15...Br.-Gen. J. G. HUNTER.
16 April '16...Br.-Gen. C. H. RANKIN.
2 May '16...Lt.-Col. F. W. DANIELL
(acting).
6 May '16...Br.-Gen. A. H. MARINDIN.
26 Mar. '18...Lt.-Col. W. A. W. CRELLIN
(acting).
7 April '18...Br.-Gen. A. CARTON DE
WIART, V.C. (wd., 20/4/18).
20 April '18...Lt.-Col. L. M. STEVENS
(acting).
23 April '18...Br.-Gen. A. J. TURNER.

106th BDE.
(new formation)

9 June '15...Br.-Gen. H. O'DONNELL.
17 Sept. '16...Lt.-Col. R. R. LAWRENSON (acting).
23 Sept. '16...Br.-Gen. H. O'DONNELL.
20 May '17...Br.-Gen. J. H. W. POLLARD.

GENERAL NOTES

The following Units also served with the 35th Division :

ARTILLERY :—131 Heavy Battery, R.G.A. (4 60-pdrs.), was raised at Lewisham on 22/1/15 and was originally intended for the 26th Division ; later on, however, the Heavy Battery was allotted to the 35th Division, and eventually the Battery went abroad independently. 131 Heavy Battery disembarked at le Havre on 9/3/16, reached Doullens on 12/3/16, and then joined XXIII H.A. Group at Etrée Wamin.

OTHER UNITS :—75th Sanitary Section joined the Division in England, went to France with the Division, and disembarked at le Havre on 1/2/16. On 9/4/17 the Sanitary Section left the Division and took over a Sanitary Area in IV Corps, Fourth Army.

35th Division Motor Ambce. Workshop went to France with the Division and disembkd. at Rouen on 29/1/16. The Workshop left Rouen on 4/2/16, and rejoined the Division at Renescure on 6/2/16. On 31/8/16 the Workshop was disbanded and the personnel and vehicles joined 35th Div. Supply Column.

The reorganization of the 35th Division on a 9-battalion basis was begun on 29/1/18 and was completed on 16/2/18 ; and the reorganization of the pioneer battalion (19/N.F.) on a 8-company basis was begun on 18/2/18 and was completed on 21/2/18.

35TH DIVISION [1]

Date	INFANTRY		Mounted Troops	ARTILLERY						Engineers	Signal Service	Pioneers	M.G. Units	Field Ambulances	Mobile Vety. Sec.	Divnl. Emplnt. Coy.	Divnl. Train
	Brigades	Battalions and attached Units		Field Artillery			Trench Mortar Btties.		Divnl. Ammn. Coln.	Field Coy.	Divnl. Signal Coy.						
				Brigades	Batteries	Bde. Ammn. Colns.	Medium	Heavy									
1915 July (England)	104th [2]; [3].	17/L.F., 18/L.F., 20/L.F., 23/Manch.	C Sqdn.,[5] 1/Lanc. Hsrs. 35th Div. Cyclist Coy.[7]	CLVII[8]........ CLVIII[9]; [8] CLIX[9] CLXIII (H.).[8]; [10]	A, B, C, D A, B, C, D A, B, C, D A (H.), B (H.), C (H.), D (H.)	CLVII B.A.C. CLVIII B.A.C. CLIX B.A.C. CLXIII (H.) B.A.C.	...	...	35th D.A.C.[6]	203rd[11] 204th[11] 205th[11]	35th[12]	19/ N.F.[13] (P.)	...	105th[14] 106th[14] 107th[14]	45th[15]	...	35th[16]
1916 February (France)	104th	17/L.F., 18/L.F., 20/L.F., 23/Manch.	C Sqdn.,[17] 1/Lanc. Hsrs. 35th Div. Cyclist Coy.[18]	CLVII[19] .... CLVIII[20] .... CLIX[21] CLXIII (H.)[22]	A, B, C, D A, B, C, D A, B, C, D A (H.), B (H.), C (H.), D (H.)	CLVII B.A.C. CLVIII B.A.C. CLIX B.A.C. CLXIII (H.) B.A.C.	...	...	35th D.A.C.[23]	203rd 204th 205th	35th	19/ N.F. (P.)	...	105th 106th 107th	45th	...	35th
	105th	15/Ches., 16/Ches., 14/Glouc., 15/Sher. For.															
	106th	17/R.S., 17/W. York., 19/ D.L.I., 18/H.L.I.															
1916 June (France)	104th	17/L.F., 18/L.F., 20/L.F., 23/Manch.; 104th Bde. M.G. Coy.;[24] 104th T.M. Bty.[25]	...	CLVII[26]; [28] CLVIII[26]; [27] CLIX[21]; [28] CLXIII[28]; [29]	A, B, C; D (H.) A, B, C; D (H.) A, B, C; D (H.) A, B, C; D (H.)	[30]	X.35[31] Y.35[31] Z.35[31]	V.35[31]	35th D.A.C.[32]	203rd 204th 205th	35th	19/ N.F. (P.)	...	105th 106th 107th	45th	...	35th
	105th	15/Ches., 16/Ches., 14/Glouc., 15/Sher. For.; 105th Bde. M.G. Coy.;[24] 105th T.M. Bty.[25]															
	106th	17/R.S., 17/W. York., 19/ D.L.I., 18/H.L.I.; 106th Bde. M.G. Coy.;[24] 106th T.M. Bty.[25]															
1917 June (France)	104th	17/L.F., 18/L.F., 20/L.F.;[33] 23/Manch.;[34] 104th M.G. Coy.;[34] 104th T.M. Bty.	...	CLVII[36] .... CLIX[36]	A, B, C; D (H.) A, B, C; D (H.)	...	X.35 Y.35 Z.35[39]	V.35[40]	35th D.A.C.	203rd 204th 205th	35th	19/ N.F. (P.)	241st[41] M.G. Coy.	105th 106th 107th	45th	282nd[42]	35th
	105th	15/Ches., 16/Ches.,[35] 14/Glouc.,[34] 15/Sher. For.; 105th M.G. Coy.;[34] 105th T.M. Bty.															
	106th	17/R.S., 17/W. York.,[37] 19/ D.L.I., 18/H.L.I.;[38] 106th M.G. Coy.;[34] 106th T.M. Bty.															

54

1918 March (France)															
104th	17/L.F., 18/L.F., 19/D.L.I.[8]	104th T.M. Bty.[21]	CLVII ....[22]	A, B, C; D (H.)	...	...	X.35[16] Y.35[17]	...	""	35th D.A.C.[18]	203rd 204th 205th[6]	35th	19/ N.F. (P.)[8]	No. 35 Bn. M.G.C.[19]	105th 106th 107th[9]
105th	15/Ches., 15/Sher. For., 4/N. Staff.	105th T.M. Bty.[21]	CLIX ....[23]	A, B, C; D (H.)											45th[10]
106th	17/R.S., 12/H.L.I., 18/ (Glasgow Yeo.) H.L.I.	106th T.M. Bty.[21]													232nd
															35th

NOTES

1 Raised as 42nd Div.; became 35th Div. on 27/4/15. 105th Bde. was raised as 125th Bde. and was renumbered on 27/4/15. 126th Bde. was transferred to (new) 30th Div. and became 91st Bde. Its place was then taken by the 112th Bde. from the original 37th (new 30th) Div. and this Bde. then became the 104th. In June 1915 the (new) 35th Div. was completed by a newly-formed Bde. which became the 106th. (127th Inf. Bde. had never been formed in the original 42nd—new 35th—Div.) The battalions were designated: 1st and 2nd South-East Lancashire, 4th Salford, and 8th City.

2 The battalions were designated: 1st and 2nd Birkenhead, West of England, and Nottingham.

3 The battalions were designated: Rosebery, 2nd Leeds, 2nd County of Durham, and 4th Glasgow. Joined Div. in England and disembkd. at le Havre on 1/2/16.

4 Coy. was formed on Salisbury Plain; disembkd. at le Havre on 29/1/16.

5 The Artillery Bdes. were designated: Aberdeen; Accrington and Burnley; Glasgow; West Ham; and the D.A.C. was designated B.E.L. The Bdes. were raised as 4-battery brigades; in ach brigade the batteries were lettered—A, B, C, D—and ach battery was a 4-gun battery. The Brigade was raised as a howitzer brigade, but on 2/12/15 the Bde. became an 18-pdr. gun brigade. The Brigade was raised as a gun brigade, but on 2/12/15 the Bde. became a 4.5" howitzer brigade.

6 The 3 Fd. Cos. were designated: Cambridge, Empire, and Dundee. They joined the Div. in Yorkshire, and they disembkd. at le Havre between 29–31/1/16.

7 The Signal Coy. was designated: Reading; it joined the Div. in Yorkshire; Secs. were allotted to Inf. Bdes. on 27/7/15. The Sig. Coy. disembkd. at le Havre between 29/1–1/2/16.

8 The Bn. was designated: 2nd Tyneside Pioneers; it joined the Div. in Yorkshire in July 1915, and disembkd. at le Havre on 30/1/18.

9 Raised for the original 35th Div. (App. 1F), the 3 Fd. Ambces. joined the new 35th Div. (note 1) on Salisbury Plain; the 3 Fd. Ambces. disembkd. at le Havre between 29–31/1/16.

10 Joined Div. on Salisbury Plain; disembkd. at le Havre on 1/2/16.

11 Train (233, 234, 235, 236 Cos., A.S.C.) joined the Div. in Yorkshire in July 1915; Train disembkd. at le Havre between 29/1–1/2/16.

12 Sqdn. left the Div. on 9/5/16, and joined VIII Corps Cav. Regt. on 10/5/16.

13 On 10/5/16 Coy. left the Div. and joined XI Corps Cyclist Bn.

14 Bde. disembkd. at le Havre on 30/1/16. On 28/5/16 D Bty. left and became A/CLXIII; and A (H.)/CLXIII joined and became D (H.)/CLVII.

15 Bde. disembkd. at le Havre on 1/2/16. On 27/5/16 D Bty. left and became B/CLXIII; and B (H.)/CLXIII joined and became D (H.)/CLVIII.

16 Bde. disembkd. at le Havre on 2/2/16. On 28/5/16 D Bty. left and became C/CLXIII; and C (H.)/CLXIII joined and became D (H.)/CLIX.

17 Bde. disembkd. at le Havre on 31/1/16. On 27 & 28/1/16 Bde. was reorganized: A (H.), B (H.), & C (H.) left and became C/XLVII, D (H.)/CLVII, and D (H.)/CLIX; and D/CLVII, D/CLVIII, & D/CLIX joined and became A, B, & C/CLXIII.

18 D.A.C. disembkd. at le Havre on 1/2/16. On 25/5/16 B.A.C.s were abolished and the D.A.C. was reorganized. Surplus personnel went to the Base.

19 M.G. Cos. joined from Grantham.

20 104th—formed at Grantham on 17/2/16; disembkd. at le Havre on 26/4/16 and joined Div. at Lestrem on 27/4/16;

105th—disembkd. at le Havre on 12/5/16 and joined Div. at Lestrem on 15/5/16;

106th—disembkd. at le Havre on 25/4/16 and joined Div. at Lestrem on 28/4/16.

21 T.M. Btles. were formed in Bdes.

104th—104/1 by 2/4/16, 104/2 by 12/5/16, and they became 104th T.M. Bty. by 28/6/16;

105th—105/1 by 18/3/16, 105/2 by 12/5/16, and they became 105th T.M. Bty. by 6/7/16;

106th—106/1 by 1/4/16, 106/2 by 4/5/16, and they became 106th T.M. Bty. by 28/6/16.

22 On 9/9/16 A/CLXIII and 1 sec. C/CLVIII joined Bde.; A/CLXIII was split up and made up A & B/CLVII to 6 guns each, and Sec. C/CLVIII made up C/CLVII to 6 guns. On 9/1/17 R. Sec., C (H.)/CLVII joined and made up D (H.)/CLVII to 6 hows.

23 On 8 and 9/9/16 C Bty. was broken up: 1 sec. joined CLVII and made up C/CLVII to 6 guns; and 1 sec. made up B/CLIX; B/CLXIII joined CLVIII and was split up to make up A and B/CLVIII to 6 guns each; and D (H.)/CLXIII joined Bde. and became C (H.)/CLVIII.

24 Between 8/1–28/2/17 CLVIII was broken up: On 8/1/17 A left and became C/XLVIII A.F.A. Bde.; R. Sec., D (H.) left and made up C (H.)/LII A.F.A. Bde. to 6 hows.; on 9/1/17 R. Sec., C (H.) left and made up D (H.)/CLVII to 6 guns.; on 10/1/17 L. Sec., C (H.) left and made up D (H.)/CLIX to 6 hows.; on 10/1/17 L. Sec. D (H.) left and made up D (H.)/LXIV A.F.A. Bde. to 6 hows.; and B left and became C/LXIV A.F.A. Bde.

NOTES—*continued*

" On 7/9/16 C/CLXIII joined Bde. and was split up to make up A and C/CLIX to 6 guns each; and 1 sec. C/CLVIII joined Bde. and made up B/CLIX to 6 guns. On 10/1/17 L. Sec. C (H.)/CLVIII joined and made up D (H.)/CLIX to 6 hows.

" Between 7–9/9/16 CLXIII was broken up: A joined CLVII and made up A & B/CLVII to 6 guns each; B joined CLVIII and. made up A & B/CLVIII to 6 guns each; C joined CLIX and made up A & C/CLIX to 6 guns each; and D (H.) became C (H.)/CLVIII.

" Medium T.M. Btles. were formed by 28/8/16.

" Heavy T.M. Bty. was formed on 12/9/16; it went into action near Arras on 25/9/16.

" On 7/2/18 Bn. drafted 13 offrs. & 319 o.r. to other Bns., sent surplus to II Corps Rft. Camp on 15/2/18, and Bn. was disbanded on 16/2/18.

" Between 6–11/2/18 Bn. drafted 31 offrs. & 630 o.r., sent surplus to No. 12 Entg. Bn. on 16/2/18, and Bn. was disbanded on 16/2/18.

" On 3 & 4/2/18 Bn. drafted 20 offrs. & 410 o.r., sent surplus to II Corps Rft. Camp, and Bn. was disbanded on 8/2/18.

" On 11/2/18 Bn. was disbanded; 12 offrs. & 250 o.r. went to 13/Glouc. (P.), 39th Div., and surplus left for II Corps Rft. Camp.

" On 16/11/17 Bn. left 35th Div., was under C.E., XIX Corps (for work on railways) from 16–30/11/17, left XIX Corps on 1/12/17, reached Acq on 5/12/17, and, amalgamated with 15/W. York. in 93rd Bde., 31st Div., on 7/12/17.

" On 8/2/18 Bn. was transferred to 104th Bde.

" On 23/9/17 Bn. absorbed 4 offrs. & 146 o.r. Glasgow Yeo., and became 18/(Glasgow Yeo.) H.L.I. (A & B Sqdns., Glasgow Yeo., had formed part of V Corps Cav. Regt., left V Corps on 23/8/17, and went to No. 21 Inf. Base Depot, Etaples; left Etaples on 23/9/17 and joined 18/H.L.I. at Aizecourt le Bas.)

" On 8/2/18 Z was broken up: Trench Mortars were handed over to X/35 and Y/35, and personnel was distributed. (Medium T.M. Btles. were reduced to two per Division, each with 4 offrs., 53 o.r., and 6 mortars.)

" On 8/2/18 V H.T.M. Bty. was disbanded: part of the personnel went to X/35 and part to V H.T.M. Bty., II Corps, the 3 9.2" Mortars were handed over to V, II Corps. (On this date H.T.M. Btles. were reduced from one per Division to one per Corps—4 offrs., 84 o.r., and 6 mortars.)

" Coy. left Grantham on 13/7/17, disembkd. at le Havre on 15/7/17, and joined Div. at Villers Faucon on 18/7/17.

" Coy. formed by 9/8/17.

" This Extra Reserve Bn. disembkd. at le Havre on 7/10/17, arrived Bapaume on 11/10/17, was attached to 167th Bde., 56th Div., from 11/10–9/11/17, and on 15/11/17 Bn. joined 106th Bde., 35th Div., at Chateau des Trois Tours. On 3/2/18 Bn. was transferred to 105th Bde.

" On 3/2/18 Bn. was transferred from 46th Bde., 15th Div., to 106th Bde., 35th Div.

" Bn. was formed between 22/2–2/3/18; it consisted of 104th, 105th, 106th, and 241st M.G. Cos.

35TH DIVISION
FORMATION, BATTLES, AND ENGAGEMENTS

This New Army Division had no existence before the outbreak of the Great War.

On the 10th December 1914 the formation of the Fifth New Army (37th–42nd Divisions) was authorized; this brought into existence the 42nd Division and its infantry brigades (125th, 126th, and 127th). In April 1915 the original Fourth New Army of six divisions (30th–35th) was broken up, so that it could be used for replacing casualties in the eighteen divisions (9th–26th) of the first three New Armies (see Appendix 1). The original Fifth New Army (37th–42nd Divisions) then became the Fourth New Army, and its six divisions were renumbered (30th–35th). In this way, on the 27th April 1915, the 42nd Division (the junior division of the original Fifth New Army) became the 35th Division (the junior division of the new Fourth New Army); at the same time its 125th Brigade was renumbered 105th. The 126th Brigade was transferred to the (renumbered) 30th Division and then became the 91st Brigade. The 126th Brigade was replaced in the 35th Division by the 112th Brigade, from the (original) 37th Division, and on arrival the 112th Brigade was renumbered and became the 104th (see Appendix 2). In June a newly-formed brigade completed the Division and was numbered 106th. (The original 127th Brigade had not been formed).

In the 104th Brigade the sub-titles of the battalions were 1st and 2nd S.E. Lancashire (17/ & 18/L.F.), Salford (20/L.F.), and 8th City (23/Manchester), this battalion had been transferred from 91st Bde., 30th Div. (p. 7). In the 105th Brigade were the 1st and 2nd Birkenhead (15/ & 16/Cheshire), West of England (14/Glouc.), and Nottingham (15/Sher. For.), and in the 106th Brigade the Rosebery (after the Earl of Rosebery—17/Royal Scots), 2nd Leeds (17/W. York.), 2nd County (19/D.L.I.), and 4th Glasgow (18/H.L.I.). The Artillery Bdes. were raised in Aberdeen, Accrington and Burnley, Glasgow, and West Ham; and the D.A.C. in Lancashire. The Field Companies were called Cambridge, the Empire, and Dundee; Reading provided the Signal Company. The sub-title of the Pioneer Battalion was 2nd Tyneside Pioneers.

As early as September 1914 it was decided that men below the official height standard of physique might be accepted for military service, and sanction was given to raise one 'Bantam' battalion; later on permission was given to raise a second, to supply wastage. The men for these two battalions came from all parts of Great Britain and Ireland and included many miners, and a third 'Bantam' battalion (28/Manchester) was transferred from the 91st Brigade, 30th Division. These three battalions of well-developed men were the nucleus of the 'Bantam Division.' Unfortunately, in a prolonged war, these islands could not supply a sufficient number of men below the average height, and of this quality, to supply the wastage of the twelve infantry battalions of a 'bantam' division. The Artillery, Engineers, and Pioneers of the 35th Division never accepted 'bantams.'

At first there was the usual shortage of uniform, equipment, and arms. On parades puttee-covered legs were often combined with bowler hats; in other cases the only outward and visible sign of a soldier might be a khaki cap, with or without a badge; and non-commissioned-officers had to be distinguished by narrow ribbon arm-bands. By January 1915, however, field training had appeared in some programmes, and musketry on miniature ranges allowed some classification. One temporary corporal, after placing a veritable barrage across the width of a landscape target, was heard to say in a hoarse whisper: "Now lads, do your best for me; its yon little windmill beside the three trees." Nevertheless, good humour, enthusiasm, and ambition enabled all ranks to surmount the initial difficulties. Great progress had been made by the end of June 1915, when the Division began to collect at Roomer Common, Marfield, Fearby, and Masham Camps, with Divisional Headquarters at Masham. In August the Division moved by rail to Salisbury Plain, to carry out the final stages of its training for the field. On the 23rd August Divisional Headquarters opened at Marlborough, moved on the 14th September to Chiseldon, and on the 11th October to Cholderton. Late in the year the Division received orders to prepare for Egypt and all ranks were issued with tropical uniforms and pith helmets. On the Plain, wearing their helmets, the 'Bantams' were said to look like overgrown mushrooms. But in a very short time the destination of the Division was changed to the Western Front, and the pith helmets were replaced by soft caps and gas-masks.

In January 1916 orders for France were received, embarkation began on the 28th January, and by 6 a.m. on the 6th February the Division completed its concentration to the eastward of St. Omer. For the remainder of the Great War the 35th Division served on the Western Front in France and Belgium and was engaged in the following operations :—

1916
BATTLES OF THE SOMME

15–17 July	**Battle of Bazentin Ridge** (105th Bde. under 18th Div.; 106th Bde. under 9th Div.) [XIII Corps, Fourth Army].
19–30 July	Fighting for Arrow Head Copse [XIII Corps, Fourth and Maltzhorn Farm Army].
19–26 August	Fighting for Falfemont Farm [XIV Corps, Fourth Army].

On the 8th December the G.O.C. 35th Division sent in a report to VI Corps on the low physical and moral standard of the infantry of the Division, consequent on the replacement of the losses in the Battles of the Somme by undersized men, who were not real ' bantams ' but merely physically undeveloped and unfit men from the towns ; whereas the original ' bantams ' were mostly sturdy, stocky miners. In consequence of the report, the A.D.M.S. of the Division was ordered to inspect the twelve infantry battalions. This inspection was carried out between the 9th–15th December, and on account of deficient physique the A.D.M.S. rejected 1439 men. On the 18th December the Brigade Commanders were informed that no more 'bantams' were to be accepted. By the 21st December, after further inspections by the G.O.C. 35th Division, the total number of ' rejects ' in the twelve battalions rose to 2784. Nevertheless a considerable number of the original ' bantams ' remained, and even at the end of the Great War many ' bantams ' were still serving in the 35th Division.

1917

Between January and the end of March the rejected men were drafted to the infantry base depots and to labour battalions. (Even so, for some months commanding officers had to exercise great watchfulness to prevent previously rejected ' bantams ' from being accepted as reinforcements). The ' rejects ' of December 1916 were replaced by men from disbanded yeomanry regiments and men who had been training at the cavalry depot. To receive this large number of reinforcements a depot battalion was formed in the Division, and it had the additional duties of putting the men through a musketry course and training the new arrivals for trench warfare as infantry.*

14–18 March	**German Retreat to the Hindenburg Line** [IV Corps, Fourth Army].

BATTLES OF YPRES

22 October	**Fighting in the Houthulst Forest** [XIV Corps, Fifth Army].
26 Oct.–4 Nov.	**Second Battle of Passchendaele** [XIV Corps until 2 p.m., 30/10 ; then XIX Corps, Fifth Army].

1918

24–30 March	**FIRST BATTLES OF THE SOMME**
24 and 25 March	**First Battle of Bapaume** [VII Corps, Fifth Army, until 4 a.m., 25/3 ; then VII Corps, Third Army].

THE ADVANCE TO VICTORY
THE FINAL ADVANCE IN FLANDERS

28 Sept.–2 Oct.	**Battle of Ypres** [XIX Corps, Second Army].
14–19 Oct.	**Battle of Courtrai** [XIX Corps, Second Army].
31 October	**Tieghem** [XIX Corps, Second Army].

---

* The first divisional sign was the appropriate one of a Bantam Cock ; but, after the reorganization of the Bantam Division in 1917, the divisional sign was changed to a circular emblem composed of seven 5s.

During the night of 1st/2nd November the 35th Division was relieved; but on the 5th the Division again took over part of the front line along the left bank of the Schelde opposite Berchem. At 5.30 a.m. on the 9th November the 106th Brigade pushed 18/H.L.I. across the river; and, when the battalion was established, the Brigade crossed and made good the foothold on the right bank. During the same morning B/CLIX crossed the Schelde by the right-hand bridge in the 41st Division area; and during the day the 104th and 105th Brigades, with two machine-gun companies and a platoon of XIX Corps Cyclists, crossed by foot-bridges. By 10.30 p.m. a pontoon bridge was completed.

On the 11th November the Division was ordered to push on to the line of the R. Dendre; and, before the Armistice brought hostilities to a close at 11 a.m., the G.O.C. entered Grammont followed by 17/Lancashire Fusiliers; the battalion at once established posts on the Dendre bridges and on the sluice.

On the 12th November the Division passed into XIX Corps Reserve and on the 18th began to move further westward. On the 27th the march westward was continued, and on the 28th H.R.H. Princess Mary took the salute of 17/Royal Scots as they marched through Ypres. By the 2nd December the Division had reached its final quarters to the north-west of St. Omer with its headquarters at Eperlecques. On the 11th December the first batch of miners left for demobilization.

During January 1919 the Division was used to quell rioting at Calais and accomplished this duty successfully. Two Brigades (104th and 105th) were left at Calais and the remainder of the Division returned to Eperlecques. Swiftly the units dwindled. On the 9th April the Artillery left for demobilization; and by the end of April 1919 the 35th Division ceased to exist. During the Great War the 35th Division lost 23,915 killed, wounded, and missing.

36TH (ULSTER) DIVISION

G.O.C.

23 September 1914	... ...	Major-General C. H. POWELL.
14 September 1915	... ...	Major-General O. S. W. NUGENT.
6 May 1918	... ...	Major-General C. COFFIN, V.C.

G.S.O.1.

20 Oct. 1914...Captain W. B. SPENDER
 (G.S.O.2, tempy. G.S.O.1.)
14 Sept. 1915...Major Hon. A. V. F.
 RUSSELL.
18 Sept. 1915...Lt.-Col. Hon. A. V. F.
 RUSSELL.
5 April 1916...Lt.-Col. C. O. PLACE
 (wounded & captured, 26/3/18).
27 Mar. 1918...Major L. CARR (acting).
1 April 1918...Lt.-Col. A. G. THOMSON.
[17 Nov. 1918...Lt.-Col. H. F. L.
 GRANT].

A.-A. & Q.-M.-G.

16 Sept. 1914...Major J. CRAIG.
29 Oct. 1914...Lt.-Col. J. CRAIG
 (sick, 7/8/15).
21 April 1915...Major G. T. DRAGE
 (acting; sick, 17/5/15).
17 May 1915...Captain E. P. GRANT
 (acting).
26 June 1915...Major G. F. CAVENDISH-
 CLARKE (acting).
4 July 1915...Lt.-Col. T. V. P.
 McCAMMON (tempy.).
3 Sept. 1915...Major H. C.
 SINGLETON (acting).
7 Sept. 1915...Major G. MEYNELL.
13 Sept. 1915...Lt.-Col. G. MEYNELL.
29 Oct. 1915...Lt.-Col. L. J. COMYN.
4 Nov. 1917...Lt.-Col. S. H. GREEN.

B.-G., R.A.

30 June 1915...Br.-Gen. J. W.
 HAWKINS.
17 Aug. 1915...Br.-Gen. H. A.
 BRENDON.
9 Oct. –
12 Dec.1915} Br.-Gen. R. J. ELKINGTON.*
10 Nov. 1915...Br.-Gen. H. J. BROCK.
23 Sept. 1918...Lt.-Col. C. F. POTTER
 (acting).
4 Oct. 1918...Br.-Gen. C. ST. L. G.
 HAWKES.

C.R.E.

22 Oct. 1914...Colonel H. FINNIS.
25 Sept. 1915...Lt.-Col. P. T. DENIS DE
 VITRÉ.
5 Sept. 1916...Lt.-Col. W. A. C. KING
 (killed, 27/5/17).
28 May 1917...Lt.-Col. A. CAMPBELL.
15 Dec. 1917...Lt.-Col. A. G. T. CUSINS.
4 April 1918...Lt.-Col. R. H.
 MACKENZIE.

---

* Commanded 56th (1st London) Division Artillery. This Divisional Artillery went to France with the 36th (Ulster) Division, and was attached to the 36th Division until 11 and 12/12/15 (see Table and note 18; and General Notes).

107th BDE.
(originally 1st Bde.)

14 Sept. '14...Br.-Gen. G. H. H.
COUCHMAN.
20 Oct. '15...Br.-Gen. W. M.
WITHYCOMBE.
(On 3/11/15, 107th Bde. (with 110th
Fd. Ambce.) was transferred to 4th
Division, for attachment).

12th BDE.*

(On 5/11/15, 12th Bde. and 10th Fd.
Ambce. joined from 4th Division, for
attachment).
 [4 Oct. '14]...Br.-Gen. F. G. ANLEY.
(On 3/2/16, 12th Bde. and 10th Fd.
Ambce. returned to 4th Division).

107th BDE.

(On 7/2/16, 107th Bde. and 110th Fd.
Ambce. rejoined from 4th Division).
[20 Oct. '15]...Br.-Gen. W. M.
WITHYCOMBE.
 8 Mar. '17...Br.-Gen. F. J. M.
ROWLEY.
 2 June '17...Br.-Gen. W. M.
WITHYCOMBE.
30 April '18...Br.-Gen. E. I. DE S.
THORPE (wd., 13/9/18).
14 Sept. '18...Lt.-Col. R. H.
MACKENZIE (acting).
23 Sept. '18...Br.-Gen. H. J. BROCK.

108th BDE.
(originally 2nd Bde.)

14 Sept. '14...Br.-Gen. G. W. HACKET
PAIN.
 4 Dec. '15...Br.-Gen. C. R. J.
GRIFFITH.
21 May '18...Br.-Gen. E. VAUGHAN.

109th BDE.
(originally 3rd Bde.)

14 Sept. '14...Br.-Gen. T. E. HICKMAN.
14 April '16...Lt.-Col. W. F. HESSEY (acting).
14 May   '16...Br.-Gen. R. G. SHUTER.
13 Jan. '17...Br.-Gen. A. ST. Q. RICARDO.
 2 Feb. '17...Lt.-Col. A. C. PRATT (acting).
 1 March '17...Br.-Gen. A. ST. Q. RICARDO.
12 Dec. '17...Lt.-Col. N. G. BURNAND (acting).
23 Dec. '17...Br.-Gen. W. F. HESSEY (injured, 16/4/18).
16 April '18...Lt.-Col. J. E. KNOTT (acting).
21 April '18...Br.-Gen. E. VAUGHAN (tempy.).
17 May   '18...Br.-Gen. W. F. HESSEY.

---

* For composition, see General Notes (opposite).

GENERAL NOTES

The following also served with the 36th (Ulster) Division :—

12th Inf. Bde. (Br.-Gen. F. G. Anley—1/K.O., 2/L.F., 2/Essex, 1/5/S. Lanc., and 10th Fd. Ambce.),	from 4th Division, was attached to the 36th (Ulster) Division from 5/11/15–3/2/16 in exchange for	107th Inf. Bde. (Br.-Gen. W. M. Withycombe— 8/R. Ir. Rif., 9/R. Ir. Rif., 10/R. Ir. Rif., 15/R. Ir. Rif., and 110th Fd. Ambce.).

Note.—During this period (5/11/15–3/2/16) 2/L.F. (12th Bde.) was attached to 108th Bde., in exchange for 11/R. Ir. Rif. ; and 2/Essex (12th Bde.) was attached to 109th Bde., in exchange for 14/R. Ir. Rif.

ARTILLERY—I LONDON, II LONDON, III LONDON, IV LONDON (H.)* BDES., B.A.C.s., and 10th D.A.C.	went to France with the 36th Div. in October 1915 and served with the 36th Div. until December 1915 (see Table and note 18).

529 (H.) Battery, R.F.A. (4, 4.5″ howitzers) disembarked at le Havre on 4/10/16 and joined CLXXII on 7/10/16 (see note 37).

36 Heavy Battery, R.G.A. was raised for the 36th Division ; but the Heavy Battery did not go overseas and was broken up at home.

INFANTRY—7/R. Irish Rifles served with 48th Bde., 16th Div., until 23/8/17, with 49th Bde., 16th Div., until 14/10/17, and joined 36th Div. on 15/10/17. On 14/11/17 Bn. (17 offrs. and 515 o.r.) was absorbed by 2/R. Ir. Rif. in 108th Bde., 36th Div. (also see note 48).

OTHER UNITS—76th Sanitary Section joined the 36th Division in England, went to France with the Division, and disembarked at le Havre on 6/10/15. On 14/4/17 the Sanitary Section left the 36th Division and took over IIIB Sanitary Area in IX Corps, Second Army.

36th Division Motor Ambce. Workshop left Grove Park on 16/9/15 and joined 36th Div. at Bordon. The Workshop left Bordon on 17/9/15, reached Belfast on 18/9/15, took over and shipped ambulances 19–22/9/15, reached Liverpool on 22/9/15, and Grove Park on 25/9/15. The Workshop left Grove Park on 29/9/15, arrived Avonmouth and shipped vehicles on 1/10/15, and personnel embarked at Southampton on 8/10/15. The Workshop reached Rouen on 4/10/15, left Rouen on 7/10/15, and joined 36th Div. at Flesselles on 8/10/15. On 9/4/16 the Workshop was disbanded and the personnel and vehicles were absorbed by 36th Div. Supply Column.

On 10/2/18 the reorganization of the 36th (Ulster) Division on a 9-battalion basis was completed ; and on 24/2/18 the pioneer battalion (16/R. Ir. Rif.) was reorganized on a 3-company basis.

---

*B (H.) and C (H.)/LVII were also temporarily serving in IV LONDON (H.) BDE. (see Table and note 18).

36TH (ULSTER) DIVISION [1]

Dates	INFANTRY — Brigades	Battalions and attached Units	Mounted Troops	ARTILLERY — Field Artillery Brigades	Batteries	Bde. Ammn. Colns.	Trench Mortar Btles. — Medium	Heavy	Divnl. Ammn. Coln.	Engineers — Field Coy.	Signal Service — Divnl. Signal Coy.	Pioneers	M.G. Units	Field Ambulances	Mobile Vety. Sec.	Divnl. Emplnt. Coy.	Divnl. Train
1914 October (Ireland)	107th [3]	8/R. Ir. Rif., 9/R. Ir. Rif., 10/R. Ir. Rif., 15/R. Ir. Rif.	1/ Service Sqdn., [5] 8/(Innis.) Dgns. 36th Div. Cyclist Coy. [6]	...[7]	...	...	...	...	...	121st [8] 122nd [8]	36th [9]	16/ R. Ir. Rif., [10] (P.)	...	108th [11] 109th [11] 110th [11]	...	...	36th [12]
	108th [4]	11/R. Ir. Rif., 12/R. Ir. Rif., 13/R. Ir. Rif., 9/R. Ir. F.															
	109th [4]	9/R. Innis. F., 11/R. Innis F., 14/R. Ir. Rif.															
1915 July (England)	107th	8/R. Ir. Rif., 9/R. Ir. Rif., 10/R. Ir. Rif., 15/R. Ir. Rif.	1/ Service Sqdn., 8/(Innis.) Dgns. 36th Div. Cyclist Coy.	CLIII; [21] CLIV (H.) [21]; [28]	A, B, C, D / A (H.), B (H.), C (H.), D (H.)	CLIII B.A.C. CLIV (H.) B.A.C.	...	...	36th D.A.C. [12]; [13]	121st 122nd 150th [14]	36th	16/ R. Ir. Rif. (P.)	...	108th 109th 110th	48th [14]	...	36th
	108th	11/R. Ir. Rif., 12/R. Ir. Rif., 13/R. Ir. Rif., 9/R. Ir. F.		CLXXII [14]; [28]	A, B, C, D	CLXXII B.A.C.											
	109th	9/R. Innis. F., 11/R. Innis. F., 14/R. Ir. Rif.		CLXXIII [14]; [28]	A, B, C, D	CLXXIII B.A.C.											
1915 October (France)	107th	8/R. Ir. Rif., 9/R. Ir. Rif., 10/R. Ir. Rif., 15/R. Ir. Rif.	1/ Service Sqdn., [16] 8/(Innis.) Dgns. 36th Div. Cyclist Coy. [17]	I LONDON [18]	1/, 2/, 3/Lond.	I LOND. B.A.C.	...	...	10th D.A.C. [13]	121st 122nd 150th	36th	16/ R. Ir. Rif. (P.) [A]	...	108th 109th 110th	48th	...	36th
	108th	11/R. Ir. Rif., 12/R. Ir. Rif., 13/R. Ir. Rif., 9/R. Ir. F.		II LONDON [19]	4/, 5/, 6/Lond.	II/LOND. B.A.C.											
	109th	9/R. Innis. F., 11/R. Innis. F., 14/R. Ir. Rif.		III LONDON [19]	7/, 8/, 9/Lond.	III/LOND. B.A.C.											
				IV LONDON (H.) [19]	10/Lond. (H.), 11/Lond. (H.); B (H.), LVII C (H.), LVII	IV LOND. (H.) B.A.C.											
1916 June (France)	107th	8/R. Ir. Rif., 9/R. Ir. Rif., 10/R. Ir. Rif., 15/R. Ir. Rif.; [18] 107th Bde. M.G. Coy.; [19] 107th T.M. Bty. [20]	...	CLIII; [21] [28]	A, B, C; D (H.)	...[28]	X.36 [34] Y.36 [35] Z.36 [35]	V.36 [37]	36th D.A.C. [38]	121st 122nd 150th	36th	16/ R. Ir. Rif. (P.)	...	108th 109th 110th	48th	...	36th
	108th	11/R. Ir. Rif., 12/R. Ir. Rif., 13/R. Ir. Rif., 9/R. Ir. F.; [22] 108th Bde. M.G. Coy.; [23] 108th T.M. Bty. [24]	...	CLIV [26]; [28]	A, B, C												
	109th	9/R. Innis. F., 11/R. Innis. F., 14/R. Ir. Rif.; [27] 109th Bde. M.G. Coy.; [28] 109th T.M. Bty. [28]		CLXXII [34]; [28] CLXXIII [34]; [28]	A, B, C; D (H.) / A, B, C; D (H.)												

	Infantry Brigades and Battalions	Artillery Brigades R.F.A.		Trench Mortar Btys.		D.A.C.	Field Coys. R.E.	Signal Coy.	Pioneers	M.G. Units	Field Ambulances	Mobile Vet. Section	Divnl. Emp. Coy.	Divnl. Train
	...	CLIII[34] ...... CLXXIII[35]	...	X.36 Y.36 Z.36[39]	V.36[38]	36th D.A.C.	121st 122nd 150th	36th	16/ R. Ir. Rif. (P.)	266th[40] M.G. Coy.	108th 109th 110th	48th	233rd[41]	36th
1917 June (France)	**107th** ...... 8/R. Ir. Rif.,[26] 9/R. Ir. Rif.,[27] 10/R. Ir. Rif.,[28] 15/R. Ir. Rif.: 107th M.G. Coy.;[36] 107th T.M. Bty. **108th** ...... 11/R. Ir. Rif.,[29] 12/R. Ir. Rif.,[30] 9/R. Ir. F.;[31] 108th M.G. Coy.;[37] 108th T.M. Bty. **109th** ...... 9/R. Innis. F., 10/R. Innis. F., 11/R. Innis. F.,[32] 14/R. Ir. Rif.;[33] 109th M.G. Coy.;[37] 109th T.M. Bty.	CLIII ...... A, B, C; D (H.) CLXXIII ...... A, B, C; D (H.)	...	X.36 Y.36	V.36	36th D.A.C.	121st 122nd 150th	36th	...	266th M.G. Coy.	108th 109th 110th	48th	233rd	36th
1918 March (France)	**107th** ...... 1/R. Ir. Rif.,[42] 2/R. Ir. Rif.,[43] 15/R. Ir. Rif.; 107th T.M. Bty. **108th** ...... 12/R. Ir. Rif., 1/R. Ir. F.,[44] 9/(N. Irish Horse) R. Ir. F.;[31] 108th T.M. Bty. **109th** ...... 1/R. Innis. F.,[45] 2/R. Innis. F.,[46] 9/R. Innis. F.; 109th T.M. Bty.	CLIII ...... A, B, C; D (H.) CLXXIII ...... A, B, C; D (H.)	...	X.36 Y.36	...	36th D.A.C.	121st 122nd 150th	36th	16/ R. Ir. Rif. (P.)	No. 36 Bn.[47] M.G.C.	108th 109th 110th	48th	233rd	36th

NOTES

[1] On 28/10/14 the Ulster Division became the 36th (Ulster) Division.

[2] Raised as 1st Bde.; on 2/11/14 it became 107th Bde. The four Bns. were the East, West, South, and North Belfast Volunteers.

[3] Raised as 2nd Bde.; on 2/11/14 it became 108th Bde. The four Bns. were the South Antrim, Central Antrim, Down, and County Armagh Volunteers.

[4] Raised as 3rd Bde.; on 2/11/14 it became 109th Bde. The four Bns. were the Tyrone, Derry, Donegal & Fermanagh, and Young Citizens Volunteers.

[5] The 1/Service Sqdn. was formed between 8/10–8/11/14 at Enniskillen.

[6] The Cyclist Coy. began to form on 18/11/14 (W.E. 200).

[7] No Artillery joined the Division in Ireland. CXLII, CXLIII, CXLIV, and CXLV (How.) Bdes., R.F.A., were to be raised for the 36th Div., but these four Fd. Arty. Bdes. were never formed.

[8] Raised with the Division, and reached Antrim on 11/11/14.

[9] Formed by 10/11/14.

[10] Bn. began to form on 2/12/14; became Divnl. Pioneer Bn. on 6/1/15.

[11] The three Fd. Ambces. were forming in Nov. 1914.

[12] The Train was formed in Nov. 1914; it consisted of 251, 252, 253, and 254 Cos., A.S.C. On 23/10/15 the Cos. became Nos. 1, 2, 3, 4 Cos., 36th Div. Train.

[13] The Artillery Bdes. were designated: Empire (CLIII & CLIV), West Ham (CLXXII), and East Ham (CLXXIII); and the D.A.C. was West Ham. The Bdes. were raised as 4-battery brigades; in each brigade the batteries were lettered—A, B, C, D—and each battery was a 4-gun battery. When the Division went to France in Oct. 1915 the Divnl. Artillery remained (temporarily in England).

[14] Joined at Antrim by March 1915.

[15] Joined Div. in England, went to France with Div., and disembkd. at le Havre on 6/10/15.

[16] 1/Service Sqdn. disembkd. at le Havre on 6/10/15; was attached to Meerut Cav. Bde., 2nd Ind. Cav. Div., 13–26/4/16. On 21/6/16 Sqdn. left 36th Div. and joined X Corps Cav. Regt.

[17] Coy. disembkd. at le Havre on 4/10/15; was attached to Meerut Cav. Bde., 2nd Ind. Cav. Div., 13–26/4/16. On 31/5/16 Coy. was broken up; half went to X Corps Cyclist Bn., and half went to 15/R. Ir. Rif. (107th Bde.).

[18] The four Artillery Bdes. and the D.A.C. went to France with 36th Div., and disembkd. at le Havre on 4, 5, & 6/10/15. On 18/11/15 B (H.) & C (H.)/LVII (H.) left 36th Div., rejoined 10th Div. at Mudros, and on 13/12/15 disembkd. at Salonika with 10th Div. I, II, III, IV (H.) Lond. Bdes. left 36th Div. in France on 11 & 12/12/15, and on 25 & 28/2/16 the 4 Bdes. rejoined the reformed 56th (1st London) Div. in France. The D.A.C. joined 56th Div. on 27/2/16 and became 56th D.A.C. (The 3 Gun Bdes. had been re-armed with 18-pdr. Q.F.s, and the four howitzer batteries with 4.5" Howitzers, in England, on their attachment to the 36th Div.)

[19] The M.G. Cos. were formed: 107th on 18/12/15 at Forceville; 108th on 26/1/16 at Ribeaucourt; and 109th on 23/1/16 at Fienvillers.

NOTES—continued

[29] T.M. Btles. were formed in Bdes.: 107th—107/1 by 1/4/16, 107/2 joined on 15/4/16, and they became 107th T.M. Bty. by 23/6/16; 108th—108/1 & 108/2 by 1/4/16, and they became 108th T.M. Bty. on 23/6/16; 109th—109/1 & 109/2 by 7/4/16, and they became 109th T.M. Bty. by 21/6/16.

[31] Bde. disembkd. at le Havre on 27/11/15 and rejoined 36th Div. On 21 & 22/5/16 D Bty. was transferred and became C/CLIV; and C (H.)/CLIV joined Bde. and became D (E.)/CLIII.

[32] Bde. disembkd. at le Havre on 1/12/15 and rejoined 36th Div. On 28/2/15 A (H.) left Bde. and joined 46th Div., became R (H.)/IV N. Mid. Bde. on 8/3/16, and on 23/5/16 became D (H.)/CCXXXI. On 21/5/16 CLIV was reorganised: B (H.), C (H.), & D (H.) left and became D (H.)/CLXXIII, D (H.)/CLIII, D (E.)/CLXXII; and D/CLXXII, B/CLXXIII, D/CLIII joined and became A, B, & C/CLIV.

[33] Bde. disembkd. at le Havre on 27/11/15 and rejoined 36th Div. On 20 & 21/5/16 D Bty. was transferred and became A/CLIV, and D (H.)/CLIV joined Bde. and became D (H.)/CLXXII.

[34] Bde. disembkd. at le Havre on 28/11/15 and rejoined 36th Div. On 21/5/16 D Bty. was transferred and became B/CLIV; and B (H.)/CLIV joined Bde. and became D (H.)/CLXXIII.

[35] D.A.C. disembkd. at le Havre on 28/11/15 and rejoined 36th Div. Between 16-18/5/16 B.A.C.s were abolished and the D.A.C. was reorganised.

[36] Medium T.M. Bties. were formed by 1/6/16.

[37] Heavy T.M. Bty. was formed by 20/6/16.

[38] These 2 Bns. amalgamated on 28/8/17 and became 8/9/R. Ir. Rif. On 7/2/18 the Bn. was disbanded: 32 offrs. & 650 o.r. were sent to other Bns., and surplus joined No. 21 Entg. Bn.

[39] Bn. ceased to form part of Bde. on 10/2/18; on 20/2/18 Bn. was disbanded and became part of No. 21 Entg. Bn.

[40] These 2 Bns. amalgamated on 13/11/17 and became 11/13/R. Ir. Rif. On 10/2/18 the Bn. left the Bde. and moved into Divnl. Res.; on 19/2/18 Bn. left 36th Div. and became No. 22 Entg. Bn. in XIX Corps.

[41] On 25/9/17 Bn. absorbed 304 o.r. of B & C Sqdns., N. Ir. Horse (X Corps Cav. Regt.); Bn. was then designated 9/(N. Irish Horse) R. Ir. F.

[42] On 4/2/18 Bn. left the Bde., moved into Divnl. Res., and sent a draft of 7 offrs. & 150 o.r. to 2/R. Innis. F. On 21/2/18 Bn. was disbanded and surplus joined No. 21 Entg. Bn.

[43] On 8/2/18 Bn. left the Bde., moved into Divnl. Res., and sent a draft of 20 offrs. & 400 o.r. to 9/R. Innis. F. On 21/2/18 Bn. was disbanded and surplus joined No. 23 Entg. Bn.

[44] On 10/2/18 Bn. left the Bde. and moved into Divnl. Res. On 18/2/18 Bn. was disbanded and surplus joined No. 23 Entg. Bn. on 21/2/18.

[45] On 14/9/16 A was broken up to complete B and C to 6 guns each; A/CLIV joined and became A/CLIII. On 13/1/17 1 sec. D (H.)/CLXXII joined and made up D (H.)/CLIII to 6 hows.

[46] Between 11-14/9/16 C Bty. was broken up and made up A and B to 6 guns each; Bde. was then broken up: A/CLIV became A/CLIII and B/CLIV became B/CLXXIII.

[47] Between 4-12/9/16 CLXXII was reorganised: C Bty. was broken up to make up A and B to 6 guns each. On 7/10/16 529 (H.) Bty. joined Bde. and became C (H.)/CLXXII on 12/10/16. Between 13-31/1/17 CLXXII was broken up: D (H.) was broken up to complete D (H.)/CLIII and D (H.)/CLXXIII to 6 hows. each; C (H.) was broken up to complete D (H.)/LXXVII and D (H.)/CXIII A.F.A. Bdes. to 6 hows. each; A/CLXXII became C/LXXVII A.F.A. Bde., and B/CLXXII became C/CXIII A.F.A. Bde.

[48] Between 11-14/9/16 B was broken up to complete A and C to 6 guns each; on 14/9/16 B/CLIV joined and became B/CLXXIII. On 13/1/17 1 sec. D (H.)/CLXXII joined and made up D (H.)/CLXXIII to 6 hows.

[49] Trench Mortars were reorganised on 11/2/18: Z was broken up and distributed between X and Y; and V Heavy T.M. Bty. was disbanded.

[50] Coy. left Grantham on 12/1/18, disembkd. at le Havre on 14/1/18, and joined Div. on 17/1/18.

[51] Coy. formed by 21/7/17.

[52] Bn. served in 25th Bde., 8th Div., until 3/2/18; the Bn. was then transferred to 107th Bde., 36th Div., and Bn. joined 107th Bde. on 4/2/18.

[53] Bn. served in 7th Bde., 3rd Div., from outbreak of Great War until 18/10/15, and from 20/10/15-13/11/17 in 74th Bde., 25th Div.; Bn. joined 108th Bde., 36th Div., on 14/11/17 and absorbed 7/R. Ir. Rif. (formerly in 48th Bde., 16th Div.). On 8/2/18 Bn. was transferred to and joined 107th Bde.

[54] Bn. served in 10th Bde., 4th Div., from outbreak of Great War until 2/8/17, joined 36th Div. on 3/8/17, and 107th Bde. on 24/8/17. On 8/2/18 Bn. was transferred to and joined 108th Bde.

[55] Bn. served in 87th Bde., 29th Div., until 5/2/18, when the Bn. was transferred to and joined 108th Bde.

[56] Bn. served in 12th Bde., 4th Div., from outbreak of Great War until 6/12/14 when Bn. was transferred to G.H.Q. Troops; served with 8th Bde., 2nd Div., from 26/1/15 until 22/7/15 when Bn. was transferred to Third Army Troops; served with 14th Bde., 5th Div., from 18/11/15 until 24/12/15 when Bn. was transferred to 96th Bde., 32nd Div. On 31/1/18 Bn. was transferred from 96th Bde., 32nd Div., to 109th Bde., 36th Div., and joined 109th Bde. on 3/2/18.

[57] Bn. was formed on 1/3/18; it consisted of 107th, 108th, 109th, and 266th M.G. Cos.

36TH (ULSTER) DIVISION

FORMATION, BATTLES, AND ENGAGEMENTS

This New Army Division had no existence before the outbreak of the Great War.

After the declaration of war with Germany there was a delay of some weeks, probably on political grounds, before the order was issued to form an Ulster Division. In the meantime, many of the volunteers from the Ulster Volunteer Force, as well as men from Ulster generally, had refused to wait ; some crossed over and enlisted in battalions forming in England, but many more joined one of the two New Army Irish divisions (10th and 16th), which were also forming at that time—all these men were lost to the Ulster Division. On the other hand, several officers joined up in Ulster, on their own responsibility, and formed their men into companies and battalions. Then came the welcome order to form the Ulster Division, with its 1st, 2nd, and 3rd Infantry Brigades, and divisional troops.

The 1st Brigade assembled at Ballykinlar and Donard Lodge Camps ; its four battalions were the East, West, South, and North Belfast Volunteers (8/, 9/, 10/, and 15/R. Ir. Rif.). The 2nd Brigade concentrated at Clandeboye Camp, and its four battalions were the South and Central Antrim (11/ and 12/R. Ir. Rif.), Down (13/R. Ir. Rif.), and County Armagh Volunteers (9/R. Ir. Fus.). The 3rd Brigade collected at Finner Camp, Ballyshannon ; its four battalions were the Tyrone (9/R. Innis. Fus.), Derry (10/R. Innis. Fus.), Donegal and Fermanagh Volunteers (11/R. Innis. Fus.), and Young Citizens Volunteers of Belfast (14/R. Ir. Rif.).

The Service Squadron was formed at Enniskillen, and the Field Companies, Signal Company, Pioneer Battalion, Field Ambulances, and Train were raised with the Division. At first it had been suggested that the Artillery should also be raised in Ulster, but this project was not proceeded with.

Divisional headquarters opened at 29 Wellington Place, Belfast, and on Wednesday the 28th October the Ulster Division was numbered 36th, but retained " Ulster " as a sub-title, and on Monday the 2nd November the three infantry brigades received the numbers 107th, 108th, and 109th (see Appendix 2). These divisional and brigade numbers were unchanged for the remainder of the service of the Division.

10,000 complete outfits were provided for the Division by private enterprise, and in mid-November 180 service rifles arrived for each battalion. But in these early days there were only about two regular officers available to help with each unit, and progressive training was made difficult owing to the lack of essential equipment.

In March 1915 the G.O.C. was informed that certain Territorial Artillery had been reserved to complete the Division, and on the 12th April the 36th (Ulster) Division was allotted to the Sixth New Army. But at this time the original Fourth New Army was broken up so as to provide reinforcements (see Appendix 1), and on the 27th April the Sixth New Army became the Fifth New Army.

In July the Ulster Division left Ireland, concentrated at Seaford, and awaited the arrival of its Artillery. It was now that the G.O.C. learned that the Territorial Artillery intended for the 36th Division had been transferred to another New Army Division, and its place would be taken by newly-raised artillery brigades, recruited in the Croydon area (CLIII & CLIV) and in East and West Ham (CLXXII, CLXXIII, & D.A.C.). The G.O.C. and G.S.O.1. motored up from Seaford to inspect these brigades and found that so far no uniform, arms, or equipment had been issued, and the men were being taught to mount and dismount on wooden horses. Shortly afterwards the artillery was moved by rail to join the Division and the first articles to appear out of the baggage wagons were these wooden horses. On arrival, the artillery was quartered at Lewes, and very soon uniforms, equipment, harness, and guns were received.

On the 20th July Field-Marshal Earl Kitchener inspected the Division at Seaford. Early in September the whole Division moved to Bordon and Bramshott, and the change of station was completed by the 14th. The last stage of the final preparation for the field was now undertaken. After a long period of strenuous and intelligent work, however, the Division had already reached a state of real efficiency, for it must be remembered that (with the exception of the artillery) the Division was composed almost entirely of Ulster Volunteers, and *sub rosa* they had been training (with some musketry) for about 18 months. It was in consequence of this early training that the rest of the Ulster Division was ready for the field before its artillery had completed its training and gun-practice ; and very shortly after arrival in the Bordon area the Division received orders to move to France and was informed that it would be accompanied overseas by the 1st London Division Artillery, T.F., and the 10th D.A.C. (see General Notes, Table, and notes 18 and 21-25).

On Sunday the 26th September the first advance party left. On Thursday the 30th September H.M. the King inspected the Ulster Division on Hankley Common ; and between the 3rd–6th October the Division crossed to France. By the 9th October concentration was completed around Flesselles (7 miles north of Amiens), and on the 13th the Ulster Division incurred its first war casualties.

For the remainder of the Great War the 36th (Ulster) Division served on the Western Front in France and Belgium and was engaged in the following operations :

1915

1916

THE BATTLES OF THE SOMME
1 and 2 July ... ... Battle of Albert [X Corps, Fourth Army].

1917

7–9 June ... ... Battle of Messines [IX Corps, Second Army].
7 June ... ... Capture of Wytschaete.

BATTLES OF YPRES
16 and 17 August ... Battle of Langemarck [XIX Corps, Fifth Army].

BATTLE OF CAMBRAI
20 and 21 November ... The Tank Attack [IV Corps, Third Army].
23–27 November ... ... Capture of Bourlon Wood [IV Corps, Third Army].
8 December ... ... The German Counter-Attack (108th Bde., with 61st Div.), [III Corps, Third Army].

1918

FIRST BATTLES OF THE SOMME

21–23 March	Battle of St. Quentin [XVIII Corps, Fifth Army].
24 and 25 March ...	Actions at the Somme Crossings [XVIII Corps, Fifth Army].
26 and 27 March ...	Battle of Rosières [XVIII Corps, Fifth Army].

BATTLES OF THE LYS

10 and 11 April	Battle of Messines (108th Bde., with 19th Div.), [IX Corps, Second Army].
13–15 April	Battle of Bailleul (108th Bde., with 19th Div.), [IX Corps, Second Army].
17–18 April	First Battle of Kemmel Ridge (108th Bde., with 19th Div.), [IX Corps, Second Army].
20 July–19 Sept.	THE ADVANCE TO VICTORY [X Corps, Second Army].

THE FINAL ADVANCE IN FLANDERS

28 Sept.–2 Oct.	Battle of Ypres [II Corps, Second Army].
14–19 October	Battle of Courtrai [II Corps, Second Army].
25 October	Ooteghem [II Corps, Second Army].

On the 27th October the 36th Division pushed on and occupied Kleineberg Ridge; on the 28th it was relieved in the front line and moved back towards the Lys valley between Courtrai and Menin, with headquarters at Belleghem. The Division was now transferred to X Corps. By the 4th November divisional headquarters and 107th and 108th Brigades moved into Mouscron (north-east of Tourcoing), and on the 9th the Division came under XV Corps. The troops were still occupying the same positions when the Armistice brought hostilities to a close at 11 a.m. on the 11th November.

The Division settled down for the winter at Mouscron (divisional headquarters, 107th and 108th Brigades, two field companies, two field ambulances, and the Train), Tourcoing (divisional artillery), Roncq (109th Brigade and one field company), and Sterrenhoek (one field ambulance). On the 7th December H.M. the King with T.R.H. The Prince of Wales and Prince Albert passed through the divisional area. During this month the troops were employed in military training and education, and 54,203 attendances were recorded at the divisional educational classes.

On the 30th and 31st January 1919 H.R.H. The Prince of Wales paid a two days' visit to the Division; and during this month about four thousand men left for demobilization. Gradually the Division dwindled, units were reduced to cadre, on the 1st June cadres were further reduced to equipment guard, and on the 29th June the Division ceased to exist. During the Great War the 36th (Ulster) Division lost 32,186 killed, wounded, and missing.

NOTE.—Marshal Foch's Message to the People of Northern Ireland (November 1928) is given in Appendix 5.

37TH DIVISION

G.O.C.

6 April 1915	Major-General COUNT GLEICHEN.*
22 October 1916	Major-General S. W. SCRASE-DICKENS (invalided, 9/11/16).
9 November 1916	Major-General H. BRUCE-WILLIAMS.

G.S.O.1.

6 April 1915...Lt.-Col. B. VINCENT.
28 Jan. 1917...Captain Sir T. R. L. THOMPSON, Bt. (acting).
1 Feb. 1917...Lt.-Col. J. G. DILL.
29 Oct. 1917...Major W. A. T. BOWLY (acting).
31 Oct. 1917...Lt.-Col. E. L. MAKIN.
5 Mar. 1918...Lt.-Col. W. A. T. BOWLY.
6 April 1918...Major W. ANDERSON (acting).
8 April 1918...Lt.-Col. P. S. ROWAN.
10 July 1918...Lt.-Col. W. PLATT.

A.-A. & Q.-M.-G.

26 April 1915...Lt.-Col. L. F. GREEN-WILKINSON.
3 Jan. 1916...Major E. I. D. GORDON (acting).
8 Jan. 1916...Lt.-Col. A. D. M. BROWNE.
25 April 1918...Lt.-Col. H. N. A. HUNTER.
24 May 1918...Lt.-Col. H. G. REID.

B.-G. R.A.

16 April 1915...Br.-Gen. S. LUSHINGTON.
17 Sept. 1915...Br.-Gen. F. POTTS.

C.R.E.

1 June 1915...Lt.-Col. H. B. DES VOEUX.
4 Oct. 1916...Major V. GILES (acting).
8 Oct. 1916...Major R. F. A. BUTTERWORTH (acting).
15 Oct. 1916...Lt.-Col. H. DE L. POLLARD-LOWSLEY.
19 June 1918...Major R. D. JACKSON (tempy.).
1 July 1918...Lt.-Col. R. D. JACKSON.

---

* By authority of H.M. the King, from 15/8/1917, Major-General Count Gleichen was known as Major-General Lord Edward Gleichen.

110th BDE.
(originally 131st Bde.)

8 April '15...Br.-Gen. E. G. T.
BAINBRIDGE.
1 June '16...Lt.-Col. E. L. CHALLENOR
(acting).
9 June '16...Br.-Gen. W. F. HESSEY.
(On 7/7/16 110th Bde. was transferred
complete to 21st Division).

63rd BDE.

(On 8/7/16 63rd Bde. was transferred
complete from 21st Division to 37th
Division).
[7 Oct. '15]...Br.-Gen. E. R. HILL.
16 Mar. '17...Br.-Gen. E. L.
CHALLENOR.
26 Sept. '18...Br.-Gen. R. OAKLEY.
21 Oct. '18...Br.-Gen. A. B. HUBBACK.

111th BDE.
(originally 132nd Bde.)

9 April '15...Br.-Gen. R. W. R.
BARNES.
(On 6/7/16 111th Bde. was attached to
34th Division).

102nd BDE.

(On 6/7/16 102nd Bde., from 34th Div.,
was attached to 37th Division).
[28 Dec. '14]...Br.-Gen. T. P. B.
TERNAN.
(On 22/8/16 102nd Bde. rejoined 34th
Division).

111th BDE.

(On 22/8/16 111th Bde. rejoined 37th
Division, from 34th Division).
[9 April '15]...Br.-Gen. R. W. R.
BARNES.
22 Nov. '16...Lt.-Col. W. W. SEYMOUR
(acting).
26 Nov. '16...Br.-Gen. C. W. COMPTON.
19 Oct. '17...Br.-Gen. S. G. FRANCIS.

112th BDE.
(originally 133rd Bde.)

12 April '15...Br.-Gen. J. MARRIOTT.
14 Sept. '15...Br.-Gen. P. M. ROBINSON.
(On 6/7/16 112th Bde. was attached to 34th Division).

103rd BDE.

(On 6/7/16 103rd Bde., from 34th Div., was attached to 37th
Division).
[4 July '16]...Br.-Gen. H. E. TREVOR.
(On 22/8/16 103rd Bde. rejoined 34th Division).

112th BDE.

(On 22/8/16 112th Bde. rejoined 37th Division, from 34th
Division).
[14 Sept. '15]...Br.-Gen. P. M. ROBINSON.
29 Nov. '16...Lt.-Col. R. P. COBBOLD (acting).
2 Dec. '16...Br.-Gen. A. ST. Q. RICARDO.
10 Jan. '17...Lt.-Col. R. P. COBBOLD (acting).
14 Jan. '17...Br.-Gen. R. C. MACLACHLAN (killed, 11/8/17).
11 Aug. '17...Lt.-Col. R. C. CHESTER-MASTER (acting).
16 Aug. '17...Br.-Gen. A. E. IRVINE.
27 Sept. '18...Br.-Gen. W. N. HERBERT.

GENERAL NOTES

The following also served with the 37th Division :—

102nd Inf. Bde. (Br.-Gen. T. P. B. Ternan–20/N.F., 21/N.F., 22/N.F., 23/N.F., 102nd M.G. Coy., 102nd T.M. Bty.); **103rd Inf. Bde. (Br.-Gen. H. E.** Trevor – 24/N.F., 25/N.F., 26/N.F., 27/N.F., 103rd M.G. Coy., 103rd T.M. Bty.); and **18/N.F. (P.),**	from 34th Division, were attached from 6/7–22/8/16 to the 37th Division, in exchange for	**111th Inf. Bde. (Br.-Gen.** R. W. R. Barnes), **112th Inf. Bde. (Br.-Gen.** P. M. Robinson), and **9/N. Staff (P.).**

ARTILLERY—502 (H.) Battery R.F.A. (4, 4.5″ howitzers)–Monmouth. Territorial Howitzers—disembkd. at le Havre on 6/10/16, left le Havre on 8/10/16, and joined CXXVI Bde.* on 9/10/16 (note 28).
37 Heavy Battery, R.G.A., was raised for the 37th Division ; but the Heavy Battery did not go overseas and was broken up at home.

MACHINE-GUN UNIT—16th Motor-Machine-Gun Battery left Bisley on 25/7/15, joined 37th Division at Perham Down on 26/7/15, and disembkd. at le Havre on 29/7/15. On 9/5/16 Battery was transferred to VII Corps, Third Army.

OTHER UNITS—37th Sanitary Section joined Division in England, disembkd. at le Havre on 1/8/15 ; between 12–20/4/17 the Section left the Division and took over a Sanitary Area in XVIII Corps, Third Army.

37th Division Motor Ambce. Workshop joined Division in England, went to France with the Division, and disembkd. at Rouen. Workshop left Rouen on 2/8/15 and rejoined Division at Eecke on 5/8/15 ; on 6/4/16 the Workshop was disbanded and absorbed by 37th Div. Supply Column.

On 21/2/18 the reorganization of the 37th Division on a 9-battalion basis was completed ; and on 28/2/18 the pioneer battalion (9/N. Staff.) was reorganized on a 3-company basis.

* CXXVI Bde., which was broken up in January 1917 (note 28), must not be confused with CXXVI A.F.A. Bde. (A & B/2/1/H.A.C. and 2/1/Warwickshire Batteries, and B.A.C.) ; CXXVI A.F.A. Bde. was formed in England in 1917 and disembkd. at Boulogne on 21/6/17.

37TH DIVISION [1]

Dates	INFANTRY — Brigades	Battalions and attached Units	Mounted Troops	ARTILLERY — Field Artillery — Brigades	Batteries	Bde. Ammn. Colns.	Trench Mortar Btts. — Medium	Heavy	Divnl. Ammn. Coln.	Engineers — Field Cos.	Signal Service — Divnl. Signal Coy.	Pioneers	M.G. Units	Field Ambulances	Mobile Vety. Sec.	Divnl. Emplnt. Coy.	Divnl. Train
1915 April (England)	110th[2, 3]; 111th[3, 4]; 112th[2, 3]	6/ Leic., 7/Leic., 8/Leic., 9/ Leic. 10/R.F., 13/R.F., 13/ K.R.R.C., 13/R.B., 8/E. 11/R. War., 6/Bedf., 8/E. Lanc., 10/L.N.L.	H.Q., M.G. Sec. & B Sqdn.[5] 1/Q.O. York. Dgns. 37th Div. Cyclist Coy.[7]	CXXIII[6]; CXXIV[6]; CXXV[6]; CXXVI (H.)[6]	A, B, C, D A, B, C, D A (H.), B (H.), C (H.); D (H.)	CXXIII B.A.C. CXXIV B.A.C. CXXV B.A.C. CXXVI (H.) B.A.C.	...	...	37th D.A.C.	152nd[8] 153rd[9] 154th[9]	37th[10]	9/N. Staf.[11] (P.)	...	48th[13] 49th[13] 50th[13]	28th[13]	...	37th[14]
1915 August (France)	110th; 111th; 112th	6/Leic., 7/Leic., 8/Leic., 9/ Leic. 10/R.F., 13/R.F., 13/ K.R.R.C., 13/R.B. 11/R. War., 6/Bedf., 8/E. Lanc., 10/L.N.L.	H.Q., M.G. Sec., & B Sqdn.[15] 1/Q.O. York. Dgns. 37th Div. Cyclist Coy.[16]	CXXIII[17]; CXXIV[18]; CXXV[19]; CXXVI (H.)[20]	A, B, C, D A, B, C, D A (H.), B (H.), C (H.); D (H.)	CXXIII B.A.C. CXXIV B.A.C. CXXV B.A.C. CXXVI (H.) B.A.C.	...	...	37th D.A.C.	152nd 153rd 154th	37th	9/N. Staf. (P.)	...	48th 49th 50th	28th	...	37th
1916 May (France)	110th[21]; 111th[22]; 112th[23]	6/Leic., 7/Leic., 8/Leic., 9/ Leic.; 110th Bde. M.G. Coy.;[24] 110th T.M. Bty.[24] 10/R.F., 13/R.F., 13/ K.R.R.C., 13/R.B.; 111th Bde. M.G. Coy.;[24] 111th T.M. Bty.[24] 11/R. War., 6/Bedf., 8/E. Lanc., 10/L.N.L.;[24] 112th Bde. M.G. Coy.;[24] 112th T.M. Bty.[24]	...	CLXXIII[17];[25] CLXXIV[18];[26] CLXV[19];[27] CLXXVI[20];	A, B, C; D (H.) A, B, C; D (H.) A, B, C; D (H.) A, B, C	...[29]	X.37[30] Y.37[30] Z.37[30]	V.37[31]	37th D.A.C.[32]	152nd 153rd 154th	37th	9/N. Staf.[33] (P.)	...	48th 49th 50th	28th	...	37th
1917 June (France)	63rd[35]; 111th; 112th	8/Linc., 8/Som. L.I., 4/ Middx., 10/Y. & L.;[36] 63rd M.G. Coy.;[37] 63rd T.M. Bty. 10/R.F., 13/R.F.,[38] 13/ K.R.R.C., 13/R.B.; 111th M.G. Coy.;[39] 111th T.M. Bty. 11/R. War.,[40] 6/Bedf., 8/E. Lanc., 10/L.N.L.;[39] 112th M.G. Coy.;[39] 112th T.M. Bty.	...	CXXIII[33]; CXIV[34]	A, B, C; D (H.) A, B, C; D (H.)	...	X.37 Y.37 Z.37[38]	V.37	37th D.A.C.	152nd 153rd 154th	37th	9/N. Staf. (P.)	247th[40] M.G. Coy.	48th 49th 50th	28th	234th[41]	37th

1918 March (France)	63rd	8/Linc., 8/Som. L.I., 4/Middx.; 63rd T.M. Bty.	CXXIII	A, B, C; D (H.)	...	X.37[15]	37th D.A.C.	152nd	37th	9/N. Staff (P.)	No. 37 Bn. M.G.C.[24]	48th	28th	234th	37th
	111th	10/R.F., 13/K.R.R.C., 13/R.B.; 111th T.M. Bty.	CXXIV	A, B, C; D (H.)		Y.37[16]		153rd				49th			
	112th	13/R.F., *6/Bedf., 1/Essex; 112th T.M. Bty.						154th				50th			
1918 June (France)	63rd	8/Linc., 8/Som. L.I., 4/Middx.; 63rd T.M. Bty.	CXXIII	A, B, C; D (H.)	...	X.37	37th D.A.C.	152nd	37th	9/N. Staff (P.)	No. 37 Bn. M.G.C.	48th	28th	234th	37th
	111th	10/R.F., 13/K.R.R.C., 13/R.B.; 111th T.M. Bty.	CXXIV	A, B, C; D (H.)		Y.37		153rd				49th			
	112th	13/R.F., 1/1/Herts.; 112th T.M. Bty.						154th				50th			

NOTES

1 Raised as 44th Div. in March 1915; became 37th Div. by 27/4/15.

2 Raised as 131st, 132nd, and 133rd Bdes.; became 110th, 111th, and 112th Bdes. by 27/4/15.

3 The 4 Bns. were raised as Army Troops Bns.: 6/Leic. for First, 7/Leic. for Second, and 8/ and 9/Leic. for Third New Army.

4 The 4 Bns. were raised as Army Troops Bns.: 10/R.F. for Second, and 13/R.F., 13/K.R.R.C., and 13/R.B. for Third New Army.

5 The 4 Bns. were raised as Army Troops Bns.: 6/Bedf. for First, and 11/R. War., 8/E. Lanc., and 10/L.N.L. for Third New Army.

6 Joined in England by 21/8/15, went to France with Div., and disembkd. at le Havre on 1/8/15.

7 Coy. was formed in the Div. by 14/5/15 and camped at Windmill Hill. Coy. disembkd. at le Havre on 30/7/15.

8 The three 18-pdr. Bdes. were raised for the (original) 31st Div. (App. 1B); when the 31st Div. was broken up the 3 Bdes. joined the Arty. Reserve, and were posted to the 37th Div. by 15/4/15. The 4.5" How. Bde. was raised for the original 32nd Div. (App. 1C); when the 32nd Div. was broken up the Bde. joined the Arty. Reserve, and it was posted to the 37th Div. as the How. Bde. by 15/4/15.

The Bdes. were 4-battery brigades; in each brigade the batteries were lettered—A, B, C, D—and each battery was a 4-gun battery.

9 The Cos. joined by 14/4/15; they disembkd. at le Havre, 31/7–1/8/15.

10 On 17/6/15 40th Div. Signal Coy. became 37th Div. Signal Coy. and joined 37th Div.

11 The Pioneer Bn. (formerly an Army Troops Bn. of Third New Army) was selected on 19/4/15 and joined Div. on 20/4/15. The Pioneer Bn. disembkd. at le Havre on 29/7/15.

12 The Fd. Ambces. joined Div. in June 1915; they had been raised for 16th (Irish) Div. The Fd. Ambces. disembkd. at le Havre, 29/7–1/8/15.

13 Joined Div. by 7/5/15; disembkd. at le Havre on 1/8/15, and concentrated with Div. on 3/8/15.

14 Train consisted of 288, 289, 290, & 291 Cos., A.S.C.; it disembkd. at le Havre, 29–31/7/15.

15 Sqdn. left Div. on 10/5/16; joined II Corps Cav. Regt. on 12/5/16.

16 Coy. left Div. on 11/5/16; joined VII Corps Cyclist Bn. on 11/5/16.

17 On 4/6/16 A Bty. was transferred and became C/CCXXVI; D Bty. then became A/CCXXIII; and B (H.)/CXXVI joined and became D (H.)/CXXIII.

18 On 4/6/16 A Bty. was transferred and became A/CXXVI; D Bty. was transferred and became B/CXXVI; C/CXXV joined and became A/CXXIV; and A (H.)/CXXVI joined and became D (H.)/CXXIV.

19 On 4/6/16 C Bty. was transferred and became A/CXXIV; D Bty. then became C/CXXV; and C (H.)/CXXVI joined and became D (H.)/CXXV.

20 On 7/2/16 D (H.) Bty. and portion of B.A.C. were transferred to 48th Div. and became D (H.)/CCXLIII (H.) and on 18/5/16 D (H.)/CCXLIII became D (H.)/CCXLII.

21 On 4/6/16 CXXVI was reorganized: A (H.), B (H.), & C (H.) Btles. left and became D (H.)/CXXIV, D (H.)/CXXIII, and D (H.)/CXXV; A & D/CXXIV joined and became A & B/CXXVI, and A/CXXIII joined and became C/CXXVI.

22 On 7/7/16 110th Bde. was transferred complete to 21st Div. in exchange for 63rd Bde. (note 32).

23 From 6/7–22/8/16 111th and 112th Bdes. & 9/N. Staff. (P.), were attached to 34th Div. in exchange for 102nd and 103rd Bdes. (see General Notes).

24 M.G. joined from Grantham:

110th—left Grantham on 24/2/16, disembkd. at le Havre on 2/3/16, joined Bde. on 4/3/16. M.G. Coy. was transferred with 110th Bde. to 21st Div. on 7/7/16 (note 21).

111th—disembkd. at le Havre on 25/2/16, joined Bde. on 4/3/16;

112th—left Grantham on 24/2/16, disembkd. at le Havre on 2/3/16, and joined Bde. on 4/3/16.

[51] T.M. Btles. were formed in Bdes.:

110th.—110/1 on 23/3/16, 110/2 by 13/5/16, and they became 110th T.M. Bty. on 13/8/16 (110th T.M. Bty. was transferred with 110th Bde. to 21st Div. on 7/7/18—note 21).

111th—111/1 & 111/2 by 3/5/16, and they became 111th T.M. Bty. by 2/7/16;

112th—112/1 by 30/3/16, 112/2 by. 15/5/16, and they became 112th T.M. Bty. by 1/7/16.

[52] On 30/8/16 B/CXXIII was broken up to complete A and C to 6 guns each; B/CXXV (completed to 6 guns by 1 sec. A/CXXV) joined CXXIII and became B/CXXIII. On 25/1/17 R. Sec. C (H.)/CXXVI joined and made up D (H.)/CXXIII to 6 hows.

[53] On 31/8/16 C/CXXIV was broken up to complete A and B to 6 guns each; C/CXXV (completed to 6 guns by 1 sec. A/CXXV) joined CXXIV and became C/CXXIV. On 25/1/17 L. Sec. C (H.)/CXXVI joined and made up D (H.)/CXXIV to 6 hows.

[54] On 31/8/16 Bde. was broken up: A. Bty. was broken up to complete B and C to 6 guns each; B then became B/CXXIII and C became C/CXXIV; D (H.) was transferred and became D (H.)/CXXVI.

[55] On 30/8/16 B Bty. was broken up to complete A and C to 6 guns each, and D (H.)/CXXIV joined and became D (H.)/CXXVI. On 9/10/16 502 (H.) Bty. (Monmouth. Terrtl. Howitzers) joined CXXVI; on 23/10/16 C Bty. became B Bty. and 502 (H.) then became C (H.)/CXXVI. On 25/1/17 C (H.)—late 502 (H.)—was broken up: R. Sec. made up D (H.)/CXXIII and L. Sec. made up D (H.)/CXXIV to 6 hows. each; A Bty. was transferred and became A/XVIII A.F.A. Bde.; B Bty. was transferred and became A/CCLXXXII A.F.A. Bde. On 28/1/17 D (H.) was broken up: R. Sec. made up D (H.)/CCLXXXII A.F.A. Bde. and L. Sec. made up D (H.)/XVIII A.F.A. Bde. to 6 hows. each; CXXVI Bde. was then broken up.

[56] Between 21–23/5/16 B.A.C.s were abolished and the D.A.C. was reorganised.

[57] The 3 Medium T.M. Bties. were formed by May 1916.

[51] The Heavy T.M. Bty. was formed on 25/5/16.

[52] On 8/7/16 63rd Bde. was transferred complete from 21st Div. to 37th Div., in exchange for 110th Bde. (note 21).

[53] On 4/2/18 the Bn. was disbanded.

[54] On 4/2/18 the Bn. was transferred to 112th Bde.

[55] On 7/2/18 the Bn. was disbanded: 32 offrs. and 650 o.r. were drafted; remdr. went to Divnl. Rft. Camp on 14/2/18, and on 21/2/18 joined No. 15 Entg. Bn.

[56] On 4/2/18 20 offrs. and 400 o.r. were transferred to 11/E. Lanc. (31st Div.); on 21/2/18, 8/E. Lanc. was disbanded and surplus joined Inf. Base Depot at Etaples.

[57] On 4/2/18 the Bn. was disbanded.

[58] On 6/2/18 Z was split up between X and Y.

[59] On 6/2/18 V H.T.M. Bty. left the Div.

[60] Coy. disembkd. at le Havre on 16/7/17 and joined Div. at Dranoutre on 19/7/17.

[61] Coy. was formed by 16/8/17.

[62] On 20/5/18 Bn. was reduced to T.C.; on 21/5/18 T.C. was transferred to 39th Div., and remdr. was absorbed by 1/Herts. (note 45).

[63] Bn. served with 88th Bde., 29th Div., until 4/2/18; Bn. was then transferred to and joined 112th Bde. on 4/2/18.

[64] Bn. was formed at Bristol Camp, Dickebusch, on 4/3/18; it consisted of 63rd, 111th, 112th, and 247th M.G. Coe.

[65] Bn. disembkd. at le Havre on 6/11/14, joined 2nd Div. (in front of Ypres) on 12/11/14, 4th (Gds.) Bde., 2nd Div., on 20/11/14, and 6th Bde., 2nd Div., on 19/8/15. Bn. was transferred to 118th Bde., 39th Div., on 29/2/16; to 116th Bde., 39th Div., on 8/2/18; and joined 112th Bde., 37th Div., on 11/5/18. On the way up to join the 112th Bde. on 11/5/18, the Bn. (about 25 offrs. & 500 o.r.) marched into an area already infected by a concentrated German gas-shell bombardment; all the Bn. became casualties, except 1 offr. & 7 o.r.; and on 12/5/18 the offr. and 5 of the 7 men had to be evacuated to the C.C.S.

[66] On 22/5/18 1/1/Herts. absorbed remdr. (30 offrs. & 650 o.r.) of 6/Bedf. (note 42).

37TH DIVISION

FORMATION, BATTLES, AND ENGAGEMENTS

This New Army Division had no existence before the outbreak of the Great War.

The Division began to form in the middle of March 1915. It was raised for the Sixth New Army and at first was numbered 44th, its infantry brigades were the 131st, 132nd, and 133rd.

On the 10th April orders were issued to break up the six divisions of the original Fourth New Army and to use the service battalions of these six divisions for training and providing reinforcements. On the 12th April it was decided that the 16th (Irish) Division should be replaced in the Second New Army by another division formed of the Army Troops battalions which had been raised for the first three New Armies; the artillery reserves would provide the artillery and the B.-G., R.A., was to be appointed at once. As soon as possible the selected division would be concentrated near Salisbury for its final training. The 44th Division was the one selected; it was at once renumbered 37th, and its Infantry Brigades became the 110th, 111th, and 112th (see Appendix 2). A divisional commander had already been appointed; on the 12th April divisional headquarters opened at Andover and the Division began to assemble. The thirteen infantry battalions were provided by the Army Troops battalions of the first three New Armies: two came from the First, two from the Second, and nine from the Third New Army. The Artillery had been raised for the original 31st and 32nd Divisions (Appendices 1B and 1C): CXXIII, CXXIV, and CXXV were raised for the original 31st Division; when that division was broken up the three field artillery brigades joined the Artillery Reserve, and by the 15th April they were posted to the 37th Division. In a similar way CXXVI, raised for the original 32nd Division, was transferred to the Artillery Reserve, and then, by the 15th April, posted as the Howitzer Brigade to the 37th Division. In June the three field ambulances were transferred from the 16th Division to the 37th. It was in this way that the Division was completed.

Collected as they were from the Army Troops battalions of the first three New Armies, the origins and early histories of the thirteen battalions differed considerably. It will suffice to give two examples. One battalion (originally raised as part of the Second New Army) was composed of City of London business staffs. Recruiting for this battalion began on the 21st August 1914 and 210 men presented themselves; six days later the strength of the unit was 1,600. At first the men paraded in all sorts of clothing: men in silk hats and morning coats fell in alongside others who wore caps and norfolk jackets. This battalion served in the 37th Division from April 1915 until the Armistice and it had 2,647 casualties. Another battalion (which was raised in September 1914 for the Third New Army) trained at first near Pokesdown and was attached to an infantry brigade. In the early days very little equipment and uniform were available and each company possessed only a few antiquated Lee-Enfield rifles. Battalion training consisted in daily route marches, lectures, and a bi-weekly attack on Foxbury Hill, varied with outpost schemes and night occupations of Hengistbury Head to repel a repeatedly-invading enemy. Guards also were posted along the shore to watch for German submarines; but it was never made clear how the enemy vessels were to be distinguished from our own submarines. In the early spring, brigade exercises began; and then came the arrival of the mules. It was noticed that the animals were unshod; thereupon the farrier-sergeant determined to remedy the matter at once, he picked up the hind leg of the nearest mule for a preliminary inspection, and—promptly disappeared.

By April 1915, however, when the various units were selected to form the 37th Division, they had all been in existence some months, and they had already succeeded in overcoming the early and very real difficulties attendant on a shortage of trained instructors, complicated by the small number of modern arms which were available, and insufficient equipment. Consequently it was only necessary to undertake the final preparation of the Division for the field.

The concentration on Salisbury Plain was completed without any loss of time, and on the 21st April divisional headquarters moved to Cholderton. Divisional training was intensive; and on the 25th June H.M. the King inspected the 37th Division on Sidbury Hill. In July the Division received orders to move to France; the advance party left on the 22nd July, embarkation began on the 28th and continued until the 81st July, and on the 2nd August the Division completed its concentration around Tilques (north-west of St. Omer).

For the remainder of the Great War the 37th Division served on the Western Front in France and Belgium and was engaged in the following operations :—

1915

1916

BATTLES OF THE SOMME*

13–18 November ... ... Battle of the Ancre [V Corps, Fifth Army].**

1917

BATTLES OF ARRAS

9–11 April ... ... First Battle of the Scarpe [VI Corps, Third Army].
11 April ... ... Capture of Monchy le Preux.
23 & 24 April ... ... Second Battle of the Scarpe [XVII Corps, Third Army].
28 & 29 April ... ... Battle of Arleux [XVII Corps, Third Army].

BATTLES OF YPRES

31 July–2 August... ... Battle of Pilckem Ridge [IX Corps, Second Army].
22–25 September ... ... Battle of the Menin Road Ridge (112th Bde., with 39th Div., X Corps, 22 & 23/9/17; & with 19th Div., IX Corps, 23–25/9/17) [Second Army].
27 Sept.–3 Oct. ... ... Battle of Polygon Wood [IX Corps, Second Army].
4 October ... ... Battle of Broodseinde [IX Corps, Second Army].
9 October ... ... Battle of Poelcappelle [IX Corps, Second Army].
12 October ... ... First Battle of Passchendaele [IX Corps, Second Army].

---

* From 6/7–22/8/16 the 111th and 112th Inf. Bdes. and 9/N. Staff. (P.) were attached to the 34th Division and took part with it in the Battles of the Somme, 1916—Battle of Albert (part), Battle of Bazentin Ridge, and Battle of Pozières Ridge (see General Notes 34th and 37th Divisions, and Engagements 34th Division).

** In the Battle of the Ancre the 63rd and 111th Inf. Bdes. served from 13/11/16 with the 63rd (R.N.) Division, and the 112th Inf. Bde. served from 13–17/11/16 with the 2nd Division (112th rejoined 37th Division on 17/11/16). At noon on 15/11/16 the 37th Division took over the 63rd (R.N.) Div. front with the 63rd and 111th Inf. Bdes. (The 37th Division held this part of the line until relieved by the 7th Division at 6 a.m., 26/11/16.) 37th Division Artillery also took part in the Battle of the Ancre (13–18/11/16), covering 63rd (R.N.) Div., from 13/11/16, and 37th Div. from 15/11/16.

1918

FIRST BATTLES OF THE SOMME

5 April ... ... **Battle of the Ancre** [IV Corps, Third Army].

THE ADVANCE TO VICTORY
SECOND BATTLES OF THE SOMME

21–23 August ... ... **Battle of Albert** [IV Corps, Third Army].

BATTLES OF THE HINDENBURG LINE

12 September ... ... **Battle of Havrincourt** [IV Corps, Third Army].
1 October ... ... **Battle of the Canal du Nord** [IV Corps, Third Army].
8 and 9 October... ... **Battle of Cambrai** [IV Corps, Third Army].
9–12 October ... ... **Pursuit to the Selle** [IV Corps, Third Army].

THE FINAL ADVANCE IN PICARDY

22–25 October ... ... **Battle of the Selle** [IV Corps, Third Army].
4 November ... ... **Battle of the Sambre** [IV Corps, Third Army].

Early on the 5th November the 5th Division passed through the 37th and the latter then concentrated and rested southward of le Quesnoy. On the 11th November the 37th Division moved back to the Bethencourt-Caudry area, and during the march it was informed that at 11 a.m. the Armistice with Germany had come into force. The units were now employed in training, education, and recreation, and on the 23rd the divisional R.E. and the pioneer battalion rejoined. On the 24th November the Division was informed that it was to move to an area north of Charleroi, and on the 1st December the march began. Between the 2nd–14th the Division halted in billets north of le Quesnoy ; the move was then continued, and on the 20th December the Division settled down in its final billets between Charleroi and the Maubeuge–Nivelles road, with divisional headquarters at Gosselies. Units were employed in educational training, and on the 26th December demobilization began.

During January 1919 demobilization and education continued. On the 15th February orders were received that the Division would gradually be reduced, and at midnight on the 24th/25th March it ceased to exist. During the Great War the 37th Division lost 29,969 killed, wounded, and missing.

38TH (WELSH) DIVISION

G.O.C.

19 January 1915	Major-General I. PHILIPPS.
9 July 1916	Major-General H. E. WATTS (tempy.).
12 July 1916	Major-General C. G. BLACKADER.
22 October 1917	Br.-Gen. E. W. ALEXANDER, V.C. (tempy.).
17 November 1917	Br.-Gen. W. A. M. THOMPSON (acting).
22 November 1917	Major-General C. G. BLACKADER (sick, 20/5/18).
20 May 1918	Br.-Gen. H. E. AP RHYS PRYCE (acting).
23 May 1918	Major-General T. A. CUBITT.

G.S.O.1.

21 April 1915...Major H. C. REES (acting).
18 Sept. 1915...Lt.-Col. H. E. AP RHYS PRYCE.
9 July 1916...Lt.-Col. C. BONHAM-CARTER (tempy.).
12 July 1916...Lt.-Col. H. E. AP RHYS PRYCE.
17 Oct. 1917...Lt.-Col. J. E. MUNBY.

A.-A. & Q.-M.-G.

25 Feb. 1915...Major P. MALCOLM (acting).
19 April 1915...Major H. E. AP RHYS PRYCE (acting).
20 Sept. 1915...Lt.-Col. C. E. WILLES.
15 Sept. 1916...Major H. M. PRYCE-JONES (acting).
18 Oct. 1916...Lt.-Col. H. M. PRYCE-JONES.
5 Dec. 1917...Lt.-Col. H. R. LEE.

B.-G., R.A.

13 July 1915...Br.-Gen. W. A. M. THOMPSON.
20 Mar. 1918...Lt.-Col. W. C. E. RUDKIN (acting).
1 April 1918...Br.-Gen. T. E. TOPPING.

C.R.E.

11 Nov. 1914...Lt.-Col. A. PEARSON.
1 Sept. 1915...Lt.-Col. E. H. DE V. ATKINSON.
16 May 1916...Lt.-Col. G. S. KNOX (sick, 1/7/16).
1 July 1916...Major I. W. LAMONBY (acting).
6 July 1916...Lt.-Col. C. G. FALCON.
22 Sept. 1916...Lt.-Col. B. S. PHILLPOTTS (wd., 2/9/17 ; died 4/9/17).
3 Sept. 1917...Major J. C. I. WOOD (acting).
8 Sept. 1917...Lt.-Col. T. E. KELSALL.
[15 Nov. 1918...Lt.-Col. M. WHITWILL].

113th BDE.
(previously 128th Bde.; originally 1st Bde.)

30 Oct. '14...Br.-Gen. O. THOMAS.
25 Nov. '15...Br.-Gen. L. A. E. PRICE-
DAVIES, V.C.
15 Oct. '17...Lt.-Col. R. O. CAMPBELL
(acting).
17 Oct. '17...Br.-Gen. H. E. AP RHYS
PRYCE.
[19 Nov. '18...Br.-Gen. A. CARTON DE
WIART, V.C.].

114th BDE.
(previously 129th Bde.; originally 2nd Bde.)

27 Oct. '14...Br.-Gen. R. H. W. DUNN.
10 Nov. '15...Br.-Gen. T. O. MARDEN.
19 Aug. '17...Br.-Gen. A. R. HARMAN.
6 Aug. '18...Br.-Gen. T. R. C. PRICE.

115th BDE.
(previously 130th Bde.; originally 3rd Bde.)

20 Nov. '14...Br.-Gen. I. PHILIPPS.
13 Feb. '15...Br.-Gen. H. J. EVANS.
30 Aug. '16...Br.-Gen. C. J. HICKIE.
7 Mar. '17...Lt.-Col. F. W. SMITH (acting).
9 Mar. '17...Br.-Gen. J. R. MINSHULL-FORD (wd., 3/6/17).
4 June '17...Lt.-Col. J. H. HAYES (acting).
9 June '17...Br.-Gen. T. G. COPE (sick, 14/7/17).
14 July '17...Lt.-Col. F. W. SMITH (acting).
19 July '17...Lt.-Col. J. H. HAYES (acting).
20 July '17...Br.-Gen. G. GWYN-THOMAS (sick, 2/4/18).
2 April '18...Lt.-Col. J. B. COCKBURN (acting).
6 April '18...Br.-Gen. A. CARTON DE WIART, V.C. (tempy.).
7 April '18...Lt.-Col. J. B. COCKBURN (acting).
16 April '18...Br.-Gen. W. B. HULKE (wd., 30/8/18).
30 Aug. '18...Lt.-Col. C. C. NORMAN (acting).
5 Sept. '18...Br.-Gen. H. D. DE PREE.

GENERAL NOTES

The following also served with the 38th (Welsh) Division :—

ARTILLERY :—

I LONDON, II LONDON, III LONDON, IV LONDON (H.) BDES., B.A.C.s, and 10th D.A.C.	Transferred from 36th (Ulster) Division on 11 and 12/12/15, this Artillery served with 38th (Welsh) Division until 1–3/1/16. The four Bdes. then rejoined the reformed 56th (1st London) Division in France on 25 and 26/2/16. The D.A.C. joined 56th Division on 27/2/16 and became 56th D.A.C. (The 3 Gun Bdes. had been rearmed with 18-pdr. Q.F.s, and the two Howitzer Batteries with four 4.5″ howitzers each, in England, before attachment to the 36th Division).

38 Heavy Battery, R.G.A. (4, 60-pdrs.) was raised for the 38th (Welsh) Division, but the Heavy Battery left the Division before the move to Winchester. 88 Heavy Battery went to France with XLII H.A.G., and disembkd. at le Havre on 30/3/16.

OTHER UNITS :—77th Sanitary Section joined the 38th Division in England, went to France with the Division, and disembkd. at le Havre on 6/12/15. On 9/4/17 the Sanitary Section left the 38th Division and took over I Sanitary Area in VIII Corps, Second Army.

38th Division Motor Ambce. Workshop. On the departure of the Meerut Division from France on 30/11/15 the Meerut Div. Supply Column, Ammunition Sub-Park, and Motor Ambce. Workshop Unit were transferred to XI Corps, and then to 38th (Welsh) Division. On 7/2/16 the Workshop Unit joined the 38th Division at Clarques. In March 1916 notification was received that the Workshop Unit would be absorbed by 38th Division Supply Column, and between 2–9/4/16 the Workshop Unit disappeared.

No. 5 (Welsh) Bacteriological Section (1 offr. & 2 o.r.) was raised for the 38th (Welsh) Division, went to France with the Division, and disembkd. at le Havre on 3/12/15. On arrival in France the Section was transferred to First Army.

On 12/2/18 the reorganization of the 38th (Welsh) Division on a 9-battalion basis was completed ; and on 19/2/18 the pioneer battalion (19/Welsh) was reorganized on a 3-company basis.

NOTE.—The 43rd Division originally included four " Bantam " battalions—18, 19/R.W.F., 12/S.W.B., and 17/Welsh. In August 1915, when the 38th (formerly 43rd) Division moved to Winchester, these four battalions remained in N. Wales ; later on 19/R.W.F.. 12 S.W.B.. and 17/Welsh joined the 40th Division and served with that division on the Western Front (see Table, 40th Division).

38TH (WELSH) DIVISION [1]

Dates	Brigades (Infantry)	Battalions and attached Units	Mounted Troops	Field Artillery Brigades	Field Artillery Batteries	Bde. Ammn. Colns.	Trench Mortar Btrs. Medium	Trench Mortar Btrs. Heavy	Divnl. Ammn. Coln.	Engineers Field Coys.	Divnl. Signal Coy.	Pioneers	M.G. Units	Field Ambulances	Mobile Vety. Sec.	Divnl. Emplnt. Coy.	Divnl. Train
1915 August (England)	113th[2]; [3] 114th[3]; [4] 115th[3]; [4]	13/R.W.F., 14/R.W.F., 15/R.W.F., 16/R.W.F. 10/Welsh, 13/Welsh, 14/Welsh, 15/Welsh 17/R.W.F., 10/S.W.B., 11/S.W.B., 16/Welsh	H.Q., M.G. Sec, & D Sqdn.,[5] R. Wilts. Yeo.[6] 38th Div. Cyclist Coy.[7]	CXIX[8]; [9]....... CXX[8]; [9]....... CXXI[9]; [9]....... CXXII (H.)[9]; [10]	A, B, C, D A, B, C, D A, B, C, D A (H.), B (H.), C (H.), D (H.)	CXIX B.A.C. CXX B.A.C. CXXI B.A.C. CXXII (H.) B.A.C.	...	...	38th D.A.C.[11]	123rd[12] 124th[12] 151st[12]	38th[13]	19/Welsh (P.)[14]	...	129th[15] 130th 131st[15]	49th[16]	...	38th[17]
1915 December (France)	113th 114th 115th	13/R.W.F., 14/R.W.F., 15/R.W.F., 16/R.W.F. 10/Welsh, 13/Welsh, 14/Welsh, 15/Welsh 17/R.W.F., 10/S.W.B., 11/S.W.B., 16/Welsh	H.Q., M.G. Sec, & D Sqdn.,[18] R. Wilts. Yeo. 38th Div. Cyclist Coy.[19]	CXIX[20]....... CXX[21]....... CXXI[22]....... CXXII (H.)[23]	A, B, C, D A, B, C, D A, B, C, D A (H.), B (H.), C (H.), D (H.)	CXIX B.A.C. CXX B.A.C. CXXI B.A.C. CXXII (H.) B.A.C.	...	...	38th D.A.C.	123rd 124th 151st	38th	19/Welsh (P.)	...	129th 130th 131st	49th	...	38th
1916 June (France)	113th 114th 115th	13/R.W.F., 14/R.W.F., 15/R.W.F., 16/R.W.F.; 113th Bde. M.G. Coy.;[24] 113th T.M. Bty. 10/Welsh, 13/Welsh, 14/Welsh, 15/Welsh; 114th Bde. M.G. Coy.;[24] 114th T.M. Bty. 17/R.W.F., 10/S.W.B., 11/S.W.B., 16/Welsh; 115th Bde. M.G. Coy.;[24] 115th T.M. Bty.	...	CXIX[25]; [26] CXX[26]; [27] CXXI[28]; [26] CXXII[27]; [29]	A, B, C; D (H.) A, B, C; D (H.) A, B, C; D (H.) A, B, C; D (H.)	[33]	X.38[30] Y.38[30] Z.38[30]	V.38[31]	38th D.A.C.[32]	123rd 124th 151st	38th	19/Welsh (P.)	...	129th 130th 131st	49th	...	38th
1917 June (France)	113th 114th 115th	13/R.W.F., 14 R.W.F., 15/R.W.F.; 16/R.W.F.; 113th M.G. Coy.;[24] 113th T.M. Bty. 10/Welsh,[34] 13/Welsh, 14/Welsh, 15/Welsh; 114th M.G. Coy.;[24] 114th T.M. Bty. 17/R.W.F., 10/S.W.B., 11/S.W.B.;[24] 16/Welsh;[24] 115th M.G. Coy.;[24] 115th T.M. Bty.	...	CXXI[35]....... CXXII[36].......	A, B, C; D (H.) A, B, C; D (H.)	...	X.38 Y.38 Z.38[37]	V.38[38]	38th D.A.C.	123rd 124th 151st	38th	19/Welsh (P.)	176th[39] M.G. Coy.	129th 130th 131st	49th	235th[44]	38th

1918 March (France)		
113th	13/R.W.F., 14/R.W.F., 16/R.W.F.; 113th T.M. Bty.	
114th	13/Welsh, 14/Welsh, 15/Welsh; 114th T.M. Bty.	
115th	2/R.W.F.,¹⁰ 17/R.W.F., 10/S.W.B.; 115th T.M. Bty.	
CXXI	A, B, C; D (H.)	
CXXII	A, B, C; D (H.)	
...		
X.38 Y.38		
...		
38th D.A.C.		
123rd 124th 151st		
38th		
19/Welsh (P.)		
No. 38 Bn., M.G.C.		
129th 130th 131st		
49th		
235th		
38th		

NOTES

¹ Raised as 43rd Div. on 10/12/14; became 38th (Welsh) Div. on 29/4/15.

² Raised as 128th, 129th, and 130th Bdes.; became 113th, 114th, and 115th Bdes. on 29/4/15.

³ 13/, 14/, & 15/R.W.F. were designated: N. Wales "Pals," Caernarvon & Anglesey, and The London Welsh; 16/R.W.F. was formed of offrs. & men surplus to the W.E. of 13/R.W.F.

⁴ The battalions were designated: 1st Rhondda, 2nd Rhondda, Swansea, and Carmarthenshire.

⁵ 17/R.W.F. was raised at Llandudno and Blaenau Festiniog; the other three were designated: 1st Gwent, 2nd Gwent, and Cardiff City.

⁶ Joined the Div. at Winchester; went to France with the Div., and disembkd. at le Havre on 4/12/15.

⁷ Formed in the Div. at Conway on 22/4/15; went to France with the Div., and disembkd. at le Havre on 3/12/15.

⁸ The Bdes. were raised as 4-battery brigades; in each brigade the batteries were lettered—A, B, C, D—and each battery was a 4-gun battery. The 4 Bdes. disembkd. at le Havre between 23-25/12/15.

⁹ These three Brigades descended as follows from the Porthcawl Batteries (see p. 87): CXIX from No. 2 Battery; CXX from No. 1 (The Cardiff) Battery; and CXXI from No. 4 Battery. The Bde. numbers (CXIX, CXX, CXXI), with all existing personnel, were transferred from the original 30th Div. (see App. 1A).

¹⁰ This Howitzer Brigade (CXXII) descended from No. 3 Battery. The Bde. number (CXXII), with all existing personnel, was transferred from the original 31st Div. (see App. 1B).

¹¹ Disembkd. at le Havre on 25/12/15.

¹² Disembkd. at le Havre between 2-4/12/15.

¹³ Disembkd. at le Havre between 2-5/12/15.

¹⁴ Pioneer Bn. had Glamorgan as a sub-title; the personnel disembkd. at Boulogne on 5/12/15, the transport went via le Havre.

¹⁵ Formed in Dec. 1914 and Jan. 1915, and designated 1st, 2nd, and 3rd; on 27/3/15 they were numbered 129th, 130th (St. John), and 131st; the 3 Fd. Ambces. disembkd. at le Havre between 2-6/12/15.

¹⁶ Sec. disembkd. at le Havre on 5/12/15.

¹⁷ Train consisted of 330, 331, 332, & 333 Cos., A.S.C.; the Train disembkd. at le Havre between 2-5/12/15.

¹⁸ Attached to 1st Cav. Div. from 2-17/4/16; left 38th Div. on 9/5/16, and joined III Corps Cav. Regt. on 11/5/16; transferred to XV Corps Cav. Regt. on 21/5/16.

¹⁹ Attached to 1st Cav. Div. from 2-17/4/16; left 38th Div. on 10/5/16, and joined XI Corps Cyclist Bn.

²⁰ On 24/5/16 A/CXIX left and became A/CXXII; D/CXIX became A/CXIX; and A (H.)/CXXII joined and became D (H.)/CXIX.

²¹ On 24/5/16 B/CXX left and became B/CXXII; D/CXX became B/CXX; and B (H.)/CXXII joined and became D (H.)/CXX.

²² On 24/5/16 C/CXXI left and became C/CXXII; D/CXXI became C/CXXI; and D (H.)/CXXII joined and became D (H.)/CXXI.

²³ Between 22-24/5/16 A (H.), B (H), and D (H.) left and became D (H.)/CXIX, D (H.)/CXX, and D (H.)/CXXI; C (H.)/CXXII became D (H.)/CXXII; and A/CXIX, B/CXX, and C/CXXI joined and became A, B, and C/CXXII.

NOTES—continued

M.G. Cos. joined from Grantham: 113th, 114th, and 115th—disembkd. at le Havre on 17/5/16, and joined the Inf. Bdes. on 19/5/16.

T.M. Btles. were formed in Bdes.:
113th—38/1 & 2 on 26/12/15, became 113/A & B on 24/1/16, became 113/1 & 2 on 16/3/16, and on 17/6/16 became 113th T.M. Bty.;
114th—38/3 & 4 on 26/12/15, became 114/A & B on 24/1/18, became 114/1 & 2 on 16/3/16, and on 17/8/16 became 114th T.M. Bty.;
115th—38/5 & 6 on 26/12/15, became 115/A & B on 24/1/16, became 115/1 & 2 on 16/3/16, and on 17/6/16 became 115th T.M. Bty.

On 28/8/16 C was split up to make up A and B to 6 guns each, and on 29/8/16 D (H.)/CXX joined and became C (H.)/CXIX. On 14/1/17 CXIX became an A.F.A. Bde.: C (H.) was split up and 1 sec. made up D (H.)/CXXI and 1 sec. made up D (H.)/CXXII to 6 hows. each; B/CLXXIX (from 39th Div. Arty.) joined and became C/CXIX; on 18/1/17 L. Sec. D (H.)/CLXXIX joined and made up D (H.)/CXIX to 6 hows.; and No. 3 Sec., 38th D.A.C. became CXIX B.A.C.

On 28 & 29/8/16 B was broken up: 1 sec. made up A/CXX to 6 guns and 1 sec. made up B/CXXII; A/CXX became A/CXXI; C/CXX joined CXXII, was made up to 6 guns by 1 sec. C/CXXII, and became C/CXXII; and D (H.)/CXX became C (H.)/CXIX. CXX was then broken up.

On 29/8/16 A was split up to make up B and C to 6 guns each; and A/CXX joined and became A/CXXI. On 14/1/17 1 sec. C (H.)/CXXI joined and made up D (H.)/CXXI to 6 hows.

Between 26-29/8/16 CXXII was reorganized: C was split up and 1 sec. C made up A to 6 guns; 1 sec. B/CXX joined and made up B/CXXII; and C/CXX joined, was made up to 6 guns by 1 sec. C/CXXII, and C/CXX then became C/CXXII. On 14/1/17 1 sec. C (H.)/CXIX joined and made up D (H.)/CXXII to 6 hows.

X and Y were formed by April 1916; Z was formed at Gorre on 5/4/16.

Formed by 28/7/16.

Between 15-21/5/16 the B.A.C.s were disbanded and the D.A.C. was reorganized.

On 6/2/18 Bn. was disbanded: 32 offrs. & 600 o.r. were drafted, and remdr. joined No. 1 Entg. Bn.

On 7/2/18 Bn. was disbanded: 16 offrs. & 300 o.r. were drafted; and remdr. (550) joined No. 1 Entg. Bn.

On 12/2/18 Bn. left 115th Bde. and became Reserve Bn.; on 27/2/18 Bn. was disbanded.

On 6/2/18 Bn. was disbanded; surplus went to No. 1 Entg. Bn.

On 9/2/18 Z was disbanded and distributed between X and Y.

On 9/2/18 V left Div. and joined V/XV Corps H.T.M. Bty.

Coy. disembkd. at le Havre on 20/3/17 and joined Div. at Poperinghe on 28/3/17.

Coy. formed in the Div. by 23/6/17.

On 4/2/18 Bn. was transferred from 19th Bde., 33rd Div., and joined 115th Bde. on 6/2/18.

Bn. was formed on 2/3/18; it consisted of 113th, 114th, 115th, and 176th M.G. Cos.

38TH (WELSH) DIVISION

FORMATION, BATTLES, AND ENGAGEMENTS

This New Army Division had no existence before the outbreak of the Great War.

On the 28th September 1914 a representative meeting held in South Wales requested permission to raise a Welsh Army Corps of two divisions. On the 10th October official sanction was given to this request; by this time, however, more than one Welsh unit had sprung into being. On the 10th December the 43rd Division was formed; at the outset the infantry brigades were numbered 1st, 2nd, and 3rd, but later on they were renumbered 128th, 129th, and 130th. On the 10th April 1915 the original Fourth New Army of six divisions (30th–35th) was broken up to supply reinforcements to the first three New Armies (see Appendix I), and on the 29th April the 43rd Division was renumbered 38th and its infantry brigades then became the 113th, 114th, and 115th (see Appendix 2). About this same time the idea of forming a Welsh Army Corps was abandoned and the 38th Division was given the sub-title Welsh. The Division now belonged to the (new) Fifth New Army.

On the 16th September 1914 Welshmen in London formed a battalion with head-quarters in Holborn; on the 29th October this unit received official recognition and became 15/R.W.F. (The London Welsh), and on the 5th December the battalion joined 128th Brigade at Llandudno. Meanwhile on the 2nd October the N. Wales " Pals " Battalion (later 13/R.W.F.) began to form at Rhyl, and on the 30th the 128th (later 113th) Brigade came into existence; the Brigadier then started to raise at Llandudno the Caernarvon & Anglesey Battalion (later 14/R.W.F.). After 13/R.W.F. joined the Brigade at Llandudno on the 18th November, 16/R.W.F. was formed mainly from the surplus personnel of 13/R.W.F.

The 129th (later 114th) Brigade included battalions with sub-titles 1st and 2nd Rhondda (10/ & 13/Welsh), Swansea (14/Welsh—the Township subscribed £7,000 for the maintenance of this battalion), and Carmarthenshire (15/Welsh). The 130th (later 115th) Brigade was formed soon afterwards; its four battalions comprised 17/R.W.F., raised around Llandudno, 10/S.W.B. (1st Gwent) composed of Monmouth-shire men (colliers and iron-workers), 11/S.W.B. (2nd Gwent), and 16/Welsh (Cardiff City). The Pioneer Battalion (19/Welsh) was known as the Glamorgan Pioneers. Until supplies of Khaki were received most of the men were clothed in Brethyn Llwyd (the Welsh grey cloth).

During 1914 several thousand recruits for the Welsh Division were collected in Cardiff. From these recruits one field battery (later A/CXX), one battalion (13/Welsh, –2nd Rhondda), and one field ambulance (2nd St. John–later 130th) were formed; the remainder were sorted out and drafted to the various arms represented in the Welsh Division.

In the Artillery no batteries (except A/CXX) were formed until the beginning of January 1915; four batteries (Nos. 1–4) were then formed at Porthcawl. The Cardiff Battery (see above) joined at Porthcawl and became No. 1 Battery. In February the four batteries moved to Pwllheli, and each was then ordered to form a second battery. In March and April each of the eight batteries was divided into two, and it was in this way that the sixteen batteries were formed for the four brigades of the Welsh Division Artillery. Three of the numbers for the field artillery brigades (CXIX, CXX, and CXXI), together with the existing personnel, were transferred to the 38th Division from the original 30th Division, when the latter was broken up (App. 1 A, note 6); and the other artillery brigade number (CXXII), together with existing personnel, was transferred from the broken-up 31st Division (App. 1B, note 7). Nevertheless each of the four brigades descended from one of the four original batteries: CXX from No. 1 (the Cardiff Battery), CXIX from No. 2, CXXII (II.) from No. 3, and CXXI from No. 4. The Artillery felt the need of equipment even more than the infantry and for some time gun-drill had to be carried out with locally improvised weapons and vehicles—at first an old pair of 'bus wheels fitted with a pole and hook was used, in order that limbering up could be practised. It was April 1915 before any horses reached the batteries.

The 123rd and 124th Field Companies were formed from 650 skilled craftsmen who had been originally included in the 13/Welsh—raised at Cardiff; and later on the 151st Field Company was formed at Abergavenny from the surplus personnel of the 123rd and 124th Field Companies.

On the 19th January 1915 Divisional Head Quarters opened at Colwyn Bay; but at this time the units were scattered from Rhyl to Abergavenny and no divisional exercises could be carried out. In June 1915 some of the units of the Welsh Division were moved to Winchester, and by August 1915 the whole Division was concentrated there. A fair proportion of officers and non-commissioned-officers with war experience were attached to the Division to assist in training it on the suitable terrain which was now available. The Division was trained principally for open warfare; it was considered that trench warfare could be better and more rapidly assimilated in France. It was not until the last fortnight, however, that sufficient rifles were received, and then everything gave place to musketry instruction and rifle shooting; before embarkation every man had been put through a course of musketry.

The Division was now warned to prepare to move to France; depot units were separated and all service units were rapidly raised to war establishment. On the 21st November the advance party left for France; and on the 29th November the 38th (Welsh) Division was reviewed on Crawley Down by H.M. the Queen accompanied by H.R.H. Princess Mary. On the 1st December the Division began to leave Winchester, but the Divisional Artillery had to remain in England during December to carry out gun-practice at Larkhill. Between the 2nd–6th December the remainder of the Division crossed to le Havre; on the 6th it completed its concentration west of Aire and joined XI Corps. Between the 23rd–25th December the Divisional Artillery disembarked at le Havre and on the 28th rejoined the Division near St. Venant; meanwhile, between 11th December 1915 and 1st January 1916, the 56th (1st London) Division Artillery had been attached to the 38th Division.

For the remainder of the Great War the 38th (Welsh) Division served on the Western Front in France and Belgium and was engaged in the following operations:

1915

1916

BATTLES OF THE SOMME

5–11 July	**Battle of Albert** [XV Corps, Fourth Army].
7–11 Jul	**Mametz Wood.**

1917

31 July–6 Aug.; 19 Aug.–11 Sept.	**BATTLES OF YPRES** [XIV Corps, Fifth Army].
31 July–2 August ...	**Battle of Pilckem Ridge** [XIV Corps, Fifth Army].

1918

FIRST BATTLES OF THE SOMME

5 April ... ... **Battle of the Ancre** [In Reserve, V Corps, Third Army].

THE ADVANCE TO VICTORY
SECOND BATTLES OF THE SOMME

21–23 August ... ... **Battle of Albert** (V Corps, Third Army).

31 Aug.–3 Sept. ... ... **Second Battle of Bapaume** (V Corps, Third Army).

BATTLES OF THE HINDENBURG LINE

12 September ... ... **Battle of Havrincourt** (V Corps, Third Army).

18 September ... ... **Battle of Epehy** (V Corps, Third Army).

5 October ... ... **Battle of the Beaurevoir Line** (V Corps, Third Army).

8 October ... ... **Battle of Cambrai** (V Corps, Third Army).

THE FINAL ADVANCE IN PICARDY

17–22 October ... ... **Battle of the Selle** (V Corps, Third Army).

4 November ... ... **Battle of the Sambre** (V Corps, Third Army).

At 6 a.m. on the 5th November the 33rd Division passed through the front line, and the 38th Division then collected in the Forest of Mormal with headquarters at Locquignol. At 9 p.m. on the 7th the 38th Division relieved the 33rd on the right of the V Corps, beyond the Sambre. During the next three days the advanced guard brigade (113th) pushed steadily forward; and when the Armistice brought hostilities to a close, at 11 a.m. on the 11th November, the brigade had its headquarters established in the suitably named Wattignies la Victoire.

On the 3rd December H.M. the King visited the Division and saw all the troops on the Aulnoye—Petit Maubeuge road. December was spent in reorganizing and training, and during the month 3000 miners left for demobilization. On the 27th December the Division began withdrawing from the Aulnoye area; and by the 14th January 1919 it had settled down in billets to the east of Amiens, with headquarters at Querrieu. During January demobilization continued and drafts left for the Army of Occupation. From the 5th–8th February H.R.H. the Prince of Wales stayed with the Division and visited all the units. During the month 2,243 left the Division for demobilization, and 644 proceeded to join the Army of the Rhine, and in March the Division lost 1438 from the same causes. In June the units were disbanded, stores were returned, and on the 17th June 1919 the Division ceased to exist. During the Great War the 38th (Welsh) Division lost 28,635 killed, wounded, and missing.

NOTES :—

A. **38th DIVISION ARTILLERY, APRIL 1918.**—Early in April 1918 the 38th Division moved from the Armentières Front to the vicinity of Albert; the Divisional Artillery, however, remained on the Lys Front. From 7–14/4/18 the 38th Division Artillery was attached to the 34th Division and took part with the 34th Division in the Battles of the Lys—Battle of Estaires (9–11/4), and Battle of Bailleul (12–14/4). On 14 and 15/4 38th D.A. served with 59th Div. in the concluding part of the Battle of Bailleul (14 & 15/4). 38th D.A. served with the 34th Div. in the First Battle of Kemmel Ridge (17–19/4); with the 25th Div. in the Second Battle of Kemmel Ridge (25 & 26/4); and in the Battle of the Scherpenberg (29/4/18) with the 25th Div. (H.Q. 38th D.A. & CXXI) and 49th Div. (CXXII). At the end of May the 38th Division Artillery rejoined the 38th Division, in reserve west of Albert.

B. In November 1918, during the Final Advance, C Sqdn. Queen's Own Oxfordshire Hussars and A Sqdn. 5th Cyclist Regt. (N. Irish Horse) were attached to the 38th Division.

39TH DIVISION

G.O.C.

23 August 1915	Major-General N. W. BARNARDISTON.
5 June 1916	Br.-Gen. G. G. S. CAREY (tempy.).
8 June 1916	Major-General R. DAWSON.
13 July 1916	Major-General G. J. CUTHBERT.
20 August 1917	Major-General E. FEETHAM.
7 March 1918	Br.-Gen. G. A. S. CAPE (acting–killed, 18/3/18).
18 March 1918	Br.-Gen. M. L. HORNBY (acting).
23 March 1918	Major-General E. FEETHAM (killed, 29/3/18).
29 March 1918	Br.-Gen. W. G. H. THOMPSON (acting).
30 March 1918	Major-General C. A. BLACKLOCK.
30 August 1918	Br.-Gen. A. B. HUBBACK (acting).
10 September 1918	Major-General N. MALCOLM.
[27 December 1918	Br.-Gen. J. H. HALL].

G.S.O.1.

14 Aug. 1915...Lt.-Col. S. T. HALLIDAY, V.C. (sick, 12/7/16).
12 July 1916...Lt.-Col. F. W. GOSSETT.
10 Oct. 1918...Captain F. J. JEBENS (acting).

A.-A. & Q.-M.-G.

30 Aug. 1915...Lt.-Col. LORD DECIES (sick, March 1916).
4 Mar. 1916...Lt.-Col. B. C. DWYER.
24 Jan. 1917...Lt.-Col. A. E. S. CLARKE.
11 Feb. 1917...Lt.-Col. A. F. STEWART.
26 July 1917...Lt.-Col. R. E. HOLMES À COURT.
21 Aug. 1918...Major J. C. COOKE (acting).
22 Oct. 1918...Major G. TAYLOR (acting).

B.-G., R.A.

21 Sept. 1915...Br.-Gen. C. E. GOULBURN.
26 Feb. 1916...Br.-Gen. R. W. FULLER.
24 Mar. 1916...Br.-Gen. G. GILLSON.
11 Oct. 1917...Lt.-Col. C. H. KILNER (acting).
18 Oct. 1917...Br.-Gen. G. A. S. CAPE (killed, 18/3/18).
18 Mar. 1918...Lt.-Col. E. W. S. BROOKE (acting).
26 Mar. 1918...Br.-Gen. W. G. H. THOMPSON.
29 Mar. 1918...Lt.-Col. E. W. S. BROOKE (acting).
30 Mar. 1918...Br.-Gen. W. G. H. THOMPSON.

C.R.E.

8 Oct. 1915...Lt.-Col. C. G. BURNABY.
31 July 1916...Lt.-Col. S. SMITH (acting).
10 Aug. 1916...Lt.-Col. L. E. HOPKINS.
26 June 1917...Major D. H. HAMMONDS (acting).
2 July 1917...Lt.-Col. H. J. COUCHMAN.
1 Nov. 1918...Major G. S. MARSTON (acting).

116th BDE.
(originally 121st Bde.)

1 April '15...Br.-Gen. J. E. WATSON.
13 April '16...Br.-Gen. M. L. HORNBY.
18 Mar. '18...Lt.-Col. W. C. MILLWARD.
(acting).
23 Mar. '18...Br.-Gen. M. L. HORNBY
(wd., 28/3/18).
23 Mar. '18...Lt.-Col. W. C. MILLWARD
(acting).
1 April '18...Br.-Gen. L. J. WYATT.
4 Nov. '18...Lt.-Col. D. J. WARD
(acting).
[18 Dec. '18...Lt.-Col. R. G. HELY-
HUTCHINSON (acting).]

117th BDE.
(new formation)

15 July '15...Br.-Gen. P. HOLLAND
(sick, 2/4/16).
2 April '16...Lt.-Col. E. B. HALES
(acting).
6 April '16...Br.-Gen. P. HOLLAND.
15 April '16...Br.-Gen. R. D. F.
OLDMAN.
5 Mar. '17...Lt.-Col. C. H. STEPNEY
(acting).
9 Mar. '17...Br.-Gen. G. A.
ARMYTAGE.
4 Oct. '18...Lt.-Col. C. C. STAPLEDEN
(acting).
7 Oct. '18...Br.-Gen. Hon. W. P.
HORE-RUTHVEN.
17 Oct. '18...Br.-Gen. C. W. COMPTON.
6 Nov. '18...Captain M. A. ELLISSEN
(acting).

On 18/11/18 the 117th Bde. was broken up and the details were dispersed.

On 19/11/18 No. 2 L. of C. Area Reception Camp (for malarial convalescents) joined 39th Div. and became 117th Bde.

117th BDE.

[19 Sept. '18]...Br.-Gen. T. S. H. WADE.

118th BDE.
(new formation)

8 July '15...Br.-Gen. W. BROMILOW.
15 April '16...Br.-Gen. T. P. BARRINGTON (sick, 7/7/16).
7 July '16...Lt.-Col. G. A. M'L. SCEALES (acting).
13 July '16...Br.-Gen. E. H. FINCH-HATTON (sick, 4/12/16).
4 Dec. '16...Lt.-Col. G. A. M'L. SCEALES (acting).
3 Feb. '17...Br.-Gen. E. H. C. P. BELLINGHAM (captured, 28/3/18).
28 Mar. '18...Lt.-Col. E. T. SAINT (acting).
3 April '18...Br.-Gen. A. B. HUBBACK.
20 Oct. '18...Lt.-Col. H. R. BROWN (acting).
22 Oct. '18...Br.-Gen. M. L. HORNBY.
6 Nov. '18...Lt.-Col. H. R. BROWN (acting).

On 4/12/18 the 118th Bde. was broken up and the details were dispersed.

On 20/9/18 the 197th Bde. left 66th Div. and was transferred to L. of C. ; on 18/11/18 the 197th Bde. joined 39th Div. (see note 59; and note on p. 97).

197th BDE.

[3 April '18...Br.-Gen. L. L. WHEATLEY.
22 Sept. '18...Lt.-Col. A. W. BLOCKLEY (acting).
1 Oct. '18...Lt.-Col. G. V. W. HILL (acting).
6 Oct. '18]...Br.-Gen. J. H. HALL.

GENERAL NOTES

The following Units also served with the 39th Division :—

INFANTRY :—10/Q.O.R.W.K. (Kent County), 11/Q.O.R.W.K. (Lewisham), 20/Middx. (Shoreditch), and 21/Middx. (Islington) joined 118th Bde. on its formation in London at the beginning of July 1915 ; and served with it until 16/10/15, when the 118th Bde. was reorganized at Aldershot. 10/Q.O.R.W.K. then joined 123rd Bde. and 11/Q.O.R.W.K. joined 122nd Bde. in the 41st Division. 20/ and 21/Middx. remained in 118th Bde. until 23/2/16 (see notes 5 and 16).

OTHER UNITS :—82nd Sanitary Section went to France with the Division and disembkd. at le Havre on 8/3/16. On 17/4/17 the Section left the Division and took over No. 8 Sanitary District, Second Army.

39th Division Motor Ambce. Workshop went to France with the Division ; disembkd. at Rouen on 5/3/16, left Rouen on 9/3/16, and joined Division on 11/3/16. On 9/4/16 the Workshop ceased to exist, and personnel and vehicles were absorbed by 39th Div. Supply Column.

On 20/2/18 the reorganization of the 39th Division on a 9-battalion basis was completed ; and by March 1918 the pioneer battalion (13/Glouc.) was reorganized on a 3-company basis.

39th Division Composite Brigade (Br.-Gen. A. B. Hubback) was formed on 10/4/18 ; it consisted of :—

> No. 1 Bn.—11/R. Suss. & 1/1/Herts. (with 1st Line Tpt. of 1/1/Herts.);
> No. 2 Bn.—13/Glouc. & 13/R. Suss. (with 1st Line Tpt. of 13/R. Suss.);
> No. 3 Bn.—formed from 117th Bde. ;
> No. 4 Bn.—formed from 118th Bde. ;
> No. 5 Bn.*—formed from 116th, 117th, 118th Bdes., & 18/Glouc. ;
> together with :—118th Light T.M. Bty. ;
> No. 4 Coy., 39th Div. Train.

39th Division Composite Bde. took part with the Second Army in the Battles of the Lys 1918. The Composite Bde. was engaged on 16/4/18 with XXII Corps on Wytschaete Ridge ; fought with XXII Corps in the First (17–19/4) and Second (25 & 26/4) Battles of Kemmel Ridge ; and was in Reserve to XXII Corps in the Battle of the Scherpenberg (29/4/18).

On 30/4/18 No. 5 Composite Bn. rejoined 39th Div. and all ranks then rejoined their Brigade details ; on 6/5/18 the remainder of the Composite Bde. rejoined 39th Div., and the Composite Bde. was then broken up.

39th Division Artillery.—R.A. Hd. Qrs., CLXXIV, CLXXXVI, and X and Y Medium T.M. Bties.,** with No. 1 Coy., 39th Div. Train. and Ammn. Sec. 39th Div. M.T. Coy.—remained in the Line, after the withdrawal of the 39th Division, and formed a sub-group under 16th Div. Arty. On 4/4/18 39th Div. Arty. (in XIX Corps) took part in the Battle of the Avre and lost 3 offrs., 70 o.r., and 110 horses. On 12–14/4/18 39th Div. Arty. was relieved in the Line and by this time it had lost : 330 all ranks, 250 horses, 5, 18-pdrs., and 2, 4.5″ hows. On 15/4/18 39th Div. Arty. was transferred to VI Corps and the two Brigades went up into the line on 29 and 30/4/18. 39th Div. Arty. remained in VI Corps until June ; was transferred to IV Corps on 19–22/6/18, to Second Army on 3/7/18, was posted to II Corps, and went into the line on 7/7/18. On 5/8/18 39th Div. Arty. was transferred to XV Corps and went into the line again on 15/8/18. On 22 and 28/8/18 39th Div. Arty. was transferred to First Army, on 28/8/18 it came under XVII Corps, and on 24/8/18 was transferred to Canadian Corps ; and, with this Corps, 39th Div. Arty. took part in The Advance to Victory, and was engaged in the Second Battles of Arras 1918 (Battle of the Scarpe, 26–30/8; and Battle of the Drocourt–Quéant Line, 2 and 3/9/18) ; The Battles of the Hindenburg Line (Battle of the Canal du Nord, 27/9–1/10 ; and Battle of Cambrai, 8 & 9/10/18) ; and the Pursuit to the Selle (9–12/10/18). Until the end of October 1918 the 39th Div. Arty. also took an active part (with the CDN. Corps) in the Final Advance in Picardy ; and, still in the CDN. Corps in November, 39th Div. Arty. was engaged in the Battle of Valenciennes (1 & 2/11/18). On 4/11/18 39th Div. Arty. was transferred to VIII Corps and joined First Army Reserve ; its active participation in the Great War had come to an end.

---

* No. 5 Composite Bn. (Lt.-Col. C. H. N. Seymour, 17/K.R.R.C.) was formed on 12/4/18, and it consisted of :—

> A Coy.⎱ provided by 117th Bde.,
> B Coy.⎰
> C Coy.—provided by 116th Bde.,
> D Coy.—provided by 118th Bde., reinforced by details of 13/Glouc. ; together with 1st Line Tpt. of 17/K.R.R.C.

** X and Y Medium T.M. Bties. were disbanded on 15/5/18 (see note 55).

39TH DIVISION [1]

Dates	INFANTRY — Brigades	Battalions and attached Units	Mounted Troops	ARTILLERY — Field Artillery Brigades	Batteries	Bde. Ammn. Colns.	Trench Mortar Btles. Medium	Heavy	Divnl. Ammn. Coln.	Engineers Field Cos.	Signal Service Divnl. Signal Coy.	Pioneers	M.G. Units	Field Ambulances	Mobile Vety. Sec.	Divnl. Emplnt. Coy.	Divnl. Train
1915 October (England)	116th[2];[3]	11/R. Suss., 12/R. Suss., 13/R. Suss., 14/Hants.	E. Sqdn.,[4] S. Irish Horse[5] 39th Div. Cyclist Coy.[7]	CLXXIV[6]	A, B, C, D	CLXXIV B.A.C.	...	...	39th D.A.C.[8]	225th[9] 227th[9] 234th[9]	39th[10]	13/ Glouc. (P.)[11]	...	132nd[15] 133rd[15] 134th[15]	50th[16]	...	39th[14]
	117th[2];[3]	16/Sher. For., 17/Sher. For., 17/K.R.R.C., 16/R.B.		CLXXIX[6]	A, B, C, D	CLXXIX B.A.C.											
	118th[2];[3]	13/E. Surr.,[12] 20/Middx.,[13] 21/Middx.,[13] 14/A. & S.H.[13]		CLXXXIV[6]	A, B, C, D	CLXXXIV B.A.C.											
				CLXXXVI (H.)[6]	A (H.), B (H.), C (H.), D (H.)	CLXXXVI (H.) B.A.C.											
1916 March (France)	116th	11/R. Suss., 12/R. Suss., 13/R. Suss., 14/Hants.	E. Sqdn.,[22] S. Irish Horse 39th Div. Cyclist Coy.[23]	CLXXIV[24]	A, B, C, D –	CLXXIV B.A.C.	...	...	39th D.A.C.	225th 227th 234th	39th	13/ Glouc. (P.)	...	132nd 133rd 134th	50th	...	39th
	117th	16/Sher. For., 17/Sher. For., 17/K.R.R.C., 16/R.B.		CLXXIX[25]	A, B, C, D	CLXXIX B.A.C.											
	118th	1/6/Ches.,[17] 1/4/B.W.,[18] 1/5/B.W.,[19] 1/1/Camb.,[20] 1/1/Herts.[21]		CLXXXIV[26]	A, B, C, D	CLXXXIV B.A.C.											
				CLXXXVI (H.)[27]	A (H.), B (H.), C (H.), D (H.)	CLXXXVI (H.) B.A.C.											
1916 June (France)	116th	11/R. Suss., 12/R. Suss., 13/R. Suss., 14/Hants.; 116th Bde. M.G. Coy.;[30] 116th T.M. Bty.[31]	...	CLXXIV[24],[39] CLXXIX[25],[40] CLXXXIV[37],[38]	A, B, C; D (H.) A, B, C; D (H.) A, B, C; D (H.)	[28]	X.39[42] Y.39 Z.39	V.39[43]	39th D.A.C.[29]	225th 227th 234th	39th	13/ Glouc. (P.)	...	132nd 133rd 134th	50th	...	39th
	117th	16/Sher. For., 17/Sher. For., 17/K.R.R.C., 16/R.B.; 117th Bde. M.G. Coy.;[32] 117th T.M. Bty.[33]		CLXXXVI (H.)[41]	A, B, C; D (H.)												
	118th	1/6/Ches., 4/5/B.W.,[34] 1/1/Camb., 1/1/Herts.; 118th Bde. M.G. Coy.;[35] 118th T.M. Bty.[36]															
1917 July (France)	116th	11/R. Suss., 12/R. Suss., 13/R. Suss.,[37] 14/Hants.; 116th M.G. Coy.[44] 116th T.M. Bty.	...	CLXXIV[39] CLXXXVI[42]	A, B, C; D (H.) A, B, C; D (H.)	...	X.39[41] Y.39[41] Z.39[41]	V.39[44]	39th D.A.C.	225th 227th 234th	39th	13/ Glouc. (P.)	228th M.G. Coy.[45]	132nd 133rd 134th	50th	236th[46]	39th
	117th	16/Sher. For., 17/Sher. For.,[39] 17/K.R.R.C., 16/R.B.; 117th M.G. Coy.[44] 117th T.M. Bty.															
	118th	1/6/Ches., 4/5/B.W.,[40] 1/1/Camb., 1/1/Herts.;[45] 118th M.G. Coy.[44] 118th T.M. Bty.															

1918 March (France)	116th	117th	118th	CLXXIV CLXXXVI	...	39th D.A.C.	...	225th 227th 234th	39th	13/ Glouc. (P.)	No. 39 Bn. M.G.C.	132nd 133rd 134th	50th	238th	39th
116th	11/R. Suss., 13/R. Suss., 116th 1/1/Herts.; T.M. Bty.			A, B, C; D (H.) A, B, C; D (H.)	...		..:				X.39 Y.39				
117th	16/Sher.For., 17/K.R.R.C., 117th T.M. 16/R.B., Bty.														
118th	1/6/Ches., 4/5/B.W., 1/1/ Camb.; 118th T.M.Bty.														

Between 16/5—1/6/18 the 39th Division was reduced to cadre

NOTES

[1] Formed at Winchester early in August 1915 as 39th Div. This Division was a new formation.

[2] On 12/7/15 authority was given to raise 116th, 117th, & 118th Inf. Bdes. (W.O.—20/Inf./728—A.G.1). 117th & 118th Bdes. were new formations; but 121st Bde. (from original 40th—later 33rd—Div.) joined 39th Div. and, on arrival, became 116th Bde.

[3] 11/, 12/, 13/R. Suss. were designated 1st, 2nd, 3rd South Down; and 14/Hants. was designated 1st Portsmouth.

[4] The Bns. were designated: Chatsworth Rifles, Welbeck Rangers, B.E.I., and St. Pancras.

[5] The Bde. was formed in London in July 1915 (see General Notes), and it was reorganized at Aldershot between 16-23/10/15; its 3 senior battalions were designated Wadsworth, Shoreditch, and Islington (20/Inf./728 of 13/10/15).

On 24/2/16 Bde. H.Q. disembkd. at le Havre, and on 29/2/16 the Bde. was reformed at Renescure (notes 15 —21).

[6] Sqdn. disembkd. at le Havre on 14/3/16, and joined Div. at Blaringhem on 17/3/16.

[7] Coy. was formed at Seaford and joined Div. at Witley on 14/11/15. Coy. disembkd. at le Havre on 4/3/16.

[8] The Bdes. and D.A.C. were raised at The Thames Ironworks, Greenwich (CLXXIV), Lee Green (CLXXIX & CLXXXVI), and Deptford (CLXXXVI & D.A.C.); on 1 & 2/10/15 they joined the Div. at Aldershot and Ewshott. The Bdes. were raised as 4-battery brigades; in each brigade the batteries were lettered—A, B, C, D— and each battery was a 4-gun battery. The 4 Bdes. and D.A.C. disembkd. at le Havre between 4-8/3/16.

[9] The 3 Fd. Cos. were formed at Marton Hall, Yorkshire, and designated Stockton on Tees; they joined the Div. at Aldershot on 7/10/15; and disembkd. at le Havre between 4-8/3/16.

[10] Formed at Norbury and designated Empire; joined the Div. at Aldershot on 29/9/15; and disembkd. at le Havre on 4/3/16.

[11] Bn. was designated Forest of Dean Pioneers. Bn. joined the Div. at Winchester on 15/8/15, and disembkd. at le Havre on 4/3/16.

[12] The Fd. Ambces. trained near Farnham, went to France with the Div., and disembkd. at le Havre between 4-7/3/16.

[13] Joined Div. at Witley on 10/11/15, and disembkd. at le Havre on 8/3/16.

[14] The Train was raised at Pangbourne and consisted of 284, 285, 286, 287 Cos., A.S.C. 287 Coy. joined the Div. at Romsey on 8/8/15, and remdr. of the Train joined at Rushmoor Camp on 27/9/15. The Train disembkd. at le Havre between 5-7/3/16.

[15] On 29/2/16 Bde. was reformed at Renescure (note 5).

[16] The four Bns. left 118th Bde. at Witley on 23/2/16. 13/R. Suss. and 14/A. & S.H. joined 120th Bde., 40th Div.; and 14/ & 21/Middx. joined 121st Bde., 40th Div.

[17] Bn. joined 15th Bde., 5th Div., on 17/12/14; G.H.Q. Troops on 1/3/15; 20th Bde., 7th Div., on 9/1/16; left on 25/2/16, and joined 118th Bde. on 29/2/16.

[18] Bn. joined 21st (Bareilly) Bde., 7th (Meerut) Div., on 4/3/15; 139th Bde., 46th Div., on 6/11/15; 44th Bde., 15th Div., on 14/11/15; 154th Bde., 51st Div., on 6/1/16; left on 25/2/16, and joined 118th Bde., on 29/2/16. On 15/3/16 Bn. amalgamated with 5/B.W. (note 19) and became 4/5/B.W.

[19] Bn. joined 24th Bde., 8th Div., on 13/11/14; became pioneers on 18/10/15; transferred to 154th Bde., 51st Div., on 6/1/16; and joined 118th Bde. on 29/2/16. On 15/3/16 Bn. amalgamated with 4/B.W. (note 18) and became 4/5/B.W.

[20] Bn. joined 27th Div. on 18/2/15; posted to 82nd Bde., 27th Div., in March 1915; transferred to VII Corps Troops on 15/11/15; and joined 118th Bde. on 29/2/16.

[21] Bn. joined 4th (Gds.) Bde., 2nd Div., on 20/11/14; transferred to 6th Bde., 2nd Div., on 19/8/15; to G.H.Q. Troops on 28/2/16; and joined 118th Bde. on 29/2/16.

[22] Sqdn. left Div. on 10/5/16 and joined I Corps Cav. Regt. on 13/5/16.

[23] Coy. left Div. on 10/5/16 and joined XV Corps Cyclist Bn. on 11/5/16.

[24] On 20/5/18 B left and became A/CLXXXVI; D then became B; and A (H.)/CLXXXVI joined and became D (H.)/CLXXIV.

[25] On 20/5/16 C left and became C/CLXXXVI; D then became C; and B (H.)/CLXXXVI joined and became D (H.)/CLXXIX.

[26] On 20/5/16 B left and became B/CLXXXVI; D then became B; and C (H.)/CLXXXVI joined and became D (H.)/CLXXXIV.

[27] On 20/5/16 A (H.), B (H.), C (H.) left and became D (H.)/CLXXIV, D (H.)/CLXXIX, and D (H.)/CLXXXIV; and B/CLXXIV, B/CLXXXIV, and C/CLXXIX and became A, B, C/CLXXXVI; D (H.) remained D (H.), as follows:—

116th—formed at Grantham on 1/3/16, disembkd. at le Havre on 16/5/16, and joined Bde. at Loisne on 18/5/16;
117th—disembkd. at le Havre on 16/5/16 and joined Bde. near Bethune on 18/5/16;
118th—formed on 21/3/16 at Walton Cappel, from M.G. Secs. of Bns. in 118th Bde.

Light T.M. Btles. were formed as follows:—
116/1 & 116/2 were formed on 9/4/16, and by 16/6/16 became 116th T.M. Bty.;
117/1 & 117/2 were formed by 15/4/16, and on 18/6/16 became 117th T.M. Bty.;
118/1 & 118/2 were formed by 7/4/16, and between 16/6-1/7/16 they became 118th T.M. Bty.

[28] The M.G. Cos. were formed and joined Bdes. as follows:

NOTES—continued

to 6 guns each; and A/CLXXXIV joined and became C/CLXXIV. On 18/1/17 D (H.) was made up to 6 hows. by R. Sec., C (H.)/CLXXIX.

On 30/11/16 C was broken up: R. Sec. made up A and L. Sec. made up B to 6 guns each; and D (H.)/CLXXIX joined and became C (H.)/CLXXIX. On 18/1/17 CLXXIX was broken up: A became A/CCLXXVII A.F.A. Bde.; B became C/CIX A.F.A. Bde.; R. Sec. C (H.) made up D (H.)/CLXXIX to 6 hows.; L. Sec. C (H.) made up D (H.)/CCLXXVII A.F.A. Bde.; and L. Sec. D (H.) made up D (H.)/CIX A.F.A. Bde. to 6 hows.; 39th D.A.C. absorbed CLXXIX A.F.A. Bde. H.Q.

At m/n. 30/11/16 CLXXXIV was broken up to make up A and B to 6 guns each; A then became C/CLXXIV and B became C/CLXXXVI; D (H.) became C (H.)/CLXXIX.

On 29/11/16 C was broken up to make up A and B to 6 guns each; and B/CLXXXIV joined and became C/CLXXXVI. On 30/1/17 D (H.) was made up to 6 hows. by L. Sec. C (H.)/CLXXIX.

X, Y, and Z were formed by 17/6/16.

V Heavy T.M. Bty. was formed on 27/8/16 at Bus en Artois, from personnel from Third Army School of Mortars.

On 20/5/16 D.A.C. was reorganized and B.A.C.s were abolishd.

On 8/2/18 Bn. was disbanded: between 8–12/2/18 15 offrs. & 449 o.r. were drafted; on 14/2/18 surplus proceeded to Rft. Camp, and on 20/2/18 joined 17/Entg. Bn.

On 20/2/18 Bn. left Div. and marched to C Camp; on 23/2/18 Bn. was disbanded and was used to form A and B Coys. in 17/Entg. Bn.

Drafts left the Bn. between 6–8/2/18; on 8/2/18 Bn. was disbanded and surplus joined 17/Entg. Bn.

On 8/2/18 Bn. was transferred from 118th Bde. to 116th Bde.

On 7/2/18 X, Y, and Z (Medium) and V (Heavy) T.M. Btles. were reorganized into X and Y (Medium) T.M. Btles.—each with six 6" Newton T.M.s.

Coy. disembkd. at le Havre on 12/7/17 and joined Div. at Poperinghe on 19/7/17.

Coy. was formed by 30/8/17.

Bn. was formed between 3–14/3/18; it consisted of 116, 117, 118, and 228 M.G. Cos. and they became A, B, C, and D Coys. On 8/4/18 D Coy. was disbanded and distributed between A, B, and C; and a composite m.g. coy. joined from 66th Div. and became D Coy. On 11/8/18 Bn. marched to Morbecque, joined 40th Div., and Bn. served for remdr. of the War with the 40th Div.

On 23/5/18 Bn. was reduced to T.C. and surplus (6 offrs. & 367 o.r.) went to Base. On 17/6/18 T.C. was transferred to 118th Bde., and proceeded to England on 30/6/18. On 15/8/18 T.C. was reformed; and on 15/10/18 went to N. Russia with 236th Bde. (late 78th Bde.).

On 23/5/18 Bn. was reduced to T.C. and surplus (3 offrs. & 132 o.r.) went to Base. On 17/6/18 T.C. was transferred to 118th Bde., disbanded on 14/8/18, and absorbed by 4/R. Suss. in 101st Bde., 34th Div.

On 9/5/18 Bn. was transferred to 112th Bde., 37th Div., and joined on 11/5/18.

On 16/5/18 Bn. was reduced to T.C. and surplus (234 o.r.) went to Base at Etaples. On 16/8/18 T.C. was transferred to 66th Div., and on 20/9/18 went to L. of C. with 197th Bde.

On 16/5/18 Bn. was reduced to T.C. and surplus (265 o.r.) went to Base. On 16/8/18 T.C. was transferred to 66th Div., and on 20/9/18 went to L. of C. with 197th Bde.

On 16/5/18 Bn. was reduced to T.C. and surplus (277 o.r.) went to Base. On 16/8/18 T.C. was transferred to 66th Div., and on 20/9/18 went to L. of C. with 197th Bde.

On 28/5/18 Bn. was transferred to 25th Div.; on 8/7/18 Bn. joined 21st Bde., 30th Div.

On 6/5/18 Bn. was reformed; and on 14/5/18 was transferred to 46th Bde., 15th Div., joined on 15/5/18, and on 5/6/18 was transferred from 46th Bde. to 44th Bde.

On 9/5/18 Bn. was transferred to 38th Bde., 12th Div., and joined on 10/5/18 at Lealvilliers.

When the Division was reduced to Cadre in May 1918 the Bde. T.M. Btles. were broken up (by 7/5/18).

On 15/5/18 X and V were disbanded; the personnel was posted to CLXXXIV, CLXXXVI Bdes., and to Third Army Rft. Camp. (Authy.—Third Army letter of 9/5/18, No. A/A/1539/5).

Between 10/4–6/5/18 Bn. was reduced to T.C., and on 6/5/18 the surplus left for Base at Etaples. On 15/8/18 T.C. was transferred to 66th Div., and joined on 16/8/18. On 20/9/18 T.C. went to L. of C. with 197th Bde.

From 10/4/18 the M.G. Bn. was attached to various divisions; and it took part with them, up to the Armistice, in the Advance to Victory. From 11/9/18 to the end of the War No. 39 M.G. Bn. served with the 40th Div.

On 18/11/18 117th Bde. was broken up and the details were dispersed. On 19/11/18 No. 2 L. of C. Area Reception Camp (for malarial convalescents) joined 39th Div. and became 117th Bde.

On 4/12/18 118th Bde. was broken up and the details were dispersed. On 18/11/18 197th Bde. (in 66th Div. until 20/9/18), with eight cadre battalions (see note to Table of T.C.s, page 97), joined 39th Div., and on 4/12/18 took the place of the 118th Bde.

The following Training Cadres served with the 39th Division (21/5–11/11/18):

	Unit	From	Reduced to Training Cadre	Served with 39th Div. From	Served with 39th Div. To	Transferred to, Absorbed by, or Disbanded	Notes
39th Div.	25/N.F.	102nd Bde., 34th Div.	15 & 16/5/18	17/6 –	16/8/18	66th Div.	On 20/9/18 to L. of C. with 197th Bde. On 9/9/18 joined 236th Bde. in England, and on 15/10/8 embkd. for N. Russia.
	13/Gr. How.	121st Bde., 40th Div.	6/5/18	17/6 –	29/6/18	74th Bde., 25th Div.	
	13/E. Surr.	119th Bde., 40th Div.	5/5/18	17/6 –	29/6/18	7th Bde., 25th Div.	On 20/9/18 to L. of C. with 197th Bde.
	7/Sher. For.	178th Bde., 59th Div.	7/5/18	15/8 –	16/11/18	116th Bde.	
	21/Middx.	119th Bde., 40th Div.	5/5/18	17/6 –	29/6/18	74th Bde., 25th Div.	
	14/H.L.I.	120th Bde., 40th Div.	6/5/18	17/6 –	16/8/18	66th Div.	On 20/9/18 to L. of C. with 197th Bde.

Bde.	Battalion	Joined from	Date	Period	Disposal	Remarks
116th Bde.	15/R. Scots	101st Bde., 34th Div.	16/5/18	17/6 – 28/7/18	XV Corps Rft. Camp	On 14/8/18 Bn. was disbanded.
	16/R. Scots	101st Bde., 34th Div.	16/5/18	17/6 – 14/8/18	Disbanded	
	18/N.F.	Pioneer Bn., 34th Div.	18/5/18	17/6 – 29/7/18	118th Bde.	On 20/9/18 to L. of C. with 197th Bde.
	23/N.F.	102nd Bde., 34th Div.	17/5/18	17/6 – 16/8/18	66th Div.	Transferred from 118th Bde.
	4/Linc.	177th Bde., 59th Div.	8/5/18	28/9 – 8/11/18	Demobilised	On 20/9/18 to L. of C. with 197th Bde.
	10/Linc.	103rd Bde., 34th Div.	18/5/18	17/6 – 16/8/18	66th Div.	On 20/9/18 to L. of C. with 197th Bde.
	7/Suff.	35th Bde., 12th Div.	19/5/18	24/5 – 16/8/18	66th Div.	On 20/9/18 to L. of C. with 197th Bde.
	4/E. York.	150th Bde., 50th Div.	15/7/18	16/8 – 6/11/18	118th Bde.	
	9/Bedf.	112th Bde., 37th Div.	20/5/18	22/5 – 31/5/18	Demobilised	
	4/Gr. How.	150th Bde., 50th Div.	15/7/18	16/8 – 9/11/18	118th Bde.	
	5/Gr. How.	150th Bde., 50th Div.	15/7/18	16/8 – 6/11/18	Demobilised	
	7/B. Staff.	7th Bde., 25th Div.	11/7/18	16/8 – 6/11/18	Demobilised	
	5/N. Staff.	176th Bde., 59th Div.	9/5/18	12/8 – 6/11/18	Demobilised	Transferred from 117th Bde.
117th Bde.	2/10/King's	122nd Bde., 57th Div.	30/4/18	27/6 – 3/8/18	Disbanded	
	4/Linc.	177th Bde., 59th Div.	8/5/18	27/6 – 27/7/18	118th Bde.	
	11/Chesh.	75th Bde., 25th Div.	17/6/18	23/6 – 3/8/18	Disbanded	
	2/5/Sher. For.	178th Bde., 59th Div.	7/5/18	26/6 – 3/8/18	Disbanded	
	5/K.R.R.C.	41st Bde., 14th Div.	27/4/18	27/6 – 3/8/18	Disbanded	
	9/K.R.R.C.	42nd Bde., 14th Div.	27/4/18	27/6 – 3/8/18	Disbanded	
	5/N. Staff.	176th Bde., 59th Div.	9/5/18	27/6 – 12/8/18	116th Bde.	
	5/D.L.I.	151st Bde., 50th Div.	15/7/18	16/8 – 9/11/18	Demobilised	
	6/D.L.I.	151st Bde., 50th Div.	15/7/18	16/8 – 6/11/18	Demobilised	
	8/D.L.I.	151st Bde., 50th Div.	15/7/18	16/8 – 6/11/18	Demobilised	
	6/Conn. Rang.	47th Bde., 16th Div.	13/4/18	27/8 – 3/8/18	Disbanded	
	8/R.B.	41st Bde., 14th Div.	25/4/18	27/6 – 3/8/18	Disbanded	
	9/R.B.	42nd Bde., 14th Div.	27/4/18	27/6 – 3/8/18	Disbanded	
	6/R.M.F.	30th Bde., 10th Div.	7/6/18	27/6 – 3/8/18	Disbanded	
118th Bde.	4/N.F.	149th Bde., 50th Div.	15/7/18	16/8 – 10/11/18	Demobilised	
	5/N.F.	149th Bde., 50th Div.	15/7/18	16/8 – 10/11/18	Demobilised	
	6/N.F.	149th Bde., 50th Div.	15/7/18	16/8 – 9/11/18	Demobilised	
	18/N.F.	Pioneer Bn., 34th Div.	18/5/18	29/7 – 15/8/18	66th Div.	
	4/Linc.	177th Bde., 59th Div.	8/5/18	27/7 – 28/9/18	116th Bde.	Transferred from 116th Bde. On 20/9/18 went to L. of C. with 197th Bde.
	6/Bedf.	112th Bde., 37th Div.	20/5/18	31/5 – 4/8/18	Disbanded	Transferred from 117th Bde.
	4/E. Lan.	198th Bde., 66th Div.	7/4/18	16/8 – 16/11/18	116th Bde.	
	11/R. Suss.	116th Bde., 39th Div.	23/5/18	17/6 – 30/6/18	25th Div.	
	13/R. Suss.	116th Bde., 39th Div.	23/5/18	17/6 – 14/8/18	Disbanded	On 9/9/18 joined 236th Bde. in England, and on 15/10/18 embkd. for N. Russia.
	9/B.W.	46th Bde., 15th Div.	19/5/18	21/5 – 17/6/18	16th Div.	On 2/7/18 joined 47th Bde., 16th Div.
	8/10/Gord. H.	44th Bde., 15th Div.	6/6/18	9/6 – 30/7/18	II Corps Rft. Camp	On 17/8/18 Bn. was disbanded.
	7/Cam. H.	44th Bde., 15th Div.	10/6/18	11/6 – 30/7/18	XIX Corps Rft. Camp	On 14/8/18 Bn. was disbanded.
	11/A. & S.H.	45th Bde., 15th Div.	9/6/18	11/6 – 30/7/18	X Corps Rft. Camp	On 26/8/18 Bn. was disbanded.

NOTE.—The following Training Cadres joined 39th Div. on 18/11/18 with 197th Bde :—18/N.F., 23/N.F., 25/N.F., 10/Linc., 13/Glouc., 16/Sher. For., 14/H.L.I., and 16/R.B. These eight T.C.s had all left 66th Div. on 20/9/18 with 197th Bde., when the 66th Bde. went to L. of C.

39TH DIVISION

FORMATION, BATTLES, AND ENGAGEMENTS

This New Army Division had no existence before the outbreak of the Great War.

The 39th Division began to form around Winchester early in August 1915. The 287 Coy., A.S.C., was the first unit to arrive, it marched from Pangbourne and reached the camp at Romsey on the 8th August. On the 14th the G.S.O.1 arrived, on the 15th the pioneer battalion (13/Glouc.) reached Standon Camp by train from Yorkshire, and on the 16th the first infantry battalion (16/R.B.) camped at Hursley Park. Winchester was selected for divisional headquarters because it was centrally placed among the scattered units, but the rent of the offices in Jewry Street had to be defrayed by the officers themselves. On the 28th September the 39th Division left Winchester and moved to Marlborough Lines, Aldershot. Up to this time only Divisional Staff, 117th Infantry Brigade (a new formation which so far consisted of only three battalions—16/Sher. For., 17/K.R.R.C., & 16/R.B.), Pioneer Battalion (13/Glouc.), and 287 Coy., A.S.C., had joined. By the 18th October all the remaining units of the Division concentrated at Aldershot, except the Divisional Squadron, the 118th Infantry Brigade, the three Field Ambulances (training near Farnham), and the Veterinary Section—the last-named unit joined on the 10th November.

The 116th Infantry Brigade was the renumbered 121st Brigade, which had been raised for the original 40th (later 33rd) Division*. The 118th Infantry Brigade was a new formation which was raised in July in London (see General Notes). On the 16th October, however, the 118th Brigade was reorganized at Aldershot (see Table), and early in November it moved to Witley, with the 39th Division. Owing to the late date when the battalions of this Brigade were raised they were still in the recruit stages of training.

Until it left for the Western Front the Division remained at Witley. During January and February 1916 the general musketry course was fired at Aldershot. Rifles, however, had only been issued a few days before and the weather was bad; nevertheless orders were received that the course was to be fired without any delay. During February the divisional artillery carried out its gun-practice on Salisbury Plain. On the 24th February the Division was to have been inspected on Hankley Common by H.M. the King and a rehearsal was held on the 23rd; but a heavy fall of snow caused the inspection itself to be cancelled.

Mobilization orders were received during February and advance parties left for France at the end of the month. The battalions of the 118th Brigade had to be left behind as they were not yet ready for service overseas. The Commander and the staff of the 118th Brigade left Witley on the 23rd February, disembarked at le Havre on the 24th, and on the 29th took over five battalions (see Table) and the 118th Brigade was then reformed at Renescure (south-east of St. Omer). Meanwhile the remainder of the Division at Witley had received orders that entrainment would begin on the 29th February; but twice the date was altered, and it was the 2nd March before entrainment actually began. The Division crossed from Southampton to le Havre and disembarkation was completed on the 8th March; by the 11th the Division had concentrated around Blaringhem in the First Army area; and on the 17th the divisional squadron joined at Blaringhem. The Division was now complete.

For the remainder of the Great War the 39th Division served on the Western Front in France and Belgium and was engaged in the following operations :—

---

* Appendix 2.

1916

BATTLES OF THE SOMME

3 September	Fighting on the Ancre [V Corps, Reserve Army].
26–28 September	Battle of Thiepval Ridge [V Corps, Reserve Army].
5 Oct.–11 Nov.* ...	Battle of the Ancre Heights [II Corps, Reserve Army, until 30/10 ; then II Corps, Fifth Army].
14 October	Capture of Schwaben Redoubt.
21 October	Capture of Stuff Trench.
18 and 14 November ...	Battle of the Ancre [II Corps, Fifth Army].

1917

BATTLES OF YPRES

31 July–2 Aug.	Battle of Pilckem Ridge [XVIII Corps, Fifth Army].
16–18 August	Battle of Langemarck [X Corps, Second Army].
20–25 September	Battle of Menin Road Ridge [X Corps, Second Army].
26 and 27 September ...	Battle of Polygon Wood [X Corps, until 10 a.m. 27/9 ; then IX Corps, Second Army].
29 Oct.–10 Nov.	Second Battle of Passchendaele [X Corps, Second Army].

1918

FIRST BATTLES OF THE SOMME

22 and 28 March ...	Battle of St. Quentin [VII Corps, Fifth Army].
24 and 25 March	Actions at the Somme Crossings (less 116th Bde.) [VII Corps, until 4.80 a.m. 25/3 ; then XIX Corps, Fifth Army].
24 and 25 March	Battle of Bapaume (116th Bde.) [VII Corps, Fifth Army, until 4 a.m. 25/8 ; then Third Army].
26 and 27 March	Battle of Rosières [XIX Corps, Fifth Army].

BATTLES OF THE LYS

16 April	Fighting on Wytschaete Ridge (39th Div. Comp. Bde.)** [XXII Corps, Second Army].
17–19 April	First Battle of Kemmel Ridge (39th Div. Comp. Bde.) [XXII Corps, Second Army].
25 and 26 April	Second Battle of Kemmel Ridge (39th Div. Comp. Bde.) [XXII Corps, Second Army].
29 April	Battle of the Scherpenberg (89th Div. Comp. Bde.) [In Reserve, XXII Corps, Second Army].

---

* By the 10th November 1916 the percentage of reinforcements in the Division was :— Officers—50% ; Other Ranks—66%.

** For its composition see General Notes.

At 11 a.m. on the 11th April divisional headquarters had opened at Eperlecques (N.W. of St. Omer). The return of the Composite Brigade on the 6th May, however, marked the end of the active operations of the 39th Division. By the 1st of June the Division was reduced to cadre*; thereafter it was engaged in supervising courses of instruction for American troops and in receiving and disposing of over forty battalions which had been reduced to training cadre (see Table on pp. 96 & 97).

Meanwhile the American 77th Division had arrived for training in the Eperlecques area and its training began on the 7th May. On the 7th June divisional headquarters moved from Eperlecques to Wolphus (on the Ardres road, 10 miles N.W. of St. Omer) and during the next two months the 30th, 78th, and 80th (American) Divisions were attached for instruction. On the 15th August divisional headquarters moved to Varengeville (on the coast, W.S.W. of Dieppe) and the infantry brigades moved to Etaples, Rouen, and le Havre. On the 1st November orders were received to demobilize the battalion training staffs of the 39th Division, and by Armistice this demobilization was nearly completed (see Table). On the 16th November orders were given to disband the 117th and 118th Brigades and to reconstitute the Division by taking over the brigade at the malarial camp at Martin Eglise and the 197th Brigade (formerly in the 66th Division); by the 19th November this had been carried out. During December the 116th Brigade moved to le Havre to form the staff of the Embarkation Camp.

In January 1919 the 197th Brigade moved to the General Base Reinforcement Depot at No. 8 Camp (le Havre). On the 5th March divisional headquarters moved to Rouen, and during June the units were gradually disbanded. On the 5th July instructions were received that the remainder of the Division was to be broken up; on the 10th July divisional headquarters closed down and the remaining officers proceeded to England in charge of records. The Division had come to an end. During its active employment in the Great War the 39th Division lost 27,869 killed, wounded, and missing.

---

* For the employment of 39th Division Artillery (April–November 1918) see General Notes

40TH DIVISION

G.O.C.

25 September 1915 ... ... Major-General H. G. RUGGLES-BRISE.
24 August 1917 ... ... Major-General J. PONSONBY.
3 July 1918 ... ... Major-General Sir W. E. PEYTON.

G.S.O.1.

15 Sept. 1915...Major F. D. FINLAY
  (acting).
25 Oct. 1915...Lt.-Col. H. A. WALKER.
13 April 1917...Lt.-Col. A. H. S. HART-
  SYNNOT (acting).
16 April 1917...Lt.-Col. W. G. CHARLES.
17 Mar. 1918...Lt.-Col. C. H. G. BLACK.

A.-A. & Q.-M.-G.

7 Sept. 1915...Lt.-Col. C. F. MOORES.

B.-G., R.A.

21 Sept. 1915...Br.-Gen. F. G. STONE.
8 April 1916...Br.-Gen. H. L. REED,
  V.C.
2 Jan. 1917...Br.-Gen. G. H. W.
  NICHOLSON.
25 Dec. 1917...Br.-Gen. C. E. PALMER.

C.R.E.

1 Nov. 1915...Lt.-Col. R. J. B. MAIR.
25 Mar. 1917...Lt.-Col. A. C. BAYLAY.
30 Nov. 1917...Lt.-Col. H. W. BECHER
  (acting).
1 Dec. 1917...Lt.-Col. G. J. P.
  GOODWIN.
30 Mar. 1918...Lt.-Col. A. C. BAYLAY.
6 June 1918...Major F. W. CLARK
  (acting).
15 June 1918...Lt.-Col. R. P.
  PAKENHAM-WALSH.
15 July 1918...Major J. E. VILLA
  (acting).
4 Aug. 1918...Lt.-Col. W. R. WILSON.

119th BDE.

(new formation)

22 July '15...Br.-Gen. R. C. STYLE.
8 May '16...Br.-Gen. C. S. PRICHARD.
16 Aug. '16...Br.-Gen. C. CUNLIFFE
  OWEN.
16 Nov. '16...Lt.-Col. E. A. POPE
  (acting).
20 Nov. '16...Br.-Gen. F. P. CROZIER.

120th BDE.

(new formation)

7 Sept. '15...Br.-Gen. Hon. C. S.
  HEATHCOTE-DRUMMOND-
  WILLOUGHBY.
15 Mar. '18...Lt.-Col. R. F. FORBES
  (acting).
23 Mar. '18...Br.-Gen. C. J. HOBKIRK.
18 Oct. '18...Br.-Gen. Hon. W. P.
  HORE-RUTHVEN.

121st BDE.

(new formation)

7 Oct. '15...Br.-Gen. J. CAMPBELL.
27 April '18...Lt.-Col. L. LLOYD (acting).
6 May '18...Br.-Gen. W. B. GARNETT.
17 Sept. '18...Br.-Gen. G. C. STUBBS.

40TH DIVISION[1]

Dates	INFANTRY Brigades	Battalions and attached Units	Mounted Troops	ARTILLERY Field Artillery Brigades	Batteries	Bde. Ammn. Colns.	Trench Mortar Btles. Medium	Heavy	Divnl. Ammn. Coln.	Engineers Field Cos.	Signal Service Divnl. Signal Coy.	Pioneers	M.G. Units	Field Ambulances	Mobile Vety. Sec.	Divnl. Emplmt. Coy.	Divnl. Train
1916 April (England)	119th[2; 3]	19/R.W.F., 12/S.W.B., 17/Welsh,[3] 18/Welsh[3]	A Sqdn.,[6] 1/R. Wilts. Yeo. 40th Div. Cyclist Coy.[7]	CLXXVIII (H.)[8]	A (H.), B (H.), C (H.), D (H.)	CLXXVIII (H.) B.A.C.[10]	...	...	40th D.A.C.[9]; [10]	224th[11] 229th[11] 231st[11]	40th[12]	12/ Gr. How.[13] (P.)	...	135th[14] 136th[14] 137th[14]	51st[15]	...	40th[16]
	120th[4]; [5]	11/K.O., 13/E. Surr.,[4] 14/H.L.I., 14/A. & S.H.,[4] 12/Suff.,[4] 13/Gr. How.,[6] 20/Middx.,[6] 21 Middx.[6]		CLXXXI[5]	A, B, C, D	CLXXXI B.A.C.[10]											
	121st[4]; [5]			CLXXXV[6]	A, B, C, D	CLXXXV B.A.C.[10]											
				CLXXXVIII[6]	A, B, C, D	CLXXXVIII B.A.C.[10]											
1916 June (France)	119th	19/R.W.F., 12/S.W.B., 17/Welsh, 18/Welsh.; 119th Bde. M.G. Coy.;[17] 119th T.M. Bty.[18]	...[6]; [5]	CLXXVIII[19]; [18]	A, B, C; D (H.)	...[18]	X.40[20] Y.40[21] Z.40[21]	V.40[22]	40th D.A.C.[10]	224th 229th 231st	40th	12/ Gr. How. (P.)	...	135th 136th 137th	51st	...	40th
	120th	11/K.O., 13/E. Surr., 14/H.L.I., 14/A. & S.H.; 120th Bde. M.G. Coy.;[17] 120th T.M. Bty.[18]		CLXXXI[18]; [20]	A, B, C; D (H.)												
	121st	12/Suff., 13/Gr. How., 20/Middx., 21/Middx.; 121st Bde. M.G. Coy.;[17] 121st T.M. Bty.[18]		CLXXXV[18]	A, B, C; D (H.)												
				CLXXXVIII[18]; [20]	A, B, C; D (H.)												
1917 June (France)	119th	19/R.W.F.,[34] 12/S.W.B.,[34] 17/Welsh,[34] 18/Welsh.; 119th M.G. Coy.;[47] 119th T.M. Bty.	...	CLXXVIII[19]	A, B, C; D (H.)	...	X.40 Y.40 Z.40[21]	V.40[22]	40th D.A.C.	224th 229th 231st	40th	12/ Gr. How. (P.)	244th[23] M.G. Coy.	135th 136th 137th	51st	237th[24]	40th
	120th	11/K.O.,[34] 13/E. Surr.,[34] 14/H.L.I., 14/A. & S.H.; 120th M.G. Coy.;[47] 120th T.M. Bty.		CLXXXI[20]	A, B, C; D (H.)												
	121st	12/Suff., 13/Gr. How., 20/Middx., 21/Middx.; 121st M.G. Coy.;[47] 121st T.M. Bty.															
1918 March (France)	119th	13/E. Surr.,[35]; [36] 18/Welsh,[36] 21/Middx.,[36]; [37] 119th T.M. Bty.[44]	...	CLXXVIII	A, B, C; D (H.)	...	X.40 Y.40 21[21]; [44]	...[44]	40th D.A.C.	224th 229th 231st	40th	12/ Gr. How.[44] (P.)	No. 40 Bn.,[47] M.G.C.	135th 136th 137th	51st	237th	40th
	120th	10/11/H.L.I.,[42] 14/H.L.I.,[42] 14/A. & S.H.;[42] 120th T.M. Bty.[44]		CLXXXI	A, B, C; D (H.)												
	121st	12/Suff.,[41] 13/Gr. How.,[43] 20/Middx.;[43] 121st T.M. Bty.[44]															

	119th	120th	121st
1918 July (France)	13/R. Innis. F.,[44] 13/E. Lanc.,[45] 12/N. Staf.;[46] 119th T.M. Bty.[53]	10/K.O.S.B.,[47] 15/K.O.Y.L.I.,[48] 11/Cam. H.,[49] 120th T.M. Bty.[54]	8/R. Irish Regt.,[50] 23/L.F.,[51] 23/Ches.;[52] 121st T.M. Bty.[55]

	40th	237th	51st	135th 136th 137th	No. 39 Bn.[34] M.G.C.	17/ Worc.[34] (P.)	40th	224th 229th 231st	40th D.A.C.	X.40[44] Y.40[44]	...	...	CLXXVIII ...... CLXXXI	...
After Reconstitution													A, B, C; D (H.) / A, B, C; D (H.)	

NOTES

[1] Formed at Aldershot in September 1915 as 40th Div. This Division was a new formation.

[2] The Inf. Bdes. were raised in 1915 as 119th, 120th, & 121st Bdes.; all three Bdes. were new formations.

[3] 17/ & 18/Welsh were designated 1/ and 2/Glamorgan.

[4] Bde. was reconstituted in Feb. 1916; on 23/2/16 13/E. Surr. and 14/A. & S.H. (from 118th Bde., 39th Div.) replaced 13/Sco. Rif. and 12/S. Lanc.

[5] Bde. was reconstituted in Feb. 1916: on 23/2/16 20/ and 21/Middx. (from 118th Bde., 39th Div.) replaced 18/Sher. For. and 22/Middx. 12/Suff. was designated East Anglian.

[6] Sqdn. joined Div. in England; disembkd. at le Havre on 5/6/16; left Div. on 20/6/16, and on 21/6/16 joined IX Corps Cav. Regt.

[7] Coy. formed in Div. in England; disembkd. at le Havre on 6/6/16; left Div. on 11/6/16, and on 13/6/16 joined Reserve Army.

[8] The Bdes. were raised at East Ham (CLXXVIII), Ashton (CLXXXI), Tottenham (CLXXXV), and Nottingham (CLXXXVIII). The Bdes. were raised as 4-battery brigades; in each brigade the batteries were lettered – A, B, C, D—and each battery was a 4-gun battery.

[9] Whilst still in England the Bdes. were reorganized: each Bde then had three four-gun 18-pdr. batteries and one four-gun howitzer battery ; to effect this reorganization, the howitzer Bde. (CLXXXVIII) exchanged a four-gun howitzer battery for a four-gun 18-pdr. battery with each of the other three Bdes. (CLXXVIII, CLXXXI, CLXXXV, CLXXXVIII). The four Bdes. disembkd. at le Havre between 2-5/6/16.

[10] The D.A.C. was raised at Hammersmith. The D.A.C. disembkd. at le Havre on 6/6/16.

[11] Whilst still in England the B.A.C.s were abolished and the D.A.C. was reorganized.

[12] Joined Div. in England and disembkd. at le Havre between 2-4/6/16. The Fd. Cos. were raised at Doncaster.

[13] Joined Div. in England and disembkd. at le Havre 2-6/6/16. The Sig. Coy. was raised at Doncaster.

[14] Joined Div. in England and disembkd. at le Havre on 2/8/16.

[15] Assembled in Dec. 1915 and trained at Tweseldown; disembkd. at le Havre on 3 & 4/6/16.

[16] Joined in England and disembkd. at le Havre on 5/6/16.

[17] The Train consisted of 292, 293, 294, and 295 Cos., A.S.C., it joined in England and disembkd. at le Havre 2-5/6/16.

[18] 119th, 120th, and 121st Bde. M.G. Cos. left Grantham on 16/6/16, disembkd. at le Havre on 17/6/16, and joined the Div. at Bruay on 19/6/16.

[19] The Light T.M. Bties. were formed: 119th by 25/6/16; 120th by 8/6/16; 121st by 15/6/16.

[20] On 1/9/16 1 sec. C/CLXXXV joined and made up A; 1 sec. C/CLXXXV made up B; and 1 sec. C/CLXXXV made up C, to 6 guns each. On 8/1/17 L. Sec. D (H.)/CLXXXI joined and made up D (H.)/CLXXVIII to 6 hows.

[21] On 1/9/16 1 sec. A/CLXXXV joined and made up A; 1 sec. B/CLXXXV made up B; and 1 sec. A/CLXXXV made up C, to 6 guns each. Between 8-12/1/17 D (H.) was broken up and reformed: L. Sec. joined CLXXVIII and made up D (H.)/CLXXVIII to 6 hows.; and D (H.)/CLXXVIII joined CLXXXI and became D (H.)/CLXXXI, made up by R. Sec. D(H.)/CLXXXI.

[22] Between 31/8-1/9/16 CLXXXV was broken up: A and 1 sec. made up CLXXXI and made up A, B, C/CLXXXI to 6 guns each; C and 1 sec. B joined CLXXVIII and made up A, B, C CLXXVIII to 6 guns each; D (H.) became C (H.) CLXXXVIII.

[23] On 1/9/16 C was broken up: 1 sec. C made up A and 1 sec. C made up B, to 6 guns each; and D (H.)/CLXXXV joined and became C (H.)/CLXXXVIII. Between 8-13/1/17 CLXXXVIII was broken up: A became A/XIV A.F.A. Bde. on 14/1/17; B became A/XV R.H.A. (Army Bde.) on 13/1/17, and on 1/6/17 was renumbered 402; C (H.) was transferred to III Corps; and D (H.) joined CLXXXI (was made up to 6 hows. by R. Sec. of the old D (H.)/CLXXXI) and then became D (H.)/CLXXXI.

[24] X, Y, and Z were formed on 25/6/16; the establnt. of each Medium T.M. Bty. was 4, 2" mortars, 2 offrs., and 23 o.r.

[25] V was formed on 4/7/16.

[26] On 6/2/18 Bn. sent 8 offrs. & 150 o.r. to 2/R.W.F. and remdr. of 19/R.W.F. left Div. and joined VI Corps Rft. Camp. On 15/2/18 19/R.W.F. was disbanded and taken into 8/Entg. Bn.

[27] On 8/2/18 Bn. drafted 11 offrs. & 250 o.r., and on 10/2/18 remdr. of Bn. left Div. and joined VI Corps Rft. Camp. On 16/2/18 Bn. was disbanded and taken into 9/Entg. Bn.

[28] Between 5-9/2/18 Bn. drafted 14 offrs. & 300 o.r., and on 9/2/18 remdr. of Bn. left Div. and joined VI Corps Rft. Camp. On 16/2/18 Bn. was disbanded and taken into 9/Entg. Bn.

[29] Between 3-7/2/18 Bn. drafted 23 offrs. & 577 o.r., and on 7/2/18 remdr. of Bn. left Div. and joined VI Corps Rft. Camp. On 17/2/18 Bn. was disbanded and taken into 9/Entg. Bn.

[30] On 16/2/18 Bn. was transferred to 119th Bde.

[31] On 5/2/18 Bn. was transferred to 119th Bde.

[32] On 6 & 7/3/18 Z was broken up and distributed between X and Y.

[33] V Heavy T.M. Bty. was broken up on 6 & 7/3/18.

[34] Coy. left Grantham on 15/7/17, disembkd. at le Havre on 16/7/17, joined Div. at Hrudecourt on 20/7/17. Formed by 13/6/17.

[35] On 5/5/18 Bn. was reduced to T.C. surplus (1 offr., 447 o.r.) went to Base. On 3/6/18 T.C. was transferred to 34th Div., on 17/6/18 to 39th Div.; and on 30/6/18 joined 7th Bde., 25th Div. In England T.C. left 25th Div. and went to Lowestoft.

[36] On 5/5/18 Bn. was reduced to T.C., surplus went to Base. On 18/6/18 T.C. joined 47th Bde. 16th Div. at Boulogne, amalgamated with 25/Welsh at N. Walsham, and 18/Welsh rejoined 47th Bde., 16th Div., at Aldershot on 7/7/18.

NOTES—*continued*

[47] On 21/4/18 Bn. drafted 2 offrs. & 200 o.r. to 1/Middx. On 5/5/18 21/Middx. was reduced to T.C., surplus (1 offr., 438 o.r.) went to Base. On 3/6/18 T.C. was transferred to 34th Div., on 17/6/18 to 39th Div., and on 30/6/18 joined 74th Bde., 25th Div. In England T.C. left 25th Div. and went to Cromer.

[48] On 1/2/18 Bn. joined 119th Bde. from 46th Bde., 15th Div.; on 16/2/18 Bn. was transferred to 120th Bde. On 6/5/18 Bn. was reduced to T.C., surplus went to Base. On 3/6/18 T.C. was transferred to 34th Div., and on 16/6'18 to 14th Div.; joined 43rd Bde. on 19/6/18, and on 21/6'18 T.C. absorbed 22/H.L.I. and became 10/H.L.I.

[49] On 6/5/18 Bn. was reduced to T.C., surplus went to Base. On 3/6/18 T.C. joined 34th Div., on 17/6/18 T.C. was transferred to 39th Div., and on 16/8/18 to 66th Div. On 20/9/18 T.C. went to L. of C. with 197th Bde.

[50] On 7/4/18 24 offrs. & 496 o.r. were drafted and remdr. of Bn. (6 offrs. & 216 o.r.) was transferred to 30th Div. On 14/5/18 Bn. was reduced to T.C., surplus went to Base. On 16/6/18 T.C. joined 14th Div., absorbed 17/A. & S.H., and on 21/6/18 joined 42nd Bde.

[51] On 6/5/18 Bn. was reduced to T.C., surplus (21 offrs. & 670 o.r.) went to Base. On 16/6/18 T.C. joined 14th Div.; T.C. absorbed 16/Suff., and on 19/6/18 joined 43rd Bde.

[52] On 6/5/18 Bn. was reduced to T.C., surplus went to Base. On 3/6/18 T.C. joined 34th Div.; on 17/6/18 T.C. was transferred to 39th Div., and joined 25th Div. on 30/6/18. Bn. was reformed in England, joined 236th Bde. (late 75th) on 9/9/18, and in Oct. 1918 went to N. Russia with 236th Bde.

[53] On 6/5/18 Bn. was reduced to T.C., surplus (4 offrs., & 670 o.r.) went to Base. T.C. was transferred on 31/5/18 to 16th Div., to 14th Div. on 16/6/18, and joined 43rd Bde.; on 20/6/18 T.C. absorbed 34/Middx.

[54] The Light T.M. Bties. were disbanded on 5/5/18.

[55] X and Y (Medium T.M. Bties.) were broken up in April 1918.

[56] Bn. was reorganized on a 3-company basis on 24/2/18—Z Coy. was broken up. On 5/5/18 the Pioneer Bn. was reduced to T.C.; surplus (10 offrs. & 350 o.r.) went to Base. On 28/6/18 T.C. was disbanded and absorbed by 17/Worc. (note 55).

[57] Bn. was formed on 25/2/18; it consisted of 119th, 120th, 121st, and 224th M.G. Cos. On 9/5/18 the M.G. Bn. was disbanded, and personnel and transport went to M.G. Base.

RECONSTITUTED DIVISION

[58] Nos. 7, 8, & 11 Garr. Gd. Bns. joined 120th Bde. on 10/6/18, and on 11/6/18 they were redesignated 13/Garr. Bn. R. Innis. F., 13/Garr. Bn. E. Lanc., and 12/Garr. Bn. N. Staff. On 15/6/18 the formation of the 3 Garr. Bns. was completed, and the 3 Garr. Bns. were then transferred to 119th Bde. On 13/7/18 the title Garrison was eliminated.

[59] Nos. 6, 9, & 10 Garr. Gd. Bns. joined 120th Bde. on 10/6/18, and on 11/6/18 they were redesignated 11/Garr. Bn. Cam. H., 10/Garr. Bn. K.O.S.B., and 15/Garr. Bn. K.O.Y.L.I. On 15/6/18 the formation of the 3 Garr. Bns. was completed, and the 120th Bde. was reconstituted with these 3 Garr. Bns. On 13/7/18 the title Garrison was eliminated.

[60] 2/Garr. Gd. Bn. R. Irish Regt. joined 178th Bde., 59th Div., on 17/5/18, was redesignated 8/Garr. Bn. R. Irish Regt. on 25/5/18, and on 20/6/18 Bn. joined 121st Bde. On 13/7/18 the title Garrison was eliminated.

[61] 4/Provl. Garr. Bn. joined 176th Bde., 59th Div., on 13/5/18, was redesignated 23/Garr. Bn. L.F. on 25/5/18, and on 19/6/18 Bn. joined 121st Bde. On 13/7/18 the title Garrison was eliminated.

[62] 23/Garr. Gd. Bn. Cheshire R. joined 178th Bde., 59th Div., on 24/5/18, became 23/Garr. Bn. Cheshire R. on 25/5/18, and on 20/6/18 Bn. joined 121st Bde. On 13/7/18 the title Garrison was eliminated.

[63] On 15/6/18 each Bde. was ordered to form one Light T.M. Bty. (estblnt.—3 offrs. & 47 o.r., with 6 mortars each). By 13/7/18 the 3 T.M. Bties. were formed.

[64] Between 1–25/7/18 X and Y (Medium T.M. Bties.) were reformed at Barly.

[65] 1/Provl. Garr. Gd. Bn. joined 176th Bde., 59th Div., on 13/5/18, and on 25/5/18 Bn. was redesignated 17/Garr. Bn. Worc. R. On 18/6/18 Bn. was transferred to 121st Bde.; on 28/6/18 Bn. absorbed T.C. of 12/Gr. How. (P.), and on 29/6/18 Bn. left 121st Bde. and became Pioneer Bn., 40th Div. On 13/7/18 the title Garrison was eliminated.

[66] On 11/9/18 No. 39 Bn. M.G.C. (from 39th Div.) joined 40th Div.; relieved No. 104 Bn. M.G.C. (see General Notes), and No. 39 Bn. M.G.C. then served with 40th Div. until the end of the War.

GENERAL NOTES

The following Units also served with the 40th Division :—

ARTILLERY :—W. Medium T.M. Battery was formed in the Division on 29/7/16 ; between 10–31/10/16 W was converted into a Heavy T.M. Bty.

INFANTRY :—13/Sco. Rif. and 12/S. Lanc. served in the 120th Bde. from its formation until Feb. 1916 (note 4). The two battalions disappeared on the reorganization of the Bde. (see Narrative).

18/Sher. For. and 22/Middx. served in the 121st Bde. from its formation until Feb. 1916 (note 5). The two battalions disappeared on the reorganization of the Bde. (see Narrative).

2/R.S.F. On 7/4/18 Bn. was transferred from 90th Bde., 30th Div., to 120th Bde., 40th Div. ; on 25/4/18 Bn. was transferred to S. African Bde., 9th Div., and joined on 26/4/18 ; and on 13/9/18 Bn. was transferred to 28th Bde., 9th Div. (Until 19/12/15 Bn. had served with 21st Bde., 7th Div.).

MACHINE-GUN UNIT :—No. 104 Bn., M.G.C., served with the Division from 24/8–16/9/18. (104 M.G.Bn. was formed at Etaples on 18/7/18 from 2/County of London Yeo. Originally designated F Battalion, it was redesignated No. 104 Bn. on 19/8/18).

OTHER UNITS :—83rd Sanitary Section joined Div. in England ; disembkd. at le Havre on 5/6/16, and concentrated at Lillers on 7/6/16. The Section left the Division on 24/4/17 and took over a Sanitary Area in the Fourth Army.

40th Div. Motor Ambce. Workshop joined Div. in England, crossed to France on 2/6/18, and concentrated at Lillers ; the Unit was then merged in 40th Div. A.S.C. workshops.

On 16/2/18 the reorganization of the 40th Division on a 9-battalion basis was completed ; and on 24/2/18 the pioneer battalion (12/Gr. How.) was reorganized on a 3-company basis.

Composite Brigades—(a) On 18/4/18 40th Division formed a **Composite Bde.** (Br.-Gen. J. Campbell*), made up as follows :—A Bn. (20/ & 21/ Middx.), B Bn. (13/Gr. How.), C Bn. (12/Suff. & 13/E. Surr.), and M.G. Coy. (from No. 40 Bn. M.G.C.) and Light T.M. Bty. (from 119th & 121st T.M. Bties.), with 224th Fd. Coy., 1 sub.-sec. S.A.A. Sec. 40th D.A.C., 137th Fd. Ambce., and No. 4 Coy., Divnl. Train.

This Composite Brigade was employed in digging the Herzeele–le Brearde Line (in front of Cassel).

(b) On 27/4/18 a second **Composite Bde.** (Br.-Gen. F. P. Crozier) was formed : A Bn. (18/Welsh), B Bn. (13/E. Surr.), and C Bn. (10/11 & 14/H.L.I.), with 1 Coy., No. 40 Bn. M.G.C., 136th Fd. Ambce., and No. 2 Coy., Divnl. Train. No. 2 Composite Bde. (under Divnl. H.Q.) was employed on digging the Poperinghe Line.

On 2/5/18 Nos. 1 and 2 Composite Bdes. were withdrawn and 40th Div. began reducing all Infantry and M.G. Units to Training Cadre ; the surplus personnel went to the Base (notes 35-47).

40th Division Artillery :—On 27/3/18, after the 40th Division had been withdrawn, the 40th Division Artillery remained in action covering part of VI Corps front, and took part in the Battle of Arras (28/3/18). From April to August 1918 40th Div. Arty. remained in VI Corps and was employed (like Army Field Artillery) to cover various divisions which held VI Corps Front Line. Still in VI Corps, 40th Div. Arty. was engaged in the **Second Battles of the Somme** (Battle of Albert, 21–23/8). On 25/8/18 40th Div. Arty. was transferred to XVII Corps and was engaged with it in the **Second Battles of Arras** (Battle of the Scarpe, 26–30/9, and Battle of the Drocourt–Quéant Line, 2–3/9) ; and in the **Battles of the Hindenburg Line** (Battle of the Canal du Nord, 27/9–1/10. and Battle of Cambrai, 8–9/10) ; and the Pursuit to the Selle (9–12/10/18).

On 13/10/18 40th Div. Arty. was relieved in the front line ; and entrained on 16/10/18 on transfer from XVII Corps, Third Army to 40th Div., XV Corps, Second Army. On 18/10/18 40th Division Artillery rejoined 40th Division at Armentières.

* Until 27/4/18, then Lt.-Col. L. Lloyd.

40TH DIVISION

FORMATION, BATTLES, AND ENGAGEMENTS

This New Army Division had no existence before the outbreak of the Great War.

Most of the earlier New Army divisions had a strictly territorial basis, at any rate so far as the infantry and pioneers were concerned; but the infantry of the 40th Division was composed of English, Welsh, and Scottish units and the pioneers were English.

Early in September 1915 the first divisional staff officer reached Stanhope Lines, Aldershot, and, within a short time, the remainder of the divisional staff assembled. Units also began to arrive, and in December 1915 the Division moved out to Blackdown, Pirbright, and Woking; it remained in this training area until it went to France.

The standard of height for an infantry soldier had been lowered before the 40th Division was formed, and the four Welsh battalions of the 119th Infantry Brigade were composed entirely of 'bantams.' The men of the other two brigades (120th and 121st) were mixed in height, but even in these two brigades there were many 'bantams.' All three infantry brigades were new formations (see Appendix 2).

The 'bantams' of the 119th Infantry Brigade were well-knit, hardy Welshmen; but the 120th and 121st Infantry Brigades contained a large proportion of under-developed and unfit men, and a drastic weeding-out became necessary. In this way one battalion, which had arrived at Aldershot 1,000 strong, was reduced by medical rejections to little over 200 men. These rejections caused delay in the training programme, but, unfortunately, the first enthusiasm for enlistment also had spent itself; the losses, therefore, could not be made good in time from the ordinary sources of supply. In the 119th Brigade the wastage due to medical rejections had been slight; but in the 120th and 121st Brigades it was estimated that only two service-able battalions could be formed from the existing four in each brigade, consequently the 120th and 121st Brigades would each require two new battalions to complete it to war establishment. To prevent the departure of the Division being indefinitely postponed, the Divisional Commander, early in 1916, recommended that four new battalions should be sent to the Division to bring it up to its full complement of men. This recommendation was approved, and the four battalions which previously formed the 118th Brigade (39th Division) were ordered to move to the 40th Division. Meanwhile, in February 1916, the original four battalions in each of the 120th and 121st Infantry Brigades were amalgamated to form two battalions for each of these two brigades. Within three days this internal reorganization was completed and two battalions in each brigade disappeared (see General Notes). Then, on the 23rd February, the four new battalions arrived and two each were alloted to the 120th and 121st Brigades. The reformation of these two brigades was finished; divisional training was intensified at once, all deficiencies were made good, and arms and equipment were completed.

After the middle of May 1916 the Division was warned to prepare to move to France. On the 25th May the Division paraded on Laffans Plain for inspection by H.M. the King. On the 27th mobilization began and was completed on the 31st. Entrainment started on the 1st June, disembarkation was carried out at le Havre between the 2nd–6th, and by 6.30 p.m. on the 9th June the Division completed concentration in the Lillers area (N.N.W. of Béthune).

For the remainder of the Great War the 40th Division served on the Western Front in France and Belgium and was engaged in the following operations :—

1916

BATTLES OF THE SOMME

14–18 November ... ...   **Battle of the Ancre** (120th Bde., under 31st Div.)
[XIII Corps, Fifth Army].

1917

14–25 March	**German Retreat to the Hindenburg Line** [XV Corps, [Fourth Army].
21; 24 & 25 April; } and 5 May }	**Capture of Fifteen Ravine; Villers Plouich; Beaucamp; and la Vacquerie** [XV Corps, Fourth Army].

BATTLE OF CAMBRAI

23–25 November	**Capture of Bourlon Wood** [IV Corps, Third Army].

1918

FIRST BATTLES OF THE SOMME

21–23 March	**Battle of St. Quentin** [VI Corps, Third Army].
24 & 25 March	**First Battle of Bapaume** [VI Corps, Third Army].

BATTLES OF THE LYS

9–11 April	**Battle of Estaires** [XV Corps, First Army].
12 & 13 April	**Battle of Hazebrouck** [XV Corps, First Army, until noon 12/4; then Second Army].

On 2/5/18 the reduction of the Division to Training Cadre began. At first Divisional Headquarters were at St. Omer (until the 4th June), then at Lederzeele until the 23rd, and after that at Renescure. Between the end of May and the middle of June all Training Cadres left the Division (notes 35/43) and six Garrison Guard Battalions joined on the 10th June; followed by four more between the 18th–20th June. On the 14th June orders were received that the 40th Division was to be reorganized; this was completed by the middle of July (see Table). In case of an emergency the 40th Division was to be prepared to hold the West Hazebrouck Line. By the 18th July the infantry brigades began to take over portions of the Front Line. Between this time and the end of the Great War the 40th Division took part in the following operations :—

THE ADVANCE TO VICTORY

28 Sept.–19 Oct.; 27 Oct.–10 Nov.	**THE FINAL ADVANCE IN FLANDERS** [XV Corps, Second Army].
28 Sept.–2 Oct.	**Battle of Ypres** [XV Corps, Second Army].

The Division remained in the front line and continued to advance; on the 18th October Croix (south of Roubaix) was occupied, and on the next day the Division was relieved in the front line at Lannoy and Leers. On the 27th October the Division again took over part of the XV Corps front line from Pecq—along the Schelde left bank—Espierres Canal. Patrols were pushed across the Schelde to reconnoitre, but no foothold on the right bank was maintained until the 2nd November. On the 8th an advance was made and Herrines was occupied. A company of XV Corps Cyclists was now attached to the 40th Division; at 3 p.m. on the 9th November Velaines was entered, an advance of 7 miles having been made since daybreak. On the 10th the front line was extended to the north; the cyclists pushed on, crossed the Rhosne, and reached the railway north-east of Anvaing. This was the furthest point reached in the final advance of the 40th Division. During the night of the 10th/11th November the 59th and 29th Divisions (XI and II Corps) joined hands in front of XV Corps and the 40th Division was withdrawn into reserve, with divisional headquarters at Lannoy. At 11 a.m. on the next day, 11th November, the Armistice brought hostilities to a close.

After the Armistice the Division rested and was employed in training and on road repair, and lectures were given on various educational subjects. On the 25th November the Division moved back and headquarters opened at Roubaix. On the 2nd December a divisional school was opened and refresher courses were given to carpenters, blacksmiths, tinsmiths, plumbers, and bricklayers; during this month pivotal men and miners left for demobilization.

During January and February 1919 demobilization continued at an increasing rate and in February all the divisional schools were closed. In March the Division was reduced to cadre strength and divisional cadre headquarters moved to Croix. Until the middle of May 1919 the 40th Division Cadre Groups remained in existence, and then they finally disappeared. The Division had come to end. During the Great War the 40th Division lost 19,179 killed, wounded, and missing.

41ST DIVISION

G.O.C.

13 September 1915 ... ... Major-General S. T. B. LAWFORD.

G.S.O.1.

18 Sept. 1915...Major E. P. DORRIEN-
SMITH (acting).
14 Jan. 1916...Lt.-Col. B. D. L. G.
ANLEY.
3 May 1917...Lt.-Col. R. G. PARKER.
1 Mar. 1918...Lt.-Col. E. A. BECK.

A.-A. & Q.-M.-G.

18 Sept. 1915...Lt.-Col. J. S. KNOX.
28 Aug. 1916...Lt.-Col. C. F. POTTER.
9 July 1917...Lt.-Col. T. S. RIDDELL-
WEBSTER.

B.-G., R.A.

8 Nov. 1915...Br.-Gen. S. LUSHINGTON
(wounded, 27/9/17).
27 Sept. 1917...Lt.-Col. G. A. CARDEW
(acting).
12 Oct. 1917...Br.-Gen. A. S. COTTON.

C.R.E.

11 Nov. 1915...Lt.-Col. W. M.
COLDSTREAM (sick, 4/5/16).
7 May 1916...Captain E. C. BAKER
(acting).
15 May 1916...Lt.-Col. E. N. STOCKLEY.
6 June 1918...Lt.-Col. A. C. HOWARD.

122nd BDE.
(new formation)

27 Sept. '15...Br.-Gen. F. W. TOWSEY.
8 June '18...Br.-Gen. S. V. P.
WESTON.

123rd BDE.
(new formation)

30 Sept. '15...Br.-Gen. C. S.
DAVIDSON.
23 Sept. '16...Br.-Gen. C. W. E.
GORDON (killed, 23/7/17).
24 July '17...Br.-Gen. W. F. CLEMSON
(tempy).
3 Aug. '17...Br.-Gen. E. PEARCE
SEROCOLD.
23 June '18...Br.-Gen. M. KEMP-WELCH.

124th BDE.
(new formation)

29 Sept. '15...Br.-Gen. W. F. CLEMSON (wd., 9/6/16).
10 June '16...Lt.-Col. EARL OF FEVERSHAM (acting).
24 June '16...Br.-Gen. W. F. CLEMSON.
24 July '17...Lt.-Col. W. C. CLARK (acting).
2 Aug. '17...Br.-Gen. W. F. CLEMSON.
21 June '18...Br.-Gen. R. L. ADLERCRON.

41st DIVISION [1]

Date	INFANTRY — Brigades	INFANTRY — Battalions and attached Units	Mounted Troops	ARTILLERY — Field Artillery — Brigades	ARTILLERY — Field Artillery — Batteries	ARTILLERY — Bde. Ammn. Colns.	ARTILLERY — Trench Mortar Btts. — Medium	ARTILLERY — Trench Mortar Btts. — Heavy	Divnl. Ammn. Coln.	Engineers — Field Cos.	Signal Service — Divnl. Signal Coy.	Pioneers	M.G. Units	Field Ambulances	Mobile Vety. Sec.	Divnl. Emplnt. Coy.	Divnl. Train
1916 April (England)	122nd [2] ; [3]	12/E. Surr., 15/Hants., 11/Q.O.R.W.K., [3] 18/K.R.R.C.	B Sqdn., [8] R. Wilts. Yeo.	CLXXXIII (H.) [3]	A (H.), B (H.), C (H.), D (H.)	CLXXXIII (H.) B.A.C.	...	...	41st D.A.C. [5]	228th [6]	41st [9]	19/ Middx. [10] (P.)	...	138th [11] 139th [11] 140th [11]	52nd [12]	...	41st [13]
	123rd [4] ; [4]	11/Q.O.R.W.K., 4 23/Middx., 20/D.L.I.	41st Div. Cyclist Coy. [7]	CLXXXVII [5]	A, B, C, D	CLXXXVII B.A.C.				233rd [6]							
	124th [5] ; [5]	10/Queen's, 26/R.F., 32/R.F., 21/K.R.R.C.		CLXXXIX [5]	A, B, C, D	CLXXXIX B.A.C.				237th [6]							
				CXC [5]	A, B, C, D	CXC B.A.C.											
1916 May (France)	122nd	12/E. Surr., 15/Hants., 11/Q.O.R.W.K., 18/K.R.R.C.	B Sqdn., [14] R. Wilts. Yeo.	CLXXXIII (H.) [3]	A (H.), B (H.), C (H.), D (H.)	CLXXXIII (H.) B.A.C.	...	...	41st D.A.C.	228th	41st	19/ Middx. (P.)	...	138th 139th 140th	52nd	...	41st
	123rd	11/Queen's, 10/Q.O.R.W.K., 23/Middx., 20/D.L.I.	41st Div. Cyclist Coy. [16]	CLXXXVII [15]	A, B, C, D	CLXXXVII B.A.C.				233rd							
	124th	10/Queen's, 26/R.F., 32/R.F., 21/K.R.R.C.		CLXXXIX [15]	A, B, C, D	CLXXXIX B.A.C.				237th							
				CXC [15]	A, B, C, D	CXC B.A.C.											
1916 June (France)	122nd	12/E. Surr., 15/Hants., 11/Q.O.R.W.K.; 122nd Bde. M.G. Coy.; [30] 122nd T.M. Bty. [31]	...	CLXXXIII [17] ; [32]	A, B, C; D (H.)	[32]	X.41 [35] Y.41 [36] Z.41 [38]	V.41 [37]	41st D.A.C. [33]	228th 233rd 237th	41st	19/ Middx. (P.)	...	138th 139th 140th	52nd	...	41st
	123rd	11/Queen's, 10/Q.O.R.W.K., 20/D.L.I.; 123rd Bde. M.G. Coy.; [34] 123rd T.M. Bty. [31]		CLXXXVII [17] ; [32]	A, B, C; D (H.)												
	124th	10/Queen's, 26/R.F., 32/R.F., 21/K.R.R.C.; 124th Bde. M.G. Coy.; [34] 124th T.M. Bty. [31]		CLXXXIX [17] ; [34]	A, B, C; D (H.)												
				CXC [17] ; [35]	A, B, C; D (H.)												
1917 June (France)	122nd	12/E. Surr., 15/Hants., [35] 11/Q.O.R.W.K., 122nd M.G. Coy.; 122nd T.M. Bty.	...	CLXXXVII [17]	A, B, C; D (H.)	...	X.41 Y.41 Z.41	V.41 [38]	41st D.A.C.	228th 233rd 237th	41st	19/ Middx. (P.)	238th [37] M.G. Coy.	138th 139th 140th	52nd	238th [11] [33]	41st
	123rd	11/Queen's, 10/Q.O.R.W.K., 23/Middx., 20/D.L.I.; 123rd M.G. Coy.; 123rd T.M. Bty.		CXC [35]	A, B, C; D (H.)												
	124th	10/Queen's, 26/R.F., 32/R.F., 21/K.R.R.C.; 124th M.G. Coy.; 124th T.M. Bty.															

Dates	Brigade	Battalions, &c.	Field Artillery Brigades		Batteries		Trench Mortar Btties.		D.A.C.	Field Coys. R.E.	Signal Coy.	Pioneers	M.G. Units	Field Ambulances	Mobile Vety. Sec.	Divnl. Emp. Coy.	Divnl. Train
1917 December (Italy)	122nd	12/E. Surr., 15/(Hants. Carabiniers) Hants., 11/Q.O.R.W.K., 18/K.R.R.C.; 122nd M.G. Coy.; 122nd T.M. Bty.	CLXXXVII	...	A, B, C; D (H.)	...	X.41	...	41st D.A.C.	228th	41st	19/Middx. (P.)	199th M.G. Coy.	138th	52nd	238th	41st
	123rd	11/Queen's, 10/Q.O.R.W.K., 23/Middx., 20/D.L.I.; 123rd M.G. Coy.; 123rd T.M. Bty.	CXC		A, B, C; D (H.)		Y.41			233rd				139th			
	124th	10/Queen's, 26/R.F., 32/R.F., 21/K.R.R.C.; 124th M.G. Coy.; 124th T.M. Bty.					Z.41			237th				140th			
1918 March (France)	122nd	12/E. Surr., 15/(Hants. Carabiniers) Hants., 18/K.R.R.C.; 122nd T.M. Bty.	CLXXXVII	...	A, B, C; D (H.)	...	X.41	...	41st D.A.C.	228th	41st	19/Middx. (P.)	No. 41 Bn. M.G.C.	138th	52nd	238th	41st
	123rd	11/Queen's, 10/Q.O.R.W.K., 23/Middx.; 123rd T.M. Bty.	CXC		A, B, C; D (H.)		Y.41			233rd				139th			
	124th	10/Queen's, 26/R.F., 20/D.L.I.; 124th T.M. Bty.								237th				140th			

NOTES

1 Formed at Aldershot in September 1915 as 41st Div. This Division was a new formation.

2 The Inf. Bdes. were raised in 1915 as 122nd, 123rd, & 124th Bdes.; all three Bdes. were new formations.

3 The Bns. were designated: Bermondsey, 2nd Portsmouth, Lewisham, and Arts & Crafts. On 16/10/15 11/Q.O.R.W.K. joined 122nd Bde. from 118th Bde. from 39th Div.

4 The Bns. were designated: Lambeth, Kent County, 2nd Football, and Westside. On 16/10/15 10/Q.O.R.W.K. joined 123rd Bde. from 118th Bde., 39th Div.

5 The Bns. were designated: Battersea, Bankers, East Ham, and Yeoman Rifles.

6 Sqdn. joined Div. before 20/11/15 at Aldershot. The Sqdn. disembkd. at le Havre on 6/5/16.

7 Coy. was formed in the Div. before 20/11/15 at Aldershot. The Coy. disembkd. at le Havre on 6/5/16.

8 The Artillery Bdes. were designated: Hampstead, Fulham, Hackney, and Wimbledon; and the D.A.C. was designated: West Ham. The Bdes. were raised as 4-battery brigades, in each brigade the batteries were lettered—A, B, C, D—and each battery was a 4-gun battery. The Divnl. Arty. disembkd. at le Havre between 2-5/5/16.

9 The 3 Fd. Cos. were designated: Barnsley, Ripon, and Reading; the Signal Coy. was designated Glasgow. The companies disembkd. at le Havre between 2-6/5/16.

10 The Pioneer Bn. was designated: 2nd Public Works, and it joined the Div. at Aldershot before 20/11/15. The Bn. disembkd. at le Havre on 2/5/16.

11 The 3 Fd. Ambces. were trained at Crookham; they went to France with the Div., and disembkd. at le Havre between 3-6/5/16.

12 The Sec. joined the Div. at Aldershot before 20/11/15; it disembkd. at le Havre on 5/5/16.

13 The Train consisted of 296, 297, 298, & 299 Coys., A.S.C.: It collected at Mytchett, went to France with the Div., and disembkd. at le Havre between 2-5/5/16.

14 Sqdn. left the Div. on 31/5/16, was attached to 2nd Cav. Div. from 1-21/6/16, and joined IX Corps Cav. Regt. on 22/6/16.

15 Coy. left the Div. on 28/5/16, and joined II Corps Cyclist Bn. that day.

16 On 27/5/16 A (H.), B (H.), & C (H.) left CLXXXIII and became D (H.)/CLXXXIX, D (H.)/CLXXXVII, and D (H.)/CXC; and D/CLXXXIX, D/CLXXXVII, and D/CXC joined and became A, B, and C/CLXXXIII; D (H.) remained D (H.)/CLXXXIII.

17 On 27/5/16 D left and became B/CLXXXIII; and B (H.)/CLXXXIII joined and became D (H.)/CLXXXVII.

18 On 27/5/16 D left and became A/CLXXXIII; and A (H.)/CLXXXIII joined and became D (H.)/CLXXXIX.

19 On 27/5/16 D left and became C/CLXXXIII; and C (H.)/CLXXXIII joined and became D (H.)/CXC.

20 122nd M.G. Coy. disembkd. at le Havre on 17/5/16 and joined 122nd Bde. on 21/5/16; 123rd M.G. Coy. disembkd. at le Havre on 17/6/16 and joined 123rd Bde. on 20/6/16; 124th M.G. Coy. disembkd. at le Havre on 17/6/16 and joined 124th Bde. on 19/6/16.

21 Bde. T.M. Btties. were formed in Bdes. as follows: 122nd—122/1 & 122/2 were formed on 20/5/16, and became 122nd T.M. Bty. by 15/6/16; 123rd—123rd T.M. Bty. was formed by 15/6/16; 124th—124/1 & 124/2 were formed by 2/6/16, and became 124th T.M. Bty. by 15/6/16.

22 Between 18-30/11/16 Bde. was broken up: R. Sec. A made up A/CLXXXVII, L. Sec. A made up B/CLXXXVII, and Sec. C made up C/CLXXXVII; B & D (H.) were transferred to CXC; and Sec. C made up C/CXC to 6 guns.

NOTES—continued

[52] On 30/11/16 A was made up to 6 guns by R. Sec. A/CLXXXIII, B was made up by L. Sec. A/CLXXXIII, and C was made up by Sec. C/CLXXXIII (note 23). D (H.)/CXC joined, was made up to 6 hows. by L. Sec. D (H.)/CLXXXVII, and became D (H.)/CLXXXVII; and R. Sec. D (H.) joined D (H.)/CLXXXIII and became D (H.)/CXC. On 5/12/16 R. Sec. of old D (H.)/CLXXXVII returned, joined L. Sec. of old D (H.)/CLXXXVII, and D (H.)/CLXXXVII was reformed; and old D (H.)/CXC then became A (H.)/CLXXXVII. On 8/1/17 D (H.)/CLXXXVII was made up to 6 hows. by 1 sec. of D (H.)/CXC.

[53] On 26 & 27/11/16 A was split up and made up B and C to 6 guns each; D (H.) remained 4 hows. On 5/12/16 old D (H.)/CXC (see note 23) joined and became A (H.)/CLXXXIX. On 8/1/17 CLXXXIX became an A.F.A. Bde., and A (H.) was transferred to CXC (note 25); on 20/1/17 1 sec. C (H.)/CCXXXVI (from 47th Div.) joined and made up D (H.)/CLXXXIX, and on 21/1/17, 34th Bty. (6th Div. until 15/2/16, then 47th Div.) joined CLXXXIX A.F.A. Bde.

[54] On 25 & 26/11/16 B/CLXXXIII joined, was made up to 6 guns by R. Sec. A/CXC, and became A/CXC; L. Sec. A/CXC made up B/CXC to 6 guns; and Sec. C/CLXXXIII joined and made up C/CXC; D (H.)/CLXXXIII joined CXC, was made up to 6 hows. by R. Sec. D (H.)/CLXXXVII, and became D (H.)/CXC; and old D (H.)/CXC was transferred to CLXXXVII (note 23). On 5/12/16 R. Sec. D (H.)/CLXXXVII left new D (H.)/CXC, returned to CLXXXVII, and old D (H.)/CLXXXVII was reformed. On 8/1/17 new D (H.)/CXC was broken up: 1 sec. left and made up D (H.)/CLXXXVII; the remaining Sec. made up A (H.)/CLXXXIX (note 24) to 6 hows., and A (H.)/CLXXXIX then became D (H.)/CXC.

[55] On 17/5/16 3 Medium (2") T.M. Btes. were formed; the personnel came from the B.A.C.s.

[56] V Heavy T.M. Bty. (240 m/m. mortars) was formed and in action by 24/7/16.

[57] At 9 a.m., 22/5/16 B.A.C.s were abolished, absorbed by D.A.C., and reformed into Nos. 1, 2, and 3 Sections, 41st D.A.C.—A Echelon.

[58] On 25/8/17 a draft of 12 offrs. & 307 o.r. 1/1/Hants. Carabiniers joined 15/Hants., and on 8/10/17 119 o.r. of the same Yeo. Regt. joined the Bn., which was then redesignated 15/(Hants. Carabiniers) Hants.

[59] On 29/10/17 V Heavy T.M. Bty. was disbanded and the personnel was absorbed by the Fd. Bties. and the D.A.C.

[21] Coy. was formed at Grantham on 18/2/17, disembkd. at le Havre on 14/7/17, and joined Div. at Abeele on 17/7/17. Coy. left 41st Div. on 1/10/17, embkd. at Marseille on 12/10/17, disembkd. at Magil on 8/11/17, reached Amara on 28/10/17, and joined 54th Ind. Inf. Bde., 18th Ind. Div., at Hayaida on 30/12/17.

[22] Coy. was formed by 16/6/17.

[23] On 16/3/18 Bn. was disbanded and drafted to 6/ & 10/Q.O.R.W.K., No. 41 M.G. Bn., and 11/Entg. Bn. On 17/3/18 Bn. was transferred to 124th Bde.

[24] On 18/3/18 Bn. was disbanded and drafted to 10/Queen's, 10/, 23/, & 28/R.F., No. 41 M.G. Bn., and 9/Entg. Bn.

[25] On 16/3/18 Bn. was disbanded and drafted to 1/, 2/, 7/, 9/, 12/, 13/, 16/, 17/, & 18/K.R.R.C., and surplus joined No. 41 M.G. Bn.

[27] In Italy Z was attached to G.H.Q. (Italy) T.M. School from 24/1-28/2/18. Z returned to France with 41st Div. in March 1918; and on 25/4/18 Z was broken up and absorbed by X and Y.

[4] Coy. served with 49th Div. from 19/12/16-29/10/17; and on 30/10/17 Coy. joined 41st Div. at Bray Dunes.

[6] The Bn. was formed at Sombrin on 17/3/18; it comprised 122nd, 123rd, 124th, and 199th M.G. Cos.

GENERAL NOTES

The following Units also served with the 41st Division:—

ARTILLERY:—86 Siege Battery, R.G.A. (2, 12" Hows. on Railway Mountings) was attached to 41st Div. at Aldershot from 1/4/16 until departure for France. The Bty. disembkd. at le Havre on 8/5/16, and joined XXVI Heavy Arty. Group on 9/5/16.

89 Siege Battery, R.G.A. (4, 9.2" Hows.) was attached to 41st Div. at Aldershot from 1/4/16 until departure for France. The Bty. disembkd. at le Havre on 30/4/16, and was attached to Canadian Corps Heavy Artillery on 1/6/16.

XIII Belgian Field Artillery Regt. (1st Group—1st, 2nd, & 3rd Bties.; 2nd Group—4th, 5th, & 6th Bties.) was attached for administration to 41st Division—1st Group under tactical command of B.G., R.A., 41st Div. and 2nd Group under tactical command of B.G., R.A., 47th Div.—from 1/1-17/5/17; XIII F.A. Regt. then left to rejoin the Belgian Army.

OTHER UNITS:—84th Sanitary Section joined Div. in England; disembkd. at le Havre on 5/5/16, and served with the Div. in France until 19/4/17, when the Sany. Sec. was transferred to Army Troops, Fifth Army.

41st Div. Motor Ambce. Workshop joined Div. in England; disembkd. at Rouen on 5/5/16, left Rouen on 10/5/16, joined Div. at Merris on 11/5/16; the Unit was then merged in 40th Div. A.S.C. workshops.

On 18/3/18 the reorganization of the 41st Division on a 9-battalion basis was completed; and on 18/3/18 the pioneer battalion (19/Middx.) was reorganized on a 8-company basis.

41ST DIVISION

FORMATION, BATTLES, AND ENGAGEMENTS

This New Army Division had no existence before the outbreak of the Great War.

The 41st Division (the junior division of the reconstituted Fifth New Army) was formed at Aldershot in September 1915. The Division was an entirely new formation (see Appendix 2); and the three infantry brigades (122nd, 123rd, and 124th) were also new formations which came into existence in September 1915. During that month and the next the battalions and divisional troops moved into the Aldershot Training Area.

The sub-titles of the four battalions of the 122nd Infantry Brigade were Bermondsey (12/E. Surrey), 2nd Portsmouth (15/Hants.), Lewisham (11/Q.O.R.W.K.), and Arts & Crafts (18/K.R.R.C.); the sub-titles of the battalions of the 123rd Brigade were Lambeth (11/Queen's), Kent County (10/Q.O.R.W.K.), 2nd Football (23/Middx.), and Wearside (20/D.L.I.); and the battalions of the 124th Brigade were called Battersea (10/Queen's), Bankers (26/R.F.), East Ham (32/R.F.), and Yeomen Rifles (21/K.R.R.C.). The Field Artillery Brigades were designated Hampstead (CLXXXIII), Fulham (CLXXXVII), Hackney (CLXXXIX), and Wimbledon (CXC); the D.A.C. was called West Ham. The sub-titles of the three R.E. Field Companies were Barnsley (228th), Ripon (233rd), and Reading (237th); the Signal Company's designation was Glasgow; and the sub-title of the Pioneer Battalion (19/Middx.) was 2nd Public Works. The majority of these units were raised by mayors of boroughs, in response to Lord Kitchener's 1915 appeal for units to be formed of groups of friends who were all associated with one locality; and as far as possible the sub-titles were selected to perpetuate the birthplaces, or origins, of the units.

Training began in earnest after the arrival of the Division in the Aldershot area. Gradually the men were equipped with a short Lee-Enfield Mark III rifle, and learned both the use and care of arms. It was impressed on them that the rifle was not merely a weapon with which to fire, but it must be cleaned and prized above all other objects. One sergeant-instructor put it very clearly: "You must take as much care of your rifle as you would of your wife. Every day rub it all over with an oily rag."

Slowly signallers, Lewis gunners, bombers, and other specialists began to appear; officers went on various courses, and some were attached for a short spell of duty in France. On one occasion the monotony of training was broken by German aircraft passing over the huts occupied by one of the battalions. On the alarm being given the commanding officer, in an excess of zeal worthy of Midshipman Easy, ordered his battalion to fall in on parade, and presented the enemy with a considerable target; fortunately no bombs were dropped.

During this period of training, route marches were numerous, as they were considered excellent for trying the endurance of the men and making them fit. These exercises were carried out in full marching order; and, in addition, in each of the leather pouches was placed an iron weight—known as 'Kitchener's chocolate'—to simulate the ammunition normally carried in the field. In the far-distant future, puzzled archaeologists may speculate about the origin of numerous iron lumps found lying in Hampshire and Surrey ditches.

The time came for intensive divisional training to be started; to facilitate this, in February 1916 the infantry brigades and the divisional troops were all concentrated in Aldershot—Divnl. Hd. Qrs., the R.F.A., and the 122nd Bde. in Marlborough Lines; the R.E., the 124th Bde., and the Pioneers in Stanhope Lines; and the 123rd Bde. in Wellington Lines.

Final preparation for service in the field was strenuously undertaken, and all deficiencies in arms and equipment were made good. On the 26th April the Division was inspected by H.M. the King, who was accompanied by Field-Marshal Lord French and General Sir A. Hunter. Mayors of boroughs and others who had assisted in raising the various units and formations were also present at this parade.

Entrainment began on May Day 1916, disembarkation in France was concluded on the 6th May, and on the 8th May the Division completed its concentration between Hazebrouck and Bailleul, in the Second Army area.

For the remainder of the Great War the 41st Division served mainly on the Western Front in France and Belgium and was engaged in the following operations:

1916

BATTLES OF THE SOMME

15–17 September ... ... Battle of Flers-Courcelette [XV Corps, Fourth Army].

4–10 October ... ... Battle of the Transloy Ridges [XV Corps, Fourth Army].

1917

7–14 June ... ... Battle of Messines [X Corps, Second Army].

BATTLES OF YPRES

31 July–2 Aug. ... ... Battle of Pilckem Ridge [X Corps, Second Army].

20–22 September ... ... Battle of the Menin Road Ridge [X Corps, Second Army].

26 Sept.–11 Nov. ... Operations on the Flanders Coast [XV Corps, Fourth Army].

On the 7th Nov., the 41st Div. was informed that it was to be transferred to the Italian Front, and on the 12th entrainment began. On the 16th November the first units detrained in the Mantua area, and by the 18th the Div. completed its concentration to the N.W. of Mantua. On the 30th November it began to take over the front line behind the Piave (N.W. of Treviso) from the Italian 1st Div. The relief was completed by 9 a.m. 2nd Dec., and the 41st Div. then formed part of XIV Corps.

1918

On the 16th January the 7th Division began to relieve the 41st Div. and the relief was completed by 10 a.m. on the 19th; the 41st Div. then passed into G.H.Q. Reserve. On the 16th Feb. the Div. began to relieve the 23rd Div. in the left sector of XIV Corps Front Line, N. of Montebelluna, and by 4 p.m. on the 18th the relief was completed. The Div. held the left sector until 10 a.m. 26th Feb., when the 23rd Div. again took it over. On the 28th Feb. the 41st Div. concentrated in the Campo S. Piero entraining area, preparatory to returning to France. On the 1st March entrainment began, and on the 9th March the Div. completed detrainment at Doullens and Mondicourt; the Div. then joined IV Corps, Third Army. Before the end of the Great War the 41st Division took part in the following operations on the Western Front:

FIRST BATTLES OF THE SOMME

22 & 23 March ... ... Battle of St. Quentin [IV Corps, Third Army].

24 & 25 March ... ... Battle of Bapaume [IV Corps, Third Army].

28 March ... ... Battle of Arras [IV Corps, Third Army].

9–29 April ... ... BATTLES OF THE LYS [VIII Corps, until 8 a.m., 13/4; then II Corps, Second Army].

1918
(continued).

ADVANCE TO VICTORY

3–6 September ... ...   **Advance in Flanders** [XIX Corps, Second Army].

THE FINAL ADVANCE IN FLANDERS

28 Sept.–2 Oct. ... ...   **Battle of Ypres** [XIX Corps, Second Army].
14–19 October ... ...   **Battle of Courtrai** [XIX Corps, Second Army].
25 October ... ...   **Ooteghem** [XIX Corps, Second Army].

On the 26th and 27th October the Division was relieved in the front line and drawn back to rest around Courtrai. On the 1st November it re-occupied part of XIX Corps Front Line and established touch with the French 41st Division on the 3rd November; on the same day the 124th Brigade pushed three Lewis Gun posts across the Schelde at Berchem bridge, but on the 4th these posts were heavily shelled and had to be withdrawn. On the 9th November, the 123rd Brigade effected the passage of the Schelde, and that night established an outpost line on the Renaix–Nukerke road, gaining touch on the left with the French 41st Division. The Division pushed on; and by 11 a.m. on the 11th November, when the Armistice brought hostilities to a close, the leading brigade (124th) had advanced through Nederbrakel and was covered by its outpost line on the high ground above Tenbosch; cyclists had reached the line of the Dendre near Grammont.

On the 12th November the 41st Division was informed that it had been selected to form part of the Army of Occupation in Germany; on the 13th it took over the out-post line of XIX Corps and established posts in Grammont. On the 14th the Division was transferred to II Corps, and on the 18th it began its advance to the Rhine. On the 28th the Division was halted astride the Dendre between Lessines and Grammont and on this day it was transferred to X Corps. On the 12th December the advance eastwards was continued through Enghien–Hal–Braine l'Alleud–Plancenoit–Marbais–Sombreffe–Temploux–north of Namur–north of Huy; the billeting area on the left bank of the Meuse was reached on the 21st December.

On the 6th January 1919 the Division began to entrain for Germany and on the 12th it took over the left sector of X Corps in the Cologne Bridgehead, with divisional headquarters in Cologne. Military, educational, and recreational training was carried out whilst the Division was on garrison duty on the Rhine, and demobilization proceeded steadily. During February and at the beginning of March some changes took place in the grouping of infantry units. Then, on the 15th March, came the big change —the British divisions in the Army of the Rhine, were renamed, and the 41st Division became the London Division. The Division was thus brought to an abrupt end. During the Great War the 41st Division lost 32,158 killed, wounded, and missing.

63RD (ROYAL NAVAL) DIVISION

G.O.C.

21 September 1914	Br.-Gen. Sir G. G. ASTON (sick, 29/9/14).
29 September 1914	Br.-General A. PARIS.
3 October 1914	Major-General A. PARIS (wounded, 12/10/16).
12 October 1916	Br.-Gen. C. H. DE ROUGEMONT (acting).
16 October 1916	Br.-Gen. C. N. TROTMAN (acting).
17 October 1916	Major-General C. D. SHUTE.
19 February 1917	Major-General C. E. LAWRIE.
30 August 1918	Major-General C. A. BLACKLOCK.

G.S.O.1.

4 Sept. 1914...Lt.-Col. A. H. OLLIVANT.
29 Feb. 1916...Major E. F. P.
SKETCHLEY (acting).
25 May 1916...Lt.-Col. C. A. KER.
28 July 1916...Lt.-Col. N. R.
DAVIDSON.
7 Aug. 1916...Lt.-Col. C. F. ASPINALL.
15 Nov. 1917...Lt.-Col. W. G. NEILSON.
8 July 1918...Lt.-Col. T. L. B. SOUTRY
(sick, 25/8/18).
25 Aug. 1918...Major W. R. MEREDITH
(acting).
26 Aug. 1918...Lt.-Col. J. H.
MACKENZIE.

A.-A. & Q.-M.-G.

[7 Aug. 1914]...Lt.-Col. H. D.
FARQUHARSON (acting).
23 Sept. 1914...Lt.-Col. H. D.
FARQUHARSON.
29 Sept. 1914...Major G. S. RICHARDSON.
30 Oct. 1914...Lt.-Col. G. S.
RICHARDSON.
21 Dec. 1915...Lt.-Col. J. D. BULLER.
12 April 1916...Major R. F. C. FOSTER
(acting).
27 May 1916...Lt.-Col. R. F. C.
FOSTER.
2 Aug. 1918...Lt.-Col. R. R. SMYTH.

B.-G., R.A.

[20 June 1916]...Br.-Gen. C. H. DE
ROUGEMONT.

(In July 1916 the Divisional Artillery
joined 63rd (R.N.) Div. in France, from
63rd (2/Northumbrian) Div.*–see Table
and notes 65–68 and 71.)

C.R.E.

[21 Aug. 1914]...Lt.-Col. A. B. CAREY.
27 May 1916...Lt.-Col. G. H.
HARRISON.
21 Dec. 1916...Major A. R. DAVIES
(acting).
28 Dec. 1916...Lt.-Col. S. H. COWAN.
19 April 1918...Major J. W. REVELL
(acting).
12 May 1918...Lt.-Col. J. A. GRAEME.

---

* On 21/7/1916 the 63rd (2/Northumbrian) Division was broken up in England (see Part 2B).

1st R. NAVAL BDE.

1 Sept. '14...Commodore W.
HENDERSON
(interned in Holland, 9/10/14).
11 Nov. '14...Br.-Gen. D. MERCER.

On 2/8/15 the Bde. became

1st BDE.

[11 Nov. '14]...Br.-Gen. D. MERCER.
28 May '16...Br.-Gen. C. L. McNAB
(sick, 21/6/16).
25 June '16...Lt.-Col. E. J. STROUD
(acting).

On 2/7/16 the Bde. (less Staff) was broken up.

On 7/7/16 3rd (R. Marine) Bde.—with Staff of 1st Bde.—became

1st (R. NAVAL) BDE.

[25 June '16]...Lt.-Col. E. J. STROUD
(acting).
16 July '16...Br.-Gen. R. E. S.
PRENTICE.

On 19/7/16 1st (R. Naval) Bde. was numbered

188th BDE.

[16 July '16]...Br.-Gen. R. E. S.
PRENTICE.
16 Dec. '17...Br.-Gen. J. F. S. D.
COLERIDGE.
[29 Nov. '18...Br.-Gen. H. NELSON].

2nd R. NAVAL BDE.

1 Sept. '14...Commodore O.
BACKHOUSE.

In July 1915 the Bde. was broken up.

On 2/8/15 the Bde. was reformed and became

2nd BDE.

[27 Oct. '14]...Br.-Gen. C. N. TROTMAN*
(sick, 20/9/15).
20 Sept. '15...Lt.-Col. E. J. STROUD
(acting).
1 Oct. '15...Br.-Gen. C. N. TROTMAN
(sick, 18/11/15).
19 Nov. '15...Lt.-Col. E. J. STROUD
(acting).
26 Jan. '16...Br.-Gen. C. N. TROTMAN.
21 May '16...Lt.-Col. L. WILSON
(acting).
27 May '16...Br.-Gen. L. F. PHILIPS.

On 7/7/16 the 2nd Bde became

2nd (R. NAVAL) BDE.

[27 May '16]...Br.-Gen. L. F. PHILIPS.

On 19/7/16 2nd (R. Naval) Bde. was numbered

189th BDE.

[27 May '16]...Br.-Gen L. F. PHILIPS.
30 Oct. '17...Br.-Gen. J. F. S. D.
COLERIDGE.
16 Dec. '17...Br.-Gen. A. M. ASQUITH
(sick, 28/2/18).
28 Feb. '18...Commander B. H. ELLIS
(acting).
1 Mar. '18...Lt.-Col. H. F.
KIRKPATRICK (acting).
6 Mar. '18...Br.-Gen. H. N. BRAY
(wd., 12/3/18).
13 Mar. '18...Lt.-Col. H. F.
KIRKPATRICK (acting).
19 Mar. '18...Br.-Gen. H. D. DE PREE.
24 Aug. '18...Commander W. M.
EGERTON (acting).
3 Sept. '18...Br.-Gen. B. J. CURLING.

---

* From Royal Marine Bde. (p. 119).

ROYAL MARINE BDE.

6 Aug. '14...Maj.-Gen. E. L. McCausland.
25 Aug. '14...Br.-Gen. Sir G. G. Aston.
24 Sept. '14...Br.-Gen. A. Paris.
29 Sept. '14...Lt.-Col. C. McN. Parsons (acting).
5 Oct. '14...Colonel A. E. Marchant (acting).
27 Oct. '14...Br.-Gen. C. N. Trotman.

On 2/8/15 the 4 R. Mar. Bns. were reformed in 2 Bns., Chatham/Deal and Portsmouth/Plymouth; the 2 Bns. were then transferred to the reformed 2nd Bde. and R. Marine Bde. then ceased to exist.

3rd (ROYAL MARINE) BDE.

(On 22 May 1916, on arrival in France, the Bde. was reformed.)
22 May '16...Lt.-Col. E. J. Stroud (acting).
25 May '16...Br.-Gen. C. N. Trotman.

On 7/7/16 3rd (R.M.) Bde.—with Staff of 1st Bde.—became 1st (R. Naval) Bde.

190th BDE.

(The 4 Bns. to form this Bde.—3 from U.K. & 1 in France—were collected in France between 9/7–21/8/16. The Bde. then replaced 3rd R. Mar. Bde.)

9 July '16...Br.-Gen. C. N. Trotman (sick, 13/9/16).
13 Sept. '16...Lt.-Col. R. J. I. Hesketh (acting).
15 Sept. '16...Lt.-Col. A. R. H. Hutchison (acting).
2 Oct. '16...Br.-Gen. C. N. Trotman (sick, 5/10/16).
5 Oct. '16...Lt.-Col. R. J. I. Hesketh (acting).
6 Oct. '16...Lt.-Col. A. R. H. Hutchison (acting).
17 Oct. '16...Br.-Gen. C. N. Trotman.
24 Oct. '16...Br.-Gen. Hon. C. J. Sackville-West (wd., 29/10/16).
29 Oct. '16...Br.-Gen. W. C. G. Heneker.
8 Dec. '16...Lt.-Col. E. P. C. Boyle (acting).
12 Dec. '16...Lt.-Col. R. J. I. Hesketh (acting).
18 Dec. '16...Br.-Gen. H. W. E. Finch.
4 June '17...Lt.-Col. J. S. Collings-Wells (acting).
10 June '17...Lt.-Col. E. F. E. Seymour (acting).
18 June '17...Lt.-Col. J. S. Collings-Wells (acting).
20 June '17...Br.-Gen. A. R. H. Hutchison.
6 June '18...Br.-Gen. W. B. Lesslie.

63RD (ROYAL NAVAL) DIVISION [1]

ORDER OF BATTLE, 1914-1918

Dates	INFANTRY — Brigades	INFANTRY — Battalions and attached Units	Mounted Troops	Field Artillery — Brigades	Field Artillery — Batteries	Bde. Ammn. Colns.	Trench Mortar Btties. — Medium	Trench Mortar Btties. — Heavy	Divnl. Ammn. Coln.	Engineers — Field Cos.	Signal Service — Divnl. Signal Coy.	Pioneers	M.G. Units	Field Ambulances	Mobile Vety. Sec.	Divnl. Emplnt. Coy.	Divnl. Train
1914 October (Antwerp)	1st R. NAVAL [2]; 2nd R. MARINE [3]	1st (Drake), 2nd (Hawke), 3rd (Benbow), 4th (Collingwood); 5th (Nelson), 6th (Howe), 7th (Hood), 8th (Anson), 9th (Chatham), 10th (Portsmouth), 11th (Plymouth), 12th (Deal)	...	...	...	...	...	...	...	R.E. Detnt. [4]	...	...	...	...	...	...	...
1915 April (Gallipoli)	1st (R. NAVAL) [5]; 2nd (R. NAVAL) [6]; 3rd (R. MARINE) [6]	Drake, Nelson, Deal [6]; Howe, Hood, Anson; Chatham, Portsmouth, Plymouth	R.N.D. Cyclist Coy. [7]	...	...	R.N.D.S.A.A. Coln. [8]	...	...	...	No. 1 Coy. [9]; No. 2 Coy. [9]	R.N.D. [9]	...	Armoured Motor M.G. Sqdn. [10]	No. 1 [9]; No. 2 [9]; No. 3 [9]	19th [11]	...	R.N.D. [11]
1915 June (Gallipoli)	1st (R. NAVAL) [12]; 2nd (R. NAVAL) [14]; [15]; 3rd (R. MARINE) [16]	Drake, Hawke, [17] Benbow, [18] Nelson; Collingwood, [19] Howe, Hood, [20] Anson; Chatham, [21] Portsmouth, [21] Plymouth, [22] Deal [14]; [21]	R.N.D. Cyclist Coy.	...	...	R.N.D.S.A.A. Coln.	...	...	...	No. 1 Coy.; No. 2 Coy.	R.N.D.	...	...	No. 1; No. 2; No. 3	19th	...	R.N.D.
1915 August (Gallipoli)	1st [13] ......; 2nd [14]; [1]	Drake, Hawke, Nelson, Hood [20]; Howe, Anson; Chatham & Deal [21]; [23] Portsmouth & Plymouth [21]; [24]	R.N.D. Cyclist Coy.	...	...	R.N.D.S.A.A. Coln.	...	...	...	No. 1 Coy.; No. 2 Coy.; No. 3 Coy. [23]	R.N.D.	...	...	No. 1; No. 2 [24]; No. 3	19th	...	R.N.D.
1915 September (Gallipoli)	1st [27] ......; 2nd [28]	Drake, Hawke, Nelson, Hood; Howe, Anson, 1/R.M., [25] 2/R.M. [26]	R.N.D. Cyclist Coy.	...	...	R.N.D.S.A.A. Coln.	...	...	...	No. 1 Coy.; No. 2 Coy.; No. 3 Coy. [23]	R.N.D.	...	...	No. 1; No. 2; No. 3	19th	...	R.N.D.
1916 March (Ægean)	1st [27] ......; 2nd [28]	Drake, Hawke, Nelson, Hood; Howe, Anson, -1/R.M., [29] 2/R.M.	R.N.D. Cyclist Coy. [30]	...	...	R.N.D.S.A.A. Coln. [31]	...	...	...	No. 1 Coy. [32]; No. 2 Coy. [32]; No. 3 Coy. [32]	R.N.D. [32]	...	...	No. 1 [31]; No. 2 [30]; No. 3 [30]	19th [33]	...	R.N.D. [32]
1916 May (France)	1st (R. NAVAL) [34]; [31]; [16]; 2nd (R. NAVAL) [17]; [38]; 3rd (R. MARINE) [41]	Drake, [34] 1/Hood, [35] 2/Hood [36]; Hawke, [34]; [35] Nelson, [34]; [35] Howe, [40]; [41] 2nd (R. Naval) Bde. M.G. Coy. [42]; Anson, [43] 1/R.M., [34] 2/R.M. [44]	R.N.D. Cyclist Coy. [45]	1/IV Home Counties [47] (H.)	1/4/Kent (H.), 1/5/Kent (H.)	1/IV Home Ctles. (H.) [47] B.A.C.	...	...	...	1st R.N., [48] 2nd R.N. [48] 3rd R.N. [48]	R.N.D. [49]	14/ Worc. [50] (P.)	...	1st (R.N.) [51]; 2nd (R.N.) [51]; 3rd (R.N.) [51]	53rd [52]	...	R.N.D. [52]

Date	Brigade	Battalions, etc.		Artillery Brigade	Batteries		T.M. Bty.	V	D.A.C.	Field Cos. R.E.		Pioneers	M.G.	Field Ambulances			
1916 July (France)	188th[44];[44]	Howe,[40];[41] Anson,[41] 1/[188th] R.M.,[41] 2/R.M.,[41] Bde. M.G. Coy.,[41] 188th T.M. Bty.[44]	...	CCXXIII[46] ...	A, B, C; D (H.)	...	X.63[49] Y.63[49] Z.63[49]	V 63[50]	63rd D.A.C.[51]	1st R.N. 2nd R.N. 3rd R.N.	63rd[52]	14/ Worc. (P.)	...	1st (R.N.) 2nd (R.N.) 3rd (R.N.)	53rd	...	63rd[72]
	189th[47]; [48]	Drake,[47] Hawke,[47] Nelson,[47] Hood,[44];[47] 189th Bde. M.G. Coy.,[44];[48] 189th T.M. Bty.[44]		CCXXV[46] ...	A, B, C; D (H.)												
	190th[44]	7/R.F.,[44] 4/Bedf.,[44] 10/ R.D.F.,[44] 1/1/H.A.C.;[44] 190th Bde. M.G. Coy.;[44] 190th T.M. Bty.[44]		CCXXVI[44] ...	A, B, C; D (H.)												
				CCXXVII[44] ...	A, B, C												
1917 June (France)	188th	Howe,[44] Anson, 1/R.M., 2/ R.M.; 188th M.G. Coy. [45];[47] Drake, Hawke, Nelson, Hood; 189th M.G.	...	CCXXIII[44] ...	A, B, C; D (H.)	...	X.63 Y.63 Z.63[44]	V.63[44]	63rd D.A.C.	247th[44] 248th[44] 249th[40]	63rd[45]	14/ Worc. (P.)	223rd[44] M.G. Coy.	148th (R.N.)[44] 149th (R.N.)[45] 150th (R.N.)[45]	53rd	253rd[45]	63rd
	189th	Coy.;[47];[45] 189th T.M. Bty.		CCXXVII[45] ...	A, B, C; D (H.)												
	190th	7/R.F., 4/Bedf., 10/R.D.F.;[45] 1/28/London;[45] 190th M.G. Coy.;[47] 190th T.M. Bty.															
1918 March (France)	188th	Anson, 1/R.M., 2/R.M.;[44] 188th T.M. Bty.	...	CCXXIII ...	A, B, C; D (H.)	...	X.63[45] Y.63[45]	..	63rd D.A.C.	247th 248th 249th	63rd	14/ Worc. (P.)	No. 63 Bn.[44] M.G.C.	148th (R.N.) 149th (R.N.) 150th (R.N.)	53rd	253rd	63rd
	189th	Drake, Hawke, Hood; 189th T.M. Bty.		CCXXVII ...	A, B, C; D (H.)												
	190th	7/R.F., 4/Bedf., 1/28/ London; 190th T.M. Bty.															
1918 May (France)	188th	Anson, R.M., 2/R. Ir. Regt.;[44] 188th T.M. Bty.	...	CCXXIII ...	A, B, C; D (H.)	...	X.63 Y.63	...	63rd D.A.C.	247th 248th 249th	63rd	14/ Worc. (P.)	No. 63 Bn. M.G.C.	148th (R.N.) 149th (R.N.) 150th (R.N.)	53rd	253rd	63rd
	189th	Drake, Hawke, Hood; 189th T.M. Bty.		CCXXVII ...	A, B, C; D (H.)												
	190th	7/R.F., 4/Bedf., 1/28 London; 190th T.M. Bty.															

NOTES

[1] The R.N. Div. was formed in England in Sept. 1914. On 29/4/16 the R.N. Div. was transferred from the Admiralty to the War Office (Authy.—79/8954 (S.D.2), d/d. 29/4/16); and on 19/7/16 the R.N. Div. became 63rd (R.N.) Div. (A.C.I. No. 1363, d/d. 8/7/16).

[2] The 2 Royal Naval Bdes. were formed in August & September 1914 and concentrated near Deal. On 5/10/14 the 2 Bdes. disembkd. at Dunkirk, reached Antwerp that night, and returned to Dover on 11/10/14.

[3] The R. Mar. Bde. was formed in Aug. 1914, landed at Ostend on 27/8/14, returned to Deal on 31/8/14. R. Mar. Bde. re-embkd. on 19/9/14, disembkd. at Dunkirk on 20/9/14, reached Cassel on 30/9/14, and arrived at Antwerp on 3/10/14. On 11/10/14 R. Mar. Bde. returned from Ostend to England. (For R.M.A. Bn., see General Notes.)

[4] R.E. Detmt. (Capt. E. H. Rooke, with 1 offr., 4 N.C.O.s, & 28 sappers) with 1 ton of explosives, means of ignition, tools, and stores, reached Dunkirk with R. Mar. Bde. on 20/9/14, and Antwerp on 3/10/14.

[5] The 2 Bdes. embkd. at Avonmouth on 28/2 & 1/3/15, reached Lemnos on 17/3/15, and disembkd. at Port Said on 26 & 27/3/15. Began re-embkn. on 12/4/15, reached Skyros on 16/4/15, demonstrated in Gulf of Xeros on 25/4/15; and on 28/4/15 began landing at Cape Helles.

[6] R. Mar. Bde. (H.Q. & Chatham and Plymouth Bns.) embkd. at Devonport on 6/2/15, reached Lemnos on 24/2/15, engaged at Kum Kale and Sedd el Bahr on 4/3/15. On 12/3/15 Bde. was reformed at Lemnos, with Chatham, Portsmouth, and Plymouth Bns.; Deal Bn. was transferred to 1st Bde. 3rd Bde. reached Port Said on 27/3/15; Bde. re-embkd. on 7/4/15, reached Lemnos on 11 & 12/4/15; reinforced Anzac Corps at Kaba Tepe from 28/4/15 until 12/5/15. On 13/5/15 the Bde. rejoined R.N. Div. and went into the line at Cape Helles on 25/5/15.

[7] Formed in England and went to Gallipoli with R.N. Div.

[8] S.A.A. Coln. joined Div. at Port Said on 26/3/15.

[9] Joined Div. in England and went to Gallipoli with R.N. Div.

[10] Joined Div. at Lemnos on 17/3/15, was engaged with Div. at Anzac and Gallipoli in April and May 1915.

[11] Vety. Sec. joined Div. at Port Said on 31/3/15.

[12] Train consisted of 275 & 279 Cos., A.S.C.; the 2 Cos. joined the Div. at Port Said on 28/3/15.

[13] On 2/8/15 the Bde. became 1st Bde.

[14] In July 1915 the Bde. was broken up. On 2/8/15 the Bde. was reformed, amalgamated with R. Mar. Bde., and became 2nd Bde.

[15] On 30/5/15 each Bn. was reorganized in 3 Cos. On 2/8/15 2nd Naval and R. Mar. Bdes. amalgamated and became 2nd Bde.

[16] On 30/5/18 Deal Bn. rejoined R. Mar. Bde. and was then reorganized in 3 Cos.

[17] On night 28/29/5/15 Bn. landed at Cape Helles and joined 1st Bde.

[18] On night 30/31/5/15 Bn. landed at Cape Helles and joined 1st Bde. On 9/6/15 Bn. was disbanded and absorbed by the other R.N. Bns.

[19] On night 29/30/5/15 Bn. landed at Cape Helles and joined 2nd. Bde. On 9/6/15 Bn. was disbanded and absorbed by the other R.N. Bns.

[20] On 2/8/15 Bn. was transferred to 1st Bde.

[21] Chatham & Deal Bns. amalgamated on 27/7/15, and joined 2nd Bde. on 2/8/15.

[22] Portsmouth & Plymouth Bns. amalgamated on 27/7/15, and joined 2nd Bde. on 2/8/15.

[23] Coy. joined the Div. at Blandford; was left behind to complete its training, and rejoined Div. in Gallipoli.

[24] On 5/8/15 No. 2 Fd. Ambc. left Gallipoli for Mudros.

[25] On 12/8/15 Chatham & Deal Bn. was renamed 1st Bn., R.M.

[26] On 12/8/15 Portsmouth & Plymouth Bn. was renamed 2nd Bn., R.M.

[27] After the Evacuation of the Bde. concentrated at Mudros on 9 & 10/1/16. Between 19/1–15/2/16 Drake and Hawke Bns. went to Imbros. On 20/1/16 Hood Bn. went to Tenedos, and on 22/2/16 Hood (less 1 Coy.) returned to Mudros.

[28] After the Evacuation of Helles the Bde. concentrated at Mudros on 9 & 10/1/16. Between 20–22/2/16 Bde. moved to Stavros (Greece)—40 miles E. of Salonika.

[29] These Units concentratd at Mudros on 9 & 10/1/16.

[30] This Fd. Coy. went to Stavros on 20/2/16.

[31] This Fd. Ambcc. went to Stavros on 22/2/16.

[32] On 18/2/16 the Sec. was transferred to 42nd (E. Lanc.) Div.

[33] 275 (H.T.) Coy. left the Div. at Mudros and was transferred to H.Q. Base, M.E.F. 279 (H.T.) Coy. went to France and joined 31st Div. Train on 15/3/16.

[34] After arrival in France, in May 1916, the Bde. was reorganized and Hawke & Nelson Bns. were transferred to 2nd Bde. On 7/7/16 the 3rd Bde. became 1st Bde. (The old 1st Bde. was broken up on 2/7/16.)

[35] Drake disembkd. at Marseille on 20/5/16.

[36] Hood disembkd. at Marseille on 20/5/16. On 1/6/16 Hood was divided to form nucleus of two Bns.—1/Hood & 2/Hood. The 2 Bns. were reamalgamated on 5/7/16 and became Hood Bn.

[37] After arrival in France, in May 1916, Bde. was reorganized. On 5/7/16 it was again reorganized and then consisted of:—

Drake, Hawke, Nelson, and Hood Bns.

[38] Hawke disembkd. at Marseille on 23/5/16.

[39] Nelson disembkd. at Marseille on 22/5/18.

[40] Howe disembkd. at Marseille on 12/5/16. Howe Bn. was transferred to 3rd Bde. on 3/7/16 (also see note 41).

[41] On 22/5/16 the Bde. was reformed at Vieulaine (on the Somme, N. of Airaines). On 7/7/16 the 3rd Bde. became 1st Bde.

[42] Anson disembkd. at Marseille on 19/5/16.

[43] 1/R.M. disembkd. at Marseille on 19/5/16.

[44] 2/R.M. disembkd. at Marseille on 12/5/16.

[45] On 28/5/16 2nd Bde. M.G. Coy. was formed in France—personnel was found by Hawke, Nelson, and Howe Bns.

[46] The Cyclist Coy. disembkd. on 23/5/16 at Marseille (from Mudros). In June 1916 the Coy. was broken up in the concentration area.

[47] Bde. (2, 4.5″ How. Btles. & B.A.C.)—formerly part of the 44th (Home Cties.) Div. Arty.—disembkd. at le Havre on 10/3/16, joined R.N. Div. in France by 9/6/16, and on 24/6/16 was numbered CCXXIII (H.); and 1/4/Kent (H.) Bty. then became A (H.) and 1/5/Kent (H.) Bty. became B (H.). On 18/7/16 A (H.)/CCXXIII became D (H.)/CCCXVIII; on 26/7/16 B (H.)/CCXXIII became D (H.)/CCCXVI, and the B.A.C. became the D.A.C. (On 31/7/16 CCCXVIII was renumbered CCXXIII—see note 65.)

[48] The Fd. Coe. disembkd. at Marseille: 1st on 22/5/16; 2nd on 20/5/16; and 3rd on 23/5/16.

[49] The Sig. Coy. disembkd. at Marseille on 23/5/16.

[50] Bn. disembkd. at le Havre on 21/6/16 and joined Div. at Bruay on 23/6/16.

[51] The Fd. Ambcs. disembkd. at Marseille: 1st on 20/5/16; and 2nd & 3rd on 23/5/16.

[52] The Sec. came from Woolwich; it disembkd. at le Havre on 31/5/16, arrived at Rouen on 2/6/16, left Rouen on 17/6/16, and joined Div. at Bruay on 18/6/16.

[53] The Train (H.Q. & 4 Cos.) joined the Div. at Mudros, prior to embkn. for France. The Train disembkd. at Marseille between 20–23/5/16; went to Abbeville for completion; and rejoined the Div. by 14/6/16. The 4 Cos. were numbered 761, 762, 763, & 764 Cos., A.S.C.

[54] On 19/7/16 1st Bde. was numbered 188th (see note 1).

[55] On 19/7/16 2nd Bde. was numbered 189th (see note 1).

[56] On 6/7/16 a new Bde. was orderd to be formed as 3rd Bde., R.N. Div. (notes 41 and 34). On 8/7/16 the Bde. Cdr. learned of the War Office that the new 3rd Bde. would be numbered 190th Bde. The Bde. completed its formation (with the Div.) between 29/6–21/8/17.

[57] This S.R. Bn. was at Falmouth on 8/7/16, disembkd. at le Havre on 24/7/16, and joined Bde. on 27/7/16.

NOTES—*continued*

" This S.R. Bn. was at Felixstowe on 8/7/16, disembkd. at le Havre on 25/7/16, and joined Bde. on 27/7/16.

" The Bn. was at Dublin on 8/7/16, disembkd. at le Havre on 19/8/16, and joined Bde. on 21/8/16.

" Bn. went to France on 18/9/14; served in 8th, 7th, 85th, & 7th Bdes., in 3rd Div., from 10/11/14-14/10/15, when Bn. was transferred to G.H.Q. Troops. On 9/7/16 Bn. joined 190th Bde. and served in the Bde. until 29/6/17, when Bn. was transferred to G.H.Q. Troops. On 25/9/18 Bn. joined 4th Gds. Bde. and served with 4th Gds. Bde. until 28/10/18; Bn. was then transferred to G.H.Q. Troops until the Armistice. On 5/11/19 Bn. reached Cologne Bridgehead and came under Second Army.

" Coy. left Grantham on 31/7/18, disembkd. at le Havre on 1/8/16, arrived at Barlin on 4/8/16, and was allotted to 188th Bde. Coy. left the Div. for the Base on 17/5/17.

" 2nd Naval Bde. M.G. Coy. (note 45) was numbered 189th on 19/7/16. Coy. left the Div. for the Base on 15/5/17.

" Coy. disembkd. at le Havre on 5/9/16, detrained at Barlin on 7/9/16, and joined 190th Bde.

" Bde. Light T.M. Bties. were formed:
188th—1st Light T.M. Bty. at Bajus on 6/7/18, became 188th on 21/7/16;
189th—2nd Light T.M. Bty. by 5/7/16, became 189th on 21/7/16;
190th—3rd Light T.M. Bty. on 14/8/16, became 190th on 25/7/16.

" CCCXVIII Bde. (formerly in 63rd, 2/Northb'n., Div.), disembkd. at le Havre on 3/7/18 and joined R.N. Div. on 5/7/16; Bde. consisted of A, B, & C Bties. (12 18-pdrs.). On 18/7/16 1/4/Kent (H.) Bty. joined from 1/IV/Home Ctics. (H.) Bde. (n. 47), and became D (H.)/CCCXVIII. On 19/7/16 number of Bde. was changed to CCXXV, and on 31/7/16 Bde. was renumbered CCXXIII. On 31/8/18 Bde. was reorganized: R. Sec. A/CCCXVI joined and made up A; L. Sec. A/CCCXVI made up B; and L. Sec. B/CCCXVI made up C, to 6, 18-pdrs. each. On 24/1/17 L. Sec. D (H.)/CCCXV joined D (H.)/CCXXIII and made up Bty. to 6 hows.

" CCCXV Bde. (formerly in 63rd, 2/Northb'n., Div.) disembkd. at le Havre on 3/7/16 and joined R.N. Div. on 5/7/16; Bde. consisted of A, B, C, and D (H.) Bties. (12, 18-pdrs. & 4, 4.5" hows.). On 31/8/16 Bde. was reorganized: C was broken up and R. Sec. made up A and L. Sec. made up B to 6, 18-pdrs. each. On 18/11/16 525 (H.) Bty. joined and became C (H.). On 24/1/17 D (H.) was broken up: L. Sec. D (H.) joined D (H.)/CCXXIII and R. Sec. D (H.)/CCCXV joined D (H.)/CCCXVII and made up Bties. to 6 hows. each. On 11/2/17 C (H.) became D (H.)/CCCXV, and R. Sec. C (H.)/CCCVIII (from 61st Div.) joined and made up D (H.) to 6 hows.; and A/CCLX (from 51st Div.) joined Bde., and became C/CCCXV: Bde. then became an A.F.A. Bde.

" CCCXVI Bde. (formerly in 63rd, 2/Northb'n., Div.) disembkd. at le Havre on 3/7/18 and joined R.N. Div. on 5/7/16; Bde. then consisted of A, B, & C Bties. (12, 18-pdrs.). On 26/7/18 1/5/Kent (H.) Bty. joined from 1/IV/Home Ctics. (H.) Bde. (n. 47) and became D (H.)/CCCXVI. On 30-31/8/16 CCCXVI was broken up: A and L. Sec. B joined CCCXIII and made up A, B, & C/CCXXIII to 6, 18-pdrs. each (n. 65); R. Sec. B made up C/CCCXVI to 6 guns and C/CCCXVI then became C/CCXXIII; and D (H.)/CCCXVI became D (H.)/CCCXVII.

" CCCXVII Bde. (formerly in 63rd, 2/Northb'n., Div.) disembkd. at le Havre on 3/7/18 and joined R.N. Div. on 5/7/16; Bde. then consisted of A, B, & C Bties. (12, 18-pdrs.). On 31/8/18 Bde. was reorganized: C was broken up and R. Sec. made up A, and L. Sec. made up B to 6, 18-pdrs. each; C/CCCXVI (made up to 6 guns by R. Sec. B/CCCXVI) joined CCCXVII and became C/CCCXVII; and D (H.)/CCCXVI also joined and became D (H.)/CCCXVII. On 24/1/17 R. Sec. D (H.)/CCCXV joined D (H.)/CCCXVII and made up Bty. to 6 hows.

" The 3 Medium T.M. Bties. joined the Div. on 5/7/18.

" On 29/7/16 1, 9.45" Heavy T.M. arrived, and the formation of a Heavy T.M. Bty. was ordered.

" D.A.C. (formerly in 63rd, 2/Northb'n., Div.) disembkd. at le Havre on 4/7/16, and joined R.N. Div. on 12/7/16.

" On 19/7/16 Coy. was numbered 63rd (see note 1).
" On 19/7/16 the Train was numbered 63rd (see note 1).

" Between 6-28/2/18 Bn. was drafted and disbanded; drafts went to Anson, 1/R.M., 2/R.M., and 7/Entg. Bns.

" 223rd M.G. Coy. left Grantham 25/4/17, disembkd. at Boulogne 28/4/17, joined Div. 2/5/17, and was posted to 189th Bde. on 8/5/17. On 12/6/17 Coy. was transferred to 188th Bde., and was renumbered 188th M.G. Coy.

" Between 8-23/2/18 Bn. was drafted and disbanded; drafts went to Drake, Hood, and 7/Entg. Bns., and surplus went to the Base.

" 224th M.G. Coy. left Grantham 25/4/17, disembkd. at Boulogne 25/4/17, joined Div. 29/4/17, and was posted to 188th Bde. on 8/5/17. On 12/6/17 Coy. was transferred to 189th Bde., and was renumbered 189th M.G. Coy.

" On 22/6/17 Bn. left 190th Bde., 63rd Div., and joined 48th Bde., 16th Div. On 13/2/18 Bn. went to VII Corps Rft. Depot, and was disbanded on 15/2/18.

" Bn. went to France on 27/10/14, formed part of G.H.Q. Troops until 28/6/17, when Bn. joined 190th Bde.

" On 1/2/17 the 3 Fd. Cos. were transferred to the Corps of R.E.; and on 18/2/17 the Fd. Cos. were numbered 247th, 248th, and 249th.

" 223rd M.G. Coy. was formed on 6/8/17 at Camiers (M.G. Corps Base Depot). From 8/8-9/9/17 Coy. trained at Camiers; on 7/9/17 Coy. joined 63rd Div. at St. Aubin and became Divnl. M.G. Coy.

" On 19/7/17 the Fd. Ambces. were numbered 148th (R.N.), 149th (R.N.), and 150th (R.N.). (Authy. A.C.I. No. 1044 of 3/7/17.)

" Coy. was formed by 2/7/17.

" On 29/4/18 1/ & 2/R.M. amalgamated and became R. Marine Bn.

" On 2/2/18 Z was broken up and distributed to X and Y.

" On 2/2/18 V Heavy T.M. Bty. was broken up and the personnel posted to X and Y.

" On 1/3/18 M.G. Bn. was formed; it consisted of 188th, 190th, and 223rd M.G. Cos.

" Bn. served in 8th Bde., 3rd Div., until 24/10/14, in 4th Div. until 22/5/16, in 22nd Bde., 7th Div., until 14/10/16, in 49th Bde., 16th Div., until 23/4/18, when Bn. joined 188th Bde., 63rd (R.N.) Div.

63RD (ROYAL NAVAL) DIVISION

GENERAL NOTES

The following Units also served with the 63rd (Royal Naval) Division :—

Commander C. R. Samson's Detnt. (400 Naval & Marine ratings—chiefly Officers and Chief Petty Officers, R.N.R.—with motor-cars and 6 aeroplanes) was at Morbecque and at the Aviation Ground, Dunkirk ; from 20/9–3/10/14 the Detnt. was attached to R. Marine Bde.

MOUNTED TROOPS—1/Q.O.O. Hsrs. disembkd. at Dunkirk on 22/9/14 and served with R.N. Div. from 29/9–3/10/14 ; the Regt. was then transferred & came under Base Cdt., Dunkirk.

ARTILLERY—525 (H.) Bty. (4, 4.5″ Hows.) disembkd. at le Havre on 11/11/16, left le Havre on 15/11/16, and joined CCCXV on 18/11/16 (note 66).

INFANTRY—R.M.A. Battalion served with R. Marine Bde. until the Bde. returned from Ostend on 31/8/14 ; it was then replaced by the Deal Bn.

1/4/K.S.L.I. went to India with 44th (Home Cties.) Div. on 30/10/14, disembkd. at Rangoon on 10/12/14, and on 10/2/15 reached Singapore (with 1 Coy. at Hong Kong from 5/4/15). Bn. left Singapore on 14/4/17 and on 29/7/17 reached le Havre (via Ceylon, Durban, Cape Town, Plymouth, and Southampton). Bn. left le Havre on 17/8/17 and joined 190th Bde., 63rd Div., at Maroeuil on 18/8/17. Bn. served with 190th Bde. from 18/8/17–4/2/18, and was then transferred to 56th Bde., 19th Div.

2/2/London
2/4/London
{ the two Bns. disembkd. at Malta on 31/12/14 and served there until August 1915. 2/2/London disembkd. at Helles on 18/10/15 and joined 2nd Bde., R.N. Div., on 14/10/15 ; 2/4/London disembkd. at Helles and joined 1st Bde., R.N. Div., on 15/10/15. The two Bns. served with the R.N. Div. until the Evacuation of Helles on 8/9/1/16 ; then they went to Alexandria (21/1/16) and were attached to the 53rd Div. The 2 Bns. disembkd. at Marseille (24/4/16) and went to Rouen. By mid-June 1916 both Bns. had been broken up and drafted.

OTHER UNITS—Sanitary Section arrived and joined R.N. Div. at Port Said on 30/8/15. This Sanitary Section did not return to France in May 1916 with R.N. Div.

63rd Sanitary Section was formed on 31/5/16 in R.N. Div. (personnel was furnished by 3rd (R.N.) Fd. Ambce.) and the Section served with 63rd (R.N.) Div. until 8/4/17 ; the Section then left the Div. and took over a First Army Sanitary Area.

On 28/2/18 the reorganization of the 63rd (R.N.) Division on a 9-battalion basis was completed ; and on 28/2/18 the pioneer battalion (14/Worc.) was reorganized on a 3-company basis.

63RD (ROYAL NAVAL) DIVISION

FORMATION, BATTLES, AND ENGAGEMENTS

The Royal Naval Division had no existence before August 1914; but the idea of assembling one dated from before the opening of the Great War. The Admiralty realized that on mobilization there would be 20–30,000 men of the Reserves of the Royal Navy for whom there would not be room on any ship of war. This surplus personnel would be sufficient to form two naval Brigades and a Brigade of Marines, available either for Home Defence or for any special purpose.

On the outbreak of the Great War the Royal Marine Brigade (4 battalions—R.M.A., Chatham, Portsmouth and Plymouth) was formed at once, and on the 27th August the Brigade landed at Ostend. Meanwhile the two Royal Naval Brigades were assembling and forming around cadres, consisting of petty officers of the Navy, instructors and sergeants of the Royal Marines, and a sprinkling of retired regular army officers. As they were formed, the eight battalions concentrated at Walmer and Betteshanger. Khaki clothing could not be provided for the naval ratings; consequently, when the men embarked for the Antwerp expedition they were still wearing their pocketless blue jumpers, and 80% went to Belgium without an issue of haversacks, mess tins, or waterbottles. Even the re-arming of the two brigades with charger-loading rifles was only completed three days before leaving for Antwerp. Although the Royal Naval Division remained under the Admiralty until April 1916 (when it was transferred to the War Office) yet, from the outset, it was wisely decided to adopt army organization for this division. But, for the Antwerp expedition, no artillery, no engineers (except Captain Rooke's detachment, see Table and note 4), no signal company, no field ambulances, and no train were available.

On the 31st August the R. Marine Bde. returned from Ostend to England, and the R.M.A.Bn. was then replaced by the Deal Bn. On the 19th September the Brigade re-embarked (2,200 strong) and on landing at Dunkirk it found there 97 London Motor Omnibuses to transport its ammunition and stores. The R. Marine Bde. reached Cassel on the 30th, and it detrained at Antwerp during the night of the 3rd/4th October. By this time, however, the outer ring of forts had already fallen and bombardment of the trenches had begun.

Orders reached Walmer at 4 a.m. on Sunday the 4th October that the two Royal Naval Bdes. were to embark that day at Dover. The means of intercommunication were limited; each battalion had only one bicycle and the horses of the mounted officers were withdrawn during the march to Dover; cases of cycles were, however, drawn at Dover, but it was only on the 8th that the machines could be unpacked and fitted up. The two R. Naval Bdes. began embarkation at 10 p.m. on the 4th, at 10 a.m. on Monday the 5th they disembarked at Dunkirk, at 8 p.m. the same day they left for Antwerp in two troop trains and a store train; and at 2.30 a.m. on the 6th October the two R. Naval Brigades reached Antwerp and joined the R. Marine Bde. in the defence of the beleagured fortress. The Royal Naval Division then took part in the following operation :—

1914

6–9 October ... ... **Defence of Antwerp** (Royal Naval Division; but R. Mar. Bde. since 4/10/14).

During the afternoon of the 6th October the 1st R. Naval Bde. reinforced the right of the R. Marine Bde.; during that night (6th/7th), however, the R.N. Division retired and occupied the trenches of the 2nd Line of Defence between Forts 1–8, with the right flank resting on the right bank of the Schelde : the 1st R. Naval Bde was on the left, the 2nd R. Naval Bde. on the right, and the R. Marine Bde. in reserve.

About m/n on the 7th/8th bombardment opened on the forts, trenches, and city ; by 6 p.m. on the 8th Forts 1, 2, and 4 had fallen and, the situation having become hopeless, the retirement from Antwerp became unavoidable. That night the withdrawal began ; the R.N. Division crossed the Schelde and marched to St. Gilles Waes. On the 9th the Division began entraining for Ostend, except about 1,500 men (chiefly belonging to the 1st R. Naval Bde. and under the Commander of that brigade) who failed to get through, crossed the Dutch frontier on the 9th, and were interned in Holland. The rest of the R.N. Division re-embarked at Ostend and reached Dover on the 11th October. The Antwerp expedition was over. The Division now settled down in England to make good its losses, complete its equipment and its training, and prepare for its next adventure.

For a time the two R. Naval Brigades were scattered about the country, wherever accommodation was available, whilst the four R. Marine battalions went to their various headquarters. So far no field artillery could be allotted to the Division ; but engineer units were formed at Walmer, and a Naval Depot (which would also act for the whole division) was opened at the Crystal Palace. Unfortunately, the requirements of the Fleet necessitated constant demands on the Division for the supply of certain ratings, all the stokers were in one company of a battalion and they were all recalled at the same time to Naval Service. By the end of the Dardanelles Campaign very few ratings with sea service still remained in the Division. This drain was peculiar to the R.N. Division and it added considerably to the difficulties of organization and training.

On the 27th November 1914 the Division began to move to an area around Blandford.

1915

By the end of January the move to the Blandford area was completed, the R. Marine Bde. being the last to arrive. The R.N. Division, however, was still very scattered ; and it is quite true to say that, in a peaceful area, the Division was never concentrated before it reached France in 1916. Nevertheless units pushed ahead as rapidly as possible with their war training and soon the improvement in their fighting efficiency became very marked.

On the 6th February R. Marine Bde. Hd. Qrs. and the Chatham and Plymouth Bns. embarked at Devonport and they reached Lemnos on the 24th February. On the 18th February orders reached Blandford for the rest of the Division to be ready to follow the R. Marine Bde. At 11.30 a.m. on the 24th the Division was inspected by H.M. the King, and on the 28th it marched to Blandford Station to entrain for Avonmouth, leaving behind Hawke, Benbow, and Collingwood Bns. and the 3rd Fd. Coy. R.E., to complete their training. The six transports sailed on the 1st March and at 5.30 a.m. on the 19th they arrived off the western shore of the Gallipoli Peninsula. On the previous day the great naval attack on the Straits had failed ; so the transports were diverted to Port Said, and by the 29th March the Division completed its disembarkation in Egypt. Here it was informed that it was to take part in the land assault of the Gallipoli Peninsula. On the 5th April the units started to re-embark, and on the 8th the transports began to leave for Mudros, each ship having a tow of lighters.

The R.N. Division then took part in the Gallipoli Campaign and was engaged in the following operations :—

25 & 26 April	**Demonstration in the Gulf of Xeros** (R.N. Div.–less Anson and Plymouth Bns.).	

BATTLES OF HELLES AND ANZAC

25 & 26 April ... ... **The Landing at Cape Helles** (Anson and Plymouth Bns.) [29th Div.].

28 April ... ... **First Battle of Krithia** (2nd R.N. Bde., and Drake and Plymouth Bns.) [R.N. Div.].

1 and 2 May ... ... **Eski Hissarlik** (2nd R.N. Bde., and Drake and Plymouth Bns.) [R.N. Div.].

6–8 May ... ... **Second Battle of Krithia** (2nd R.N. Bde., under General d'Amade ; and Drake and Plymouth Bns., under Composite Division*).

28 April–12 May ... ... **Defence of Anzac** (3rd R. Mar. Bde. (less Plymouth Bn.), and Nelson and Deal Bns.) [1st Aus. Div., until 1/5 ; then N.Z. & A. Div., Anzac Corps].

2 May ... ... **The Chessboard** (3rd R. Mar. Bde. (less Plymouth Bn.), and Nelson and Deal Bns.) [Anzac Corps.]

4 June ... ... **Third Battle of Krithia** (R.N. Div.) [VIII Corps].

1916

7–Night 8/9 January **Evacuation of Helles** (R.N. Div.) [VIII Corps].

After the evacuation, the Division at first went to Mudros ; and between the 19th January and the 20th February Drake and Hawke Bns. went to Imbros, Hood Bn. to Tenedos, and the 2nd Brigade (with No. 3 Field Company and No. 1 Field Ambulance) to Stavros. Whilst the Division was on garrison duty in the Ægean, reinforcements arrived to replace the wastage incurred in the Gallipoli Campaign.

In April it was decided to bring the troops to France and the Division was then transferred from the Admiralty to the War Office (see Table, note 1). During May the move from the Ægean to France was carried out, and between the 12th–23rd May the units all disembarked at Marseille (see Table and notes). After arrival in France the Division was completed with Artillery, Trench Mortars, Machine Guns, and Train (see Table), and on the 19th July the Division received a number and henceforward became the 63rd (Royal Naval) Division, and the Infantry Brigades were numbered 188th, 189th, and 190th. For the remainder of the Great War the 63rd (R.N.) Division served on the Western Front in France and Belgium and was engaged in the following operations :—

BATTLES OF THE SOMME

13–15 November ... ... **Battle of the Ancre** [V Corps, Fifth Army].

1917

20 Jan.–27 Feb. ... ... **Operations on the Ancre** [II Corps, Fifth Army].

17 & 18 February ... **Miraumont** [II Corps, Fifth Army].

BATTLES OF ARRAS

23 & 24 April ... ... **Second Battle of the Scarpe** [XIII Corps, First Army].

28 & 29 April ... ... **Battle of Arleux** [XIII Corps, First Army].

BATTLES OF YPRES

26 Oct.–5 Nov. ... ... **Second Battle of Passchendaele** [XVIII Corps, Fifth Army].

30 & 31 Dec. ... ... **Welch Ridge** [V Corps, Third Army].

---

* For Composite Division, see Appendix 4.

1918

FIRST BATTLES OF THE SOMME

21–23 March	Battle of St. Quentin [V Corps, Third Army].
24 & 25 March	First Battle of Bapaume [V Corps, Third Army].
5 April	Battle of the Ancre [V Corps, Third Army].

THE ADVANCE TO VICTORY
SECOND BATTLES OF THE SOMME

21–23 August	Battle of Albert [IV Corps, Third Army].

SECOND BATTLES OF ARRAS

2 & 3 September ...	Battle of the Drocourt-Quéant Line [XVII Corps, Third Army].

BATTLES OF THE HINDENBURG LINE

27 Sept.–1 Oct.	Battle of the Canal du Nord [XVII Corps, Third Army].
8 October	Battle of Cambrai [XVII Corps, Third Army].
8 October	Capture of Niergnies.

THE FINAL ADVANCE IN PICARDY

7 November	Passage of the Grande Honnelle [XXII Corps, First Army].

On the 8th November the Division advanced rapidly ; by 10 p.m. on the 9th its foremost troops were east of the Mons–Maubeuge road, and on the 10th the Mons–Binche railway was reached. The Mons–Givry road was the divisional objective for the 11th; the advance started early, and by 11 a.m., when the Armistice brought hostilities to a close, divisional headquarters had opened at Harveng.

On the 13th November the Division was informed that it would not accompany the force selected to advance into Germany; on the 15th it was transferred from the XXII Corps to the VIII Corps. On the 17th the Army of Occupation advanced and passed through the outpost line and the divisional outposts were withdrawn. On the 26th the Division began to move back towards Valenciennes.

On the 5th December H.M. the King visited the Division ; and during this month miners and key-men left for demobilization. During January 1919 the Division dwindled steadily. By the end of the month a total of 3875 had been demobilized and this number had swollen to 7047 by the end of February. Thus the Division shrunk to cadre, and in April 1919 its eventful career came to an end. During the Great War the 63rd (Royal Naval) Division lost 47,953 killed, wounded, and missing.

APPENDICES

1; 1A, 1B, 1C, 1D, 1E, 1F;
2, 3, 4, & 5.

AUGMENTATION OF THE ARMY.

FORMATION AND STORY OF THE ORIGINAL FOURTH NEW ARMY, 1914–1915.

The first mention of the original Fourth New Army occurs in Army Order 389 issued on the 14th September 1914. This Order stated that, on formation, the Fourth New Army would consist of the 27th–32nd Divisions. But, before the time came to carry this out, it was found that the battalions withdrawn from the overseas garrisons in India, China, Hong Kong, Singapore, and Egypt, together with one Territorial Force battalion (5/Royal Scots), would form three additional regular divisions—27th, 28th, and 29th—consequently the numbering of the divisions to form the Fourth New Army had to be changed.

On the 8th October 1914 instructions were issued that each Reserve and Extra Reserve battalion of the Infantry of the Line should form a Service battalion, provided that the parent battalion was not thereby reduced to a strength below 1,500 all ranks. In this way it was expected that the necessary number of Service battalions could be raised for the Fourth New Army. These Service battalions were to remain in Coast Defences until accommodation for them could be provided at the new training centres, and a War Office letter of the 25th October gave the composition of the eighteen brigades which were to form the infantry of the six divisions of the Fourth New Army. This letter was followed in November 1914 by an Army Order (20/3551) which stated that approval had been given for the further addition to the Army of a Fourth New Army of six divisions (30th–35th). This Order gave the full organization and composition of the six new divisions and detailed all the units. The infantry brigades were to be formed in Coast Defences and to remain there until they received orders to move to training centres.*

On the 19th November the composition of the infantry of the Fourth New Army was cancelled and another substituted (actually the alterations only affected the three infantry brigades of the 30th Division). At the same time it was notified that brigadiers would shortly be appointed to all the infantry brigades of the Fourth New Army.**

On the 5th December the training centres were selected for the field artillery and infantry of the divisions : two divisions would be in hutted camps at Cannock Chase, and the other four divisions at Prees Heath (Shropshire), Oswestry, Rhyl, and Clipstone (Notts.). The heavy batteries and their ammunition columns would remain at Woolwich, the field companies and signal companies would be assembled at Buxton and Shrewsbury, and the field ambulances at Llandrindod Wells.

On the 16th January 1915 it was notified that the number of field companies in each division would be raised from two to three.*** The immediate and direct consequence of this alteration was that the 30th–35th Divisions lost all their field companies, as the twelve on their establishment were ordered to be transferred to

---

*This Army Order never received a number and never got beyond proof stage. As there was no likelihood of the Army Order being issued, on 19/2/15 an order was given that the type should be distributed.

**The brigadiers, with the dates of their appointment, are shown on the Tables (1A–1F) with their brigades.

***20/Engineers/4940—A.G.1.

APPENDIX I.

corresponding divisions (21st–26th) of the Third New Army to complete the new numbers. This transfer was carried out early in February (see Tables and notes, Appendices 1A–1F). It was intended to raise three new field companies for each of the six divisions of the Fourth New Army, but this had not been done before the divisions were broken up in April 1915.

The principal reason for the dispersal of the six divisions (30th–35th) was the urgent need to provide trained reinforcements for the eighteen divisions of the first three New Armies when they took the field.

In consequence of this need for trained reinforcements, a decision was reached on the 10th April 1915 that the service battalions of the Fourth New Army should be reconstituted as reserve battalions, and used for providing and training reinforcements; henceforward they would be known as 2nd-reserve battalions. The infantry brigades would become Reserve Infantry Brigades and be renumbered—1st–18th (see Tables and notes given in Appendices 1A–1F). In this way terminated, in England, the brief life of the original Fourth New Army and its six divisions (30th–35th).

The lack of officers and trained instructors, as well as the shortage of guns, rifles, horses, transport, equipment, and uniforms which had been experienced by nearly all the divisions of the first three New Armies (see Narratives in Part 3A), were naturally felt in increasing severity by all the six divisions of the original Fourth New Army. Even in April 1915 they were still in an elementary stage of training, due entirely to these deficiencies. Indeed on the 10th April, when these six divisions disappeared, though infantry brigade staffs had been appointed in each division, no divisional commanders, no staff officers, either "G" or "Q", no divisional artillery commanders had been selected; four C.R.E.s,* however, had been appointed.

The six divisions, even at the end of their service, were little more than a collection of eighteen infantry brigades, composed largely of men who were still recruits for all practical purposes, and recruits who were not even armed with modern weapons; the artillery, signal companies, field ambulances, and trains were in a no more advanced state of preparation for war. It is not difficult to appreciate the wisdom of the decision to break up these six divisions, to use certain of the units to complete other divisions,** and to turn the infantry brigades and battalions into reserve formations for providing the reinforcements which would soon be so urgently needed.

After the original Fourth New Army had been broken up the Fifth New Army became the Fourth New Army, and its six divisions (37th–42nd) were renumbered (30th–35th).***

---

*The four divisions and their C.R.E.s were as follows: 31st Division (Lt.-Col. S. C. Babington), 32nd Division (Lt.-Col. C. W. Davy), 33rd Division (Lt.-Col. P. J. J. Radcliffe), and 34th Division (Major A. E. Panet).

**See Tables and notes (Appendices 1A–1F).

***See Appendix 2.

30TH DIVISION

ORDER OF BATTLE, 1914-1915

30TH DIVISION [1]

Dates	INFANTRY		Mounted Troops	ARTILLERY					Engineers		Pioneers	Field Ambulances	Divnl. Train
				Field Artillery			Heavy Battery	Divnl. Ammn. Coln.		Signal Service			
	Brigades	Battalions		Brigades	Batteries	Bde. Ammn. Colns.			Field Cos.	Divnl. Signal Coy.			
1914 December (England)	89th² (Br.-Gen. H. P. Leach—4/12/14)	15/N.F., 11/Gr. How., 16/ D.L.I., 17/D.L.I.	30th Div. Cyclist Coy.	CXVIII⁵·⁶; CXIX⁵·⁶; CXX⁵·⁶; CXXI (H.)⁵·⁶	A, B, C, D A, B, C, D A, B, C, D A (H.), B (H.), C(H.), D (H.)	CXVIII B.A.C. CXIX B.A.C. CXX B.A.C. CXXI (H.) B.A.C.	30 H.B. & Hy. Bty. A.C.	30th D.A.C.	97th⁷ 98th⁷	30th	...	90th⁸ 91st⁸ 92nd⁸	30th
	90th³ (Br.-Gen A. J. A. Wright—28/11/14)	13/W. York., 9/E. York., 11/K.O.Y.L.I., 11/Y. & L.											
	91st⁴ (Br.-Gen. F. C. Godley—7/12/14)	9/Linc., 11/Duke's, 14/Sher. For., 14/Manch.											

On 10/4/15 the 30th Division was broken up.

NOTE—The composition of the Infantry Brigades is the amended composition of 19/11/14 (p. 131).

The formation of the Fourth New Army was approved in an Army Order issued in November 1914, and the units of the 30th Division began to form forthwith. On the 10th April 1915 the divisions of the Fourth New Army were broken up; the three infantry brigades of the 30th Division became Reserve Infantry Brigades, and henceforward the 12 Service battalions became 2nd-reserve battalions and were used for training recruits and providing reinforcements.

NOTES

[1] The formation of the Division was approved on 5/11/14. On 10/4/15 the Division was broken up in England.

[2] On 10/4/15 89th Bde. became 1st Reserve Inf. Bde.

[3] On 10/4/15 90th Bde. became 2nd Reserve Inf. Bde.

[4] On 10/4/15 91st Bde. became 3rd Reserve Inf. Bde.

[5] The Bdes. were raised to form 4-battery brigades; each battery was to be a 4-gun battery; and in each brigade the batteries were lettered—A, B, C, D.

[6] After the break-up of the 30th Div, CXIX, CXX, & CXXI (with existing personnel) joined 38th (Welsh) Div. In England, and went to France with 38th Div.—CXXI (H.) became an 18-pdr. brigade. (CXVIII (How.) Bde. was formed at Woolwich on 16/2/15—see General Notes, 11th Div., Part 3A, p. 21.)

[7] On 30/1/15 the two Fd. Cos. were transferred to 21st Div. at Chesham.

[8] In November 1915 the three Fd. Ambccs. joined the new 32nd Div. (formerly 39th Div.).

31st DIVISION

ORDER OF BATTLE, 1914-1915

31st DIVISION [1]

Dates	INFANTRY		MOUNTED TROOPS	ARTILLERY						ENGINEERS		SIGNAL SERVICE	PIONEERS	FIELD AMBULANCES	DIVNL. TRAIN
	Brigades	Battalions		Brigades	Field Artillery		Bde. Ammn. Colns.	Heavy Battery	Divnl. Ammn. Coln.	Field Cos.		Divnl. Signal Coy.			
					Batteries										
1914 December (England)	92nd [2] (Br.-Gen. G. H. C. Colomb—1./12/14)	14/K.R.R.C., 15/K.R.R.C., 14/R.B., 15/R.B.	31st Div. Cyclist Coy.	CXXII [4, 7]; CXXIII [5, 6]; CXXIV [6, 8]; CXXV (H.) [9, 10]	A, B, C, D		CXXII B.A.C. CXXIII B.A.C. CXXIV B.A.C. CXXV (H.) B.A.C.	31 [New] H.B. [10] & Hy. Bty. A.C.	31st D.A.C.	99th [10] 100th [10]		31st	...	93rd [11] 94th [11] 95th [11]	31st
	93rd [3] (Br.-Gen. W. H. H. Waters—1/12/14)	9/Queen's, 9/Q.O.R.W.K., 14/Midx., 15/Midx.			A, B, C, D										
	94th [3] (Br.-Gen. J. R. M. Dalrymple-Hay —28/11/14)	10/Norf., 10/Suff., 11/L.N.L. [5] 9/Bedf.,			A (H.), B (H.), C (H.), D (H.)										

On 10/4/15 the 31st Division was broken up.

The formation of the Fourth New Army was approved in an Army Order issued in November 1914, and the 31st Division began to form forthwith. On the 10th April 1915 the divisions of the Fourth New Army were broken up; the three infantry brigades of the 31st Division became Reserve Infantry Brigades, and henceforward the 12 Service battalions became 2nd-reserve battalions and were used for training recruits and providing reinforcements.

NOTES

[1] The formation of the Division was approved on 5/11/14. On 10/4/15 the Division was broken up in England.

[2] On 10/4/15 92nd Bde. became 4th Reserve Inf. Bde.

[3] On 10/4/15 93rd Bde. became 5th Reserve Inf. Bde.

[4] On 10/4/15 94th Bde. became 6th Reserve Inf. Bde.

[5] On 28/11/14 11/L.N.L. replaced 12/Essex (to 106th Bde., 35th Div.).

[6] The Bdes. were raised to form 4-battery brigades; each battery was to be a 4-gun battery; and in each brigade the batteries were lettered—A, B, C, D.

[7] After the break-up of the 31st Div., CXXII (with existing personnel) joined 38th (Welsh) Div. in England. Bde. then became a 4.5" How. Bde., and it went to France with 38th Div.

[8] In April 1915, CXXIII, CXXIV, & CXXV (H.), with existing personnel, joined the new 37th Div., and went to France with 37th Div. (CXXV became an 18-pdr. Bde.) The Bdes. disembkd. in France in July 1915.

[9] 31 [New] Hy. Bty. was renumbered 132 Hy. Bty. 132 Hy. Bty. disembkd. at le Havre (with 60 pdrs.) on 21/3/16, and joined IX H.A.G. on 31/3/16.

[10] In Feb. 1915 the two Fd. Cos. were transferred to the 22nd Div.

[11] On 27/11/15 the three Fd. Ambces. joined the new 31st Div. (formerly 38th Div.) at Larkhill.

31 Hy. Bty., R.G.A. (4, 60-pdrs.) was serving with the 4th Div. at the outbreak of the Great War; in Aug. 1914 the 31 Hy. Bty. went to France. 31 Hy. Bty. rejoined the 4th Division on 9/9/14 in France.

32ND DIVISION

ORDER OF BATTLE, 1914-1915

32ND DIVISION [1]

Dates	INFANTRY		Mounted Troops	ARTILLERY					Engineers	Signal Service	Pioneers	Field Ambulances	Divnl. Train
				Field Artillery			Heavy Battery	Divnl. Ammn. Coln.	Field Cos.	Divnl. Signal Coy.			
	Brigades	Battalions		Brigades	Batteries	Bde. Ammn. Colns.							
1914 December (England)	95th [3] ...... (Br.-Gen. G. A. Mills—1/12/14)	9/Buffs, 14/R.F., 15/R.F., 10/E. Surr.	32nd Div. Cyclist Coy.	CXXVI [7];[8]	A, B, C, D	CXXVI B.A.C.	32 H.B. & Hy. Bty. A.C.	32nd D.A.C.	101st [10] 102nd [10]	32nd	...	96th [11] 97th [11] 98th [11]	32nd
	96th [3] ...... (Br.-Gen. J. E. W. S. Caulfield—30/11/14)	10/Leic.[5] 13/Hants, 9/O. & B.L.I., 9/R. Berks		CXXVII [7];[8]	A, B, C, D	CXXVII B.A.C.							
	97th [4] (Br.-Gen. F. P. English—30/11/14)	12/R. War.,[6] 13/R. War., 10/R. Suss., 13/H.L.I.		CXXVIII [7];[8] ...... CXXIX (H.) [7];[9]	A, B, C, D A (H.), B (H.), C(H.), D (H.)	CXXVIII B.A.C. CXXIX (H.) B.A.C.							

On 10/4/15 the 32nd Division was broken up.

The formation of the Fourth New Army was approved in an Army Order issued in November 1914, and the units of the 32nd Division began to form forthwith. On the 10th April 1915 the divisions of the Fourth New Army were broken up; the three infantry brigades of the 32nd Division became Reserve Infantry Brigades, and henceforward the 12 Service battalions became 2nd-reserve battalions and were used for training recruits and providing reinforcements.

NOTES

The formation of the Division was approved on 5/11/14. On 10/4/15 the Division was broken up in England.

[2] On 10/4/15 95th Bde. became 7th Reserve Inf. Bde.

[3] On 10/4/15 96th Bde. became 8th Reserve Inf. Bde.

[4] On 10/4/15 97th Bde. became 9th Reserve Inf. Bde.

[5] Bn. was transferred from 97th Bde. on 12/12/14.

[6] Bn. was transferred from 96th Bde. on 12/12/14.

[7] The Bdes. were raised to form 4-battery brigades; each battery was to be a 4-gun battery; and in each brigade the batteries were lettered—A, B, C, D.

[8] After the break-up of the 32nd Div., CXXVI (with existing personnel) in April 1915 was transferred to the new 37th Div. in England. Bde. became a 4.5" How. Bde., and went to France with 37th Div. in July 1915.

[9] CXXVII, CXXVIII, & CXXIX (H.) Bdes. were never formed. In Aug. 1915, however, the numbers were used for three Howitzer Brigades which were formed for the 4th, 8th, and 27th Divisions.

[10] On 1/2/15 the two Fd. Cos. were transferred to the 23rd Div. at Aldershot.

[11] In June 1915 the 3 Fd. Ambces. joined the new 32nd Div. (formerly 39th Div.); on 2/11/15 the 3 Fd. Ambces. were transferred to the new 30th Div. (formerly 37th Div.), and they served with the 30th Div. for the remainder of the Great War.

33RD DIVISION

ORDER OF BATTLE, 1914-1915

33RD DIVISION ¹

Dates	INFANTRY		Mounted Troops	ARTILLERY					Engineers	Signal Service	Pioneers	Field Ambulances	Divnl. Train
	Brigades	Battalions		Field Artillery			Heavy Battery	Divnl. Ammn. Coln.	Field Cos.	Divnl. Signal Coy.			
				Brigades	Batteries	Bde. Ammn. Colns.							
1914 December (England)	98th¹ (Br.-Gen. J. M. Gordon—7/12/14) 99th¹ (Br.-Gen. P. Holland—5/12/14) 100th (Br.-Gen. H. D. McIntyre—1/12/14)	9/Som. L.I., 12/Worc., 13/Worc., 13/Sher. For. 10/K.O., 10/E. Lanc., 10/S. Staff, 10/N. Staff. 11/Devon, 11/E. Surr., 14/H.L.I.,³ 14/A. & S.H.⁴	33rd Div. Cyclist Coy.	CXXX⁵ ...... CXXXI⁵ ...... CXXXII⁵ ...... CXXXIII (H.)	A, B, C, D A, B, C, D A, B, C, D A (H.), B (H.), C(H.), D (H.)	CXXX B.A.C. CXXXI B.A.C. CXXXII B.A.C. CXXXIII (H.) B.A.C.	33 H.B. & Hy. Bty. A.C.	33rd D.A.C.	103rd⁷ 104th⁷	33rd	...	99th⁸ 100th⁸ 101st⁸	33rd

On 10/4/15 the 33rd Division was broken up.

The formation of the Fourth New Army was approved in an Army Order issued in November 1914, and the units of the 33rd Division began to form forthwith. On the 10th April 1915 the divisions of the Fourth New Army were broken up; the three infantry brigades of the 33rd Division became Reserve Infantry Brigades, and henceforward 10 of the 12 Service battalions (see note 5) became 2nd-reserve battalions and were used for training recruits and providing reinforcements.

NOTES

¹ The formation of the Division was approved on 5/11/14. On 10/4/15 the Division was broken up in England.

² On 10/4/15 98th Bde. became 10th Reserve Inf. Bde.

³ On 10/4/15 99th Bde. became 11th Reserve Inf. Bde.

⁴ On 10/4/15 100th Bde. became 12th Reserve Inf. Bde.

⁵ These two battalions had not joined 100th Bde. by 10/4/15. 14/H.L.I. and 14/A. & S.H. joined 120th Bde., 40th Div., and served in France with 40th Div.

⁶ The Bdes. were to be raised as 4-battery brigades; each battery was to be a 4-gun battery; and in each brigade the batteries were to be lettered—A, B, C, D.*

⁷ In Feb. 1915 the two Fd. Cos. were transferred to the 24th Div.

⁸ By Oct. 1915 the three Fd. Ambcrs. had joined the new 33rd Div. (formerly 40th Div.).

NOTE:

Actually the four Fd. Arty. Bdes. were not formed. After the 33rd Div. had been broken up the numbers were used for Bdes. formed for the 28th, 3rd Canadian, 29th, and 11th Divisions. (CXXX, CXXXI, & CXXXII, were formed between 8/9/15-8/3/16; CXXXIII was formed at el Ferdan between 26/4-31/5/16 for the 11th Division.)

34TH DIVISION

ORDER OF BATTLE, 1914-1915

34TH DIVISION [1]

Dates	INFANTRY			ARTILLERY					Engineers		Pioneers	Field Ambulances	Divnl. Train
				Field Artillery			Heavy Battery	Divnl. Ammn. Coln.		Signal Service			
	Brigades	Battalions	Mounted Troops	Brigades	Batteries	Bde. Ammn. Colns.			Field Cos.	Divnl. Signal Coy.			
1914 December (England)	101st[2] .... (Br.-Gen. S. B. Jameson—4/12/14) 102nd[3] .... (Br.-Gen. R. B. Fell—29/11/14) 103rd[4] .... (Br.-Gen. G. de S. De Lisle—28/11/14)	12/Sco. Rif., 11/B.W., 10/ Sea. H., 8/Cam. H. 14/R.S., 9/K.O.S.B., 7/ Dorset, 8/Wilts. 16/R.F., 14/W.York., 9/ D.C.L.I., 8/Northn.	34th Div. Cyclist Coy.	CXXXIV[5] ...... CXXXV[5] ...... CXXXVI[5] ...... CXXXVII (H.)[5]	A, B, C, D A, B, C, D A, B, C, D A (H.), B (H.), c (H.), D (H.)	CXXXIV B.A.C. CXXXV B.A.C. CXXXVI B.A.C. CXXXVII (H.) B.A.C.	34 H.B. & Hy. Bty. A.C.	34th D.A.C.	105th[6] 106th[6]	34th	...	102nd[7] 103rd[7] 104th[7]	34th

On 10/4/15 the 84th Division was broken up.

NOTES

[1] The formation of the Division was approved on 5/11/14. On 10/4/15 the Division was broken up in England.

[2] On 10/4/15 101st Bde. became 13th Reserve Inf. Bde.

[3] On 10/4/15 102nd Bde. became 14th Reserve Inf. Bde.

[4] On 10/4/15 103rd Bde. became 15th Reserve Inf. Bde.

[5] The Bdes. were to be raised as 4-battery brigades; each battery was to be a 4-gun battery; and in each brigade the batteries were to be lettered—A, B, C, D. (Actually the brigades were never formed.)

[6] In Feb. 1915 the two Fd. Cos. were transferred to the 25th Div.

[7] Between 8-10/11/15 the three Fd. Ambcs. joined the new 34th Div. (formerly 41st Div.).

The formation of the Fourth New Army was approved in an Army Order issued in November 1914, and the units of the 34th Division began to form forthwith. On the 10th April 1915 the divisions of the Fourth New Army were broken up; the three infantry brigades of the 34th Division became Reserve Infantry Brigades, and henceforward the 12 Service battalions became 2nd-reserve battalions and were used for training recruits and providing reinforcements.

137

35TH DIVISION

ORDER OF BATTLE, 1914-1915

35TH DIVISION [1]

Dates	INFANTRY		Mounted Troops	ARTILLERY				Divnl. Ammn. Coln.	Engineers	Signal Service	Pioneers	Field Ambulances	Divnl. Train
				Field Artillery			Heavy Battery		Field Cos.	Divnl. Signal Coy.			
	Brigades	Battalions		Brigades	Batteries	Bde. Ammn. Colns.							
1914 December (England)	104th[2] .... (Br.-Gen. M. Q. Jones—9/12/14) 105th[3] .... (Br.-Gen. C. M. Brunker—1/12/14) 106th[4] .... (Br.-Gen. E. H. Rodwell—29/11/14)	12/R.W.F., 9/S.W.B., 12/ Welsh, 9/K.S.L.I. 15/King's, 16/King's, 14 Ches., 10/S. Lanc 10/Bedf., 11/Glouc., 12/ Essex,[5] 13/A. & S.H.	35th Div. Cyclist Coy.	CXXXVIII[6] ...... CXXXIX[6] ...... CXL[6] ...... CXLI (H.)[6]	A, B, C, D A, B, C, D A, B, C, D A (H.), B (H.), C (H.), D (H.)	CXXXVIII B.A.C. CXXXIX B.A.C. CXL B.A.C. CXLI (H.) B.A.C.	35 [New] H.B.[7] & Hy. Bty. A.C.	35th D.A.C.	107th[8] 108th[8]	35th	...	105th[9] 106th[9] 107th[9]	35th

On 10/4/15 the 35th Division was broken up.

The formation of the Fourth New Army was approved in an Army Order issued in November 1914, and the units of the 35th Division began to form forthwith. On the 10th April 1915 the divisions of the Fourth New Army were broken up; the three infantry brigades of the 35th Division became Reserve Infantry Brigades, and henceforward the 12 Service battalions became 2nd-reserve battalions and were used for training recruits and providing reinforcements.

NOTES

[1] The formation of the Division was approved on 5/11/14. On 10/4/15 the Division was broken up in England.

[2] On 10/4/15 104th Bde. became 16th Reserve Inf. Bde.

[3] On 10/4/15 105th Bde. became 17th Reserve Inf. Bde.

[4] On 10/4/15 106th Bde. became 18th Reserve Inf. Bde.

[5] On 28/11/14 12/Essex replaced 11/L.N.L. (to 94th Bde., 31st Div.).

[6] The Bdes. were to be raised as 4-battery brigades; each battery was to be a 4-gun battery; and in each brigade the batteries were to be lettered—A, B, C, D. (Actually the brigades were never formed.)

[7] 35 [New] Hy. Bty. was renumbered 133 Hy. Bty.* In England 133 Hy. Bty. was attached to 32nd. Div. (p. 23). 133 Hy. Bty. disembkd. at le Havre (with 60-pdrs.) on 27/5/16, and joined XLVIII H.A.G. on 29/5/16.

[8] On 30/1/15 the two Fd. Cos. were transferred to the 26th Div.

[9] By Oct. 1915 the three Fd. Ambces. had joined the new 35th Div. (formerly 42nd Div.).

---

* 35 Hy. Bty., R.G.A. (4, 60-pdrs.) was serving with the 2nd Div. at the outbreak of the Great War; in Aug. 1914 the 35 Hy. Bty. went to France with the 2nd Div.

APPENDIX 2

Formation of the Divisions for the Fourth and Fifth New Armies

(30TH—41ST DIVISIONS)

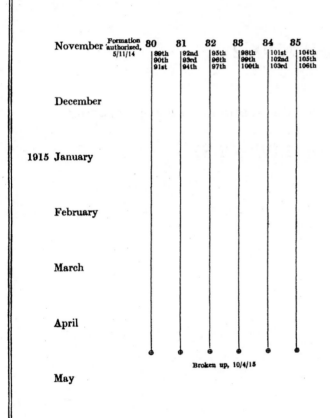

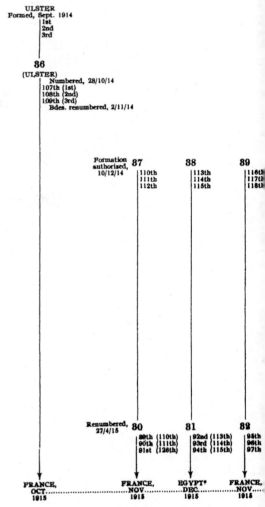

1914 September

October

November

December

1915 January

February

March

April

May

ULSTER
Formed, Sept. 1914
1st
2nd
3rd

36
(ULSTER)
Numbered, 28/10/14
107th (1st)
108th (2nd)
109th (3rd)
Bdes. renumbered, 2/11/14

Formation
authorized,
5/11/14

80
89th
90th
91st

81
92nd
93rd
94th

82
95th
96th
97th

83
98th
99th
100th

84
101st
102nd
103rd

85
104th
105th
106th

Formation
authorized,
10/12/14

87
110th
111th
112th

88
113th
114th
115th

89
116th
117th
118th

Broken up, 10/4/15

Renumbered,
27/4/15

80
89th (110th)
90th (111th)
91st (126th)

81
92nd (113th)
93rd (114th)
94th (115th)

82
95th
96th
97th

FRANCE,
OCT.
1915

FRANCE,
NOV.
1915

EGYPT*
DEC.
1915

FRANCE,
NOV.
1915

NOTES—

89th, 101st, etc., are infantry brigades.
Original numbers of infantry brigades are given in brackets, thus : (110th), (120th), etc.
(N.F.) is New Formation.
121st Inf. Bde. (of the original 40th Division) became 116th Inf. Bde. in the new 39th Division.
127th Inf. Bde. (of the original 42nd Division) was not formed.

FOR THE FOURTH AND FIFTH NEW ARMIES
41ST DIVISIONS)

40
119th
120th
121st

41
122nd
123rd
124th

42
125th
126th
127th (not formed)

43
[WELSH]
Formed, 10/12/14
128th (1st)
129th (2nd)
130th (3rd)

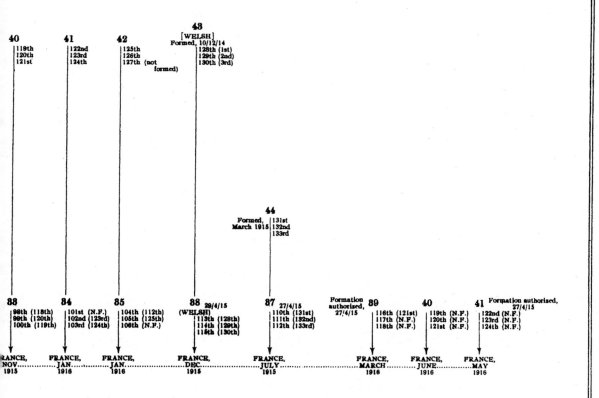

44
Formed, March 1915
131st
132nd
133rd

33
98th (118th)
99th (120th)
100th (119th)

FRANCE, NOV. 1915

34
101st (N.F.)
102nd (123rd)
103rd (124th)

FRANCE, JAN. 1916

35
104th (112th)
105th (125th)
106th (N.F.)

FRANCE, JAN. 1916

38
(WELSH) 29/4/15
113th (128th)
114th (129th)
115th (130th)

FRANCE, DEC. 1915

37 27/4/15
110th (131st)
111th (132nd)
112th (133rd)

FRANCE, JULY 1915

Formation authorised, 27/4/15

39
116th (121st)
117th (N.F.)
118th (N.F.)

FRANCE, MARCH 1916

40
119th (N.F.)
120th (N.F.)
121st (N.F.)

FRANCE, JUNE 1916

41 Formation authorised, 27/4/15
122nd (N.F.)
123rd (N.F.)
124th (N.F.)

FRANCE, MAY 1916

* 31st Div. went first to Egypt (disembkn. was completed in January 1916).
In March 1916 the 31st Div. was transferred to France.

141

APPENDIX 3

Summary of Divisions from Great Britain and Ireland
1914-1918

A ... ... Number of Divisions
B ... ... Service of Divisions

A. Number of Divisions

	In Great Britain & Ireland on 1st August 1914	Formed by Great Britain & Ireland during the Great War 1914–1918	TOTAL
CAVALRY DIVISIONS ... ... (1st–3rd)	... (see NOTE)	3	3
MOUNTED DIVISIONS ... (1st, 2nd, 2nd/2nd, 4th, & Yeo. Mtd.)	... (see NOTE)	5	5
REGULAR DIVISIONS ... ... (Gds.; 1st–8th ; 27th–29th)	6	6	12
NEW ARMY DIVISIONS ... (9th–26th ; 30th–41st)	...	36**	36
TERRITORIAL FORCE DIVISIONS (42nd–69th)*	14	14	28
OTHER DIVISIONS ... ... (63rd (R.N.), & 71st–75th)	...	6	6
TOTAL ...	20	70	90

NOTE.—On 1/8/14 there were also in Great Britain & Ireland :—

    5 Cavalry Brigades,

    14 Mounted Brigades (T.F.), &

    3 Infantry Brigades (T.F.)

GREAT BRITAIN AND IRELAND
918

B. Service of Divisions

	Served Overseas in Theatres of War	Went to India	Served at Home	TOTAL
CAVALRY DIVISIONS ... ... (1st–3rd)	3	...	...	8
MOUNTED DIVISIONS ... (1st; 2nd; 2nd/2nd; 4th; & Yeo. Mtd.)	2	...	3	5
REGULAR DIVISIONS ... ... (Gds.; 1st–8th; 27th–29th)	12	...	...	12
NEW ARMY DIVISIONS ... (9th–26th; 30th–41st) ...	30	...	6**	86
TERRITORIAL FORCE DIVISIONS (42nd–69th)*	19	8	6	28
OTHER DIVISIONS ... ... (63rd (R.N.), & 71st–75th)	3	...	3	6
TOTAL ...	69	8	18	90

NOTES.—74th DIVISION (formed at el'Arish) was composed entirely of British units; 75th DIVISION (also formed at el'Arish) was partly completed by Indian units (see Part 2B, pp. 117–130).

70th DIVISION (209th, 210th, and 211th Infantry Brigades) was never formed.

* Includes 63rd (2nd NORTHUMBRIAN) DIVISION.
** The original 30th–35th DIVISIONS were broken up in April 1915 (see Appendices 1 and 2).

APPENDIX 4

Composite Division (Temporary) Helles, 5—17/5/1915

COMPOSITE DIVISION (TEMPORARY)—HELLES, 5-17/5/1915

G.O.C.   MAJOR-GENERAL A. PARIS.
G.S.O.1. Lt.-Col. A. H. OLLIVANT.

COMPOSITE BDE.

(Lt.-Col. H. G. CASSON)

Drake Bn.,
Plymouth Bn., R.M.L.I. ;
and attached, from 4—10/5/15,
1/L.F. (from 86th Bde., 29th Div.).

and   Bde. Sec., Aus. Div. Sig. Coy.

Bde. was replaced at 8 a.m. on 10/5/15 by

2nd ROYAL NAVAL BDE.

(Commodore O. BACKHOUSE)

Howe Bn.,
Hood Bn.,
Anson Bn. ;
with attached,
Drake Bn.,
Plymouth Bn., R.M.L.I.

2nd AUSTRALIAN INF. BDE. (VICTORIA)

(Colonel J. W. M°CAY
(wd, 9/5/15) ;
then
Lt.-Col. W. K. BOLTON)

5/Bn.,
6/Bn.,
7/Bn.,
8/Bn. ;

NEW ZEALAND INF. BDE.

(Colonel F. E. JOHNSTON)

Auckland Bn.,
Canterbury Bn.,
Otago Bn.,
Wellington Bn. ;

and   Bde. Sec., N.Z. & A. Div. Sig. Coy.

DIVISIONAL TROOPS

R.N. Div. Cyclist Coy.,
No. 1 (R.N.) Field Coy.,
No. 2 (R.N.) Field Coy.,

R.N. Div. Sig. Coy.,
Detnt., Armoured Motor M.G. Sqdn.

On 5/5/15 the Composite Division was formed at Helles (Gallipoli).

The Composite Division was engaged in the **Second Battle of Krithia** (6-8/5/15). On 7-9/5/15 125th (Lanc. Fus.) Inf. Bde. (Br.-Gen. H. C. Frith) & 127th (Manchester) Inf. Bde. (Br.-Gen. N. Lee)—from 42nd (East Lanc.) Div.—were attached to the Composite Division.*

On 17/5/15 the Composite Division was broken up at Helles, and brigades, etc., rejoined their own divisions.

*For the composition of 125th & 127th Inf. Bdes. see Tables of 42nd (E. Lanc.) Div. in **Part 2A.**

MARSHAL FOCH'S MESSAGE TO THE PEOPLE OF NORTHERN IRELAND—NOVEMBER 1928.

" I saw beneath the surface of the tragic events that we know by the name of the Battle of the Somme. I knew that the task set the Ulster Division was an impossible one, but there are moments in war when it is necessary to attempt the impossible for reasons that are not visible on the surface.

" The attack of the Ulster Division on the Somme, in that terrible July of twelve years ago, was such a moment. I saw something of the operations, and nothing moved me more than the sublime heroism of those men of Ulster.

" The task set them was impossible, but they came nearer to achieving the impossible, in my opinion, than any other body of men I have ever seen. They gave their lives freely ; by the sacrifice, they made possible the great victory we are celebrating this week-end.

" When the moment of silence comes, my mind goes back over the whole battle front as I knew it at different periods ; but outstanding is the vision that rests with me of those immortal men of your Ulster Division as they faced death in its ugliest form, because they had grasped the grim truth that their sacrifice was required to lay the foundation of our subsequent victories.

" I do not know of any troops on the Somme who suffered more than the Ulster Division, and yet when they had emerged from their Calvary their morale was as high as ever it had been ; and, had we given the word, those men would have gone into the fray again determined to conquer or die."

INDEX OF FORMATIONS

BRIGADES AND DIVISIONS

BRIGADES

Artillery—
R.F.A.—

LVII (H.), 63, fn.* ; 64 ; 65 (note 18).
CXVIII, 133.
CXIX, 84 ; 87 ; 88 ; 133.
CXX, 84 ; 87 ; 88 ; 133.
CXXI, 84, 85 ; 87 ; 88 ; 89, note A ; 133.
CXXII, 84, 85 ; 87 ; 88 ; 89, note A ; 134.
CXXIII, 74, 75 ; 77 ; 78 fn.** ; 134.
CXXIV, 74, 75 ; 77 ; 78 fn.** ; 134.
CXXV, 74 ; 77 ; 134.
CXXVI, 73, & fn.* ; 74 ; 77 ; 78 fn.** ; 135.
CXXVII, 135.
CXXVIII, 135.
CXXIX (H.), 135.
CXXX, 136.
CXXXI, 136.
CXXXII, 136.
CXXXIII (H.), 136.
CXXXIV, 137.
CXXXV, 137.
CXXXVI, 137.
CXXXVII (H.), 137.
CXXXVIII, 138.
CXXXIX, 138.
CXL, 138.
CXLI (H.), 138.
CXLII, 65 (note 7).
CXLIII, 65 (note 7).
CXLIV, 65 (note 7).
CXLV (H.), 65 (note 7).
CXLVIII, 4, 5 ; 7.
CXLIX, 4, 5 ; 7.
CL, 4 ; 7.
CLI, 4 ; 7.
CLII, 43 ; 44, 45 ; 48.
CLIII, 64, 65 ; 67 ; 68 ; 69.
CLIV, 64 ; 67 ; 68.
CLV, 11 ; 14 ; 17 ; 18 ; 23 ; 24 ; 26 ; 28.
CLVI, 34, 35 ; 37.
CLVII, 54, 55 ; 57.
CLVIII, 54 ; 57.
CLIX, 54, 55 ; 57 ; 59.
CLX, 43 ; 44, 45 ; 48.
CLXI, 11 ; 14 ; 17 ; 18 ; 21 ; 24, 25 ; 26 ; 28.
CLXII, 34, 35 ; 37.
CLXIII, 54 ; 57.
CLXIV, 11 ; 14 ; 17 ; 18 ; 21 ; 24 ; 26 ; 28.
CLXV, 11 ; 14, 15 ; 18 ; 21 ; 24 ; 27 ; 28.
CLXVI, 34 ; 37.
CLXVII, 34 ; 37.
CLXVIII, 11 ; 14 ; 17 ; 18 ; 21 ; 24, 25 ; 26 ; 28.
CLXIX, 11 ; 13, and fn.* ; 14 ; 18 ; 21 ; 24 ; 27 ; 28.
CLXX, 11 ; 14, 15 ; 18 ; 21 ; 24 ; 27 ; 28.
CLXXI, 11, 14 ; 18 ; 21 ; 24 ; 27 ; 28.
CLXXII, 63 ; 64 ; 67 ; 68.
CLXXIII, 64, 65 ; 67 ; 68 ; 69.
CLXXIV, 93 ; 94, 95 ; 98.
CLXXV, 43 ; 44 ; 48.
CLXXVI, 44 ; 48.

R.F.A.—(Continued)

CLXXVIII, 102, 103 ; 105.
CLXXIX, 94 ; 98.
CLXXXI, 102, 103 ; 105.
CLXXXIII, 110 ; 113.
CLXXXIV, 94 ; 98.
CLXXXV, 102.
CLXXXVI, 93 ; 94, 95 ; 98.
CLXXXVII, 110, 111 ; 113.
CLXXXVIII, 102.
CLXXXIX, 110 ; 113.
CXC, 110, 111 ; 113.
CCXXIII, 121 ; 127.
CCCXV, 121 ; 124 ; 127.
CCCXVI, 121 ; 127.
CCCXVII, 121 ; 127.
CCCXVIII, see CCXXIII, note 05, page 123.

Cheshire, 23.
I East Anglian, 33 ; 37.
II East Anglian, 33 ; 37.
III East Anglian (How.), 33 ; 37.
IV East Anglian, 33 ; 37.
1/IV Home Counties (How.), 120.
I London, 63 ; 64 ; 68 ; 83 ; 88.
II London, 63 ; 64 ; 68 ; 83 ; 88.
III London, 63 ; 64 ; 68 ; 83 ; 88.
IV London (How.), 63 ; 64 ; 68 ; 83 ; 88.
I Welsh (How.), 23.
II Welsh, 23.
IV Welsh, 23.
XIII Belgian Field Artillery Regt., 112.

Infantry Brigades—

4th Guards, 12 ; 13 ; 15 ; 16 ; 19.
12th, 62 ; 63.
14th, 22 ; 24, 25 ; 28.
19th, 32 ; 34, 35 ; 38.
21st, 2 ; 4, 5 ; 9.
63rd, 72 ; 74, 75 ; 78 fn.**.
89th (originally 110th), 2 ; 4, 5 ; 7 ; 9 ; 140.
90th (originally 111th), 2 ; 4, 5 ; 7 ; 105, 140.
91st (originally 126th), 2 ; 4 ; 7 ; 57 ; 140, 141.
92nd (originally 113th), 12 ; 14, 15 ; 17 ; 19 ; 140.
92nd (Composite), 13.
93rd (originally 114th), 12 ; 14, 15 ; 17 ; 140.
94th (originally 115th), 12 ; 13 ; 14 ; 17 ; 140.
94th (Yeomanry), 12 ; 13 ; 15 ; 16.
95th (originally 116th), 22 ; 24 ; 27 ; 140.
96th (originally 122nd), 22 ; 24, 25 ; 27 ; 28 ; 48 ; 140, 141.
97th (originally 117th), 22 ; 24, 25 ; 27 ; 28 ; 140.
98th (originally 118th), 27 ; 32 ; 34, 35 ; 37 ; 141.
99th (originally 120th), 32 ; 34 ; 37 ; 141.
100th (originally 119th), 32 ; 33 ; 34, 35 ; 37 ; 38 ; 141.
101st (new formation), 42 ; 44, 45 ; 48 ; 49 ; 141.

153

Infantry Brigades—(Continued)

102nd (originally 123rd), 42; 43; 44, 45;
  48; 49; 72; 73; 75 n. 22; 141.
103rd (originally 124th), 42; 43; 44, 45;
  48; 49; 72; 73; 75 n. 22; 141.
104th (originally 112th), 7; 52; 54, 55; 57;
  59; 140, 141.
105th (originally 125th), 52; 54, 55; 57; 58;
  59; 141.
106th (new formation), 52; 54, 55; 57; 58;
  59; 141.
107th (originally 1st Bde.), 62; 63; 64, 65;
  67; 69; 140.
108th (originally 2nd Bde.), 62; 63; 64, 65;
  67; 68; 69; 140.
109th (originally 3rd Bde.), 62; 63; 64, 65;
  67; 69; 140.
110th (originally 131st), 72; 74; 77; 141.
111th (originally 132nd), 42; 43; 49 fn.*;
  72; 73; 74, 75; 77; 78 fns.*, & **; 141.
112th (originally 133rd), 42; 43; 49 fn.*;
  72; 73; 74, 75; 77; 78; 78 fn.*, & **;
  141.
113th (previously 128th; originally 1st Bde.),
  82; 84, 85; 87; 89; 141.
114th (previously 129th; originally 2nd Bde.),
  82; 84, 85; 87; 141.
115th (previously 130th; originally 3rd Bde.),
  82; 84, 85; 87; 141.
116th (originally 121st), 37; 92; 93; 94, 95;
  97; 98; 99; 100; 141.
117th (new formation), 92; 93; 94, 95; 97;
  98; 100; 141.
118th (new formation), 92; 93; 94, 95; 97;
  98; 100; 141.
119th (new formation), 101; 102, 103; 106;
  107; 141.
120th (new formation), 101; 102, 103; 105;
  106; 107; 141.
121st (new formation), 101; 102, 103; 105;
  106; 107; 141.
122nd (new formation), 109; 110, 111; 113;
  141.
123rd (new formation), 109; 110, 111; 113;
  115; 141.
124th (new formation), 109; 110, 111; 113;
  115; 141.
125th (Lancashire Fusilier), 148, 149.
127th (Manchester), 148, 149.
188th, 118; 121; 127.
189th, 118; 121; 127.
190th, 119; 121; 124; 127.
197th, 92; 96 (note 59); 97; 100.
1st (Royal Naval), 118; 120; 124; 125; 126;
  127.
2nd (Royal Naval), 118; 120; 124; 125;
  126; 127; 148.
3rd (Royal Marine), 119; 120; 124; 125;
  126; 127.
Composite Bde. (Helles), 148.
1st Composite (40th Div.), 105.
2nd Composite (40th Div.), 105.
21st Composite, 3; 9.
30th Composite, 3; 88.
39th Composite, 93; 99; 100.
92nd Composite, 13.
2nd Australian (Helles), 148, 149.
New Zealand (Helles), 149.
South African, 105.
Commdr. Samson's Detnt., 124.

Infantry Brigades of (original) Fourth New Army—

89th, 132; 133; 140.
90th, 132; 133; 140.

Infantry Brigades of (original) Fourth New Army—(Continued)

91st, 132; 133; 140.
92nd, 132; 134; 140.
93rd, 132; 134; 140.
94th, 132; 134; 140.
95th, 132; 135; 140.
96th, 132; 135; 140.
97th, 132; 135; 140.
98th, 132; 136; 140.
99th, 132; 136; 140.
100th, 132; 136; 140.
101st, 132; 137; 140.
102nd, 132; 137; 140.
103rd, 132; 137; 140.
104th, 132; 138; 140.
105th, 132; 138; 140.
106th, 132; 138; 140.

DIVISIONS

30th (originally 37th), 1—9; 7; 132; 140.
31st (originally 38th), 11—19; 17; 132; 140.
32nd (originally 39th), 21—29; 27; 132; 140.
33rd (originally 40th), 31—39; 37; 132; 141.
34th (originally 41st), 41—50; 48; 132; 141.
35th (originally 42nd), 7; 51—59; 57; 132;
  141.
36th (Ulster), 61—69; 67; 140; 151.
37th (originally 44th), 71—79; 77; 141.
38th (Welsh—originally 43rd), 81—89; 87;
  141.
39th (new formation), 91—100; 96; 97; 98;
  100; 141.
40th (new formation), 83, Note; 101—108;
  106; 141.
41st (new formation), 109—115; 113; 141.
63rd (2nd/Northumbrian), 117.
63rd (Royal Naval), 117—128; 125, 126;
  127; 148, 149.
Composite Div. (Helles), 127; 148, 149.

Divisions of the (original) Fourth New Army—

30th, 7; 131; 132; 133; 140.
31st, 7; 131; 132; 134; 140.
32nd, 7; 131; 132; 135; 140.
33rd, 7; 131; 132; 136; 140.
34th, 7; 131; 132; 137; 140.
35th, 7; 131; 132; 138; 140.

ADDITIONAL UNITS

Heavy Batteries, R.G.A.—

11 (Hull), 3.
30, 133.
31, 134 fn.*.
31 (New), 134, and note 9.
32, 135.
33, 136.
34, 137.
35, 138 fn.*.
35 (New), 138, and note 7.
36, 63.
37, 73.
38, 83.
124 (2nd Hull), 13.
125, 3.
126, 33; 37.
130, 43.
131, 53.
132, 134 (note 9).
133, 23; 138 (note 7).

Siege Batteries, R.G.A.—

86, 112.
89, 112.
545, 3.

Infantry Battalions (attached—but not training cadres)—

14/A. & S.H., 3.
5/Conn. Rang., 47.
12/K.O.Y.L.I. (P.), 13.
1/4/K.S.L.I., 124.
6/Leins., 47.
2/2/London, 124.
2/4/London, 124.
20/Middx., 93.
21/Middx., 93.
22/Middx., 105.
2/L.N.L., 13.
12/L.N.L. (P.), 23.
10/Q.O.R.W.K., 93.
11/Q.O.R.W.K., 93.
2/R.D.F., 13.
7/R.D.F., 13 fn.***.
6/R. Innis. F., 47.
5/R. Ir. F., 3.
7/R. Ir. Rif., 63.
R.M.A. Bn., 124.
2/R.M.F., 13.

Infantry Battalions—(*Continued*)

6/R.M.F., 13 fn.**.
2/R.S.F., 105.
18/R.W.F., 83, Note.
19/R.W.F., 83, Note.
1/6/Sco. Rif., 33.
13/Sco. Rif., 105.
18/Sher. For., 105.
12/S. Lanc., 105.
12/S.W.B., 83, Note.
17/Welsh, 83, Note.

Machine-Gun Battalions—

39, 95 ; 103.
104, 105.

Motor-Machine-Gun Batteries—

16th, 73.
19th, 3 ; 33.

Mounted Units—

N. Irish Horse, 23 ; 65 ; 66, note 31 ; 89, note B.
Q.O.O. Hsrs. 89, note B ; 124.

155

CORRIGENDA

HISTORY OF THE GREAT WAR 1914-1918
ORDER OF BATTLE OF DIVISIONS

PART 1.

PAGE 29. *Note* 17. After 3/9/15 add (from 16th Div. Arty.).

PAGE 34. *Under 2nd Brigade.* The last 2 entries should read :
26 Sept. '18...Lt.-Col. D. G. JOHNSON (acting).
5 Oct. '18...Br.-Gen. G. C. KELLY.
„   *Under 3rd Brigade.* The last entry should read :
6 Oct. '18...Br.-Gen. E. G. ST. AUBYN.

PAGE 37. *Note* 12, *1st line.* 29/3/15 should read, 24/8/15.

PAGE 42. *Under 99th Brigade.* The first entry should read :
[19 Dec. '14]...Br.-Gen. R. O. KELLETT.

PAGE 45. *Note* 9. 15/12/15 should read, 20/12/15.
„   *Note* 33. Add : Attached to 66th Div., 16/7-7/11/17.

PAGE 50. *Under 76th Brigade.* The first entry should read :
[21 July '15]...Br.-Gen. E. ST. G. PRATT.

PAGE 53. *Note* 13. After to add, 63rd Bde.,
„   *Note* 16. After to add, 62nd Bde.,
„   *Note* 17. 2/3/15 should read 25/11/14.
„   *Note* 21. 10/2/16 should read, 15/4/16.

PAGE 61. *Note* 9, *line* 2. 21/5/15 should read, 29/5/15.

PAGE 66. *Under 14th Bde.,* seventh entry. Crompton should read Compton.

PAGE 67. *Under entry* against 2/R. Innis. F.
30/12/15 should read 24/12/15.

PAGE 69. *Note* 29, *line* 2. Delete all the note after A/CCC ; and substitute,
joined XXVIII from 60th Div., and became A/XV on 21/1/17 ;
A/CXXVI joined XXVIII and became A/XXVIII.

PAGE 70. *Under* 1916. Battles of the Somme.
add as second entry,
29 July ... Capture of Longueval [XV Corps, Fourth Army].

PAGE 85. *Note* 18. After the date add, (from 16th Div.).
„   *Note* 19, *line* 2. Alter 24/1/16 to 29/1/16.

PAGE 89. *Under B.-G., R.A.* add these two entries :
>>> 25 Mar., 1918...Br.-Gen. E. S. HOARE NAIRNE (tempy.).
>>> 27 Mar., 1918...Br.-Gen. J. W. F. LAMONT.

PAGE 93. *Note* 16, *line* 2. in Jan. 1916 should read, joined on 5/3/16.

PAGE 95. *Under* 1918. In the entry dealing with the Battle of the Aisne, delete the last square bracket and full stop, and add, until 29/5 ; then Fifth (French) Army].

PAGE 107. *Under Artillery.* Add this additional entry at end :
>>> Heavy Arty. Bde., R.G.A. (71st & 121st Hy. Bties.) left Woolwich on 13/2/15, disembkd. at le Havre on 15/2/15, and joined 28th Div. on 17/ & 18/2/15. Hy. Arty. Bde. left 28th Div. on 6/4/15 and became IX Hy. Arty. Bde... R.G.A.

PAGE 109. *Note* 48. Add at end of note :
>>> 366 joined CCLXVIII (74th Div.) on 11/9/17.

PAGE 112. *April* 1920, *Column* 3, *2nd line.* Russel's should read, Russell's.

PART 2A.

PAGE 44. *Under* 1914, *Column* 3 add in Devon & Cornwall Bde., after 4/D.C.L.I., 5/D.C.L.I.*

PAGE 45. *Note* 14, *line* 2. 25/6/17 should read, 18/8/17.

PAGE 46. *General Notes.* Add at end :
>>> *NOTE.*—For service in India, 5/D.C.L.I. was replaced by 6/Devon.; but part of 5/D.C.L.I. was used to complete 4/D.C.L.I. for service overseas.

PAGE 51. *Note* 20, *line* 7. After reached add, le

PAGE 57. *Note* 4, *line* 2. 25/6/17 should read, 18/8/17.
,, *Note* 5, *line* 2. Delete 25/6/17 and rest of note. Substitute :
>>> 20/8/17. The Bn. was disbanded 3–18/8/18.

PAGE 98. *Under B.-G., R.A.* After the entry dated 17 Mar. 1918 add :
>>> 22 Mar. 1918...Br.-Gen. E. S. HOARE NAIRNE (tempy.).

PAGE 100. *Under* 1918. In the entry dealing with the Battle of the Aisne, delete the last square bracket and full stop, and add :
>>> until 29/5 ; then Fifth (French) Army].

PAGE 105. *Note* 30, *line* 2. D(H.) should read, C(H.)
,, *Note* 43, *line* 11. C/LXXXI should read, C/LXXXVI.

PAGE 131. *Under* 1915. Last line delete full stop and add :
; 162nd Bde. also went on 30/12/15.
,, *Under* 1916. In second line, after, Cairo ; add :
162nd Bde. rejoined on 1/2/16,

PAGE 137. *Note* 57, *line* 1. 2/5/L.N.L. should read 4/5/L.N.L.

PAGE 142. *Under 2nd London Bde.* Delete last entry, dealing with 9 Sept. '14, and
substitute these two entries :
9 Sept. '14...Colonel C. MATTHEY (acting).
21 Sept. '14...Br.-Gen. W. C. G. McGRIGOR.

PAGE 145. *Note* 40, *line* 1. 23/3/15 should read, 23/3/16.
,, ,, *line* 2. 30/5/15 should read, 30/5/16.
,, *Note* 52, *line* 2. 11th should read, 30th.

PART 2B.

PAGE 21. *Note* 41, *line* 3. 15/6/18 should read, 19/6/18.

PAGE 37. *Note* 33. 52nd Bde., 17th Div. should read, 103rd Bde., 34th Div.

PAGE 53. *Note* 34, *Line* 5. Delete reference to D(H.), and substitute :
D(H.) did not go to France.

PAGE 62. *Under* 1915 (*August*) *3rd Column, line* 8 (of units) 2/6/Soc. Rif. should read,
2/6/Sco. Rif.

PAGE 72. *1st Column, eleventh entry*
6/York. should be, 6/Gr. How.
,, *4th Column, eighteenth line*
opposite to entry of 7/Sher. For.
15/6 should be, 19/6

PAGE 79. *Under* 1918, *December, 214th Bde.*
1/4/Buffs. should read, 4/Buffs. (R.) ;
,, and
1/4/R.W.F. should read, 4/R.W.F. (R.).

PAGE 80, *Note* 40, *line* 1. Delete Special and after Reserve add, T.F.

PART 3A.

PAGE 147. *Note* 12, *line* 3. 17/11/15 should read, 20/11/15,

Lightning Source UK Ltd.
Milton Keynes UK
UKOW03f1126141114

241613UK00001B/19/P